Digital Design Principles and Computer Architecture

EDWARD KARALIS

PRENTICE HALL

Upper Saddle River, New Jersey   ***Columbus, Ohio***

Library of Congress Cataloging-in-Publication Data

Karalis, Edward.
    Digital design principles and computer architecture / Edward Karalis.
       p. cm.
    Includes bibliographical references and index.
    ISBN 0–13–374588–0
    1. Digital integrated circuits—Design and construction.
    2. Computer architecture.   I. Title.
TK7874.65.K37   1996
004.2′56—dc20   96–13543
                                   CIP

Cover Image: ©Norman Rothschild/International Stock
Editor: Charles E. Stewart, Jr.
Production Editor: Christine M. Harrington
Design Coordinator: Jill E. Bonar
Cover Designer: Brian Deep
Production Manager: Laura Messerly
Marketing Manager: Debbie Yarnell

This book was set in Times Roman by The Clarinda Company and was printed and bound by Book Press. The cover was printed by Phoenix Color Corp.

 © 1997 by Prentice-Hall, Inc.
Simon & Schuster/A Viacom Company
Upper Saddle River, New Jersey 07458

All rights reserved. No part of this book may be reproduced, in any form or by any means, without permission in writing from the publisher.

Printed in the United States of America

10 9 8 7 6 5 4 3 2 1

ISBN: 0-13-374588-0

Prentice-Hall International (UK) Limited, *London*
Prentice-Hall of Australia Pty. Limited, *Sydney*
Prentice-Hall of Canada, Inc., *Toronto*
Prentice-Hall Hispanoamericana, S. A., *Mexico*
Prentice-Hall of India Private Limited, *New Delhi*
Prentice-Hall of Japan, Inc., *Tokyo*
Simon & Schuster Asia Pte. Ltd., *Singapore*
Editora Prentice-Hall do Brasil, Ltda., *Rio de Janeiro*

To the memory of my parents
Eftihios and Aphrodite

PREFACE

The proliferation of digital devices has affected every aspect of contemporary life. The invention of the transistor in 1948 paved the way for the steady evolution of digital logic, which culminated in the development of the microprocessor during the early seventies. Design criteria were constantly redefined to keep up with the fast pace of changing technology, and they were primarily cost-driven.

Initially, the goal of digital design was to minimize the number of discrete transistors per gate. When small scale integration (SSI) provided several gates in one package, the goal shifted toward reducing the number of gates used. Medium scale integration (MSI) made possible complete functional blocks in one package; the emphasis was then placed on lowering the package count. Large scale integration (LSI) enabled designers to contain a complete device in one package. Thus, the effort was refocused on reducing input and output lines needed by the package itself. Very large scale integration (VLSI) has resulted in devices that require computer-aided engineering tools and techniques to achieve flexible and high-performance designs.

With the advent of the microprocessor, a new array of options became available, revolutionizing the digital design process and its scope. This programmable universal logic module can be used by designers in a variety of applications by simply giving it different sets of commands. New design goals were developed as well, such as processing speed, data throughput, and memory size.

Today we are standing at the dawn of a new era in which microprocessors enable us to plan an endless list of sophisticated applications. Personal computers, loaded with elaborate programs, enable users to perform myriad tasks, the types of which are limited only by their imagination. Computer networking makes possible rapid information exchanges, ranging in form from simple messages to high-resolution graphics.

The main objective of this text is to present a comprehensive yet concise treatment of the underlying concepts and building blocks that make up today's digital components and systems. Conceptual coverage includes the relevant analytical tools and design methodologies. "Building blocks" are the various integrated devices, modules, and their signal interactions. An attempt is made to provide a balance of theory, application, and functional-level examples so as to make the material technology-independent.

Each chapter explains the essential principles of a specific topic and can therefore stand alone. Chapter 1 presents a quantitative treatment of digital arithmetic, binary codes, and switching algebra, which are used throughout the text. Combinational networks are discussed in Chapter 2, which also presents design examples spanning the evolution of digital devices. Sequential networks, both synchronous and asynchronous, are presented in Chapter 3, along with design examples of all levels of integration. Microprocessors are introduced in Chapter 4, in which architectures, functions, memory, timing and control, and I/O are defined. Microprocessor software is explained in Chapter 5. This discussion covers data structures, algorithms, programming concepts, languages, and development tools. Microprocessor interfacing is presented in Chapter 6, in which polling, interrupts, devices, and controllers are discussed. Microprocessor-based design fundamentals are given in Chapter 7. Design of both hardware and software is covered, using both conventional and multitasking approaches. Microprocessor communications are outlined in Chapter 8. Channels, modems, terminals, and protocols are explained. An overview of microprocessor networks is provided in Chapter 9. Local area networks, the OSI reference model, and various standards are included in the discussion. The various signal conversions required between the microprocessor and the real world are described in Chapter 10. Signal analysis techniques are presented in Chapter 11, along with examples of sampling, filtering, and transform algorithms. Chapter 12 deals with arbitrary signal synthesis methods.

This text can be used by both students and professionals to gain or review digital design knowledge. Each chapter is filled with equations, figures, and tables for quick reference. Also, numerous examples are also provided as an aid in understanding the material.

It is a formidable task to acknowledge and give due credit to all those who, directly or indirectly, contributed to the completion of this work. In order to avoid the embarrassment of omitting anyone, I want to thank collectively all those who have made this book possible. I am especially grateful to Eric Alphonsi, Jack McFadden, Dave Miller, and Dave Guerrino for their knowledge and inspiration.

E. Karalis

BRIEF CONTENTS

CONTENTS

1

MATHEMATICAL BACKGROUND

The nucleus of a digital system is the *binary digit,* or *bit,* which can take one of two possible states, the true or the false. A true state is assigned a logical one and a false state is assigned a logical zero. However, the physical meaning of a specific bit can be any one of a number of events, such as the presence of a signal, the closure of a switch, a certain voltage level, or an arithmetic digit. The material in this chapter deals with the grouping of binary digits to form number representations, arithmetic operations, coding assignments, and relationships that form the basis of digital systems. The chapter objectives are as follows: (1) define the positional number system notation, (2) explain number conversions from one base to another, (3) discuss binary arithmetic operations, (4) cover both fixed and floating point calculations, (5) present the main binary codes, and (6) provide an overview of Boolean algebra, which forms a common thread throughout the text.

1.1 NUMBER SYSTEM NOTATION

A number N is represented by an ordered set of symbols called digits. Each digit represents a unit quantity, and its position determines the weight it contributes to the overall value. For example, the number 124.5 can be expressed as the sum of $100 + 20 + 4 + 0.5$. Taking this a step further, it can be written as the sum of the digit-weight products or, $1 \times 10^2 + 2 \times 10^1 + 4 \times 10^0 + 5 \times 10^{-1}$. Each digit is multiplied by a weight value, in this case 10 raised to an exponent. The exponent's value is dependent on the corresponding digit's relative position. In the decimal number system, there are ten unique digits, 0–9. The number of unique digits, in this case ten, is called the *base* or *radix*. In general, the following expression can be used to define the positional number system notation:

$$N = d_{n-1}r^{n-1} + d_{n-2}r^{n-2} + \cdots + d_1r^1 + d_0r^0 + d_{-1}r^{-1} \\ + d_{-2}r^{-2} + \cdots + d_{-m}r^{-m}$$

(1.1)

where N represents the actual number value

   d_i the individual digits

   r the radix or base

   n the number of integral digits

   m the number of fractional digits

The equation can also be written in a compact form as, $N = d_{n-1} \cdots d_1 d_0 . d_{-1} d_{-2} \cdots d_{-m}$. A period, placed between the d_0 and d_{-1} digits, separates the number into its integral and fractional parts and is called the radix point. The digits to the left of the radix point make up the integral part of the number, and those to the right make up its fractional part. The leftmost digit is known as the most significant digit (MSD), and the rightmost is known as the least significant digit (LSD). The radix of a number determines how many permissible symbols can be used as digits in the number. A number represented in this notation can be a real number, an integer, or a fraction, depending upon the values of n and m, respectively. Example 1.1 illustrates positional notation.

EXAMPLE 1.1   Express the number 135.25 as a summation of products consisting of individually weighted digits.

$$N = d_2 \times 10^2 + d_1 \times 10^1 + d_0 \times 10^0 + d_{-1} \times 10^{-1} + d_{-2} \times 10^{-2}$$
$$N = 1 \times 10^2 + 3 \times 10^1 + 5 \times 10^0 + 2 \times 10^{-1} + 5 \times 10^{-2} = 135.25$$

In general, for a given radix r number system, there are r possible symbols available for use as digits. It is common practice to append r as a subscript to a number for clarity. It is technically suitable to use binary digits to represent and store numbers in a digital system, where each bit position can assume two values, 0 or 1. In addition, there are two other popular radix systems, the octal and the hexadecimal. The *octal*, or base 8, system uses digits 0–7, and they can be easily converted to a binary format as an ordered set of three bits each. This is possible because the number of combinations of such a set becomes $2^3 = 8$, which equals the number of symbols each octal digit can assume. The *hexadecimal*, or base 16, system uses digits 0–9 and letters A–F to represent the sixteen possible symbols each digit can assume. By the same argument, each hexadecimal digit can be converted to a binary format as a set of four ordered bits, since $2^4 = 16$. The binary system has a widespread use for representing numbers in digital storage media, since each bit can represent the two stable states, 0 and 1, of the basic digital storage cell. A given binary number can be easily converted to its decimal format, which becomes the summation of the powers of 2, corresponding to the individual bit-weight products of the given binary number N_2. The subscript indicates a number representation in base 2 notation. Example 1.2 illustrates a binary-to-decimal conversion.

TABLE 1.1
Base r notation

$r = 10$	$r = 2$	$r = 8$	$r = 16$
0	0000	0	0
1	0001	1	1
2	0010	2	2
3	0011	3	3
4	0100	4	4
5	0101	5	5
6	0110	6	6
7	0111	7	7
8	1000	10	8
9	1001	11	9
10	1010	12	A
11	1011	13	B
12	1100	14	C
13	1101	15	D
14	1110	16	E
15	1111	17	F

EXAMPLE 1.2

Given $N_2 = (11010.011)_2$, convert it to base 10 notation.

$$N_2 = (11010.011)_2$$

$$N_{10} = d_4 \times 2^4 + d_3 \times 2^3 + d_2 \times 2^2 + d_1 \times 2^1 + d_0 \times 2^0 + d_{-1} \times 2^{-1} + d_{-2} \times 2^{-2} + d_{-3} \times 2^{-3}$$

$$N_{10} = 1 \times 2^4 + 1 \times 2^3 + 0 \times 2^2 + 1 \times 2^1 + 0 \times 2^0 + 0 \times 2^{-1} + 1 \times 2^{-2} + 1 \times 2^{-3}$$

$$N_{10} = 16 + 8 + 2 + 0.25 + 0.125 = (26.375)_{10}$$

Binary digits, grouped as an ordered set of bits, are used in every digital computer storage medium for representing various types of information. A group of four bits is commonly known as a *nibble,* a group of eight bits is called a *byte,* and a group of sixteen is referred to as a *word*. It should be noted that a number of any base can be represented by a binary number in a digital computer memory. The maximum number of bits k required to represent each digit of that number is defined by the relation $k = \lceil \log_2 n \rceil$, where n stands for the number of permissible symbols used as digits in that number. The number of bits k is defined as the smallest integer equal to or greater than the bracketed expression. In the case of a hexadecimal number, the bracketed expression becomes 4; in the case of a decimal number it becomes 3.32, which is rounded off to the integer 4. Table 1.1 provides a tabulation of the four prevalent base number system representations.

1.2 BASE CONVERSIONS

The information stored in a digital computer memory is nothing more than fixed-length one and zero patterns contained in individual cells. A *cell* is a storage element that contains one bit of information. In order for the data to be meaningful to a user, they must often be converted from one format to another. The basic approaches used in the conversion process are the repeated division by r_2 method and the repeated multiplication by r_2 method. The division method is suitable in the case where an integer number of base r_1 is converted to base r_2. The multiplication method applies in the case where a number of base r_2 is converted to base r_1. In both cases base r_1 is greater than base r_2. When converting from base r_2 to base 10, however, the sum of the individual digit-weight products method is more direct. The specific types of conversion discussed below illustrate these and other approaches.

Binary-to-Decimal

To convert a binary integer into a decimal number, the sum of the individual digit-weight products method is used. Let N be a five-bit binary integer. The corresponding base 10 integer is calculated by

$$N_{10} = d_4 2^4 + d_3 2^3 + d_2 2^2 + d_1 2^1 + d_0 2^0 \tag{1.2}$$

Using the equation above, we start with the most significant bit (MSB) of the number and multiply it by its weight, in this case 16. Then the next lower significant bit-weight product is evaluated and added to the previous product. This process is continued until the least significant bit (LSB) product is added to the partial product sum. Example 1.3 illustrates the binary-to-decimal integer conversion.

EXAMPLE 1.3　　Given an integer binary number $N_2 = (10101)_2$, convert it to its decimal equivalent.

$$N_{10} = d_4 \times 2^4 + d_3 \times 2^3 + d_2 \times 2^2 + d_1 \times 2^1 + d_0 \times 2^0$$
$$N_{10} = 1 \times 2^4 + 0 \times 2^3 + 1 \times 2^2 + 0 \times 2^1 + 1 \times 2^0$$
$$N_{10} = (16 + 4 + 1)_{10}$$
$$N_{10} = (21)_{10}$$

To convert a binary fractional number into a decimal fraction, the same method is used. Let N be a four-digit binary fractional number. The corresponding base 10 fractional number is calculated by

$$N_{10} = d_{-1} 2^{-1} + d_{-2} 2^{-2} + d_{-3} 2^{-3} + d_{-4} 2^{-4} \tag{1.3}$$

In the above equation, we start with the most significant bit of the number and multiply it by its weight, in this case 0.5. Then the next lower significant bit-weight product is evaluated and added to the previous product. This process is continued until the least significant bit product is evaluated and added to the partial product sum. Example 1.4 illustrates the fractional binary-to-decimal conversion.

EXAMPLE 1.4

Given a fractional binary number $N_2 = (0.1010)_2$, convert it to its decimal equivalent.

$$N_{10} = d_{-1} \times 2^{-1} + d_{-2} \times 2^{-2} + d_{-3} \times 2^{-3} + d_{-4} \times 2^{-4}$$
$$N_{10} = 1 \times 2^{-1} + 0 \times 2^{-2} + 1 \times 2^{-3} + 0 \times 2^{-4}$$
$$N_{10} = (0.5 + 0.125)_{10}$$
$$N_{10} = (0.625)_{10}$$

In the case of a real binary number, the procedure above is applied to the integral and fractional parts, respectively.

Decimal-to-Binary

To convert a decimal integer into a binary number, the division by r_2 method is employed. In this case the decimal base is r_1 and the binary base is r_2. Let N be a decimal integer to be converted into an n bit binary number. The number can be rewritten as a polynomial of order $n - 1$, as shown below:

$$N = d_{n-1}2^{n-1} + \cdots + d_2 2^2 + d_1 2^1 + d_0 2^0 \tag{1.4}$$

This equation is then divided by 2, and the result is

$$\frac{N}{2} = Q_1 + d_0 2^{-1} \tag{1.5}$$

where $Q_1 = d_{n-1}2^{n-2} + \cdots + d_2 2^1 + d_1 2^0$

The result contains the remainder d_0 divided by 2. The process is repeated successively until the quotient Q_i becomes zero. The resulting remainders become the bits of the binary number representing the decimal integer. Example 1.5 illustrates the decimal-to-binary integer conversion.

EXAMPLE 1.5

Given a decimal integer $N_{10} = (27)_{10}$, convert it to its binary equivalent.

Q_i	b_i
$27 \div 2 = 13$	$b_0 = 1$
$13 \div 2 = 6$	$b_1 = 1$
$6 \div 2 = 3$	$b_2 = 0$
$3 \div 2 = 1$	$b_3 = 1$
$1 \div 2 = 0$	$b_4 = 1$

$$N_2 = b_4 b_3 b_2 b_1 b_0 = (11011)_2$$

To convert a decimal fractional number into a binary fraction, the multiplication by r_2 method is used. Let N be a decimal fraction expressed as a polynomial of order $-m$, as shown below:

$$N = d_{-1}2^{-1} + d_{-2}2^{-2} + \cdots + d_{-m+1}2^{-m+1} + d_{-m}2^{-m} \tag{1.6}$$

The equation above is then multiplied by 2, and the result is

$$2N = d_{-1} + M_1 \tag{1.7}$$

where $M_1 = d_{-2}2^{-1} + \cdots + d_{-m+1}2^{-m} + d_{-m}2^{-m+1}$

The resulting integer d_{-1} becomes the most significant bit. The process is repeated successively until the fractional product M_i becomes zero. In general this is not always possible, since a finite fraction in one base system may not be representable as a finite fraction in another base system. In such a case, the ending criterion will be the number of bits desired or the required accuracy. Example 1.6 illustrates the decimal fraction-to-binary conversion.

EXAMPLE 1.6

Given two decimal fractional numbers $N_{10} = (0.125)_{10}$ and $P_{10} = (0.150)_{10}$, convert them to their binary equivalents.

	$N_{10} = (0.125)_{10}$			$P_{10} = (0.150)_{10}$		
	M_i	b_i		M_i	b_i	
	$0.125 \times 2 = 0.250$	$b_{-1} = 0$		$0.150 \times 2 = 0.3$	$b_{-1} = 0$	
	$0.250 \times 2 = 0.500$	$b_{-2} = 0$		$0.300 \times 2 = 0.6$	$b_{-2} = 0$	
	$0.500 \times 2 = 1.000$	$b_{-3} = 1$		$0.600 \times 2 = 1.2$	$b_{-3} = 1$	
	$0.000 \times 2 = 0.000$	$b_{-4} = 0$		$0.200 \times 2 = 0.4$	$b_{-4} = 0$	
				$0.400 \times 2 = 0.8$	$b_{-5} = 0$	
	$N_2 = (001)_2$			$0.800 \times 2 = 1.6$	$b_{-6} = 1$	
				$0.600 \times 2 = 1.2$	$b_{-7} = 1$	
				$0.200 \times 2 = 0.4$	$b_{-8} = 0$	
				$P_2 = (00100110)_2$		

In the case of a real decimal number, the conversion procedures above are applied to the integral and fractional parts, respectively. Table 1.2 provides the powers of 2 for values of n from 0 to 15 and can be used for quick conversions.

Binary-to-Octal and -Hexadecimal

To convert a binary number to its octal equivalent, all that is required is a simple three-bit grouping format, starting at the radix point. In the case where an exact grouping of three is not possible, the remaining bits are augmented with zeros to produce an exact group. Then, each

TABLE 1.2
Binary powers of n

n	2^n	2^{-n}
0	1	1.0
1	2	0.5
2	4	0.25
3	8	0.125
4	16	0.0625
5	32	0.0312
6	64	0.0156
7	128	0.00781
8	256	0.00390
9	512	0.00195
10	1,024	0.000976
11	2,048	0.000488
12	4,096	0.000244
13	8,192	0.000122
14	16,284	0.000061
15	32,568	0.0000305

group of three is evaluated in base 2 arithmetic as a positive integer, and the result becomes the equivalent octal digit. The binary-to-octal conversion procedure is illustrated in Example 1.7.

EXAMPLE 1.7

Given the real binary number $N_2 = (10101.01101)_2$, convert it to its octal equivalent.

$$N_2 = (10101.01101)_2$$
$$N = 010 \ 101.011 \ 01$$
$$N = 010 \ 101.011 \ 010$$
$$N_8 = d_1 d_0.d_{-1} d_{-2} = (25.32)_8$$

To convert a binary number to its hexadecimal equivalent, the procedure above can be used, but with four-bit groupings, so that all sixteen possible hexadecimal digit combinations are represented. Example 1.8 illustrates a binary-to-hexadecimal base conversion.

EXAMPLE 1.8

Given a real binary number $N_2 = (11101.011011)_2$, convert it to its hexadecimal equivalent.

$$N_2 = (11101.011011)_2$$
$$N = 0001 \ 1101.0110 \ 11$$
$$N = 0001 \ 1101.0110 \ 1100$$
$$N_{16} = d_1 d_0.d_{-1} d_{-2} = (1D.6C)_{16}$$

The three- and four-bit grouping procedures demonstrated above can be applied in reverse in order to convert an octal or hexadecimal number to its binary equivalent form. That is, each octal or hexadecimal digit is rewritten as a group of three or four bits, respectively, with the resulting leading and/or trailing zeros deleted. The octal-to-binary conversion procedure is detailed in Example 1.9.

EXAMPLE 1.9

Given the octal number $N_8 = (135.75)_8$, convert it to its binary equivalent.

$$N_8 = d_2 d_1 d_0 . d_{-1} d_{-2} = (135.75)_8$$
$$N_2 = (001\ \ 011\ \ 101.111\ \ 101)_2$$
$$N_2 = (1011101.111101)_2$$

The hexadecimal-to-binary conversion procedure is detailed in Example 1.10.

EXAMPLE 1.10

Given a hexadecimal number $N_{16} = (1D.AC)_{16}$, convert it to its binary equivalent.

$$N_{16} = d_1 d_0 . d_{-1} d_{-2} = (1D.AC)_{16}$$
$$N_2 = (0001\ \ 1101.1010\ \ 1100)_2$$
$$N_2 = (11101.101011)_2$$

Decimal-to-Octal and -Hexadecimal

To convert a decimal number to its octal or hexadecimal equivalent form, a number of methods can be used. For example, the multiplication by r_2 or division by r_2 method can be applied to any two base number systems. In this case r_2 would be 8 or 16, and the multiplication or division process would be a function of the number to be converted and the direction of the conversion. If, however, the given decimal number is converted to its binary format as an intermediate step, it becomes an easier task to derive the final octal or hexadecimal representation. This base conversion approach is illustrated in Example 1.11.

EXAMPLE 1.11

Given the decimal number $N_{10} = (27.125)_{10}$, find its octal and hexadecimal equivalent forms.

$$N_{10} = (27.125)_{10}$$
$$N_2 = (11011.001)_2 \text{ (intermediate conversion to base two)}$$
$$N = 011\ \ 011.001$$
$$N_8 = d_1 d_0 . d_{-1} = (33.1)_8$$
$$N_2 = (11011.001)_2$$
$$N = 0001\ \ 1011.0010$$
$$N_{16} = d_1 d_0 . d_{-1} = (1B.2)_{16}$$

Conversion from an octal or hexadecimal base system to a decimal base system may also be performed using the multiplication by r_2 and the division by r_2 methods. Once again r_2 would be either 8 or 10, depending on the number and the direction of the conversion process. However, positional notation can be used to produce an elegant solution to the problem. In this approach each octal or hexadecimal digit is multiplied by its corresponding weight, using positional notation, and the partial products are summed to produce the equivalent decimal number. Example 1.12 illustrates the sum of digit-weight products method.

EXAMPLE 1.12   Given the octal number $N_8 = (33.1)_8$ and the hexadecimal number $N_{16} = (1B.2)_{16}$, find their decimal equivalent forms.

$$N_8 = (33.1)_8$$
$$N_{10} = 3 \times 8^1 + 3 \times 8^0 + 1 \times 8^{-1}$$
$$N_{10} = (24 + 3 + 0.125) = (27.125)_{10}$$
$$N_{16} = (1B.2)_{16}$$
$$N_{10} = 1 \times 16^1 + 11 \times 16^0 + 2 \times 16^{-1}$$
$$N_{10} = (16 + 11 + 0.125) = (27.125)_{10}$$

It should be noted that in hexadecimal-to-decimal conversion, the decimal equivalent number of each hexadecimal digit is used to facilitate the conversion process.

1.3 ARITHMETIC OPERATIONS

The four basic arithmetic operations of addition, subtraction, multiplication, and division can be carried out in any defined base number system. Digital information is stored in memory, using binary format of either one or zero. The emphasis here will be on base 2 arithmetic so as to gain a better understanding of bit manipulation in a digital computer. Let A and B represent two single-bit binary numbers and C represent the result of the particular operation. All the possible combinations for each of the four operations are computed below.

$A + B = C$			Carry	$A - B = C$			Borrow	$A \times B = C$			$A \div B = C$		
0	0	0	0	0	0	0	0	0	0	0	0	0	*
0	1	1	0	0	1	1	1	0	1	0	0	1	0
1	0	1	0	1	0	1	0	1	0	0	1	0	*
1	1	0	1	1	1	0	0	1	1	1	1	1	1

*Undefined

Binary addition and subtraction operations are rather straightforward and are based on the rules above. Example 1.13 illustrates binary addition and subtraction procedures.

EXAMPLE 1.13

Given the binary number $A = 10101.10$ and the binary number $B = 01011.01$, find the sum $A + B$ and the difference $A - B$.

$A = 10101.10$ $(21.50)_{10}$ (augend)	$A = 10101.10$ $(21.50)_{10}$ (minuend)
$B = 01011.01$ $(11.25)_{10}$ (addend)	$B = 01011.01$ $(11.25)_{10}$ (subtrahend)
$S = 100000.11$ $(32.75)_{10}$ (sum)	$D = 1010.01$ $(10.25)_{10}$ (difference)

Binary multiplication can be accomplished in several ways. The conventional method is to perform a straightforward operation using the rules above. Another approach is to use the multiplication-by-2 property of a binary number, which is equivalent to displacing all bits one place to the left, also called *left shift* operation. This operation can be verified using positional notation. Yet another approach is to add the larger number to itself a number of times specified by the value of the smaller number, with the result equaling the product of the two. The last two approaches are feasible for computer implementation. The three binary multiplication approaches are detailed in Example 1.14, in which binary integers are used for clarity.

EXAMPLE 1.14

Given the binary number $A = 1101$ and the binary number $B = 101$, find their product $A \times B$ using the three methods discussed above.

(a) Conventional

$A = 1101$ $(13)_{10}$ (multiplicand)
$\times B = 101$ $(5)_{10}$ (multiplier)

```
  1101
  0000    Partial Products
+1101
```

1000001 $(65)_{10}$ Product

(b) Left Shift and Add

$$13 \times 5 = A \times B$$
$$13 \times 4 + 13 \times 1 = (1101)_2 \times 4 + (1101)_2 \times 1$$
$$52 + 13 = (110100 + 1101)_2$$
$$65 = (1000001)_2$$

(c) Add B Times

```
  1101
  1101
  1101
  1101
+1101
```

1000001

Binary division can also be performed in several ways. The conventional method is to perform longhand division using the binary division rules. Another way is to use the divide-by-2 property of a binary number, by performing a simple *right shift* operation on it, which is the opposite of a left shift. This operation can be verified by the use of positional notation. Yet another approach is to subtract the smaller number from the larger number as many times as is necessary for the result to become zero or less than the smaller number, in which case it becomes a nonzero remainder. The number of successive subtractions becomes the quotient. The last two approaches are feasible for computer implementation. The three binary division approaches are illustrated in Example 1.15, in which binary integers are used for simplicity.

EXAMPLE 1.15 Given the binary number $A = 1000001$ and $B = 1101$, find the quotient $A \div B$ using the three methods discussed above. Note that the number of bits in A is $m = 7$ and in B is $n = 4$.

<table>
<tr><td colspan="2" align="center">(a) Conventional</td><td colspan="2" align="center">(b) Right Shift and Subtract</td></tr>
</table>

(a) Conventional

```
              101 (quotient)
(divisor) 1101)1000001 (dividend)
             −01101
              011
              0110
              01101
              1101
              0000
```

(b) Right Shift and Subtract

$A \div B$

$A \div B \times 8$ (adjust divisor)

$65 < 104$ (shift right) $b_3 = 0$

$65 > 52$ (subtract and shift right) $b_2 = 1$

$13 < 26$ (shift right) $b_1 = 0$

$13 = 13$ (subtract and shift right) $b_0 = 1$

$0 = \dfrac{13}{2}$ (Done)

(c) Subtract x Times

```
 1000001
−  1101
 ───────
 110100
−  1101
 ───────
 100111
−  1101
 ───────
 011010
−  1101
 ───────
 001101
−  1101
 ───────
   0000
```

The examples above illustrate the four basic arithmetic operations applied to binary numbers. An algorithm, or a set of rules, necessary to perform each operation can be formulated based on the various procedures used. It is also possible to streamline the operations by reducing them to a set of steps requiring either all additions or additions with directional shifts. This can be accomplished by the use of complement arithmetic, which makes it possible to subtract two numbers by adding one to the complement of the other. Hence, the subtraction operation in ordinary subtraction and division is replaced by complement addition. The concept of complements is discussed in the next section.

1.4 FIXED-POINT ARITHMETIC

To represent a binary integer in digital memory, it is necessary to make provisions for its sign. A simple approach is to use the *sign and magnitude* notation of a binary number. Given a digital memory word of n bits, n is designated as the MSB and defines the sign. The remaining number of bits, 0 through $n - 1$, are used to represent the magnitude of the number. An MSB of zero represents a positive number and an MSB of one represents a negative number. Given a binary number represented by a row of m digits, of which k are valued as ones at a given time, the number of unique combinations that can result is defined by $N = 2^m$. The number of unique combinations, N, becomes the summation of the combinations formed by m things taken k at a time. For example, given a word of 16 bits, the number of different values it can represent in sign and magnitude notation is 2^{16} or 65,536. This represents a range of $\pm 32,767$ possible values that can be assigned. In general, the sign and magnitude notation can be expressed in terms of positional notation, using an extra significant digit to represent the sign of the number, formed by the remaining digits. In the case of a binary number the expression becomes

$$N = s + d_{n-1}2^{n-1} + d_{n-2}2^{n-2} + \cdots + d_1 2^1 + d_0 2^0 \tag{1.8}$$

where $s = 0, 1$

  $d = 0, 1$

For example, the sign and magnitude representation of the number 19_{10} is $N_2 = 0 + 1 \times 2^4 + 0 \times 2^3 + 0 \times 2^2 + 1 \times 2^1 + 1 \times 2^0 = (010011)_2$.

The concept of complements facilitates arithmetic operations. Given a number N in base r represented as an ordered set of k digits, the *base complement* of N is defined as $\overline{N} = r^k - N$. In other words, the complement of a number in a given base is defined as the maximum value number minus the number. By the same token the complement of a digit is the digit obtained by subtracting the digit from the maximum value digit $(r - 1)$ in that base r system. The reduced base complement of a number N in base r represented by k digits can also be defined as $\overline{M} = r^k - N - 1$. These two complement definitions are better known, in the binary base system, as *two's complement* and *one's complement,* respectively. Example 1.16 shows the procedure for deriving the two's complement of a binary number.

EXAMPLE 1.16

Given the binary number $N = 0110$, find its two's complement notation.

$$\overline{N} = r^k - N = 2^k - N = 2^4 - N = 10000 - 0110 = 1010$$

The one's complement representation basically takes the two's complement procedure one step further and subtracts a one from the two's complement representation of the number. The one's complement procedure is shown in Example 1.17.

EXAMPLE 1.17

Given the binary number $N = 0110$, find its one's complement notation.

$$\overline{M} = r^k - N - 1 = 2^k - N - 1 = 2^4 - N - 1 = (10000 - 0110) - 0001 = 1001$$

From the results of Example 1.17, it becomes apparent that the one's complement notation of a binary number is equivalent to interchanging all zeros with ones, and all ones with zeros, in the original number. Based on this observation, it becomes easier to derive the one's complement notation of a number by a simple bit complementation and then add a one to it in order to derive the two's complement representation. Thus for $N = 0111$, the one's complement becomes 1000 and the two's complement, 1001. From the results of Example 1.16 it can be observed that the two's complement notation of a binary number is equivalent to simply complementing all bits to the left of the rightmost "1" in the original number.

Binary number representation in the sign and magnitude, one's complement, and two's complement notations differs somewhat. All three notations use the sign bit in order to determine whether a number is positive or negative. Positive numbers are represented identically in all three notations. Negative numbers in the sign and magnitude notation are identical to the positive in magnitude. Negative numbers in one's complement notation are the exact complements of the positive. Negative numbers in two's complement notation are the one's complements plus one. Table 1.3 provides the representation of negative binary numbers, 0 through 15, in these three notation systems. A decimal point is shown after the sign bit for clarity.

It should be noted that the decimal point is implied when the number is stored in a digital memory medium.

TABLE 1.3
Fixed-point notation

Decimal	Binary	Signed	One's Complement	Two's Complement
0	0000	1.0000	0.0000	0.0000
−1	0001	1.0001	1.1110	1.1111
−2	0010	1.0010	1.1101	1.1110
−3	0011	1.0011	1.1100	1.1101
−4	0100	1.0100	1.1011	1.1100
−5	0101	1.0101	1.1010	1.1011
−6	0110	1.0110	1.1001	1.1010
−7	0111	1.0111	1.1000	1.1001
−8	1000	1.1000	1.0111	1.1000
−9	1001	1.1001	1.0110	1.0111
−10	1010	1.1010	1.0101	1.0110
−11	1011	1.1011	1.0100	1.0101
−12	1100	1.1100	1.0011	1.0100
−13	1101	1.1101	1.0010	1.0011
−14	1110	1.1110	1.0001	1.0010
−15	1111	1.1111	1.0000	1.0001

Another useful concept is that of the *modulus*, which pertains to the capacity of measurement in a given system or unit of measurement. For example, a two-digit decimal counter is a device capable of counting from 0 to 99 or 100 different events, hence it is modulo 100. This counter, therefore, cannot distinguish between a number, a, less than one hundred and a number, b, greater than one hundred. This can be stated as "b is congruent to a modulo 100." In general, the modulus m of a set of ordered digits k in a given base r is defined as $m = r^k$. The following equation provides a general relationship of congruence:

$$a = b \bmod m \cdot i,$$

where $i = 1, 2, \ldots, l.$

Modulo addition is defined as the summation of two numbers a and b, with respect to a given modulus, obtained by ignoring any resulting carry digits. The concepts of modulus and modulo addition are expanded upon in Example 1.18.

EXAMPLE 1.18

Given $b = 100$ and $m = 30$, find all the congruences, and perform modulo 30 additions on the last two.

$$a = b \bmod m \cdot i \qquad i = 1, 2, \ldots, l$$
$$a = 100 \bmod 30 \cdot i \qquad i = 1, 2, 3$$
$$a = 70, 40, 10$$
$$(40 + 10) \bmod 30 = 20$$

Sign and Magnitude

To add two numbers with the same sign in this notation, simply add the magnitudes and assign the same sign to the result. The procedure used to add two numbers with opposite signs depends on whether the magnitude of the augend is greater or less than the addend value. If the augend is greater, we first complement the magnitude portion of the addend and perform an addition with the augend; then the resulting end-around-carry bit is added to the LSB of the sum, and the sign of the augend is repeated for the result. If the augend is less than or equal to the addend, we first complement the magnitude portion of the addend and perform an addition with the augend; then we complement the result and assign it the sign of the addend. The sign and magnitude addition and subtraction procedures are illustrated in Example 1.19.

EXAMPLE 1.19

Given two numbers $A = 5$ and $B = 3$, perform addition on them using sign and magnitude notation in base 2 arithmetic exhausting all sign, augend, and addend permutations.

0.0101 (+5)	0.0101 (+5)	1.0101 (−5)	1.0011 (−3)
0.0011 (+3)	1.0011 (−3)	0.0011 (+3)	0.0101 (+5)

0.1000 (+8)	0101	0101	0011
	+ 1100 (complement)	+ 1100 (complement)	+ 1010 (complement)

	0001	0001	1101
	+ 1 (carry)	+ 1 (carry)	

	0.0010 (+2)	1.0010 (−2)	0.0010 (+2)
			(complement)

1.0101 (−5)	0.0011 (+3)
1.0011 (−3)	1.0101 (−5)

1.1000 (−8)	0011
	+ 1010 (complement)

	1101

	1.0010 (−2) (complement)

One's Complement

A positive number in one's complement notation is represented by its true binary magnitude, preceded by a positive sign bit of zero. A negative number in one's complement notation is represented by its complemented binary magnitude, preceded by a negative sign bit of one. The procedure to add two numbers in one's complement notation is basically to sum the magnitudes and the signs. If an end-around-carry bit occurs during the addition of the signs, it is added to the LSB of the magnitude sum. If the augend and the addend have the same sign, a resulting sum of the opposite sign indicates an *overflow* condition, which means the answer is beyond the capacity of the number of bits used to represent it. By the use of one's complement notation for binary numbers, it is possible to perform subtraction by adding the one's complement representation of the subtrahend to the minuend. This is the equivalent of changing the sign of the subtrahend and adding it to the minuend. Example 1.20 illustrates the addition and subtraction procedures for one's complement operations.

EXAMPLE 1.20	Given two numbers $A = 3$ and $B = 5$, perform binary addition on them in one's complement representation exhausting all sign, augend, and addend permutations.

0.0101 (+5)	0.0101 (+5)	1.1010 (−5)	1.1100 (−3)
0.0011 (+3)	1.1100 (−3)	0.0011 (+3)	0.0101 (+5)

0.1000 (+8)	0.0001	1.1101 (−2)	0.0001
	+ 1 (carry)		+ 1 (carry)

	0.0010 (+2)		0.0010 (+2)

0.0011 (+3)	1.1010 (−5)
1.1010 (−5)	1.1100 (−3)
———	———
1.1101 (−2)	1.0110
	+ 1 (carry)
	———
	1.0111 (−8)

Two's Complement

A positive number in two's complement notation is represented by its true binary magnitude, preceded by a positive sign bit of zero. A negative number in two's complement notation is represented by a negative sign bit of one, preceding the incremented by one complemented magnitude. Adding two numbers in two's complement notation is done by adding the numbers and their sign bits and disregarding any resulting end-around-carry bit. When the augend and the addend have the same sign, a resulting sum of the opposite sign indicates an overflow condition. Using two's complement notation for a binary number, it is possible to perform subtraction by adding the two's complement representation of the subtrahend to the minuend. This equivalence relation is expressed as

$$N_1 + \overline{N}_2 = N_1 + (2^k - N_2) = (N_1 - N_2) + 2^k \tag{1.9}$$

Since the resulting number exceeds the maximum capacity of k bits representation, the sign overflow bit is ignored. Hence, $N_1 + \overline{N}_2 = N_1 - N_2$. Example 1.21 illustrates the binary procedure for performing two's complement operations.

EXAMPLE 1.21 Given two numbers $A = 5$ and $B = 3$, perform binary addition on them in two's complement representation exhausting all sign, augend, and addend permutations.

0.0101 (+5)	0.0101 (+5)	1.1011 (−5)	1.1101 (−3)
0.0011 (+3)	1.1101 (−3)	0.0011 (+3)	0.0101 (+5)
———	———	———	———
0.1000 (+8)	0.0010 (+2)	1.1110 (−2)	0.0010 (+2)

0.0011 (+3)	1.1011 (−5)
1.1011 (−5)	1.1101 (−3)
———	———
1.1110 (−2)	1.1000 (−8)

The use of complement representation for binary numbers reduces binary arithmetic operations to a series of additions and shift operations, thus eliminating the need for subtraction. From the previous discussion, it becomes obvious that two's complement representation is the easiest to implement for addition and subtraction operations, followed by one's complement and then sign and magnitude notations. Fixed-point notation, by its very nature, is limited to integer number arithmetic operations.

1.5 FLOATING-POINT ARITHMETIC

To represent a real binary number in a digital memory medium, it is convenient to use scientific notation. In this notation system, a given number is defined by a fractional value called the *mantissa* and an integer value called the *exponent*. The value of a real number in such a notation is enumerated using the following equation:

$$N = M \times 2^e$$

where

$$0.5 \leq M < 1 \text{ for } +N; \; -0.5 \geq M > -1 \text{ for } -N \tag{1.10}$$

The given number, N, is the product of the normalized mantissa, M, and the binary base, $r = 2$, raised to the power of the exponent, e. A *normalized mantissa* is obtained by adjusting the exponent value to place the mantissa within the ranges in Equation 1.10. For example, $N = 0.10101 \times 2^3 = (0.5 + 0.125 + 0.03125) \times 8 = (5.25)_{10}$. The number of bits used to define the mantissa determines the resolution or precision of the real number. The number of bits defining the exponent determines the range of values that a real number can assume. Single precision and double precision refer to the number of digital words used to store the mantissa, hence the precision of the represented real number. The benefit of such a notation is that both very large and very small numbers can be represented in a compact format. However, arithmetic operations in this notation are more elaborate and require more time to execute than in other notations.

When the value of the exponent becomes too large to be contained within the allowable number of bits, an overflow condition occurs. Conversely, when the value of the exponent becomes too small to allow representation of the number, an underflow condition occurs. A normalized mantissa of one or greater is an *overflow* and a normalized mantissa of less than one-half is an *underflow* condition for a positive real number. Example 1.22 illustrates these concepts using a binary word to represent real numbers.

EXAMPLE 1.22

Given a binary word with seven bits (n) for the exponent and nine bits (m) for the mantissa, define the largest and smallest possible real numbers that can be represented in floating-point format. Also, find the largest and smallest numbers that can be defined using fixed-point notation.

(a) Using floating-point notation

The maximum value for M is defined as $1 - 2^{m-1} = 1 - 2^8 = 0.11111111$.
The maximum value for e is defined as $2^{n-1} - 1 = 2^{7-1} - 1 = 2^6 - 1 = 63$.
Hence, the largest positive number is $N = 0.11111111 \times 2^{63} \approx 2^{63}$, and the smallest definable positive number is $N = 0.10000000 \times 2^{-63} = 2^{-64}$.
The largest negative number is $N = 1.10000000 \times 2^0 = -2^{-1}$, and the smallest definable negative number is $N = 1.11111111 \times 2^{-63}$.

(b) Using fixed-point notation

The maximum value for $N = 2^{15} - 1 = 32,767$.
The minimum value for $N = 2^0 = 1$.

In the example the mantissa range is a signed quantity, as is the exponent range. Hence, the MSB bits are reserved for the sign. The mantissa and the exponent can be presented in any one of the three fixed-point notations discussed in section 1.4. However, two's complement notation facilitates the complex procedures required to perform the arithmetic operations. The absolute value for the greatest mantissa range is, therefore, calculated as $1 - 2^{m-1}$ or $1 - 2^8$, and smallest is simply 2^{-1} or $\frac{1}{2}$. Using scientific notation representation, in base ten, the greatest mantissa range is 0.99999999 and the smallest is 0.1. The maximum exponent value is calculated as $2^{n-1} - 1$ or $2^6 - 1 = 63$, and the minimum value as simply 2^0 or 1.

It should be noted that the range expansion available in floating-point notation results from the basic definition of a given number as $N = M \times 2^e$ where $e = 2^{n-1}$. Consequently, using the same set of bits to define a number in fixed-point notation results in a much smaller range, which is defined as $N = 2^p$ where $p = m + n - 1$. The exponentiation function is relatively easy to implement with simple shift and add operations, since it is the summation of the powers of two.

Floating-Point Calculations

To add or subtract two numbers using floating-point notation, it is necessary to perform an alignment of the exponents so that they are both made equal prior to the operation. This is accomplished by first picking the larger of the two numbers and then shifting the mantissa of the smaller to the right until the exponents are equal, a procedure called *scaling*. Then the result is *normalized*. Given two numbers $P = M_1 \times 2^a$ and $Q = M_2 \times 2^b$, the following equations are used for addition and subtraction operations.

$$P \pm Q = [M_1 \pm M_2 \times 2^{-(a-b)}] \times 2^a \qquad \text{where } a > b \qquad \text{(1.11)}$$
$$P \pm Q = [M_2 \pm M_1 \times 2^{-(b-a)}] \times 2^b \qquad \text{where } b > a \qquad \text{(1.12)}$$

Example 1.23 illustrates floating-point addition and subtraction.

EXAMPLE 1.23 Given $P = 0.1000 \times 10^3$ and $Q = 0.1000 \times 10^2$, find their sum and difference.

$$P + Q = [0.1000 + (0.1000) \times 2^{-(3-2)}] \times 2^3$$
$$P + Q = [0.1000 + (0.0100)] \times 2^3 = 0.1100 \times 2^3$$
$$P - Q = [0.1000 - (0.0100)] \times 2^3 = 0.0100 \times 2^3 = 0.1000 \times 2^2$$

Multiplication in floating-point notation requires no initial alignment of the exponents. A product of two numbers is formed by multiplying the mantissas and adding the exponents.

Given the numbers $P = M \times 2^a$ and $Q = M_2 \times 2^b$, their product is derived by the use of the following equation:

$$P \times Q = [M_1 \times M_2] \times 2^{(a+b)} \qquad (1.13)$$

The resulting product is normalized, and the exponent value is adjusted accordingly.

Division in floating-point notation requires no initial alignment of the exponents. A quotient of two numbers is formed by dividing their mantissas and subtracting their exponents. Given two numbers $P = M_1 \times 2^a$ and $Q = M_2 \times 2^b$, their quotient is defined by the following equation:

$$P \div Q = \left[\frac{M_1}{M_2}\right] \times 2^{(a-b)} \qquad (1.14)$$

Example 1.24 shows floating-point multiplication and division.

EXAMPLE 1.24

Given $P = 0.1000 \times 10^3$ and $Q = 0.1000 \times 10^2$, find their product and quotient.

$$P \times Q = (0.1000)(0.1000) \times 2^{3+2} = 0.01000 \times 2^5 = 0.1000 \times 2^4$$
$$P \div Q = [(0.1000)/(0.1000)] \times 2^{3-2} = 1.0 \times 2^1 = 0.10 \times 2^2$$

A round-off operation may be performed on the results to minimize the effect of truncation due to the finite word length.

1.6 BINARY CODES

A binary code is a unique assignment of one and zero bit combinations that represents a symbol. A symbol may be a numeral, a letter, or a special character representation in a digital format. In general, if a digit can represent n symbols, then k digits result in n^k different arrangements. Similarly, when n symbols are taken r at a time, with order dependence, the number of resulting permutations is defined as $_nP_r = n!/(n - r)!$, where the term $n! = n \times n - 1 \times n - 2 \times \ldots \times 1$. Finally, if n symbols are taken r at a time, independent of ordering, the number of combinations is defined as $_nC_r = {_nP_r}/r!$, where $r!$ is the number of order-independent permutations. Example 1.25 further illustrates these concepts.

EXAMPLE 1.25

Given a three-digit decimal number, calculate the number of total arrangements, the number of permutations, and the number of combinations possible.

$$n = 10 \text{ symbols}, \ k = 3 \text{ digits}, \text{ and } r = 3 \text{ symbols}$$
$$n^k = 10^3 = 10 \times 10 \times 10 = 1,000$$
$$_nP_r = n!/(n - r)! = 10!/(10 - 3)! = 10!/7! = 10 \times 9 \times 8 = 720$$
$$_nC_r = {_nP_r}/r! = 720/r! = 720/(3 \times 2) = 120$$

In the first case, the number 1,000 defines all the possible codes generated by a three-digit decimal number. In the second case, the number 720 defines all the possible permutations generated by a ten-symbol decimal number, taken three symbols at a time. And finally, the number of possible combinations is one hundred and twenty, since there are 3! order-independent permutations.

A geometric representation of an n-bit binary code is possible by defining a given binary digit combination as a point in space. In the case of one bit, two such combinations are possible, thus defining a line. In the case of two bits, four such combinations are possible, and they form a square in a plane. The total number of possible combinations formed by a three-bit code is eight, and they define the vertices of a cube in 3-space. In general, a set of n-bit combinations results in 2^n unique assignments and can be used to define the vertices of a cube in n-space. In addition, the numbers of unique subcubes formed by a k bit code ($k < n$), contained in an n cube, is defined by $s = 2^n/2^k$. The *distance* between two vertices in an n cube is defined as the number of bit positions that they differ by. A distance of one between two vertices forms an edge or a straight line. In general, the distance between two such vertices, representing two code combinations in a set, can be calculated by $d = \Sigma\,(p_i \oplus q_i)$, where $p_i \oplus q_i$ represents addition modulo two, which is addition of the p_i and q_i bits without a carry operation, and where the Σ symbol represents a summation over the two n-bit numbers, P and Q.

Binary-Coded Decimal Code

A binary-coded decimal (BCD) code is convenient for representing decimal numbers in digital memory. In order to represent the ten allowable symbols of each decimal digit, a minimum of four bits is required, since $2^4 = 16$. This results in six unused combinations, which can be used to detect errors in the code. In general, using sixteen combinations, taken ten at a time, it is possible to form $_nC_r = 16!/(16 - 10)!10! = 8008$ different such codes. The four-bit code used to represent a decimal number is the so-called 8421, or natural weighted BCD code, because each bit position corresponds to its natural binary value. The following equation defines the natural weighted BCD code representation of an arbitrary decimal number.

$$N_{BCD} = \sum_{i=0}^{n-1} d_i 10^i \qquad (1.15)$$

where $d_i = 8b_3 + 4b_2 + 2b_1 + 1b_0$

n = the number of decimal digits

The representation of a decimal number in BCD notation is further illustrated in Example 1.26.

EXAMPLE 1.26   Given the three-decimal digit number $N_{10} = (312)_{10}$, find its natural weighted BCD code representation.

$N_{10} = (312)_{10} = (300 + 10 + 2)_{10}$

$N_{10} = (8 \times 0 + 4 \times 0 + 2 \times 1 + 1 \times 1) \times 10^2 + (8 \times 0 + 4 \times 0 + 2 \times 0 + 1 \times 1)$
$\times 10^1 + (8 \times 0 + 4 \times 0 + 2 \times 1 + 1 \times 0) \times 10^0$

$$N_{10} = (3) \times 10^2 + (1) \times 10^1 + (2) \times 10^0$$
$$N_{BCD} = [0011]\,[0001]\,[0010]$$

It is quite possible to perform binary addition using BCD notation in groups of four bits starting with the LSD. However, when a BCD sum exceeds nine, or produces a carry, then the number 6 is added to normalize the result. The resulting carry is added to the next significant digit. Example 1.27 provides a BCD addition operation.

EXAMPLE 1.27

Given two BCD numbers $N = 1001$ and $M = 0101$, find their sum.

$$N + M = 1001 + 0101 = 1110 \text{ (exceeds nine)}$$
$$N + M = 1110 + 0110 \text{ (six)} = [0001]\,[0100]$$

Another interesting four-bit code is the 2421 weighted one. This particular code is referred to as a self-complementing code in that its one's complement expression is equal to the nine's complement of the decimal number it represents. This feature is very attractive in cases in which binary arithmetic is to be performed using BCD notation, eliminating the need for subtraction.

Gray Code

Using Gray code representation for natural binary numbers, also known as a unit distance code, any two consecutive numbers differ by only one bit position. Gray code originated in the encoding of a rotating shaft position. Since the sequence is known in advance, any deviations from it indicates an encoding error condition. A binary number can be converted to its Gray code equivalent by the positional summation of the modulo two additions on the adjacent bits. This process is explained with the following equation:

$$G_n = \sum_{i=0}^{n-1} (B_i \oplus B_{i+1}) \times 2^i \tag{1.16}$$

In the case of $n = 4$, we have the following expressions:

$$G_0 = B_0 \oplus B_1$$
$$G_1 = B_1 \oplus B_2$$
$$G_2 = B_2 \oplus B_3$$
$$G_3 = B_3 \oplus B_4 = B_3$$

By the same token, a given Gray code number can be converted to its natural binary format with the positional summation of the modulo two additions of all the higher order bits, using each bit as a reference. This is explained in the following equation:

$$B_n = \sum_{i=0}^{n-1} B_i \times 2^i \qquad \text{where } B_i = G_i \oplus G_{i+1} \oplus \cdots \oplus G_n \tag{1.17}$$

TABLE 1.4
Binary-coded decimal numbers

Decimal	Binary	Gray	BCD (8421)	BCD (2421)
0	0000	0000	0000 0000	0000 0000
1	0001	0001	0000 0001	0000 0001
2	0010	0011	0000 0010	0000 0010
3	0011	0010	0000 0011	0000 0011
4	0100	0110	0000 0100	0000 0100
5	0101	0111	0000 0101	0000 1011
6	0110	0101	0000 0110	0000 1100
7	0111	0100	0000 0111	0000 1101
8	1000	1100	0000 1000	0000 1110
9	1001	1101	0000 1001	0000 1111
10	1010	1111	0001 0000	0001 0000
11	1011	1110	0001 0001	0001 0001
12	1100	1010	0001 0010	0001 0010
13	1101	1011	0001 0011	0001 0011
14	1110	1001	0001 0100	0001 0100
15	1111	1000	0001 0101	0001 1011

In the case of $n = 4$, we have the following expressions:

$$B_0 = G_0 \oplus G_1 \oplus G_2 \oplus G_3$$
$$B_1 = G_1 \oplus G_2 \oplus G_3$$
$$B_2 = G_2 \oplus G_3$$
$$B_3 = G_3 \oplus G_4 = G_3$$

The calculations above assume that the nonexistent bits of B_4 and G_4 are assigned the value of zero. Table 1.4 contains the various coded representations of decimal numbers, zero through fifteen, for comparison.

Character Codes

To represent alphabetical characters and other printable symbols in a digital memory, it is necessary to use enough bits to cover all possible combinations. There are two popular codes available: the seven-bit American Standard Code for Information Interchange (ASCII) and the eight-bit Extended Binary Coded Decimal Interchange Code (EBCDIC). These codes are referred to as character codes since they have enough combinations, 128 and 256, to represent not only the upper- and lower-case alphabetical characters, but the ten decimal digits as well. In addition, they can represent all the typewriter symbols and other nonprintable symbols used for information interchange protocols. The EBCDIC code was developed by IBM, which is its primary user. The ASCII code was developed by the American National Standards Institute

(ANSI) and is used widely among the digital system industry and its users. Since the ASCII code has only seven bits, it can be stored in one byte, with one spare bit that is often used for parity check.

Parity is used for error detection during information exchange via a noisy medium or channel. That is, if an ASCII code is received with the opposite parity to the one with which it was sent, an error will occur. There are two types of parity, even and odd. *Parity* is derived by the modulo two addition of the bits, with the spare bit assuming a value such that the whole byte has either an even or an odd number of ones. The parity derivation is achieved using the following equation:

$$P(x) = X_7 \oplus X_6 \oplus X_5 \oplus X_4 \oplus X_3 \oplus X_2 \oplus X_1 \oplus X_0 \qquad \textbf{(1.18)}$$

where $P(x) = 0$ for even parity

$P(x) = 1$ for odd parity

X_7 = parity bit

$X_6 \ldots X_0$ the specific ASCII code

For example, if $A = 1000001$ was assigned odd parity, it would become $A = 11000001$. If it was received as $C = 11000011$, an error is probable since the parity is even. Table 1.5 lists all possible ASCII code combinations. These consist of 96 printable characters and 32 control characters.

TABLE 1.5
American Standard Code for Information Interchange (ASCII)

$X_3X_2X_1X_0$	$X_6X_5X_4$							
	000	001	010	011	100	101	110	111
0000	NUL	DLE	SP	0	@	P	`	p
0001	SOH	DC1	!	1	A	Q	a	q
0010	STX	DC2	"	2	B	R	b	r
0011	ETX	DC3	#	3	C	S	c	s
0100	EOT	DC4	$	4	D	T	d	t
0101	ENQ	NAK	%	5	E	U	e	u
0110	ACK	SYN	&	6	F	V	f	v
0111	BEL	ETB	'	7	G	W	g	w
1000	BS	CAN	(	8	H	X	h	x
1001	HT	EM	)	9	I	Y	i	y
1010	LF	SUB	*	:	J	Z	j	z
1011	VT	ESC	+	;	K	[	k	{
1100	FF	FX	,	<	L	\	l	|
1101	CR	GS	–	=	M	]	m	}
1110	SO	RS	.	>	N	^	n	~
1111	SI	US	/	?	O	—	o	DEL

1.7 BOOLEAN ALGEBRA

Boolean algebra is the language of digital systems. It was first defined by the English mathematician George Boole (1815–1864). In *Boolean algebra* the variables can only assume one of two values. These values are designated as true and false or one and zero. The algebra is developed from a set of postulates based on a set of elementary ideas with arbitrary conditions. Using the postulates as a basis, a set of algebraic properties is derived and the fundamental theorems of Boolean algebra are generated to form a working set of rules.

Boolean algebra can be represented in at least three different forms: the algebra of sets, the algebra of logic, and switching algebra. The algebra of sets is defined for a set S of E elements belonging to that set and forms the basis of theoretical discussions. The algebra of logic is defined using propositions and forms the basis of algorithm design. Switching algebra is defined using the binary state of a switching variable and forms the basis of digital systems analysis and synthesis. The following discussion elaborates on these concepts.

Fundamental Definitions

A *set* is a collection of objects, called elements, which makes up that set. Specific symbols are used to define relations between the elements of the set. The equals sign (=) defines that two elements A and B in the set are identical. The *union* (+) operation on two elements A and B is defined as their logical summation. The *intersection* (·) operation on two elements A and B is defined as the logical product of the two elements. Finally, the *complement* (‾) of an element A is defined as that which does not belong to A and is written as $\overline{A}$. The following definition $A + \overline{A} = 1$ is called the *universe* element and consists of all elements in the set. The complement of the previous definition, or $(A + \overline{A}) = 0$, is called the *empty* or *null* element, and it means that no elements are in that set. These concepts are better illustrated by the use of Venn diagrams. A *Venn diagram* is a square box depicting a set of elements. An element in the set is represented by a circle area inside the square. A shaded area inside the Venn diagram represents element relationships in a given set. Figure 1.1 presents Boolean algebra definitions using Venn diagrams.

Propositional logic is defined using expressions consisting of true or false statements. The following terminology is used to define relations between logical statements. The equals sign defines that two logical statements are identical. The OR operation on two logical statements A and B is defined as an expression that becomes true when either A, B, or both statements are true. The AND operation on two logical statements A and B is defined as an expression that becomes true

a) A b) $A + B$ c) $A \cdot B$ d) $A + \overline{A}$ e) $\overline{A + \overline{A}}$

FIGURE 1.1
Boolean algebra definitions.

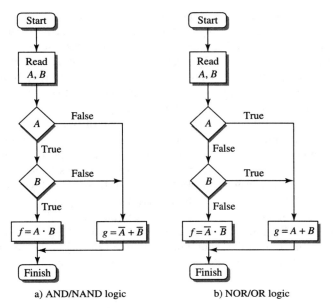

a) AND/NAND logic   b) NOR/OR logic

FIGURE 1.2
Flowchart definitions of logical expressions.

only when A and B are both true. The complement or ($\overline{}$) operation on a logical statement A is defined as that which is opposite of A or $\overline{A}$. Thus, if A is true, then $\overline{A}$ is false, and vice-versa. A *flowchart* is a graphically depicted sequence of steps used to define an algorithmic solution to a problem. It consists of geometrical shapes representing the various operations required in each step. Figure 1.2 illustrates how the above propositional logic definitions are used to define a flowchart solution. Figure 1.2a takes the two logical statements, A and B, and examines their values. If both are true, the AND function is produced; otherwise the NAND complement function is produced. Similarly, Figure 1.2b examines the two statements, and if either one is true, the OR function is produced; otherwise the NOR complement function is produced.

    Switching variables are defined as having two states, the true and the false. These states can represent a myriad of physical events. The OFF or ON condition of a switch and the presence or absence of a signal are the primary true and false events used in actual digital systems. The digits 0 and 1 are used to symbolize the two states of a switching variable. These variables are used to describe logic circuits that form the basis of digital systems. The equals sign defines that two switching variables A and B are identical. The OR operation on two switching variables A and B is defined as a one if either A, B, or both are one, and defined as zero otherwise. The AND operation on two switching variables A and B is defined as a one if both A and B are one, and zero if this condition is not met.

    The complement or NOT operation on a switching variable A is defined as $\overline{A}$. The result is zero if A is one, and one if A is a zero. These operations can be performed on more than two variables at a time. Hence, a systematic procedure can be used to tabulate all the possible variable combinations and their corresponding values, yielding a *truth table*. For a given number of n switching variables a truth table of 2^n rows is generated.

Another interesting concept is that of the positive and negative logic conventions. If the true state is represented by a binary one and the false state is represented by a binary zero, then the *positive logic* convention is used. If however, the true state is represented by a binary zero and the false state by a binary one, then the *negative logic* convention is used. The choice of different logic conventions for the same set of conditions results in different truth tables. Table 1.6 presents these concepts, and it can be observed that a positive logic OR operation corresponds to a negative logic AND operation, and vice-versa.

The circuit realization of these operations can take one of two forms, either solid state switch- or logic gate-based. Figure 1.3 illustrates the two possible realizations of the truth tables in Table 1.6 using positive and negative logic conventions. The positive logic convention defines an open switch condition as logic zero and a closed switch as logic one. The negative logic convention defines the exact opposite. In Figure 1.3a the positive logic is implemented, using normally open switches. In Figure 1.3b negative logic is implemented, using normally closed switches. Figures 1.3c and 1.3d use logic gate symbols, for positive and negative logic, respectively, to define the circuit realizations. A *gate* is a two-valued logic device that provides an output of 1 or 0 as a function of the input binary variable values. For the positive logic convention, *false* is defined as logic zero and *true* as logic one. The opposite holds for the negative logic convention.

Switching Algebra Rules

Thus far we have defined four symbols used with switching variables, the equals sign, the OR operator, the AND operator, and the complement operator. Using these symbols, a set of primitive functions or rules can be defined on one or more switching variables.

$$X = f(A, B)$$
$$X_1 = \overline{A}(\text{COMPLEMENT, NOT, INVERT})$$
$$X_2 = A + B(\text{OR})$$
$$X_3 = A \cdot B(\text{AND})$$

TABLE 1.6
Positive and negative logic truth tables

Positive Logic				Negative Logic			
ABC	NOT	OR	AND	ABC	NOT	AND	OR
000	1	0	0	111	0	1	1
001	1	1	0	110	0	0	1
010	1	1	0	101	0	0	1
011	1	1	0	100	0	0	1
100	0	1	0	011	1	0	1
101	0	1	0	010	1	0	1
110	0	1	0	001	1	0	1
111	0	1	1	000	1	0	0

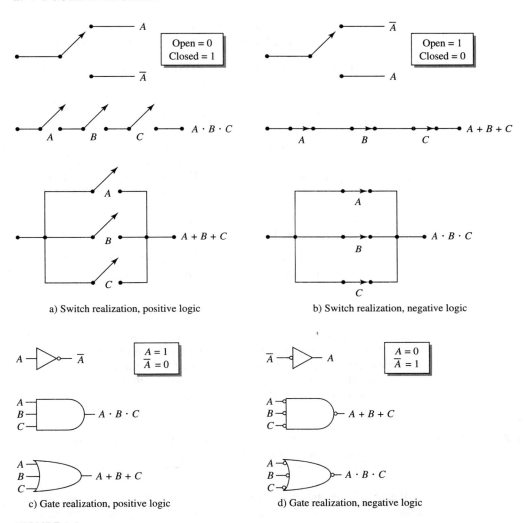

FIGURE 1.3
Circuit realization of switching variable operations.

The rules of precedence in switching algebra are the same as those in ordinary algebra. Parentheses have the highest priority, followed by the AND or binary product operation, followed by the OR or binary sum operation. Similarly, the basic properties of ordinary algebraic expressions apply to switching algebra as well.

1. $A \cdot B = B \cdot A$ and $A + B = B + A$ (commutative)
2. $A \cdot (B \cdot C) = (A \cdot B) \cdot C$ and $A + (B + C) = (A + B) + C$ (associative)
3. $A \cdot (B + C) = (A \cdot B) + (A \cdot C)$ and $A + (B \cdot C) = (A + B) \cdot (A + C)$ (distributive)

The following set of postulates represents a set of independent conditions imposed upon the fundamental definitions and forms the basis of the elementary theorems of switching algebra:

1. $A = 1$ if $A \neq 0$ 2. $A = 0$ if $\bar{A} = 1$ 3. $0 + 0 = 0$
   $A = 0$ if $A \neq 1$ $A = 1$ if $\bar{A} = 0$ $0 \cdot 0 = 0$
4. $1 + 1 = 1$ 5. $0 + 1 = 1$ 6. $\bar{0} = 1$
   $1 \cdot 1 = 1$ $0 \cdot 1 = 0$ $\bar{1} = 0$

Using the set of postulates shown above, the elementary theorems of switching algebra are deduced. Shown below, these theorems form a set of working rules that can be applied to switching functions and logical expressions. The symbols 1 and 0 refer to the universe and null elements, respectively, and the literals define the switching variables.

1. $A + 0 = A$ 2. $A + 1 = 1$ 3. $A + A = A$ 4. $A + \bar{A} = 1$
   $A \cdot 0 = 0$ $A \cdot 1 = A$ $A \cdot A = A$ $A \cdot \bar{A} = 0$

5. $(\overline{\bar{A}}) = \bar{A}$ 6. $A \cdot (A + B) = A$ 7. $(\overline{A + B}) = \bar{A} \cdot \bar{B}$ 8. $AB + \bar{A}C + BC$
   $(\overline{\bar{A}}) = A$ $A + (A \cdot B) = A$ $(\overline{A \cdot B}) = \bar{A} + \bar{B}$ $= AB + \bar{A}C (A + B)$
                                                                                                $\cdot (\bar{A} + C) \cdot (B + C)$
                                                                                                $= (A + B) \cdot (\bar{A} + C)$

These elementary theorems can be proven by the use of either a Venn diagram or perfect induction, which uses a truth table to verify both sides of the equals sign. The primary uses of the theorems are to prove switching algebra identities and to simplify expressions involving switching variable functions. Example 1.28 uses the method of perfect induction to prove Theorem 7, by comparing all possible variable combinations.

EXAMPLE 1.28

Prove Theorem 7 using the method of perfect induction. By exhaustive comparison of the corresponding truth tables (Table 1.7), it can be seen that Theorem 7 is valid.

If each OR operator in an expression is replaced by the AND operator, and AND by OR, then the resulting expression becomes the *dual* of the original. In addition, if the original expression or theorem is true, then the dual becomes true as well. A related concept is that of complementation of an expression. This concept is an extension of duality and is defined in

TABLE 1.7
Proof of Theorem 7

AB	$A + B$	$\overline{A + B}$	$\bar{A} \cdot \bar{B}$	$A \cdot B$	$\overline{A \cdot B}$	$\bar{A} + \bar{B}$
00	0	1	1	0	1	1
01	1	0	0	0	1	1
10	1	0	0	0	1	1
11	1	0	0	1	0	0

TABLE 1.8
Three variable function definitions

Logic	Positive	Dual	Complement	Negative	
Function	AND	OR	NAND	OR	
ABC	f_p	f_d	f_c	ABC	f_n
000	0	0	1	111	1
001	0	1	1	110	1
010	0	1	1	101	1
011	0	1	1	100	1
100	0	1	1	011	1
101	0	1	1	010	1
110	0	1	1	001	1
111	1	1	0	000	0

Theorem 7, better known as *De Morgan's theorem*. Given an expression, we can derive its *complement expression* by first replacing each OR operator by the AND operator (and AND by OR) and then replacing each switching variable by its complement form. These concepts are brought together in Table 1.8, where a positive logic convention switching function $f(A, B, C)$ is used to define its dual, complement, and negative logic convention equivalent forms.

The basic three-variable, positive convention, switching function is defined as $f_p(A, B, C) = A \cdot B \cdot C$, or the AND function. To derive its dual, the AND operators are changed to OR operators. Hence, the dual becomes $f_d(A, B, C) = A + B + C$, or the OR function. The complement function of the basic function $f_p(A, B, C)$ is derived by first changing the AND operators to OR operators and then complementing the switching variables. Thus, $f_c(A, B, C) = \overline{A \cdot B \cdot C} = \overline{A} + \overline{B} + \overline{C}$, by the application of De Morgan's Theorem, and the resulting function is called the NAND function. An alternative method for deriving the complement of a function is to invert the values of the output function as listed in the truth table. Finally, using the negative logic convention, $f_n(A, B, C) = \overline{\overline{A} \cdot \overline{B} \cdot \overline{C}} = A + B + C$, the positive AND becomes a negative OR function.

Switching Function Representation

A switching function of two or more switching variables is defined as a set of rules that assigns one or zero values to the resulting variable combinations. In general, given n variables, the number of unique variable combinations becomes $N = 2^n$. Given a truth table representation of N variable combinations, the reasoning above can be applied twice to show that there are $M = 2^N$ possible ways of assigning one or zero values to N combinations that define a function. For example, given two switching variables, there are $N = 2^2 = 4$ possible combinations. This results in $M = 2^4$, or sixteen definable functions. These functions are illustrated in Figure 1.4, where the basic logic equation is given along with a Venn diagram representation, a truth table definition, and its basic logic symbol. A *logic symbol* shows the input and output variable topology of a given logic function.

For $n = 3$ we have a total of 2^8 or 256 possible functions available. Listing all such functions is quite a task. In addition, as n increases, the function complexity becomes difficult to

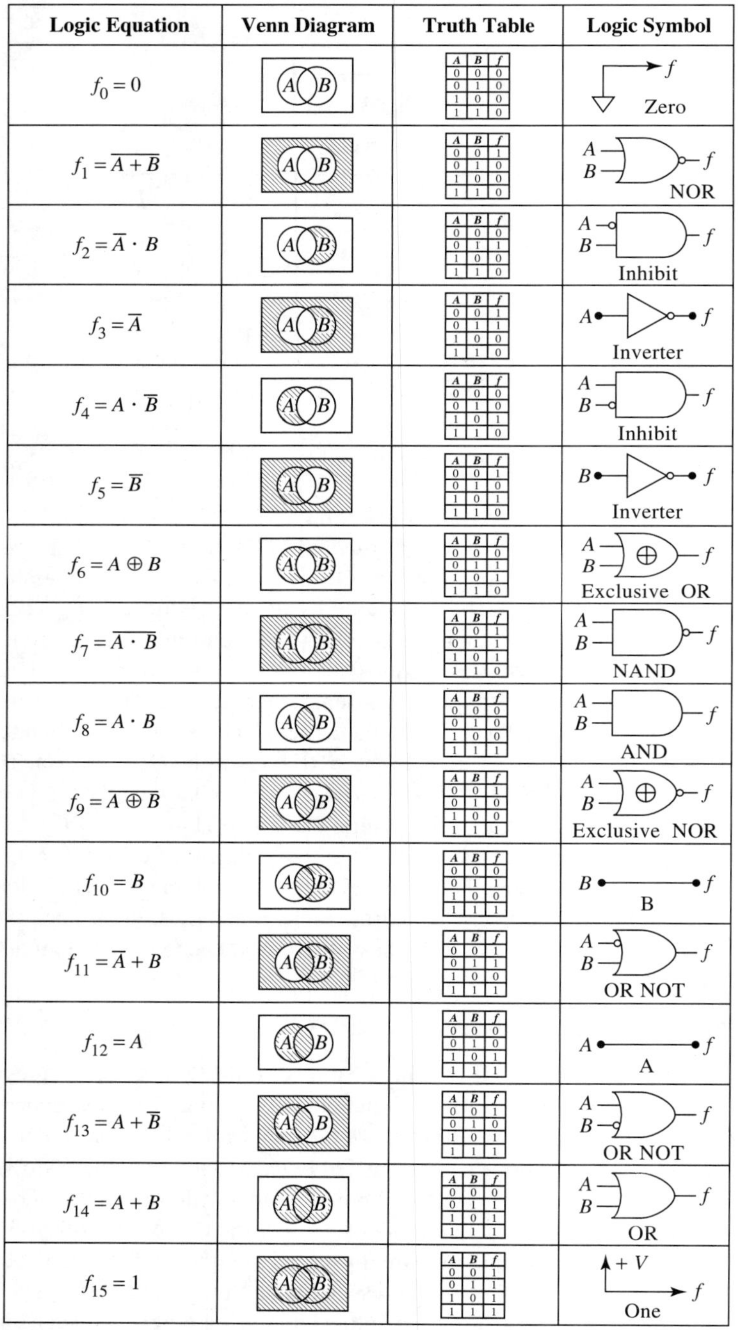

Logic Equation	Venn Diagram	Truth Table	Logic Symbol
$f_0 = 0$		$A\,B\,f$: 0 0 0 / 0 1 0 / 1 0 0 / 1 1 0	Zero
$f_1 = \overline{A + B}$		$A\,B\,f$: 0 0 1 / 0 1 0 / 1 0 0 / 1 1 0	NOR
$f_2 = \overline{A} \cdot B$		$A\,B\,f$: 0 0 0 / 0 1 1 / 1 0 0 / 1 1 0	Inhibit
$f_3 = \overline{A}$		$A\,B\,f$: 0 0 1 / 0 1 1 / 1 0 0 / 1 1 0	Inverter
$f_4 = A \cdot \overline{B}$		$A\,B\,f$: 0 0 0 / 0 1 0 / 1 0 1 / 1 1 0	Inhibit
$f_5 = \overline{B}$		$A\,B\,f$: 0 0 1 / 0 1 0 / 1 0 1 / 1 1 0	Inverter
$f_6 = A \oplus B$		$A\,B\,f$: 0 0 0 / 0 1 1 / 1 0 1 / 1 1 0	Exclusive OR
$f_7 = \overline{A \cdot B}$		$A\,B\,f$: 0 0 1 / 0 1 1 / 1 0 1 / 1 1 0	NAND
$f_8 = A \cdot B$		$A\,B\,f$: 0 0 0 / 0 1 0 / 1 0 0 / 1 1 1	AND
$f_9 = \overline{A \oplus B}$		$A\,B\,f$: 0 0 1 / 0 1 0 / 1 0 0 / 1 1 1	Exclusive NOR
$f_{10} = B$		$A\,B\,f$: 0 0 0 / 0 1 1 / 1 0 0 / 1 1 1	B
$f_{11} = \overline{A} + B$		$A\,B\,f$: 0 0 1 / 0 1 1 / 1 0 0 / 1 1 1	OR NOT
$f_{12} = A$		$A\,B\,f$: 0 0 0 / 0 1 0 / 1 0 1 / 1 1 1	A
$f_{13} = A + \overline{B}$		$A\,B\,f$: 0 0 1 / 0 1 0 / 1 0 1 / 1 1 1	OR NOT
$f_{14} = A + B$		$A\,B\,f$: 0 0 0 / 0 1 1 / 1 0 1 / 1 1 1	OR
$f_{15} = 1$		$A\,B\,f$: 0 0 1 / 0 1 1 / 1 0 1 / 1 1 1	One

FIGURE 1.4

Sixteen functions of two binary variables.

handle. However, the elementary functions of two variables serve as the building blocks for developing generalized n-input variable logic symbols to represent an arbitrary n switching variable function.

Thus far the switching functions have been defined using the summation of products method. Each product consists of all n switching variables, which occur only once in either their true or complemented states. The products are called *minterms,* and each such product defines a unique combination of n variables in the truth table. Such a function notation is called a *sum-of-products* (SOP) representation of a switching function. The rule for forming each minterm is to represent a one value in the truth table with the true form of the corresponding variable and a zero value in the truth table with the complemented form of the corresponding variable.

Another way of defining switching functions uses the product of summations method. Each sum or factor consists of all n switching variables, which occur only once in either their true or their complemented state. These sums are called *maxterms,* and each such sum defines a unique combination of n variables in the truth table. Such a function notation is called a *product-of-sums* (POS) representation of a switching function. The rule for forming each maxterm is to represent a one value in the truth table with the complemented form of the corresponding variable and a zero value in the truth table with the true form of the corresponding variable. Example 1.29 illustrates the SOP and POS function definition methods.

EXAMPLE 1.29

Given the two functions $f_1(A, B) = A \cdot B$ and $g_2(A, B) = A + B$, define their POS and SOP forms, respectively.

$f_1(A, B) = A \cdot B$ is given as a single SOP expression

$g_1(A, B) = (A + B) \cdot (A + \overline{B}) \cdot (\overline{A} + B)$ becomes the POS expression

$g_2(A, B) = A + B$ is given as a single POS expression

$f_2(A, B) = (\overline{A} \cdot B) + (A \cdot \overline{B}) + (A \cdot B)$ becomes the SOP expression

TABLE 1.9
Truth table for Example 1.29

AB	AND	OR
00	0	0
01	0	1
10	0	1
11	1	1

Therefore, it is possible to express a switching function in two different forms, known as the *SOP canonical form* and the *POS canonical form,* consisting of either minterm or maxterm expressions, respectively. The resulting expression of a function definition has a direct relation to realization complexity, size, and cost associated with the physical circuit implementation. In general, a switching function of n variables has 2^n possible minterms and maxterms, which correspond to the unique combinations of the associated truth table tabulation. In the case of three switching variables, there are eight possible minterms and eight possible maxterms, and they are defined in Table 1.10.

TABLE 1.10
Canonical forms of a three-variable function

	SOP Definition			*POS Definition*	
#	ABC	Minterm	#	ABC	Maxterm
0	000	$m_0 = \overline{A} \cdot \overline{B} \cdot \overline{C}$	0	000	$M_0 = A + B + C$
1	001	$m_1 = \overline{A} \cdot \overline{B} \cdot C$	1	001	$M_1 = A + B + \overline{C}$
2	010	$m_2 = \overline{A} \cdot B \cdot \overline{C}$	2	010	$M_2 = A + \overline{B} + C$
3	011	$m_3 = \overline{A} \cdot B \cdot C$	3	011	$M_3 = A + \overline{B} + \overline{C}$
4	100	$m_4 = A \cdot \overline{B} \cdot \overline{C}$	4	100	$M_4 = \overline{A} + B + C$
5	101	$m_5 = A \cdot \overline{B} \cdot C$	5	101	$M_5 = \overline{A} + B + \overline{C}$
6	110	$m_6 = A \cdot B \cdot \overline{C}$	6	110	$M_6 = \overline{A} + \overline{B} + C$
7	111	$m_7 = A \cdot B \cdot C$	7	111	$M_7 = \overline{A} + \overline{B} + \overline{C}$

It is also possible to represent a resulting truth table of n variable combinations in a graphical format, known as the Karnaugh map, which is easier to visualize and interpret than the Venn diagram. A *Karnaugh map* is a diagram that contains 2^n square cells, which represent all the possible combinations of n switching variables. An arbitrary function of n switching variables can be defined and mapped using a one-to-one correspondence between the variable combinations, which define the minterms or maxterms, and the associated cells in the Karnaugh map. The diagram is Gray code assignment, and the map is thought to be a two-dimensional mapping of a toroidal surface. In other words, the adjacency principle extends past the edges of the map so that the top and bottom row cells and the left and right column cells form corresponding adjacencies. The principal use of the map is to perform switching function minimization using the distributive property and Theorem 4 repeatedly. The minterm AND operators ($\cdot$) may be omitted for clarity.

For instance, if a function is defined on the map as $f(A, B, C) = ABC + AB\overline{C}$, then by definition it is mapped in two adjacent cells on the Karnaugh map and using the distributive property, $f(A, B, C) = AB(C + \overline{C})$. Consequently, applying Theorem 4, $f(A, B, C) = AB(1) = AB$. Similarly, if a function is defined on the map as $g(A, B, C) = (\overline{A} + \overline{B} + \overline{C}) \cdot (\overline{A} + \overline{B} + C)$, then using the distributive property, $g(A, B, C) = (\overline{A} + \overline{B}) + (C \cdot \overline{C})$. By applying Theorem 4, $g(A, B, C) = (\overline{A} + \overline{B}) + (0) = (\overline{A} + \overline{B})$. Given an n variable function, m variables can be eliminated from each minterm (or maxterm) for every 2^m adjacencies formed in the Karnaugh map, where m is less than n. Figure 1.5 illustrates Karnaugh map definitions for one, two, three, and four switching variables.

The literal expression in each cell defines the represented minterm, and the integer subscript is its decimal equivalent number. A *literal* is a switching variable instance of either its true or its complemented state. The SOP canonical form, used to represent an arbitrary function of n switching variables, can be expressed in the following closed form equation:

$$f(\text{SOP}) = \sum_{i=0}^{2^n-1} m_i \tag{1.19}$$

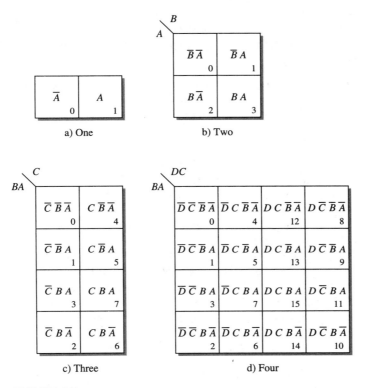

FIGURE 1.5
Karnaugh map definitions for switching variables.

where each possible m_i minterm assigns a value of one to f(SOP), and the i index becomes its decimal equivalent number. Similarly, the POS canonical form, used to represent an arbitrary function of n switching variables, can be expressed in the following closed form equation:

$$g(POS) = \prod_{i=0}^{2^n-1} M_i \tag{1.20}$$

where each possible M_i maxterm assigns a value of zero to g(POS), and the i index becomes its decimal equivalent number. It can be deduced from these equations that a function expressed in SOP form cannot have more than $2^n - 1$ minterms; otherwise, it is defined for all possible combinations and it becomes a trivial function. Likewise, a function expressed in POS form cannot have more than $2^n - 1$ maxterms, or it is defined for all possible combinations and becomes a trivial function. In addition, the logical sum of a function f and its complement $\bar{f}$ equals one ($f + \bar{f} = 1$). Also, the logical product of a function g and its complement $\bar{g}$ equals zero ($g \cdot \bar{g} = 0$). Usually the SOP form is used to define a function f on a Karnaugh map. However, the POS form can also be used to define a function, either directly or by defining the complement of f and then using De Morgan's theorem to derive g. The concepts above are elaborated in Example 1.30.

EXAMPLE 1.30

Given the function $f(C, B, A) = m_2 + m_4 + m_6$, find its complement $\bar{f}(C, B, A)$ and define $g(C, B, A)$ and $\bar{g}(C, B, A)$ using the Karnaugh map in Figure 1.5c. Then minimize the functions.

From Figure 1.6a we get

$$f(C, B, A) = m_2 + m_4 + m_6, \text{ and } g(C, B, A) = M_0 \cdot M_1 \cdot M_3 \cdot M_5 \cdot M_7$$

Similarly, from Figure 1.6b we get

$$\bar{f}(C, B, A) = m_0 + m_1 + m_3 + m_5 + m_7, \text{ and } \bar{g}(C, B, A) = M_2 \cdot M_4 \cdot M_6$$

1. $f(C, B, A) = m_2 + m_4 + m_6 = (\overline{C}B\overline{A}) + (C\overline{B}\overline{A}) + (CB\overline{A})$
   $= (m_2 + m_6) + (m_4 + m_6) = B\overline{A} + C\overline{A}$
2. $\bar{f}(C, B, A) = m_0 + m_1 + m_3 + m_5 + m_7 = (\overline{C}\,\overline{B}\overline{A}) + (\overline{C}\,\overline{B}A) + (\overline{C}BA) + (C\overline{B}A)$
   $+ (CBA)$
   $= (m_1 + m_3 + m_5 + m_7) + (m_0 + m_1) = A + \overline{C}\,\overline{B}$
3. $g(C, B, A) = M_0 \cdot M_1 \cdot M_3 \cdot M_5 \cdot M_7$
   $= (C + B + A) \cdot (C + B + \overline{A}) \cdot (C + \overline{B} + \overline{A}) \cdot (\overline{C} + B + \overline{A}) \cdot (\overline{C} + \overline{B} + \overline{A})$
   $= (M_1 \cdot M_3 \cdot M_5 \cdot M_7) \cdot (M_0 \cdot M_1) = \overline{A}(C + B)$

Also, $g(C, B, A) = (\overline{\bar{f}(C, B, A)}) = \overline{A}(C + B)$ using De Morgan's Theorem.

4. $\bar{g}(C, B, A) = M_2 \cdot M_4 \cdot M_6 = (C + \overline{B} + A) \cdot (\overline{C} + B + A) \cdot (\overline{C} + \overline{B} + A)$
   $= (M_2 \cdot M_6) \cdot (M_4 \cdot M_6) = (\overline{B} + A) \cdot (\overline{C} + A)$

Also,

$$\bar{g}(C, B, A) = \overline{f(C, B, A)} = (\overline{B} + A) \cdot (\overline{C} + A)$$

using De Morgan's theorem.

From the preceding example, it becomes apparent that $f + \bar{f} = 1$ and $g \cdot \bar{g} = 0$. Also, it should be noted that by using De Morgan's theorem it is possible to reduce the effort required to minimize these functions. It was also shown that $g(C, B, A) = \overline{\bar{f}(C, B, A)}$ and $\bar{g}(C, B, A) = \overline{f(C, B, A)}$, where $f(C, B, A)$ is the SOP form and $g(C, B, A)$ is the POS form definition of the given switching function. Therefore, a given canonical form function can be minimized and expressed in *standard form*. This subset, standard form, may not contain every minterm or maxterm. In addition, each reduced minterm or maxterm may not include every variable. The reduced minterms are called *P-terms* and the reduced maxterms are called *S-terms*.

Switching Function Realization

The most common realization of an arbitrary switching function is in terms of logic gates. The mapping of a function into physical gate devices is referred to as *realization*. When the function is expressed in its canonical form, then the number of gates required is directly proportional to the number of terms. Similarly, the number of inputs per gate is directly proportional to the number of literals per term. When minimization is performed on the canonical form expression of an arbitrary function, it becomes possible to eliminate terms and literals, as shown in Exam-

0	1
0	4
0	0
1	5
0	0
3	7
1	1
2	6

1	0
0	4
1	1
1	5
1	1
3	7
0	0
2	6

a) Map for f and g b) Map for $\bar{f}$ and $\bar{g}$

FIGURE 1.6
Karnaugh maps for Example 1.30.

ple 1.30, thus reducing the complexity of the resulting logic gate realization. It is possible to use a set of gates to realize any arbitrary function of n variables. Such a set of gates is called *functionally complete*. The elementary set of operators AND, OR, and NOT forms a functionally complete set, since switching algebra is based on these elementary operations. Realization of canonical form expressions of a function results in a two-level gate network. The SOP standard form is defined as the sum of products; hence the P-terms are realized using AND gates with their outputs feeding into an OR gate. Conversely, the POS standard form is defined as the product of sums; hence the S-terms are realized using OR gates with their outputs feeding into an AND gate. Example 1.31 depicts these concepts.

EXAMPLE 1.31 Given $f(A, B) = \bar{A}B + A\bar{B}$ and $g(A, B) = (A + \bar{B}) \cdot (\bar{A} + B)$, realize the functions using AND, OR, and NOT gates.

Figure 1.7a shows the realization of $f(A, B) = \bar{A}B + A\bar{B}$. This function is realized using two AND gates, one for each P-term, followed by an OR gate to form the sum. The NOT, or inverter, gates are needed to provide the complements of A and B variables. Figure 1.7b shows the realization of $g(A, B) = (A + \bar{B}) \cdot (\bar{A} + B)$. This function is realized using two OR gates, one for each S-term, followed by an AND gate to form the product. Also, the two NOT gates are needed to provide

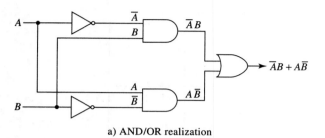

a) AND/OR realization

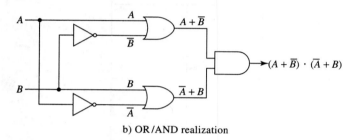

b) OR/AND realization

FIGURE 1.7
Function realization for Example 1.31.

the complement of A and B variables. It should be noted that a true two-level gate network can be obtained only if the variables A and B are available in both their true and complemented forms.

The ideal realization process is to use a single gate type to implement the canonical form switching function expression. Two such functionally complete gates exist: the NAND gate, which implements the relationship $f(A, B) = \overline{A \cdot B}$, and the NOR gate, which implements the relationship $g(A, B) = \overline{A + B}$. The NAND gate can be proven functionally complete if it can be shown that it can realize the three elementary operations AND, OR, and NOT. First, by applying Theorems 3 and 5 and letting $A = B$, we get

$$f(A, B) = \overline{A \cdot B}$$
$$f(A, A) = \overline{A \cdot A} = \overline{A}$$
$$f(B, B) = \overline{B \cdot B} = \overline{B}$$

Second, by the relationship above and Theorems 5 and 7, we get

$$f(A, B) = \overline{A \cdot B}$$
$$f(A, B) = \overline{((\overline{A \cdot A}) \cdot (\overline{B \cdot B}))} = \overline{((\overline{A}) \cdot (\overline{B}))} = A + B$$

Finally, by the function and Theorems 3 and 7, we get

$$f(A, B) = \overline{A \cdot B}$$
$$f(A, B) = \overline{((\overline{A \cdot B}) \cdot (\overline{A \cdot B}))} = (A \cdot B) + (A \cdot B) = A \cdot B$$

The NOR gate can be proven functionally complete if it can be shown that it can realize the three elementary operations AND, OR, and NOT. First, by applying Theorems 3 and 5 and letting $A = B$, we get

$$g(A, B) = \overline{A + B}$$
$$g(A, A) = \overline{(A + A)} = \overline{A}$$
$$g(B, B) = \overline{(B + B)} = \overline{B}$$

Second, by the relationship above and Theorems 5 and 7, we get

$$g(A, B) = \overline{A + B}$$
$$g(A, B) = \overline{((\overline{A + B}) + (\overline{A + B}))} = (A + B) \cdot (A + B) = A + B$$

Finally, by the function and Theorems 3 and 7, we get

$$g(A, B) = \overline{A + B}$$
$$g(A, B) = \overline{((\overline{A + A}) + (\overline{B + B}))} = \overline{((\overline{A}) + (\overline{B}))} = A \cdot B$$

Example 1.32 illustrates the use of NAND and NOR gates for realization of canonical form switching functions.

EXAMPLE 1.32

Given $f(A, B) = \overline{A}B + A\overline{B}$ and $g(A, B) = (A + \overline{B}) \cdot (\overline{A} + B)$, realize the functions using NAND and NOR gates.

From Figure 1.8a we get $f = \overline{((\overline{A} \cdot B) \cdot (A \cdot \overline{B}))}$, and using Theorem 7 twice it becomes $f = \overline{(A + \overline{B}) \cdot (\overline{A} + B)} = (\overline{A} \cdot B) + (A \cdot \overline{B})$. Similarly, from Figure 1.8b we get $g = \overline{((\overline{A + \overline{B}}) + (\overline{\overline{A} + B}))}$, and by applying Theorem 7 twice it becomes $g = \overline{((\overline{A} \cdot B) + (A \cdot \overline{B}))} = (A + \overline{B}) \cdot (\overline{A} + B)$. The NAND gate implementation results in an SOP canonical form. Using the NOR gate implementation results in a POS canonical form. Again it should be noted that if the true and complemented forms of the switching variables are available then the realization becomes a true two-level gate network. It is interesting to note that the realized functions in Example 1.32 are better known as exclusive OR and NOR, respectively, for $f(A, B) = A \oplus B = (\overline{A} \cdot B) + (A \cdot \overline{B})$, and $g(A, B) = \overline{A \oplus B} = (A + \overline{B}) \cdot (\overline{A} + B) = (\overline{A} \cdot \overline{B}) + (A \cdot B)$ using the distributive property and Theorem 4. As it turns out, $f(A, B)$ and $g(A, B)$ are both complements and duals of each other. The exclusive OR function is rather versatile because of its unique properties, and it is widely used in digital systems. Its two most often used properties are $A \oplus 1 = \overline{A}$, $A \oplus 0 = A$ and $f(A, A \oplus B) = B$. Using the first property variable, complementation is achieved, and using the second, it is possible to derive one of the variables from the generated function.

It is also possible to realize functions with a greater than two-level gate network. Such an implementation results in a mix of gate types, and performance will be reduced. The finite amount of time it takes an input variable change to appear at the gate's output is called *propagation delay, t_p*. The cumulative delay, over several gate levels, limits the maximum network operating speed.

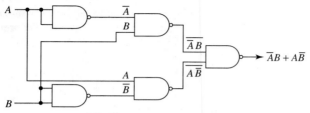

a) NAND/NAND realization

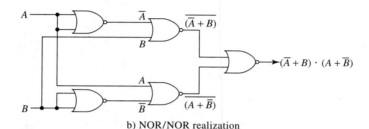

b) NOR/NOR realization

FIGURE 1.8
Function realization for Example 1.32.

PROBLEMS

1.1 Convert the binary integers $A = 11001011$ and $B = 00110100$ to their decimal equivalents.

1.2 Convert the binary fractions $A = 0.11001011$ and $B = 0.00110100$ to their decimal equivalents.

1.3 Convert the decimal numbers $A = 250$ and $B = 355$ to their binary equivalents.

1.4 Convert the decimal fractions $A = 0.250$ and $B = 0.355$ to their binary equivalents.

1.5 Convert the binary numbers $A = 10100110$ and $B = 01011001$ to their octal equivalents.

1.6 Convert the binary numbers $A = 10100110$ and $B = 01011001$ to their hexadecimal equivalents.

1.7 Convert the octal numbers $A = 127$ and $B = 255$ to their binary equivalents.

1.8 Convert the hexadecimal numbers $A = A2B$ and $B = 3CD$ to their binary equivalents.

1.9 Convert the decimal numbers $A = 1234$ and $B = 4321$ to their octal equivalents.

1.10 Convert the decimal numbers $A = 1234$ and $B = 4321$ to their hexadecimal equivalents.

1.11 Convert the octal numbers $A = 1234$ and $B = 4321$ to their decimal equivalents.

1.12 Convert the hexadecimal numbers $A = 1234$ and $B = 4321$ to their decimal equivalents.

1.13 Given two binary numbers $A = 01111000$ and $B = 00101000$, find their sum $A + B$ and their difference $A - B$.

1.14 Given two binary numbers $A = 01111000$ and $B = 00101000$, find their product $A \times B$.

1.15 Given two binary numbers $A = 01111000$ and $B = 00101000$, find their ratio $A \div B$.

1.16 Given two binary numbers $A = 01111000$ and $B = 00101000$, find their one's and two's complements.

1.17 Given two decimal numbers $A = 48$ and $B = 13$, convert to binary numbers and find their difference $A - B$ using two's complement arithmetic.

1.18 Given $f(A, B, C) = m_0 + m_3 + m_5 + m_6$, find its dual and its complement.

1.19 Given $g(A, B, C) = M_0 \cdot M_3 \cdot M_5 \cdot M_6$, find its dual and its complement.

1.20 Realize a four-bit binary-to-gray code encoder, and a gray-to-binary decoder using exclusive-OR gates.

REFERENCES

Bartee, T. C. *Digital Computer Fundamentals.* New York: McGraw-Hill, 1977.

Chu, S. *Digital Computer Design Fundamentals.* New York: McGraw-Hill, 1962.

Mano, M. Morris. *Digital Logic and Computer Design.* Englewood Cliffs, NJ: Prentice-Hall, 1979.

Scott, N. R. *Electronic Computer Technology.* New York: McGraw-Hill, 1970.

2

COMBINATIONAL NETWORKS

A *combinational network* is the realization of a switching function, Y, whose values at a given instant are determined solely by the combined values of the input switching variables, X_i, at that instant. That is, $Y = f(X_i)$. There are two basic processes associated with combinational networks, network analysis and network synthesis. A realized network can be analyzed to derive the switching variable logic equations. Given a set of logic equations, the synthesis process is used to realize a network. The objectives of this chapter are as follows: (1) to define network analysis and synthesis tools and techniques, (2) to explain SSI-level design methodology, (3) to present MSI-level building block–based design, (4) to cover LSI-level module-based design approaches, and (5) to provide an overview of VLSI-level module design using ABEL.

2.1 NETWORK ANALYSIS

Network analysis is performed on a given combinational circuit by writing down the resulting expressions for each logic gate function, starting from the input and progressing towards the output. The resulting overall expression may be further simplified using Boolean algebra theorems. The analysis process is illustrated in Example 2.1.

EXAMPLE 2.1   Given the combinational circuit of Figure 2.1a, derive its input-output relationships, and simplify the resulting functions.

The process begins by writing the equation for each gate output, starting from left to right. As such, each function becomes the composite of the gated input switching variables. Next the Boolean algebra theorems are used to simplify each function's expression.

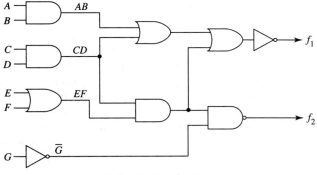

a) Combinational network

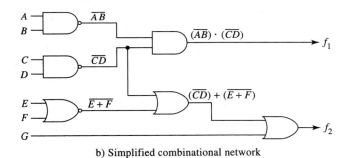

b) Simplified combinational network

FIGURE 2.1
Combinational network for Example 2.1.

Applying the above process to Figure 2.1a, the expression for f_1 becomes

$$f_1 = \overline{[(A \cdot B) + (C \cdot D)] + [(C \cdot D) \cdot (E + F)]} \text{ by inspection}$$
$$f_1 = \overline{[(A \cdot B) + (C \cdot D)]} \cdot \overline{[(C \cdot D) \cdot (E + F)]} \text{ using Theorem 7}$$
$$f_1 = [(\overline{A \cdot B}) \cdot (\overline{C \cdot D})] \cdot [(\overline{C \cdot D}) + (\overline{E + F})] \text{ using Theorem 7}$$
$$f_1 = [(\overline{A} + \overline{B}) \cdot (\overline{C} + \overline{D})] \cdot [(\overline{C} + \overline{D}) + (\overline{E} \cdot \overline{F})] \text{ using Theorem 7}$$
$$f_1 = [(\overline{A} + \overline{B}) \cdot (\overline{C} + \overline{D})] + [(\overline{A} + \overline{B}) \cdot (\overline{C} + \overline{D}) \cdot (\overline{E} \cdot \overline{F})] \text{ by the distributive property}$$
$$f_1 = [(\overline{A} + \overline{B}) \cdot (\overline{C} + \overline{D})] = (\overline{A \cdot B}) \cdot (\overline{C \cdot D}) \text{ using Theorems 6 and 7}$$

Similarly, from Figure 2.1a the expression for f_2 becomes

$$f_2 = \overline{[(C \cdot D) \cdot (E + F)] \cdot \overline{G}} = [(\overline{C} + \overline{D}) + (\overline{E} \cdot \overline{F})] + G$$
$$f_2 = (\overline{C} + \overline{D}) + (\overline{E} \cdot \overline{F})] + G = (\overline{C \cdot D}) + (\overline{E + F}) + G$$

Based on the simplified expressions for f_1 and f_2, the network shown in Figure 2.1b will perform the same function.

The following observations can be made from the analysis example. First, the gate levels were reduced from four to three, and then the number of required gates was reduced from nine to six. It should be noted, however, that the type of gates used was confined to the two-input type. It is possible to further reduce the logic complexity by the use of gates with more inputs. This is accomplished by using a three-input OR gate to realize f_2, thus reducing the number of gates used to five. In the example, each function shares a term or gate from the other function. In summary, this simple analysis example brings into focus some of the basic constraints and limitations associated with logic gate realization of switching variable functions. As has been shown, it becomes possible to simplify the switching function expressions, which results in a better realization with fewer gates and gate levels. These reductions have a direct impact on the operating speed of the network, since they eliminate one gate level, and on the implementation cost of the required gates and interconnections.

Figure 2.2 defines the well-known functions of three switching variables, in both positive and negative logic conventions. The basic logic equation is provided along with the Venn diagram representation. A truth table definition and the corresponding logic symbol are also presented.

A truth table consisting of input variable combinations is used to define each corresponding output function. A given row of input combinations in the truth table is assigned a decimal equivalent number N, known as the *binary state*, by using natural binary weights, where

$$N = \sum_{i=0}^{n-1} d_i x 2^i \ ; \ d_i = 0,1 \tag{2.1}$$

For example, the binary state $d_3 d_2 d_1 d_0 = 1010$ is assigned the decimal number 10. It should be noted that as the number of inputs increases, the associated function complexity increases drastically.

In the general case, a combinational network of n-input switching variables and m-output switching functions can be analyzed using the stimulus-response method. A systematic stimulation of the inputs, using consecutive increasing binary states, produces an output response for each output function. Hence, a truth table can be easily constructed that represents an exhaustive cause-and-effect relationship between the input and output. The output column of each function is scanned in order to derive its minterms. These are all the input states that produce a one in the function's output column. Finally, the function's equation is written as a summation of its minterms. Function minimization techniques will be covered in the next section. The stimulus-response method of combinational analysis is illustrated in Example 2.2.

In this example, the three functions are listed as a summation of their minterms; it is just as easy, however, to list them as a product of their maxterms. The minterm notational subscript corresponds to the binary input combination number. In addition, it becomes apparent in the truth table that each input variable has a cyclic pattern whose length is equal to its binary weight, or 2^i, where i is the relative bit position. Each column in the truth table is also known as a *designation number*. Looking at the function equations, it becomes obvious that there is sharing of minterms among the functions. This redundancy is used to reduce the total number of required terms in the combinational network. In general, common minterms may exist for pairs, triples, or n-tuples of output functions.

a) Positive logic

Logic Equation	Venn Diagram	Truth Table	Logic Symbol
$f = A \cdot B \cdot C$	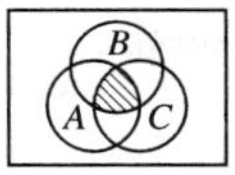	A B C f 0 0 0 0 0 0 1 0 0 1 0 0 0 1 1 0 1 0 0 0 1 0 1 0 1 1 0 0 1 1 1 1	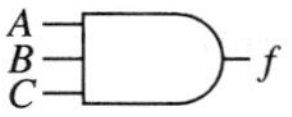 A, B, C → AND → f
$f = A + B + C$	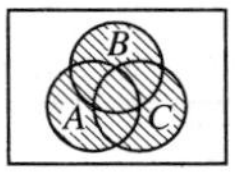	A B C f 0 0 0 0 0 0 1 1 0 1 0 1 0 1 1 1 1 0 0 1 1 0 1 1 1 1 0 1 1 1 1 1	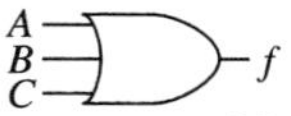 A, B, C → OR → f
$f = \overline{A \cdot B \cdot C}$	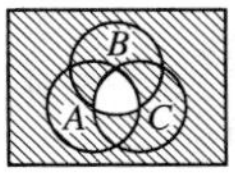	A B C f 0 0 0 1 0 0 1 1 0 1 0 1 0 1 1 1 1 0 0 1 1 0 1 1 1 1 0 1 1 1 1 0	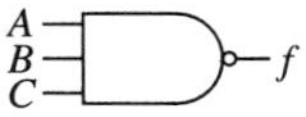 A, B, C → NAND → f
$f = \overline{A + B + C}$	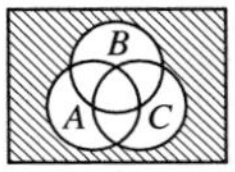	A B C f 0 0 0 1 0 0 1 0 0 1 0 0 0 1 1 0 1 0 0 0 1 0 1 0 1 1 0 0 1 1 1 0	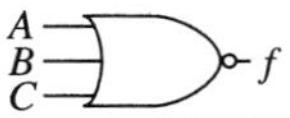 A, B, C → NOR → f

a) Positive logic

b) Negative logic

Logic Equation	Venn Diagram	Truth Table	Logic Symbol
$f = A + B + C$	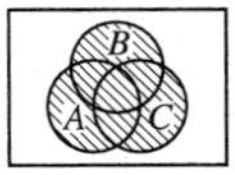	A B C f 1 1 1 1 1 1 0 1 1 0 1 1 1 0 0 1 0 1 1 1 0 1 0 1 0 0 1 1 0 0 0 0	 A, B, C → OR → f
$f = A \cdot B \cdot C$	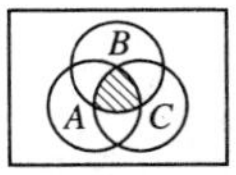	A B C f 1 1 1 1 1 1 0 0 1 0 1 0 1 0 0 0 0 1 1 0 0 1 0 0 0 0 1 0 0 0 0 0	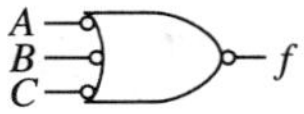 A, B, C → AND → f
$f = \overline{A + B + C}$	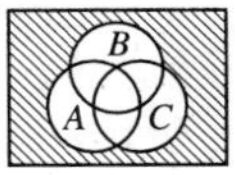	A B C f 1 1 1 0 1 1 0 0 1 0 1 0 1 0 0 0 0 1 1 0 0 1 0 0 0 0 1 0 0 0 0 1	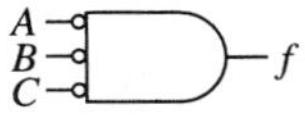 A, B, C → NOR → f
$f = \overline{A \cdot B \cdot C}$	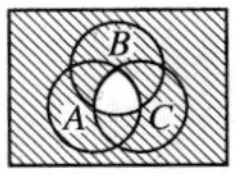	A B C f 1 1 1 0 1 1 0 1 1 0 1 1 1 0 0 1 0 1 1 1 0 1 0 1 0 0 1 1 0 0 0 1	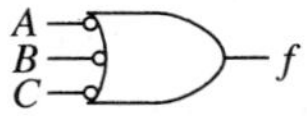 A, B, C → NAND → f

b) Negative logic

FIGURE 2.2
Basic functions of three switching variables.

EXAMPLE 2.2

Given a generalized combinational network of $n = 4$ and $m = 3$, defined in Table 2.1, derive the three resulting function equations.

$$X = m_3 + m_7 + m_8 + m_{12} + m_{15} = (\overline{D}\,\overline{C}BA) + (\overline{D}CBA) + (D\overline{C}\,\overline{B}\,\overline{A}) + (DC\overline{B}\,\overline{A}) + (DCBA)$$

$$Y = m_1 + m_5 + m_9 + m_{12} + m_{14} = (\overline{D}\,\overline{C}\,\overline{B}A) + (\overline{D}C\overline{B}A) + (D\overline{C}\,\overline{B}A) + (DC\overline{B}\,\overline{A}) + (DCB\overline{A})$$

$$Z = m_3 + m_7 + m_{11} + m_{15} = (\overline{D}\,\overline{C}BA) + (\overline{D}CBA) + (D\overline{C}BA) + (DCBA)$$

TABLE 2.1

Truth table for Example 2.2

Binary State	DCBA	X	Y	Z
0	0000	0	0	0
1	0001	0	1	0
2	0010	0	0	0
3	0011	1	0	1
4	0100	0	0	0
5	0101	0	1	0
6	0110	0	0	0
7	0111	1	0	1
8	1000	1	0	0
9	1001	0	1	0
10	1010	0	0	0
11	1011	0	0	1
12	1100	1	1	0
13	1101	0	0	0
14	1110	0	1	0
15	1111	1	0	1

2.2 NETWORK SYNTHESIS

Combinational network synthesis solves the input-output specification problem by realizing a combinational network with the minimum number of gates necessary to perform the required function(s). In general, we have n specified input variables and m resulting output functions using the stimulus-response relationship. An input matrix of n columns and 2^n rows can be defined that represents all the input combinations. In this matrix each column forms a unique designation number and each row defines a unique input state. Similarly, an output matrix of m columns and 2^n rows can be defined, in which each column represents an output function and each row defines a unique output state, based on a fixed input-output state relationship. Each input state can be converted to its decimal equivalent number, which is then used as a subscript to uniquely identify its associated minterm or maxterm. Each output function column can be graphed on the Karnaugh map and minimized to either an SOP or a POS form. The resulting equations are used to realize the required combinational network.

An important concept in the synthesis problem is the unspecified or *"don't care" conditions,* which result either because these input combinations will never occur or because if they do occur, the resulting output states are of no concern. The "don't care" conditions provide flexibility in the design process, since they can be assigned arbitrary states to facilitate the minimization effort. The synthesis process is further illustrated in Example 2.3.

EXAMPLE 2.3

Given a truth table relationship of four input variables and three output functions, as shown in Table 2.2, realize the required combinational networks using AND and OR gates. Provide both the SOP and POS forms, and use the Karnaugh map for function minimization.

From the truth table definition we get the SOP form as

$$X = m_3 + m_6 + m_{11} + m_{12}$$
$$Y = m_1 + m_6 + m_{10} + m_{15}$$
$$Z = m_2 + m_3 + m_6 + m_{12}$$

Similarly, the complement SOP form becomes

$$\overline{X} = m_0 + m_1 + m_2 + m_4 + m_5 + m_7 + m_8 + m_{10} + m_{13} + m_{14} + m_{15}$$
$$\overline{Y} = m_0 + m_2 + m_3 + m_5 + m_7 + m_8 + m_{11} + m_{13} + m_{14}$$
$$\overline{Z} = m_0 + m_1 + m_4 + m_5 + m_7 + m_8 + m_9 + m_{10} + m_{15}$$

and the "don't care" terms are

$$d_x = d_9$$
$$d_y = d_4 + d_9 + d_{12}$$
$$d_z = d_{11} + d_{13} + d_{14}$$

TABLE 2.2
Truth table for Example 2.3

Binary State	DCBA	X	Y	Z
0	0000	0	0	0
1	0001	0	1	0
2	0010	0	0	1
3	0011	1	0	1
4	0100	0	d	0
5	0101	0	0	0
6	0110	1	1	1
7	0111	0	0	0
8	1000	0	0	0
9	1001	d	d	0
10	1010	0	1	0
11	1011	1	0	d
12	1100	1	d	1
13	1101	0	0	d
14	1110	0	0	d
15	1111	0	1	0

From Figure 2.3a, b, and c, we get the following simplified expressions for the SOP form of the functions:

$$X = m_6 + m_{12} + (m_{11} + m_3)$$
$$X = \overline{D}CB\overline{A} + DC\overline{B}\,\overline{A} + (D\overline{C}BA + \overline{D}\,\overline{C}BA)$$
$$X = \overline{D}CB\overline{A} + DC\overline{B}\,\overline{A} + \overline{C}BA$$
$$Y = m_{10} + m_{15} + (m_1 + d_9) + (m_6 + d_4)$$
$$Y = D\overline{C}B\overline{A} + DCBA + (\overline{D}\,\overline{C}\,\overline{B}A + D\overline{C}\,\overline{B}A) + (\overline{D}\,CB\overline{A} + DCB\overline{A})$$
$$Y = D\overline{C}B\overline{A} + DCBA + \overline{C}\,\overline{B}A + C B\overline{A}$$
$$Z = (m_2 + m_3) + (m_6 + d_{14}) + (m_{12} + d_{13})$$
$$Z = (\overline{D}\,\overline{C}B\overline{A} + \overline{D}\,\overline{C}BA) + (\overline{D}\,CB\overline{A} + DCB\overline{A}) + (DC\overline{B}\,\overline{A} + DC\overline{B}A)$$
$$Z = \overline{D}\,\overline{C}B + CB\overline{A} + DC\overline{B}$$

From Figure 2.3d, e, and f, we get the simplified expressions, listed below, for the SOP form of the complement functions. The POS form is then derived using De Morgan's theorem.

$$\overline{X} = (m_0 + m_2 + m_{10} + m_8) + (m_0 + m_1 + m_5 + m_4) + (m_5 + m_7 + m_{15} + m_{13})$$
$$\qquad + (m_{15} + m_{14})$$
$$\overline{X} = (\overline{D}\,\overline{C}\,\overline{B}\,\overline{A} + \overline{D}C\overline{B}\,\overline{A} + D\overline{C}\,\overline{B}\overline{A} + DC\overline{B}\,\overline{A}) + (\overline{D}\,\overline{C}\,\overline{B}\overline{A} + \overline{D}\,\overline{C}\,\overline{B}A + \overline{D}C\overline{B}\,\overline{A} + D\overline{C}\,\overline{B}\,\overline{A})$$
$$\qquad + (\overline{D}C\overline{B}A + \overline{D}CBA + DCBA + DC\overline{B}A) + (DCBA + DCB\overline{A})$$
$$\overline{X} = \overline{C}\,\overline{A} + \overline{D}\,\overline{B} + CA + DCB$$
$$(\overline{\overline{X}}) = X = (C + A) \cdot (D + B) \cdot (\overline{C} + \overline{A}) \cdot (\overline{D} + \overline{C} + \overline{B}),\ \text{using De Morgan's theorem}$$
$$\overline{Y} = (m_0 + m_2) + (m_3 + m_{11}) + (m_5 + m_7) + (m_{14} + d_{12}) + (m_8 + d_9 + m_{13} + d_{12})$$
$$\overline{Y} = (\overline{D}\,\overline{C}\,\overline{B}\,\overline{A} + \overline{D}\,\overline{C}B\overline{A}) + (\overline{D}\,\overline{C}BA + D\overline{C}BA) + (\overline{D}C\overline{B}A + \overline{D}CBA) + (DCB\overline{A} + DC\overline{B}\,\overline{A})$$
$$\qquad + (D\overline{C}\,\overline{B}\overline{A} + D\overline{C}B\overline{A} + DCB\overline{A} + DC\overline{B}\,\overline{A})$$
$$\overline{Y} = (\overline{D}\,\overline{C}\,\overline{A} + \overline{C}B\overline{A} + \overline{D}CA + DC\overline{A} + D\overline{B})$$
$$(\overline{\overline{Y}}) = Y = (D + C + A) \cdot (C + \overline{B} + \overline{A}) \cdot (\overline{D} + \overline{C} + \overline{A}) \cdot (\overline{D} + \overline{C} + A) \cdot (\overline{D} + B)$$
$$\overline{Z} = (m_0 + m_1 + m_4 + m_5) + (m_{10} + d_{11} + m_8 + m_9) + (m_5 + m_7 + m_{15} + d_{13})$$
$$\overline{Z} = (\overline{D}\,\overline{C}\,\overline{B}\,\overline{A} + \overline{D}\,\overline{C}\,\overline{B}A + \overline{D}C\overline{B}\,\overline{A} + \overline{D}C\overline{B}A) + (D\overline{C}B\overline{A} + D\overline{C}BA + D\overline{C}\,\overline{B}\,\overline{A} + D\overline{C}\,\overline{B}A)$$
$$\qquad + (\overline{D}C\overline{B}A + \overline{D}CBA + DCBA + DCB\overline{A})$$
$$\overline{Z} = (\overline{D}B) + (D\overline{C}) + (CA)$$
$$(\overline{\overline{Z}}) = Z = (D + B) \cdot (\overline{D} + C) \cdot (\overline{C} + \overline{A})$$

In the preceding example, the three-output functions were individually minimized using the Karnaugh map. Both the functions and their complements were used to derive the product-of-sums and sum-of-products expressions. For the realization it was assumed that the input variables are available in both their true and complemented forms. Looking at the equations, it appears that the SOP versions produces a better overall solution to the synthesis problem, in terms of gate count. Specifically, the SOP X function requires one less gate than the POS form, and the same applies for the Y function as well. The SOP function Z uses the same number of

0	0	1	0
0	4	12	8
0	0	0	d
1	5	13	9
1	0	0	1
3	7	15	11
0	1	0	0
2	6	14	10

a) X map

0	d	d	0
0	4	12	8
1	0	0	d
1	5	13	9
0	0	1	0
3	7	15	11
0	1	0	1
2	6	14	10

b) Y map

(continued)

FIGURE 2.3
Karnaugh maps for Example 2.3.

0	0	1	0
0	4	12	8
0	0	d	0
1	5	13	9
1	0	0	d
3	7	15	11
1	1	d	0
2	6	14	10

c) Z map

1	1	0	1
0	4	12	8
1	1	1	d
1	5	13	9
0	1	1	0
3	7	15	11
1	0	1	1
2	6	14	10

d) $\overline{X}$ map

FIGURE 2.3 *(continued)*

1	d	d	1
0	4	12	8
0	1	1	d
1	5	13	9
1	1	0	1
3	7	15	11
1	0	1	0
2	6	14	10

e) $\overline{Y}$ map

1	1	0	1
0	4	12	8
1	1	d	1
1	5	13	9
0	1	1	d
3	7	15	11
0	0	d	1
2	6	14	10

f) $\overline{Z}$ map

FIGURE 2.3 *(continued)*

gates, but requires more inputs per gate. It should be noted that the AND and OR logic gates can be substituted with NANDs and NORs, depending on which realization is chosen. Additional simplification may be possible by the use of minterm sharing between the output functions. This can reduce both the number of required gates and their number of inputs. This concept is illustrated in Example 2.4.

EXAMPLE 2.4

Using the function expressions in Example 2.3, realize the minimized functions using minterm sharing.

$$X = m_3 + m_6 + m_{11} + m_{12} + d_9$$
$$Y = m_1 + m_6 + m_{10} + m_{15} + d_4 + d_9 + d_{12}$$
$$Z = m_2 + m_3 + m_6 + m_{12} + d_{11} + d_{13} + d_{14}$$

These three functions are placed on one Karnaugh map in Figure 2.4, using the convention XYZ. It should be noted that m_6 and m_{12} are shared by all three functions. As such they are excluded from the minimization process and are added separately to all three functions. This results in the following simplified expressions:

$$X = (m_3 + m_{11}) + (m_{11} + d_9) = (\overline{D}\,\overline{C}BA + D\overline{C}BA) + (D\overline{C}BA + D\overline{C}\,\overline{B}A) = \overline{C}BA + D\overline{C}A$$
$$Y = m_1 + m_{10} + m_{15} = \overline{D}\,\overline{C}\,\overline{B}A + D\overline{C}B\overline{A} + DCBA$$
$$Z = (m_2 + m_3) = (\overline{D}\,\overline{C}B\overline{A} + \overline{D}\,\overline{C}BA) = \overline{D}\,\overline{C}B$$

XYZ

000	0d0	1d1	000
0	4	12	8
010	000	00d	dd0
1	5	13	9
101	000	010	10d
3	7	15	11
001	111	00d	010
2	6	14	10

FIGURE 2.4
Karnaugh map for Example 2.4.

The following terms are shared by all three functions:

$$XYZ = m_6 + m_{12} = \overline{DCB}\overline{A} + DC\overline{B}\,\overline{A}$$

In the resulting SOP realization the gate count is reduced by two, simply by taking into account the existing common minterms and the "don't care" conditions specified by the requirements. In general, this method may or may not produce any further simplification.

Design Tools and Techniques

The Karnaugh map is a powerful design tool for function minimization with up to six input switching variables. The functional expressions are simplified systematically by defining a minimization procedure using the properties of the map to arrive at an elegant realization.

A host of assumptions and special terminology form the basis for the procedure. First, the Karnaugh map is used to plot the minterms of a function to be minimized. Second, the map is thought of as a continuous surface called a *toroid*. Any two minterms that vary in only one variable position are said to be adjacent; in other words, m_i and m_j are adjacent if m_i contains X_i and m_j contains $\overline{X}_i$ with all other variables identical. For example, in Figure 2.5 cells 36 and 44 are physically and logically adjacent since $F\overline{E}DC\overline{B}\overline{A}$ and $F\overline{E}D\overline{C}\overline{B}\overline{A}$ differ only in the variable D. Similarly, cells 8 and 40, and 2 and 18 are adjacent, based on the Karnaugh map definitions. Also, cells 0, 16, 32, and 48 form an adjacent set.

It should be noted that a minterm is a P-term that contains all the literals of an n variable function. Any product term or minterm I is an *implicant* of a function f if when $I = 1, f$ assumes a value of 1. For example, for $f(A, B, C, D) = AB + \overline{A}BD$ we have the following implicants: $AB, \overline{A}BD, AB\overline{C}, ABC, AB\overline{D}, ABD, AB\overline{C}D, ABC\overline{D}, AB\overline{C}D$, and $ABCD$. A *prime implicant* of a function f is an implicant that cannot be reduced any further by the adjacency rule $AB + A\overline{B} = A$. For example, for $f(A, B, C, D)$ both AB and $\overline{A}BD$ are prime implicants of f, but $ABC\overline{D}$ and $AB\overline{C}D$ are not. An *essential prime implicant* is one that contains one or more product terms that are not included in any other prime implicants. For example, AB and $\overline{A}BD$ are essential prime implicants, but $AB\overline{C}$ and $AB\overline{D}$ are not. A *minimal cover* for the switching function f consists of all the essential prime implicants, plus the smallest number of prime implicants necessary to represent the function. As was stated earlier, two adjacent minterms eliminate one switching variable, and, in general, 2^k mutual adjacencies eliminate k variables. This also results in the elimination of one or more minterms. This relationship can be restated as $k = \log_2 n$ where $k = 0, 1, 2, 3, \ldots$ is the number of eliminated variables and $n = 1, 2, 4, 8, \ldots$ is the number of adjacent cells combined on a Karnaugh map.

Using the principles discussed above, the following procedure can be used to derive a minimal cover for an arbitrary switching function definition:

1. Plot all minterms of the function on the n-dimensional Karnaugh map, including all "don't care" conditions.
2. Combine adjacent cells on the map to form the largest possible n-tuples, by using the relationship $k = \log_2 n$ and by judiciously assigning values to any "don't care" minterms. Eliminate k switching variables from combined minterms to form the prime implicants.

FED (columns) \ CBA (rows)

$\bar F\bar E\bar D\bar C\bar B\bar A$ 0	$\bar F\bar E\bar D C\bar B\bar A$ 4	$\bar F\bar E D C\bar B\bar A$ 12	$\bar F\bar E D\bar C\bar B\bar A$ 8	$\bar F E D\bar C\bar B\bar A$ 24	$\bar F E D C\bar B\bar A$ 28	$\bar F E\bar D C\bar B\bar A$ 20	$\bar F E\bar D\bar C\bar B\bar A$ 16
$\bar F\bar E\bar D\bar C\bar B A$ 1	$\bar F\bar E\bar D C\bar B A$ 5	$\bar F\bar E D C\bar B A$ 13	$\bar F\bar E D\bar C\bar B A$ 9	$\bar F E D\bar C\bar B A$ 25	$\bar F E D C\bar B A$ 29	$\bar F E\bar D C\bar B A$ 21	$\bar F E\bar D\bar C\bar B A$ 17
$\bar F\bar E\bar D\bar C B A$ 3	$\bar F\bar E\bar D C B A$ 7	$\bar F\bar E D C B A$ 15	$\bar F\bar E D\bar C B A$ 11	$\bar F E D\bar C B A$ 27	$\bar F E D C B A$ 31	$\bar F E\bar D C B A$ 23	$\bar F E\bar D\bar C B A$ 19
$\bar F\bar E\bar D\bar C B\bar A$ 2	$\bar F\bar E\bar D C B\bar A$ 6	$\bar F\bar E D C B\bar A$ 14	$\bar F\bar E D\bar C B\bar A$ 10	$\bar F E D\bar C B\bar A$ 26	$\bar F E D C B\bar A$ 30	$\bar F E\bar D C B\bar A$ 22	$\bar F E\bar D\bar C B\bar A$ 18
$F\bar E\bar D\bar C B\bar A$ 34	$F\bar E\bar D C B\bar A$ 38	$F\bar E D C B\bar A$ 46	$F\bar E D\bar C B\bar A$ 42	$F E D\bar C B\bar A$ 58	$F E D C B\bar A$ 62	$F E\bar D C B\bar A$ 54	$F E\bar D\bar C B\bar A$ 50
$F\bar E\bar D\bar C B A$ 35	$F\bar E\bar D C B A$ 39	$F\bar E D C B A$ 47	$F\bar E D\bar C B A$ 43	$F E D\bar C B A$ 59	$F E D C B A$ 63	$F E\bar D C B A$ 55	$F E\bar D\bar C B A$ 51
$F\bar E\bar D\bar C\bar B A$ 33	$F\bar E\bar D C\bar B A$ 37	$F\bar E D C\bar B A$ 45	$F\bar E D\bar C\bar B A$ 41	$F E D\bar C\bar B A$ 57	$F E D C\bar B A$ 61	$F E\bar D C\bar B A$ 53	$F E\bar D\bar C\bar B A$ 49
$F\bar E\bar D\bar C\bar B\bar A$ 32	$F\bar E\bar D C\bar B\bar A$ 36	$F\bar E D C\bar B\bar A$ 44	$F\bar E D\bar C\bar B\bar A$ 40	$F E D\bar C\bar B\bar A$ 56	$F E D C\bar B\bar A$ 60	$F E\bar D C\bar B\bar A$ 52	$F E\bar D\bar C\bar B\bar A$ 48

FIGURE 2.5
Six-variable Karnaugh map.

3. Make a list of all prime implicants obtained in step 2 and separate all the essential prime implicants from the list.
4. Using the reduced list of prime implicants, find the minimum set necessary to cover the function.
5. Find the minimal cover consisting of the essential prime implicants plus the minimum subset of prime implicants found in step 4.

It is possible that more than one minimized solution can be derived with this procedure. The procedure can also be extended to derive a minimal cover for multiple-output functions by also obtaining the common prime implicants of two or more functions, as described in Example 2.4. In addition, it is possible to define prime implicants for the logical product of two or more functions that can be used to achieve simplification. In general, a prime implicant exists for either the X or Y function, but may exist for both X and Y, and this rule can be extended to m such functions. The Quine–McCluskey method for finding the prime implicants of a switching function uses a systematic procedure to tabulate the prime implicants, starting with the minterms and using the expression $AB + A\overline{B} = A$ repeatedly. The basic steps for this method are outlined below:

1. List all function minterms and group them by the number of 1s they contain.
2. Form minterm pairs that differ by one variable to create a new term with one less variable, and replace them with it.
3. Repeat step 2 until no new terms can be formed. The resulting set of terms is the prime implicant list of the function.
4. Form a table using the original minterms to define the columns and the resulting prime implicant to define the rows. The relationship between each minterm and a given prime implicant is indicated by an x entry to the appropriate table location.
5. Using the table, determine the essential prime implicants by inspection. Find a minimal cover consisting of the essential prime implicants and a small subset of additional prime implicants.

The procedures above are illustrated in Example 2.5. The SOP function is defined using the minterm combination numbers.

EXAMPLE 2.5

Minimize the function $f(\text{SOP}) = (0, 2, 3, 7, 8, 10, 11, 13)$, using the Karnaugh map and Quine–McCluskey methods.

a) Karnaugh map method

Using the Karnaugh map in Figure 2.6, the minimized function expression becomes

$$f = (0, 2, 8, 10) + (3, 7) + (10, 11) + 13$$
$$f = \overline{C}\overline{A} + \overline{D}BA + D\overline{C}B + DC\overline{B}A$$

b) Quine–McCluskey method

STEP 1: Find prime implicants.

Minterm	Term	Term
0 0000	0, 2 00_0	0, 2, 8, 10 _0_0
2 0010	0, 8 _000	
8 1000	2, 3 001_	
3 0011	2, 10 _010	
10 1010	8, 10 10_0	
7 0111	3, 7 0_11	
11 1011	3, 11 _011	
13 1101	10, 11 101_	

STEP 2: Find minimal cover using Table 2.3.

$$f = (13) + (3, 7) + (10, 11) + (0, 2, 8, 10) = DC\overline{B}A + \overline{D}BA + D\overline{C}B + \overline{C}\,\overline{A}$$

1	0	0	1
0	4	12	8
0	0	1	0
1	5	13	9
1	1	0	1
3	7	15	11
1	0	0	1
2	6	14	10

FIGURE 2.6
Karnaugh map for Example 2.5.

TABLE 2.3
Minterms table for Example 2.5

Prime Implicants	0	2	3	7	8	10	11	13
*13								x
0, 8	x				x			
2, 3		x	x					
2, 10		x				x		
*3, 7			x	x				
3, 10			x			x		
3, 11			x				x	
+10, 11						x	x	
+0, 2, 8, 10	x	x			x	x		
Minimal Cover	+	+	*	*	+	+	+	*

* = essential prime implicant
+ = additional prime implicant

Both methods yield the same minimal function. These methods can be extended to handle multiple-output function minimization. In addition, they can be readily implemented as logic minimization programs. The covering problem remains one of heuristic algorithm solutions that find near-minimum solutions most of the time.

The iterated consensus is another method of finding the prime implicants of a switching function. This method consists of applying the Consensus Theorem, $AB + \overline{A}C + BC = AB + \overline{A}C$, repeatedly. The advantage of this method is that it does not require the switching function to be in its minterm form.

Oversimplification may result in *static hazards* or glitches under certain input combinations because of unequal propagation path delays of the various input switching variables as they go through the different gate levels, creating race conditions. A switching function $f = AB + \overline{A}C$ will exhibit a 1-0-1 momentary logic state transition when A changes from 0 to 1 or vice-versa, and the variables B and C are both 1. This type 1 static hazard can be eliminated by picking a near-minimal cover for $f = AB + \overline{A}C + BC$ instead. Similarly, the function $g = (A + B) \cdot (\overline{A} + C)$ will go through a 0-1-0 momentary logic state transition when A changes from 0 to 1 or vice-versa, and the variables B and C are both 0. This type 2 static hazard can also be eliminated by choosing a near-minimal cover for $g = (A + B) \cdot (\overline{A} + C) \cdot (B + C)$ instead. Static hazard elimination also results in no *dynamic hazards,* which are hazards that produce logic function errors.

A combinational network can be represented in at least four different formats: a truth table, a set of logic equations, a logic diagram, and a timing diagram. *Logic equations* provide a concise definition of a given function. The *logic diagram* provides a pictorial representation of a logic function using interconnected logic symbols. A *timing diagram* shows the logic state versus timing relationship of a function. These types of representation are shown in Example 2.6.

EXAMPLE 2.6

A binary half-adder, whose truth table is provided in Table 2.4, is a logic circuit that has two input switching variables $A, B,$ and two output functions S, C. Using the truth table, derive the logic equations, logic diagram, and timing diagram for this network.

TABLE 2.4
Truth table for Example 2.6

A B	S	C
0 0	0	0
0 1	1	0
1 0	1	0
1 1	0	1

The following equations are derived from the truth table:

$$S = \overline{A}B + A\overline{B} = A \oplus B$$
$$C = A \cdot B$$

Using the above equations, the logic diagram is presented in Figure 2.7a, using an exclusive-OR gate and an AND gate. Figure 2.7b illustrates the two input variable states' and the corresponding S and C functions' timing relationships.

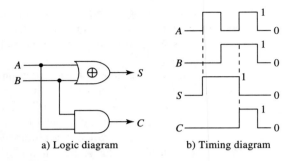

a) Logic diagram   b) Timing diagram

FIGURE 2.7
Half adder diagrams for Example 2.6.

Initially, with the introduction of small scale integration (SSI) logic devices, emphasis was placed on finding a cover that required the smallest number of P-terms or gates. Later, with the advent of medium scale integration (MSI) logic devices, the emphasis was shifted to finding a cover that required the smallest number of literals or interconnections among the various functional building blocks. With the development of large scale integration (LSI) devices, the emphasis on minimization was relaxed as long as the function could be implemented using one LSI module; otherwise, heuristic techniques were used to "fit" the function inside the LSI device. The very large scale integration (VLSI) devices relax all the above constraints, and the emphasis is placed on performance enhancement.

2.3 SSI COMBINATIONAL DESIGN

Small scale integration implements one to ten gates in a single integrated circuit (IC) chip, with an average pin-to-gate ratio of three to one. The physical devices come in a dual inline package (DIP). There are usually one to four identical gates in each DIP, constrained by the pin limitation of the package, which is usually fourteen pins, including power and ground. The gate functions may be Quad two-input OR, AND, NOR, NAND, or exclusive-OR type, with four gates per package. In addition, hex inverter gates are available for variable complementation; six gates are contained per package. The Karnaugh map is an ideal tool for simplifying switching variable expressions of up to six variables, in order to minimize the number of DIP packages for SSI logic implementation. Example 2.7 illustrates the use of SSI devices to implement a full-adder arithmetic network.

EXAMPLE 2.7 Design a two-binary-digit full-adder network, defined in Table 2.5, using SSI devices. From Figure 2.8a, the simplified S function expression becomes

$$S = A\overline{B}\,\overline{C}_N + \overline{A}B\overline{C}_N + \overline{A}\,\overline{B}C_N + ABC_N$$
$$S = (A\overline{B} + \overline{A}B)\overline{C}_N + (\overline{A}\,\overline{B} + AB)C_N$$
$$\text{Let } X = (A\overline{B} + \overline{A}B) = (A \oplus B)$$
$$\overline{X} = (\overline{A\overline{B} + \overline{A}B}) = (\overline{A \oplus B}) = \overline{A}\,\overline{B} + AB$$
$$S = X\overline{C}_N + \overline{X}C_N = X \oplus C_N = (A \oplus B) \oplus C_N$$

TABLE 2.5
Truth table for Example 2.7

$A\,B\,C_N$	S	C_{N+1}
0 0 0	0	0
0 0 1	1	0
0 1 0	1	0
0 1 1	0	1
1 0 0	1	0
1 0 1	0	1
1 1 0	0	1
1 1 1	1	1

From Figure 2.8b, the simplified C_N function expression becomes

$$C_{N+1} = \overline{A}BC_N + A\overline{B}C_N + AB\overline{C}_N + ABC_N$$
$$C_{N+1} = (\overline{A}B + A\overline{B}) \cdot C_N + (AB\overline{C}_N + ABC_N)$$
$$C_{N+1} = (A \oplus B) \cdot C_N + (A \cdot B)$$

The solution requires two exclusive-OR gates, two AND gates, and one OR gate. A closer look at Examples 2.6 and 2.7 reveals a certain regularity. That is, two half-adder net-

0	1	0	0
0	4	12	8
1	0	0	0
1	5	13	9
0	1	0	0
3	7	15	11
1	0	0	0
2	6	14	10

a) S map

FIGURE 2.8
Karnaugh maps for Example 2.7.

0	0	0	0
0	4	12	8
0	1	0	0
1	5	13	9
1	1	0	0
3	7	15	11
0	1	0	0
2	6	14	10

b) C_{N+1} map

FIGURE 2.8 (continued)

works cascaded together, with the addition of an OR gate, perform the full-adder function. This is illustrated in Figure 2.9a. Here each half-adder is represented by a functional block diagram for clarity. Similarly, the basic full-adder network can be cascaded to make an n-bit parallel binary-adder network, as shown in Figure 2.9b.

The binary numbers A and B consist of two binary digits each. The subscripted notation is used to differentiate between the individual bits of the number. A combinational logic network can be defined, using a truth table, for each of the basic mathematical operations using binary numbers. Each such implementation will provide a fixed arithmetic network capable of performing a fast mathematical operation on two binary numbers with a fixed number of bits. Looking at the half-adder implementation, such an operation requires one Quad two-input exclusive-OR package and one Quad two-input NAND package, using NAND/NAND versus AND/OR logic for the carry function. Similarly, the full two-bit adder implementation requires a Quad two-input exclusive-OR and two Quad two-input NAND packages.

Another useful arithmetic function is the magnitude comparator. Given n binary-digit switching variables A and B, we can define three operations upon them: $A = B$, $A > B$, and $A < B$. These are collectively called the magnitude comparison function. Example 2.8 uses the two-bit variables A and B to implement the magnitude comparator logic with SSI packages.

EXAMPLE 2.8

Given $A = A_1A_0$ and $B = B_1B_0$, realize their functions $A = B$, $A > B$, and $A < B$, as defined in Table 2.6, using SSI logic.

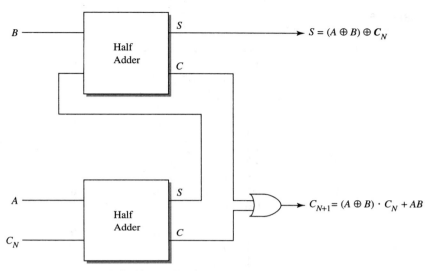

a) Full adder combinational network using half adders

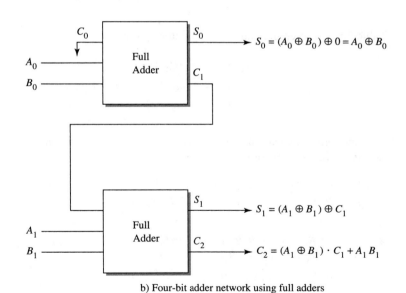

b) Four-bit adder network using full adders

FIGURE 2.9
Binary adder realization techniques.

TABLE 2.6
Truth table for Example 2.8

$B_1B_0A_1A_0$	f_1 $(A = B)$	f_2 $(A > B)$	f_3 $(A < B)$
0 0 0 0	1	0	0
0 0 0 1	0	1	0
0 0 1 0	0	1	0
0 0 1 1	0	1	0
0 1 0 0	0	0	1
0 1 0 1	1	0	0
0 1 1 0	0	1	0
0 1 1 1	0	1	0
1 0 0 0	0	0	1
1 0 0 1	0	0	1
1 0 1 0	1	0	0
1 0 1 1	0	1	0
1 1 0 0	0	0	1
1 1 0 1	0	0	1
1 1 1 0	0	0	1
1 1 1 1	1	0	0

From Table 2.6, the three magnitude comparator functions become

$$f_1 = m_0 + m_5 + m_{10} + m_{15}$$
$$f_2 = m_1 + m_2 + m_3 + m_6 + m_7 + m_{11}$$
$$f_3 = m_4 + m_8 + m_9 + m_{12} + m_{13} + m_{14}$$

The three functions above are mapped in Figure 2.10 as f_1, f_2, f_3. From Figure 2.10, the simplified function expressions become,

$$f_1 = m_0 + m_5 + m_{10} + m_{15}$$
$$f_1 = \overline{B_1}\overline{B_0}\overline{A_1}\overline{A_0} + B_1\overline{B_0}A_1\overline{A_0} + \overline{B_1}B_0\overline{A_1}A_0 + B_1B_0A_1A_0$$
$$f_2 = (m_2 + m_3 + m_6 + m_7) + (m_1 + m_3) + (m_3 + m_{11})$$
$$f_2 = (\overline{B_1}\overline{B_0}A_1\overline{A_0} + \overline{B_1}\overline{B_0}A_1A_0 + \overline{B_1}B_0A_1\overline{A_0} + \overline{B_1}B_0A_1A_0) + (\overline{B_1}\overline{B_0}\overline{A_1}A_0$$
$$+ \overline{B_1}\overline{B_0}A_1A_0) + (\overline{B_1}\overline{B_0}A_1A_0 + B_1\overline{B_0}A_1A_0)$$
$$f_2 = \overline{B_1}A_1 + \overline{B_1}\overline{B_0}A_0 + \overline{B_0}A_1A_0$$
$$f_3 = (m_8 + m_9 + m_{12} + m_{13}) + (m_4 + m_{12}) + (m_{12} + m_{14})$$
$$f_3 = (B_1\overline{B_0}\overline{A_1}\overline{A_0} + B_1\overline{B_0}\overline{A_1}A_0 + B_1B_0\overline{A_1}\overline{A_0} + B_1B_0\overline{A_1}A_0) + (\overline{B_1}B_0\overline{A_1}\overline{A_0}$$
$$+ B_1B_0\overline{A_1}\overline{A_0}) + (B_1B_0\overline{A_1}\overline{A_0} + B_1B_0A_1\overline{A_0})$$
$$f_3 = B_1\overline{A_1} + B_0\overline{A_1}\overline{A_0} + B_1B_0\overline{A_0}$$

The implementation of the two-bit magnitude comparator network requires seven DIP packages: one hex inverter, three Dual four-input NAND, two Triple three-input NAND, and

$f_1 f_2 f_3$

100	001	001	001
0	4	12	8
010	100	001	001
1	5	13	9
010	010	100	010
3	7	15	11
010	010	001	100
2	6	14	10

FIGURE 2.10
Karnaugh map for Example 2.8.

one Quad two-input NAND. It should be noted that it is possible to further simplify the $f_1 = (A = B)$ switching function by using mixed gate design. As such,

$$f_1 = \overline{B}_1\overline{B}_0\overline{A}_1\overline{A}_0 + \overline{B}_1 B_0 \overline{A}_1 A_0 + B_1 \overline{B}_0 A_1 \overline{A}_0 + B_1 B_0 A_1 A_0 = \overline{B}_1\overline{A}_1(\overline{B}_0\overline{A}_0 + B_0 A_0)$$
$$+ \; B_1 A_1(\overline{B}_0\overline{A}_0 + B_0 A_0)$$
$$f_1 = (\overline{B}_0\overline{A}_0 + B_0 A_0) \cdot (\overline{B}_1\overline{A}_1 + B_1 A_1) = \overline{(B_0 \oplus A_0)} \cdot \overline{(B_1 \oplus A_1)}$$

The resulting expression can be realized with two two-input exclusive-NOR gates that feed a two-input AND gate. This is an improvement over the five four-input NANDs needed to realize the initial expression.

A different type of logic operation is applied in the majority logic combinational network. Given a number of input switching variables ($n \geq 3$), a majority function is defined such that its output is one for every input combination that has more 1 states than 0 states. Majority logic is used in redundant designs for reliable operations. Example 2.9 uses five-input switching variables to define and implement a majority logic network using SSI packages.

EXAMPLE 2.9

A five-input majority function $f(A, B, C, D, E)$ produces a 1 output if three or more input variables are 1. Otherwise the output is 0. Minimize and realize this network using SSI logic.

$$f(\text{SOP}) = (7, 11, 13, 14, 15, 19, 21, 22, 23, 25, 26, 27, 28, 29, 30, 31)$$

Figure 2.11 is used to simplify the majority logic function that results in the following expression:

$$f = (m_7 + m_{15}) + (m_{11} + m_{15}) + (m_{13} + m_{15}) + (m_{14} + m_{15}) + (m_{22} + m_{30})$$
$$+ (m_{28} + m_{30}) + (m_{30} + m_{31} + m_{27} + m_{26}) + (m_{21} + m_{23} + m_{31} + m_{29})$$
$$+ (m_{19} + m_{23}) + (m_{25} + m_{27})$$

$$f = (ABC\overline{E}) + (ABD\overline{E}) + (ACD\overline{E}) + (BCD\overline{E}) + (\overline{A}BCE) + (\overline{A}CDE)$$
$$+ (BDE) + (ACE) + (AB\overline{D}E) + (A\overline{C}DE)$$

Implementing the minimization process, using the Karnaugh map, the resulting P-term of two adjacent cells, m_i and m_j, is defined as m_i with the corresponding weighted literal $(j - i)$ deleted where $j > i$. For example $(m_7 + m_{15})$, $i = 7, j = 15$, and $j - i = 8$; thus the literal D is deleted from the minterms and $(ABC\overline{D}\,\overline{E})_7 + (ABCD\overline{E})_{15} = (ABC\overline{E})$. This technique is applied repeatedly in mutually adjacent cell pairs. The resulting network requires one hex inverter, five Dual four-input AND, one Triple three-input OR, and one Quad two-input OR DIP package.

The following combinational networks provide controllable selection of input switching variables and form the fundamental building blocks of combinational logic design. The first network is called a *multiplexer,* and it selects one out of two or more input variables at its output. In the case of two switching variables A and B, we define a third binary control variable X, such that when X is true, B is selected at the output and when X is false, A is selected instead.

0	0	0	0	0	1	0	0
0	4	12	8	24	28	20	16
0	0	1	0	1	1	1	0
1	5	13	9	25	29	21	17
0	1	1	1	1	1	1	1
3	7	15	11	27	31	23	19
0	0	1	0	1	1	1	0
2	6	14	10	26	30	22	18

FIGURE 2.11
Karnaugh map for Example 2.9.

Similarly, we can define a second network called a *demultiplexer,* which distributes an input switching variable A to one of two outputs, depending on the state of the binary control variable X. These two networks are detailed in Example 2.10.

EXAMPLE 2.10

Given two switching variables A and B and the control variable X, realize the selector function defined in Table 2.7 and distributor function defined in Table 2.8.

TABLE 2.7
Selector truth table for Example 2.10

X	B	A	f_1
0	0	0	0
0	0	1	1
0	1	0	0
0	1	1	1
1	0	0	0
1	0	1	0
1	1	0	1
1	1	1	1

TABLE 2.8
Distributor truth table for Example 2.10

X	A	f_2	f_3
0	0	0	0
0	1	1	0
1	0	0	0
1	1	0	1

From Figure 2.12a, the simplified expression for the selector function becomes

$$f_1 = \overline{X} \cdot A + X \cdot B$$

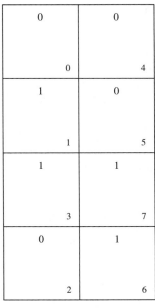

a) Selector map   b) Distributor map

FIGURE 2.12
Karnaugh maps for Example 2.10.

Similarly, from Figure 2.12b, the simplified expression for the distributor function becomes

$$f_2 = \overline{X} \cdot A$$
$$f_3 = X \cdot A$$

These two logic networks can be generalized as a 2^n-to-1 selector, multiplexer, and a 1-to-2^n distributor, demultiplexer, respectively.

The next two logic networks are defined as decoder and encoder functions. For example, a 2-to-4 decoder function takes two input switching variables, A and B, and provides four output functions, one for each input combination. In general, for n-input switching variables, 2^n output functions are defined. Also, a 4-to-2 encoder function takes four input switching variables A, B, C, D and provides two output functions, which define the four mutually exclusive inputs. In general, for 2^n-input switching variables, n output functions are defined. Example 2.11 illustrates the realization of these two networks using SSI packages.

EXAMPLE 2.11

Realize a 2-to-4 decoder and a 4-to-2 encoder as defined in Tables 2.9 and 2.10, respectively. From Table 2.9, the decoder function expressions are derived by inspection as

$$f_1 = \overline{B} \cdot \overline{A}$$
$$f_2 = \overline{B} \cdot A$$
$$f_3 = B \cdot \overline{A}$$
$$f_4 = B \cdot A$$

From Figure 2.13a, the simplified expression for f_5 becomes

$$f_5 = (m_4 \cdot d_{12}) + (m_8 \cdot d_{12})$$
$$f_5 = (\overline{D}C\overline{B}\overline{A} + DC\overline{B}\overline{A}) + (D\overline{C}\overline{B}A + DC\overline{B}A) = C\overline{B}\overline{A} + DB\overline{A}$$

And from Figure 2.13b, the simplified expression for f_6 becomes

$$f_6 = (m_2 + d_6 + d_{10} + d_{14}) + (m_8 + d_{10})$$
$$f_6 = (\overline{D}\,\overline{C}B\overline{A} + \overline{D}CB\overline{A} + D\overline{C}B\overline{A} + DCB\overline{A}) + (D\overline{C}\,\overline{B}A + D\overline{C}B\overline{A}) = B\overline{A} + D\overline{C}\overline{A}$$

TABLE 2.9 Decoder truth table for Example 2.11	$B\ A$	$f_1\ f_2\ f_3\ f_4$
	0 0	1 0 0 0
	0 1	0 1 0 0
	1 0	0 0 1 0
	1 1	0 0 0 1

TABLE 2.10 Encoder truth table for Example 2.11	$D\ C\ B\ A$	$f_5\ f_6$
	1 d d d	0 0
	0 1 d d	0 1
	0 0 1 d	1 0
	0 0 0 1	1 1

The majority of SSI-based combinational networks can be handled with the truth table definition and minimized on the Karnaugh map and by the judicious use of any "don't care" conditions.

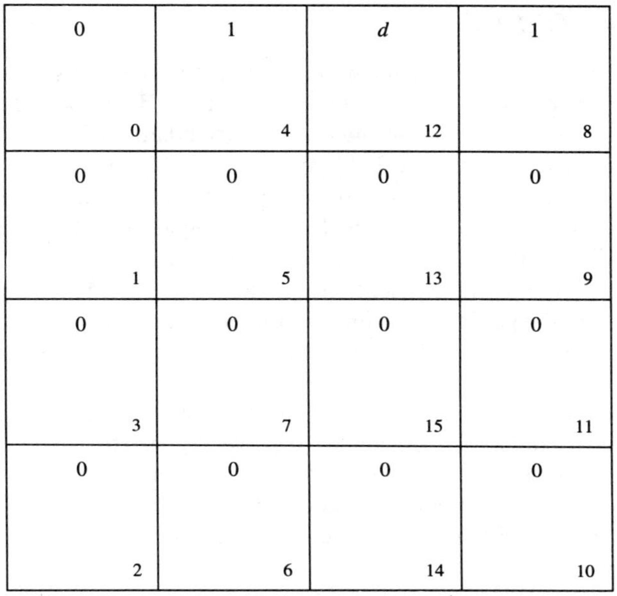

0	1	d	1
0	4	12	8
0	0	0	0
1	5	13	9
0	0	0	0
3	7	15	11
0	0	0	0
2	6	14	10

a) f_5 map

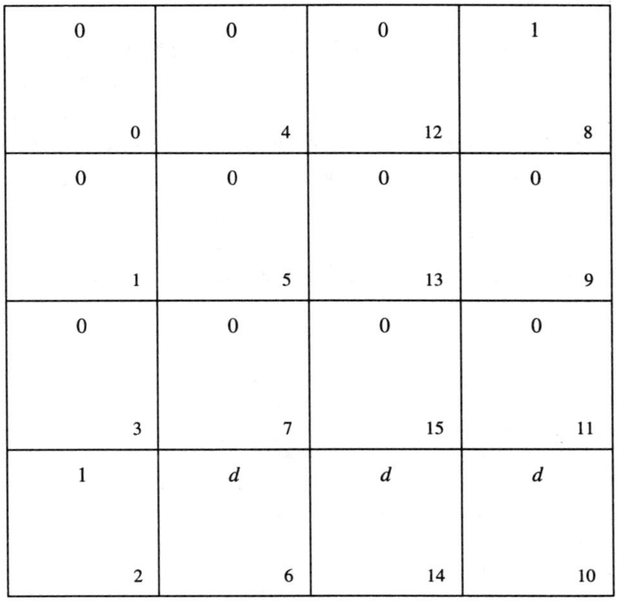

0	0	0	1
0	4	12	8
0	0	0	0
1	5	13	9
0	0	0	0
3	7	15	11
1	d	d	d
2	6	14	10

b) f_6 map

FIGURE 2.13
Karnaugh maps for Example 2.11.

2.4 MSI COMBINATIONAL DESIGN

Medium scale integration implements from ten to one hundred gates in a single integrated circuit package. The average pin-to-gate ratio is two to one. These IC packages contain a complete combinational network that has been minimized by standard methods and is limited by the number of available pins, which is usually sixteen. The MSI packages form complete functional building blocks that can be used to implement combinational logic designs, bypassing standard minimization methods. In addition, these packages have expansion logic that enables them to be cascaded and to accommodate more variables. The SSI packages can serve a useful function by providing any necessary logic, outside the MSI packages, that can be distributed as needed in the particular design. MSI logic modules include multiplexers, demultiplexers, encoders, decoders, magnitude comparators, binary adders, and arithmetic logic units (ALUs).

The primary use of multiplexers is providing input variable selection. However, a multiplexer can be thought of as a universal logic module capable of generating any of the 2^N, $N = 2^n$ functions of n variables. There are two common techniques available to accomplish this, the n-variable method and the $n - 1$, or folding, method. The n-variable method is a rather straightforward one, based on the multiplexer function equation. For example, an eight-to-three multiplexer equation becomes

$$f = A_0\overline{X}_0\overline{X}_1\overline{X}_2 + A_1 X_0\overline{X}_1\overline{X}_2 + A_2\overline{X}_0 X_1\overline{X}_2 + A_3 X_0 X_1\overline{X}_2 + A_4\overline{X}_0\overline{X}_1 X_2 + A_5 X_0\overline{X}_1 X_2$$
$$+ A_6\overline{X}_0 X_1 X_2 + A_7 X_0 X_1 X_2$$

The logic expression is a summation of all its minterms. Hence, by selectively enabling or disabling each minterm that is, by making the appropriate A_i a fixed one or zero state, any function of three switching variables can be implemented. The *folding method* uses an $n - 1$ input multiplexer to implement any n-input variable function by mapping the nth input variable at the A_i inputs. Example 2.12 demonstrates the folding method.

EXAMPLE 2.12 Using an eight-input multiplexer, apply the folding method to map the four-variable function defined in Table 2.11.

TABLE 2.11
Truth table for Example 2.12

DCBA	f	DCBA	f
0000	0	1000	0
0001	1	1001	1
0010	0	1010	0
0011	1	1011	1
0100	0	1100	0
0101	1	1101	0
0110	0	1110	0
0111	0	1111	1

Using Table 2.11, the four-variable function can be written in SOP form as shown below:

$$f = \overline{DC}\,\overline{B}A + \overline{DC}BA + \overline{D}C\overline{B}A + D\overline{C}\overline{B}A + D\overline{C}BA + DCBA$$

$$f = (m_1 + m_3 + m_5 + m_9 + m_{11} + m_{15})$$

An eight-input multiplexer has three control input variables X_0, X_1, X_2. The input variables are mapped as follows: $A = X_0, B = X_1, C = X_2$. The Karnaugh maps of Figure 2.14a and b are used to determine the connections for the other multiplexer inputs, as a function of variable D.

Let the ith cell of the three-variable Karnaugh map represents the $A_{i^{th}}$ input to the multiplexer. Then, comparing the two maps and combining the results, we construct Table 2.12.

The multiplexer function is basically a logic-controlled n-position selector switch. Conversely, a demultiplexer can be thought of as an n-position distribution switch. For example, a one-to-eight demultiplexer switches the input variable A to one of the eight selected outputs. The MSI demultiplexer module implements the following eight function expressions:

$$f_0 = A\overline{X}_0\overline{X}_1\overline{X}_2 \qquad f_3 = AX_0X_1\overline{X}_2 \qquad f_6 = A\overline{X}_0X_1X_2$$
$$f_1 = AX_0\overline{X}_1\overline{X}_2 \qquad f_4 = A\overline{X}_0\overline{X}_1X_2 \qquad f_7 = AX_0X_1X_2$$
$$f_2 = A\overline{X}_0X_1\overline{X}_2 \qquad f_5 = AX_0\overline{X}_1X_2$$

a) $D = 0$ map   b) $D = 1$ map

FIGURE 2.14
Karnaugh maps for Example 2.12.

TABLE 2.12
Multiplexer input table for Example 2.12

A_i Input	$D = 0$ Map	$D = 1$ Map	Input Value
A_0	0	0	0
A_1	1	1	1
A_2	0	0	0
A_3	1	1	1
A_4	0	0	0
A_5	1	0	$\overline{D}$
A_6	0	0	0
A_7	0	1	D

An encoder module provides for decimal- or BCD-to-binary conversion. It is used, for example, after a calculator keyboard entry. The standard implementation is that of a priority encoder, where the active input switching variable with the highest prefix is encoded regardless of the other variable states. For example, for an eight-to-three priority encoder, if A_5 was active, logic one, and A_6 and A_7 were inactive, then the decoded output would be $B_0 \overline{B}_1 B_2$ or 5, regardless of the states of the A_0–A_4 input switching variables.

A decoder module provides for binary-to-decimal or binary-to-BCD conversion. For example, it is used before a calculator display. In addition, a decoder can serve as a generalized code conversion device with n-input variables, and a number of outputs ranging from n to 2^n. A well-known application is that of the hex–to–seven-segment decoder function used to convert a hexadecimal to a seven-segment display format. Example 2.13 demonstrates this particular code conversion.

EXAMPLE 2.13

Define the truth table for a hexadecimal–to–seven-segment decoder function, using Figure 2.15 as reference.

FIGURE 2.15
Seven-segment display for Example 2.13.

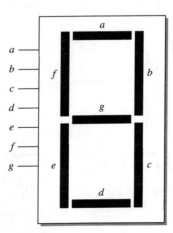

Using Figure 2.15, the hexadecimal–to–seven-segment display functions may be found by inspection (see Table 2.13). As such, each input variable combination activates one or more segments to display the hexadecimal digit.

TABLE 2.13
Truth table for Example 2.13

DCBA	a	b	c	d	e	f	g	Display
0000	1	1	1	1	1	1	0	0
0001	0	1	1	0	0	0	0	1
0010	1	1	0	1	1	0	1	2
0011	1	1	1	1	0	0	1	3
0100	0	1	1	0	0	1	1	4
0101	1	0	1	1	0	1	1	5
0110	0	0	1	1	1	1	1	6
0111	1	1	1	0	0	0	0	7
1000	1	1	1	1	1	1	1	8
1001	1	1	1	0	0	1	1	9
1010	1	1	1	0	1	1	1	A
1011	0	0	1	1	1	1	1	B
1100	1	0	0	1	1	1	0	C
1101	0	1	1	1	1	0	1	D
1110	1	0	0	1	1	1	1	E
1111	1	0	0	0	1	1	1	F

TABLE 2.14
Truth table for ALU module

Function Selection				Arithmetic Operation	Logic Operation
X_3	X_2	X_1	X_0	$X_4 = 0$	$X_4 = 1$
0	0	0	0	A	$\overline{A}$
0	0	0	1	A Plus 1	$\overline{A + B}$
0	0	1	0	A Plus $\overline{B}$	$\overline{A}B$
0	0	1	1	-1	0
0	1	0	0	A Plus $A\overline{B}$	$\overline{AB}$
0	1	0	1	$(A + B)$ Plus AB	$\overline{B}$
0	1	1	0	$(A - B) - 1$	$A \oplus B$
0	1	1	1	A Plus AB	$A\overline{B}$
1	0	0	0	A Plus B	$\overline{A} + B$
1	0	0	1	$(A + \overline{B})$ Plus AB	$\overline{A \oplus B}$
1	0	1	0	$(AB) - 1$	B
1	0	1	1	A Plus A	$A \cdot B$
1	1	0	0	$(A + B)$ Plus A	1
1	1	0	1	$(A + \overline{B})$ Plus A	$A + B$
1	1	1	0	$A - 1$	$A + \overline{B}$
1	1	1	1	$B - 1$	A

Actual MSI decoder modules may have two more control input variables, one for producing a blank output and another for testing the display by displaying an unconditional numeral 8.

A magnitude comparator module provides for the equal, less, or greater tests of two four-bit binary numbers, A and B. In addition, it accepts inputs from other comparator outputs for cascading capability.

A binary adder module performs the binary addition operation on two four-bit binary numbers, A and B, and provides the sum and carry functions. In addition, it accepts a carry from other binary adders for cascading capability.

An arithmetic logic unit (ALU) is one of the largest MSI modules, packaged in a twenty-four pin DIP. ALUs are capable of performing either sixteen arithmetic operations or sixteen logical operations on two four-bit binary numbers, A and B. In addition to the general function outputs, the carry input and output are also provided for cascading ALUs as multiples of four-bit binary variables. Table 2.14 is a truth table for a typical ALU module. The MSI-based ALU has five control inputs, X_4–X_0, to specify the mode and operation. The arithmetic operations are

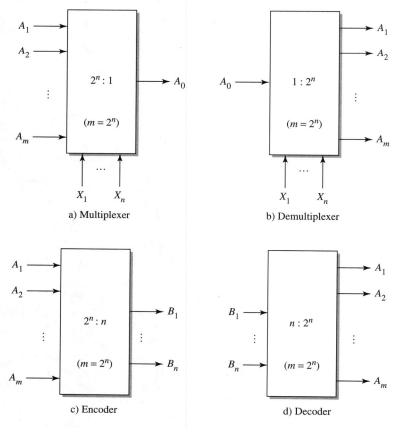

FIGURE 2.16
Fundamental combinational networks.

defined in two's complement arithmetic. The logic operations consist of the sixteen elementary functions. Also, the difference between a logical OR ($+$) and an arithmetic plus is the carry operation of the latter.

The four generalized combinational networks that have widespread use in MSI logic design are illustrated in Figure 2.16. It should be pointed out that the difference between a decoder and a demultiplexer is the extra input variable in the demultiplexer network. A decoder can be also viewed as a minterm generator logic network.

MSI-based combinational logic design requires virtually no logic minimization. All such procedures are incorporated into the specific MSI functional building block at the time of development. The resulting MSI modules perform a complete logic function operation on n variables at a time. In addition, they have the capability, via extra built-in logic, to be cascaded so that a multiple of n-variable logic network can be implemented easily. Thus, the basic problem remains that of interconnections among the various modules. The generalized devices, shown in Figure 2.16, can provide an answer by using the inherent parallel-to-serial and serial-to-parallel conversion capabilities of the multiplexer/demultiplexer pair. Another important concept is that of *tri-state logic,* where in addition to the logic zero and one states, a third state is defined, called *Hi-Z,* which provides a condition that results in a high-impedance or virtually open output. Tri-state logic is useful for *bused networks,* in which two or more outputs are tied together but only one is enabled at any given time. This logic eliminates the need for multiplexing.

2.5 LSI COMBINATIONAL DESIGN

Large scale integration has further increased device logic densities. LSI packages usually contain one hundred to one thousand gates and may have twenty-eight, forty, or sixty-four pins. The pin-to-gate ratio is a fractional number. As with the SSI and MSI configurations, there are standard LSI building blocks available for general-purpose applications. These LSI combinational networks are mainly in read-only memory (ROM) form. These are one-time programmable devices. A ROM is a physical realization of a truth table, such that each row of the $n \times 2^n$ truth table represents a unique input variable combination and results in a permanent and unique n-bit output pattern. In addition to the standard available LSI modules, two other types are available, the semicustom logic and the custom logic. Figure 2.17 depicts the various types of digital logic building blocks available. These span the available levels of integration.

LSI standard logic modules have been optimized and are used in large quantities for code conversion and look-up table applications. LSI semicustom logic devices give more design flexibility, at the expense of reduced logic density, by providing a programmable architecture.

Programmable logic devices (PLDs) consist of an AND function array cascaded to an OR function array, where either or both arrays may be user-programmable. When neither array is programmable, we have hardwired and random logic. A programmable AND followed by a fixed OR array results in the Programmable array logic (PAL)® device. (PAL is a registered trademark of Monolithic Memories Inc.) A fixed AND array followed by a programmable OR array results in a programmable read-only memory (PROM) device. A programmable AND array without an OR array results in a programmable gate array (PGA) device. Finally, a programmable AND array followed by a programmable OR array results in a programmable logic array (PLA) device.

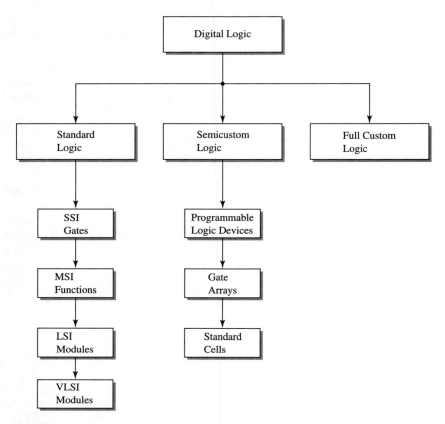

FIGURE 2.17
Digital logic categories.

PROMs are either one-time or multiple-time programmable by the user. One-time programmable PROMs have a fusible link that becomes either an open or a short circuit. PROMs that can be reprogrammed are available as erasable (EPROMs) or electrically erasable (EEPROMS). EPROMs need to be removed from the actual circuit for erasure and reprogramming. EEPROMS can be reprogrammed in the circuit by a rewrite operation.

Gate arrays consist of a semifinished IC that contains a set of regular gate patterns, arranged in various logic combinations. The device manufacturer uses the customer's requirements to complete the design, by developing an interconnection mask that configures the various gates, which enables the device to perform the specified function.

Standard cells differ from gate arrays in that instead of starting with a semicustom chip, the cell definitions exist in software form within a computer memory. Each standard cell is defined by a set of functional, electrical, and physical parameters. These predefined cells, logic building blocks, are selected and interconnected according to the designer's logic circuit diagrams. This process takes place in the computer, prior to chip manufacturing, and it results in a higher logic density compared to gate array designs.

TABLE 2.15
PLD configurations

Device	AND Array	OR Array
PGA	Programmable	None
PAL	Programmable	Fixed
PROM	Fixed	Programmable
PLA	Programmable	Programmable

Full custom LSI designs give the circuit designer total control of the design to achieve logic optimization, performance, and density, and therefore have the highest implementation cost.

Table 2.15 lists the possible programmable logic device configurations, using a generalized AND/OR array PLD architecture. Figure 2.18 depicts a typical internal logic organization for the most flexible programmable logic device, the PLA. Each input variable is buffered and has the true and complemented logic states connected, via the programmable matrix, to an AND gate array effectively creating "don't care" conditions. Similarly, the individual AND gate outputs are buffered and have their true and inverted logic states connected, via a second programmable matrix, to an OR gate array, effectively creating another set of "don't care" conditions. The number of AND gates, M, corresponds to the number of P-terms in a given switching function, and the number of OR gates, N, corresponds to the number of output functions possible. Given a particular PLA with a finite number of inputs, AND gates, and OR gates, any generalized combinational network can be embedded within the device, subject to these limitations. The PLA has built-in programming logic capability for one-time programming. Once the specified combinational network has been minimized, using standard methodology, the resulting P-term expressions for each output variable are programmed into the device as required, starting with the AND array and followed by the OR array. The programming process for each AND gate input literal electrically disconnects the undesired state of that literal. Similarly, the programming process for the OR array electrically disconnects the complemented output of the selected AND array gate. The extra AND and OR gates are left intact with each input literal having both states

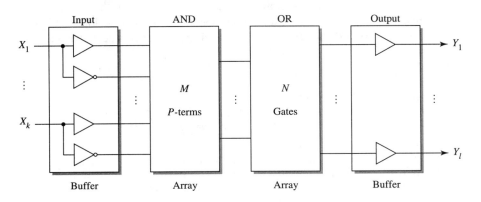

FIGURE 2.18
PLA device organization.

tied to the matrix. This has the same effect as disconnecting all inputs for possible future programming in case of error or function expansion. In practice, PLAs come with many more AND gates than either inputs or output OR gates in order to facilitate implementation of multiple functions. Also, the output buffer has a programmable active level option.

Standard Module

The ROM module is used extensively for code conversions, such as ASCII-to-EBDIC and vice-versa. Also, it serves as a look-up table for mathematical or trigonometric functions in high-speed applications. Another interesting application is that of high-speed alphanumeric character generation for visual displays or printers. A character-generator ROM can produce any of the 128 ASCII characters in a fixed-element matrix, usually a five-column–by–seven-row format. This is accomplished by first providing it the specific ASCII code, as an input variable combination, and then providing an increasing consecutive input pattern to generate the output display character, either a row or a column at a time. The binary equivalent ASCII input code can be seen as an address field in the fixed AND matrix, selecting a fixed-bit pattern in the output OR matrix. The input AND matrix consists of an $n \times 2^n$ array, and the preprogrammed OR matrix consists of a $2^n \times m$ array. Each unique 2^n-input combination address field results in a unique output m-bit pattern.

Table 2.16 lists the contents of a column scan character ROM, starting at a base address specified by the binary equivalent of the ASCII character "E." The output row bits, d_7–d_0, produce the letter "E," while the column address bits, A_2, A_1, A_0, are incremented from zero to five.

Table 2.17 lists the contents of a row scan character ROM, starting at the base address specified by the ASCII character "E." The output column bits, d_5–d_0, produce the letter "E," while the row address bits, A_2, A_1, A_0, are incremented from zero to seven.

Looking at the two character-generation schemes, in both instances the ASCII character binary equivalent is applied to the device for the duration of the scan. The column scan method is suitable for visual displays, whereas the row scan method is suitable for printer applications. It should be noted that the scanning occurs at the LSB locations of the character's base address. Thus, for the case of ASCII character "E," the input base address is 1000101000, or hexadecimal 228, and the character is stored between 228 and 22D for the column and 228 and 22F for the row scans, respectively. Also, in both scan methods the base input address results in an all-zero output for producing the necessary spacing between adjacent characters.

TABLE 2.16

Column scan truth table for "E"

A_9	A_8	A_7	A_6	A_5	A_4	A_3	A_2	A_1	A_0	d_7	d_6	d_5	d_4	d_3	d_2	d_1
1	0	0	0	1	0	1	0	0	0	0	0	0	0	0	0	0
1	0	0	0	1	0	1	0	0	1	1	1	1	1	1	1	1
1	0	0	0	1	0	1	0	1	0	1	0	0	1	0	0	1
1	0	0	0	1	0	1	0	1	1	1	0	0	1	0	0	1
1	0	0	0	1	0	1	1	0	0	1	0	0	1	0	0	1
1	0	0	0	1	0	1	1	0	1	1	0	0	1	0	0	1

TABLE 2.17
Row scan truth table for "E"

A_9	A_8	A_7	A_6	A_5	A_4	A_3	A_2	A_1	A_0		d_5	d_4	d_3	d_2	d_1
1	0	0	0	1	0	1	0	0	0		0	0	0	0	0
1	0	0	0	1	0	1	0	0	1		1	1	1	1	1
1	0	0	0	1	0	1	0	1	0		1	0	0	0	0
1	0	0	0	1	0	1	0	1	1		1	0	0	0	0
1	0	0	0	1	0	1	1	0	0		1	1	1	1	1
1	0	0	0	1	0	1	1	0	1		1	0	0	0	0
1	0	0	0	1	0	1	1	1	0		1	0	0	0	0
1	0	0	0	1	0	1	1	1	1		1	1	1	1	1

PROM Module

The PROM LSI module is a user-programmable device, programmable either one time or multiple times (with an EPROM version). It consists of a fixed AND logic array that performs an n-to-2^n decoder function, which selects a $2^n \times m$ OR programmable logic array. Each of the 2^n possible input combinations represents a unique input state in the corresponding truth table, and each of the 2^n possible m-output bit patterns represents the resulting output switching variables based on a predefined input-output functional relationship. Each input variable combination is also called the PROM input address, which selects a stored m-bit pattern, also known as data bits. It should be noted that given an n-input PROM, an increase to $n + 1$ results in an AND array of 2^{n+1}, that is, it doubles in size. Similarly, given an m-output PROM, an increase to $m + 1$ results in an extra OR array column of 1×2^n size.

A PROM can be seen as an exhaustive minterm decoder, in which each address location corresponds to one minterm. When selecting adjacent minterm locations, it is possible to create static hazards due to unequal propagation delays through the various signal paths. For example, given a function $f_1 = m_j + m_k = X_4 X_3 X_2 \overline{X}_1 + X_4 \overline{X}_3 X_2 \overline{X}_1$, since logic minimization is not possible in the fixed AND array, each time f_1 is selected, the X_3 variable transition may generate a static hazard. To ensure that such hazard conditions are avoided, the device manufacturer specifies a timing relationship between input and output behavior known as a *timing diagram*. The concepts above are illustrated in Figure 2.19.

In Figure 2.19a the generalized PROM AND/OR matrix array sizes are defined with a specific 4×3 PROM size, detailed in Figure 2.19b, where the "$\times$" indicates the intact programmable connections or links. The input-output timing relationship is provided in Figure 2.19c. For any X_i input variable transition, we define a t_h, or *hold time*, during which the X_i must be held in a stable state for an output transition to occur. Also, the t_a, or *access time*, is defined as the time from the last input variable transition to the time at which the output variables have reached their new stable states.

The programming of a PROM is a straightforward procedure, in which a given state table is mapped one-to-one into a particular device, provided its size is equal to or greater than the state table definition of the required generalized combinational network. The programming is accomplished by selecting an address location and providing the corresponding output bit pattern to the output pins and then providing a control pin signal to select the programming mode of operation. After the programming is accomplished, the on-chip programming logic is disabled by hardwiring the control pin. The device is then ready for its intended use. However, if

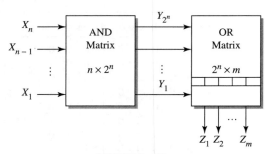

a) PROM size $2^n \times m$

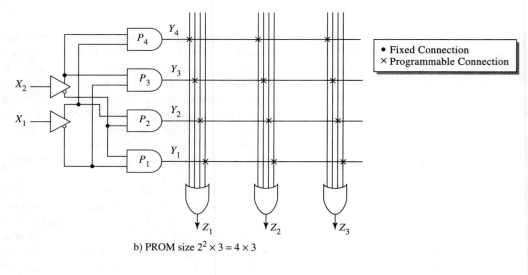

• Fixed Connection
× Programmable Connection

b) PROM size $2^2 \times 3 = 4 \times 3$

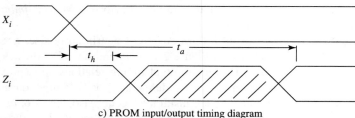

c) PROM input/output timing diagram

FIGURE 2.19
PROM size and timing definitions.

a set of minimized switching function equations, in standard form, is programmed into a PROM, it is necessary to expand them into their canonical form prior to the programming sequence. This is accomplished by the repeated use of Theorem 4. Example 2.14 elaborates on this method.

EXAMPLE 2.14 Given the three functions f_1, f_2, f_3 of the four input variables X_4, X_3, X_2, X_1, derive their truth table format for PROM implementation.

$$f_1 = \overline{X}_4 X_3 \overline{X}_2 \overline{X}_1 + \overline{X}_4 X_1 + X_4 \overline{X}_3$$
$$f_2 = \overline{X}_3 \overline{X}_2 X_1 + X_3 X_1 + X_4 X_2 X_1$$
$$f_3 = X_2 X_1 + X_4 X_2 + X_3 X_2 \overline{X}_1$$

Starting with

$$f_1 = \overline{X}_4 X_3 \overline{X}_2 \overline{X}_1 + \overline{X}_4 X_1 + X_4 \overline{X}_3$$
$$f_1 = \overline{X}_4 X_3 \overline{X}_2 \overline{X}_1 + [\overline{X}_4 X_1 (X_3 + \overline{X}_3) \cdot (X_2 + \overline{X}_2)] + [X_4 \overline{X}_3 (X_2 + \overline{X}_2) \cdot (X_1 + \overline{X}_1)]$$
$$f_1 = \overline{X}_4 X_3 \overline{X}_2 \overline{X}_1 + \overline{X}_4 X_3 \overline{X}_2 X_1 + \overline{X}_4 X_3 \overline{X}_2 X_1 + \overline{X}_4 \overline{X}_3 X_2 X_1 + \overline{X}_4 X_3 X_2 X_1 + X_4 \overline{X}_3 \overline{X}_2 \overline{X}_1$$
$$\quad + X_4 \overline{X}_3 \overline{X}_2 X_1 + X_4 \overline{X}_3 X_2 \overline{X}_1 + X_4 \overline{X}_3 X_2 X_1$$
$$f_1 = m_4 + m_1 + m_5 + m_3 + m_7 + m_8 + m_9 + m_{10} + m_{11}$$

Similarly,

$$f_2 = \overline{X}_3 \overline{X}_2 X_1 + X_3 X_1 + X_4 X_2 X_1$$
$$f_2 = m_1 + m_9 + m_7 + m_5 + m_{11} + m_{13} + m_{15}$$

and

$$f_3 = X_2 X_1 + X_4 X_2 + X_3 X_2 \overline{X}_1$$
$$f_3 = m_3 + m_7 + m_{11} + m_{15} + m_{10} + m_{14} + m_6$$

The three resulting function minterms are listed in Table 2.18.

TABLE 2.18
Truth table for Example 2.14

State	X_4 X_3 X_2 X_1	f_1	f_2	f_3
0	0 0 0 0	0	0	0
1	0 0 0 1	1	1	0
2	0 0 1 0	0	0	0
3	0 0 1 1	1	0	1
4	0 1 0 0	1	0	0
5	0 1 0 1	1	1	0
6	0 1 1 0	0	0	1
7	0 1 1 1	1	1	1
8	1 0 0 0	1	0	0
9	1 0 0 1	1	1	0
10	1 0 1 0	1	0	1
11	1 0 1 1	1	1	1
12	1 1 0 0	0	0	0
13	1 1 0 1	0	1	0
14	1 1 1 0	0	0	1
15	1 1 1 1	0	1	1

PAL Module

The PAL LSI module consists of a programmable AND logic array and a fixed OR logic array. The PGA is a special case of the PAL device in that it does not have an OR logic array. These devices are useful for providing SSI and MSI logic designs in one package, thus eliminating external interconnections. The programmable feature allows the design of a selective decoder, at the expense of the AND array size. Figure 2.20 illustrates the architecture of the PGA and PAL devices. The PGA finds uses in selecting minterm decoding applications, since each AND gate has n inputs and can be programmed to sense any one of the 2^n possible input combinations. The PAL is used to realize arbitrary minimized functions of n-input variables. Both devices are limited by their inputs, outputs, and AND array size. The generalized PGA equation for the function f_i in Figure 2.20a becomes

$$f_i = (\overline{X}_2 + \overline{I}_4) \cdot (X_2 + \overline{I}_3) \cdot (\overline{X}_1 + \overline{I}_2) \cdot (X_1 + \overline{I}_1) \tag{2.2}$$

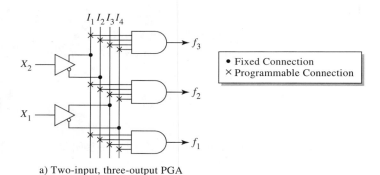

a) Two-input, three-output PGA

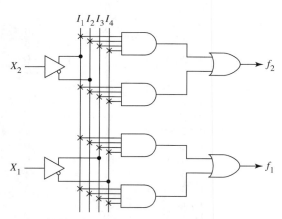

b) Two-input, four AND, two-output PAL

FIGURE 2.20
PGA and PAL device architectures.

which defines the unprogrammed state of the PGA and forms the basis for realizing any minterm containing all input variables.

The generalized PAL equation for the function f_i in Figure 2.20b becomes

$$f_i = \sum_{j=1}^{M=2} [(\overline{X}_2 + \overline{I}_4) \cdot (X_2 + \overline{I}_3) \cdot (\overline{X}_1 + \overline{I}_2) \cdot (X_1 + \overline{I}_1)]_j \qquad (2.3)$$

which defines the unprogrammed state of the PAL. This state is used as a basis for realizing an arbitrary function of n input by m output variables within the limitations of the dedicated AND array size, M. The $\overline{I}_k$ literal denotes a unique programmable link in each AND logic gate input. Initially all such links are present and are represented by 0 in the equations above. During the programming process the unwanted links are eliminated and represented by 1 in the equations above. Example 2.15 elaborates on the programming process of a PAL device.

EXAMPLE 2.15

Given a PAL device with three inputs, nine AND gates, and three outputs, derive the programming equations for the functions f_1, f_2, f_3. Assume that each OR output gate has three dedicated AND gates.

$$f_1 = m_1 + m_2 + m_3$$
$$f_2 = m_4 + m_5 + m_6$$
$$f_3 = m_1 + m_5 + m_7$$

The PAL expression for each m_i is as follows:

$$m_i = [(\overline{X}_3 + \overline{I}_6) \cdot (X_3 + \overline{I}_5) \cdot (\overline{X}_2 + \overline{I}_4) \cdot (X_2 + \overline{I}_3) \cdot (\overline{X}_1 + \overline{I}_2) \cdot (X_1 + \overline{I}_1)]$$

where $\overline{I} = 0$ for connection
       $\overline{I} = 1$ for break

For example,

$$m_1 = [(\overline{X}_3 + 0) \cdot (X_3 + 1) \cdot (\overline{X}_2 + 0) \cdot (X_2 + 1) \cdot (\overline{X}_1 + 1) \cdot (X_1 + 0)]$$
$$m_1 = [(\overline{X}_3) \cdot (1) \cdot (\overline{X}_2) \cdot (1) \cdot (1) \cdot (X_1)] = \overline{X}_3\overline{X}_2X_1$$

Thus,

$$f_1 = [(\overline{X}_3 + 0) \cdot (\overline{X}_2 + 0) \cdot (X_1 + 0)] + [(\overline{X}_3 + 0) \cdot (X_2 + 0) \cdot (\overline{X}_1 + 0)] + [(\overline{X}_3 + 0) \cdot (X_2 + 0) \cdot (X_1 + 0)]$$
$$f_1 = \overline{X}_3\overline{X}_2X_1 + \overline{X}_3X_2\overline{X}_1 + \overline{X}_3X_2X_1$$

Similarly,

$$f_2 = X_3\overline{X}_2\overline{X}_1 + X_3\overline{X}_2X_1 + X_3X_2\overline{X}_1$$

and

$$f_3 = \overline{X}_3\overline{X}_2X_1 + X_3\overline{X}_2X_1 + X_3X_2X_1$$

Since the PAL device has a fixed OR logic array, the logic minimization process is limited to single-output function realization methods only. That is to say, no P-term sharing is possible with PAL architecture, since each output OR gate has dedicated AND gates hardwired to it via the OR matrix.

PLA Module

The PLA LSI device consists of a programmable AND array cascaded to a programmable OR array. This provides flexibility and maximum minimization capability prior to embedding of the desired function into the PLA device. The PLA has a selective input decoder, as opposed to the exhaustive PROM input decoder, because of its programmable AND matrix. It has selectable concurrent output capability, as opposed to the fixed dedicated PAL outputs, because of its programmable OR matrix. It also has the ability to incorporate "don't care" conditions for logic minimization.

Figure 2.21 illustrates the internal architectures of a two-input, five-AND gate, three-output PLA device. The generalized equation of the function f_i in Figure 2.21 becomes

$$f_i = \sum_{j=1}^{M=5} C_{ij} \cdot M_j \tag{2.4}$$

where C_{ij} represents the connection from the jth AND gate output to the ith OR gate input, and the M_j term is defined as

$$M_j = [(\overline{X}_2 + \overline{I}_4) \cdot (X_2 + \overline{I}_3) \cdot (\overline{X}_1 + \overline{I}_2) \cdot (X_1 + \overline{I}_1)]_j \tag{2.5}$$

and defines the jth unprogrammed AND logic gate. The C_{ij} term assumes a one state for connection and a zero state for no connection. Similarly, the $\overline{I}_k$ links assume a zero state for connection and a one state for no connection. If both the true and complemented inputs are connected to a given AND gate, then the corresponding literal becomes a "don't care." In addition, if an AND gate with all its true and complemented inputs is connected to an OR gate input, it becomes a "don't care" P-term, which does not interfere with the logic and can be programmed at a later time if required. A "don't care" P-term and a disconnected P-term have no effect in the PLA logic function realization. However, the "don't care" P-term can be used at a later time to either correct a logic error or modify the embedded function.

As with all programmable logic, the PLA comes with a fixed number of inputs, outputs, and P-terms that can be used to realize an arbitrary $n \times m$ input-output combinational network. If the particular functions fit within one PLA device, then further logic minimization is meaningless. However, there are instances in which the number of required P-terms is not enough to realize the specified combinational network. A brute force solution would be to use the tri-state capability of these devices, in which one output from one device is used to enable the other device. Using this capability, the inputs and the outputs are tied together and the number of P-terms are doubled. If the number of P-terms required exceeds the actual number of P-terms by a small number, then it is possible to apply heuristic minimization methods, such as minterm sharing, and reduce them so that one PLA solution is possible. In some PLAs it is possible to

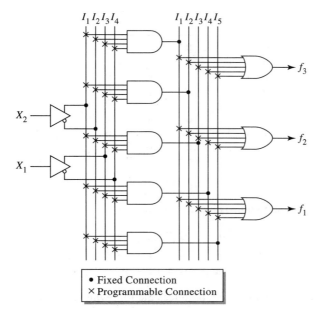

FIGURE 2.21
PLA device architecture.

select the active level of the outputs as either low or high, by an extra programming step, which is useful for implementing the complement of a function that may require fewer P-terms for inherent minimization. In general, it is always possible to use multiple-output function minimization algorithms to produce simultaneous minterm and literal minimization, prior to embedding the specified functions into a PLA device. Example 2.16 illustrates the use of a PLA device for a multiple-output function realization.

EXAMPLE 2.16

Given a PLA device with three inputs, six AND gates, and three outputs, define the programming expressions for the following three functions:

$$f_1 = m_1 + m_2 + m_3$$
$$f_2 = m_4 + m_5 + m_6$$
$$f_3 = m_1 + m_5 + m_7$$

(a) Brute force yields

$$f_1 = m_1 + m_2 + m_3 = P_1 + P_2 + P_3$$
$$f_2 = m_4 + m_5 + m_6 = P_4 + P_5 + P_6$$
$$f_3 = m_1 + m_5 + m_7 = P_7 + P_8 + P_9$$

TABLE 2.19
Truth table for Example 2.16

X_3 X_2 X_1	f_1	f_2	f_3
0 0 0	0	0	0
0 0 1	1	0	1
0 1 0	1	0	0
0 1 1	1	0	0
1 0 0	0	1	0
1 0 1	0	1	1
1 1 0	0	1	0
1 1 1	0	0	1

b) Minterm sharing, as shown in Table 2.19, results in

$$f_1 = m_1 + m_2 + m_3 = P_1 + P_2 + P_3$$
$$f_2 = m_4 + m_5 + m_6 = P_4 + P_5 + P_6$$
$$f_3 = m_1 + m_5 + m_7 = P_1 + P_5 + P_7$$

(c) Individual function minimization, produces the following expressions:

$$f_1 = (\overline{X}_3\overline{X}_2X_1 + \overline{X}_3X_2X_1) + (\overline{X}_3X_2\overline{X}_1 + \overline{X}_3X_2X_1)$$
$$f_1 = \overline{X}_3X_1 + \overline{X}_3X_2 = P_1 + P_2$$
$$f_2 = (X_3\overline{X}_2\overline{X}_1 + X_3\overline{X}_2X_1) + (X_3\overline{X}_2\overline{X}_1 + X_3X_2\overline{X}_1)$$
$$f_2 = X_3\overline{X}_2 + X_3\overline{X}_1 = P_3 + P_4$$
$$f_3 = (\overline{X}_3\overline{X}_2X_1 + X_3\overline{X}_2X_1) + (X_3\overline{X}_2X_1 + X_3X_2X_1)$$
$$f_3 = \overline{X}_2X_1 + X_3X_1 = P_5 + P_6$$

Table 2.20 provides a tabular format of the PLA programming parameters. Each P-term is associated with the input variables and the output function. For instance, P_4 uses X_3 and $\overline{X}_1$ and is connected to f_2, where a 1 indicates a true variable and a 0 indicates a complemented variable connection. The dashes (-) indicate that no connection is present.

The specified PLA has six P-terms, but a brute force solution requires nine P-terms, and thus it is P-term–limited. A heuristic solution, using minterm sharing, requires seven P-terms, and is therefore also P-term–limited. Individual output function minimization requires six P-terms; hence it is an acceptable solution in this case. In general, if no solution is found applying the methods above, then a multiple-output systematic minimization algorithm serves as the last approach before using two PLAs.

For one-of-a-kind designs, such minimization methods are not cost-effective. In volume production applications, however, every effort should be made, including function complementation, to minimize the number of PLA devices required for a given network realization. PLAs are an LSI alternative to SSI-hardwired logic solutions, since they provide the same flexibility without any external interconnections. LSI is not the end for logic configurations, but rather the beginning of a new era for digital system realization approaches.

TABLE 2.20
PLA programming table

P-Term	Input X_3 X_2 X_1	Output f_1 f_2 f_3
P_1	0 – 1	1 – –
P_2	0 1 –	1 – –
P_3	1 0 –	– 1 –
P_4	1 – 0	– 1 –
P_5	– 0 1	– – 1
P_6	1 – 1	– – 1

2.6 VLSI COMBINATIONAL DESIGN

Very large scale integration (VLSI) logic modules have equivalent logic densities of over one thousand gates. They come in various packages, with the number of pins ranging from fifty-two to more than two hundred. There are three common packages available, the pin-grid array (PGA), the plastic j-lead chip carrier (PLCC), and the quad flat pack (QFP). The last two are used with surface-mount technology designs. The modules achieve reduced size of products, low interconnection costs, higher operating speeds, increased reliability, and flexible designs.

There are two basic VLSI user specific integrated circuit (USIC) approaches, the complex PLDs (CPLDs) and the field programmable cell arrays (FPCAs). The CPLD is made up of simple, PAL-based, PLD building blocks that can be interconnected via a central programmable crosspoint matrix. High-performance CPLDs employ a cross-grid network of distributed signal paths, which span the length and width of the chip. There are dedicated input signal pins with selectable level and polarity options. In addition, the programmable signal pins can be configured as static inputs/outputs or as dynamic, bidirectional I/Os. The FPCAs consist of a universal logic cell array. Each logic cell is of either look-up table– or multiplexer logic–based design. The cells are capable of generating any Boolean function of n variables, where n is between 2 and 8. The area between the cells is used to route orthogonal signal paths of segments of various lengths. Strategically located switches along each path can be configured to connect any two cells on the chip. Each signal pin can be configured as either input, output, or bidirectional, with selectable level and polarity.

Two main device configuration options are available, one-time-programmed and reprogrammable. The former uses either fusible metal links that are selectively blown open or dielectric layer antifuse links that are selectively shorted. Reprogrammable devices use either (EPROM)/(EEPROM) switches or static random access memory (SRAM) storage elements. The fuse-based devices provide higher speeds at the expense of lower density and limited testability. The antifuse-based devices provide high speed and increased density with limited testability. The reprogrammable devices provide increased density and full testability but have lower operating speeds.

The programmable folded gate array (PFGA), shown in Figure 2.22, is a hybrid architecture that uses one gate per logic cell and a central interconnection matrix. This novel architecture relaxes the two-level AND/OR logic PLD structure constraints. It can efficiently implement either single-level or multiple-level logic designs. The device consists of two basic

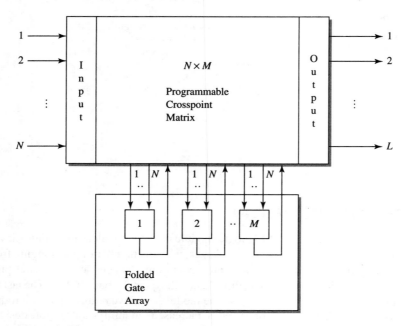

FIGURE 2.22
PFGA device architecture.

sections, the folded gate array and the programmable crosspoint matrix. The array consists of M identical N-input logic gates. The logic function is either NAND or NOR for maximum design flexibility. The matrix provides selective links that can connect the various gate inputs and outputs to each other. There are L dedicated output gates, which leaves $M–L$ available gates for internal logic use. This arrangement provides for efficient utilization of every gate in the device. Example 2.17 illustrates the realization of a comparator function, using both PLD and PFGA architectures.

EXAMPLE 2.17	Given a two-bit magnitude comparator, determine the function expressions for PLD and PFGA structure realizations. Figure 2.23a shows the AND/OR logic PLD realization. The comparator expression is

$$f(A, B) = [(A_0 \cdot B_0) + (\overline{A}_0 \cdot \overline{B})] \cdot [(A_1 \cdot B_1) + (\overline{A}_1 \cdot \overline{B}_1)]$$

Figure 2.23b depicts the NAND/NAND logic PFGA realization. The expression becomes

$$f(A, B) = \overline{\overline{[(A_0 \cdot B_0) \cdot (\overline{A}_0 \cdot \overline{B}_0)} \cdot \overline{(A_1 \cdot B_1) \cdot (\overline{A}_1 \cdot \overline{B}_1)}]}$$

Using De Morgan's theorem repeatedly, it can be shown to be identical to the previous one. Similarly, Figure 2.23c shows the NOR/NOR logic PFGA realization. The resulting expression is

$$f(A, B) = \overline{\overline{[(A_0 + B_0) + (\overline{A}_0 + \overline{B}_0)} + \overline{(A_1 + B_1) + (\overline{A}_1 + \overline{B}_1)}]}$$

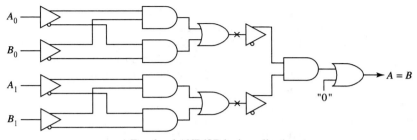

a) Two-level AND/OR logic realization

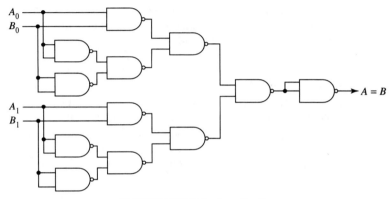

b) NAND/NAND logic realization

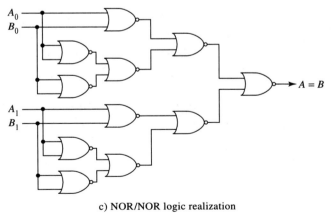

c) NOR/NOR logic realization

FIGURE 2.23
Two-bit comparator logic for Example 2.17.

In order to realize the logic using AND/OR two-level logic, it becomes necessary to exit the chip twice, wasting two input pins. This makes the device input-limited and can result in the inability to fit the logic into a single device. It also wastes OR terms, which are a precious commodity in a fixed-OR gate with PAL architecture. In contrast, the flexible array structure of the PFGA implements the design within the device without wasting any pins or gates.

In practice, VLSI devices tax the capacity of the most adept designer. For this reason software-based design tools have been developed to make the task easier and less tedious. One such popular tool is the Advanced Boolean Expression Language (ABEL)™ developed by Data I/O Corporation. ABEL uses the PRESTO logic minimization algorithm, which was developed by D. W. Brown. It is a high-level language that provides a uniform and device-independent syntax. ABEL features structured design constructs and accepts several input formats. It supports macros and directives to enhance productivity. It has a set of keywords that are combined with operators to produce statements; keywords include *title, module, device, equations, pin, input, output, test__vectors,* and *end.* Table 2.21 lists some of the operator symbols and their meanings.

A design can be entered as a schematic, as a netlist describing interconnected symbols, as a truth table, or as Boolean equations. Once the design is defined, it becomes the source file to the language compiler. First, syntax checking takes place, followed by conversion to Boolean equations format. Next, logic minimization is performed and a JEDEC output file is produced. The acronym JEDEC stands for Joint Electronic Device Engineering Council and is the name of an ASCII output file standard used for device programming and test vector creation. The file uses functional simulation to verify that a design is realizable with a specified device. In addi-

TABLE 2.21
ABEL definitions

Symbol	Meaning	Example
=	Unconditional	A = 1;
:=	Conditional	ELSE A with B := 1;
==	Relational	y3 := (Sel == 3) & En;
.x.	Don't Care	1, .x., 0;
x	Hex	xE;
^b	Binary Vector	^b1010101;
[ ]	Set	[X1, X2, X3]
→	Set Assignment	[X1, X2, X3] → Sel;
"	Comments	"Begin
;	Statement Delimiter	A = 0;
!	NOT	!A
#	OR	A # B
&	AND	A & B
!#	NOR	A !# B
!&	NAND	A !& B
$	XOR	A $ B
''	String	'Abel'

tion, the source and object printable files are generated, along with the specific device pin designations. The JEDEC file is used by the device programmer to configure the selected device. The last step is to in-circuit test the device and perform timing analysis.

The two-bit comparator logic design can be used to illustrate the salient features of an ABEL source file, using Boolean equations. In this case there are five inputs, two two-bit pairs, one enable, and a single output. When the corresponding input values match, the output becomes high; otherwise it remains low. The added enable input is used to control the output tri-state buffer. The following example is a listing of an ABEL source file for the comparator logic:

EXAMPLE 2.18

Develop the ABEL source file for a two-bit comparator logic function.

```
module    comparator
title    '2-bit comparator;
device   'PLD;
     A0, A1, B0, B1    pin 1,2,3,4;
     Equal   pin 5;
     Enable   pin 6;
     Input   =[A0, A1, B0, B1];
     Output   =[Equal];
     H,L,Z   =1,0,Z;
equations
     Output = ((A0 & B0) # (!A0 & !B0)) & (A1 & B1) # (!A1 & !B1))
             & Enable;
test__vectors
        ([Enable, Input] → Output)
     [L, ^b0000] → Z;
     [H, ^b0000] → 1;
     [L, ^b0101] → Z;
     [H, ^b0101] → 1;
     [L, ^b1010] → Z;
     [H, ^b1010] → 1;
     [L, ^b1111] → Z;
     [H, ^b1111] → 1;
end
```

"Module" defines the logic function. "Title" provides a descriptive name. "Device" specifies the target programmable device name. The signal names are associated with device pins. The input and output signal sets are declared. The device states L, H, Z are assigned values, then the logic function equation is provided in ABEL syntax. Finally, a set of test vectors is specified for logic verification.

VLSI devices are currently becoming available that challenge the designer's intuition while relaxing existing logic density limitations. Novel architectures use regular geometric logic building blocks along with reconfigurable interconnection matrices and I/O functions. Such devices can achieve generalized multi-input, multioutput, and multilevel logic networks, and they are reprogrammable. These new approaches are known as user specific integrated circuit designs. They achieve the complexity of a digital-printed circuit card, with embedded configuration capability and increased function flexibility. These features provide for versatile designs in a broad spectrum of applications.

PROBLEMS

2.1 Draw the SOP realization of Example 2.3 using AND/OR logic.

2.2 Draw the POS realization of Example 2.3 using AND/OR logic.

2.3 Draw the SOP realization of Example 2.4 using NAND/NAND logic.

2.4 Draw the full-adder realization of Example 2.7, using XOR, AND, and OR logic.

2.5 Determine the truth table for a half subtracter, and realize it using AND/OR and NOT logic.

2.6 Determine the truth table for a full subtracter, and realize it using AND/OR and NOT logic.

2.7 Draw the comparator function of Example 2.8, using NAND/NAND logic.

2.8 Determine the truth table for a three-variable positive logic XOR function, and write its SOP and POS forms.

2.9 Draw the majority logic function of Example 2.9, using AND/OR logic.

2.10 Determine the truth table for a three-variable positive logic majority function, and write its SOP and POS forms.

2.11 Determine the truth table for a three-variable negative logic exclusive-NOR function, and write its SOP and POS forms.

2.12 Determine the truth table for a three-variable negative logic minority function, and write its SOP and POS forms.

2.13 Draw the selector and distributor logic of Example 2.10, using NAND and AND logic, respectively.

2.14 Draw the decoder and encoder functions of Example 2.11, using AND and NAND logic, respectively.

2.15 Draw the four-variable function of Example 2.12, using an 8:1 multiplexer module.

2.16 Design a 32:1 multiplexer, using 8:1 modules, without tri-state capability.

2.17 Design a 32:1 multiplexer, using 8:1 modules, with tri-state capability.

2.18 Place the function of Table 2.18 on the Karnaugh map, and derive the simplified expressions.

2.19 A man needs to cross a river with a goat, a wolf, and a bag of corn. His boat can only hold him and two other items. Determine the valid combinations to get across, such that the goat does not eat the corn and the wolf does not eat the goat, if they are left unattended on the same bank.

2.20 A gas furnace controller has the following cycle. When the thermostat calls for heat, the spark generator and pilot valve are activated, provided the limit switch is closed. When the pilot flame sense switch closes, it energizes the main gas valve and disables the spark generator. When the temperature switch closes, the blower motor starts, provided the cover sense switch is closed. When the thermostat heat setting is satisfied, it disables the pilot and main gas valves. The blower motor stays on until the temperature switch opens. Realize this control logic using AND, OR, and NOT gates. Hint: Let closed = 1 and open = 0.

REFERENCES

Blakesley, Thomas R. *Digital Design with Standard MSI and LSI.* New York: John Wiley, 1975.

Exel. *EEPROM Data Book.* San Jose, CA: Exel, 1988.

Intel. *Programmable Logic Handbook.* Santa Clara, CA: Intel, 1990.

Maley, G. A., and Earle, J. *The Logic Design of Transistor Digital Computers.* Englewood Cliffs, NJ: Prentice-Hall, 1963.

Marcovitz, A. B., and Pugsley, J. B. *An Introduction to Switching System Design.* New York: John Wiley, 1971.

Monolithic Memories, Inc. *Bipolar LSI Databook.* Sunnyvale, CA: Monolithic Memories, 1982.

Pellerin, D. B. *Digital Design Using ABEL.* Englewood Cliffs, NJ: Prentice Hall, 1994.

Signetics: *Integrated Fuse Logic Data Manual.* Sunnyvale, CA: Signetics, 1983.

————. *PLD Data Manual.* Sunnyvale, CA: Signetics, 1989.

Texas Instruments, Inc. *TTL Logic Data Book.* Dallas, TX: Texas Instruments, 1993.

3

SEQUENTIAL NETWORKS

A *sequential network* is a switching function realization whose output values are dependent on the current input X and the previously stored state y. Therefore, a sequential function Z is defined as $Z = f(X, y, t)$, where t is the time variable. As in the case of a combinational network, either one can systematically input a stimulus and record the output response, or given an input-output relationship, the sequential network can be realized.

A combinational network can be viewed as a parallel n-input network, where one of the 2^n possible input combinations is applied simultaneously and results in a time-independent output. In contrast, a sequential network is seen as a serial input network where a specific k-input variable combination is applied to it over a finite interval, where $1 \leq k < n$, and results in a time dependent relationship. This requires that a storage device be used to produce an output as a function of the present and previous input states. The objectives of this chapter are as follows: (1) to define network analysis and explain synchronous and asynchronous network synthesis, (2) to present SSI-level design methodology, (3) to cover MSI-level building block designs, (4) to discuss LSI-level module design approaches, and (5) to provide an overview of VLSI-level module design, using ABEL and VHDL.

3.1 NETWORK ANALYSIS

A basic concept in sequential networks is the delay operation. A delay operation shifts a switching variable function X one unit in time, denoted as τ. Thus, $X(t) = X(t + \tau)$ may not hold true if the state of the variable X is changed during the unit interval τ. The delay notation is useful in defining the basic memory or storage element in a sequential network, also known as a *flip-flop*.

Another important concept is the *clock*, which is a sequential circuit for the generation of a stable reference signal called a *square wave*. The time interval of a repeating pattern is called the *period, T,* and its reciprocal is known as the *fundamental clock frequency*. The signal's active time, t_d, divided by its period is called the *duty cycle* and for a square wave is always $\frac{1}{2}$. The active time interval is called a *pulse* and is bounded by a *leading edge* and a *trailing edge*. A *level* is a signal whose duration is several pulse intervals of the same unit length. A sequential network is called *synchronous* if a clock is used as an additional input variable to control its operation. An *asynchronous* sequential network has no clock input. These concepts are illustrated in Figure 3.1.

A sequential network consists of a combinational network and a digital memory made up of flip-flops for storing the previous states. A *flip-flop* is a logic device capable of storing one binary digit of information. It may have one or more inputs. It has two outputs, known as the Q and $\bar{Q}$. Its next state, $Q(t + \tau)$, is a function of the present state $Q(t)$ and the present input $X(t)$, where τ represents the inherent delay of the device caused by its finite signal propagation time from input to output. In the case of a synchronous flip-flop, the input-output relationship is defined in terms of clock pulses that provide synchronization at the expense of operational speed, since the clock period must be greater than the delay interval τ of the flip-flop. Therefore, we have the next state $Q_{n+1}(t_{n+1})$, at clock pulse t_{n+1}, as a function of the present state $Q_n(t_n)$ and the present input $X_n(t_n)$ at the clock pulse t_n.

Starting with a sequential network in the form of a logic diagram, it is possible to write a set of recursive logic equations by inspection, as in the case of combinational networks. In the case of large networks, a systematic stimulus-response tabulation results in the *state transition table,* which lists every possible input and present state combination and the resulting next state output values. A compact form of this table, the *function table,* lists every input variable combination and defines the next state values in terms of $1, 0$, or present state Q. Also the "don't care" states d are included. In some instances certain input variable combinations result in undetermined next

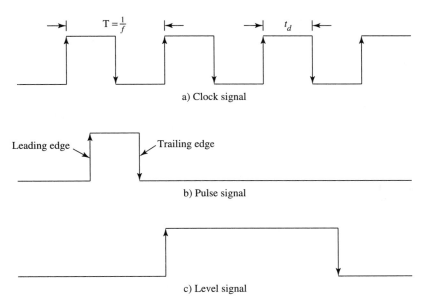

a) Clock signal

b) Pulse signal

c) Level signal

FIGURE 3.1
Basic digital timing definitions.

states *x,* and an effort is made to avoid those combinations. A *timing diagram* can be constructed to illustrate the transition table states as a function of time. In addition, a *state flow diagram* can be defined that provides a graphic representation of the sequential network. States are represented with circles, and transitions are shown as lines connecting the states.

There are four basic flip-flop types: the RS, the T, the D, and the JK. The RS flip-flop can be either asynchronous or synchronous. The T, D, and JK flip-flops are basically synchronous. The RS flip-flop can be converted to synchronous operation by gating its inputs with a clock signal.

The JK flip-flop is considered the universal type since it can be easily configured to emulate any of the other three types. The D and JK flip-flops also have asynchronous inputs to set their initial state, Q, to either 0 or 1. An RS flip-flop consists of two cross-coupled gates, both of which are either NAND or NOR. A pair of two-input NOR gates can be configured by taking the output of one and providing it as an input to the other. The remaining input of each gate is used to place the device in either of its two binary states. The following example provides a detailed analysis of a NOR-gate RS flip-flop.

EXAMPLE 3.1
Given the RS flip-flop logic symbol, logic, timing, and state flow diagrams in Figure 3.2, define the state transition and function tables.

The following recursive equations are derived by inspection using the logic diagram shown in Figure 3.2b.

$$\overline{Q} = \overline{Q + S} = \overline{Q} \cdot \overline{S}$$
$$Q = \overline{\overline{Q} + R} = Q \cdot \overline{R}$$
$$\text{For } R = S = 1, Q = \overline{Q}$$

These equations show that for $R = S = 0$, there is no change in output, Q. Also, if $S = 1$ and $R = 0$, then $Q = 1$, and if $S = 0$ and $R = 1$, then $Q = 0$. For $R = S = 1$, the outputs Q and $\overline{Q}$ are equal, which is contradictory and should be avoided. The timing diagram of Figure 3.2c serves as a vehicle to derive the state transition table. Conversely, the transition table can be used as a basis for producing the timing diagram. The state transition table (Table 3.1) is placed on the Karnaugh map of Figure 3.3, and the simplified state transition function equation becomes

$$Q(t + \tau) = S \cdot \overline{R} + \overline{R} \cdot Q(t)$$

TABLE 3.1
State transition table for Example 3.1

$Q(t)$	R	S	$Q(t + \tau)$
0	0	0	0
0	0	1	1
0	1	0	0
0	1	1	d
1	0	0	1
1	0	1	1
1	1	0	0
1	1	1	d

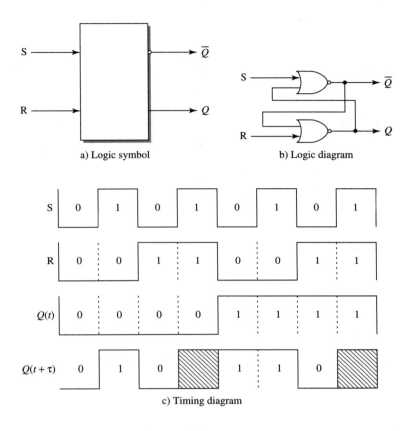

a) Logic symbol

b) Logic diagram

c) Timing diagram

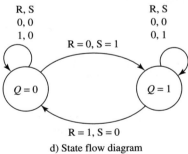

d) State flow diagram

FIGURE 3.2
RS flip-flop definitions for Example 3.1.

FIGURE 3.3
State transition function map for Example 3.1.

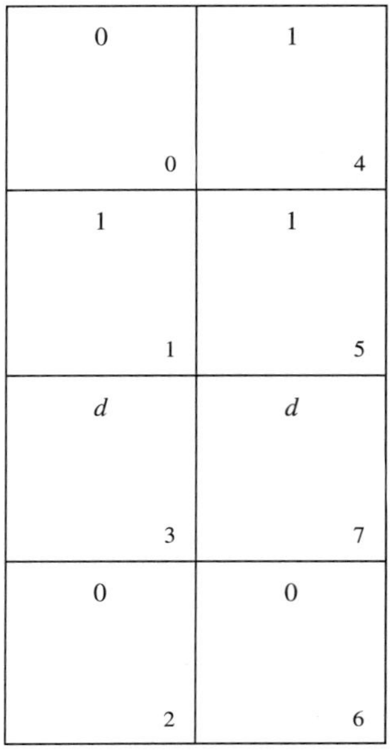

0	1
0	4
1	1
1	5
d	d
3	7
0	0
2	6

Using the two forbidden input combinations, it can be further simplified to

$$Q(t + \tau) = S + \overline{R} \cdot Q(t)$$

The function table (Table 3.2) is a condensed state transition table and can be derived from the state flow diagram of Figure 3.2d. The state flow diagram illustrates the two stable states of the RS flip-flop and all the stable and unstable transitions from each state. Starting with the $Q = 0$ state, an $S = 1$ input will produce a transition to the $Q = 1$ state. Similarly, starting with the $Q = 1$ state, an $R = 1$ input will produce a transition to the $Q = 0$ state.

The T, or toggle, flip-flop has a single input, T, and two outputs, Q and $\overline{Q}$, whose states alternate as T changes from 0 to 1. The following example illustrates the operation of the T flip-flop.

TABLE 3.2
Function table for Example 3.1

R S	$Q(t + \tau)$
0 0	$Q(t)$
0 1	1
1 0	0
1 1	d

EXAMPLE 3.2

Analyze the operation of the T flip-flop shown in Figure 3.4, and define its state transition and function tables.

The T flip-flop can be realized using an RS flip-flop and two AND gates. The state transition function equation, $Q(t + \tau)$, can be found by inspection from the logic diagram of Figure 3.4b and the transition function of the RS flip-flop, by substituting $S = \overline{Q} \cdot T$ and $R = Q \cdot T$, in $Q(t + \tau) = S + \overline{R} \cdot Q(t)$.

The state transition table, Table 3.3, can be generated from the transition function $Q(t + \tau) = \overline{Q(t)} \cdot T + Q(t) \cdot \overline{T} = T \oplus Q(t)$. It can be condensed to form the function table of Table 3.4. The state transition and function tables can also be derived from the timing and state flow diagrams, respectively, shown in Figures 3.4c and d.

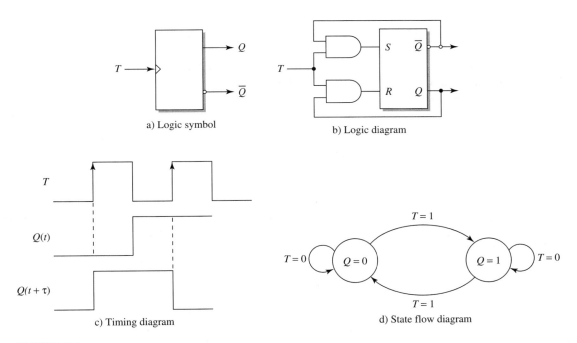

a) Logic symbol

b) Logic diagram

c) Timing diagram

d) State flow diagram

FIGURE 3.4
T flip-flop definitions for Example 3.2.

TABLE 3.3
State transition table for Example 3.2

$Q(t)$	T	$Q(t + \tau)$
0	0	0
0	1	1
1	0	1
1	1	0

TABLE 3.4
Function table for Example 3.2

T	$Q(t + \tau)$
0	$Q(t)$
1	$\overline{Q}(t)$

The D, or data, flip-flop has two inputs, the D and the clock, and two complementary outputs, Q and $\overline{Q}$. The state of its Q output follows that of an input at the time of the clock signal's transition from low to high and is delayed by the device propagation time, τ. Hence, the state transition function becomes $Q(t + \tau) = D(t) \cdot CLK$. The D-type latch is a similar device that changes its output state when the clock input is in a high state and retains that value when the clock input is in a low state. The following example provides an analysis for a D-type latch.

EXAMPLE 3.3 Perform an analysis on the D latch device illustrated in Figure 3.5, and define its state transition and function tables.

FIGURE 3.5
D flip-flop definitions for Example 3.3.

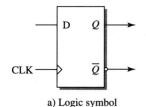

a) Logic symbol

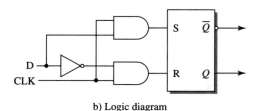

b) Logic diagram

CLK = 1, D = 1

CLK, D
0, 0
0, 1 $Q = 0$ $Q = 1$ CLK, D
0, 0
0, 1

CLK = 1, D = 0

c) State flow diagram

TABLE 3.5
State transition table for Example 3.3

Q_n	CLK	D	Q_{n+1}
0	0	0	0
0	0	1	0
0	1	0	0
0	1	1	1
1	0	0	1
1	0	1	1
1	1	0	0
1	1	1	1

The D latch can be realized using an RS flip-flop, two two-input AND gates, and an inverter. The state transition function equation, $Q(t + \tau)$, can be found by inspection from the logic diagram of Figure 3.5b and the transition function of the RS flip-flop, by substituting $S = D \cdot CLK$ and $R = \overline{D} \cdot CLK$ in $Q(t + \tau) = S + \overline{R} \cdot Q(t)$. This results in $Q_{n+1} = D \cdot CLK + D \cdot Q_n + \overline{CLK} \cdot Q_n$, where n and $n + 1$ are the present and next state indices. The equation can be further simplified to $Q_{n+1} = D \cdot CLK + \overline{CLK} \cdot Q_n$, by applying Theorem 8. Using this equation, the state transition table (Table 3.5) can be generated and condensed to form the function table (Table 3.6).

Next, the state transition table is plotted on the Karnaugh map in Figure 3.6, and the resulting state transition function equation is confirmed. The state flow diagram of Figure 3.5c can also be used to derive the function table contents.

FIGURE 3.6
State transition function map for Example 3.3.

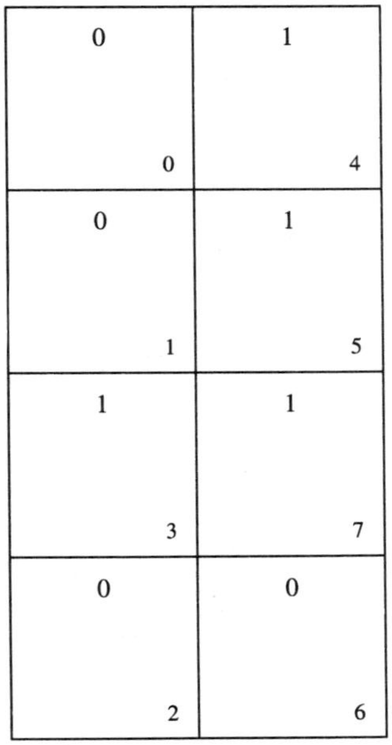

TABLE 3.6
Function table for Example 3.3

CLK	D	Q_{n+1}
0	0	Q_n
0	1	Q_n
1	0	0
1	1	1

The JK flip-flop solves the ambiguity problem of the RS flip-flop, when both the R and S inputs are in the 1 or high state. This flip-flop has three inputs, the J, the K, and the clock, and two complementary outputs, Q and $\overline{Q}$. The following example provides a detailed analysis for a positive edge, clock transition, triggered JK flip-flop.

EXAMPLE 3.4

Analyze the edge-triggered JK flip-flop shown in Figure 3.7, and derive its state transition and function tables.

FIGURE 3.7
JK flip-flop definitions for Example 3.4.

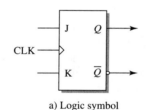

a) Logic symbol

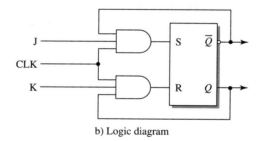

b) Logic diagram

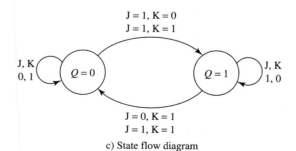

c) State flow diagram

TABLE 3.7
State transition table for Example 3.4

Q_n	J K	Q_{n+1}
0	0 0	0
0	0 1	0
0	1 0	1
0	1 1	1
1	0 0	1
1	0 1	0
1	1 0	1
1	1 1	0

The JK flip-flop can be realized using an RS device and two three-input AND gates. The state transition function equation $Q(t + \tau)$ can be found by inspection from the logic diagram of Figure 3.7b, and the transition function of the RS flip-flop, by substituting $S = \overline{Q}_n \cdot J$ and $R = Q_n \cdot K$, in $Q(t + \tau) = S + \overline{R} \cdot Q(t)$. This results in $Q_{n+1} = \overline{Q}_n \cdot J + \overline{Q_n \cdot K} \cdot (Q_n)$, which can be simplified to $Q_{n+1} = \overline{Q}_n \cdot J + Q_n \cdot \overline{K}$. Using this equation, the state transition table of Table 3.7 can be tabulated and condensed to form the function table of Table 3.8. Next, the transition table is plotted on the Karnaugh map of Figure 3.8, and the resulting state transition function is verified. The state flow diagram of Figure 3.7c can be used to verify the function table. When J = K = 1, the flip-flop will change state or toggle. If, instead, the JK flip-flop changes states during the clock level, then the transition function becomes $Q_{n+1} = \overline{Q}_n \cdot J \cdot CLK + Q_n \cdot \overline{K} + Q_n \cdot \overline{CLK}$.

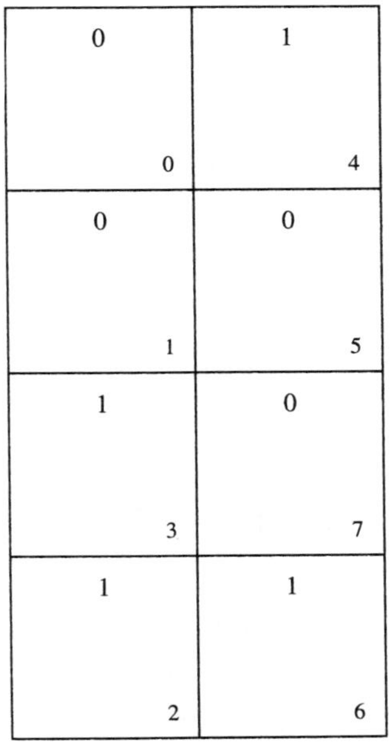

FIGURE 3.8
State transition function map for Example 3.4.

TABLE 3.8
Function table for Example 3.4

J K	Q_{n+1}
0 0	Q_n
0 1	0
1 0	1
1 1	$\bar{Q}_n$

The JK flip-flops are ideal for cascading to accomplish various sequential functions. When two or more flip-flops are cascaded, the Q and $\bar{Q}$ outputs of the first flip-flop are connected to the J and K inputs, respectively, of the second flip-flop. Their clock inputs are connected to the same clock source, as shown in Figure 3.9. The J and K input states of the first flip-flop will cause a next state transition, Q_{n+1}, to occur on the next clock input pulse. Because of the inherent path delays of the first flip-flop outputs and the clock signal, a race condition can occur, causing the second flip-flop to sense Q_{n+1} instead of Q_n. A *race condi-*

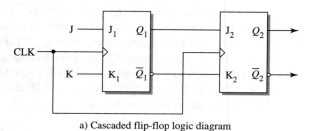

a) Cascaded flip-flop logic diagram

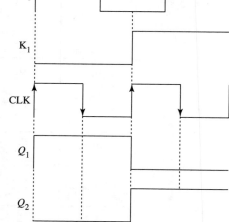

b) Cascaded flip-flop timing diagram

FIGURE 3.9
Cascaded flip-flops.

tion occurs when two or more signals arrive at the flip-flop's inputs at different times, because of different path delays, and cause the wrong output state to occur. A race condition is avoided by using two flip-flops in cascade configured as a unit, one using the true clock and the other the complemented, to produce one *master-slave flip-flop stage*. First, the master is isolated from the slave and the input states are transferred to the master J and K inputs. Second, the inputs of the master flip-flop are inhibited, and its output state is transferred to the J and K inputs of the slave flip-flop. This clock pulse controlled sequence eliminates any race conditions. It is shown in Figure 3.10.

There are two timing definitions associated with the next state transitions, both referenced to the clock input signal. These are the input setup and the input hold times. The *input setup time*, t_s, refers to the time required for an input signal to be in a stable state prior to the clock signal. The *input hold time* t_h refers to the time required for an input signal to remain in a stable state after the clock signal. For the edge-triggered devices the reference point is the clock's active transition state. For the pulse-triggered devices the reference point becomes the clock pulse. Both devices exhibit an inherent *propagation delay time* t_p from input to output transitions. Commercially available JK flip-flops incorporate asynchronous set and reset inputs,

FIGURE 3.10
Master-slave flip-flop principle.

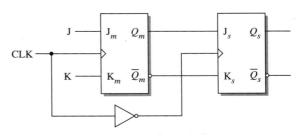

a) Master-slave flip-flop logic diagram

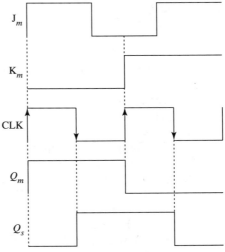

b) Master-slave flip-flop timing diagram

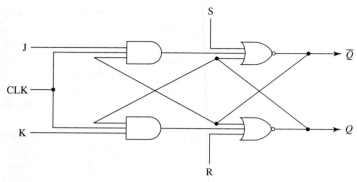

a) JK flip-flop logic diagram

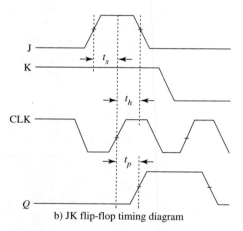

b) JK flip-flop timing diagram

FIGURE 3.11
General purpose JK flip-flop diagrams.

which can be used to preset the device to a known state prior to operation. These definitions are illustrated in Figure 3.11.

Table 3.9 lists the various JK flip-flop modes of operation. The upward arrow represents the input clock transition. The d and x entries indicate the "don't care" inputs and undetermined state, respectively.

The JK generalized flip-flop, illustrated in Figure 3.11a, can be used as a basis to realize clocked T-, D-, or RS-type devices using simple external interconnections. Starting with the state transition function, $Q_{n+1} = J \cdot \overline{Q}_n + \overline{K} \cdot Q_n$, and letting $J = K = T$, we obtain $Q_{n+1} = T \cdot \overline{Q}_n + \overline{T} \cdot Q_n = T \oplus Q_n$ as is shown in Figure 3.12a. Similarly by letting $J = D$ and $K = \overline{D}$, we get $Q_{n+1} = D \cdot \overline{Q}_n + D \cdot Q_n = D \cdot (\overline{Q}_n + Q_n) = D$, as shown in Figure 3.12b. Finally, the asynchronous RS flip-flop operation is integrated into the JK device, as shown in Figure 3.12c.

Flip-flops are usually defined in terms of the specific input(s) required to cause a predefined next state transition. This specification format is called the *excitation table,* and it is use-

TABLE 3.9
JK flip-flop modes

Mode	CLK	S	R	J	K	Q
Synchronous	↑	0	0	0	0	Q
	↑	0	0	0	1	0
	↑	0	0	1	0	1
	↑	0	0	1	1	$\overline{Q}$
Asynchronous	d	1	0	d	d	1
	d	0	1	d	d	0
	d	1	1	d	d	x

ful in deriving the state transition function in a specific flip-flop–based sequential network design. The excitation tables for the various flip-flop types are compiled in Table 3.10.

These basic flip-flops have prolific uses as the fundamental building blocks of sequential networks. They can be grouped together, in n-bit blocks, to form storage registers capable of transferring n independent information bits simultaneously at each common clock transition. In addition, they can be cascaded in n-bit lengths, with a common clock source, such that each information bit would require n clock periods in order to transfer from the first to the nth flip-flop stage. The former register transfer mode is known as parallel-in, parallel-out mode and the latter as serial-in, serial-out mode. Using external combinational logic, it is possible to achieve two hybrid modes of data transfer: parallel-in, serial-out and serial-in, parallel-out. Furthermore, it is possible to control the direction of the serial transfer modes. A right shift register transfers each incoming bit from the ith to the $i^{th} + 1$ flip-flop state. A left shift register does the reverse.

Another flip-flop application results in the binary counter, which is used for counting the number of information bits transferred over a period of time. Such counters can be defined to perform consecutive integer bit increment or decrement operations, in natural binary format,

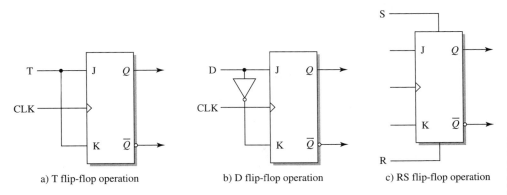

a) T flip-flop operation   b) D flip-flop operation   c) RS flip-flop operation

FIGURE 3.12
JK flip-flop configuration options.

TABLE 3.10
Flip-flop excitation table

State Transition		RS-FF		T-FF	D-FF	JK-FF	
Present State	Next State	R	S	T	D	J	K
0	0	d	0	0	0	0	d
0	1	0	1	1	1	1	d
1	0	1	0	1	0	d	1
1	1	0	d	0	1	d	0

such that an n flip-flop counter has a counting capacity of 2^n bits. Using external combinational logic, it is also possible to define any specific modulo M counter, $n \leq M \leq 2^n$, or any arbitrary counting sequence. The decimal and Gray code counters are just two examples of such definitions. Also, it is possible to define synchronous (parallel) or asynchronous (ripple) mode of counter state transitions. In summary, flip-flops form the basis for sequential network storage element design.

3.2 NETWORK SYNTHESIS

A sequential network consists of a combinational network and a memory device made up of delay- or storage-type elements. The memory device is used to store information on the present state of the network. The combinational network is used to define the next state transition and output functions. A combinational network accepts in parallel any one of the $2^n = N$ possible input combinations, at its n input terminals, and produces a simultaneous output response. In contrast, the sequential network accepts serially either one input value at a time over N input time frames or k input values at a time over t time intervals, such that $k \times t = N$. Figure 3.13

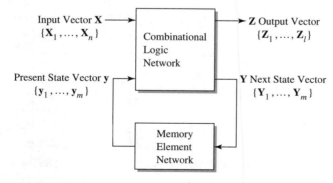

FIGURE 3.13
Sequential network block diagram.

illustrates a generalized sequential network configuration. Each received input sequence is combined with the present input state of the network to produce the next state, which is used to update the present memory state. An output function is also produced. This scheme reduces the complexity of an n-input combinational network to a much smaller sequential network that arrives at the same solution over a period of time.

The combinational logic network accepts n input switching variables (X-vector) and m present state variables (y-vector) and generates m next state variables (Y-vector) and l output variables (Z-vector). The next state variables are a function of the input variables and the present state variables (also known as internal variables), or $Y = f(X, y)$. Similarly, the output variables are a function of the input variables and the present state variables, or $Z = h(X, y)$. The relationship between Y_i and y_i is defined as $Y_i(t) = y_i(t + \tau)$ for asynchronous networks and $Y_i(n) = y_i(n + 1)$ for synchronous networks, where τ represents the memory device inherent delay and n the clock interval. The functional description of a sequential network is represented in a state table format in Table 3.11.

The *state table* consists of a next state transition tabulation and an output function tabulation, such that a given next state entry Y_{ij} is a function of the ith present state and the jth present input entry in the next state table. For example, the present state C and the input X_2 result in the next state B. Similarly, the output functions are defined in terms of present states and present inputs. For example, a present state C and a present input variable X_2 produce the output variable Z_1 and the next state B. The state table can be converted into an equivalent state flow diagram, which is basically a directed graph (digraph) representation of the sequential state table. Here the *vertices,* or circles, represent the present or internal states, and the *edges,* or directional lines, represent the various state transitions. The convention is for a literal, representing the state, to be written inside each vertex and an X_i / Z_j notation to label each edge of the resulting digraph. The corresponding state flow diagram, for Table 3.11, is presented in Figure 3.14.

There are two X-vector input sequences that can be defined for a given state flow diagram. The first is known as the *Eulerian trail,* and this specific sequence will exercise every next state transition represented by an edge in the flow diagram. However, it may not be possible to define such a sequence for all state flow diagrams. The criterion for definition is that the number of input edges must equal the number of output edges for each vertex in the directed graph. The Eulerian trail is useful for finding failures in a given network. The second sequence is known as the *Hamiltonian path,* and it transitions through all the states by going through each state only once. This sequence is useful for network synchronization. Both of these sequences are defined with an initial starting state as the reference. Thus, using state A as the starting point, the input sequence $\{X_1 X_1 X_1 X_3 X_2 X_3 X_3 X_2 X_2 X_2 X_3 X_1\}$ exercises all possible next

TABLE 3.11
State table definition

Present State	Next State			Output Function		
Input Vector ->	X_1	X_2	X_3	X_1	X_2	X_3
A	C	B	A	Z_1	Z_2	—
B	A	C	B	Z_1	$Z_1 Z_2$	—
C	D	B	D	Z_1	Z_1	Z_2
D	C	D	A	Z_2	—	Z_1

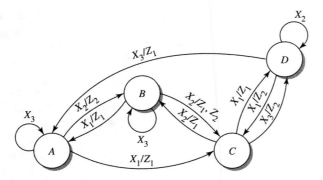

FIGURE 3.14
State flow diagram definition.

state transitions and returns to state A at the completion of this Eulerian trail. Again using state A as the reference, the input sequence $\{X_2 X_2 X_1 X_3\}$ causes a transition to every state and returns to state A at the completion of this Hamiltonian path.

Sequential networks can be classified as either clocked, synchronous or unclocked, asynchronous. The synchronous networks use a stable clock source as a reference to define when the inputs and present states may change, such that the correct next states and outputs are produced at each clock pulse interval. Asynchronous networks depend on the sequential nature of the input variables to cause the correct next states and outputs and restrict the number of simultaneous input changes to one. In both network types the inputs may be either pulses or levels.

Sequential networks can also be classified in terms of their output function definition as either Mealy or Moore type. The *Mealy type* network output function is defined in terms of both the input and state variables as $Z = f(X, y)$, and it is a pulse output. The *Moore type* network output function is defined only in terms of the present state variables as $Z = h(y)$, and it is a level output. In the Mealy state flow diagram, the output function is shown to occur during state transitions. In the Moore state flow diagram, the output is shown to occur only at present states. Since Mealy networks can produce an output at every state transition, they require fewer state

TABLE 3.12
Sequential network configurations

Synchronous Network		
Input	Output	Type
Pulse or Level	Pulse	Mealy
Pulse or Level	Level	Moore

Asynchronous Network			
Input	Output	Type	Mode
Pulse or Level	Pulse	Mealy	Pulse
Pulse or Level	Level	Moore	Pulse
Level	Level	Moore	Fundamental

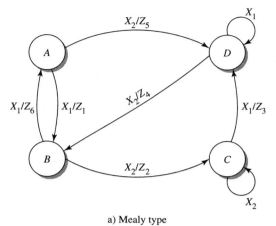

a) Mealy type

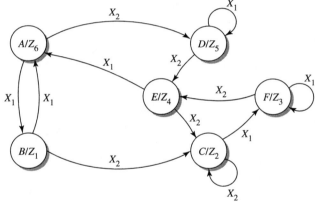

b) Moore equivalent

FIGURE 3.15
Mealy/Moore network transformation.

variables than equivalent Moore networks. A Mealy type can be transformed into a Moore type by using additional states to produce the extra output variables. Figure 3.15a illustrates a Mealy network, and Figure 3.15b shows the equivalent Moore type.

There are six output variables in the four-state Mealy network, which are produced during specific state transitions. The equivalent Moore type consists of six states, in order to produce the corresponding output variables. Table 3.12 lists the various sequential network configurations, based on the above definitions.

The synchronous type networks are commonly implemented using pulse inputs. Also, the asynchronous *pulse mode* networks are normally realized using pulse inputs. The *fundamental mode* networks can only be defined using level inputs and outputs, and therefore exist only as Moore types.

Synchronous

Sequential network models can be defined for either a Mealy or a Moore type network. The synthesis procedure almost is the same for both, the only difference being in output function definition. For the same problem specification the Moore type may require more states than its Mealy counterpart. The memory device elements may consist of D-, T-, or JK-type clocked flip-flops. The particular memory element used has a direct effect on the next state transition function complexity. The D and T types result in comparable complexity. From the excitation table of Table 3.10, it can be deduced that D-type flip-flops are preferable for 1-to-0 transitions and T-type flip-flops for 1-to-1 transitions. The JK type results in the next state transition function of lowest complexity, at the expense of an additional state variable input per device.

The timing relationships between the state variable transitions and the reference clock must be defined such that the setup and hold timing requirements of the flip-flops are satisfied in order for the correct next state transition to occur. In other words, the next state transition function inputs to the flip-flops must be stable at each clock transition. In general, a next state can become one out of 2^n possible states, where n is the number of input variables. That is to say, multiple-input variable transitions are permissible. Since the next state transition function $Y = f(X, y)$ depends upon both present states and inputs, it is imperative that no input variable transitions occur at the reference clock transitions. All such transitions must occur between clock transitions. In practice this can be achieved by synchronizing the input variables with the reference clock, using edge-triggered D flip-flops, and maintaining pulse widths greater than the clock period.

The synthesis process for a synchronous sequential network starts with a functional specification statement that describes the problem. From this functional description a state flow diagram is constructed that reflects all the possible input sequences. Next, the state flow diagram is converted into a state table format. The state table, which consists of the next state and output function matrices, is examined systematically to determine the existence of any *equivalent states*. Two states, s_i and s_j, are said to be equivalent if they produce the same outputs under all possible input combinations. Equivalent states are combined into one, and this results in a reduced state table that has as many states or rows as the number of unique input sequences to be memorized. By the same token, a reduced state table may result in a smaller number of required memory devices. The literal entries in the state table, representing generalized states, are then assigned a unique binary code in such a manner as to reduce the complexity of the resulting next state transition function. This procedure is called *encoded state assignment*. Given k flip-flops, each capable of two distinct states, it is possible to uniquely represent N states or rows in a reduced state table with k flip-flops, such that $N \leq 2^k$. The number of possible ways to assign $M = 2^k$ combinations to N states becomes the number of permutations $_M P_N$. Not all of these assignments are unique, however. There are 2^k possible state variable complementations and $k!$ reorderings, which results in duplicate assignments. Thus, the total number of assignments is reduced by the product $(2^k \cdot k!)$ and becomes the number of combinations $_M C_N = [_M P_N]/[(2^k \cdot k!)]$. For example, if $k = 2$ and $N = 4$, then $_M P_N = 24$ and $_M C_N = 3$. The unique number of available assignments grows exponentially as the number of states increases linearly.

A brute force method of trying out all possible unique assignments in order to produce the minimal next state transition function is not only tedious but also impractical. Certain basic concepts are available, however, that can be used to develop heuristic algorithms that produce near-minimal solutions most of the time. These concepts depend on the inherent properties of the state table definition to produce an efficient state assignment that results in a reduced next state transition function.

The first such property is called the *state adjacency block* (SAB), defined as a group of states that under a common input X_i result in the same next state. Such a block is called complete if it consists of 2^k states, where k is an integer defining the order of the block. In general, r state variables are needed to represent N states such that $r = \lceil \log_2 N \rceil$, where r is the smallest integer equal to or greater than the bracketed expression. This relationship may result in available spare codes that can be used to create complete SABs. It may also be possible to combine two complete SABs of the same n^{th} order and create one of the $n + 1$ order. The object is to create as many complete SABs as possible, with the judicious use of any "don't care" states, and then combine the SABs and assign mutually adjacent codes to the states in each block.

The second property is known as the *input adjacency block* (IAB), defined as a group of repeated states occurring under mutually adjacent input codes. Any "don't care" input combinations may be used to facilitate the formation of complete IABs. The adjacencies may be useful in further reducing next state transition function complexity after the actual state assignment. For such adjacencies to be effective, they must be independent from the state adjacency set expressions.

The SAB and IAB concepts form the basis of the encoded state assignment process:

1. Assign the all-zero code to the state with the maximum number of occurrences in the state table.
2. Combine as many SABs as possible to generate higher-order SABs, giving priority to those SABs with the higher repetition number.
3. Assign mutually adjacent codes to the higher-order SABs, such that they are consistent with the lower-order ones on the Karnaugh map.
4. Use any resulting IABs to further reduce the next state transition function expression.

After the state assignment is completed and incorporated into the reduced state table, the specific flip-flop excitation table is used to define the next state transition matrix. The *next state transition matrix* is an encoded state table with next state entries for a specific flip-flop device. The next state transition function is then derived from this matrix. The *next state transition function* converts the sequential problem into a combinational one by listing each next state as a function of a unique present state and a combination of input variables, $y_i x_i$. The output function truth table is generated in a similar manner. Finally, the simplified expressions for the **Y** next state variables and the **Z** output variables are represented in a logic diagram.

The synthesis process for a synchronous sequential network is summarized in the following steps:

1. Derive the state flow diagram, using the functional specification.
2. Derive the state table from the state flow diagram.
3. Reduce the state table by combining equivalent states.
4. Make an efficient state assignment on the reduced state table by the judicious use of its adjacency properties.

5. Derive the next state transition matrix, using the state assignment and the specific flip-flop excitation table.
6. Derive the next state and output function truth tables using the next state transition matrix and the output matrix.
7. Simplify the individual state variable next state transition function in step 5 and the output function in step 6, using the Karnaugh map or an algorithm.
8. Draw the resulting sequential network logic diagram.

Example 3.5 illustrates the synthesis process above using a two-input, two-output variable sequential network that recognizes two distinct input sequences and produces the appropriate output function. The functional specification requires that the inputs and outputs are pulses; hence the network must be a Mealy type.

EXAMPLE 3.5

A synchronous sequential network is required that will recognize the simultaneous input sequences X_2X_1, where $X_1 = 11001$ and $X_2 = 01100$, and that will produce an output pulse Z_1. Also, where $X_1 = 11010$ and $X_2 = 01101$, the network must produce an output pulse Z_2. Realize the resulting network using D-type flip-flops.

Figure 3.16 is a state flow diagram representation of the functional description. The state flow diagram is a graphical representation of every possible input sequence outcome. The state table is a compact representation of a state flow diagram; Table 3.13 is the state table definition

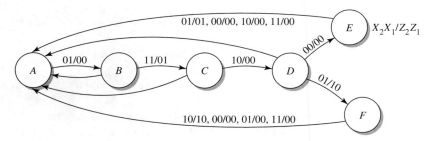

FIGURE 3.16
State flow diagram for Example 3.5.

A		E	
	0		4
F		D	
	1		5
C		d	
	3		7
B		d	
	2		6

FIGURE 3.17
State assignment map for Example 3.5.

for this problem. Table 3.14 contains the available SABs and IABs, which are placed on the Karnaugh map of Figure 3.17 to derive the encoded state assignment. Table 3.15 lists all the resulting mutually adjacent state codes. Using the state table and the state assignment, binary codes are assigned to a set of variables to uniquely identify the number of states. In this example there are six states; hence, $r = \lceil \log_2 6 \rceil = 3$. The three state variables, $y_3 y_2 y_1$, are capable of representing a total of eight states. This results in two "don't care" states that are used to simplify the next state transition function. The generalized state A was assigned the all zero code, since it has the highest number of occurrences.

Assigning the binary codes to the generalized states of Table 3.13 and using the D flip-flop excitation table results in the next state transition matrix, listed in Table 3.16. The next state transition function matrix for a D-type flip-flop is generated directly from the state assign-

TABLE 3.13
State table definition for Example 3.5

Present State	Next State Matrix Input (X_2X_1) 00 01 10 11	Output (Z_2Z_1) Matrix Input (X_2X_1) 00 01 10 11
A	A B A A	00 00 00 00
B	A A A C	00 00 00 00
C	A A D A	00 00 00 00
D	E F A A	00 00 00 00
E	A A A A	00 01 00 00
F	A A A A	00 00 10 00

TABLE 3.14
Adjacency blocks for Example 3.5

SAB	Input (X_2X_1)	Next State	IAB
A, B, C, E, F	00	A	A, B
B, C, E, F	01	A	A, C
A, B, D, E, F	10	A	A, D
A, C, D, E, F	11	A	A, E
			A, F

TABLE 3.15
State assignment for Example 3.5

State	y_3 y_2 y_1
A	0 0 0
B	0 1 0
C	0 1 1
D	1 0 1
E	1 0 0
F	0 0 1
G	1 1 0
H	1 1 1

TABLE 3.16
Next state transition matrix for Example 3.5

Present State	State Code y_3 y_2 y_1	Next State $Y_3Y_2Y_1$ (X_2X_1) 00	01	10	11	Output Z_2Z_1 (X_2X_1) 00	01	10	11
A	0 0 0	000	010	000	000	00	00	00	00
B	0 1 0	000	000	000	011	00	00	00	00
C	0 1 1	000	000	101	000	00	00	00	00
D	1 0 1	100	001	000	000	00	00	00	00
E	1 0 0	000	000	000	000	00	01	00	00
F	0 0 1	000	000	000	000	00	00	10	00
G	1 1 0	ddd	ddd	ddd	ddd	00	00	00	00
H	1 1 1	ddd	ddd	ddd	ddd	00	00	00	00

ment definition, since the excitation requirements are identical with the desired next states. The code-assigned next state transition and output matrices are organized in a truth table format, which in essence transforms the synthesis process into an $(n + m) \times (m + l)$ combinational network design problem. The next state transition and output functions, shown in Table 3.17, are derived from the next state transition matrix. Next the functions are placed on a Karnaugh

TABLE 3.17
Next state transition and output functions for Example 3.5

Minterm Number	Present State X_2 X_1 y_3 y_2 y_1	Next State Y_3 Y_2 Y_1	Output Z_2 Z_1
5	0 0 1 0 1	1 0 0	0 0
6	0 0 1 1 0	d d d	0 0
7	0 0 1 1 1	d d d	0 0
8	0 1 0 0 0	0 1 0	0 0
12	0 1 1 0 0	0 0 0	0 1
13	0 1 1 0 1	0 0 1	0 0
14	0 1 1 1 0	d d d	0 0
15	0 1 1 1 1	d d d	0 0
17	1 0 0 0 1	0 0 0	1 0
19	1 0 0 1 1	1 0 1	0 0
22	1 0 1 1 0	d d d	0 0
23	1 0 1 1 1	d d d	0 0
26	1 1 0 1 0	0 1 1	0 0
30	1 1 1 1 0	d d d	0 0
31	1 1 1 1 1	d d d	0 0

map, and the reduced next state transition and output function expressions are used to realize the sequential network logic diagram.

The Karnaugh map of Figure 3.18 is used to simplify the next state transition function, resulting in the following expressions:

$$Y_1 = (m_{13} + d_{15}) + (m_{19} + d_{23}) + (m_{26} + d_{30}) = \overline{X}_2 X_1 y_3 y_1 + \overline{X}_2 X_1 y_2 y_1 + \overline{X}_2 X_1 y_3 \overline{y}_1$$
$$Y_2 = m_8 + (m_{26} + d_{30}) = \overline{X}_2 X_1 \overline{y}_3 \overline{y}_2 \overline{y}_1 + \overline{X}_2 X_1 y_3 \overline{y}_1$$
$$Y_3 = (m_5 + d_7) + (m_{19} + d_{23}) = \overline{X}_2 \overline{X}_1 y_3 y_1 + X_2 \overline{X}_1 y_2 y_1)$$

The output function expressions, written by inspection from Table 3.17, are provided below:

$$Z_1 = m_{12} = \overline{X}_2 X_1 y_3 \overline{y}_2 \overline{y}_1$$
$$Z_2 = m_{17} = X_2 \overline{X}_1 \overline{y}_3 \overline{y}_2 y_1$$

The sequential network in the previous example represents a generic synchronous sequence detector that may be used in myriad applications—electronic locks, dual access control mechanisms, or remote control synchronizers, just to name a few. The input sequence specification can also be represented by the decimal equivalent of the $X_2 X_1$ combinations, or $I_1 = 13201$ and $I_2 = 13212$. The same sequence detector can be implemented as a Moore-type

$Y_3 Y_2 Y_1$

000	000	000	010	000	000	000	000
0	4	12	8	24	28	20	16
000	100	001	000	000	000	000	000
1	5	13	9	25	29	21	17
000	ddd	ddd	000	000	ddd	ddd	101
3	7	15	11	27	31	23	19
000	ddd	ddd	000	011	ddd	ddd	000
2	6	14	10	26	30	22	18

FIGURE 3.18
Next state transition function map for Example 3.5.

sequential network, where the outputs are only functions of the stable states. Hence the outputs become levels rather than pulses.

In order to satisfy the required flip-flop setup and hold times so as to avoid unpredictable state transitions, the input variables are synchronized with the present state variables using input storage latches. The input variable pulse widths should be at least equal to the reference

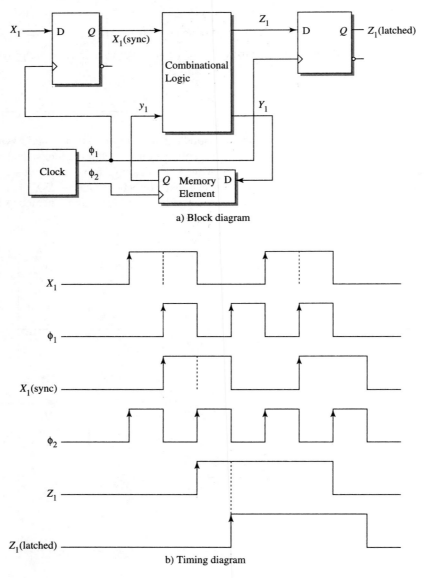

a) Block diagram

b) Timing diagram

FIGURE 3.19
Input/output signal conditioning.

clock period, in order to ensure reliable operation. In order to eliminate any output variable transient signals due to inherent combinational network race conditions, the output variables may be latched as well, using additional flip-flops. A two-phase clock can be used to latch the inputs and outputs at ϕ_1 and the state transitions at ϕ_2. Figure 3.19a illustrates these techniques in a block diagram. Figure 3.19b provides a detailed timing diagram of sequential network operation. The input variable signal X_1 is latched using the leading edge of ϕ_1 and is synchronized with the internal state variable y_1. The next state transition variable Y_1 is latched with the leading edge of ϕ_2. Finally, the output variable Z_1 is latched on the following leading edge of ϕ_1.

In summary, the clock in a synchronous sequential network controls the next state transition function such that all changes occur simultaneously at each clock edge. Input variable synchronization ensures that input transitions satisfy the timing requirements of the network, thus eliminating the possibility of erroneous state transitions. Output variable latching eliminates the chance of transients resulting from inherent network race conditions. Using a two-phase clock, a fixed delay is introduced between the input and output. This fixed delay equals one-half the reference clock period.

Asynchronous

These sequential networks are characterized by the absence of a reference clock that controls the transitions. Each state transition is instead initiated by an input variable signal change. The pulse mode networks require that no two pulses occur simultaneously, although they can occur at any time, and the next input pulse occurs after the network has reached a stable state. Each input pulse results in a next state transition, leading to a new stable state. A *stable state* is defined as one that remains at a given value until the next input pulse arrives. An input pulse must be wide enough to cause the next state transition but narrow enough not to interfere with the pulse transition occurring after that at either the same or a different input pin. The pulse mode asynchronous network model can be defined as either Mealy or Moore type. For example, vending machines can be represented as Mealy type, with the inserted coins representing the input pulses and the dispensed items representing the pulse outputs. A highway toll-collecting machine can be represented as a Moore type, with the inserted coins representing the pulse inputs and the green light representing the level output, which is reset after the vehicle passes through the toll area.

The pulse mode asynchronous synthesis process is a variation of the synchronous network synthesis. The input variable constraints provide for consistent next state transitions, which are latched with RS- or T-type flip-flops. Since the absence of a pulse is related to a stable condition, only true input variable literals appear in the network definition. The input pulses act as the reference clock in the synchronous networks, ensuring controlled next state and output variable generation.

The synthesis process for a pulse mode asynchronous sequential network is outlined in the following steps:

1. Derive the state flow diagram from the functional specification.
2. Derive the state table, using the state flow diagram.
3. Reduce the state table by combining any equivalent states.
4. Provide a state assignment that will result in a reduced next state transition function.

5. Derive the next state transition matrix, using the state assignment and the specific flip-flop excitation table.
6. Derive the next state and output function truth tables using the next state transition matrix, and the output matrix.
7. Simplify the individual state variable next state transition functions in step 5 and the output functions in step 6, using a Karnaugh map or an algorithm.
8. Draw the resulting sequential network logic diagram.

Example 3.6 illustrates the synthesis process, using a Mealy-type stamp-dispensing machine.

EXAMPLE 3.6   A stamp-dispensing machine is able to release one 25¢ stamp at a time. It accepts nickels, dimes, and quarters in any order, and it will give 5¢ change if three dimes are inserted. If after a subtotal of 10¢ or more a quarter is inserted, the machine returns all the coins without releasing a stamp. Realize this pulse mode sequential network using T-type flip-flops.

FIGURE 3.20
State flow diagram for Example 3.6.

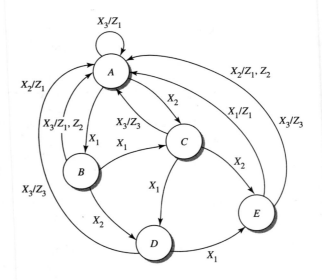

TABLE 3.18
State table definition for Example 3.6

Coin Input	Present State	Next State X_1 X_2 X_3	Output $(Z_3Z_2Z_1)$ X_1 X_2 X_3
0	A	B C A	000 000 001
5¢	B	C D A	000 000 011
10¢	C	D E A	000 000 100
15¢	D	E A A	000 001 100
20¢	E	A A A	001 011 100

FIGURE 3.21
State assignment for Example 3.6.

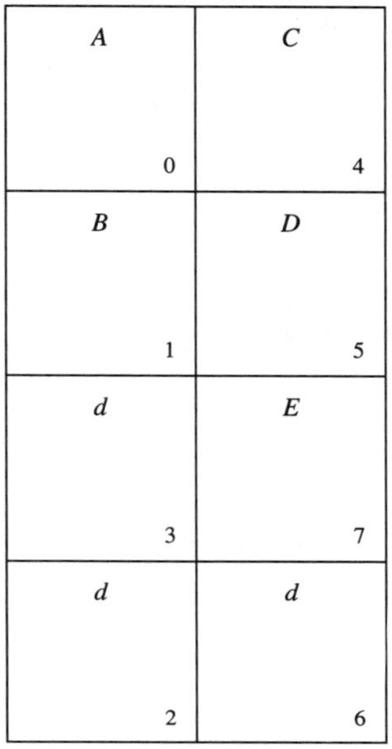

A	C
0	4
B	D
1	5
d	E
3	7
d	d
2	6

Let $X_1 = 5¢$, $X_2 = 10¢$, $X_3 = 25¢$, $Z_1 =$ stamp output, $Z_2 = 5¢$ return, and $Z_3 =$ coin return.

Figure 3.20 is the state flow diagram for the stamp-dispensing machine. The state table is derived from the state flow diagram and listed in Table 3.18. The Karnaugh map of Figure 3.21 is used to derive the encoded state assignment. The resulting encoded states are substituted in the truth table, along with the D and T flip-flop excitation tables, to provide the next state transition matrices listed in Table 3.19.

TABLE 3.19
Next state transition matrices for Example 3.6

PS	y_3 y_2 y_1	N/S D-Matrix X_1 X_2 X_3	N/S T-Matrix X_1 X_2 X_3
A	0 0 0	001 100 000	001 100 000
B	0 0 1	100 101 000	101 100 001
C	1 0 0	101 111 000	001 011 100
D	1 0 1	111 000 000	010 101 101
E	1 1 1	000 000 000	111 111 111
F	0 1 1	ddd ddd ddd	ddd ddd ddd
G	0 1 0	ddd ddd ddd	ddd ddd ddd
H	1 1 0	ddd ddd ddd	ddd ddd ddd

The next state transition and output functions are derived from Table 3.19 by inspection and placed on four-variable Karnaugh maps. The simplified next state transition function expressions, T_1, T_2, and T_3, become

$$T_1 = X_1\bar{y}_3 + X_1\bar{y}_1 + X_1y_2 + X_2y_3 + X_3y_1$$
$$T_2 = X_1y_3y_1 + X_2y_2 + X_2y_3\bar{y}_1 + X_3y_2$$
$$T_3 = X_1y_2 + X_1\bar{y}_3y_1 + X_2y_1 + X_2\bar{y}_3 + X_3y_3$$

Similarly, the output function expressions become

$$Z_1 = X_1y_3y_2y_1 + X_2y_3y_1 + X_3\bar{y}_3\bar{y}_2$$
$$Z_2 = X_2y_3y_2y_1 + X_3\bar{y}_3\bar{y}_2y_1$$
$$Z_3 = X_3y_3\bar{y}_2 + X_3y_3y_1$$

In summary, the state flow diagram follows from the word statement of the problem. The resulting state table is in its reduced form, and an efficient state assignment is made to generate the next state transition and output function matrices. Since five out of the possible eight states are used, it is possible to further reduce the next state transition function by the judicious assignment of the three "don't care" states. The next state transition function was derived for a T-type memory device. The output function is independent of memory device selection.

The fundamental mode asynchronous sequential networks are defined for level inputs and outputs. This model of network can only exist as a Moore type. The concept of *total state,* associated with this type of network, defines the network state as the combination of all present states and present input values. The input-level changes can occur at any time, but only one input variable change associated with an output variable change can occur at a time. This sequential network architecture uses delay elements between the present and next state variable terminals, and the delay element value must exceed the minimum propagation path delay of the combinational section. This constraint ensures that no essential hazards occur that could cause erroneous state transitions. *Essential hazards* originate from a single input variable change but arrive at the output at different times due to unequal path delays. The emphasis in the fundamental mode network state assignment is to make certain, as in the case of inputs, that each state-to-state transition causes a single state variable value change. In other words a coding scheme, such as Gray code, is required to eliminate critical races. A *critical race* occurs when the order of the multiple state variable changes, during state transitions, determines the next stable state. A *stable next state* is one that occurs consistently under the same present state and input combination. If such a coding scheme is not possible, then an assignment can be found that produces noncritical races or cycles. *Cycles* consist of a set of specific intermediate unstable state transitions that reach a stable final state. *Noncritical races,* even though they are order-dependent upon the multiple state variable changes, will always arrive at the correct next stable state. An alternative approach is to use any "don't care" states, or define an additional state variable to produce additional ones, in order to obtain dual adjacent coding for each state flow table row, such that all row transitions become adjacent.

The fundamental mode sequential network synthesis process begins with the conversion of the functional specification into the state flow diagram. The state flow diagram is represented by a stable table variant, which is referred to as the *state flow table*. This table is prepared by assigning one stable state per row, which is indicated by an underlined literal, and an output defined for that state. Multiple-input variable changes are assigned "don't care" states in the state flow table, since they are unspecified. The concept of compatible states is used to reduce the state flow table by row combining. Two states s_i and s_j are said to be compatible if for every input X_i the same output results when their outputs are specified. The state flow table is reduced using a *merger diagram*. This can be presented as a graph whose vertices consist of all the stable states and whose edges represent all possible compatible sets of states. Merging is possible if two or more rows can be combined into one. Such a condition occurs when there are no conflicting state entries for the same input combinations. Once a reduced state flow table is derived, a state assignment is chosen that produces single state variable changes for each state-to-state transition. Since the total state is defined as the sum of input and present state combinations, it becomes possible to reduce the total number of state variables required to distinguish each state, provided that the state assignment goal is achieved with fewer state variables. Next, the state transition matrix and the output truth table are compiled. The next state variable and output function expressions are minimized on the Karnaugh map, and the resulting logic diagram is drawn. In practice the next state variable outputs are connected directly to the present state variable inputs. If any essential hazards occur, however, the path is broken and gates are inserted to increase the feedback delay.

The synthesis process can be summarized in the following steps:

1. Derive the state flow diagram from the functional specification.
2. Derive the state flow table from the state flow diagram.
3. Reduce the state flow table by combining rows.
4. Choose a state variable assignment that results in correct next states.
5. Derive the next state transition and output matrix by substituting the assigned state variable codes into the reduced state flow table from step 3.
6. Derive the next state transition and output function truth tables using the matrix derived in step 5.
7. Minimize the next state transition and output functions.
8. Draw the resulting sequential network logic diagram.

Example 3.7 illustrates the synthesis process.

EXAMPLE 3.7

A sequencer is required for an elevator car so that it can stop at any of four floors, one at a time, and provide express service to and from the fourth and the first floors. Two input variables, X_2X_1, are defined for floor selection. An output function, Z, is defined to indicate the direction of travel. Realize the specified sequential network.

The state flow diagram of Figure 3.22 is constructed from the word statement definition of the problem. The diagram represents all possible transitions resulting from the encoded input variable combinations. Table 3.20 lists the input variable encoding. Next the state flow table is created, such that there is only one stable state and one corresponding input definition per row (Table 3.21). The underlined literals represent stable states. The plain literals represent unstable state transitions, and the dashes (-) represent forbidden "don't care" states resulting from

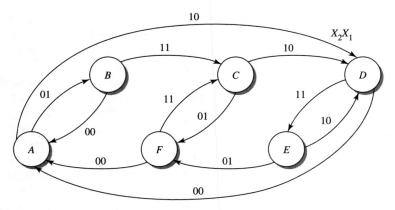

FIGURE 3.22
State flow diagram for Example 3.7.

multiple-input variable transitions. The merger diagram of Figure 3.23 is used to derive the reduced flow table, Table 3.22. The table contains multiple stable states per row, which are dis-
tinguishable by the different input combinations and which define the total state. The stable
state outputs are also specified.

TABLE 3.20
Input encoding for Example 3.7

Floor	X_2 X_1
1	0 0
2	0 1
3	1 1
4	1 0

TABLE 3.21
State flow table for Example 3.7

Present State	Next State 00 01 11 10	Output Z
$\underline{A}$	$\underline{A}$ B — D	1
$\underline{B}$	A $\underline{B}$ C —	1
$\underline{C}$	— F $\underline{C}$ D	1
$\underline{D}$	A — E $\underline{D}$	0
$\underline{E}$	— F $\underline{E}$ D	0
$\underline{F}$	A $\underline{F}$ C —	0

TABLE 3.22
Reduced flow table for Example 3.7

y_2	y_1	00	01	11	10
0	0	$\underline{A}$, 1	$\underline{B}$, 1	C	D
0	1	A	$\underline{F}$, 0	$\underline{C}$, 1	D
1	1	A	F	$\underline{E}$, 0	$\underline{D}$, 0
1	0	A	F	E	D

FIGURE 3.23
Merger diagram for Example 3.7.

$$A \text{———} B$$
$$C \text{———} F$$
$$D \text{———} E$$

A given state is stable if $Y_i = y_i$ for the same input value X_i. Each stable state is assigned a unique code. Unstable states are assigned the code of their corresponding stable states, regardless of their relative row location. The next state transition matrix consists of the corresponding total state, which defines each state flow table entry. The next state transition matrix of Table 3.23 is derived from the reduced state flow table by substituting the unique state assignment. The transition matrix is used to tabulate the next state transition and output functions. The functions are then placed on four-variable Karnaugh maps for minimization. The resulting simplified next state transition expressions are

$$Y_1 = X_2 + y_1 X_1 + y_2 X_1$$
$$Y_2 = X_2 \overline{X}_1 + y_2 X_2$$

Similarly, the output function expression is

$$Z = \overline{y}_2 \overline{y}_1 \overline{X}_2 \overline{X}_1 + \overline{y}_2 \overline{y}_1 \overline{X}_2 X_1 + \overline{y}_2 y_1 X_2 X_1$$

In the previous example, the state flow table was reduced to three rows, requiring two state variables. The extra state variable combination is used to reduce the next state transition function and to eliminate any critical races by the judicious assignment of "don't care" states. In the reduced table (Table 3.22), the first column forms a noncritical race condition. This is because stable state $\underline{A}$ is always reached when starting from an unstable state A, while $y_2 y_1 = 11$, independent of the order in which the state variables, $y_2 y_1$, change. Starting from an unstable state D while $y_2 y_1 = 00$, the same holds true for column four and its stable state $\underline{D}$. Column three represents the ideal case in which there are no races or cycles that transition through one or more unstable states. Column two displays a cycle starting from an unstable state F while $y_2 y_1 = 10$ to stable state $\underline{F}$. However, if the "don't care" state of the last row is chosen as B, then a critical race condition occurs. Specifically, starting with $y_2 y_1 = 11$, if y_2 changed first, the correct stable state $\underline{F}$ would be reached. If y_1 changed first, the incorrect stable state $\underline{B}$ would be reached instead. In state flow table rows, if the input variables, $X_2 X_1$, change simultaneously, the sequencer enters an unstable state that would inevitably lead to a stable next state. The relationship between the initial and final stable states is such that, given simultaneous input

TABLE 3.23
Next state transition matrix for Example 3.7

y_2	y_1	00	01	11	10
0	0	00, 1	00, 1	01	11
0	1	00	01, 0	01, 1	11
1	1	00	01	11, 0	11, 0
1	0	00	01	11	11

variable changes, the sequencer skips over the next adjacent state. Hence, when the single input variable change rule is violated, the elevator skips floors. One may use this property to make either odd or even floor stops.

3.3 SSI SEQUENTIAL DESIGN

A typical sequential SSI logic configuration consists of a sixteen-pin DIP package that contains two flip-flop devices. They may be RS-, D-, or JK-type storage elements, and together with the combinational logic, they form the basis for sequential network designs. These devices are used as the building blocks for storage registers, shift registers, and counters.

A *storage register* consists of a group of n flip-flops that are clocked simultaneously, using a common reference clock. This enables parallel transfers of an n-bit wide data word in and out of the register. This register type is known as parallel-in, parallel-out.

A *shift register* consists of n cascaded flip-flops that are clocked simultaneously, using a common reference clock. This arrangement enables serial data transfers in and out of the register. Thus, an n-bit data word would require n clock pulses to perform a serial transfer, versus one pulse using a parallel-in, parallel-out register. This shift register type is known as serial-in, serial-out. Shift registers can also be defined for serial-in, parallel-out and vice-versa, and with either left or right shift direction. A circular shift register is formed by connecting the last flip-flop output to the first flip-flop input. Figure 3.24 illustrates the above concepts, using D-type flip-flops. The data storage register of Figure 3.24a stores the states of the X_i input variables at each clock pulse. The shift register of Figure 3.24b stores the state of X_{IN} in the first flip-flop on the first clock pulse. At each clock pulse thereafter, each state is transferred to the next cascaded flip-flop. The right/left shift register of Figure 3.24c uses combinational logic to control the shift direction of the input. The X_R data input is used, in conjunction with DIR $= 1$, for right-shift operation. The X_L data input is used, in conjunction with DIR $= 0$, for left-shift operation. The shift register in Figure 3.24d has parallel-input data-loading capability. The flip-flops have asynchronous set and reset inputs that are used for parallel data loading, as defined by the truth table. If the Q_i flip-flop outputs are also available at the IC package pins, then parallel data-out transfers are also possible. In addition, the outputs can have tri-state capability. When all the features above are combined in one design, the result is a universal shift register.

Shift registers can also be easily configured, with combinational logic feedback to the first stage, for counting internal states. The simple feedback of the last stage output to the first stage input forms the *ring counter*. This counter is capable of counting n distinct states, one for each stage, and requires no decoding. However, it leaves $2^n - n$ unused states. If an inverter is placed in the feedback path, a twisted ring or *Johnson counter* results, which is capable of counting $2n$ states. In practice, additional combinational logic is placed in the feedback path in order to guarantee self-starting capability in one of the valid counting states. It is also possible to define a combinational feedback, consisting of cascaded exclusive-OR (XOR) gates, that enables the shift register to count up to $2^n - 1$ states. This shift register is commonly referred to as a *maximum length sequence* (MLS) counter. Figure 3.25 illustrates these shift register configurations. The ring counter configuration of Figure 3.25a generates a four-length state sequence. Similarly, the Johnson counter configuration of Figure 3.25b generates an eight-length sequence. The sequences above must be initialized in any one of the valid states in the se-

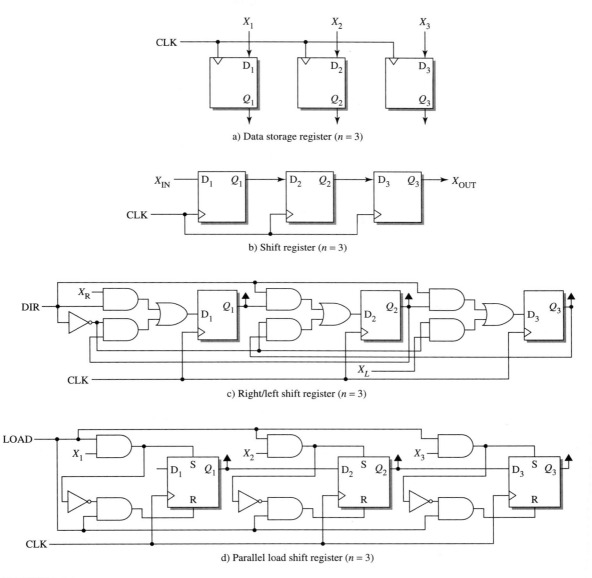

a) Data storage register ($n = 3$)

b) Shift register ($n = 3$)

c) Right/left shift register ($n = 3$)

d) Parallel load shift register ($n = 3$)

FIGURE 3.24
Flip-flop register configurations.

quence. The ring counter shown in Figure 3.25c is capable of generating a four-length state sequence from any initial state. This is achieved by the use of feedback logic to detect the two initial invalid states that cause a lockup condition. A *lockup condition* occurs when the counter enters in an unused state and stays there indefinitely. A NOR gate is used to force the counter into the 1 state when it detects the invalid states 0 and 8, respectively. The shift register configura-

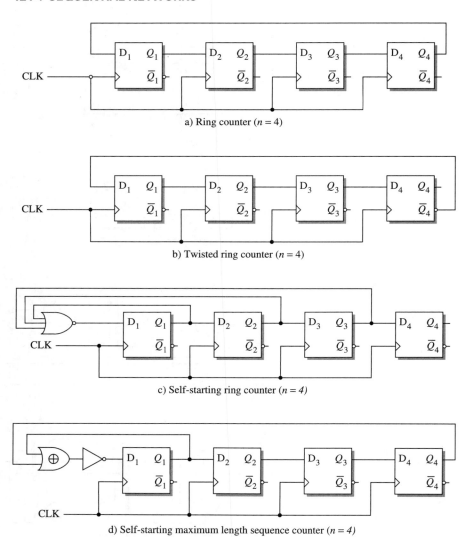

a) Ring counter ($n = 4$)

b) Twisted ring counter ($n = 4$)

c) Self-starting ring counter ($n = 4$)

d) Self-starting maximum length sequence counter ($n = 4$)

FIGURE 3.25
Shift register sequence generation.

tion of Figure 3.25d results in a self-starting maximum-length sequence counter. The outputs of stages 1 and 4 are fed back to the input, via an XOR gate, to produce a sixteen-state sequence. The NOT gate ensures that a starting state of 0 will not lock up the sequence. Another application of flip-flops is counter designs, which are capable of either sequencing consecutively through each possible state or, with external combinational logic, of following a repeatable arbitrary state sequence. In general, n flip-flops can count 2^n possible combinations or internal counter states. Conversely, N states can be counted by $\lceil \log_2 N \rceil = n$ flip-flops.

There are two general counter types, the asynchronous, or ripple, and the synchronous, or parallel. Asynchronous counters use a clock pulse only to toggle the first-stage flip-flop. The remaining stages use their outputs as clock inputs to their adjacent stage. The asynchronous counter configuration has an operating speed limitation that is a function of the number of stages. For an n-stage ripple counter, with uniform propagation delay t_p in each stage, the maximum operating clock frequency equals $f \leq 1/(nt_p)$. In other words, its counting speed cannot exceed the time it takes for an input transition to ripple through to the last stage, hence the name ripple counter. Synchronous counters provide a common clock in every stage and a look-ahead-carry combinational network to eliminate ripple and to speed up counting. This configuration

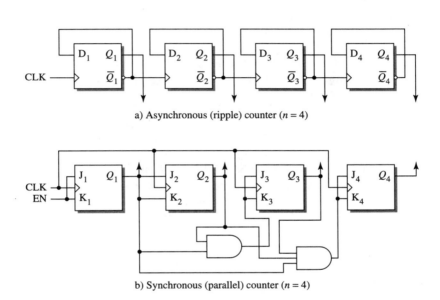

a) Asynchronous (ripple) counter ($n = 4$)

b) Synchronous (parallel) counter ($n = 4$)

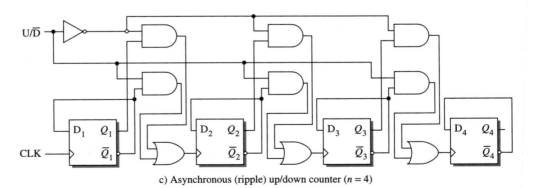

c) Asynchronous (ripple) up/down counter ($n = 4$)

FIGURE 3.26
Binary counter configurations.

has an operating speed limited by the sum of one-stage propagation delay and the parallel carry gate delay t_g. Thus, for an n-stage parallel counter the maximum operating frequency becomes $f \le 1/t_p + 1/t_g$. A counter can be defined to count from its all-zero to its all-one state, and vice-versa, using external up/down control logic. Also, an n-stage counter can be realized with any modulus value up to 2^n, by decoding the desired state to reset the counter. These various configurations are illustrated in Figure 3.26.

All three counters have one thing in common: the count occurs in the natural binary consecutive sequence. Figure 3.26a shows a realization of a four-stage binary ripple counter, using D flip-flops with feedback to achieve the equivalent of a T-type device. Figure 3.26b uses JK flip-flops, in a T configuration mode, and external logic to sense the occurrence of multiple 0-to-1 transitions for the look-ahead-carry function. In addition, a count enable input is present and can be used for controlled count operations. Figure 3.26c illustrates the concept of an up/down count sequence, which is achieved by selecting the cascaded configuration's true or complemented outputs for clock inputs. A counter can incorporate this feature, along with parallel load capability, by the use of additional combinational logic.

Synchronous counters, in addition to their speed advantage, can be configured to count in any arbitrary sequence. There are two approaches available, the indirect and direct. The indirect approach uses a binary synchronous counter and decoder to transform each counter state into the desired state sequence. The direct approach uses a storage register and a combinational network to transition through the desired state sequence. With an indirect approach the desired state in the sequence would be $Y_j = f(Y_i)$. With a direct approach the desired state would be $Y_i = f(y_i, t)$. That is, either a combinational or an *autonomous* sequential network, which requires no input variables, can be used to achieve an arbitrary sequence counter. The autonomous sequential network is faster operationally. The two arbitrary sequence counter approaches are illustrated in Figure 3.27. The indirect or arbitrary sequence emulation method shown in Figure 3.27a reduces the problem to a combinational multi-input, multi-output func-

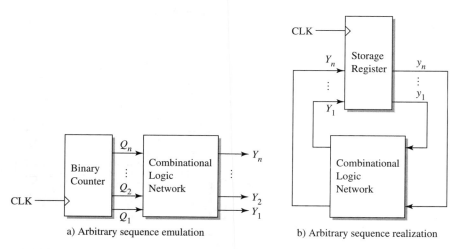

a) Arbitrary sequence emulation

b) Arbitrary sequence realization

FIGURE 3.27
Arbitrary sequence synthesis methods.

tion solution. The direct or arbitrary sequence realization method shown in Figure 3.27b is similar to a typical synchronous sequential network synthesis problem. For an n-stage counter, 2^n unique states can be decoded to produce any desired output sequence, provided it does not exceed the capacity of the existing counter.

Example 3.8 illustrates the arbitrary sequence emulation process.

EXAMPLE 3.8

Given a four-stage binary counter, derive the combinational network needed to produce the following arbitrary sixteen-state sequence:

$$1, 3, 5, 7, 9, 11, 13, 15, 0, 4, 6, 8, 10, 12, 14, 15$$

For $n = 4$, the number of possible states becomes sixteen. Table 3.24 lists the required state decoder function definition. The input columns consist of the natural binary counter sequence. The output columns define the corresponding arbitrary state sequence. The four output functions, Y_4, Y_3, Y_2, Y_1, are placed on a four-variable Karnaugh map, and the resulting decoder logic expressions are

$$Y_1 = \overline{D} + (C \cdot B \cdot A)$$
$$Y_2 = (\overline{D} \cdot A) + (D \cdot C \cdot B) + (D \cdot C \cdot \overline{A}) + (D \cdot B \cdot \overline{A})$$
$$Y_3 = (\overline{D} \cdot B) + (C \cdot B) + (B \cdot \overline{A}) + (D \cdot \overline{B} \cdot A)$$
$$Y_4 = C + (D \cdot B \cdot A)$$

TABLE 3.24
State decoder definition for Example 3.8

Input D C B A				Output Y_4 Y_3 Y_2 Y_1			
0	0	0	0	0	0	0	1
0	0	0	1	0	0	1	1
0	0	1	0	0	1	0	1
0	0	1	1	0	1	1	1
0	1	0	0	1	0	0	1
0	1	0	1	1	0	1	1
0	1	1	0	1	1	0	1
0	1	1	1	1	1	1	1
1	0	0	0	0	0	0	0
1	0	0	1	0	1	0	0
1	0	1	0	0	1	1	0
1	0	1	1	1	0	0	0
1	1	0	0	1	0	1	0
1	1	0	1	1	1	0	0
1	1	1	0	1	1	1	0
1	1	1	1	1	1	1	1

From this example it can be deduced that the desired count sequence states must be equal to those of the counter. If the desired sequence contained fewer states, feedback logic would be needed to adjust the modulus of the counter. Since the counter and the desired arbitrary sequence lengths are equal, a multi-output truth table is generated, and the individual output functions are simplified on a Karnaugh map. Note that the repeated state in the desired arbitrary count, 15, was successfully decoded, since the total number of states was within the capacity of the binary counter.

The arbitrary sequence realization method can be applied to either single or repeated state occurrences by providing k extra flip-flops for up to 2^k combined repetitions. Thus, $n + k$ flip-flops can realize a maximum of 2^n unique states and 2^k state repetitions. This method is more flexible and is similar to the synchronous sequential network synthesis, without the input variables.

The synthesis process is outlined in the following steps:

1. Derive the state function diagram from the functional specification.
2. Develop the state transition table from the state transition diagram.
3. Calculate the number of n flip-flops required, based on the number of unique states in the sequence, using the state transition table.
4. Calculate the number of k flip-flops required, based on the number of repeated states in the state transition table.
5. Using the state transition table, tabulate a truth table, specifying the next state variables as a function of the present state variables.
6. Using the truth table from step 5 and the excitation table of the specific flip-flop type, develop a next state transition matrix.
7. Simplify the resulting next state variable functions on the Karnaugh map, using any resulting "don't care" states to further reduce complexity.
8. Draw the resulting sequential network logic diagram.

Example 3.9 illustrates the synthesis procedure above, with repeated and "don't care" states, using D-type flip-flops to facilitate the next state transition function.

EXAMPLE 3.9

The following arbitrary count sequence is required:

$$0, 3, 5, 7, 3, 2, 1, 4$$

Realize a sequential network using D-type flip-flops.

The number of states $N = 7$; hence the number of required flip-flops $n = \lceil \log_2 7 \rceil = 3$. The number of repeated states $k = 1$, and the total number of flip-flops becomes $n + k = 4$. The state transition table (Table 3.25) is derived from the problem statement. Next, the state transition function is tabulated in Table 3.26, using natural binary assignment for the defined state sequence.

The following "don't care" state assignment is chosen to minimize the functions and to eliminate lockup conditions, so that self-starting sequence capability is in place.

$$S_6, S_{14}, S_{15} \rightarrow 11; \; S_{10} \rightarrow 1; \; S_8 \rightarrow 3; \; S_{12} \rightarrow 0; \; S_9 \rightarrow 4; \; S_{13} \rightarrow 7$$

TABLE 3.25
State transition table for Example 3.9

Present State	Next State
0	3
1	4
2	1
3	5
4	0
5	7
6	d
7	11
8	d
9	d
10	d
11	2
12	d
13	d
14	d
15	d

TABLE 3.26
State transition function for Example 3.9

State Number	Present $y_4\ y_3\ y_2\ y_1$				Next $Y_4\ Y_3\ Y_2\ Y_1$			
0	0	0	0	0	0	0	1	1
1	0	0	0	1	0	1	0	0
2	0	0	1	0	0	0	0	1
3	0	0	1	1	0	1	0	1
4	0	1	0	0	0	0	0	0
5	0	1	0	1	0	1	1	1
6	0	1	1	0	d	d	d	d
7	0	1	1	1	1	0	1	1
8	1	0	0	0	d	d	d	d
9	1	0	0	1	d	d	d	d
10	1	0	1	0	d	d	d	d
11	1	0	1	1	0	0	1	0
12	1	1	0	0	d	d	d	d
13	1	1	0	1	d	d	d	d
14	1	1	1	0	d	d	d	d
15	1	1	1	1	d	d	d	d

Substituting the above assignment into Table 3.26 and performing function minimization using a four-variable Karnaugh map results in the following next state transition function expressions:

$$Y_1 = \bar{y}_3\bar{y}_1 + y_3y_1 + y_3y_2 + \bar{y}_4y_2$$
$$Y_2 = \bar{y}_3\bar{y}_2\bar{y}_1 + y_3y_1 + y_3y_2 + y_4y_2y_1$$

$$Y_3 = \bar{y}_4\bar{y}_3y_1 + \bar{y}_2y_1$$
$$Y_4 = y_3y_2$$

In the previous example there are seven unique states, which can be counted with three flip-flops. In addition, there is one repeated state, 3, that requires an extra flip-flop for a total of four flip-flops. The state transition function is tabulated using the state transition table and is simplified on the Karnaugh map. The judicious assignment of the "don't care" states contributes to the function complexity reduction and also assures a self-starting count sequence capability. Normally, the counter has to be initialized to one of the states in the sequence. However, with careful "don't care" state assignment it will always transition into the desired sequence after several clock cycles, which eliminates a lockup condition. The state transition occurs in a controlled sequence and produces the desired state sequence. Each transition takes place at the occurrence of each reference clock pulse. The repetition rate and periodicity of the clock can be altered by a control logic network in order to satisfy the functional requirements of the specific application.

Because of its cyclic nature, a simple traffic light sequencer can be realized using a binary counter, with appropriate combinational logic to control the signal sequence. There are four basic states to be remembered, which are used to control the six individual traffic light signals. Let us assume that the street side has a green light and the road side has a red light. A finite time later the street side switches to yellow, while the road side remains red. A short time later the signals switch such that the street side is red and the road side, green. A fixed time later the road side switches to yellow, while the street side remains red. Then the cycle repeats itself. This basic count sequence can be controlled by providing clock pulses at the proper interval and repetition rate. Example 3.10 illustrates these concepts.

EXAMPLE 3.10

Realize a traffic light controller that has a 20-second street side green, a 10-second roadside green, and a 5-second yellow for both sides. Table 3.27 lists the state and output definitions consistent with the problem statement. The state transition and output functions of Table 3.28 are derived from Table 3.27, by using natural binary state assignment.

The state transition function can be realized using a two-stage binary counter. The six output function expressions, derived from Table 3.28 by inspection, are provided below:

$$Z_1 = \bar{y}_2 \qquad\qquad Z_4 = y_2$$
$$Z_2 = \bar{y}_2 y_1 \qquad\qquad Z_5 = y_2 y_1$$
$$Z_3 = \bar{y}_2 \bar{y}_1 \qquad\qquad Z_6 = y_2 \bar{y}_1$$

Figure 3.28 illustrates the required control timing to sequence the two-stage binary counter. The minimum time interval is five seconds—the yellow light duration—and this is chosen as the reference clock period. The control timing can be realized by indirect emulation, or direct synthesis. The emulation method uses a modulo 8 binary counter, with appropriate decoder logic, to generate the following control timing expression:

$$Z = (\bar{y}_3\bar{y}_2\bar{y}_1 + y_3\bar{y}_2\bar{y}_1 + y_3\bar{y}_2 y_1 + y_3y_2 y_1) \cdot \text{CLOCK}$$

TABLE 3.27
State definitions for Example 3.10

State		A		B		C		D		
Road	Street	Road	Street	Road	Street	Road	Street	Road	Street	Signal
Z_1	Z_4	On		On			On		On	Red
Z_5	Z_2				On			On		Yellow
Z_6	Z_3		On			On				Green

TABLE 3.28
State transition and output functions for Example 3.10

Present State	$y_2 \ y_1$	Next State	Z_1	Z_2	Z_3	Z_4	Z_5	Z_6
A	0 0	B	1	0	1	0	0	0
B	0 1	C	1	1	0	0	0	0
C	1 0	D	0	0	0	1	0	1
D	1 1	A	0	0	0	1	1	0

The previous example goes through the complete design process of the sequencer, and control timing logic, for a simple fixed-cycle traffic light controller. Initially the six different light signals are designated as Z_1 through Z_6, and the four possible states are defined. Next, the state transition table and output matrix are defined. The state assignment for the two state variables becomes the natural binary counter sequence. Finally, the six output functions are simplified, and the control timing diagram is developed. Since the smallest interval in the cycle is 5 seconds (the yellow light duration), 5 seconds is used as the reference clock repetition rate. The overall cycle time is the sum of the four state durations, or a total of 40 seconds. An eight-state binary counter with a 5-second clock period repeats its timing cycle every 40 seconds. A three-stage, modulo 8 binary counter can be used, with a decoder, to emulate the desired control timing. Alternatively, a set of three flip-flops, with feedback logic, can be used to realize the desired control timing. It should be noted that the control timing output is gated with the reference clock in order to generate the pulse width necessary to cause the sequencer state transitions. Since the problem was approached in a modular fashion, it is possible to redesign the control timing network independent of the light sequencer. During initialization it is necessary to have the sequencer and the control timing synchronized, in order to generate predictable traffic light transitions. This is achieved by starting the sequencer in state A (street side green and road side red) and the control timing in its initial state so as to maintain the required time interval for each light signal. This condition can be reached easily by providing power-on reset capability, which forces the logic to those states. The SSI sequential design provides solutions to small sequential realization problems. A larger problem can be broken into smaller parts that are more manageable. In this way a modular solution is achieved.

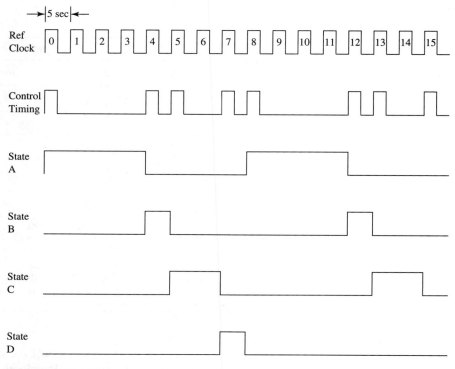

FIGURE 3.28
Control timing for Example 3.10.

3.4 MSI SEQUENTIAL DESIGN

MSI sequential network configurations consist mainly of sixteen-pin DIP packages that contain a complete functional logic building block. The logic has been minimized for optimum packing density and contains built-in "hooks" that enable the designer to cascade or expand the specific function using minimal external SSI logic. Typical functions include counters, latches, and storage and shift registers. Asynchronous counter packages are available with either single or dual, four-stage, binary or decimal counting functions. Synchronous counters are available only with a single, four-stage, binary or decimal counting function.

Options include synchronous or asynchronous parallel loading, up/down counting, and synchronous or asynchronous reset capabilities. Latches are available, as either four or eight per package, that store input states when the clock level changes from high to low. Storage registers are available, as either four or eight per package, that contain edge-triggered flip-flops with optional tri-state outputs and master reset capabilities. Shift registers are available, in packages of four or eight, with up to four possible data load/transfer modes plus optional directional shift and tri-state outputs.

MSI sequential building blocks open up new possibilities for designers to provide quick and elegant solutions, while bypassing the tedious task of logic minimization. For example, a synchronous four-stage up/down counter, with parallel load capability, can be configured as a variable-modulus down counter. It can also be cascaded with similar counters to produce a programmable-modulus divide-by-N counter, where $1 \leq N \leq 2^n - 1$ and n is the total number of flip-flop stages. In this mode of operation, starting with the all-ones state, the counter output frequency is related to its input clock frequency by $f_{OUT} = f_{IN}/N$. In the count-up mode of operation, starting with the 0 state, the relationship becomes $f_{OUT} = f_{IN}/(2^n - 1 - N)$, where $0 \leq N \leq 2^n - 2$. In both cases N represents the parallel input data value in positional notation.

Figure 3.29 illustrates a typical four-stage synchronous up/down binary counter with parallel load capability. This functional building block comes as a sixteen-pin DIP package: fourteen for dedicated input/output functions and two for voltage and ground connections. The D_1–D_4 inputs are for parallel data load operation, enabled by an active high signal on the LD input. This feature enables the counter state to be preset to any value. The load operation can be asynchronous or synchronous. If synchronous, it is gated with the reference clock. The Q_1–Q_4 outputs provide the state of each individual flip-flop. The U/$\overline{D}$ input controls the count direction when the $\overline{EN}$ input is low and a clock is present. The TC output signal becomes high during the terminal count state, 15 or 0. The TP output becomes high under the same condition, but only for the duration of one clock pulse. In Figure 3.29a the device is configured for down counting, and each time it reaches minimum count, state 5 is loaded into it. Thus, after the first cycle, the device produces an output every five clock pulses, making it a modulo 5 counter. Similarly, in Figure 3.29b the same device is configured for up counting, and each time the counter reaches its maximum count, state 5 is loaded into it. Therefore, after the first cycle, the device produces an output every ten clock pulses, making it a modulo 10 counter.

A binary counter can be cascaded with a decoder MSI module to produce timing signals that can be gated with external input variables to generate control timing patterns. This concept is illustrated in Figure 3.30. A modulo 8 counter is cascaded with a 3-to-8 decoder to produce eight repeatable time slots, corresponding to the individual counter states. These outputs are combined with input control variables to generate an arbitrary control timing pattern. In this case the pattern becomes $f_1 = X_0 Y_0 + X_1 Y_4 + X_2 Y_7$, where the three Y_i output timing variables are gated with three X_i input control variables to produce a controlled timing pattern, dependent on the input variable states as shown in Figure 3.30a. The actual timing signals, at various points in the network, are shown in Figure 3.30b, along with f_1, for $X_0 = X_1 = X_2 = 1$.

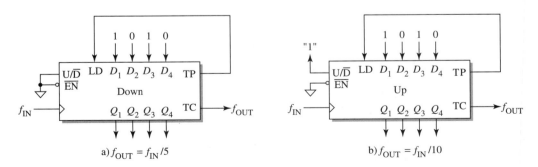

a) $f_{OUT} = f_{IN}/5$ b) $f_{OUT} = f_{IN}/10$

FIGURE 3.29
Variable modulo counter configurations.

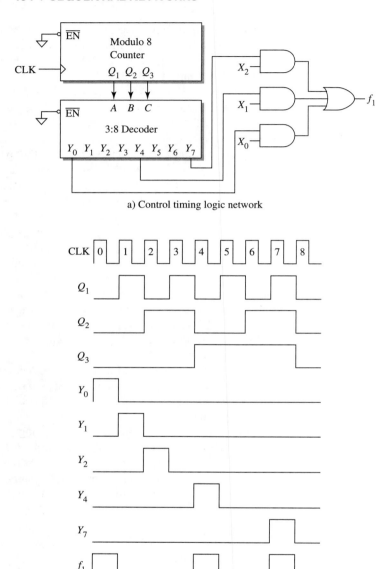

a) Control timing logic network

b) Control timing diagram

FIGURE 3.30
Control timing generation.

Another interesting counter-based design is that of a keyboard encoder function. In this configuration a counter is used, along with a decoder and multiplexer, to sense the relative position of a matrix-type keypad entry. The basic logic diagram is shown in Figure 3.31. The basic keypad consists of sixteen switches, arranged in a 4×4 matrix. The modulo 16 binary counter outputs are

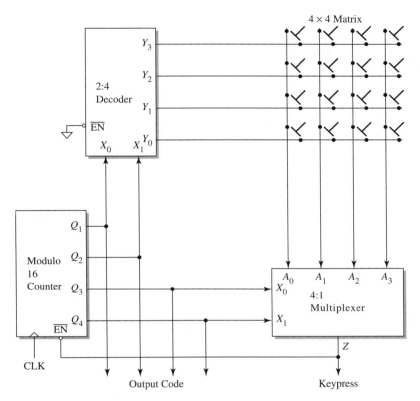

FIGURE 3.31
Keyboard encoder logic network.

used to scan the matrix one row at a time, via the decoder module, and sense a keypress operation through the multiplexer output. If at any instant a key is pressed, when the counter reaches the state corresponding to that X, Y position, the resulting multiplexer output signal Z becomes high and freezes the count at that state until the key is released. The keypress signal is used to store the counter state in a register for possible code conversion. The clock frequency must be at least thirty-two times the operator speed in order to capture a worst-case keypress operation, that is, when the counter is sixteen states away from the corresponding pressed key state.

A simple consecutive state sequence controller can be realized using counter, multiplexer, and decoder modules. In this configuration the counter provides the individual states; the multiplexer controls the counter state transitions, based on the control input variable states; and the decoder provides a unique output variable for each individual counter state. The state flow diagram and the resulting sequential network logic diagram are shown in Figure 3.32, which depicts a Mealy-type network using level inputs and pulse outputs.

The state flow diagram has eight generalized states that are assigned to eight consecutive binary counter states. The eight input variables are fed into the multiplexer module where the specific variable is sensed, at the corresponding counter state, and if true, the counter is enabled to transition

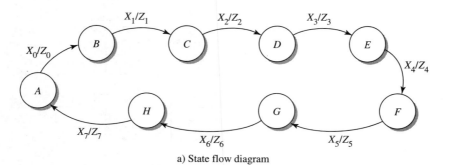

a) State flow diagram

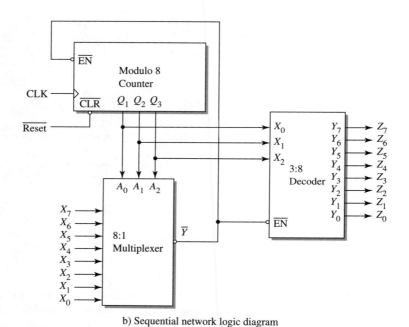

b) Sequential network logic diagram

FIGURE 3.32
Consecutive state sequence controller.

on the next clock pulse. In addition, a decoder module is enabled to generate the output signal. The output variables become true during state transitions. The input variables must remain true for at least two, but fewer than eight, clock periods in order to guarantee reliable sequence operation.

This simple sequencer can be made more flexible by adding an encoder module to provide arbitrary sequence transitions based on the input variable states. The encoder eliminates multiple-input variable state conflicts by the use of weighted priority. This sequence controller operates in the same fashion as the previous one. However, the encoded input variable state change is loaded into the counter, using a two-phase clock, and becomes the next transition state. If the input variable changes are increasing consecutively, then it operates as the simple sequencer. If the changes are arbitrary, however, the counter state transitions to the corresponding encoded input variable state at clock phase two. The output function occurs, as before, during state transitions. If a second decoder is added to provide state decoding, however, a hybrid Mealy/Moore-type network results.

Binary counters can be used to implement delay- and watchdog-type timers. A *delay timer* is loaded with a binary value at the beginning and then decremented until it reaches terminal count. The elapsed time depends on the initial counter value and the reference clock rate. A *watchdog timer* is loaded constantly with a binary value, using a monitored repetitive signal input. At the first absence of the signal the counter begins to decrement, and if the monitored signal does not occur within the preset delay interval, terminal count is reached. The delay timer provides absolute delay counts, and the watchdog provides relative delay counts. These two timers are explained further in Example 3.11.

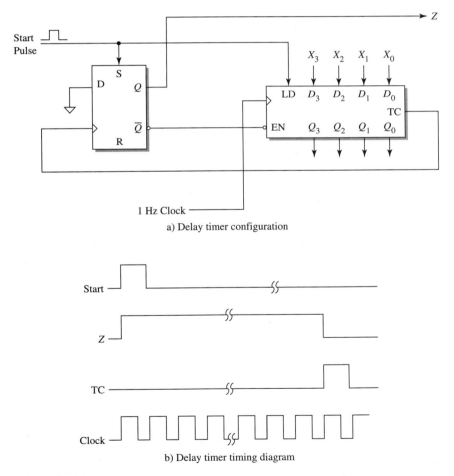

a) Delay timer configuration

b) Delay timer timing diagram

FIGURE 3.33
Delay timer realization for Example 3.11.

EXAMPLE 3.11

Realize a delay timer and a watchdog timer with a programmable preset delay of 1 to 15 seconds, using MSI presetable counter modules.

The delay timer is realized using an asynchronous load, four-stage, binary down counter and a flip-flop, as shown in Figure 3.33a. The corresponding timing diagram is illustrated in Figure 3.33b. The start pulse loads the delay value into the counter and sets the flip-flop, which enables counter operation. When the terminal count is reached, the flip-flop is reset, which disables counter operation. The output variable Z is used to measure the delay interval. Using a 1-Hz clock and a programmable-modulus counter, it is possible to generate adjustable delays.

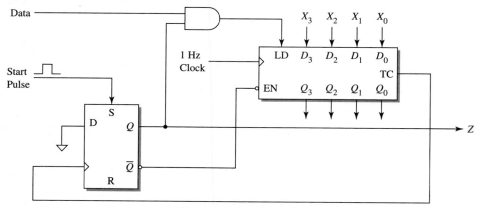

a) Watchdog timer configuration

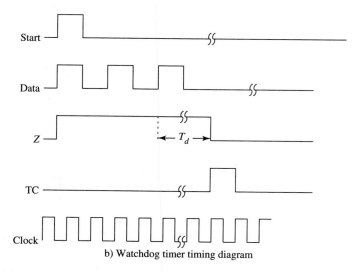

b) Watchdog timer timing diagram

FIGURE 3.34

Watchdog timer realization for Example 3.11.

The watchdog timer is realized with the addition of an AND gate, as shown in Figure 3.34a. The corresponding timing diagram is illustrated in Figure 3.34b. At the start pulse the delay value is loaded into the counter, when data is true, thus enabling the counter. The counter will start decrementing between the true data intervals; however, as long as its delay value exceeds the input data signal rate, no terminal count will be reached. When the data input becomes inactive, the counter decrements to 0 and resets the flip-flop, which disables the count and changes the state of the output variable Z.

Another MSI building block of interest is the shift register. Shift registers perform two major functions, digital delay generation, and parallel/serial data format conversions. A simple pulse delay function can be implemented to delay or stretch an input pulse signal, by n clock pulses, via a shift register.

The concepts of pulse delay and pulse stretch are illustrated in Figure 3.35, where the input signal pulse width is less than or equal to one clock pulse duration. The pulse delay function, shown in Figure 3.35a, is realized using a control input signal to parallel load a binary 1 into the first stage, which is then shifted through n stages to create a time delay $t_d = n \times T$, illustrated in the timing diagram of Figure 3.35b, where n is the number of stages and T is the reference clock period. The pulse stretch function, illustrated in Figure 3.35c, uses a flip-flop that is set by the control input signal. After n clock pulses, it is reset and the pulse cycle is repeated. It should be noted that the Q_N shift register output provides the pulse delay output, and the flip-flop output, Q_A, provides the pulse stretch function, as illustrated in the timing diagram of Figure 3.35d.

Shift registers are best suited for parallel-to-serial or serial-to-parallel data-formatting applications. For example, an n-stage shift register can accept n serial data bits, one at a time, and then parallel transfer them to another storage register. Likewise, an n-bit shift register can be parallel loaded with n bits and can then transfer them serially after n clock pulses. The parallel/serial formats evolved for economic reasons, and transfer speed is compromised for circuit simplicity and lower costs. The shift register data format modes are depicted in Figure 3.36. The serial-to-parallel mode operation, shown in Figure 3.36a, uses the serial-in shift register input to enter the serial data, using a reference clock. Every n clock pulses the shift register contents are transferred to the cascaded n-bit storage register. A modulo N counter generates the control signal. Similarly, the parallel-to-serial mode operation, shown in Figure 3.36b, uses the shift register Shift/$\overline{\text{Load}}$ input to parallel transfer n data bits into the register. When the Shift/$\overline{\text{Load}}$ input state is changed to high, the data bits are shifted out after n clock pulses. The shift register can also be configured as a circular shift register, simply by connecting the serial data output to its D_{IN} input pin. Thus, when an n-bit data word is loaded into the device and shifted by n clock pulses, it will end up in the same initial position. A shift register can also be used as a basis for realizing an n-bit serial input pattern recognizer. Here the serial data is shifted into the device and a combinational network, connected to the n output stages, provides the match output function. Example 3.12 illustrates the use of shift registers to perform simultaneous pulse delay and stretch operations.

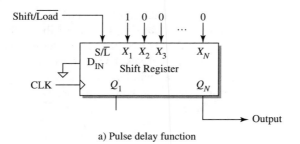

a) Pulse delay function

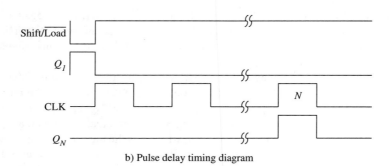

b) Pulse delay timing diagram

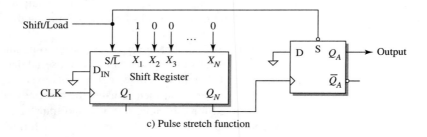

c) Pulse stretch function

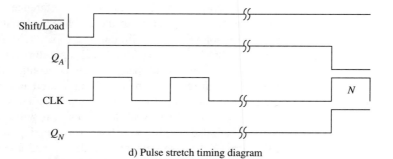

d) Pulse stretch timing diagram

FIGURE 3.35
Shift register applications.

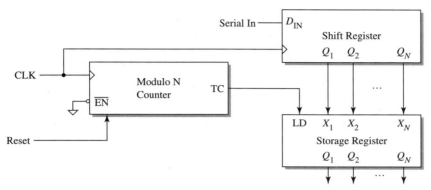

a) Serial-to-parallel mode

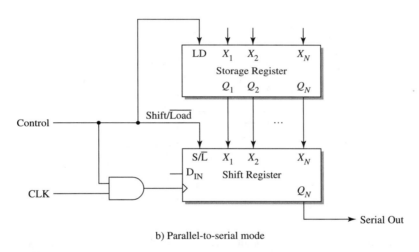

b) Parallel-to-serial mode

FIGURE 3.36
Shift register data format modes.

EXAMPLE 3.12

Realize a shift register–based network that will delay a pulse by 2 seconds and stretch it 4 seconds.

The delay-pulse network is realized with an eight-stage shift register and a D-type flip-flop. Figure 3.37a illustrates the delay/stretch network configuration logic diagram. Figure 3.37b shows the delay/stretch network timing diagram.

In the previous example, a control input signal loads a binary digit into the first shift register stage. The bit is then shifted two stages to the Q_2 output. It is then used to set the flip-flop output. The same bit is shifted an additional four stages to the Q_6 output, and then it is used to reset the flip-flop output. The reference clock has a 1-second period; thus, a 2-second–delayed pulse of 4-second duration is available at the flip-flop output, Q. The MSI-based design

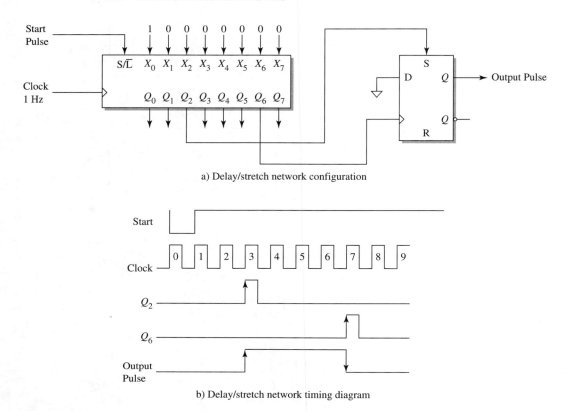

a) Delay/stretch network configuration

b) Delay/stretch network timing diagram

FIGURE 3.37
Delay network realization for Example 3.12.

provides for quick and elegant solutions because of the inherent design features of the modules and their flexibility. The design becomes a rather intuitive process.

3.5 LSI SEQUENTIAL DESIGN

This form of sequential design is based on the standard LSI modules, with memory. Memory may be provided externally, using MSI modules, or it may be integrated—buried—in a device. A module with integrated memory is known as a programmable sequential logic device (PSLD). Both asynchronous and synchronous sequential networks can be defined and realized using LSI logic configurations. The combinational portion can consist of a PAL, or PLA structure, and the sequential part can be a group of storage registers. The PAL structure, with fixed P-term allocation, provides higher logic speed and density than the PLA, with programmable P-term allocation. The PSLDs offer design flexibility via built-in features, such as programmable flip-flops and selectable active output states. Programmable flip-flops are used for the next state transition function, and selectable active output states are used for output function minimization.

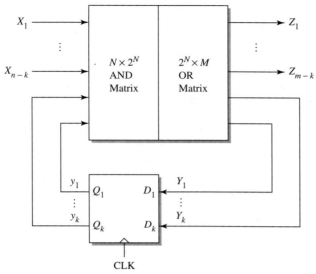

a) Synchronous sequential network

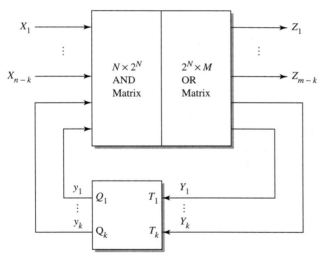

b) Asynchronous sequential network

FIGURE 3.38
PROM-based sequential network models.

A PROM-based sequential network can be realized more easily than a network based on discrete SSI logic, because of the regular geometry characteristics of PROM-based networks. A typical PROM consists of n inputs and m outputs and contains $2^n \times m$ bits of stored information. The fixed $n \times 2^n$ input AND matrix serves as an address decoder, which accesses each of the 2^n total m-bit words in the programmable output OR matrix. The exhaustive n-input decoder makes the next state transition function complexity independent of state assignment, since every possible state–next state transition is built into the AND matrix structure. Since PROMs are input- and output-limited, it becomes necessary to restrict the memory element types to either D or T flip-flops, since they require only one excitation input each. Thus, for a sequential network of k state variables, the maximum number of inputs is limited to $n - k$ and the maximum number of output variables, to $m - k$. It is therefore possible to realize either synchronous or asynchronous pulse mode sequential networks, with an arbitrary state assignment, by embedding the resulting next state transition and output function truth tables into the PROM OR matrix. In the case of asynchronous fundamental mode sequential networks, there is no need for memory elements. Rather, upon completion of state assignment, the next state transition outputs are tied directly into the present state input variables. Figure 3.38 illustrates the two PROM-based sequential logic networks. The effect of increasing the input variables by one results in an AND matrix of 2^{n+1}, or double in size. Similarly, increasing the output functions by one results in an OR matrix with an extra output column, $m + 1$. Clearly, the PROM size, and therefore cost, increases drastically with the number of extra required inputs. The use of an MSI encoder module for input variables and a decoder for output functions relaxes the input/output limitations of a PROM-based sequential network design.

Example 3.13 illustrates a PROM-based sequential logic network design, using a Mealy-type model.

EXAMPLE 3.13

Given the state table definition of a Mealy-type synchronous sequential network in Table 3.29, derive a PROM-based circuit realization, and the state flow diagram.

An arbitrary state assignment is chosen, and the resulting next state transition matrix is provided in Table 3.30. The PROM-based sequential network logic block diagram is shown in Figure 3.39a. The state flow diagram, illustrated in Figure 3.39b, is derived from the initial state table definition.

TABLE 3.29
State table definition for Example 3.13

Present State	Next State 00	01	10	11	Output 00	01	10	11
A	A	C	D	B	Z_1	Z_2	Z_3	Z_2
B	D	B	E	F	Z_3	Z_1	Z_2	Z_3
C	F	A	B	D	Z_2	Z_1	Z_3	Z_2
D	D	A	C	B	Z_3	Z_2	Z_1	Z_1
E	B	F	A	E	Z_1	Z_3	Z_2	Z_1
F	B	C	D	A	Z_2	Z_2	Z_3	Z_3

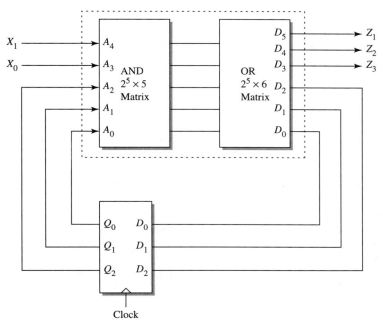

a) Sequential network logic block diagram

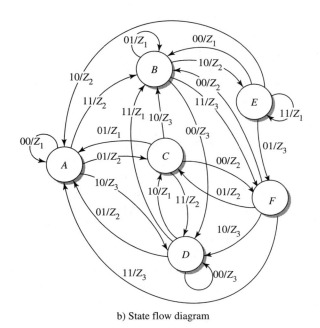

b) State flow diagram

FIGURE 3.39
PROM-based realization for Example 3.13.

TABLE 3.30
Next state transition matrix for Example 3.13

State Code	Present State $y_2\ y_1\ y_0$	Next State 00	01	10	11
A	0 0 0	000	010	011	001
B	0 0 1	011	001	100	101
C	0 1 0	101	000	001	011
D	0 1 1	011	000	010	001
E	1 0 0	001	101	000	100
F	1 0 1	001	010	011	000

In the previous example a natural binary code is assigned to the generalized entries of the state table, and a multi-output function truth table can systematically be constructed that defines the next state transition and output functions in terms of present state and input variable combinations. The resulting table has twenty-four rows, or six states times four input combinations per state. Also, there are six outputs, or three state variables and three outputs. This requires a five-input–by–six-output PROM. A five-input PROM has $2^5 = 32$ available addresses in the AND matrix, which access a thirty-two–location, six-bit–wide OR matrix. Since only twenty-four addresses are required for the next state and output functions, the eight unused locations are left blank. Each new next state transition and output function row entry in the multi-output truth table requires one PROM address. In the state flow diagram shown in Figure 3.39b, each edge is represented by a unique output OR matrix location, which is programmed with the corresponding row output function values in the truth table. This type of realization, called *total state decoding,* is well suited to PROM-based sequential network designs.

Control timing can be easily generated using a PROM to store the timing sequence and a counter to cycle through each address location, as shown in Figure 3.40. A binary counter is used whose modulus equals the timing sequence length. The PROM is chosen such that its address capacity is equal to or greater than the timing sequence length. Also, its OR matrix width must be equal to or greater than the number of individual timing signals required. The PROM output is transferred to a storage register, using the inverted reference clock, to compensate for the inherent PROM propagation path delay. Therefore, the clock pulse width must be greater than the maximum data access time of the PROM. It should be noted that registered-output PROMs also exist; these provide added flexibility.

Table 3.31 lists an address-versus-data definition to realize a specific timing sequence, which can be programmed directly into an 8 × 6 PROM.

PSLDs have either a PAL- or a PLA-based combinational logic structure and built-in memory that consists of either fixed or programmable flip-flops. PAL geometry has a programmable-input AND matrix and a fixed-output OR matrix, which is the opposite of PROM architecture. The programmable AND matrix provides for P-term minimization. The number of connected P-terms per output is fixed, and they may be either equally or unequally allocated. The function minimization is constrained by the number of P-terms available per output. Unequal static P-term allocation accommodates individual function complexity. PLA geometry, with programmable AND and OR matrices, allows total flexibility, since dynamic allocation makes efficient use of all the P-terms. Both types of device are pin-limited; therefore, input encoding and output decoding may be used if required. Figure 3.41 illustrates a PSLD-based sequential network using optional external MSI modules to compensate for inherent device limitations.

FIGURE 3.40
PROM-based control timing generation.

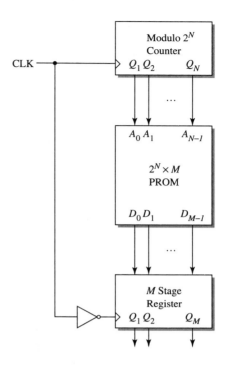

The PSLD can handle up to l input and k output variables. The internal PLA logic has $n = l + p$ inputs, $m = k + p$ outputs, and a fixed number of P-terms. The memory portion has a total of p storage devices, with programmable connections to the PLA structure. An optional input encoder and an output decoder are capable of increasing the variable capacity to 2^l and 2^k, respectively, provided they are mutually exclusive.

Because of its programming flexibility, PLSD architecture can support either synchronous- or asynchronous-type sequential networks. The design procedure can be relaxed to exclude logic minimization, provided the function can be embedded into the device. If the resulting expressions cannot fit into it, because of P-term limitations, either a heuristic or a rigorous

TABLE 3.31
PROM programming table ($n = 3$, $m = 6$)

Location	PROM Address A_2 A_1 A_0	Data Output Word D_5 D_4 D_3 D_2 D_1 D_0
0	0 0 0	0 1 0 1 0 1
1	0 0 1	1 0 1 0 1 0
2	0 1 0	0 1 0 1 0 1
3	0 1 1	0 1 1 0 0 0
4	1 0 0	1 1 0 1 1 1
5	1 0 1	1 0 1 0 0 1
6	1 1 0	0 1 0 0 1 0
7	1 1 1	0 0 1 1 1 0

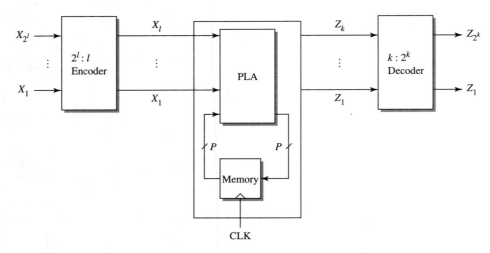

FIGURE 3.41
PSLD block diagram.

minimization is performed, depending on the degree of mismatch. In either case a sequential network design can be embedded into the PSLD, avoiding costly external logic interconnections. Example 3.14 illustrates the use of state adjacency blocks (SABs) to derive a specific state assignment (in contrast to an arbitrary assignment) that will result in a minimized next state transition function suitable for embedding.

EXAMPLE 3.14

Find a state assignment for the state table in Table 3.32, using SABs and D-type flip-flops. Derive the next state transition expressions, using P-term assignment.

Table 3.33 lists the existing SAB pairs, which produce the same next state under a common input variable combination, X_i. A single IAB is also identified. The resulting SAB-based state assignment is presented in Figure 3.42. Table 3.34 provides the next state transition matrix that results from the specific state assignment.

Table 3.35 lists a unique consecutive P-term assignment to each next state transition variable Y_i, for D-type flip-flop realization.

TABLE 3.32
State table for Example 3.14

Present State	Next State 00	01	10	11
A	A	C	D	B
B	D	B	E	C
C	E	A	B	C
D	A	E	B	D
E	C	A	C	E

TABLE 3.33
SAB and IAB definitions for Example 3.14

SAB	X_i	Next State
A,D	00	A
C,E	01	A
C,D	10	B
B,C	11	C

IAB	X_i/X_j	Next state
E,C	00/10	C

TABLE 3.34
Next state transition matrix for Example 3.14

Present y_2 y_1 y_0	Next State $Y_2Y_1Y_0$ 00	01	10	11
0 1 1	011	000	010	001
0 0 1	010	001	100	000
0 0 0	100	011	001	000
0 1 0	011	100	001	010
1 0 0	000	011	000	100

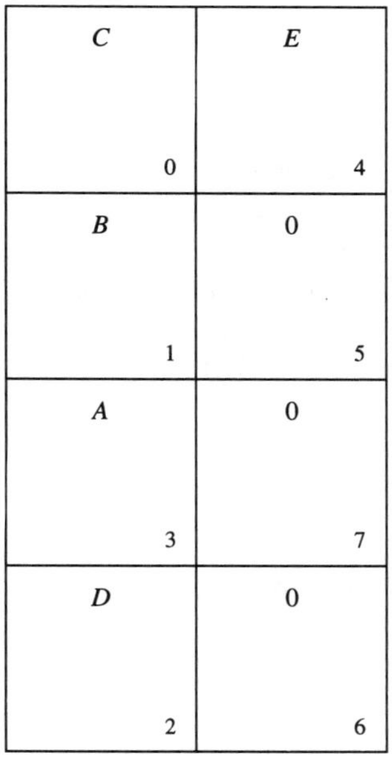

FIGURE 3.42
State assignment for Example 3.14.

TABLE 3.35
P-term assignment for Example 3.14

Present $y_2\ y_1\ y_0$	Next State $Y_2Y_1Y_0$ 00	01	10	11
0 1 1	P_1	—	P_7	P_{10}
0 0 1	P_2	P_4	P_8	—
0 0 0	P_3	P_5	P_9	—
0 1 0	P_1	P_6	P_9	P_{11}
1 0 0	—	P_5	—	P_{12}

The resulting next state transition function expressions become

$$Y_0 = P_1 + P_4 + P_5 + P_9 + P_{10}$$

$$Y_1 = P_1 + P_2 + P_5 + P_7 + P_{11}$$

$$Y_2 = P_3 + P_6 + P_8 + P_{12}$$

In the previous example, a state table column scan produces four complete SABs and a row scan finds an IAB. Next, the state assignment procedure results in mutually exclusive adjacent SAB coding, with the most often recurring state, C, assigned the all-zeros code. Using D-type flip-flops, a transition to a 0 next state requires no excitation input. This results in a savings of five P-terms. In addition, the SAB coding reduces the number of required P-terms by three. The IAB contribution of one P-term reduction is masked by the state C coding. This specific state assignment reduces the required P-terms from twenty to twelve. The next state transition function expressions are derived for each state variable Y_i as the sum of individual P_j's, where the index j represents the P-term number. The PLA structure supports P-term sharing among the outputs.

The next example illustrates a PLA-based traffic controller with four modes of operation. First, a normal light control cycle is defined as follows: street side, 36 seconds green; road side, 20 seconds green; and 4 seconds yellow for both. Second, a road side 4-seconds–delayed green operation is defined by reducing the green light interval for each side by 2 seconds. Third, a flashing street-side yellow and a flashing road-side red are defined. Fourth, a flashing street-side red and a flashing road-side yellow are defined. The flashing interval for modes three and four is 2 seconds. These modes are to be controlled by external input variables, and a provision for mode selection is required. The control timing is to be programmed into a PROM, so that the various intervals can be modified easily.

EXAMPLE 3.15

Realize a PSLD-based traffic light controller with the following modes of operation:

Mode 1: Normal Cycle   Green (3) = 36 sec
Green (6) = 20 sec
Yellow (2, 5) = 4 sec

Mode 2: Delayed Green   Green (3) = 34 sec
Green (6) = 18 sec

Delayed Green (6) = 4 sec
Yellow (2, 5) = 4 sec

Mode 3: Flashing Y/R   Yellow (2)/Red (1) = 2 sec
Mode 4: Flashing R/Y   Red (4)/Yellow (5) = 2 sec

Then provide the required control timing, using a PROM-based design.

Figure 3.43a provides the light-numbering convention and each state definition in pictorial representation. Figure 3.43b shows the state flow diagram derived from the problem definition. Table 3.36 lists the reduced state table, produced by combining states *E* and *F*.

Table 3.37, a tabulation of the available SABs, uses the two don't care states, *H* and *J*, to make complete blocks.

Figure 3.44 provides the resulting state assignment. The most frequently occurring next state, *G*, is assigned the all-zeros code.

The next state transition matrix can now be defined. Next, P-term assignment for D-type flip-flops is derived by inspection from the transition matrix. The resulting next state transition function expressions are

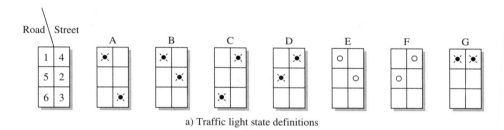

a) Traffic light state definitions

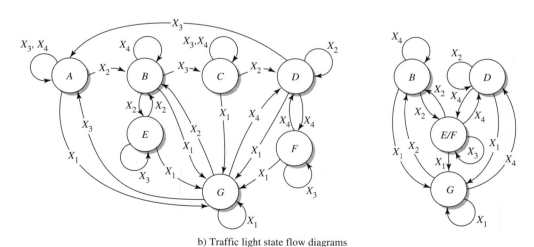

b) Traffic light state flow diagrams

FIGURE 3.43
State flow diagram for Example 3.15.

TABLE 3.36
Reduced state table definition for Example 3.15

Present State	X_1 X_2 X_3 X_4	Z_1	Z_2	Z_3	Z_4	Z_5	Z_6
A	G B A A	1	0	1	0	0	0
B	G E C B	1	1	0	0	0	0
C	G D C C	0	0	0	1	0	1
D	G D A E	0	0	0	1	1	0
E	G B E D	0	0	0	0	0	0
G	G B A D	1	0	0	1	0	0
H	d d d d						
J	d d d d						

$$Y_0 = P_1 + P_2 + P_5 + P_6 + P_8 + P_9 + P_{10}$$
$$Y_1 = P_1 + P_3 + P_5 + P_8 + P_9 + P_{11}$$
$$Y_2 = P_1 + P_4 + P_7 + P_8$$

Similarly, the output functions are derived by inspection of Table 3.36. The resulting output function expressions, state decoders, are

$$Z_1 = A + B + G = P_{12} + P_{13} + P_{14}$$
$$Z_2 = B = P_{13}$$
$$Z_3 = A = P_{12}$$
$$Z_4 = C + D + G = P_{15} + P_{16} + P_{14}$$
$$Z_5 = D = P_{16}$$
$$Z_6 = C = P_{15}$$

The resulting traffic light controller block diagram is shown in Figure 3.45. The design requires 16 P-terms, eleven for the next state transitions and five for the output functions, Z_1–Z_6. The two input variables, X_1 and X_0, are used to provide the four possible combinations. The three D flip-flops store the next state variables at the positive clock edge.

Using the state flow diagram of Figure 3.43b, the PROM-based control timing logic variable sequences for the four modes are defined and listed in Table 3.38. The initial traffic control sequencer state is *G;* both sides have a red light condition, to ensure orderly transitions between modes.

TABLE 3.37
SAB definitions for Example 3.15

SAB	X_i	Next State
A, G, E, H	X_2	B
C, D	X_2	D
A, D, G, J	X_3	A
B, C	X_3	C
E, G	X_4	D

G		A	
	0		4
E		H	
	1		5
C		B	
	3		7
D		J	
	2		6

FIGURE 3.44
State assignment for Example 3.15.

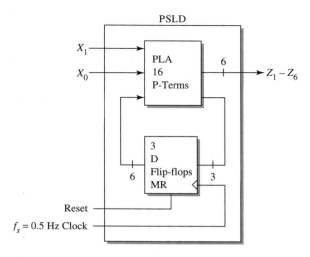

FIGURE 3.45
Traffic light controller block diagram for Example 3.15.

TABLE 3.38
Control timing PROM table for Example 3.15

Mode Address	Normal $D_7 D_6$	Delayed $D_5 D_4$	Flashing Y/R $D_3 D_2$	Flashing R/Y $D_1 D_0$
0	X_3	X_3	X_2	X_4
1	X_3	X_3	X_2	X_4
.	X_3	X_3	X_2	X_4
.	X_3	X_3	X_2	X_4
.	X_3	X_3	X_2	X_4
16	X_3	X_3	X_2	X_4
17	X_3	X_2	X_2	X_4
18	X_2	X_4	X_2	X_4
19	X_4	X_3	X_2	X_4
20	X_3	X_3	X_2	X_4
.	X_3	X_3	X_2	X_4
.	X_3	X_3	X_2	X_4
.	X_3	X_3	X_2	X_4
27	X_3	X_3	X_2	X_4
28	X_3	X_2	X_2	X_4
29	X_3	X_2	X_2	X_4
30	X_2	X_1	X_2	X_4
31	X_2	X_1	X_2	X_4

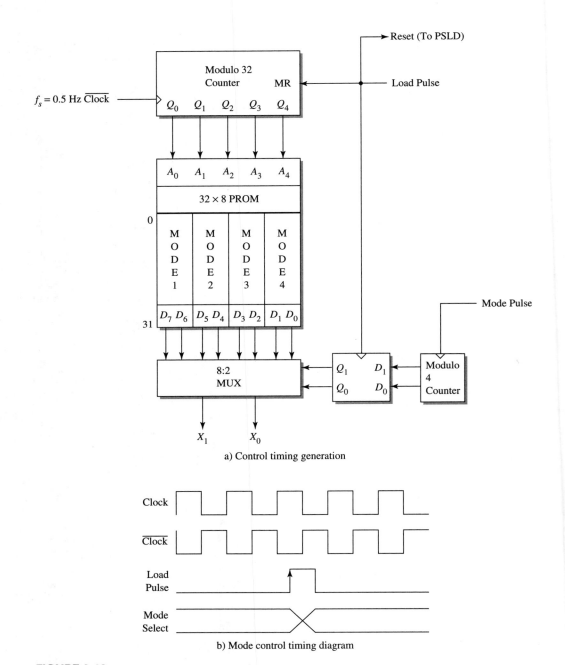

a) Control timing generation

b) Mode control timing diagram

FIGURE 3.46
PROM-based control generation for Example 3.15.

The control timing generation logic is shown in Figure 3.46a. The table is embedded into a 32×8 PROM, and a modulo 32 counter cycles through it, using a 0.5-Hz clock, every 64 seconds. The mode selection is achieved using a multiplexer, in conjunction with a register and a modulo 4 counter. Figure 3.46b illustrates the associated mode selection timing diagram. The mode can be changed asynchronously, by loading the selected mode state into the register. The register load pulse is applied to the modulo 32 counter and also resets the sequencer to its initial state, G, to prevent any traffic accidents. At the same time register outputs are used to select the new mode, via the multiplexer. The variables D_j and D_i become the PSLD control input variables that generate the mode sequence. Also, the modulo 32 counter is updated with the inverted clock to avoid output glitches based on the propagation delays.

The traffic light controller definition in the previous example was based on a synchronous, Moore-type sequential network. From the sequencer definition it can be deduced that, for both the normal and delayed modes, the basic cycle length is 64 seconds. The state flow diagram required seven states to completely define the four modes of operation. Six output functions were needed, one for each individual light signal. A reduced state table was formed by combining the generalized states E and F into one, namely E. The table was used to search for SABs and IABs, in order to derive an efficient state assignment. A column scan produced five SABs, and a row scan found no IABs. Next, the state assignment was performed, using a Karnaugh map, and the two spare states were used to generate two higher-order SABs, (A, D, G, J) and (A, G, E, H), for further simplification. The next state transition and output function expressions were defined using the PLA P-terms. The specific SAB-based state assignment resulted in eleven, out of a maximum of twenty-four, P-terms to define the next state transition function. The output function required another five, bringing the total P-term requirement to sixteen. The resulting logic was embedded into the PLA portion of the PLSD, along with three D-type flip-flops for the memory section.

The traffic light controller required a clock input, a reset input, and two input variables for the sequence generation. Also, six outputs were produced to control the light signals. The control timing was inferred from the state flow diagram and state table definitions and programmed into a 32×8 PROM. A 64-second timing cycle was generated using a 2-second reference clock input. The basic cycle length can be varied by changing the clock period, and the individual light interval can be altered by reprogramming the control PROM. It should be noted that a 128×4 PROM can be used instead, to eliminate the need for a multiplexer. Using this approach, the four modes are programmed in consecutive address blocks and the mode select inputs become the higher-order PROM address bits.

3.6 VLSI SEQUENTIAL DESIGN

VLSI logic modules with integrated flip-flop register elements are tailored for sequential designs. The basic CPLD and FPCA architectures are augmented with a programmable output section, which can be configured in several modes. The bypass mode defaults to combinational output logic. The sequential mode can be configured either as level-sensitive latch or edge-sensitive flip-flop register. Either an active high or an active low polarity can be selected. In addition, programmable feedback to the combinational logic section results in sequential network realization.

The basic CPLD logic is called a block. It is made up of a simple PAL structure, followed by a programmable I/O section, as shown in Figure 3.47a. The dedicated dual polarity inputs provide signal sense options to the programmable AND matrix. The matrix provides P-term allocation capability, either by assigning them to or sharing them with other logic blocks in the device. The selectable polarity OR section is used to minimize the number of actual gates required to implement a given function. This is accomplished by judiciously implementing the complement of a function using De Morgan's theorem. The programmable output can be configured as a selectable polarity combinational or sequential output. The storage element in the

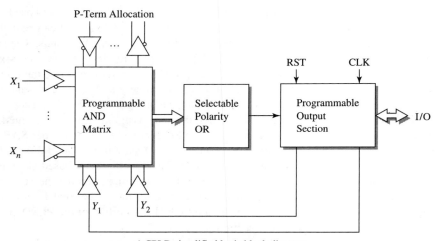

a) CPLD simplified logic block diagram

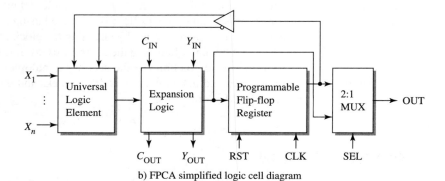

b) FPCA simplified logic cell diagram

FIGURE 3.47
VLSI module logic unit architecture.

output section can be configured as a latch or generic flip-flop. In other words, a D-, T-, or JK-type register can be selected. A prudently selected flip-flop will reduce the number of required P-terms in a sequential network design. The I/O pins can be programmed statically as either input or output, and dynamically for bidirectional I/O signals. The programmable feedback supplies the AND matrix with a choice of combinational, registered, or external input signal. This feature efficiently allocates pin functions and supports sequential machine functions.

The basic FPCA logic unit is depicted in Figure 3.47b. The universal logic element can generate any function of n-input variables. The expansion logic is used either to widen the n-input logic function or to support cascaded arithmetic and counter designs. The programmable flip-flop register can be configured as either level- or edge-sensitive. It also provides a feedback path to the logic element. The output multiplexer provides a selectable combinational or a registered output. Finally, all control inputs have a selective active sense polarity option.

Table 3.39 lists the salient features of VLSI sequential PLD architectures. The CPLDs have anywhere from 20 to 200 pins and operate with clock speeds of 50 to 125 MHz. The equivalent gate circuit complexity ranges from 1,000 to 5,000, combined into 32 to 256 logic blocks. The device clock can be either global synchronous or local asynchronous. The combinational logic is an AND/OR structure, and its programming method is EPROM/EEPROM-based. The devices use low-power, medium-density complementary metal oxide semiconductor (CMOS) technology, with high gate count, high-granularity logic blocks. There is a central

TABLE 3.39
PLD device architecture comparison

Feature	CPLD	FPCA	HPLD
Package	PLCC/QFP/PGA	PLCC/QFP/PGA	PLCC/QFP/PGA
Pin Count	20–200	52–250	80–300
Clock Speed	50–125 MHz	25–150 MHz	30–130 MHz
Gate Count	1,000–5,000	1,000–10,000	1,000–15,000
Blocks/Cells	32–256	200–1,300	200–1,500
Clock Source	Global/Local	Global/Local	Global/Local
Logic Type	AND/OR	Multiplexer/Table	Table
Program Method	EPROM/EEPROM	Programmable Link/SRAM	SRAM
Technology	CMOS	CMOS	CMOS
Granularity	High	Low/Medium	Medium
Logic Density	Medium	High	High
Connectivity	Central matrix	Distributed	Distributed
Path Routing	Continuous	Segmented	Continuous
Advantages	Predictable delays	Expandable logic	Predictable delays
	Wide gates	Flexible I/O	Flexible logic
	P-term allocation	FF register–rich	FF register–rich
Constraints	Rigid logic	Unpredictable delays	External RAM
	Fixed I/O	Narrow gates	
	FF register–limited	External memory	

programmable crosspoint matrix that provides continuous signal paths to all logic blocks. The device advantages are predictable delays, wide input gates, and P-term allocation. The constraints are rigid logic structure, fixed I/O pins, and flip-flop register limitation.

FPCAs have anywhere from 52 to 250 pins, with clock speeds of 25 to 150 MHz. The equivalent usable gate count ranges from 1,000 to over 10,000, distributed over 200 to 1,300 logic cells. The device clock can be either global or local to each cell. The combinational logic is either multiplexer- or lookup-table–based, and it is configured with either programmable links or SRAM-controlled distributed transistor switches. The devices use low-power, high-density CMOS technology, with low- to medium-granularity logic cells. A distributed, segmented-path routing network can interconnect the various cells. The device advantages are expandable logic, flexible I/O pin allocation, and flip-flop register richness. The constraints are unpredictable delays, narrow gate functions, and external memory required for the SRAM based devices.

A hybrid PLD (HPLD) architecture, which combines the best features of CPLDs and FPCAs, provides high density, high speed, and medium-granularity logic elements. It has predictable delays, flexible logic with register-rich topology, and allocatable I/O pins. Since it is internally SRAM-programmable, it requires an external memory to hold its logic configuration.

The low-end PLD devices can be supported with ABEL. The design entry method can be a state flow diagram, next state transition equations, or tables. ABEL is limited by the number of state transitions and their paths. Figure 3.48 is a hybrid model, four-state, sequential network state flow diagram. There are two realization options available, the encoded and decoded state assignment methods. In general, the encoded state assignment method requires $m = \log_2 \lceil M \rceil$ flip-flop registers and $n + m$ wide input gates. The *decoded state assignment* method requires M flip-flop registers, one per state, with only $n + 1$ wide input gates.

For CPLD implementation, the encoded state approach is preferred because CPLDs have high-granularity blocks with wide gates, but are flip-flop register–limited. For FPCA imple-

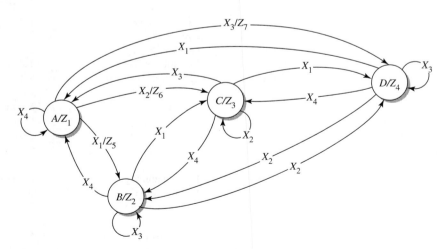

FIGURE 3.48
Hybrid model sequential network.

mentation, the decoded state method is preferred because the low-granularity, narrow gate, and flip-flop register–rich structure makes for efficient device use. Since the encoded state method has been used extensively in previous sections, the decoded state method will be highlighted in the following example.

EXAMPLE 3.16

Realize the sequential network specified by the state flow diagram of Figure 3.48, using the decoded state assignment method.

The state table definition, shown in Table 3.40, is derived directly from the state flow diagram.

The next state transition function expressions are written from the state table by inspection:

$$A = A \cdot X_4 + B \cdot X_4 + C \cdot X_3 + D \cdot X_1$$
$$B = A \cdot X_1 + B \cdot X_3 + C \cdot X_4 + D \cdot X_2$$
$$C = A \cdot X_2 + B \cdot X_1 + C \cdot X_2 + D \cdot X_4$$
$$D = A \cdot X_3 + B \cdot X_2 + C \cdot X_1 + D \cdot X_3$$

For decoded state assignment, one flip-flop per state, the following expressions result:

$$Q_1 = A, Q_2 = B, Q_3 = C, Q_4 = D$$
$$Q_1 = Q_1 \cdot X_4 + Q_2 \cdot X_4 + Q_3 \cdot X_3 + Q_4 \cdot X_1$$
$$Q_2 = Q_1 \cdot X_1 + Q_2 \cdot X_3 + Q_3 \cdot X_4 + Q_4 \cdot X_2$$
$$Q_3 = Q_1 \cdot X_2 + Q_2 \cdot X_1 + Q_3 \cdot X_2 + Q_4 \cdot X_4$$
$$Q_4 = Q_1 \cdot X_3 + Q_2 \cdot X_2 + Q_3 \cdot X_1 + Q_4 \cdot X_3$$

Similarly, the output function expressions become

$$Z_1 = Q_1 \qquad Z_2 = Q_2 \qquad Z_3 = Q_3 \qquad Z_4 = Q_4$$
$$Z_5 = Q_1 \cdot X_1 \qquad Z_6 = Q_1 \cdot X_2 \qquad Z_7 = Q_1 \cdot X_3$$

TABLE 3.40
State table for Example 3.16

Present State	Next State X_1 X_2 X_3 X_4				State Outputs Z_1 Z_2 Z_3 Z_4				Outputs X_1 X_2 X_3 X_4			
A	B	C	D	A	1	0	0	0	Z_5	Z_6	Z_7	0
B	C	D	B	A	0	1	0	0	0	0	0	0
C	D	C	A	B	0	0	1	0	0	0	0	0
D	A	B	D	C	0	0	0	1	0	0	0	0

The hybrid sequential machine ABEL source file is derived in the following example, using the state flow diagram equations entry method.

**EXAMPLE
3.17** Develop the ABEL source file for Example 3.16.

```
module    hybrid
title    `sequential machine´;
device   `FPCA´;
    Q1, Q2, Q3, Q4              pin 1, 2, 3, 4;
    X1, X2, X3, X4, clock       pin 5, 6, 7, 8, 9;
    Z1, Z2, Z3, Z4, Z5, Z6, Z7 pin 10, 11, 12, 13, 14, 15, 16;
    fset = [Q1, Q2, Q3, Q4];
    H, L = 1, 0;
    "State Numbers
    A = 1  B = 2  C = 4  D = 8;
state_diagram fset;
    State A:
    Z1 = 1;
    IF (X1) THEN B WITH Z5 := 1;
    ELSE IF (X2) THEN C WITH Z6 := 1;
    ELSE IF (X3) THEN D WITH Z7 := 1;
    ELSE IF (X4) THEN A;
    State B:
    Z2 = 1;
    IF (X1) THEN C;
    ELSE IF (X2) THEN D;
    ELSE IF (X3) THEN B;
    ELSE IF (X4) THEN A;
    State C:
    Z3 = 1;
    IF (X1) THEN D;
    ELSE IF (X2) THEN C;
    ELSE IF (X3) THEN A;
    ELSE IF (X4) THEN B;
    State D:
    Z4 = 1;
    IF (X1) THEN A;
    ELSE IF (X2) THEN B;
    ELSE IF (X3) THEN D;
    ELSE IF (X4) THEN C;
test_vectors ([X1, X2, X3, X4, clock] -> [fset, Z1, Z2, Z3,
Z4, Z5, Z6, Z7])
    [0, 0, 0, 1, H] -> [A, 1, 0, 0, 0, 0, 0, 0];
    [1, 0, 0, 0, H] -> [B, 0, 1, 0, 0, 1, 0, 0];
    [0, 0, 1, 0, H] -> [B, 0, 1, 0, 0, 0, 0, 0];
    [1, 0, 0, 0, H] -> [C, 0, 0, 1, 0, 0, 0, 0];
    [0, 1, 0, 0, H] -> [C, 0, 0, 1, 0, 0, 0, 0];
    [1, 0, 0, 0, H] -> [D, 0, 0, 0, 1, 0, 0, 0];
```

```
[0, 0, 1, 0, H] -> [D, 0, 0, 0, 1, 0, 0, 0];
[1, 0, 0, 0, H] -> [A, 1, 0, 0, 0, 0, 0, 0];
[0, 1, 0, 0, H] -> [C, 0, 0, 1, 0, 0, 1, 0];
[0, 0, 1, 0, H] -> [A, 1, 0, 0, 0, 0, 0, 0];
[0, 0, 1, 0, H] -> [D, 0, 0, 0, 1, 0, 0, 1];
[0, 0, 0, 1, H] -> [C, 0, 0, 1, 0, 0, 0, 0];
[0, 0, 0, 1, H] -> [B, 0, 1, 0, 0, 0, 0, 0];
[0, 1, 0, 0, H] -> [D, 0, 0, 0, 1, 0, 0, 0];
[0, 1, 0, 0, H] -> [B, 0, 1, 0, 0, 0, 0, 0];
[0, 0, 0, 1, H] -> [A, 1, 0, 0, 0, 0, 0, 0];
```
end

The ABEL source file starts with the *module* and *title* keywords, followed by *device* specification. The logic signals are associated with the device pins, and constant declarations are made. The keyword *state_diagram* is used to begin the state flow diagram equations design entry. Each of the four states is separately defined. The output function value associated with each state is provided. The IF-THEN-ELSE statements are used to completely specify transitions as functions of present state and input values. Also, the output functions are defined within each state. Finally, the *test_vectors* keyword is used to start the test vector sequence necessary to verify the design.

In general, the high-end PLD devices are used in an electronic design automation (EDA) environment, where computer-aided engineering (CAE) tools are used to achieve device-independent digital logic designs. There are three distinct design phases: entry, synthesis, and verification. The Electronic Design Interchange Format (EDIF) standard is a common thread in the design phases. EDIF provides a netlist entry file that describes components and their interconnections. A specific device family compiler is used to perform synthesis, using logic partitioning, fitting, interconnection, and minimization techniques. An output EDIF file is generated, with functional and timing data, to perform design verification by simulation and by actual device programming.

The Very High Speed Integrated Circuit (VHSIC) Description Language (VHDL) is defined by the Institute of Electrical and Electronics Engineers (IEEE) standard 1076 for high-level modeling and simulation of digital hardware designs. A related standard, IEEE 1164, specifies component interconnection data. The purpose of the standard is to support hierarchical, portable, and reusable component methodology. A component can be of system-, module-, device-, circuit-, or gate-level design. Components can be described in terms of their behavior or their structure. The behavioral model is used to provide component functional description, and the structural model is used for component logic and timing definitions. Tools exist to transform a graphical problem description into VHDL format. The language uses the following principal building blocks: entity, architecture, process, package, and configuration. The *entity* is used to define the component's external interface and can be viewed as its symbol. The *architecture* is used to define the component's internal structure such as data flow, logic, or timing. The *process* is used within the architecture body to define each entity's function. The *package* is a predefined function or procedure in the VHDL library. The *configuration* is used to define a specific instance of a component. Table 3.41 lists some of the VHDL symbols and their meanings.

TABLE 3.41
VHDL definitions

Symbol	Meaning	Example
=	Equal	set = '1'
/=	Not equal	Count /= 0
:	Declaration	signal d : in;
:=	Unconditional	n := n + 1;
<=	Conditional	else q <= '1';
--	Comment	--Begin
;	Statement delimiter	end;
and	AND	(j and k = '1');
or	OR	(a or b = '1');
not	NOT	a <= not 'q';
' '	Value	'1'
" "	String	"Timeout"

The following simple example shows the listing of a structural VHDL file for a JK flip-flop device. It defines both synchronous and asynchronous operations.

EXAMPLE 3.18

Develop a structural VHDL source file for the JK flip-flop device.

```
library ieee;
use ieee.std_logic_1164.all;
entity jkff is
port
  (signal set, rst, j, k: in std_logic;
  signal q: out std_logic);
end jkff;
architecture sequential of jkff is
begin
  process (set, rst, clk, j, k, q);
  begin
  if (set = `0´) and (rst = `0´) then
    if ((clk = `1´) and (j = `0´) and (k = `0´)) then q <= `q´;
    end if;
    if ((clk = `1´) and (j = `1´) and (k = `0´)) then q <= `1´;
    end if;
    if ((clk = `1´) and (j = `0´) and (k = `1´)) then q <= `0´;
    end if;
    if ((clk = `1´) and (j = `1´) and (k = `1´)) then q <= not
    `q´;
    end if;
  elseif (set = `1´) or (rst = `1´) then
    if (set = `1´) and (rst = `0´) then q <= `1´;
    end if;
```

```
        if (set = `0´) and (rst = `1´) then q <= `0´;
        end if;
        if (set = `1´) and (rst = `1´) then report ("State")ERROR;
        end if;
      end if;
    end process;
  end sequential;
```

The file consists of the IEEE library definition, the entity, and the architecture blocks. The library is a predefined package of functions to be used with this component. The entity block defines the input and output interfaces. The architecture contains a process that defines the state flow diagram of a JK flip-flop.

VLSI-based sequential design provides even greater design flexibility by offering programmable logic and memory, integrated solutions, and novel architectures. These USICs provide complexity and performance capabilities limited only by the designer's ingenuity. EDA tools hide device complexity and achieve a seamless operation.

PROBLEMS

3.1 Realize the sequential network of Example 3.5 as a Moore type, and define its state flow diagram and state table.

3.2 Using Table 3.19, define the next state transition and output functions, and place them on a Karnaugh map.

3.3 Realize the pulse mode sequential network of Example 3.6 using RS flip-flops and the same state assignment.

3.4 Using Table 3.23, define the next state transition and output functions, and place them on a Karnaugh map.

3.5 Using Figure 3.25b, determine the state sequences starting with states 0 and 2, respectively.

3.6 Using Figure 3.25d, determine the resulting maximum-length sequence starting with state 0.

3.7 Using Table 3.24, place the four-output functions on a Karnaugh map and draw the decoder logic diagram, using AND/OR gates.

3.8 Using Table 3.26 and the associated don't care states assignment, place the function on a Karnaugh map and simplify it. Draw the resulting flow diagram.

3.9 Realize the control timing for Example 3.10 using indirect and direct synthesis, with D-type flip-flops. Hint: Use a state assignment such that $Z = Y_1$.

3.10 Using Figure 3.29, design a modulo 143 counter, using both up and down count modes.

3.11 Convert Figure 3.32 into an arbitrary sequence controller by adding an 8-to-3 priority encoder and a two-phase clock. Hint: Increment counter at $\phi 1$ and load it at $\phi 2$.

3.12 Using tables 3.29 and 3.30, derive the next state transition and output functions for Example 3.13.

3.13 Derive the next state transition matrix and the unique P-term assignment for Example 3.15.

3.14 Find the Eulerian trail and the Hamiltonian path of Figure 3.39b, starting with state A.

3.15 Find the Eulerian trail and the Hamiltonian path of Figure 3.48, starting with state A.

3.16 Using the truth table developed in Problem 2.19, realize the counter logic, using direct synthesis to generate the valid sequence.

3.17 Using the counter description of Problem 2.20, draw the state flow diagram and the associated state transition table.

REFERENCES

Actel. *FPGA Data Book.* Sunnyvale, CA: Actel, 1994.

Altera. *Data Book.* San Jose, CA: Altera, 1993.

IC Applications Staff of TI Inc. *Designing with TTL Integrated Circuits.* New York: McGraw-Hill, 1971.

Kohavi, Z. *Switching and Finite Automata Theory.* New York: McGraw-Hill, 1970.

Marcus, M. P. *Switching Circuits for Engineers.* Englewood Cliffs, NJ: Prentice-Hall, 1962.

McCluskey, E. J. *Introduction to the Theory of Switching Circuits.* New York: McGraw-Hill, 1965.

Nagle, H. Troy, Jr., B. D. Carroll, and J. David Irwin. *An Introduction to Computer Logic.* Englewood Cliffs, NJ: Prentice-Hall, 1975.

Papachristou, C., and E. Karalis. "On Realization and Emulation of Sequential Machines using PLAs." Proceedings of the 1977 Conference on Information Sciences and Systems. *Johns Hopkins University Conference Proceedings* Volume 11, pp. 219–225 (March 1977).

Perry, Douglas, L. *VHDL.* 2nd ed. New York: McGraw-Hill, 1993.

Texas Instruments. *LSI Logic Data Book.* Dallas, TX: Texas Instruments, 1993.

———. *Programmable Logic Data Book.* Dallas, TX: Texas Instruments, 1990.

Wakerly, John F. *Digital Design Principles and Practice.* Englewood Cliffs, NJ: Prentice-Hall, 1994.

Xilinx. *The PGA Data Book.* San Jose, CA: Xilinx, 1988.

4

MICROPROCESSOR HARDWARE

A microcomputer unit (MCU) is a structured sequential network made up of one or more LSI building blocks. It accepts binary input data, performs computations, makes decisions, and stores and outputs the results. *Data* refers to information, represented in binary format, suitable for MCU interpretation. A microcomputer consists of four essential functional blocks: the central processing unit (CPU), the memory, and the input and output (I/O) ports. The microprocessor unit (MPU) is a CPU element fabricated on a single LSI chip, and it forms the hub of a microcomputer unit. The MPU performs numerical computations, logical operations, and control and timing functions. All MPU processes are controlled by a specific set of instructions, which, when organized in a logical fashion, make up the *stored program*, which accomplishes a specific function. An instruction set, available in every MPU, can be used to write an arbitrary program in order to solve a well-defined problem. This feature transforms the MPU into a universal logic module (ULM) capable of performing any conceivable logic operation, once it has been appropriately programmed. The particular program resides in memory, and the required data are either stored or entered, from an input port, as needed. The MPU reads an instruction from memory, decodes it, and performs the required operation upon the specified data. The result is either stored in memory or sent to an output port for external communications.

The MPU is made up of three distinct sections: the arithmetic and logic unit (ALU), the storage registers, and the control and timing section. The ALU performs all arithmetic, logic, and bit-manipulation operations on data accessed from memory, storage registers, or input ports. These operations include elementary arithmetic computations, fundamental logic functions, and the shifting, rotating, and complementing of bits. Status bits, known as *flags,* are usually associated with arithmetic and logic operations and indicate the presence of certain conditions. These include overflow, underflow, carry, zero, and sign change. The storage registers provide temporary hold for data before, during, and after ALU operations. In addition, memory addresses, intermediate results, and status codes may reside in storage registers during program execution. The control and timing section decodes, executes, and synchronizes microprocessor operations using an external reference clock signal.

The microcomputer elements are interconnected by a network of signal paths, known as the *bus,* which facilitates information transfer among all elements. There are three different types of buses: the bidirectional data bus, the unidirectional address bus, and the bidirectional control and timing bus. The number of bits in the data bus is used to classify microprocessors as eight-, sixteen-, or thirty-two–bit types. The number of address bits n can range from ten to thirty-two. They provide the MPU with the ability to access a maximum of $N = 2^n$ unique memory locations.

MPUs come in a variety of physical packages, with the number of I/O pins ranging from 28 to 168. These connect the buses with other functional blocks.

The objectives of this chapter are as follows: (1) to define the major MPU architectures, (2) to explain the various functional MPU description models, (3) to discuss memory architecture and organization, (4) to present timing and control structures and sequences, and (5) to cover I/O data transfer methods.

4.1 ARCHITECTURE DEFINITIONS

Microcomputer architecture refers to the performance and functional relationships among the components that make up a system. The classic *von Neumann architecture* defines a computer in terms of four units: the memory, which stores instructions and data; the ALU, which performs arithmetic and logical operations on the data; the control unit, which executes the instructions; and the I/O, which provides external communications. The ALU and control units are collectively referred to as the central processing unit (CPU). When implemented on the same IC package, the CPU is called the microprocessor unit (MPU).

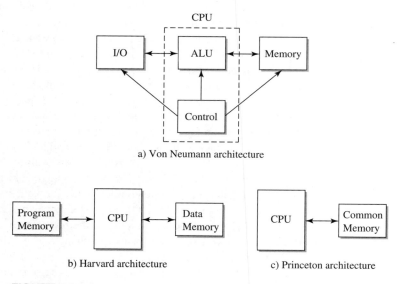

a) Von Neumann architecture

b) Harvard architecture

c) Princeton architecture

FIGURE 4.1
MCU architectures.

There are two basic memory configuration approaches. The first uses separate instruction and data memories over a dual bus. The second uses a common instruction and data memory over a single bus. The former is known as the Harvard and the latter as the Princeton architecture. These architectures are illustrated in Figure 4.1. The *Harvard architecture* features two separate memories that communicate with the CPU via two independent signal paths, or buses, providing concurrent information transfer. The *Princeton architecture* uses a common memory that provides the capability for instruction modification. MPU-based architectures use variations of these two configurations.

The two prevalent types of implementation are the single-bus and the dual-bus types. Single-bus architecture connects the MPU to the memory and I/O using the same bus. Dual-bus architecture uses two separate buses. Storage can also take two different forms: random access memory (RAM) or read-only memory (ROM). The RAM makes it possible to read or write information, and it can be used for both instruction and data storage. The ROM can be used only to read information and is better suited for instruction or table lookup storage. Figure 4.2 illustrates the two types of bus implementation.

The bus consists of address, data, and control signal lines. There are two methods for MPU and memory communications. The first method is the sequential instruction fetch and execute mode. This results in an idle ALU during the fetch cycle and an idle memory during the execution cycle. The second method uses a *pipeline architecture*. This eliminates the inefficiency of an idle ALU by fetching the next instruction while the current one is executing, providing concurrent operation. To achieve this operation it is necessary to insert a data storage register between the memory and the MPU. These two approaches are illustrated in Figure 4.3. The pipeline method increases processor throughput by reducing idle time from the sum of the system component setup and propagation delays to the worst-case delay of the slowest element in the pipeline.

The MPU depends on an external clock signal to perform its functions. The basic clock period, defined as the reciprocal of its frequency, is called the *clock cycle*. The MPU *machine cycle* is made up of several clock cycles and may be fixed or variable, depending on the design. A machine cycle is used either to perform internal machine operations or to accomplish external bidirectional data transfers to memory or I/O ports. An *instruction cycle* consists of one or more machine cycles. The first part of the cycle is referred to as the *fetch phase,* during which an instruction is obtained from memory or an I/O device. The second part of the cycle is called the *execution phase,* in which the control unit generates the necessary step sequence to perform the required operation. Execution involves the ALU when the source and destination

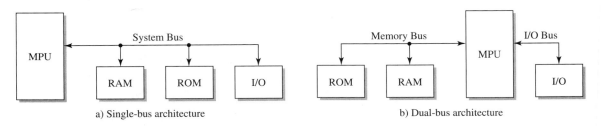

a) Single-bus architecture   b) Dual-bus architecture

FIGURE 4.2
MCU bus implementations.

FIGURE 4.3

MPU/memory interface modes.

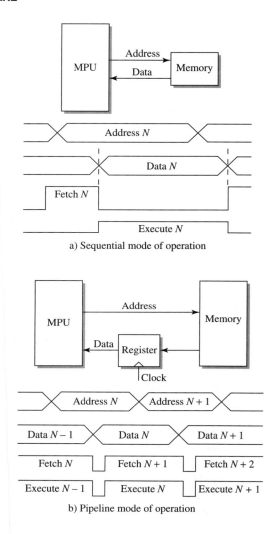

a) Sequential mode of operation

b) Pipeline mode of operation

addresses of the actual data are specified in the instruction fields. A typical MPU instruction may require one to several successive machine cycles for completion. A group of instructions organized in a manner that causes an MPU to perform a specified task is called a program. Figure 4.4 illustrates the various MPU cycles. The depicted instruction cycle, consisting of the fetch and execution phases, requires four machine cycles. Each machine cycle is composed of four clock cycles, although these numbers may vary for different instructions. A conventional microprocessor is called a single instruction single data (SISD) type, or scalar processor, since each executed instruction operates on one set of data at a time.

Microprocessors are classified according to their data word size as eight-, sixteen-, or thirty-two–bit machines. Some eight-bit devices are integrated with on-chip memory and I/O logic to form single-chip microcomputers. These are well suited for small dedicated controllers

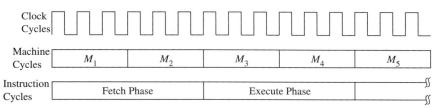

FIGURE 4.4
Instruction cycle definition.

that can be embedded into a larger system. The eight-bit devices provide a fairly large repertoire of instructions and are suitable for general-purpose applications. The sixteen-bit devices come with sophisticated instructions, which make them suitable for data-processing applications. The thirty-two–bit devices have enhanced architectures that support multitasking operations so that multiple programs can run concurrently.

Microprocessors are also available as either single- or multiple-chip implementations. The single-chip devices have a fixed address and data word size. They come with a fixed optimized instruction set that can be used to develop software for general-purpose applications. The multiple-chip devices consist of two or more bit-slices that can be cascaded to produce variable length address and data word sizes. The instruction set is defined by the designer and can be customized for a specific application. These devices come with limited support hardware and software, but they provide speed and flexibility. In contrast, single-chip devices come with many support IC devices and software support packages but operate at a slower speed.

Microprocessor models fall under two broad categories, the accumulator-based and the register-based. The accumulator-based performs all ALU operations using one dedicated register, called *accumulator,* to first store one of the operands and then the result. The register-based performs all ALU operations using a set of registers to specify source and destination of the operands and result storage. An accumulator-oriented MPU may have one or two dedicated registers to store data before and after ALU operations. The register-oriented MPU relaxes this requirement by providing software controlled assignment of data registers.

Contemporary MPU designs optimize the overall operational performance using separate instruction fetch and execution units. The fetch unit is designed to minimize the number of memory access cycles needed by the execution unit. The execution unit is designed to minimize the number of steps needed to complete a single instruction. The first microprocessor architectures were accumulator-based designs. These were followed by the register-based designs, which offered improved programming flexibility. As data word lengths grew to thirty-two bits, contemporary-design MPU architectures became both feasible and necessary to support high-performance applications scenarios.

Single-Chip MCU

This architecture combines the CPU, memory, and I/O functions into one integrated circuit module. Most single-chip MCUs have eight-bit word size and are accumulator-based designs. Figure 4.5 is a functional block diagram of a representative single-chip microcomputer.

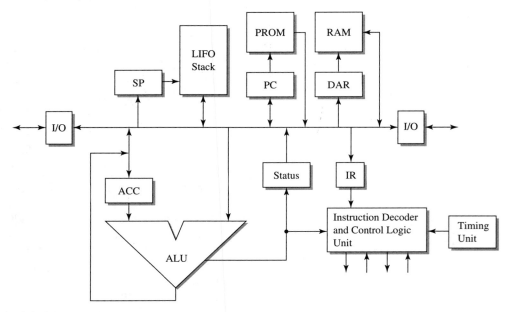

FIGURE 4.5
Single-chip MCU functional block diagram.

All functional units are configured with a common internal bus, which requires that they have tri-state output logic for bidirectional data transfers. This arrangement is a single-bus architecture that uses separate program and data memories on the same system bus. The instructions reside in the programmable ROM (PROM) and the data elements are stored in the RAM. The program consists of individual instructions, each occupying one or more PROM locations, that direct the MCU to perform a logical sequence of operations necessary to accomplish a specific task. The RAM is used to store initial data elements, intermediate values, and the final results. The I/O ports provide external communications to peripheral devices, which serve as the human interface. These devices perform input data formatting, recognizable by the MCU, and display output results in a meaningful manner. The timing unit provides a stable reference clock, which forms the basis for the machine cycle. During the instruction fetch phase, the program counter (PC) contents are used as the PROM address to provide a specific memory location. The memory location contents are then loaded into the instruction register (IR). The PC contents are incremented to provide the next memory address. Next, during the execution phase, the instruction is decoded and the control logic unit generates the required sequence of events to complete the specified operation. During the execution phase there may be a need to perform data transfers to memory or I/O ports, in addition to ALU processing. The accumulator register (ACC) serves as the source and destination for one of the operands, which is processed by the ALU. The data address register (DAR) is used to access the RAM data memory locations for read or write operations. The status register stores the states of the various conditions arising from ALU data operations. The last-in-first-out (LIFO) memory, or *stack,* and its associated stack pointer (SP) are used for storing the return address to the main program

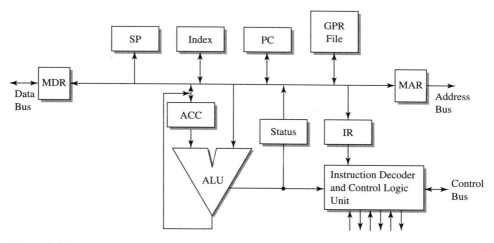

FIGURE 4.6
Accumulator-based MPU block diagram.

flow sequence, for cases in which the return address is altered as a result of internal or external conditions.

Accumulator-Based MPU

This microprocessor architecture dedicates at least one register as the source or destination of data associated with ALU operations and memory transfers. These registers are referred to as accumulators. Figure 4.6 is a functional block diagram of a typical accumulator-based design. These usually have eight- or sixteen-bit-wide data words. The internal architecture centers around a common data bus that facilitates information transfers among the various functional units. This configuration is a Princeton type design that uses a common memory for both program and data elements. The memory address register (MAR) is used to provide an address location to an external memory or I/O device. The memory data register (MDR) serves as a bidirectional buffer for external data transfers. The general purpose register (GPR) file is used for temporary data storage during program execution, minimizing the need for memory read/write operations for intermediate results. The index register provides an alternative source of memory addressing, for programming flexibility. The SP register is used to access a software-controlled LIFO stack located in external memory. The remaining elements serve the same function as those in single-chip MCUs. Accumulator-based designs require several machine cycles per instruction execution.

Register-Based MPU

A register-based MPU has a generalized accumulator-based design. As such, any of the registers in the GPR file can be assigned as accumulator by the software. The GPR file may contain anywhere from four to two hundred and fifty six registers. Figure 4.7 illustrates a representative

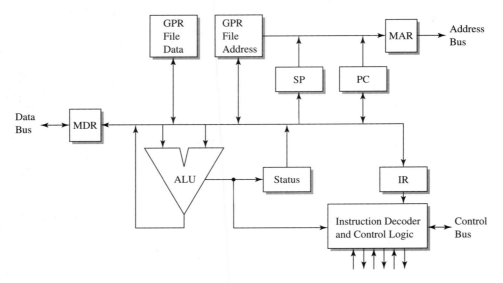

FIGURE 4.7
Register-based MPU block diagram.

register-based design, with a common information bus structure. Such designs have either sixteen- or thirty-two-bit data word size. They usually contain two GPR files, one for data and another for address storage. The GPR data file registers may be used either as accumulators or as temporary data storage. The GPR address file registers may be used as base, index, or additional stack pointer registers, for wide memory addressing flexibility. In addition, a separate address bus has been incorporated to enhance processor throughput capability. Register-based designs, also called load-and-store designs, usually require one machine cycle per instruction.

Contemporary-Design MPU

The next microprocessor evolution resulted in two functional block definitions within the same IC, the fetch and execution units, respectively.

The fetch unit acts as a buffer to the execution unit and interfaces with the external main memory and I/O devices. The fetch unit contains a cache, a memory management unit (MMU), and a bus interface unit (BIU). The *cache* is a small, high-speed memory located between the MPU and the main memory. Its purpose is to increase processor throughput by storing frequently used main memory instructions and data and to prefetch additional instructions by predicting instruction branching. *Static branching* refers to the fixed instruction code sequence loaded in memory. *Dynamic branch prediction* uses the MPU logic to forecast probable branches and provide the correct next address, thereby maintaining a uniform execution unit pipeline flow. The cache is organized with an address tag field and a corresponding contents field. All instructions and data read from main memory are entered into the cache. *Write back* refers to the MPU sending all write data to the cache until a new set is requested from the main memory. *Write through* refers to the MPU always sending all write data to both the cache and main memory. *Direct mapped* refers to the technique of storing main memory data blocks at the same cache location. *Fully associative* refers to the technique of storing main memory data blocks at different cache locations. Direct mapped results in fast data search times, with frequent read caching. Fully associative results in moderate data search times and less read caching. A hybrid technique, called *n*-way set associative, combines the best features of both. A *unified cache* combines instructions and data into one, and a *dual cache* uses a separate memory for each.

The MMU controls the available main memory by providing memory mapping, allocation, and protection mechanisms. The intent is to minimize main memory access response times and maintain high-speed bus transfers. Memory mapping translates MPU-logical addresses into physical memory locations. This feature is used to support virtual memory addressing. The *virtual memory* techniques transform the cache, main, and secondary memories into one contiguous address space. When this is done, the main memory appears larger than normal to the MPU. Memory allocation can be accomplished by dynamically assigning fixed-size pages or variable-size segments. Individual program modules are swapped in and out of main memory on a demand basis. The protection mechanism maintains program boundaries and provides controlled access to other memory areas, for data integrity. The bus interface unit (BIU) provides control and timing signals to achieve external memory I/O data transfers.

The execution unit consists of a register file, an ALU for integer arithmetic, and a floating point unit (FPU), which operate in parallel. Figure 4.8 is a simplified functional block diagram of a contemporary-design MPU. These features along with the pipelined paths enhance instruction execution.

A number of novel features are found in contemporary-design MPU architectures. A *modified Harvard architecture* refers to a common memory using dedicated instruction and data buses and a pipelined address bus. *Superscalar* refers to an MPU with multiple independent ALUs. This feature achieves multiple instruction execution per machine cycle. A complex instruction set computer (CISC) has the conventional large number of variable-length instructions. A reduced instruction set computer (RISC) has the contemporary small number of uniform-length instructions. Modern MPU designs are hybrid architectures that combine the best features of both models to provide overall optimum performance.

The following are two examples of contemporary MPU architectures: (1) a CISC pipelined MPU with an instruction prefetch queue; a unified, direct-mapped, write-through

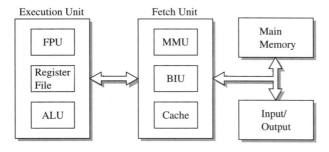

FIGURE 4.8
Contemporary-design MPU block diagram.

cache, to enhance a Princeton architecture; an integer ALU with an independent FPU for math intensive applications, and an MMU to support virtual memory management, allocation, and protection, using variable-size segments; (2) a RISC load-and-store superscalar MPU with a dual two-way associative, write-back cache to support a modified Harvard architecture; a dynamic branch prediction unit for maintaining the flow to the instruction decoder unit; dual ALUs for enhanced multiple-instruction execution; an independent FPU for improved numeric data performance; and an MMU to support virtual memory management, with variable-size segments and fixed-size pages. These hybrid MPUs are single-chip designs that contain several million transistors, housed in 100+ pin grid array (PGA) packages. They have a thirty-two-bit-wide address bus for up to four gigabytes of physical and up to sixty-four terabytes of virtual memory addressing. Also, the thirty-two–bit data bus width supports eight-, sixteen-, and thirty-two-bit operands. They operate with clock speeds of 50 to 100 MHz and can perform 80 to 100 million instructions per second (mips).

Bit-Slice MPU

This architecture consists of at least two integrated circuit modules, the register arithmetic and logic unit (RALU) and the microcode sequencer unit. The RALU has built-in logic to enable cascading for expanding the data word size to enhance performance. Figure 4.9 illustrates a typical bit-slice MPU architecture.

In this simplified configuration the microcode sequencer, together with the control store and register, is similar to the control unit of conventional architectures. The use of a control store PROM to determine the command sequence required to execute each memory instruction

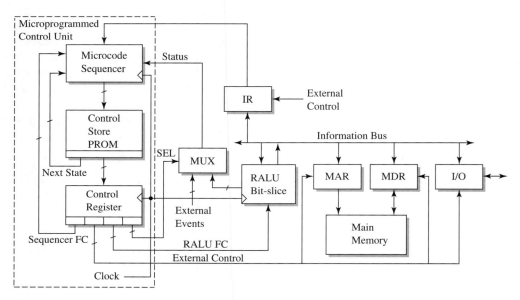

FIGURE 4.9
Bit-slice architecture block diagram.

is called *microprogramming*. A microprogrammed MCU can be configured by adding external memory, with associated registers and I/O connected via a common information bus structure. The main program memory contains an ordered set of instructions and data, which are manipulated by the RALU in the sequence provided by the microprogrammed control unit. This technique can be viewed as a machine within a machine, where a main program memory instruction is loaded into the IR register and then decoded as a starting address for the control store PROM. This results in a series of microinstructions executed by the microcode sequencer, as directed by the control and status inputs from the control store PROM and RALU, respectively. The specific main program memory instruction is completed at the end of each microprogram execution sequence. The control store PROM is followed by a pipeline register to speed throughput. This is achieved by overlapping the fetch and execution phases, which otherwise would take place sequentially. The internal RALU architecture has been optimized to minimize the number of machine cycles required per instruction.

Figure 4.10 provides a detailed block diagram of a representative bit-slice RALU device. The heart of the device consists of a two-operand ALU. The ALU is preceded by a multiplexer module that selects two out of the four possible input sources, which are external input data, accumulator, RAM A, and RAM B. Several internal data buses facilitate data transfer operations from source to destination. The dual-port RAM can address two simultaneous output data locations for read operations, but only one data address location can be written to at a time. The shifter unit provides cascadable, bidirectional one-bit shift operations. The cascadable ALU provides status outputs as a result of arithmetic or logic operations. The RALU requires an external reference clock source and an input function code that defines each operation and the source and destination of data.

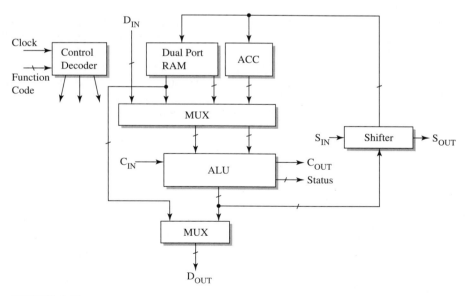

FIGURE 4.10
RALU functional block diagram.

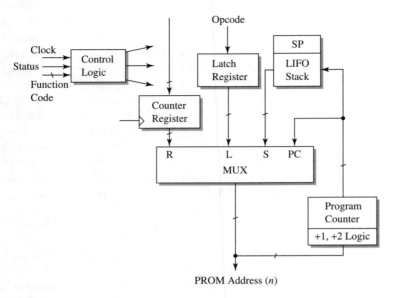

FIGURE 4.11
Microcode sequencer block diagram.

The microcode unit architecture, shown in Figure 4.11, has been tailored to generate the next control store PROM address in response to the input function code. The next address is obtained from one of four possible sources: the program counter (PC), the latch register (L), the stack (S), or the counter register (R). The program counter has built-in incrementing logic for sequential memory location access capability. The latch register is used to store the starting address of each machine instruction. The stack is used to store the next address location following the execution of a subprogram, which may change due to the occurrence of either an external or internal condition. The stack can also be used to store the next address location following a program iteration instruction. The counter register is used to access a nonsequential memory address location from the control store PROM in response to either a conditional or an unconditional instruction.

MPU Element Functions

A typical microprocessor consists of three essential elements, the ALU, the various registers, and the control logic, which are integrated into one functional unit. The ALU forms the heart of the MPU and performs all arithmetic and logic operations on the input data. The ALU consists of a basic adder that is augmented by a shifter, a complementer, and a Boolean logic section. These basic functions enable the processor to perform binary and unary operations, including addition, subtraction, increment, decrement, complement, negate, shift, and rotate. The fundamental Boolean function operations, such as AND, OR, XOR, and NOT, are also available.

The ALU generates status bits or flags to indicate certain conditions that result from arithmetic and logic operations. These include the Z, N, F, and C status bits. The Z bit is set when the result of an arithmetic operation equals zero. The N bit is used to indicate the sign resulting from an arithmetic operation. The F bit is set when the result of an arithmetic operation exceeds the value range limit of the accumulator—an overflow condition. The C bit is set to indicate that a carry operation is needed during addition or subtraction. These bits are usually stored in the status register.

The accumulator is used to store the data element to be operated upon during the instruction execution phase. In accumulator-based designs, this register serves as both the source and the destination of the operand. A typical instruction may require the contents of the accumulator to be operated with those of another register, memory location, or external input and the results placed in the accumulator. In addition, the accumulator serves as an intermediate buffer for data transfers to and from memory or I/O port. Register-based designs use the register file as a scratch pad memory to store intermediate results. This reduces the number of memory transfer cycles, which improves throughput and algorithm efficiency.

The program counter is used to keep track of the next instruction address. The instructions are normally kept in sequential address locations. Thus, at the end of each instruction cycle, the PC is incremented and its contents are used to load the MAR to fetch the next instruction. In some cases, however, such as a jump or branch instruction, the PC contents are modified by that instruction. The jump instruction can be either conditional or unconditional. If conditional, the PC contents are either incremented by one or replaced by the provided jump address, based upon the condition test status. If the jump instruction is unconditional, the PC contents are replaced by the provided address value. Similarly, the branch instruction can be either conditional or unconditional. The PC contents are augmented by an offset value for a true condition or incremented by one for a false condition. A jump to subroutine instruction requires that the next consecutive address location be saved and the PC be loaded with the provided jump address. This can be easily accomplished by storing the next address value in the stack. The provided jump address is used to access a subroutine.

A *subroutine* is a small standalone program, which may be executed as many times as required by the main program. The last subroutine instruction places the stack contents into the PC, and thus returns the processor to the correct location in the main program sequence. A subroutine can be designed to call another subroutine, which is known as *nesting*. The level of subroutine nesting is limited by the depth of the stack. For example, a ten-location LIFO stack can support up to ten levels of nesting. The SP register contains a value corresponding to the current stack location.

The IR register is used to store the instructions as they are fetched from memory. First, the PC contents are transferred into the MAR to specify the particular instruction memory location. Next, the contents of that location are loaded into the MDR and then transferred into the IR for decoding. If the instruction is contained in a single memory location, then the MPU transitions into the execution phase. Otherwise, a second fetch is performed in order to obtain the remaining instruction. The GPR file is used as either an address- or data-storing space by the MPU to enhance its performance.

The control and timing unit generates the proper sequence of signals necessary to fetch and execute each instruction. It also maintains coordination among the various elements and generates the next address as a function of the internal status or external conditions. The external conditions or *interrupts* are initiated by asynchronously occurring events and serve to improve MPU efficiency. They are handled like subroutines and can be nested, using priority schemes, to enhance MPU performance.

Data transfers between the MPU and the outside world are accomplished either by memory-read and -write or I/O operations. A memory-read operation takes the contents of a memory location, specified by the MAR, and places them in the accumulator register inside the MPU. A memory-write operation takes the contents of the accumulator and places them in a memory location, specified by the MAR. The I/O operation is similar, but an interface device is used instead of memory. A memory-read operation into the IR becomes an instruction fetch and may be followed by a memory or input data read operation to provide the operands for instruction execution. During the execution phase a specific operation, defined by the instruction, is interpreted and carried out. The resulting data, if any, may be transferred to memory or an output port with memory-write or output operation, respectively.

4.2 FUNCTIONAL DESCRIPTION

A typical microprocessor is organized using three primary signal types: address, data, and control. These signals are combined into three distinct buses. The address bus is made up of M unidirectional signal paths, which are used to specify the data locations. A maximum of 2^M unique locations can be defined with an address word of M bits in width. The data bus consists of N bidirectional signal paths, where N is the data word size. Both the address and the data bus signals have tri-state capability, which gives the MPU operating mode flexibility. In some MPUs, due to pin limitations, some of the address signal lines are multiplexed with the data signal lines and require external logic for demultiplexing. The control bus consists of all the signals necessary to accomplish the various internal and external operations. Also, voltage and ground pins are provided to supply electrical power to the device.

Block Diagram Model

An MPU can be defined in a block diagram by grouping and labeling the various signals and indicating their direction of flow. Figure 4.12 is a generic MPU functional block diagram that identifies the signal types. The reference clock signal is essential in the overall MPU operation. The *reset signal* is used to place the MPU in a known internal state. The *halt signal* is used to freeze MPU operation by gating the input clock signal. The interrupt control lines are used to sense external asynchronous events that request the attention of the MPU. The processor function code indicates a specific MPU mode, such as read, write, interrupt, internal, or halt. The bus control lines handle external device requests for bus access to perform direct memory access (DMA). In the DMA mode, a device can perform data transfers to and from memory, bypassing the MPU. The I/O control lines are used to achieve data transfers between the MPU and memory or other external devices. The data bus bandwidth determines the maximum data transfer rate as a function of the bus width in bits and MPU cycle time. The transfer rate is expressed in millions of bytes per second (mbps).

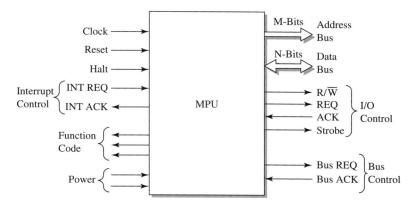

FIGURE 4.12
Typical MPU functional block diagram.

The read and write operations for exchanging data between the MPU and memory or I/O can be either synchronous or asynchronous with respect to the MPU reference clock. An MPU can be designed to operate with either one or both data transfer modes. The asynchronous transfer mode offers a speed advantage over the well-defined synchronous mode. Figure 4.13 consists of two timing diagrams that illustrate the two data transfer modes. Figure 4.13a shows read and write MPU operations using the synchronous data transfer mode. The first half of the cycle details a data-write operation. The address bus signals are activated, from their tri-state condition. The address bus contains the valid location for the MPU data to be written, indicated by a low level on the R/$\overline{\text{W}}$ control line. Next the address pulse signal is generated by the MPU and is used by the external device to latch the valid address. Also at this point, the data bus is activated and valid data appear and are transferred to a location, specified by the address bus, at the trailing edge of the address pulse. The second half of the data transfer operation is a data-read operation. Again, the address bus signals are activated, from their tri-state condition. The R/$\overline{\text{W}}$ control signal is at a high level, indicating a read operation. The address bus contains the valid location from which data will be read into the MPU. The MPU address pulse signal is used by the device to latch the valid address and place the data on the data bus, which now becomes an input path. The input data must be valid on the trailing edge of the address pulse signal. This type of data transfer method necessitates that the speed of the external device, whether memory or I/O, closely matches that of the MPU. In order to accommodate slower devices, MPUs have an additional input signal, called ready, which is controlled by the device to effectively stretch the address pulse width. Device access time variations of less than one I/O clock cycle do not contribute to processor throughput.

Figure 4.13b illustrates read and write MPU operations using the asynchronous data transfer mode. The MPU shown in Figure 4.12 features this type of data transfer mode. Again, the first half of the cycle shows a write operation and the second half, a read operation. Initially, the address bus signals are activated. Then the MPU address strobe signal indicates when they are stable. Next, the MPU sends a data request signal, declaring valid data available, to the external device. The external device responds with a data acknowledge signal to confirm a successful data transfer. Finally, the external device disables its acknowledge signal to mark the

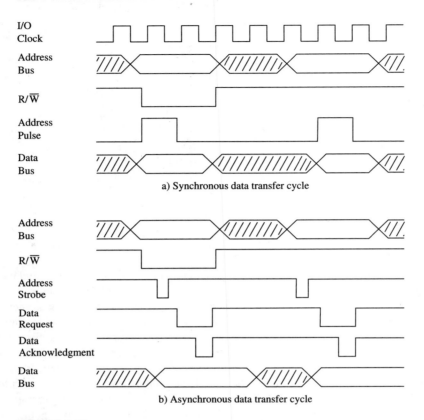

FIGURE 4.13
Data transfer timing diagrams.

end of the write operation. The read operation is performed in a similar manner, with the exception that the R/$\overline{W}$ signal is at a high level and the device acknowledge signal indicates that valid data are available to be transferred to the MPU. This data transfer mode takes advantage of external device access variations to increase processor throughput.

Register Model

An MPU can also be described in terms of its register transfer operations, known as register model representation. Figure 4.14 depicts a typical accumulator-based MPU register model. The accumulator is normally used to hold operands prior to an arithmetic or logical operation and to receive the results. The instruction register is used to hold the operation code (opcode) portion of the instruction word, after it is fetched from memory. The status register is used to hold the state of several ALU flag bits. The general-purpose register is used as temporary storage for either instructions or data. A cascaded group of such registers can form a queue within the MPU. The index register is used by the MPU to facilitate various addressing modes. This is accomplished by either using its contents or combining them with the program counter to form

FIGURE 4.14
Microprocessor register model.

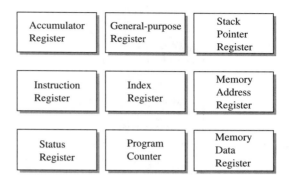

the next memory address. The program counter is used to store the memory address location of the current instruction. The stack pointer is used to store the address of the memory region designated as a LIFO stack. It is incremented during a PUSH stack operation and decremented during a POP stack operation. The memory address and data registers act as buffers between the MPU and the external memory or I/O device.

An instruction sequence flow diagram is used in conjunction with the register model definition to illustrate the various steps for a particular instruction. The simplified sequence flow diagram shown in Figure 4.15 provides a better understanding of the sequential nature of MPU operation and highlights some of its salient features. The sequence begins by the PC contents being loaded into the MAR, which specifies the memory address location and initiates a read operation. Then the PC contents are incremented. Next, the contents of the memory location, which make up the instruction opcode, are loaded into the IR register. Then the contents of the IR are transferred into the control unit. The opcode is decoded to determine, first, if any external memory data are required and second, the type of instruction. If additional operands are required from memory, a second memory read operation is performed and the PC is incremented. The read data are placed in the accumulator. Then a determination is made, based on the opcode, whether the read data are the actual operand or the memory address of the operand. In the former case, the sequence proceeds to determine the instruction type, and in the latter case, a third memory read operation is performed to retrieve the operand.

Two general types of instructions are defined, the normal and the test. Normal instructions are instructions that require no changes to the basic program flow as it exists in memory. For example, after a STEP instruction is executed, the above sequence repeats. A SUBR instruction causes the execution of a smaller program, called a subroutine, within the main program. For this to happen, two things must take place. The PC contents must be loaded into the stack, and the GPR contents, specifying the subroutine starting address, must be loaded into the PC. The INTR instruction, which interrupts the processor, is activated by an external event condition. Again, the PC contents are loaded into the stack, and the GPR register contents, specifying the interrupt routine starting address, are loaded into the PC. The last instruction of both the SUBR and INTR routines is the RTN, which stands for "return to main program." The RTN instruction causes the contents of the stack location, indicated by the SP register, to be loaded into the PC. This operation places the MPU in the main program flow. A JUMP instruction results in an unconditional jump to a specified point in the main program and causes the contents of the GPR, specifying the new program location, to be loaded into the PC. If none of the above

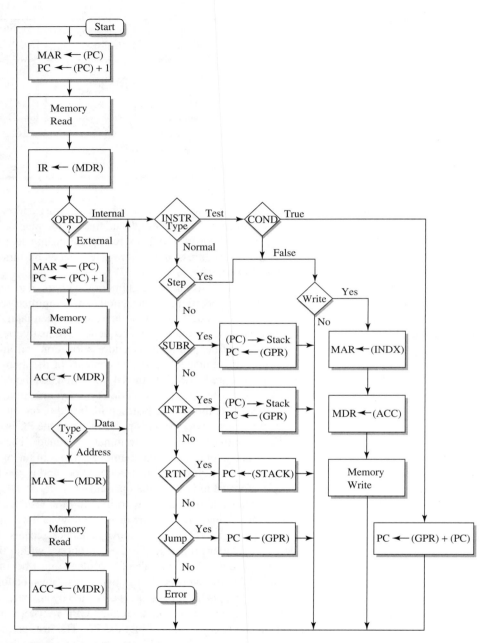

FIGURE 4.15
MPU instruction sequence flow diagram.

instructions is decoded, an internal error condition occurs and appropriate action is taken by the MPU based on the particular implementation.

A test-type instruction requires that a program flow change take place if a specified condition becomes true, prior to execution, for that particular instruction. If the specific condition test is true, then the normal program flow is altered and the GPR contents are added to the PC contents, resulting in a conditional branch. If, however, the condition test is false, then the sequence of flow defaults to that of a STEP instruction. When an instruction requires a memory-write operation, the index register contents are loaded into the MAR, specifying the address location, and the accumulator contents are loaded into the MDR. The I/O read and write operations are similar to the memory operations. The loading of the GPR and index registers is done either as part of the instruction fetch phase or as a result of the execution phase.

Instruction Set

Each operation performed by the MPU is uniquely specified by the bit pattern of each instruction. Every instruction contains the opcode and additional required information, such as addressing mode, operand address, immediate operand, or result destination address. The collection of all the various commands that an MPU recognizes is called the instruction set. This set constitutes a powerful tool for solving a wide spectrum of problems. As such, a group of instructions is arranged in a logical sequence dictated by the solution of the specific problem. Instructions are classified in four general categories as data transfer, arithmetic and logic, program control, and special types.

Data transfer instructions include operations such as moving data within the MPU registers or between external memory and a specific MPU register. Typical data transfer instructions include MOVE, EXCHANGE, READ, WRITE, INPUT, and OUTPUT. The MOVE instruction is used to accomplish data transfers among registers and/or memory. The EXCHANGE instruction is used to swap the contents of two specified locations. The READ and WRITE instructions are used exclusively for memory operations. The INPUT and OUTPUT instructions are used in conjunction with external interface devices.

Arithmetic-type instructions include the four basic operations for adding, subtracting, multiplying, and dividing two numbers. Magnitude comparison, increment, decrement, inversion, and negation instructions fall in the same group. Typical instructions include ADD, SUB, MULT, DIV, COMP, INC, DEC, INV, and NEG. The ADD instruction sums two numbers A, B to form the result $C = A + B$. Similarly, the SUB, MULT, and DIV instructions generate the difference, product, and quotient, respectively, of two numbers. The COMP instruction compares two numbers and provides a greater than, equal to, or less than result status. The INC and DEC instructions add or subtract one, respectively, from the contents of a register or memory location. The INV instruction produces the one's complement of a number. The NEG instruction generates the two's complement of a number.

Logic-type instructions include Boolean, SHIFT, ROTATE, and bit-manipulation operations. Boolean instructions perform the basic NOT, AND, OR, XOR, and INHIBIT functions. The SHIFT and ROTATE instructions are defined as directional, one-bit transpositions within a register. The basic difference between them is that in the SHIFT instruction, the LSB (MSB) is lost after each operation, but in the ROTATE operation the LSB becomes MSB, or vice-versa, depending on the specified direction. The ROTATE instruction is equivalent to a circular SHIFT. Bit manipulation can be easily achieved with the Boolean instructions, which provide for maximum flexibility at the individual bit level. Example 4.1 illustrates some of these operations.

EXAMPLE 4.1

Given an eight-bit operand $A = b_7b_6b_5b_4b_3b_2b_1b_0 = 10101101$, perform the following operations:

1. INC: $A = 10101110$, where $A = A + 1$
2. DEC: $A = 10101100$, where $A = A - 1$
3. INV: $A = 01010010$, where $A = \overline{A}$
4. NEG: $A = 01010011$, where $A = \overline{A} + 1$
5. SHIFT L: $A = 01011010$, where $A = b_6b_5b_4b_3b_2b_1b_00$
6. SHIFT R: $A = 01010110$, where $A = 0b_7b_6b_5b_4b_3b_2b_1$
7. ROT L: $A = 01011011$, where $A = b_6b_5b_4b_3b_2b_1b_0b_7$
8. ROT R: $A = 11010110$, where $A = b_0b_7b_6b_5b_4b_3b_2b_1$
9. SET b_1: $A = 10101111$, where $A = A + B$, and $B = 00000010$
10. RESET b_2: $A = 10101001$, where $A = A \cdot B$, and $B = 11111011$
11. FLIP b_3: $A = 10100101$, where $A = A \oplus B$, and $B = 00001000$
12. SIFT b_5: $A = 00100000$, where $A = A \cdot B$, and $B = 00100000$

The previous example illustrates twelve basic operations on an eight-bit operand. The INC and DEC operations increment or decrement the operand by one. The INV operation inverts the state of every operand bit, resulting in the one's complement. The NEG operation inverts the state of each bit and adds one to the result, producing the two's complement. The SHIFT L operation shifts each bit one position to the left, resulting in a zero in position b_0. Similarly, SHIFT R shifts each bit one position to the right, resulting in a zero in position b_7. The ROT L operation performs a circular left shift, resulting with b_7 in the b_0 position. The ROT R operation shifts each bit one position to the right, resulting with b_0 in the b_7 position. A SET function operation is used to OR a specific bit position of the operand with a constant whose corresponding bit value equals one. The RESET function operation is used to AND a specific bit position of the operand with a constant whose corresponding bit is zero. To FLIP or toggle a specific bit position, an XOR function operation is performed instead. Finally, the SIFT operation is used to isolate the value of a specific bit position by performing an AND function operation. Bit-manipulation instructions are useful in analyzing the individual bit positions within a data word to make elementary decisions for determining the flow of control.

The third type of MPU instructions are program control instructions, which are used to alter the program execution sequence. Program control instructions include STEP, BRANCH, JUMP, SUBR, INTR, and RTN. The STEP operation is the default action taken by an instruction and results in the PC being incremented to the next consecutive location, following current instruction execution. The BRANCH instruction modifies the PC contents by adding an offset value, depending on an internal condition test outcome. The JUMP instruction loads the PC with a value that may or may not depend on an internal condition test outcome. A SUBR instruction transfers the PC contents to the next available stack location, prior to loading the

TABLE 4.1
Program control instruction tests

Test Name	Equation	Test Name	Equation
CARRY SET	$C = 1$	$(ACC) > 0$	$Z + (N \oplus F) = 0$
CARRY CLEAR	$C = 0$	$(ACC) < 0$	$(N \oplus F) = 1$
OVERFLOW	$F = 1$	$(ACC) \geq 0$	$(N \oplus F) = 0$
NO OVERFLOW	$F = 0$	$(ACC) \leq 0$	$Z + (N \oplus F) = 1$
NEGATIVE	$N = 1$	$(ACC) > (B)$	$(C + Z) = 0$
POSITIVE	$N = 0$	$(ACC) < (B)$	$(N \oplus F) = 1$
$(ACC) = 0$	$Z = 1$	$(ACC) \geq (B)$	$C = 0$
$(ACC) \neq 0$	$Z = 0$	$(ACC) \leq (B)$	$(C + Z) = 1$

SUBR address in the PC. The INTR instruction results in a similar operation as a result of an asynchronous external condition. The RTN instruction transfers the last entry of the stack into the PC such that normal program execution sequence can resume. This group of instructions controls the program execution sequence using a set of conditions that are made up using the status register bits. Table 4.1 lists a typical set of condition tests that can be defined within an instruction opcode. The primary instructions that contain one of these tests in their opcode are BRANCH and JUMP. These tests are performed within the control unit and range from a simple status bit value check to the evaluation of a Boolean expression. The test result determines the next instruction address source. If no test is specified in the opcode, then a step operation is used to obtain the next address. It should be noted that the same test equation is used to determine the outcome of more than one condition test.

The fourth type of MPU instruction, known as special instructions, are used to control the MPU itself. Such instructions include RESET, HALT, NOP, ILLEGAL, STATUS, and MODE. A RESET instruction is used to initialize the MPU registers to a known state. A HALT instruction serves to freeze MPU operation and place the data and address buses in a Hi-Z state. A NOP operation results in an idle instruction cycle. The ILLEGAL instruction is activated as a result of an invalid opcode and results in the execution of an error-recovery subroutine. The STATUS instruction places the contents of the status register into the accumulator for possible bit manipulation. Finally, the MODE instruction is used to switch the MPU state from restricted to unrestricted access and vice-versa. The MPU instruction set is tailored to the hardware organization such that programming flexibility and execution speed are optimized.

Addressing Modes and Formats

The MPU has the inherent capability for multiple addressing modes, which enables it to speed execution time and optimize data transfer operations. Linear address, also known as physical address, uses a single register value to define a memory location. This feature supports addressing mode–independent instructions, also called orthogonal instructions. Logical address, also known as virtual address, uses the sum of two register values to define a memory location.

Seven basic addressing modes are available: implied, inherent, immediate, direct, indirect, relative, and indexed. No address is specified in the *implied mode;* rather, the instruction infers an internal MPU operation, and no operand is required. Instructions such as RESET, HALT, and RETURN are implied mode addressing instructions. *Inherent addressing* specifies the operand location within the MPU in a single instruction word. Internal register operations and control instructions use this addressing mode. *Immediate addressing* specifies no operand address; instead, the operand is located in the memory location immediately following the instruction word. This mode is used to transfer data constants for register initialization or condition testing. *Direct,* or absolute, *addressing* specifies the operand address in the next consecutive location following the instruction word. This is a general-purpose instruction addressing mode that may require multiple words in order to span the memory range in MPUs with fewer than thirty-two bits. The

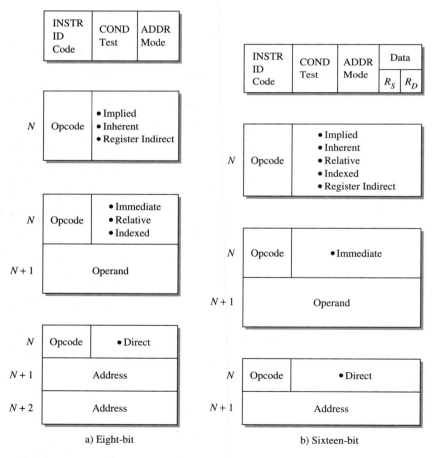

a) Eight-bit   b) Sixteen-bit

FIGURE 4.16
Instruction formats.

indirect addressing mode uses the contents of a specified general purpose internal MPU register to specify the memory address at which the actual operand is stored. This addressing mode reduces the instruction length by extending the MPU fetch cycle to derive the next address. *Relative addressing* provides an offset value in the next consecutive memory location, following the instruction word, which when added to the PC contents becomes the next operand address. This addressing mode provides flexibility by making program relocation possible within the available memory space. *Indexed addressing* adds the operand found in the next consecutive memory location following the instruction word to the contents of a designated general-purpose register to derive the next operand address. The instruction contains the operand in MPUs with greater than eight bits. This mode is useful in accessing tables or arrays stored in sequential address locations. A variation of this scheme, known as page addressing, divides the memory into a number of fixed segments called pages. The designated register is called the page register, and the operand found either in the current or in the next consecutive memory location specifies the location within the page. The addressing modes above can be classified as either absolute or computed. Implied, inherent, immediate, direct, and indirect addressing are absolute addressing modes. Relative and indexed addressing are computed modes, since they necessitate address calculation by the ALU. For immediate, direct, and relative addressing, the PC is used as the reference point. Indirect addressing uses the contents of an internal register for the address value. Indexed addressing uses the contents of an internal register for the base address value plus an offset.

Instruction formats depend on the MPU design and available addressing modes. All instructions contain an opcode field that defines the main function, identifies any condition tests, and specifies the addressing mode. The remaining instruction fields consist of either operand address information or the actual operand. Figure 4.16 outlines the various instruction formats required to achieve the basic addressing modes, in both eight- and sixteen-bit data word sizes. Example 4.2 illustrates the address derivation procedures for the inherent, immediate, direct, indirect, relative, and indexed addressing modes.

EXAMPLE 4.2

Given a sixteen-bit MPU, define the ADD instruction operation using the various addressing modes.

1. Inherent Addressing
   PC(n):ADD R_i $\qquad$ ACC = (ACC) + (R_i)
   This instruction adds the ACC contents to the R_i contents and places the sum in the ACC.
2. Immediate Addressing
   PC(n):ADD # $\qquad$ ACC = (ACC) + 100
   PC(n + 1):100
   This instruction adds the ACC contents to the next memory location contents, which is 100, and places the sum in the ACC.
3. Direct Addressing
   PC(n):ADD X $\qquad$ ACC = (ACC) + (X)
   PC(n + 1):X
   This instruction adds the ACC contents to the memory location, X, contents and places the sum in the ACC.

4. Indirect Addressing

PC(n):ADD @R$_i$ ACC = (ACC) + ((R$_i$))

This instruction adds the ACC contents to the contents of a memory location, whose address is specified by the R$_i$ contents, and places the sum in the ACC.

5. Relative Addressing

PC(n):ADD + 100   ACC = (ACC) + (n + 100)

This instruction adds the ACC contents to a memory location, specified by the PC contents plus an offset, and places the sum in the ACC.

6. Indexed Addressing

PC(n):ADD + 100@R$_i$ ACC = (ACC) + ((R$_i$) + 100)

This instruction adds the ACC contents to the contents of a memory location, specified by the sum of the R$_i$ contents plus an offset, and places the sum in the ACC.

A first-in-first-out (FIFO) queue is formed using a group of contiguous memory locations for sequentially storing and retrieving data in the same order. A LIFO stack is formed by using a group of contiguous memory locations for sequentially storing and retrieving data in reverse order. Figure 4.17 illustrates the two structures.

For the FIFO operation, separate read and write address pointers are used to access the locations. In both read and write, the pointer value is used to access the FIFO location, and then it is incremented. The read pointer, R, value cannot exceed the write pointer, W, value. The LIFO operation uses a single address pointer, SP, for both read and write. In the case of read,

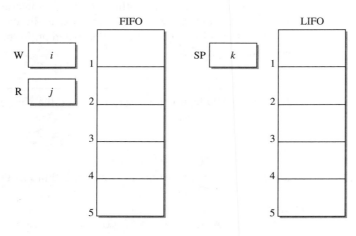

- WRITE Operation
  1. W(i)
  2. $i = i + 1$
- READ Operation
  1. R(j)
  2. $j = j + 1$

- WRITE Operation
  1. SP(k)
  2. $k = k + 1$
- READ Operation
  1. $k = k - 1$
  2. SP(k)

FIGURE 4.17
FIFO and LIFO definitions.

the SP value is used to access the LIFO, and then it is incremented. In the case of write, the SP value is first decremented, and then it is used to access the LIFO. If the allocated memory size equals the pointer modulus, then these two structures become circular and require no limit checks. A FIFO is used to store prefetched consecutive instructions from a slower memory, which enhances throughput and achieves overlapped instruction cycle operation. It can also serve as a buffer between the MPU and a slower interface device to compensate for the speed differential. The LIFO serves several functions within the MPU. It is primarily used to store the internal register contents, or MPU state, during a subroutine or interrupt. It can also be used to transfer addresses and/or data from the main program to a subroutine.

4.3 MEMORY

Any medium that is used to store a binary digit state, such that it can be retrieved by the MPU, is referred to as memory. The basic memory cell is capable of storing a single data bit. Memory can be formatted in bits, nibbles, bytes, or words. A memory can be classified according to its function, contents retention, and data access method. Memory speed, cost per bit, and power dissipation are typical parameters associated with definition and performance comparison. Speed is measured in terms of read and write cycle times. The read cycle consists of the address-to-data access time plus the output data propagation delay time. The write cycle time consists of the address-to-location access time plus the input data set-up and hold times.

Three basic memory types are available: semiconductor-based, magnetic, and optical medium–based. Figure 4.18 classifies the commonly available memory devices. The semiconductor-based devices fall under two categories, random access and sequential access. Random-access memories include the read-only (ROM) and the read/write (RAM) types. The magnetic medium–based devices also fall under two categories, tape and disk. Magnetic tape memories are accessed sequentially; magnetic disk memories are accessed in a hybrid mode. The optical medium–based devices are either read or read/write types and are similar to magnetic disks. The bit-storage density is lowest for semiconductor-based and highest for optical-based devices. There is roughly an order of magnitude difference between the semiconductor and magnetic or the magnetic and optical storage densities. As a result the semiconductor-based devices are used for main memory and the other two are used for secondary storage.

Architecture

Semiconductor-Based Memory Architectures Semiconductor-based memories have proliferated in terms of function, content retention, access, and versatility. A ROM is initially programmed with a fixed data pattern that can be accessed repeatedly. Since its contents retention is permanent, the ROM is known as a *nonvolatile memory*. ROMs are custom-programmable at the factory, during the fabrication process. They are bipolar-based and can achieve read-access times of 25 nsec. ROMs are usually programmed by use of a configuration mask during the final metalization step, which results in the highest bit-storage density available.

A PROM provides user flexibility by enabling the designer to define the state of each individual bit cell. PROMs are bipolar-based, one-time fuse-programmable devices. They can achieve read-access times of 35 nsec. Each memory bit cell has a fusible link that provides a

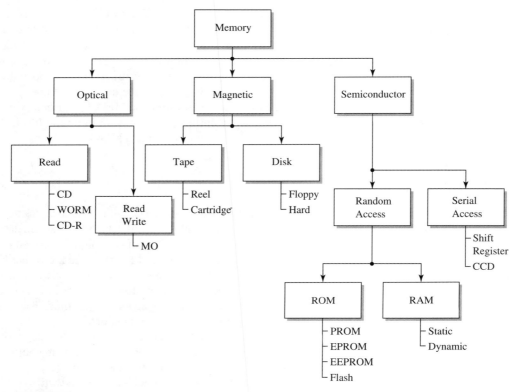

FIGURE 4.18
Memory device classification.

one-time choice to define its state as either 1 or 0. These links, along with the built-in programming logic, reduce the device bit density.

An EPROM provides the capability to erase its contents, using an ultraviolet (UV) light source for reprogramming. EPROMs are CMOS-based programmable devices that can be programmed a byte at a time by altering their internal transistor threshold turn-on voltage level. They have a clear plastic window for erasure. They can be reprogrammed by first exposing them to a UV light source for about 20 minutes.

The EEPROM, in contrast to the EPROM, is a CMOS in-circuit reprogrammable device, also programmable a byte at a time. When a design change is required, the new data are overwritten in the device.

Figure 4.19 presents the block diagram definitions associated with the above device architectures. Figure 4.19a shows a typical ROM/PROM architecture that consists of an input address buffer and associated n-to-2^n decoder logic, the $2^n \times m$ bit storage matrix, and output buffers with tri-state output select ($\overline{OS}$) for bus interface. In addition, a chip select ($\overline{CS}$) input is provided for multiple-device cascading to increase storage capacity.

Figure 4.19b depicts a sample EPROM/EEPROM architecture definition. It has a similar structure that also provides a bidirectional I/O data path to facilitate reprogramming. The

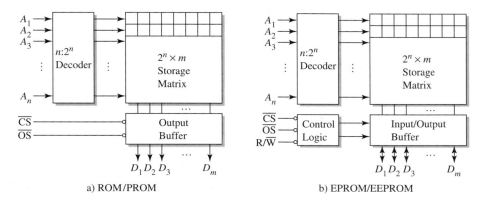

a) ROM/PROM   b) EPROM/EEPROM

FIGURE 4.19
Read-only memory block diagram.

EPROM device package has a transparent window on top of the storage matrix to accommodate data erase operations. Its control logic provides an additional read/write ($R/\overline{W}$) input for device programming and data direction selection. The EEPROM device incorporates additional timing, address, and data latching circuitry to enable its in-circuit data erase/modify capability. Read-only memories are immune to data loss during power interruption or failure. As such, they are used primarily for storing fixed program instructions, referred to as *firmware*. They are optimized for read operations and thus exhibit fast access and read cycle times.

Flash EEPROMs combine the best features of the EPROM/EEPROM devices. They achieve the high bit density of the EPROM, using one transistor per bit versus two, and the in-circuit programmability of the EEPROM. This combination trades the byte-erase capability of the EEPROM for the density advantage of the EPROM. As such, the entire memory cell array contents are erased simultaneously. The write operation uses hot electron injection, by creating a strong electric field and trapping the electrons in a floating CMOS transistor gate. The erase operation creates a reverse electric field that pulls the trapped electrons off the floating CMOS transistor gate, using the Fowler-Nordheim tunneling effect. A Flash memory block diagram is shown in Figure 4.20. Flash EEPROMs are slated to replace magnetic storage media because they provide faster access times and more reliable operation. Table 4.2 lists the main non-volatile memory parameters.

The random access memory (RAM) is designed for high-speed read and write operations. Since its contents retention is temporary, it is referred to as a *volatile memory*. Power interruption results in the permanent loss of any stored data. RAMs can be further classified as either static (SRAM) or dynamic (DRAM). SRAMs use flip-flops as the basic storage cells, while DRAMs use capacitive elements. The SRAM consists of four to six bipolar transistor elements, which form a flip-flop storage cell. It can achieve read-access times of about 20 nsec. The basic DRAM storage consists of a CMOS transistor–controlled capacitive element. It can achieve read-access times of about 60 nsec. The DRAM requires periodic data restore operations, known as *refresh,* to compensate for device limitations. The refresh process restores the capacitive element charge to its original level, thus retaining the stored data.

FIGURE 4.20
Flash EEPROM block diagram.

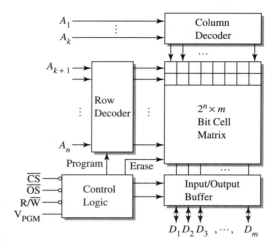

Figure 4.21 is a typical block diagram definition for RAMs. The static memory architecture depicted in Figure 4.21a consists of the basic storage matrix, a decoder, an I/O buffer, and a control logic similar to that of an EEPROM device. The static memory architecture has faster read-access and operation cycle times than a comparable dynamic memory. At the same time it requires more power and has lesser bit-storage density. A common feature of semiconductor memories is the ability to access any next address location in the same amount of time, regardless of the present address value. This feature is also known as *random access* capability.

The dynamic memory architecture, shown in Figure 4.21b, consists of the basic bit storage matrix, control and timing, refresh counter, the row and column decoders, and the I/O buffers. Dynamic memory is bit-organized, as opposed to byte-organized static memory. Each row bit cells must be refreshed every several milliseconds, or the stored information will be lost. Each R/$\overline{\text{W}}$ cycle automatically refreshes all data bits in the selected row. However, there is no guarantee that all row addresses will be accessed within the refresh period. A typical row refresh cycle lasts about 150 nsec. For a 1,024-row DRAM, it would take over 150 μsec to

TABLE 4.2
Nonvolatile memory parameters

Parameter	PROM	EPROM	EEPROM	Flash EEPROM
Write mode	Bit	Byte	Byte	Byte
Write time	10 μsec	100 μsec	5 msec	10 μsec
Write method	Fuse	Hot electron	Electron tunneling	Hot electron
Erase mode	N/A	Entire array	Byte	Entire array
Erase time	N/A	20 min	5 msec	1 sec
Erase method	N/A	UV light	Electron tunneling	Electron tunneling
Maximum cycles	One	1,000	100,000	10,000
Read time	35 nsec	100 nsec	150 nsec	120 nsec
Bit density	Low	Highest	Medium	High

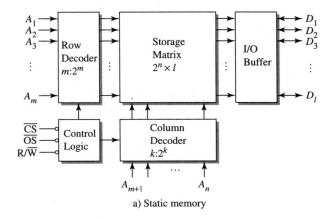

a) Static memory

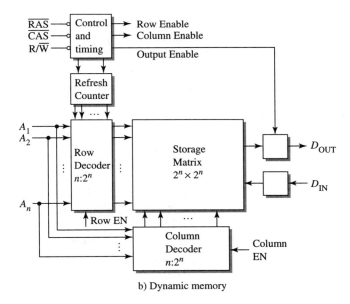

b) Dynamic memory

FIGURE 4.21
Random access memory block diagrams.

complete the refresh operation. The two basic refresh modes are the burst and the distributed. The burst mode performs an entire array refresh, using the row address strobe ($\overline{\text{RAS}}$) input and an external row address counter, by input cycling the row address lines at a periodic refresh rate. This mode makes the memory unavailable during the refresh interval, which may constitute unacceptable performance. Distributed refresh performs single consecutive address reads, which cuts the refresh interval by a factor equal to the number of rows. This mode uses the column address strobe ($\overline{\text{CAS}}$) and $\overline{\text{RAS}}$ input signals to increment the internal refresh counter. During the refresh operation, the output data line is held in a Hi-Z state.

RAM architecture enables dynamic content modification by the MPU. The RAM is used mainly to store programs and data, referred to as *software*. DRAM devices make up the main MPU memory, since they provide high density and moderate access times. In high-performance designs, a static memory acts as a high speed buffer, or cache, between the MPU and the main memory to enhance the overall throughput. The available semiconductor-based storage technologies optimize one or more associated parameters. These include power dissipation, bit density, storage capacity, and address access time. The typical PROM capacity is 128 Kbits, with an access time of 35 to 50 nsec. The typical EEPROM capacity is 512 Kbits, with an access time of 70 to 150 nsec. The typical SRAM has a capacity of 64 Kbits, with an access time of 15 to 45 nsec. The typical DRAM has a capacity of 4 Mbits, with an access time of 60 to 100 nsec.

Magnetic-Based Memory Architectures   Magnetic surface–based memory devices provide permanent retention of written data. This nonvolatile medium is used for both short-term and long-term data storage and retrieval. There are two basic implementation methods available, magnetic tape and magnetic disk.

Magnetic tape consists of a mylar tape, coated with a suitable oxide film, that retains induced magnetization pulses representing binary bit states. This bulk storage system consists of a stationary read/write head that either induces or senses magnetic patterns as the tape travels past it at a uniform rate. This configuration results in variable data access times, due to the sequential nature of the information storage. The time it takes to retrieve the next data block depends on the tape distance between the current and next locations. The bit pattern is arranged so that the data is stored and retrieved using a common read/write head assembly unit. Depending on the tape width and head design, data may be stored in either bit or byte increments. The parameters associated with magnetic tape storage are capacity, speed, access time, transfer rate, and bit density.

The two basic storage formats are shown in Figure 4.22. The bit-oriented format in Figure 4.22a starts with a bit pattern that provides the beginning of block (BOB) marking. This is followed by a serial bit field that makes up the stored data block. Next, a bit pattern specifies the block ID number. This is followed by the block check sequence (BCS) field. Then, another bit pattern defines the end of block (EOB) marking. If multiple data blocks are stored on the same tape at different times, they are separated by a blank tape segment, known as the interrecord

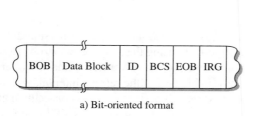

a) Bit-oriented format

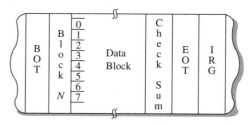

b) Byte-oriented format

FIGURE 4.22
Magnetic tape formats.

gap (IRG). This is required to compensate for the electromechanical tape transport characteristics. The bit-oriented format tape comes in a molded cartridge. The tape is organized in parallel tracks, up to thirty-two in number, that are accessed sequentially by a moving read/write head assembly. The tape motion reverses for every other track, to speed up the operation. Each track is divided into segments, and each segment is subdivided into data blocks. A tape block contains up to 512 bytes of information. For example, a cartridge tape has a length of 300 feet and a storage density of 1,040 bits per inch (bpi). It can store 120 Mbytes of data, on thirty-two tracks. The resulting data transfer rate is 158,000 bits per second (bps), with a tape speed of 150 inches per second (ips). The storage time becomes about 13 minutes.

The byte-oriented format in Figure 4.22b consists of eight parallel tracks that provide character-by-character storage. A block of characters is called a *record*. A group of records forms a *data file*. A BOT character is used to indicate the beginning of a data block, followed by a block ID number. Next, a contiguous group of bytes makes up the block, followed by a checksum field. The *checksum* value is the addition modulo two of all bytes in the data block and is used for error checking. As such, if the stored and computed checksums match, the data are assumed to be valid. The EOT character marks the end of a data block. Consecutive data blocks are separated with an IRG as well. The byte-oriented format tape comes on a variable-diameter reel. For example, a reel tape may have a length of 2,400 feet and a storage density of 6,250 bpi. It can store 180 Mbytes of data, on eight tracks. The resulting data transfer rate is 1.5 Mbps, with a tape speed of 250 ips. The storage time becomes about 2 minutes. In practice byte-oriented format tapes have an extra track for individual byte parity check.

A magnetic disk consists of a flat, circular surface coated with a suitable oxide layer in which data bits are stored in the form of selective magnetization. This storage method requires a movable read/write head assembly that either induces or senses magnetic patterns on a rotating surface. The ability to rapidly position the head anywhere over the spinning disk results in an enhanced sequential access storage medium. There are two types of disks available, the flexible or floppy, and the rigid or hard. The hard disks are usually stacked for greater storage capacity. The parameters associated with these storage media are the same as those of magnetic tape.

A floppy disk is formatted into concentric ring sections, called *tracks,* on both sides. The corresponding tracks on the two sides form a *cylinder*. Each floppy may have as many as eighty tracks per side, with each track divided into nine, fifteen, or eighteen equal-length wedges, called *sectors*. Each sector is capable of storing 128, 256, or 512 bytes. A hard-sectored disk requires a single physical mark to indicate the beginning of each track. Data are stored on disk in fixed-length blocks. When a block length is shorter than the particular sector length, the remaining space is zero-filled. Similarly, when the block size exceeds the sector length, two or more sectors are used, as required. Normally the bit-storage density is lowest on the outer track and gradually increases to a maximum on the inner track. A soft-sectored disk can be formatted with variable sector lengths, from track to track, to provide the most efficient use of the available storage area. This results in a uniform-density disk, independent of track location, with greater storage capacity.

Figure 4.23a depicts the floppy disk organization. Figure 4.23b provides a detailed view of the track format. A reference point is established by the physical index mark that indicates the beginning of each track. The index mark is surrounded by two gap areas. A sector is a soft-

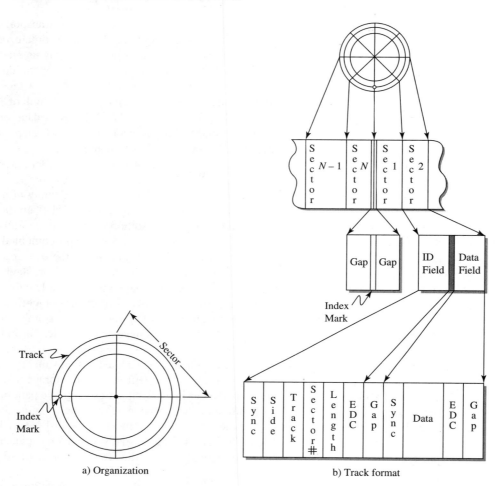

FIGURE 4.23
Floppy disk characteristics.

ware unit, and a single bit change anywhere in it necessitates a complete rewrite operation. A sector consists of a contiguous arc section made up of individual bit cell spaces, which is divided into an ID field and a data field that are separated by a gap. The gap is a buffer zone between the consecutive fields and sectors. It serves to either facilitate read/write operations or compensate for speed variations. The sync data at the beginning of each field provide disk rotation control. The side data specify which side of the disk is accessed. The track number, sector number, and data length information uniquely identify each storage area on the disk. The EDC data provide error-detection and correction capability, ensuring data integrity in the ID field. The gap following the EDC marks the start of the data field, which contains the actual stored data for that sector and has its own EDC information.

The disk storage capacity in bytes is determined with the following equation:

$$C = T_m \cdot S_n \cdot S_l \cdot 2 \qquad\qquad (4.1)$$

where T_m is the number of tracks per side, S_n is the number of sectors per track, and S_l is the sector length in bytes.

For example, a double-sided floppy disk with forty tracks and nine sectors per side and 512 bytes per sector has a total storage capacity of 368,640 bytes, or 360 KB. If a typewritten page consists of forty lines, with eighty characters per line, then the disk has a capacity of over one hundred pages. The $5\frac{1}{4}''$ floppy disk drives rotate at 360 rpm and have access times of 100 to 200 msec. They support two storage capacities, 360 KB and 1.2 MB. Data transfer rates are in the order of 500 Kbits per second, with storage densities of up to 3,000 bpi. Similarly the $3\frac{1}{2}''$ floppy disk drives rotate at 600 rpm and support two storage densities as well, 720 KB and 1.44 MB.

A hard disk drive uses a constant angular velocity, which results in concentric circles with sectors getting larger from the center to the circumference of the disk. Hard disk drives are usually composed of several stacked $3\frac{1}{2}''$ platters spinning at 3,600 rpm. The average *seek time* is the time it takes the head to travel one-third of the distance across the tracks. The average *latency time* is the time it takes for the disk to make half a revolution. The typical access time equals the sum of the average seek and latency times. The typical data transfer rate is 5 million bits per second (Mbps), with storage densities of up to 9,000 bpi. A typical hard disk access time equals 10 msec (seek), plus 8 msec (half of a revolution at 3600 rpm), or 18 msec.

Optical-Based Memory Architectures Optical medium–based memory technology uses specially coated disks. The actual recording medium is sandwiched between two plastic layers. The compact disk (CD) is analogous to the semiconductor ROM in the sense that it is a read-only device and is used for bulk data storage. A CD-ROM drive uses a CD of approximately 4.7'' in diameter. It uses constant linear velocity, nominally 3,600 rpm, which results in fixed-size sectors spiraling out from center to circumference and forming more than 20,000 tracks. The typical access time is 300 msec, with a data transfer rate of 300 thousand bytes per second (KBps). The data storage capacity is 650 MB, or about the capacity of 450 $3\frac{1}{2}''$, 1.44 MB disks. The compact disk is made of a polycarbonate material with a thin reflective aluminum layer, which is covered with a clear protective layer. The data bits are stamped into each track as a series of tiny *pits*. The remaining reflective areas are called *lands*. As a low-power laser beam illuminates each track, the pits diffuse the light while the lands reflect it. At the same time, a photodiode senses the reflections and reproduces the data stream.

The write once read many (WORM) disk is analogous to the semiconductor PROM, since it can be programmed once in the field. The WORM drive uses $5\frac{1}{4}''$ CDs. The typical access time is 450 msec, with a data transfer rate of 150 KBps and a data storage capacity of 650 MB. The WORM write process focuses a high-power laser beam through the plastic layer and onto the recording material, which results in localized heating and burns a tiny pit on a selected surface spot. The read process uses a weak laser beam to illuminate the surface, while a photodiode senses the reflectivity changes corresponding to a presence or absence of a pit. Thus, the presence or absence of a pit is used to represent a one or zero, respectively.

A recordable CD (CD-R) uses a 4.7″ CD for one-time recording. The typical access time is 280 msec, with a data transfer rate of 300 KBps and a data storage capacity of 650 MB. The CD-recordable disk is similar to a regular CD, with two differences. First, the polycarbonate is coated with a film of polymer dye, and then a reflective gold layer is added. The write mode uses a high-power laser beam to make tiny marks on the film that represent data bits. The read mode is similar to that used in CD-ROM operation. The recorded disk can be read by any CD-ROM drive.

The magneto-optical (MO) disk consists of a material that has a uniform magnetic orientation at room temperature. The magneto-optical drive uses $5\frac{1}{4}$″ disks with a magneto-optical film covered by clear polycarbonate layer. The typical access time is 30 msec, with a data transfer rate of 600 KBps and a data storage capacity of 650 MB. Operation is based on a magneto-optical interaction called the Kerr effect. Light reflected off of a magnetic surface is rotated in a direction consistent with its magnetic orientation. Blank disks come with a uniform magnetic polarization. The initial write process focuses a high-power, pulsed laser beam on a selected surface spot, which heats up to its Curie point. At the same time, a weak uniform magnetic field is applied to reverse the spot's magnetic orientation. When the spot cools down, it retains the new magnetic orientation. The read process focuses a weak laser beam to illuminate each track, while a photodetector senses the reflected light polarity to determine its rotation. Hence, the positive or negative reflected beam rotation is used to represent ones or zeros, respectively. The write cycles are preceded by an erase cycle, which returns the recording material to its initial magnetic orientation.

Organization

Computer memory can be either address-oriented or content-oriented. Address-oriented memory uses a unique n-bit input code to identify each data location within the memory. Content-oriented memory uses an m-bit input data word in order to find a possible match at one or more memory locations.

Address-oriented memories exist with sequential, random, or list-access mechanisms. In sequential access memories, a given cell access time is a function of its physical location. This depends on the relative distance from the present to the next desired position. The average access time for any given cell is one-half the maximum access time. Examples of sequential memory include shift register, tape, and disk-type storage. In random-access memories, each cell is accessed independently of its physical location, within a fixed interval. Random-access memories are primarily semiconductor based, such as PROMs, EEPROMs, and RAMs. List-oriented memories use a pointer register whose contents specify the next data location. Linear list-access memories use one or two such pointers for incremental data access. These memories include FIFO queues and LIFO stacks. Linked list-access memories use one or two pointers, or links, per stored data element to indicate the location of the next data element. These memories can be single, double, or circular linked types. Figure 4.24 shows the various address-oriented memory access mechanisms available. Random-access memories have uniform access times because they employ an exhaustive address decoder to select each data element location, as shown in Figure 4.24a. Sequential access results in nonuniform access times because of the unequal distance between any two data element locations, as shown in Figure 4.24b. Linear list access imposes constraints on the order of data transfers, as shown in Figure 4.24c.

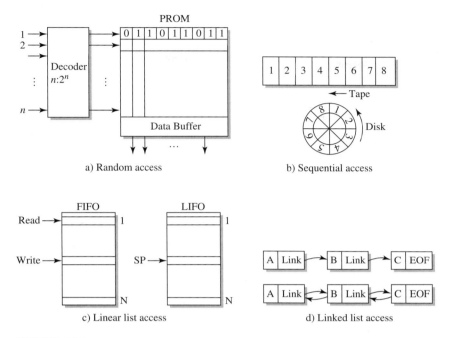

FIGURE 4.24
Memory access methods.

The FIFO queue has a Read PTR and a Write PTR, whose relationship is defined as | Write PTR | ≥ | Read PTR | ≤ N, where N is the maximum FIFO size. In other words, the absolute value of the Write PTR must be equal to or greater than the absolute value of the Read PTR. Similarly, the LIFO stack has an SP that indicates the position of the last access. It is defined as | SP | ≤ N, where N is the maximum LIFO size. Linked list access deviates from other list-access mechanisms in that it uses pointers to connect noncontiguous storage locations and forms a logical memory organization, as shown in Figure 4.24d. There are two link methods, the single and the double. The single method provides only forward links, and the double method provides reverse links as well.

Content-oriented memories exist as either associative-type or cell array–type devices. Figure 4.25 illustrates the internal organization of these memories. The associative or content addressable memory (CAM) shown in Figure 4.25a consists of an input register, a mask register, a storage array, and a match register. The input register stores the external data word. The mask register selects individual bits, within the word, for comparison. The match register provides an output based on the input and mask register contents. This organization achieves fast logic operations and magnitude comparisons. The cell array memory shown in Figure 4.25b consists of regular-pattern memory cells, with built-in control logic and uniform interface to adjacent cells. This organization has applications in high-speed logic design and two-dimensional graphics. The basic input-output relationship for a CAM device is expressed as $Y_j = M_i \cdot (X_i \cdot A_{ij} + \overline{X}_i \cdot A_{ij})$, where Y_j represents a match register output bit, X_i the corresponding input bit, and M_i the associated mask register bit. The A_{ij} term specifies the stored bit value to be compared with X_i.

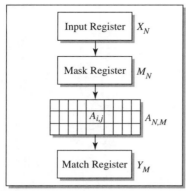

a) Associative memory

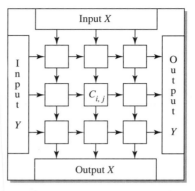

b) Cell array memory

FIGURE 4.25
Data-oriented memory organization.

Similarly, the cell array device operation can be defined as $X_{n+1} = f(x_n, y_n)$ and $Y_{n+1} = g(x_n, y_n)$, where f and g are the two output functions for each set of inputs. The term $C_{i,j}$ defines a cell.

Semiconductor-based memories can be easily tested using the walk method and the gallop method. Both systematically perform a write operation followed by a read on each memory location. The *walk test* performs n such operations per location, where n represents the number of bits. Each written value can be expressed as $V(i) = 2^i$, for $i = 0, 1, 2, 3, \ldots, n - 1$. This test ensures that reliable single-bit transitions occur between adjacent memory cells. The *gallop test* ensures that reliable multiple-bit transitions occur between adjacent memory cells. This requires only two read/write operations per memory cell. The basic bit patterns used for this test are either ones followed by zeros or alternating ones and zeros. For a data word, these patterns become $(FFFF/0000)_{16}$ and $(5555/AAAA)_{16}$, respectively. The RAM memories may also incorporate an additional bit in each location to provide dynamic parity checking of each stored data element. Magnetic medium–based memories use built-in error-detection and correction methods that result in additional storage overhead.

4.4 TIMING AND CONTROL

The control unit performs instruction decoding and generates internal timing and sequences to accomplish the specific operations. The control logic requires a reference clock to sequence and coordinate all internal and external events necessary for a specific task. An instruction cycle consists of the fetch and execute phases, which in turn require one or more machine cycles. The reference clock has a period T, which is measured between any two consecutive and consistent pulse transitions. The reference clock period forms the smallest time unit for measuring the machine-cycle interval. The timing circuitry uses the reference clock to derive multiple-phase clock pulses. Each clock phase signal forms a pulse train, which is shifted in time relative to the other phases. Multiple-phase signals are used for concurrent and pipelined control operations. Figure 4.26 illustrates these concepts.

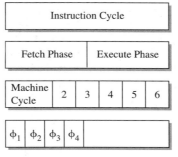

a) Processor cycles

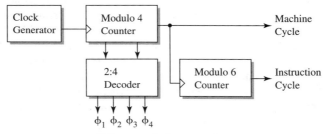

b) Processor timing generation

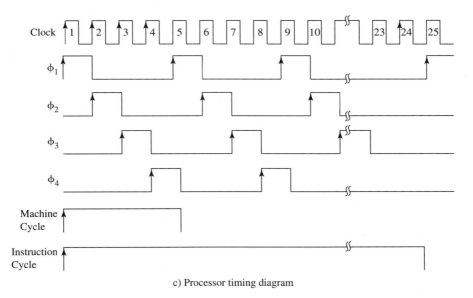

c) Processor timing diagram

FIGURE 4.26
Processor timing definition.

Figure 4.26a defines an instruction cycle that is made up of the fetch and execution phases. Each phase consists of three machine cycles, and there are four clock phases per cycle. Figure 4.26b is a block diagram of the timing circuitry. The reference clock derives a modulo 4 counter to generate the machine-cycle interval. A 2-to-4 decoder provides the four clock phases by decoding the counter states. A modulo 6 counter generates the instruction cycle interval using the machine-cycle signal as its clock input. Figure 4.26c shows the actual timing diagram for this particular timing circuitry.

Control Structures

The control unit accepts and decodes the contents of the MPU instruction register. The resulting code is used to combine the input signals with the timing logic to produce the required output control signals and accomplish the defined operation. The control unit receives external input signals such as clock, reset, acknowledge, and interrupt along with internal status and conditions. The control and timing matrix combines these with the specific decoded opcode and generates all internal control signals for the ALU, registers, stack, and data transfer operations. In addition, the matrix provides external control signals such as read, write, address strobe, and request, and it provides a processor function code. The instruction decoder consists of an n-to-2^n combinational logic network, where n is the opcode field width in bits. The required timing logic is a variation of Figure 4.26, and it incorporates a counter with a decoder to produce a complete set of time slots within the instruction cycle. The internal and external in-

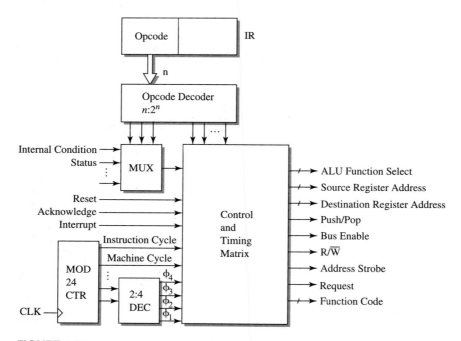

FIGURE 4.27
Control unit simplified block diagram.

put signals are applied selectively to the control and timing matrix by gating and multiplexing them. The matrix consists of hardwired random logic, which is optimized for overall instruction execution performance.

A simplified functional block diagram of the control unit is shown in Figure 4.27. The opcode decoder controls the proper gating of the timing and selection of the internal and external input signals for each particular instruction. The internal condition status multiplexer selects the opcode-specified condition for testing to control the program flow. The reset, acknowledge, and interrupt inputs are enabled, by the logic, at the proper instruction cycle time slot so as to generate the corresponding control signals. The timing logic consists of a counter and a decoder module and provides every possible timing signal required by the control matrix for each instruction cycle. The resulting control signals provide all required output pulses or levels as functions of the opcode, status, and various inputs, synchronized with the timing logic. In general, a control matrix output Z_k is defined using the connectivity matrix S_{jk} and the individual control P-term gates P_j by the following equation:

$$Z_k = \sum_{j=1}^{M} S_{jk} \cdot P_j \qquad (4.2)$$

where M = the total number of control gates

k = the particular control output, 1 to L, and

S_{jk} = 0 or 1

Also, each P-term is defined by

$$P_j = \prod_{i=1}^{n} X_i \oplus a_i \qquad (4.3)$$

where n = the number of inputs, and

a_i determines the polarity of each input variable, X_i

For instance if $M = 8$ and $n = 4$, a given output Z_3 can be defined as a summation of five out of eight possible P-terms, each made up of four input variables.

$$Z_3 = P_1 + P_3 + P_4 + P_5 + P_7$$
$$Z_3 = \overline{X}_4\overline{X}_3\overline{X}_2X_1 + \overline{X}_4\overline{X}_3X_2X_1 + \overline{X}_4X_3\overline{X}_2\overline{X}_1 + \overline{X}_4X_3\overline{X}_2X_1 + \overline{X}_4X_3X_2X_1$$

After each output signal is defined, the resulting multi-input, multi-output combinational network is minimized and implemented with random logic, for maximum instruction throughput. This approach is referred to as the conventional method and results in a fixed instruction set MPU.

Another approach to control unit design, known as microprogramming, was presented by M. V. Wilkes in 1951. Microprogramming presents a flexible and dynamic method for control unit design using a highly organized architecture, such as a PROM, to store the step sequence necessary to perform the operations of each instruction. There are two basic implementations, the horizontal and the vertical. Horizontal microprogramming uses one or more wide microcode words to execute an instruction by providing one bit for each output control signal. Each microcode word results in one microcycle operation. Vertical microprogramming combines and encodes control bits and may use added hardware to reduce the microcode memory size. Each microcode word results in several microcycles. The microcode memory or control store contains data words with several dedicated fields. Microprogramming enables the designer to customize the instruction set and provides the means for easy modifications in the future.

The microprogrammed control unit, shown in Figure 4.9 (see page 174), consists of a microcode sequencer, a control store PROM, and a control register. The basic operation begins with the current instruction opcode in the IR. The opcode points to the starting address of the corresponding control store microcode sequence required to perform the instruction. The microcode sequencer has several different input sources, such as the internal status and external event condition tests, the next microcode address, and the function code specifying the current operation. The control store PROM contains the microcode sequences needed to execute the MPU instruction set. Each microcode word has five basic fields: the next state, the sequencer function code, the external control, the RALU function, and the condition test select. The control register enables pipelined operation. Thus, while the A(n) microcode word is processed, the A(n + 1) is accessed from the control store. A common high-speed clock provides the necessary timing. The microcode sequencer can generate the next consecutive address, jump to a specific address conditionally or unconditionally, repeat the execution of one or more microcode words, or invoke a subroutine prior to calculating the next microcode address. These features provide flexibility and control store size reduction. The control unit can be viewed as an MPU within an MPU executing a series of elementary operations for each higher-level instruction.

The microcode sequencer, shown in Figure 4.11 (see page 176), is made up of a counter register, a latch register, a program counter, and a LIFO stack. These provide four different next address sources, via the built-in multiplexer, to the control store PROM. The control logic coordinates all internal operations, as defined by the function code and the selected test signal. The control store of Figure 4.9 consists of an $n \times m$ PROM, sectioned into five control fields. The next state field is used for either conditional or unconditional transfers within the control store. The function code field determines which microinstruction will be executed by the sequencer. The external control field provides the necessary signals for memory and I/O operations. The RALU function code field controls register-to-register transfers, stack manipulation, and ALU operations. The condition test select field picks either an internal or an external event status, for elementary decision making. The widths of the external and internal control fields depend on the microprogramming method, with the upper limit being the actual number of required control signals. The function code field width is determined by the number of available microinstructions. The condition test select field width depends on the total number of internal status and external event signals that can be tested by the sequencer. In general, an n-bit field defines 2^n possible codes. The next state field width depends on the control store size.

To achieve a better understanding of the control unit, let us define a hypothetical microinstruction set. Using this as a vehicle, several generic control sequences can be defined that are similar at all levels of computer operation. The representative microinstruction set is listed in Table 4.3. The STEP microinstruction is the most common, and it requires no condition testing. The associated next state field is not used. The sequencer increments its internal PC by one to form the address of the next microinstruction. The SKIP microinstruction requires a condition test, such as those in Table 4.1 (see page 185), for the sequencer to determine the next microinstruction address. The select field specifies the condition test whose state is provided, via the external multiplexer, to the sequencer status input. The internal and external control fields provide the required bit states. If the tested condition is true, the sequencer increments its PC by two; otherwise, it increments by one. The resulting PC value becomes the next microinstruction address. The JMPL microinstruction requires no condition test or next state field. The sequencer latch register contents, pointing to the beginning of a microcycle, are loaded into the PC and become the next microinstruction address. The JMPR microinstruction uses the counter register contents, provided by the next state field, to load the PC for the next microinstruction address. The JPCL microinstruction requires a condition test. The select field specifies the particular condition. The next microinstruction address becomes either the latch register contents or the incremented PC contents, for a true or a false test result, respectively. The JPCR microinstruction is similar to that of the JPCL. The next microinstruction address becomes either

TABLE 4.3
Microinstruction set definitions

Code					Next Address Source		Sequencer Operation	
X_3	X_2	X_1	X_0	Name	TEST = T	TEST = F	TEST = T	TEST = F
0	0	0	0	STEP	PC	PC	INC (PC)	INC (PC)
0	0	0	1	SKIP	PC	PC	PC = (PC) + 2	INC (PC)
0	0	1	0	JMPL	L	L	PC = (L)	PC = (L)
0	0	1	1	JMPR	R	R	PC = (R)	PC = (R)
0	1	0	0	JPCL	L	PC	PC = (L)	INC (PC)
0	1	0	1	JPCR	R	PC	PC = (R)	INC (PC)
0	1	1	0	BRCL	L	PC	PC = (L) + (PC)	INC (PC)
0	1	1	1	WAIT	PC	PC	INC (PC)	PC = (PC)
1	0	0	0	LOAD	PC	PC	LD R; INC (PC)	LD R; INC (PC)
1	0	0	1	LOOP	PC	PC	PUSH (PC); INC (PC)	PUSH (PC); INC (PC)
1	0	1	0	STOP	PC	STACK	INC (PC); POP STACK	PC = (STACK)
1	0	1	1	END	PC	STACK	INC (PC); POP STACK	R = (R) − 1; PC = (STACK)
1	1	0	0	JSR	R	R	PUSH (PC) + 1; PC = (R)	PUSH (PC) + 1; PC = (R)
1	1	0	1	JCR	R	PC	PUSH (PC) + 1; PC = (R)	INC (PC)
1	1	1	0	RTS	STACK	STACK	POP STACK; PC = (STACK)	POP STACK; PC = (STACK)
1	1	1	1	RST	PC	PC	PC = 0	PC = 0

the counter register contents, for a true test, or the incremented PC contents, for a false. The BRCL microinstruction performs a conditional relative jump. The next microinstruction address becomes the sum of the PC and the latch register contents for a true test or the PC contents for a false. The WAIT microinstruction requires a condition test field. The selected condition test result determines the next microinstruction address. Thus, a false test uses the PC contents and a true uses the incremented PC contents. The microinstructions above provide for sequential, conditional, and unconditional microprogram control flow.

The following microinstructions provide for fixed or variable microprogram sequence iterations and conditional or unconditional subroutines. The LOAD microinstruction requires a next state field. The next state field is transferred into the counter register, and the next microinstruction address becomes the incremented PC contents. The LOOP microinstruction pushes the current PC value into the stack and uses the incremented PC contents for the next address. The STOP microinstruction requires a condition select field. A selected condition true test results in a pop stack operation, and the incremented PC contents become the next address. A false test transfers the current stack location contents into the PC to form the next address. The END microinstruction is similar to the STOP, but requires no select field. Instead, the sequencer performs an internal zero status test on the counter register contents. A true test enables a pop stack operation, and the incremented PC contents become the next address. Similarly, a false test results in decrementing of the counter register contents and use of the current stack location contents for the next address. The JSR requires neither a next state nor a condition select field. First, the sequencer increments the PC contents and performs a push stack operation. Next, the counter register contents are transferred to the PC and form the next address. The JCR microinstruction requires a condition select field. If the test is true, the functions are the same as for the JSR. However, if the test is false, then the incremented PC contents become the next address. The RTS microinstruc-

TABLE 4.4
Control store internal organization

Address	Next State	Function	External	RALU	Select
0		JMPL			
P		STEP			
		STEP			
	S	JSR			
		SKIP			
		STEP			
P + 5		RST			
Q		LOOP			
		STEP			
		STOP			
Q + 3		RST			
S		STEP			
		WAIT			
		STEP			
S + 3		RTS			

tion requires no next state or condition select fields. First, a pop stack operation is performed. Next, its current location contents are transferred to the PC to form the next address. The RST microinstruction "zeroizes" the PC contents to form the next address.

Control Sequences

The microinstruction set is used to execute the MPU instructions by creating exhaustive combinations of microcode sequences to achieve the higher-level functions. Table 4.4 lists a typical

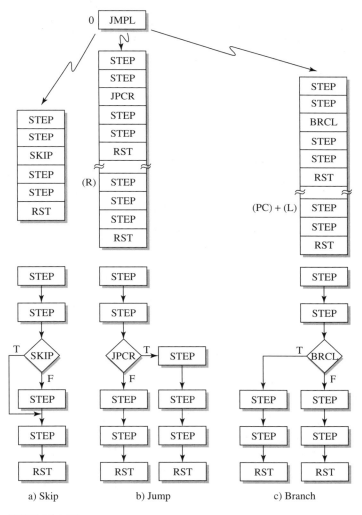

FIGURE 4.28
Conditional transfer structures.

control store organization that reflects various microinstruction sequences. The control store PROM location zero contains an unconditional jump microinstruction (JMPL), which serves to access any internal control sequence, using the provided opcode field. A typical sequence is shown, starting at location P, which uses a subroutine. The subroutine is located at address S, and its last microinstruction, RTS, returns flow of control to the main sequence. A second sequence, at location Q, serves to perform a conditional loop operation. It should be noted that both sequences use the RST microinstruction to transfer control to location zero and process the next opcode-specified sequence. Sequence complexity varies according to the specific MPU instruction.

The following discussion elaborates on several basic control sequences that may arise as a result of the MPU instruction execution process. A simple block sequence can be formed using a group of consecutive STEP-type microinstructions and an RST for the transfer of control. Figure 4.28 illustrates three conditional transfer of control structures, using the SKIP, JPCR, and BRCL microinstructions. A simple skip control sequence can be formed by inserting a SKIP between two STEP types to create conditional execution of the next microinstruction. Figure 4.28a provides a control store function code sequence, with the corresponding control

FIGURE 4.29
Loop control structures.

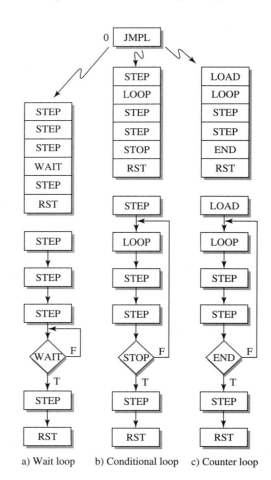

a) Wait loop   b) Conditional loop   c) Counter loop

flow diagram. The rectangular and diamond-shaped blocks are used to represent action and decision points, respectively. An elementary conditional jump sequence is formed in a similar manner. Such a sequence selects either a consecutive or a nonconsecutive execution path. A sample conditional jump sequence is shown in Figure 4.28b, along with a control flow diagram for clarity. Lastly, a conditional branch sequence selects one of two possible execution paths. A detailed illustration of a sample branch sequence is provided in Figure 4.28c.

An iteration or control loop enables the cyclic repetition of microinstructions until a certain condition becomes true. Loop control sequences can be constructed using the WAIT, LOOP, STOP, and END microinstructions. There are three basic forms: the wait loop, the conditional loop, and the counter loop. Figure 4.29 illustrates the three control sequences. A wait loop control sequence results in the conditional execution of the same microinstruction and is useful for delay generation or external event synchronization. Figure 4.29a illustrates the sequence and its corresponding control flow diagram. A conditional loop sequence performs a consecutive group of microinstructions a number of times, as determined by a condition test status. This control sequence is shown in Figure 4.29b, along with the control flow diagram.

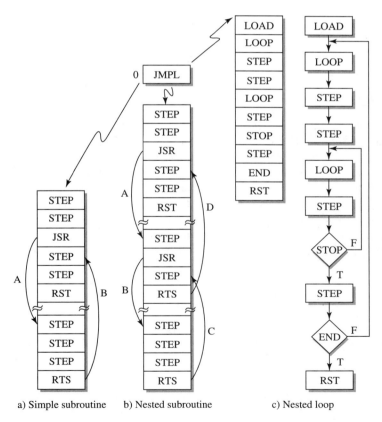

a) Simple subroutine   b) Nested subroutine   c) Nested loop

FIGURE 4.30
Simple and nested control structures.

The counter control sequence performs a consecutive group of microinstructions a number of times, as determined by the initial value of the counter register. The sequence and control flow diagram is shown in Figure 4.29c.

Simple subroutines, nested subroutines, and nested loops are also possible. The simple subroutines use the JSR and RTS microinstructions to access and return flow of control, respectively. Nesting results when a microprogram control sequence either accesses or uses another control sequence as part of its execution. Nesting is possible using the push and pop operations on the microcode sequencer stack. Figure 4.30 illustrates these control sequences. A simple subroutine is accessed from the main control sequence via the JSR microinstruction. Conditional access is also possible using the JCR instead. Figure 4.30a illustrates this control structure, using arrows to show the flow of control. A nested subroutine results when a first subroutine accesses a second, as shown in Figure 4.30b. The number of nested levels is limited by the depth of the sequencer stack. The control flow sequence order is depicted with arrows. A nested loop sequence consists of a basic loop sequence that contains a second loop, as shown in Figure 4.30c. The control store map and its associated control flow diagram are provided for clarity. The outside main loop is formed using the LOAD, LOOP, and END microinstructions. The inside conditional loop is formed with the LOOP and STOP microinstructions. These elementary control structures are a representative sample of the various possible control sequences, using the microinstruction set given in Table 4.3. They give insight into the overall operation of the control unit that performs MPU instruction decoding and generates the appropriate internal and external control sequences.

4.5 INPUT/OUTPUT

The I/O section of the MPU serves to communicate with the outside world. The prevalent medium for transmitting and receiving data is a network of signal paths, known as the bus, which provides interconnection among the various devices. The MPU bus consists of three distinct groups of signals: the address, the data, and the control lines. The MPU output address lines are used to specify the unique memory location at which an exchange will take place. The bidirectional data lines serve to transfer the data between the MPU and memory or an external device. At any single time interval, only a single data word can occur on the bus. This means that only a single device can act as the data source for any given transfer, and usually only a single data destination device will be enabled on the bus at any given time. Figure 4.31 is a typical

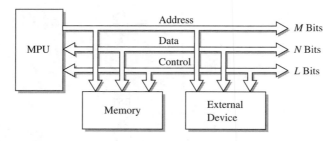

FIGURE 4.31
MPU system bus block diagram.

MPU system bus block diagram. There are *M* address bits capable of specifying up to 2^M unique address locations, with *N* bidirectional data bit paths. The MPU control signals vary from processor to processor, but there are generic similarities of control functions.

There are two basic I/O exchange methods, the synchronous and the asynchronous. A synchronous bus design requires that the MPU I/O instruction execution speeds be closely matched to the memory and device access times. Asynchronous bus design allows for slower memory and I/O devices to perform data transfers with the MPU. Figure 4.32 provides a more detailed representation of the two bus designs. The synchronous bus transfer method, depicted in Figure 4.32a, operates as follows. First, the MPU places an address value on the address lines. Second, it sets the state of the R/$\overline{W}$ signal for either an input or an output data transfer. Third, the Address Pulse control signal indicates when the address value is stable and valid. Fourth, the data word is placed on the data lines. The I/O clock provides for memory and MPU data transfer synchronization.

The asynchronous data transfer shown in Figure 4.32b operates in a similar manner, but the I/O clock is no longer needed. Synchronization is instead achieved with the Data Request and Data Acknowledge interactive signals. The Data Request signal is asserted by the MPU, and the memory responds with the Data Acknowledge signal to complete the transfer cycle. This enables the MPU to perform data exchanges with slower-speed memories. Data exchanges are controlled by the MPU; thus the memory must be ready whenever the MPU requests an I/O operation.

MPU bus designs use two basic approaches for I/O device addressing. The first, called memory-mapped I/O, does not differentiate between memory and I/O address locations. The second, called I/O-mapped I/O, provides separate addresses for memory and I/O address space. The memory-mapped I/O approach results in a simple bus design with the capability of interfacing to a virtually unlimited number of I/O devices. In addition, common instructions are used, which provide software flexibility and simplified MPU architecture and achieve high transfer rates. However, it also results in decreased memory addressing capability and requires fast access times and complicated I/O device designs. I/O-mapped I/O provides total memory addressing capability, buffered data transfers to accommodate slower devices, and simplified I/O device designs. However, it requires additional control signals and special I/O instructions. This results in complicated MPU designs and reduced software flexibility. In addition, some processor designs multiplex some of their address lines with the data lines to reduce the number of pins, which results in added I/O interface complexity and reduced throughput.

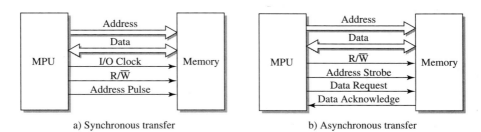

a) Synchronous transfer   b) Asynchronous transfer

FIGURE 4.32
MPU-to-memory transfer block diagram.

Data Transfer Methods

There are three basic processor-to-device communication methods available: programmed I/O, interrupt I/O, and device I/O.

Programmed I/O operations are controlled by the stored program. Each data word transfer requires the execution of an I/O instruction. Figure 4.33 is a typical MPU-to-device interconnection block diagram. The device contains four internal registers: command, status, input, and output. The MPU can make unconditional transfers to the command register in order to configure the device for a specific mode of operation. Consequently, the MPU can read the contents of the device status register, at any time, to determine if the device is ready to send or receive data. Two types of programmed I/O transfers are possible, unconditional and conditional. The former type requires that the device has the ability to exchange data upon MPU demand. The conditional type requires that the MPU query the device to determine if it is ready to perform a data exchange. Conditional transfers sacrifice valuable MPU time if the device is slow or if multiple devices are queried.

Interrupt I/O operations are controlled by the device. Hence, when the device is ready to send or receive data, it sends an interrupt request signal to the MPU, which acts as an alert. In response, the MPU replies with an interrupt acknowledge signal and proceeds with the required data transfer action. This results in a more efficient data exchange process, but it requires additional hardware control signals. The interrupt method actually causes the MPU to suspend its current program execution sequence and process the external request instead. Upon completion, the MPU reverts to its normal program execution mode. In addition, there are processor-generated interrupts, such as hardware error, instruction error, and program interrupts or traps. A hardware error interrupt may result from a bus or power failure. An instruction error interrupt may result from an illegal instruction. A trap condition interrupt may result from a divide-by-zero or similar operation.

Interrupts are classified using two parameters: the layer or level and the importance or priority. A single-level, single-priority interrupt type is referred to as *polled*. With polled interrupts, each device must be queried by the MPU to determine the requesting source. The device scanning order is determined by the MPU software and can be altered to provide some flexibility. This interrupt method requires minimal additional hardware, but it is more time-consuming as the number of devices increases. Figure 4.34 is a diagram of a typical polled interrupt configuration. The particular active device enables the request line to the MPU, indicating a pending interrupt. In response, the MPU sends an acknowledge to the devices and proceeds, in a predetermined order, to read the status register of each device to identify the requesting device.

A single-level, multiple-priority interrupt type is known as *vectored*. Each device enables the MPU to automatically select the required subroutine to service its request. The device pri-

FIGURE 4.33

MPU-to-device interconnection block diagram.

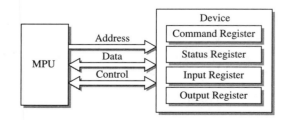

FIGURE 4.34
Polled interrupt block diagram.

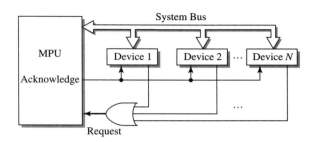

ority is fixed, which results in reduced flexibility. This interrupt scheme provides faster exchanges but requires additional hardware. Figure 4.35 depicts a typical vectored interrupt hardware configuration. A vectored interrupt system has the ability to distinguish and provide an interrupt service routine to the MPU for each specific interrupt. In this configuration, the active device enables the request line to the MPU, and at the same time its relative priority is mapped into an address vector, via a priority encoder. When the MPU sends an acknowledge, the vector is loaded on the data bus and is used to invoke the corresponding interrupt service routine. In the case of simultaneous interrupt requests, the priority encoder resolves any contention in a controlled manner.

The multiple-level, single-priority interrupt type is called a *daisy chain,* as a result of the cascaded device interconnection scheme. This method results in a hardware tradeoff between the MPU and the external interrupt logic. Each device has a fixed priority, determined by the chaining sequence, and is assigned to a unique level. Hence, the device electrically closest to the MPU has the highest priority. Figure 4.36 illustrates a typical daisy chain interrupt scheme. The MPU acknowledge, which acts as an interrupt enable, is passed serially from one device to the next and results in an interlock mechanism. A requesting device sends a signal to the MPU that is mapped into a unique address or autovector by the encoder. This signal also inhibits acknowledge to the lower-priority devices. The autovector is used by the MPU to invoke the corresponding interrupt service routine. It should be noted that this scheme results in one priority per level.

Use of a multiple-level, multiple-priority interrupt type results in extensive external hardware but accommodates many more devices with multiple priorities per level. The highest-

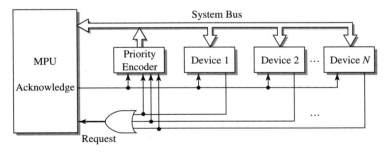

FIGURE 4.35
Vectored interrupt block diagram.

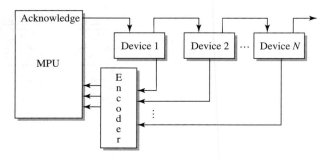

FIGURE 4.36
Daisy chain interrupt block diagram.

priority requesting device is represented by an address vector on the data bus that selects the corresponding service routine. Figure 4.37 shows a typical hardware implementation for this interrupt method. Using this scheme, a total of N devices can be supported using M priority encoders. Each encoder converts 2^k inputs into k interrupt requests for a total of $2^k \cdot M = N$ external devices. The M priority encoders are daisy chained to provide an absolute overall device priority order. Each of the k interrupt requests, representing the priority number for that level, are inputs to a logic network that generates an address vector for each device. Also, each of the encoders provides an active status input to the interrupt-level priority encoder and, in turn, to the MPU. Thus, the relative highest-level interrupt code is provided to the MPU to indicate an

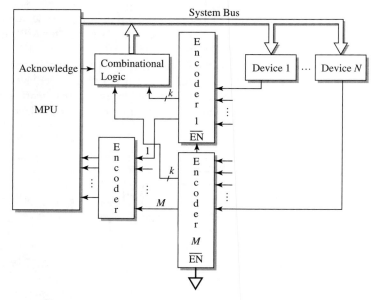

FIGURE 4.37
Multiple-level and priority interrupt block diagram.

external device request. When the MPU sends an acknowledge, the appropriate vector number is placed, by the interrupt logic, on the data bus. This vector is used by the MPU to invoke the corresponding interrupt service routine.

An interrupt process generally consists of the following steps:

1. Sense the interrupt request.
2. Save the current MPU state onto the stack.
3. Determine the interrupt vector number.
4. Generate the interrupt vector address.
5. Perform the interrupt routine.
6. Restore the MPU state.
7. Return to the main program.

Interrupt request sensing is usually performed at a specific point within the instruction cycle and is not necessarily performed on all instructions. MPUs contain an interrupt mask register whose size is a function of the number of interrupts. Hence, an MPU can control external interrupt requests by suitable programming. A multiple-level interrupt MPU can use the register to dynamically alter priorities by judicious programming.

Once the interrupt is sensed, the current MPU state, that is, the contents of the essential registers, must be saved. This may be done by context switching or by placing the contents on the stack. *Context switching* is feasible for single-interrupt processing where a secondary register set is used to store the MPU state using a single instruction. Multiple-interrupt or nested-interrupt processing necessitates the use of a stack to preserve the request order. A higher-priority interrupt can preempt an ongoing lower-priority service routine. However, selective masking can prevent this from occurring. The number of nested interrupt levels depends on the depth of the stack and the number of MPU registers needed to define its state. The interrupt mask register is used to inhibit specific interrupt requests and is program-controlled. There are, however, interrupts such as hardware error, system reset, and power failure that have the highest priority and cannot be masked or inhibited. In addition, there are software-generated requests for conditions that require a break in the normal program flow. As a result, the required service routine is invoked, and upon completion the normal program resumes at the breakpoint. These internal interrupt requests result from illegal instructions or status register conditions such as overflow or divide-by-zero. An internal address vector table contains the starting address for each interrupt service routine. Once invoked, the service routines operate similarly to program subroutines, although they are initiated by asynchronous events rather than normal instruction execution, as in the case of subroutines.

Device I/O uses direct memory access (DMA) as a method of transferring the data of a device directly to and from memory. As such, data exchanges occur without using the MPU's internal architecture. Thus, instead of transferring a single data word from memory to an MPU register and then to the device, creating a bottleneck, data is sent directly via the information bus. Usually, large blocks of data are sent at a time, which results in high-speed transfers. External devices or peripherals are connected to the MPU and memory via the bus. Figure 4.38 is a typical DMA configuration block diagram. This transfer method requires additional hardware to control the data exchanges. The MPU usually provides the necessary control parameters to the DMA controller via the bus. These parameters include memory starting location, number of

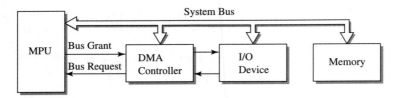

FIGURE 4.38
Direct memory access block diagram.

data words, and the device address. When DMA occurs, the MPU is in an idle state, with all address and relevant control signals in a tri-state condition. Hence the DMA controller must provide all the essential address and control bus signals. The DMA controller contains a set of registers for data status and control functions; these registers are initiated by the MPU. Thus, when the requesting device signals the controller for a data transfer, all the parameters are present to determine the source, destination, block size, and data direction. In turn, the controller enables the bus request signal to the MPU, which responds, when ready, with a bus grant signal yielding system control. At this point, the DMA controller generates the appropriate signals to perform the data transfer. Upon completion, the DMA controller disables its bus request signal and, in turn, the MPU drops its bus grant signal. This results in the MPU taking control of the bus for normal operation. Hence, suspension of normal operation allows the devices to gain bus control and perform memory I/O operations without altering the internal MPU state.

In short, programmed I/O provides for basic data transfers. Interrupt I/O results in improved data transfers. Device I/O achieves optimum data transfers.

Data Transfer Modes

There are two basic data transfer modes, the parallel I/O and the serial I/O. Parallel transfers occur between the MPU and the device, using the bus as the exchange medium. In general, data buffering may be required to provide speed synchronization and data length conversion. This is illustrated in Figure 4.39a. For simplicity, only an output data transfer that uses a data register between the MPU and the device is shown. The control logic satisfies the MPU address and handshake requirements. In addition, it generates selective control signals to the data register and completes the transfer, using the SEND control signal and sensing the device READY status. An input data transfer would be handled in a similar manner. In either case, the data register compensates for the different data lengths and transfer rates of the MPU and device. A second data register can be inserted, between the MPU and device, to enhance throughput, which is known as *double buffering*. This results in the MPU loading one register while the contents of the other are transferred to the device. In essence a pipeline architecture is formed, whose throughput equals the slowest element in it. A similar arrangement can be designed for input data transfers.

Serial data transfers result when the contents of a data register are required to be sent one bit at a time, using a shift clock. For maximum throughput, such an operation requires a buffer register and a shift register between the MPU and the serial device. This is shown in Figure 4.39b. The control logic provides the link between the MPU and the shift register. A data word

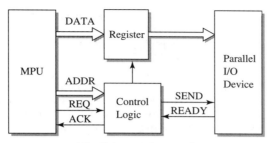

a) Parallel output data transfer

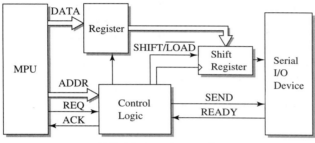

b) Serial output data transfer

FIGURE 4.39
Data transfer modes.

is placed in the buffer register once every n shift clock pulses. The data word is then transferred to the shift register using the SHIFT/$\overline{\text{LOAD}}$ control signal. The control logic may "wrap" the data word with Start and Stop bits, creating asynchronous formats. The control logic provides the SEND control signal to the device. The device returns the READY status signal to control the data flow. Serial data transfer is used in long-distance data exchanges, where a trade-off between speed and circuit complexity is desired.

PROBLEMS

4.1 Determine the range capability of the following address bus widths: eight, sixteen, twenty, and thirty-two.

4.2 Determine the range of integer values that can be represented with eight-, sixteen-, and thirty-two-bit word sizes.

4.3 Given a 50 MHz clock, determine the time interval of a machine cycle that requires four clock periods. Also, determine the fetch and execution intervals that take three and five machine cycles, respectively.

4.4 Given an eight-bit operand A = 10100101, perform the following independent operations: INC, DEC, INV, and NEG.

4.5 Given an eight-bit operand B = 11011011, perform the following independent operations: SHIFT L, SHIFT R, ROT L, ROT R.

4.6 Given an eight-bit operand C = 11001100, perform the following independent operations: SET b_0 and b_4, RESET b_2 and b_6, FLIP b_1 and b_5, and SIFT b_0 and b_7.

4.7 Verify that the equation $Z + (N \oplus F) = 1$ is a complete test for the ACC ≤ 0 condition, using two's complement arithmetic. Derive the equivalent truth table and draw the logic diagram.

4.8 Verify that the equation $Z + (N \oplus F) = 0$ is a complete test for the ACC > 0 condition, using two's complement arithmetic. Derive the equivalent truth table and draw the logic diagram.

4.9 Given a 16-bit MPU with PC = 200, ACC = 100, and R = 25, describe the SUB instruction operation using inherent addressing.

4.10 Given a 16-bit MPU with PC = 200, ACC = 100, and the data word equals 50, describe the SUB instruction operation using immediate addressing.

4.11 Given a 16-bit MPU with PC = 200, ACC = 100, X = 300, and the contents of location 300 equal 55, describe the SUB instruction operation using direct addressing.

4.12 Given a 16-bit MPU with PC = 200, ACC = 100, R = 450, and the contents of location 450 equal 35, describe the SUB instruction operation using indirect addressing.

4.13 Given a 16-bit MPU with PC = 200, ACC = 100, the offset value equals 75, and the contents of location 275 equal 15, describe the SUB instruction operation using relative addressing.

4.14 Given a 16-bit MPU with PC = 200, ACC = 100, R = 280, the offset pointer value equals 30, and the contents of location 310 equal 30, describe the SUB instruction operation using indexed addressing.

4.15 Determine the maximum storage capacities of a high-density $5\frac{1}{4}''$ floppy disk and a high-density $3\frac{1}{2}''$ floppy disk.

4.16 A hard disk is rotating at 6,000 rpm. Its head assembly can scan the tracks in 24 msec. Determine its typical access time.

4.17 A FIFO and a LIFO memory have the following initial pointer values: W(i) = 4, R(j) = 3, and SP(k) = 5. Determine the pointer values after five write and three read operations.

REFERENCES

AMD. *Bipolar Microprocessor Logic and Interface Data Book.* Sunnyvale, CA: AMD, 1983.

Bishop, Ron. *Basic Microprocessors and the 6800.* New Rochelle, NJ: Hayden, 1979.

Intel. *Components Handbook.* Santa Clara, CA: Intel, 1978.

———. *Microprocessor Handbook.* Santa Clara, CA: Intel, 1990.

———. *Memory Components Handbook.* Santa Clara, CA: Intel, 1990.

Johnson, D. E., J. L. Hilburn, and P. M. Julich. *Digital Circuits and Microcomputers.* Englewood Cliffs, NJ: Prentice Hall, 1979.

Korn, G. A. *Microprocessors and Small Digital Systems for Engineers and Scientists.* New York: McGraw-Hill, 1977.

Mick, J. R. and J. Brick. *Bit Slice Microprocessor Design.* New York: McGraw-Hill, 1980.

Morse, S. P. *The 8086 Primer: An Introduction to Its Architecture, System Design and Programming.* Rochelle Park, NJ: Hayden, 1980.

Motorola. *The 68000 Microprocessor User's Manual.* Phoenix, AZ: Motorola, 1980.

National Semiconductor. *Memory Handbook.* Santa Clara, CA: National Semiconductor, 1992.

"Optical Technologies." *Byte* (14)10:228–264 (October 1989).

Short, Keneth L. *Microprocessors and Programmed Logic.* Englewood Cliffs, NJ: Prentice Hall, 1981.

Texas Instruments. *MOS Memory Data Book.* Dallas, TX: Texas Instruments, 1993.

5

MICROPROCESSOR SOFTWARE

The MPU requires that a program resides in memory and contains a logical sequence of instructions. The MPU fetches and executes these, one at a time, in order to perform the specified operations. *Software* is the means and methodology used for defining operations suitable for computer implementation. This includes computer languages, programs, and associated documents. Software provides the means by which a specific MPU architecture can be adapted to various applications of dissimilar nature and scope. The process begins with a problem that requires an MPU-based solution. Next, the problem is analyzed and partitioned into logical segments suitable for algorithm development. The *algorithm* is a sequence of MPU operations that arrives consistently at the required solution in a finite number of steps. Then the data formats are defined for internal processing and I/O transfers, consistent with the solution approach. Each algorithm is usually converted into a flowchart for clarity. The flowchart is a symbolic representation of the actual algorithm outlining the step sequence necessary to solve a problem. Once the data formats and algorithms have been defined, they are converted into a group of MPU instructions that become the program. When a program is executed, it provides the solution to a specified problem. A complete instruction set is defined for each MPU, providing the basis for program coding. Each instruction defines a different operation and specifies the values or locations of the operands. Once completed, a program is tested to verify accuracy and consistency. If discrepancies are found, the program goes through a debugging phase in which latent faults are detected, located, and corrected. Such faults can be attributed to either algorithm design or coding errors. Once a program is verified, it is usually stored in a nonvolatile memory and is then referred to as *firmware*. The input/output data associated with the program reside in volatile memory to provide flexibility and to facilitate information transfers. Software documentation allows for life-cycle support of the program by providing an audit trail to use for making future revisions and for pinpointing any design flaws. The objectives of this chapter are as follows: (1) to define simple data types, data structures, and algorithms; (2) to explain the various programming methodologies; (3) to cover low-level language programming techniques, (4) to review high-level languages; and (5) to discuss systems software and operating system concepts.

5.1 DATA STRUCTURES AND ALGORITHMS

For information to be processed, it must be defined and organized into data types compatible with MPU architectures. A bit is the most primitive data form and indicates a logic state within the MPU. An event status can be represented by a single bit, also known as a *flag.* A group of four bits forms a *nibble,* which can be used to define a hexadecimal digit. A group of eight bits forms a *byte* and can represent an ASCII character. A group of sixteen bits forms a *word,* which is used to define generalized data formats. A group of contiguous data words forms a *block,* which may reside either in RAM or in a disk sector. In software terminology, words are associated with *fields* that make up *records.* Multiple data records are organized in *files.* A disk contains a collection of data files, stored in tracks, which are organized for easy access and form a *database.*

Data types are organized in four major groups: scalar, structured, linear list, and linked list. *Scalar data* can assume a range of values and are defined with a fixed number of bits. Table 5.1 lists most common scalar data types along with their associated parameters. Logical data are used in conjunction with Boolean operators to provide for condition testing. The operators can be extended to nibble, byte, and integer size. However, the outcome depends solely on the corresponding bits of the two operands. In addition, masking techniques enable the selection of one or more specific bits within a data word, by inhibiting the rest, to provide testing flexibility. BCD data are used for representing decimal digits within the MPU. Hex data provide an efficient way of creating and displaying a four-bit string for machine language programming. Character data are used for generalized information exchange between the MPU and the external world. These consist of alphanumeric and other special symbols. Integer data are used to represent fixed-point numbers and are available in either single-word or double-word format. Real data are used to represent floating-point numbers and are also available in two formats. Arithmetic, logical, and bit-manipulation instructions can operate on all of the scalar data types.

Structured data are made up of scalar data and are arranged into blocks. There are two basic variations, the array and the record. An *array* consists of similar scalar data, such as integers, and has a unique name, starting location, and size. In general, an array can be defined with one or more dimensions, each with a different size. A one-dimensional array forms a lookup table; a two dimensional array forms a matrix relationship between two input variables. A *record* is a table of dissimilar contiguous scalar data arranged in various fields. Each record

TABLE 5.1
Scalar data type definitions

Data Type	Size	Range	Format
Logical	1	0–1	d_0
BCD	4	0–9	$d_3d_2d_1d_0$
Hex	4	0–15	$d_3d_2d_1d_0$
Character	8	0–255	$d_7d_6d_5d_4d_3d_2d_1d_0$
Integer	N	$2^N - 1$	Sign, magnitude
Double integer	$2N$	$2^{2N} - 1$	Sign, magnitude
Real	N	$\pm 2^{\pm K}$	Sign, exponent, mantissa
Double real	$2N$	$\pm 2^{\pm L}$	Sign, exponent, mantissa

TABLE 5.2
Array structure

Address	Data
N	1
$N + 1$	3
$N + 2$	5
$N + 3$	7
$N + 4$	9
$N + 5$	11
$N + 6$	13
$N + 7$	15
$N + 8$	17
$N + 9$	19

is defined using a name, location, size, and field contents. Table 5.2 lists an example of the array structure data type. The array contains all odd consecutive integers between 1 and 20. This results in a lookup table representation of data within the MPU such that a unique value is stored in each address location. Table 5.3 lists an example of the record data type. The record contains typical employee data arranged in a logical sequence of fields of varying length in a contiguous memory block.

Linear lists are formed using a table in conjunction with one or more address pointers. This results in sequential store and retrieve data operations. The most common linear lists are the *stack* and *queue,* and these are used to form other variations. The stack results in a LIFO buffer and is used extensively for subroutine and interrupt processing. A stack is associated with a name, size, location, and pointer. A queue results in a FIFO buffer with an input write pointer and an output read pointer. If the pointers are not reset and their maximum range is defined as modulo N, where N is the list size, then it becomes a circular buffer. Two queues can be combined to form a *dequeue,* which permits read and write operations from either side. Figure 5.1 illustrates the linear list data structures. The FIFO buffers enable high-speed data ex-

TABLE 5.3
Record structure

	Name	
Number	Street	
City		State
Zip	Phone number	
Social security number		
Salary		Dependents
Annual leave		Sick leave
Badge number	Title	

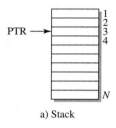

a) Stack

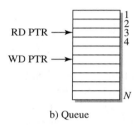

b) Queue

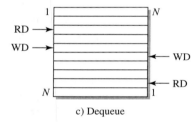

c) Dequeue

FIGURE 5.1
Linear list data structures.

changes between the MPU and an external device. They also compensate for differences in data transfer rates between two information exchanging media. For reliable operation, the read pointer must always lag behind the write pointer value.

   Linked list data structures are formed using noncontiguous memory locations that are interconnected with link pointers. Single linked lists provide forward access capability. Double linked lists have a forward and a backward link pointer for each data element to provide for bidirectional access. A circular linked list results when the last element link points to the first element. A linked list is associated with a name, location, size, and individual element link pointers. Another example of a linked list structure is the *binary tree*. Its initial data element is called the *root*. Each subsequent element location is known as a *node*. Each element is associated with two pointers, the left and the right. This definition results in a hierarchical data structure that is symmetrical about the root. Trees are used to store information organized in a logical manner. Figure 5.2 illustrates the linked list representations above. Linked list struc-

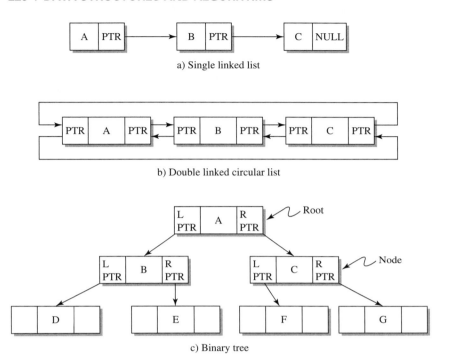

FIGURE 5.2
Linked list data structures.

tures require sequential access to individual elements within the list, but they are easily expanded.

Flowcharting Techniques

An algorithm is a logical sequence of elementary operations that outlines the solution to a specific problem in a finite number of steps. The process of creating an algorithm begins with problem definition, followed by problem analysis. Next, rules are established and then converted into a concise procedure for solving the problem. To be successful, an algorithm must possess certain properties, including finiteness, conciseness, consistency, and reliability. The number of steps in an algorithm determines its speed and efficiency. Precise definition results in optimal coding of the procedure. Repeatability of results is essential. Dependable operation, within the range of parameter values, is of utmost importance to its usefulness.

There are various types of algorithms, classified by the problem-solving technique used. A *closed form algorithm* produces an exact solution using direct computation. An *open form algorithm* produces an approximate solution using numerical methods. A *decomposition algorithm* breaks the whole problem down into smaller, more manageable problems. A *heuristic algorithm* arrives at the correct solution using adaptive trial-and-error techniques. A *brute force*

TABLE 5.4
Algorithm definitions

Type	Example Problems	Comments
Closed form	Convert °C to °F	Exact solution
Open form	Compute natural log expression	Approximate solution
Decomposition	Determine area of complex polygon	Small, regular shapes
Heuristic	Perform long division	Trial and error
Brute force	Find largest array element	Exhaustive search

algorithm uses exhaustive search to find the best solution to a specific problem. Table 5.4 lists an example problem for each algorithm type. The conversion of a temperature value expressed in degrees Celsius to degrees Fahrenheit is achieved by the use of the following equation and results in an exact solution:

$$°F = °C \cdot 1.8 + 32 \tag{5.1}$$

The computation of the natural log expression e^x requires a series expansion of the following equation and results in an approximate solution:

$$e^x = 1 + x + \frac{x^2}{2!} + \frac{x^3}{3!} + \ldots + \frac{x^n}{n!} \tag{5.2}$$

where n is the number of terms.

Thus, a decision has to be made regarding accuracy to determine the number of terms needed. This decision is a compromise between accuracy and computation speed. The area of a complex polygon can be computed by first subdividing it into smaller shapes with known area formulas. For example, the area of one irregular shape may be the sum of the areas of a rectangle, a triangle, and a square. Hence, the expression for the area becomes the following equation:

$$A = A_1(\text{rectangle}) + A_2 (\text{triangle}) + A_3 (\text{square}) = a_1 \cdot b_1 + \frac{1}{2} (a_2 \cdot b_2) + a_3^2 \tag{5.3}$$

An example of a heuristic algorithm is the long division process. A trial-and-error method is used to determine the quotient, whose value is adjusted based on the remainder value. Finally, finding the largest array element requires an exhaustive search and test of each element, resulting in a brute force solution.

Algorithms are usually expressed in flowchart format for clarity. A *flowchart* is a graphical representation of a series of operations using geometrical figures as symbols. Flowcharts can be used at all levels of software development. At the initial problem definition and analysis level, a flowchart shows in general terms what needs to be done. At the selected algorithm design and development level, a flowchart describes how problem requirements will be satisfied. The program level flowchart uses symbolic MPU instructions to represent detailed, step-by-step actions.

FIGURE 5.3
Basic flowchart symbols.

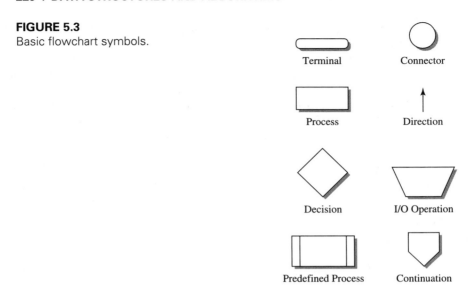

Terminal

Connector

Process

Direction

Decision

I/O Operation

Predefined Process

Continuation

Figure 5.3 shows the most common symbols used to construct flowcharts. The terminal symbol is used to denote the beginning or the end of a procedure. The rectangle process symbol specifies an operation to be performed, which is written within the rectangle. The diamond decision symbol indicates a program flow control step; the direction that the process takes next is based on the defined test result. The predefined process symbol represents a subroutine or function that is described in detail elsewhere in the flowchart. The connector symbol is used in

TABLE 5.5
Register transfer language definition

Element Type	Meaning
Operand symbols	*Data source/destination*
Letters A, B, C, etc.	Register
Letters X, Y, Z	Variable
Acronyms ACC, PC, etc.	Special register
Numerals 1, 2, 3, etc.	Constant value
Qualifier symbols	*Selective attributes*
Parentheses ( )	Contents
Indexes i	Individual element
#	Immediate value
@	Indirect value
Operator symbols	*Functions*
$+, -, \cdot, \div, *$	Add, subtract, multiply, divide, exponent
$\rightarrow, \leftrightarrow$	Direction, exchange
$\wedge, v, \oplus, \sim$	AND, OR, XOR, NOT
$>, <, \neq, =$	Greater than, less than, not equal to, equal to

lieu of lines to show program flow between places in the flowchart. The arrow symbol shows the direction of program flow. The trapezoid I/O symbol defines an external transfer operation. The continuation symbol denotes the connectivity of flowcharts on successive pages.

Flowcharts define overall algorithm functions during initial development, and they establish program module relationships and interactions. In addition, they illustrate the logical sequence of steps for the programmer and serve as a debugging tool during test and verification.

At the program level, the use of a set of operands, qualifiers, and operators, known as Register Transfer Language (RTL), results in MPU instruction clarity. Table 5.5 provides a list of the most common elements in RTL and their meanings.

The following example illustrates the use of RTL and flowcharts to develop and document an algorithm.

EXAMPLE 5.1

Using the formula °F = (1.8) · °C + 32, develop a design-level flowchart and a programming-level flowchart that define a procedure that takes the temperature in degrees Celsius, converts it to degrees Fahrenheit, and outputs both values.

The high-level flowchart shown in Figure 5.4a defines the major steps involved in entering, calculating, and displaying the results. The detail-level flowchart shown in Figure 5.4b out-

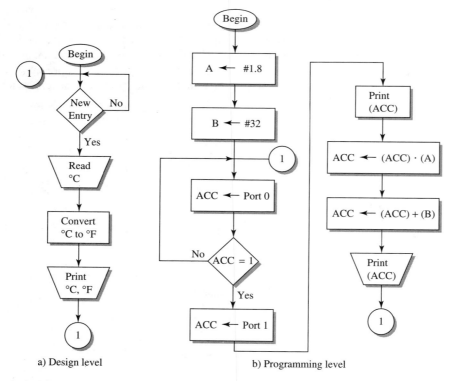

a) Design level

b) Programming level

FIGURE 5.4
Flowchart for Example 5.1.

lines, in RTL, each individual MPU operation required to perform the temperature conversion using the provided formula.

Linear List Operations

Two common operations associated with linear lists are searching and sorting. *Searching* is used to determine the presence or absence of a particular type of element value within the list. *Sorting* is used to arrange the elements of the list in either ascending or descending order according to their values.

There are three common search methods: the linear, the binary, and the hashing or randomizing. *Linear search* scans each element in sequence until either a match is found or the whole list is scanned. *Binary search* uses a trial-and-error technique. It can be used only with ordered lists. The first search location becomes the midpoint, and the element's relative location is determined. The search then proceeds to either the top or the bottom half of the list. This process is repeated with midpoints assigned in successively smaller sections until either a match occurs or the whole list is scanned. Binary search is faster than the linear search method. Search time for both methods is a function of the list size. The average and maximum search times for these search methods can be derived with the following equations:

$$\text{Linear:} \quad T_{\text{avg}} = k \cdot [(N + 1)/2] \quad \text{and} \quad T_{\text{max}} = k \cdot N \tag{5.4}$$

$$\text{Binary:} \quad T_{\text{avg}} = k \cdot \log_2 (N - 1) \quad \text{and} \quad T_{\text{max}} = k \cdot \log_2 (N + 1) \tag{5.5}$$

where N denotes the list size and k is a proportionality constant.

The *hashing* or randomizing search method relaxes the time-to-size dependency by using the actual element to derive its storage location. This necessitates more storage and is therefore useful only for large lists. The basic relationship between the element value and its address location is given in the following equation:

$$A(e) = e \cdot (\text{mod } P) + k \tag{5.6}$$

where e is the element value, P is a large integer, and k is a small integer.

Thus, a unique address is derived for each address value. The parameters are selected so as to eliminate addressing conflicts and hits, and to provide a contiguous memory block.

The linear search algorithm design flowchart is shown in Figure 5.5. The first step initializes the table pointer to the starting location and sets the finish variable to 0. Then the new element is read and compared in sequence to each element on the list. If at any point a match is found, the search is terminated and the match variable is set. Otherwise, the search continues until the whole list is scanned and the process halts.

The binary search algorithm is more involved, since it uses a trial-and-error technique to define each new search location. Figure 5.6 depicts the binary search design flowchart for lists containing elements in ascending order of magnitude. The procedure begins by initializing the lower limit (LL) to 1, the upper limit (UL) to N, and the finish variable to 0. The new element is then read and placed in temporary storage. The first test establishes the table's midpoint; it

FIGURE 5.5
Linear search design flowchart.

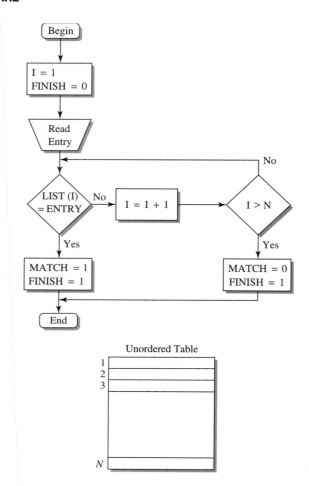

Unordered Table

may also terminate the search if an out-of-bounds condition occurs. The next two steps test the limits according to the relative positional order of the entry element for the next iteration. If neither of the above test conditions are true, the element is found, and the match and finish variables are set. The final test checks for the value of the finish variable and terminates the procedure when its value becomes 1.

An unordered table can be sorted prior to a binary search operation. There are three basic sorting methods: selection, exchange, and insertion. *Selection sort* takes the first table element and switches it with the smallest one. Then it takes the second table entry and switches it with the next smallest one. The process continues until all the table elements are arranged in an ascending order of magnitude. The *exchange sort* compares successive adjacent table elements and swaps them if they are not in ascending order. The process repeats until the whole table is in ascending order. The *insertion sort* searches the table from top to bottom sequentially until an element is found to be out of order. Next, the element is placed in its proper location and the remaining elements are shifted one place within

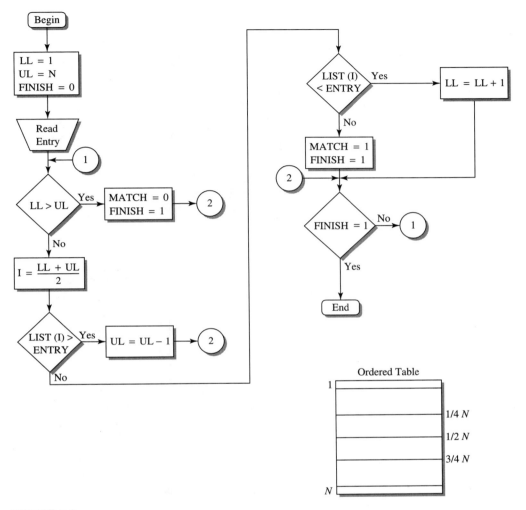

FIGURE 5.6
Binary search design flowchart.

the table. The process continues until all elements are arranged in ascending order. The minimum number of comparisons is $N - 1$ and the maximum is $N \cdot [(N - 1)/2]$, where N is the table size. Hence, the average and maximum times for the above sort procedures become

$$T_{avg} = k \cdot (N - 1) \text{ and } T_{max} = k \cdot N^2 \tag{5.7}$$

where k is a constant.

Table 5.6 details the three sorting methods.

TABLE 5.6
Sorting methods

Selection Sort					Exchange Sort							Insertion Sort			
2	1	1	1	1	2	2	2	2	2	2	1	2	1	1	1
5	5	2	2	2	5	3	3	3	1	1	2	5	2	2	2
3	3	3	3	3	3	5	1	1	3	3	3	3	5	3	3
1	2	5	4	4	1	1	5	5	5	4	4	1	3	5	4
6	6	6	6	5	6	6	6	4	4	5	5	6	6	6	5
4	4	4	5	6	4	4	4	6	6	6	6	4	4	4	6

FIGURE 5.7
Selection sort design flowchart.

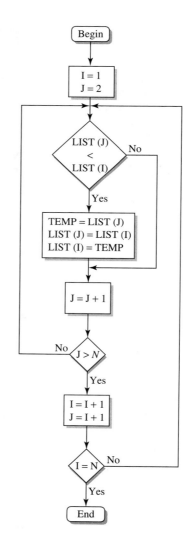

The selection sort design flowchart is shown in Figure 5.7. The first step sets the two address pointers to 1 and 2. Next, the first element is compared against every other element in the table. If an element is out of order, a switch takes place. Then the *I* index variable is incremented and the second element is compared to all others. The process continues until *I* = *N,* which signals the completion of the procedure.

The exchange sort design flowchart is shown in Figure 5.8. This is also called *bubble sort,* since elements of lesser magnitude flow toward the top of the table. The procedure begins with the two table pointers set to 1 and 2. Next, the two adjacent elements are checked for relative order and swapped if necessary. Then the next two consecutive table elements are tested. The process continues until all elements have been compared once. When the table is ordered, the index *I* becomes equal to *N* and the procedure is completed. If the table is not ordered, additional passes are performed until all elements are placed in ascending order.

The sorting and searching algorithms can be easily extended to two-dimensional arrays by treating each column or row in the array as a one-dimensional table. For example, a two-dimensional array is formed by *M* tables, each of which is *N* elements long. They are defined as

FIGURE 5.8

Exchange sort design flowchart.

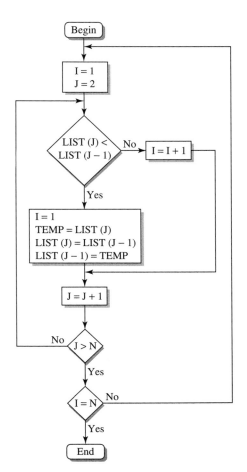

A(I, J), where the I index defines the table row number (1 to N) and the J index defines the table number (1 to M). Similarly, three-dimensional array structures can be formed by P two-dimensional arrays and are defined as A(I, J, K), where K is the specific array layer number (1 to P). For $P = 1$, the three-dimensional array defaults to a two-dimensional one. Similarly, for $M = 1$, a two-dimensional array defaults to a one-dimensional table. Also, for $N = 1$, a one-dimensional table becomes a scalar.

Two useful array operations are searching for the maximum or minimum element and comparing the elements of two similar arrays for matchings. Figure 5.9 illustrates these two operations, using two-dimensional arrays. The 5 × 4 array is scanned to determine its largest element value. This is located at A(4, 3) and equals 12, as shown in Figure 5.9a. The two 4 × 4 host and target arrays are compared element by element for possible value matchings. The resulting match array shows six element matches, indicated by an element value of 1. Figure 5.10 shows a design flowchart for the largest array element search and the array element comparison algorithms. The search procedure begins by comparing the first array element, NEXT(1, 1), to every other one in column one, followed by column 2, until the whole array is scanned. At each comparison the element of larger magnitude is placed in the MAX location and the corresponding NEXT(I, J) indices are stored in K and L, respectively. When the whole array is searched, indicated by $I > N$, the procedure terminates and the largest array element value resides in MAX. Its actual array location is specified by the corresponding K and L index values.

The array element comparison procedure systematically compares every element in the host array with the corresponding element in the target array. If their values are equal, the corresponding location in the match array is set to 1; otherwise it is set to 0. Also, the total vari-

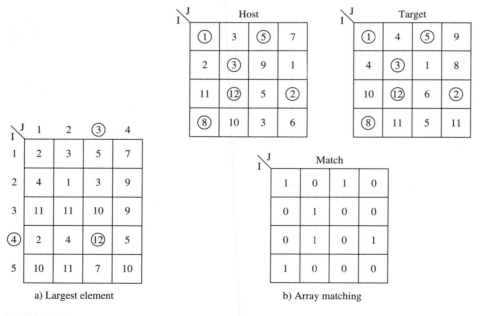

a) Largest element

b) Array matching

FIGURE 5.9
Two-dimensional array operations.

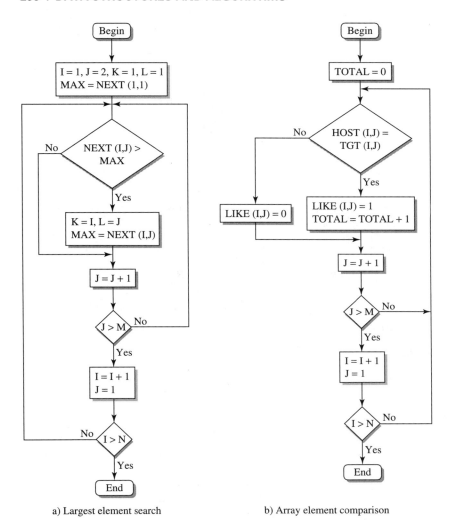

a) Largest element search   b) Array element comparison

FIGURE 5.10
Array algorithms design flowcharts.

able is incremented to track the number of matches. When the complete array is scanned, the match array contains all matched locations, and the total variable value provides their actual number.

Linked List Operations

The two main linked list operations are element insertion and element deletion. Appending an element to the list is a special case of insertion in which the new element is placed at the end of the list.

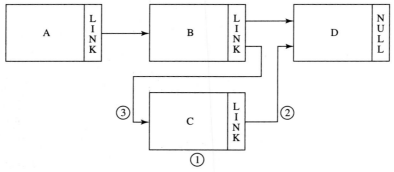

a) Insert operation

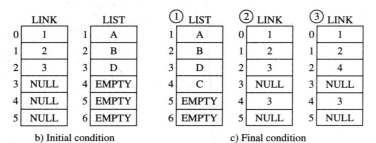

b) Initial condition   c) Final condition

FIGURE 5.11
Linked list insert procedure.

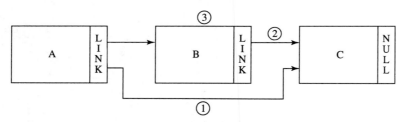

a) Delete operation

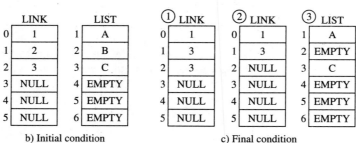

b) Initial condition   c) Final condition

FIGURE 5.12
Linked list delete procedure.

Insertion is a three-step procedure, once the location is determined. The process is detailed in Figure 5.11. The initial list contains three elements, A, B, and D. The new element C is to be inserted in its proper order, in this case between elements B and D. The first step is to store C into an empty list location. The second step is to link the new element to its next successive element, D. The third step is to provide a new link from the previous element B to the new element C. This last action removes the old link between B and D.

The deletion procedure also requires three steps, once the specific element is located within the list. The procedure is detailed in Figure 5.12. The element B is to be deleted from the sample list. Step 1 provides a link from the previous element A to the next element C, bypassing B. Step 2 eliminates the existing link from B to C, replacing it with the *Null symbol,* indi-

FIGURE 5.13
Linked list operations flowchart.

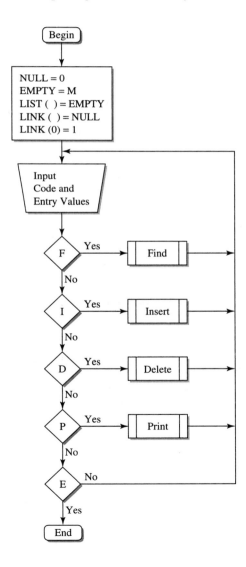

cating the end of the list. Step 3 overwrites the location of B with an *Empty symbol,* so that the location becomes available for future insertions.

In addition to insertion and deletion, linked list operations may require that a specific element be found or that the list be displayed. Figure 5.13 provides a high-level flowchart outlining linked list operations.

The initial linked list operation sets the list elements to Empty and the links to Null. The Empty status value equals $M;$ hence the list element values range from 0 to $M - 1$. Similarly, the Null value equals 0; thus the link pointer values range from 1 to N. Also, the first link pointer value is set to 1, and the first element is stored in the corresponding location. Next, the input operation provides the function code and the entry value. The function symbol is tested to determine the required operation on the Entry element.

Figure 5.14 presents each step of the FIND linked list operation in detail. The FIND procedure first sets the link pointer to 0 and then resets the two status variables. Next, it compares the Entry value to each list element in sequence, until either a match is found or the whole list is scanned. If a match is found, the Match variable is set. If the scan is completed with no match, the Sorry variable is set instead.

The INSERT procedure, as represented in Figure 5.15, does a linear search of the list in order to locate the first Empty status location. This location may be empty initially or because of a previous delete operation. Once the empty location is found, its index I is stored in Empty. Next, the linked list is searched sequentially, using the link pointer, to determine the relative position of the new Entry value. Once this is established, the Entry value is placed in the list location specified by the Empty variable. Then a link pointer is created that points from the new

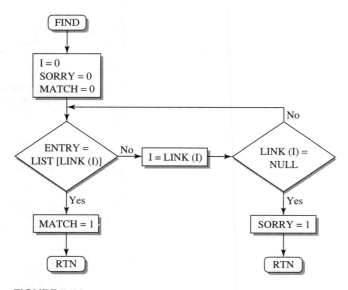

FIGURE 5.14
FIND procedure design flowchart.

FIGURE 5.15
INSERT procedure design flowchart.

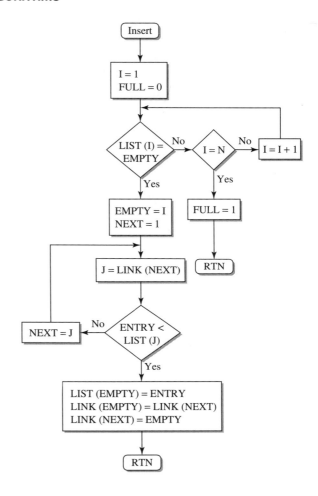

to the next ordered list element, and the previous element link changed to point to the new Entry element. If no empty location is found, the Full variable is set and the procedure is terminated.

The DELETE procedure, shown in Figure 5.16a, performs a sequential link pointer search on the list to determine the presence of the Entry element. If such a value exists, a link is defined between the previous and next elements, with respect to the Entry element. Next, the link between the entry and the next element is deleted. Finally, the Entry element location in the list is changed to Empty status. If the Entry element is not found, then the Sorry variable is set and the procedure is terminated.

The PRINT procedure, in Figure 5.16b, scans the list sequentially, using the link pointer, and transfers each element to an output device. This is repeated until the Null symbol is encountered, indicating the end of the list.

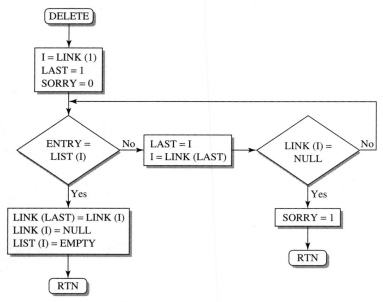

a) DELETE procedure design flowchart

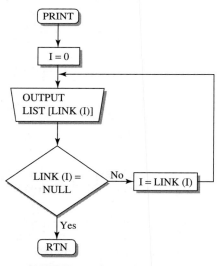

b) PRINT procedure design flowchart

FIGURE 5.16
DELETE and PRINT procedures design flowcharts.

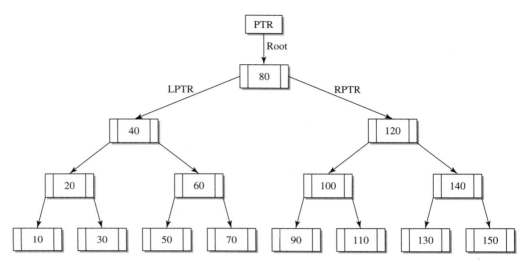

FIGURE 5.17
Balanced binary tree with ordered elements.

The binary search can be easily extended to balanced binary tree structures that contain elements in ascending order of magnitude. Such a structure is illustrated in Figure 5.17. A balanced binary tree possesses a symmetry about the root. The data ordering is such that locations reached with the RPTR (right pointer) contain a greater magnitude element then those reached with the LPTR (left pointer) at the same level. This arrangement is conducive to the binary search algorithm detailed in Figure 5.18. The search starts at the root, which is the equivalent of an ordered table midpoint. The Entry element is compared with the root element to determine its relative position within the structure. If the Entry element is smaller, the search is directed to the LPTR. If the Entry element is larger, the search is shifted to the RPTR. In either case the pointer is checked for a Null value signifying the end of an unsuccessful search. The process is repeated, using successive approximation, until either a match occurs or the element is not found. If a successful search occurs, the variables Finish and Match are set to 1 prior to termination.

5.2 PROGRAMMING CONCEPTS

Software development is a cyclic process that consists of several phases. It starts with the functional requirements phase, which defines what needs to be done. Next, the design specification phase outlines how the task is going to be accomplished. The *program design phase* incorporates the selected algorithm into the solution and codes detailed solution steps into MPU instructions. The debugging phase checks the resulting program code for syntax and logic errors. The *verification phase* exercises the program to determine if it satisfies the functional requirements and does not contain any design flaws. Often a program change to correct an error results

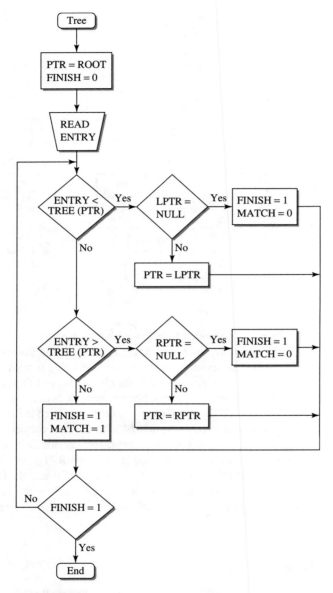

FIGURE 5.18
Binary tree search algorithm design flowchart.

in new errors elsewhere in the program. The *program maintenance phase* provides the necessary corrections and possible enhancements as a result of the verification phase.

A well-known technique for software development is the *top-down method*. This is a systematic approach for the design and development of large computer programs. The process is initiated at the requirements level, which is used to derive design parameters. Then it proceeds to the detailed definition and stepwise refinement of the next lower levels. Each level contains a group of functional entities that form individual modules. Each such module accepts an input set of data and produces a corresponding output set, consistent with the module definition. The requirements analysis uses an order of definition from general to specific. The top-down method uses hierarchical structures with specific rules that dictate module design order, independence, interactions, and interfacing. The actual module implementation order, set via program coding, may occur in either top-down or bottom-up sequence, although top-down is the preferred approach.

For example, an integer list representing the scores of a class test needs to be arranged in ascending order of magnitude. From the problem statement it becomes obvious that there are three basic requirements: first, input the list; second, perform sorting; and third, output the result. The analysis level explains how these requirements will be satisfied. First, a keyboard input device will be used to input the test scores. Next, a selection sort algorithm will be used to arrange the table contents in an ascending numerical order. Lastly, the table contents will be sent, one element at a time, to an output device for hard copy. The design level provides detailed design flowcharts for each of the three tasks. These flowcharts are used to develop the actual program. Then the program is coded. The program code consists of a logical sequence of instructions that direct the MPU to accomplish each task. Table 5.7 lists the top-down method software development levels.

This process is known as functional decomposition. The requirements level describes the problem conditions and assumptions in a clear manner, so a precise outline of what needs to be done can be created. The analysis level examines the requirements, selects the proper algo-

TABLE 5.7
Top-down programming concepts

Requirements	Input scores
	Sort score
	Output scores
Analysis	Enter scores via the keyboard
	Use selection sort algorithm
	Output ordered table to printer
Design	Keyboard entry flowchart
	Selection sort flowchart
	Printer output flowchart
Coding	INIT module
	MAIN module
	ENTRY module
	SORT module
	PRINT module

rithm, and explains how each task will be accomplished. The design level provides detailed procedures in flowchart format. The program level converts the procedures into MPU instructions.

The two basic test approaches are the *white box* and the *black box*. The white box approach is logic-based and assumes detailed knowledge of the program. The black box approach is data-based and depends strictly on the input and output data relationships. Program verification testing ensures that the final program satisfies the initial requirements.

Structured Programming

A program is developed using basic building blocks known as logic control structures. These structures have one entry point and one exit point. They are combined to form functional elements of code, which are called *units*. Each such unit can be designed, coded, and tested independently. The units are integrated to form a *module*. A set of modules makes up the final program as a cohesive and well-defined structure. The benefits of this approach are reliability and maintainability. There are three elementary logic structure types: the *sequence,* the *decision,* and the *iteration*. These structures are described using English-like statements that form the Program Design Language (PDL) method for designing and developing software.

Figure 5.19 illustrates the sequence logic structure format. The sequence block represents a group of fundamental tasks such as assignment of value or mathematical operation. The flow of control goes from process A to process B unconditionally. Each process may consist of several instructions.

The decision logic structure enables either a conditional two-way branch or an *m*-way selection for the next executing instruction. Figure 5.20 shows the various decision logic structures, using flowcharts and their equivalent *structured diagrams*. The IF-THEN-ELSE structure provides conditional control based on the outcome of condition A. If the test result is true, then process B is executed; otherwise process C is selected. The IF-THEN structure is a special case of the IF-THEN-ELSE in that no operation results when the condition A test result is false. The CASE OF I structure provides conditional selection of execution of a process as a function of the index *I* value.

FIGURE 5.19
Sequence structure definition.

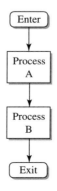

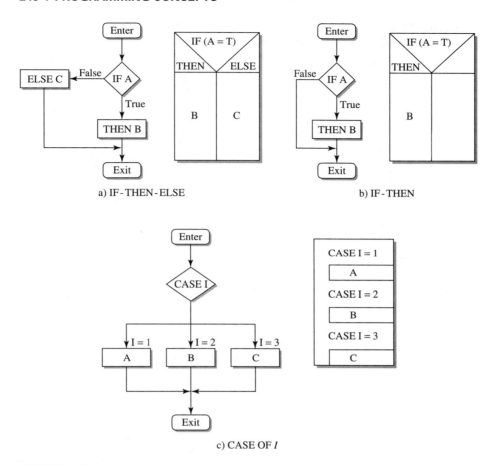

FIGURE 5.20
Decision control structure definitions.

There are three versions of the iteration logic control structure: DO-WHILE, DO-UNTIL, and PROCESS-UNTIL. These are illustrated in Figure 5.21. The DO-WHILE performs a test on condition A, and if its outcome is true, it transfers control to B. Process B transfers control to condition A, and the test is repeated. This sequence continues until the test result of condition A becomes false. The minimum number of process B executions is zero. The DO-UNTIL sequence is the reverse of DO-WHILE because process B is executed prior to performing a test on condition A. This results in a minimum number of one execution for process B. PROCESS-UNTIL is similar to DO-UNTIL, but in addition process C is executed if the condition A test result is false. This control structure is useful for executing a code sequence, contained in B, a fixed number of times. For example, if process C is incrementing an index i and condition A is testing for $i = N$, then process B will be executed N times.

These seven control structure definitions are used as a basis in the design and development of software intended to accomplish a specified task. Figure 5.22 illustrates a structured

FIGURE 5.21
Iteration control structure definitions.

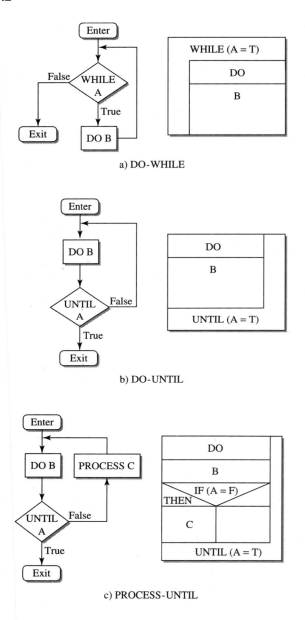

a) DO-WHILE

b) DO-UNTIL

c) PROCESS-UNTIL

program as a combination of elementary control structures. Both flowchart and structured diagram forms are presented. The sample program is a composite of several control structures, but it contains only one entry point and exit point. Thus, the entire program can be represented as one high-level sequence control structure. The searching and sorting algorithms discussed earlier can be easily represented using PDL and structured diagrams. The linear search procedure is presented in Figure 5.23. The basic algorithm uses a DO-WHILE, an IF-THEN-ELSE,

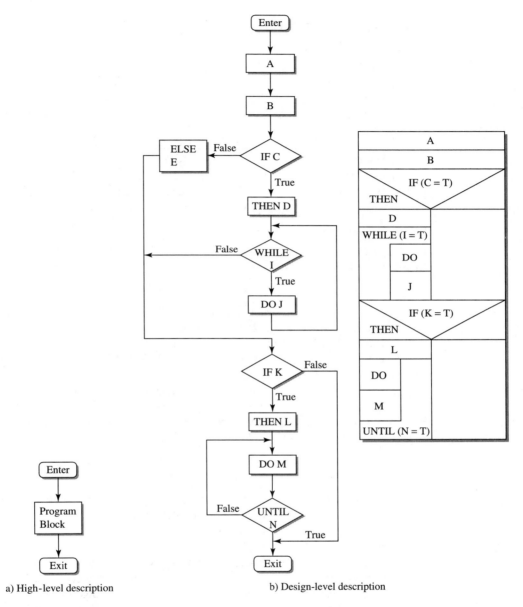

FIGURE 5.22
Structured program description.

a) High-level description

b) Design-level description

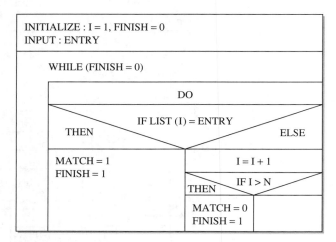

FIGURE 5.23
Linear search structured diagram.

and an IF-THEN control structure. Next the binary search algorithm is presented, using the same format, in Figure 5.24. The algorithm uses a DO-WHILE, an IF-THEN-ELSE, and a nested IF-THEN-ELSE control structure. The selection sort algorithm is illustrated in Figure 5.25. This algorithm requires a nested DO-WHILE and an IF-THEN logic control structure.

Structured diagrams provide a compact definition of algorithms, for the design and development of programs. In addition, English-like description of logic control structures, with PDL, results in a concise and clear representation of each module. Thus, modules can be analyzed and modified prior to actual program coding.

Programming Tools

Program implementation is achieved through the systematic application of a framework of software constructs that provide the transition from design to realization. These basic tools include the flag, the register, the counter, the timer, the table, the stack, the queue, and the subroutine.

A *flag* is used to provide status information from one part of a program to another. For example, an interrupt routine sets a status flag to indicate the source and nature of an asynchronous event. The main program code performs a status test to determine if an interrupt has occurred. Upon detecting a specific interrupt flag, this routine directs the flow of control to the corresponding service routine and resets the flag. A *register* is an extension of the flag in that it can be used to store a group of individual flags. Also, it provides temporary storage for either addresses or data during program execution.

A *counter* is formed using a register, the contents of which are incremented to signify the occurrence of an event. The counter's value is used by the main program for decision making. An iteration counter is used to keep track of program execution loops. Its contents may be pre-

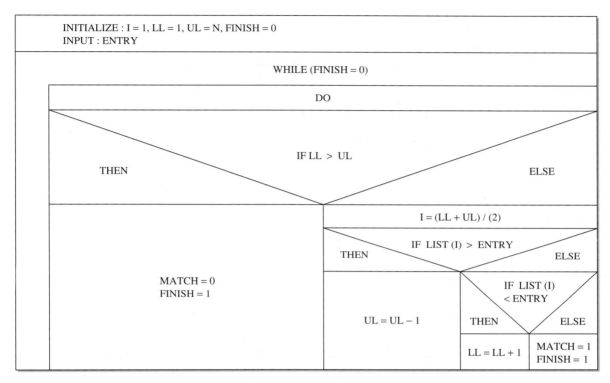

FIGURE 5.24
Binary search structured diagram.

set, incremented, or decremented by one or more loop instructions so as to provide program flexibility. A *timer,* formed in a similar fashion, is used to keep track of periodic time intervals or to provide precise time delays. Figure 5.26 illustrates an event counter and a delay timer. The event counter may be formed by incrementing the contents of a register each time an input variable A equals an integer value $K,$ signifying the occurrence of a specific event. If N such occurrences take place, the variable limit is set to 1. The initial register, $I,$ is set to 0 elsewhere in the program. The delay timer consists of an iterative loop that increments the contents of a register, the initial value of which is 0, until it reaches a preset value. The Delay variable is set to 1 to indicate the completion of the delay interval. The variable N can be changed to provide for variable delays.

A *table* is formed using a contiguous set of memory locations to store an array of data. A table is useful in speeding up operations by providing a stored versus a calculated solution. Another application of tables is the generation of address vectors within a program, illustrated in Figure 5.27. An entry code is read and its value is compared to an offset value constant. If a match occurs, a pointer is formed as the sum of the entry code and the PC contents. The pointer is used to access table location X, which contains a JMP instruction to the corresponding routine. The invoked routine performs the function selected by the entry code. The

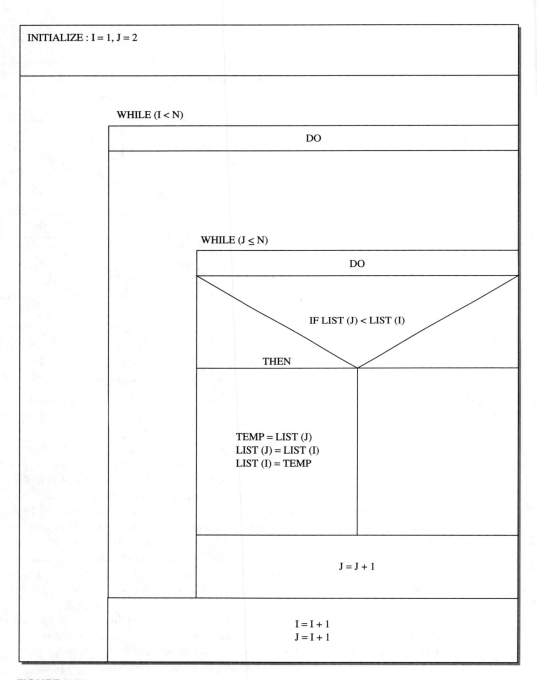

FIGURE 5.25
Selection sort structured diagram.

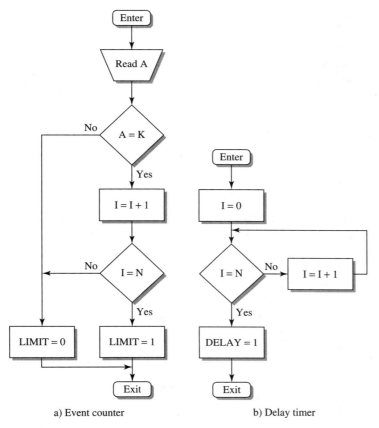

a) Event counter   b) Delay timer

FIGURE 5.26
Programming tool definitions.

last instruction in each routine transfers flow of control to a predetermined point in the main program.

The *stack* is essential for performing subroutines and interrupt functions. It is used to store the MPU state prior to such processing. In addition, stack-oriented MPU architectures store both operands and operators together, to speed up computations. Such a format is known as Reverse Polish Notation (RPN) and is shown in Table 5.8. Evaluation of the algebraic expression is performed using the stack.

The *queue* is used as a buffer between two unequal speed devices to provide increased throughput. Register-oriented MPU architectures prefetch instructions in a pipeline queue, as shown in Table 5.9. The evaluation of the algebraic expression is achieved with the use of three registers. The A register holds the intermediate and final results. Registers B and C provide the memory address locations at which the variables reside. The final result is stored at a memory location indicated by the contents of register D.

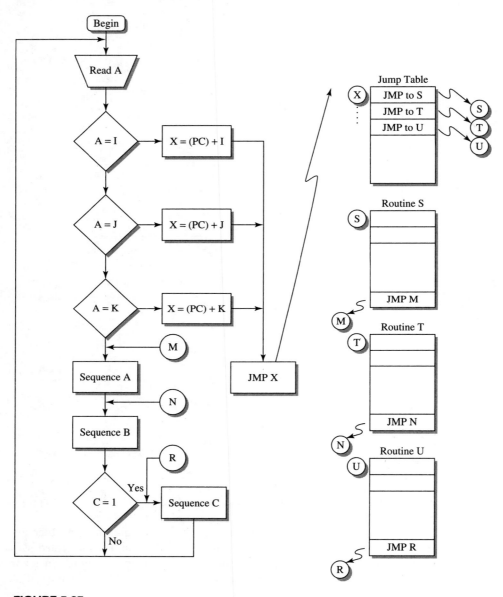

FIGURE 5.27
Jump table definition.

The *subroutine* is a sequence of instructions that can be invoked from different places within the main program. This feature eliminates code redundancy and results in efficient use of memory. The CALL instruction transfers control from the main program to the subroutine. Similarly, the RETURN instruction transfers control from the subroutine to the main program.

TABLE 5.8
Stack-oriented process

Equation	Stack	Operation
(A * B) + C = D	A	A
	B	A, B
	.	A · B
	C	A · B, C
	+	A · B + C
	D	A · B + C, D
	=	A · B + C = D

TABLE 5.9
Register-oriented process

Equation	Memory	Operation
A * B + C = D	MPY A, B	(A) · @ (B) → A
	ADD A, C	(A) + @ (C) → A
	STORE D, A	(A) → @ (D)

This operation is illustrated in Figure 5.28. The main program makes three separate calls to subroutine X. In each case, after the subroutine is executed, the flow of control returns to the next consecutive main program instruction.

The two fundamental subroutine types are the *iterative* and the *recursive*. Iterative subroutines proceed by repeating an operation several times until the desired result occurs. Recursive subroutines proceed by defining an operation in terms of itself in order to produce the desired result. These two approaches are illustrated in Figure 5.29. The POWER subroutines

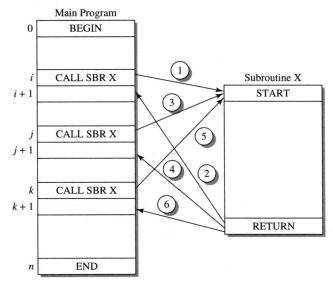

FIGURE 5.28
Subroutine operation block diagram.

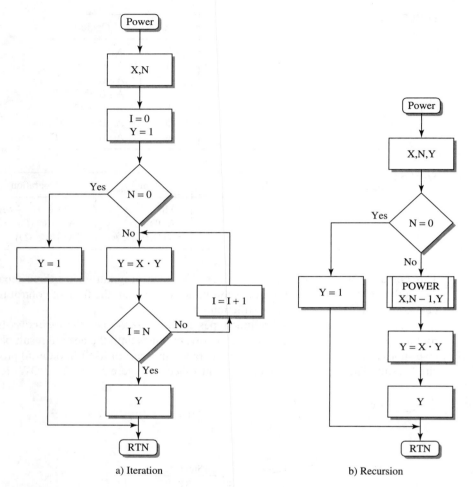

FIGURE 5.29
Subroutine implementations.

evaluate the Nth power of an input variable X. The main program provides the X and N variables to the subroutine. The iterative approach implements a loop that computes the expression $Y = X \cdot Y$ a total of N times, starting with $Y = 1$. During each pass, the previous value of Y is multiplied by the X variable value to generate the new intermediate result. On the Nth pass the Y variable value is returned to the main program. The recursive approach differs in that the POWER routine calls itself N times, to create an N-level nested subroutine. This requires additional stack space, which results in slower operation. Many problems, however, have recursive solutions by nature, making the approach attractive. The Nth call results in a special case of $N = 0$ that starts the actual computation of the expression $Y = X \cdot Y$, with Y set initially to 1. Then it proceeds to the next level, and the process continues until all N levels are completed. Upon completion, as in the case of the iterative approach, the Y variable value is returned to the main program.

Program Definitions

A program is made up of individual blocks of code and data that reside in memory and perform specific functions. A typical set of logically organized modules is shown in Figure 5.30, using block diagram representation. All major program modules are represented as blocks, and their relationships are shown as directional lines. The program initialization vector is accessed each time the MPU program counter is reset. The vector points to the start of the initialization routine. This routine is used to preset and configure MPU internal registers and external I/O devices prior to main program execution. Upon completion, the flow of control goes to the built-in-test (BIT) routine. This routine performs systematic diagnostic operations on the MPU, memory, and other bus interface devices to determine their readiness status. Upon successful completion, the flow of control goes to the main program code block. This usually consists of a large loop structure that performs conditional test and branch operations. Each branch operation is directed via a jump table, for program flexibility, to a specific routine to accomplish the selected task. Program routines invoke one or more subroutines that are defined during the design phase for code efficiency. During main program execution, interrupts can occur at any time. Such interrupts can be either internal or external, and single or nested. The stack is used for both subroutines and interrupts, and it is the limiting factor in determining the number of

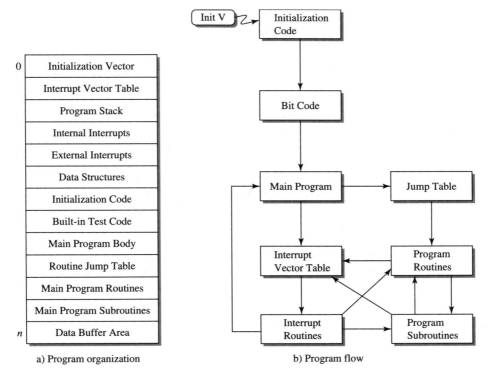

a) Program organization   b) Program flow

FIGURE 5.30
Program definition block diagrams.

nesting levels. The data structures are used and may be modified in the course of program execution. The data buffer area is used for temporary data storage and I/O transfers. The program organization depicted in Figure 5.30a, presented for discussion purposes, shows the physical memory locations of each individual program module. The program flow diagram detailed in Figure 5.30b represents the functional interaction among the various modules, which in unison constitute a standalone program. A single program residing inside the MPU memory transforms it into a dedicated, application-specific machine and provides an efficient solution to a well-defined problem.

5.3 LOW-LEVEL LANGUAGES

Machine language provides MPU-specific binary code, which is decoded and executed to perform a specific task. This elementary program level uses the MPU's instruction set to create an object code that resides in a fixed area in memory. Assembly language is a set of mnemonics, symbols, labels, and data that are used to generate a program with statements. These statements define the operations and the operand values. This is known as a *source code* and is quite readable. The source code is used as the input to an assembler, or translator program, which outputs consistent binary code called the *object code*. Assembly-language programming provides relocatable object code within the MPU memory.

Machine Language

An MPU accomplishes a specified task by executing a logical sequence of instructions, called a program, that are stored in memory. It fetches, decodes, and executes them one at a time. These primitive instructions are stored in binary form using the machine language programming method. Instructions are classified as either single-word or multiple-word types. Single-word instructions require one memory location; multiple-word instructions require two or more. Multiple-word instructions also require multiple fetch cycles, prior to execution, which reduces MPU efficiency.

Machine-language programming develops a logical sequence of binary code, using the MPU instruction set, and stores it into memory. This approach is useful for small programs, but it requires that the programmer has in-depth knowledge of the specific MPU architecture. The following discussion serves to illustrate the process. A program is required to transfer fifty consecutive data words from an external device into memory, starting at address location 100. Such a program is called a bootstrap loader and is used to initialize an MPU prior to main program execution. Table 5.10 lists a sample machine-language program designed to accomplish this task. The sample program assumes an eight-bit MPU. It uses MPU register B to store the starting address location and register C to store the number of words to be transferred. In general, writing a machine language program is a tedious task, and the process is susceptible to induced errors.

An enhancement to binary code format groups binary bits to form a compact hexadecimal equivalent code. This technique speeds up coding and makes it easier to detect induced errors. However, hex coding does not provide any additional meaning to the instruction for user comprehension. Thus, the programmer is forced either to memorize or to contin-

TABLE 5.10
Machine-language program definition

Instruction Number	Instruction Location	Binary Code	Comments
1	1	10010001	LOAD STATUS ADDR 5 100
	2	01100100	INTO REG B
2	3	10010010	LOAD NUMBER OF WORDS 5 50
	4	00110010	TO BE SENT INTO REG C
3	5	11001010	INPUT DEV STAT IN ACC
4	6	11100000	SKIP IF (ACC) ≠ 0
5	7	10110101	JUMP TO LOC FIVE
6	8	11001011	INPUT WORD IN ACC
7	9	10100001	STORE (ACC) AT @ (B)
8	10	00110001	INCREMENT (B)
9	11	01000010	DECREMENT (C)
10	12	11000010	LOAD (C) IN ACC
11	13	11010101	IF (ACC) ≠ 0 JUMP TO LOC FIVE
12	14	11110000	STOP

uously refer to a manual for each machine instruction. Also, the resulting program is inflexible in that it will only work properly when stored in a specific memory area. For instance, instruction 5, in location 7, does an unconditional jump to location 5. This requires that the program starting address be at location 1. Using this absolute reference addressing scheme, the program must be modified each time it is loaded at a different starting address. The corresponding hex format instruction notation for the sample program is listed in Table 5.11 for comparison.

The program begins by loading the address value of 100 into the MPU register B to specify the starting memory location for the fifty words. This instruction occupies two memory locations. The first part, 91_{16}, specifies the operation and associated register. The second part, 64_{16}, is the hex value for decimal 100. The second instruction loads the number of words to be transferred into the C register. This instruction is also made of two parts. The first part, 92_{16}, defines the operation and associated register. The second part, 32_{16}, is the hex number for decimal 50. The remaining instructions occupy a single memory location. The third instruction

TABLE 5.11
Hex notation program definition

Instruction Location	Hex Code	Instruction Location	Hex Code
1	91	8	CB
2	64	9	A1
3	92	10	31
4	32	11	42
5	CA	12	C2
6	E0	13	D5
7	B5	14	F0

reads the device status into the accumulator register. The fourth instruction does a conditional test and skips the next instruction if the accumulator contains a nonzero value. The fifth instruction is used to set up a control loop. Repeated execution of instructions 3 through 5 occurs until a nonzero device status is obtained, indicating a valid input data word. The sixth instruction transfers the valid input data word from the device to the accumulator. The seventh instruction transfers the accumulator contents into a memory location specified by an address value in register B. The eighth instruction increments the contents of register B by one, to provide the memory address for the next valid input data word. The ninth instruction decrements the contents of register C by one, to keep track of the actual number of word transfers. The tenth instruction loads the contents of register C into the accumulator. The eleventh instruction tests the zero flag of the accumulator for true condition, to terminate the program. The twelfth instruction stops the MPU PC from incrementing.

Assembly Language

Assembly language is a second-level programming method that employs mnemonic symbols to describe the function of each instruction. A *mnemonic* is an acronym used to represent each machine instruction and provide a quick identification of the operation it performs. Address locations are represented by one or more alphanumeric characters, known as *labels,* to enable relative branch and jump addresses and to facilitate flexible and relocatable programs. In addition, groups of characters, or *strings,* are used to create operand symbols for defining variables and data constants, which speeds up program revisions. Thus, assembly language is a collection of mnemonics, labels, and symbols that conform to a set of rules for developing a source code program. The source code serves as the input to the assembler program. The *assembler* is a program that translates mnemonic source code into machine object code. This process consists of three steps: converting mnemonics into opcode, assigning actual address values to labels, and substituting a data value for each symbol.

Assembly-language programming is useful for small- to medium-size programs that require frequent revisions and that must be relocatable. These programs are also suitable for time critical operations. Assemblers provide special features to enhance and streamline the coding process. For example, symbolic mathematical expressions are evaluated and result in a single data value at assembly time. Assembler-specific instructions, known as *directives,* are used to control operation, and they result in no related object code. Directives provide flexibility by permitting selective assembly of individual routines or the defining and allocating of memory space. Furthermore, shorthand notation for a group of instructions, known as a *macro,* can be defined for frequently used functions. Hence, a macro-defined instruction can be repeated as required within a program, and the assembler will each time generate the equivalent code.

Table 5.12 provides a comparison between machine-language and assembly-language programming. After close examination of the table, one can conclude that assembly language programs are self-documenting and easier to follow because of their symbolic content. Also, address labels make the program relocatable within the available memory. Furthermore, address and data constants can be easily changed to accommodate program starting location and size. The depicted program consists of twelve instruction mnemonics. Each instruction provides an insight into the actual operation performed by the MPU. The LDB instruction performs a "load immediate data" operation into the internal B register. The value specifies the

TABLE 5.12

Comparison of machine and assembly language

Instruction Number	Instruction Location	Machine Code	Assembly Code	Comments
1	1	91	LDB #100	LOAD B WITH
	2	64		VALUE OF 100
2	3	92	LDC #50	LOAD C WITH
	4	32		VALUE OF 50
3	5	CA	START LDA X1	LD (X1) IN ACC
4	6	E0	SNZ	SKP IF (ACC) ≠ 0
5	7	B5	JMP START	JMP TO START
6	8	CB	LDA X2	LD (X2) IN ACC
7	9	A1	STA @B	STO (ACC) @ (B)
8	10	31	INC B	INCR (B)
9	11	42	DEC C	DECR (C)
10	12	C2	LDA C	LOAD (C) IN ACC
11	13	D5	JNZ START	JMP IF ACC ≠ 0
12	14	F0	END	END PROGRAM

starting memory location for the transferred data storage. The LDC instruction directs the MPU to load its internal C register with the number of required word transfers. The previous instruction formats contain a mnemonic part and the immediate value, denoted by the # symbol, found in the next consecutive memory address. The LDA instruction, which has the address label START, loads the contents of X1 location in the accumulator. The SNZ instruction is a conditional skip type. The JMP instruction is an unconditional jump type and contains a symbolic operand. This, in conjunction with the two previous instructions, forms a conditional loop structure. The LDA instruction loads the contents of X2 location in the accumulator. The STA instruction performs a B register indirect store operation of the accumulator contents. The INC and DEC instructions modify the contents of the B and C registers, respectively. The INC instruction increments the contents of B by one to specify the address value for the next input data word. The DEC instruction decrements the contents of C by one to keep track of the number of data words transferred. The LDA instruction loads the contents of C into the accumulator. The JNZ instruction provides a conditional jump to the address label START, to repeat the data word transfer cycle until the contents of C equal 0. The END instruction terminates this program and stops execution.

Assembly-language instruction format consists of four distinct fields: label, mnemonic, operand, and comment. The label field must be present when another instruction, within the program, is referenced to this instruction. The mnemonic field is essential for each instruction since this field defines instruction operation. The operand field provides the permissible options for each specific instruction. The comment field serves to clarify the scope of each individual instruction within the program. Table 5.13 illustrates these field definitions. The table starts with the directive ORG, which commands the assembler to set the MPU program counter at a starting address of 100. The DATA directive indicates to the assembler that data definition follows. The EQU directives instruct the assembler to assign the specified data values to the corresponding symbolic operands X and Y. Next, two data values are loaded into the A register, used

TABLE 5.13
Assembly language notation

Label	Mnemonic	Operand	Comment
	ORG	100	SET PC = 100
	DATA		OPERAND DEF
X	EQU	50	INITIAL VALUE
Y	EQU	200	STARTING ADDRESS
LOOP	LDA	X	LD X INTO A
	LDB	Y	LD Y INTO B
	STA	@B	STORE (ACC) @ (B)
	INC	B	B = (B) + 1
	DEC	A	A = (A) − 1
	JNZ	LOOP	JUMP IF (A) > 0
	END		PROGRAM HALT

as an accumulator, and the B register. The X data value, which is stored in A, serves as the initial value for a table containing consecutive, decreasing integers. The Y data value, which is stored in B, defines the starting address memory location of the table. The control loop is used to store each integer in consecutive, decreasing order until the contents of A equal 0. The END directive specifies program completion to the assembler. The program will reside in memory starting at address 100 and will generate a table of consecutive, decreasing integers, beginning with fifty. The table is located between address 200 and 250. Address labels and operand symbols provide program modification flexibility. Also, the ORG directive easily relocates the entire program.

Assembler Functions

The assembler is a standalone program used to translate a source code program in symbolic notation into an object code program. It allows instruction references within the program by permitting the use of defined names and labels. Also, it allows storage location references by the use of symbolic address names. It provides for expression evaluation, which results in a single operand value. It contains macro symbols, which represent a specific sequence of source code as a single mnemonic entry. Using the directives, it is possible to achieve conditional assembly of selected program modules during program development and debugging phases.

The assembler program performs five basic operations on a source code program. First, it assigns a memory location address to each instruction mnemonic. Second, it converts mnemonics into opcodes. Third, it assigns numerical values to instruction labels such that they match the instruction address. Fourth, it evaluates and assigns operand values to each instruction. The operands are specified either explicitly as immediate data or implicitly as symbols for addresses and mathematical expressions. Fifth, it generates the object code in the specific machine format. The directives are mnemonics that control assembler operations but generate no object code. The source program comments are provided for clarity and are ignored by the assembler. The assembler generates a symbol table that contains each address label or data symbol and its corresponding value, which is used for cross-reference during the assembly process.

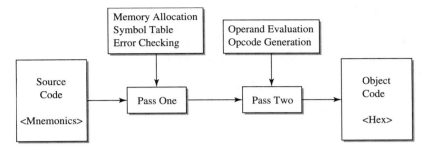

FIGURE 5.31
Two-pass assembler operation.

Most assemblers are implemented using a two-pass technique, and as a result the source code is processed twice. The overall assembly process is illustrated in Figure 5.31. During the first pass the following steps take place:

1. Assign memory space to each mnemonic.
2. Allocate the correct number of memory words for each instruction.
3. Store each instruction label and its assigned address value.
4. Store each symbol name and its defined value.
5. Perform error check on each mnemonic.
6. Perform duplication check on instruction labels.
7. Allocate memory space as specified by the assembler directives.

During the second pass the following steps occur:

8. Convert instruction mnemonics into specific MPU opcode.
9. Determine operand values using the symbol table or by expression evaluation.
10. Perform operand error check.
11. Derive object code.

There are some basic requirements associated with the source program. For instance, each label and symbol must be uniquely defined using alphanumeric characters. Mnemonics are reserved for opcode definitions only. The instruction LDA #Y $=$ M$\cdot$X+B illustrates the expression evaluation feature of an assembler. The expression Y $=$ M$\cdot$X+B is evaluated first, and the result is loaded into the A register. A macro can be defined, using the START MACRO and END MACRO directives, respectively. The macro symbol RANGE can be used to insert a group of instructions each time it is listed. Hence, a Macro instruction RANGE,X can be predefined to produce the following code sequence:

Macro Definition	Comments
LDA X	Load Acc With (X)
MPY X+1	Multiply (Acc) $\cdot$ (X+1) $\rightarrow$ Acc
ADD X+2	Add (Acc) + (X+2) $\rightarrow$ Acc
STA R1	Store (Acc) $\rightarrow$ R1

This code sequence takes three consecutively stored numbers, beginning with location X, and calculates the expression $Y = M \cdot X + B = (X) \cdot (X+1) + (X+2)$. Then it stores the result in the R1 internal register. Other directives are available for conditional assembly, memory allocation, and printout format. The assembler printout listing contains the input source code, output object code, symbol table, and any errors detected during assembly. The listing format is arranged in the following seven fields: instruction number, address, object code, label, mnemonic, operand, and comment. The instruction number serves as a reference for each line of code. The address field specifies the memory location of each machine-level instruction. The object code field contains the resulting assembly instruction opcode and operand, in hexadecimal notation. The remaining four fields are a duplication of the source code as provided by the programmer. The following example illustrates a typical assembly-level program using two operands, for source and destination, respectively.

EXAMPLE 5.2

Assembly-language system initialization program

```
X       EQU   1000H      DEFINE SYMBOLIC OPERANDS
P0      EQU   1005H
P1      EQU   1010H
P2      EQU   1015H
P3      EQU   1016H
        ORG   1020H      SPECIFY PROGRAM STARTING ADDRESS
INIT    MOV   #3AH, P0   CONFIGURE DEVICE A
        MOV   #51H, P1   CONFIGURE DEVICE B
        MOV   #3FH, P2   CONFIGURE DEVICE C
POLL    MOV   P3, R1     XFER DEV C STATUS TO R1
        AND   #01H, R1   MASK ALL BITS EXCEPT ZERO
        COMP  #01H, R1   IS BIT ZERO SET?
        JPZ   POLL       REPEAT LOOP IF NOT SET
        MOV   X, R2      LOAD R2 WITH X
TEST    MOV   #55H, @R2  WRITE 55H TO LOC SPEC BY (R2)
        MOV   @R2, R1    READ CONTENTS SPEC BY (R2) IN R1
        COMP  #55H, R1   COMPARE (R1) TO 55H
        JNE   FAIL       IF NOT EQUAL JMP TO FAIL
        MOV   #AAH, @R2
        MOV   @R2, R1
        COMP  #AAH, R1
        JNE   FAIL
        DEC   R2         R2 = (R2) - 1
        JNZ   TEST       IF R2 ≠ 0 JUMP TO TEST
PASS    JMP   MAIN       JUMP TO MAIN PROGRAM
FAIL    JMP   FAIL       LOCKUP
MAIN    CLR   R1         CLEAR (R1)
        —     —
```

The previous example program brings out the salient features of assembly language programming. The EQU directive assigns numerical values to the symbolic operands used in the source program. The ORG directive sets the initial MPU program counter value to the starting address location of the object program. The INIT label is used to identify the first line of source code for clarity. The next three consecutive MOV instructions transfer immediate operand values to predefined symbolic device addresses. These serve to properly configure the three external devices. The POLL address label defines and forms a control loop structure. The operation performs device status reading to determine its readiness. This involves bit masking and compare functions, which are carried out by the AND and COMP instructions, respectively. This process is conditionally repeated, via the JPZ instruction, until the device status bit is set. The next instruction transfers the X symbol value into the R2 register. The R2 contents specify the starting address location for the memory test portion of the program. The test writes a data word of 55_{16} into the first memory location, then reads it into R1 and compares them. Next, the process repeats itself using a data word of AA_{16} instead. If the data match, it proceeds to the next memory location; otherwise it jumps to the label FAIL, which is an infinite loop. These two data values test each memory location for multiple adjacent bit transitions. The DEC and JNZ instructions keep track of the tested memory locations and terminate the test successfully. Finally, the PASS address label points to the JMP instruction, which provides an unconditional branch to the main program.

Assembly-language programming provides self-documenting capability. This makes feasible programs of a few thousand lines of code, as compared to a few hundred lines for machine language. The labels and symbols provide program clarity, flexibility, and relocation capability. Macros result in redundant program code compression. However, assembly language is MPU-specific and requires familiarity with hardware architecture for efficient code generation.

5.4 HIGH-LEVEL LANGUAGES

A high-level language is designed with English-like statements and a set of rules to achieve MPU-independent, general problem solutions. There are four major statement types: specification, assignment, program control, and I/O. Each statement may contain one or more of the following: expressions, variables, constants, operators, and keywords or tokens.

The source program serves as the input to a translator program, known as the *compiler,* which converts each individual statement into several machine language instructions. A compiler provides a complete program conversion prior to execution. Some high-level languages use an *interpreter program* to convert and execute one source statement at a time.

High-level language programming results in portable, reliable, maintainable, and self-documenting programs with built-in error-handling mechanisms. The advantages these features offer are offset by additional memory requirements and slower execution times. The objective of high-level languages is to allow the programmer to focus on the actual problem-solving task. The translator program handles the burden of the resulting internal manipulations and housekeeping chores of the specific MPU architecture. The equation $Y = M \cdot X + B$ becomes a one-line statement in high-level language notation. The compiler uses this equation to derive a set of assembly-level instructions, consistent with the specific MPU, that accomplishes the desired function. A typical set of resulting statements is listed below:

```
LDA  #M
MPY  #X
ADD  #B
STA  Y
```

First, the value of M is loaded into the accumulator. Next, the contents of the accumulator are multiplied by the X value and the result is stored in the accumulator. Then the value B is added to the accumulator contents. Finally, the result is stored in memory location Y. These steps assume that the MPU has an MPY instruction; otherwise a multiplication subroutine must be written in assembly language.

Several high-level languages are available, each tailored for a specific area of application. FORTRAN is the first major high-level language developed for scientific and engineering applications. FORTRAN stands for Formula Translation and was developed in the 1950s. The language has since gone through several revisions, with the FORTRAN-77 version incorporating structured programming capability. The language contains an extensive function library to facilitate mathematical calculations and uses a compiler program to produce MPU-specific object code. BASIC is another prolific high-level language that supports user interaction. This is accomplished via the use of an interpreter translator program to reduce program execution time. The acronym BASIC stands for Beginner's All-purpose Symbolic Instruction Code. Introduced in the 1960s, the language is relatively easy to learn, yet it contains powerful features. It has also gone through several revisions that have provided various enhancements, including string manipulation, structured programming, subroutines, graphics, and compiler implementation. Pascal is yet another general-purpose high-level language. Introduced in the 1970s, it features structured programming concepts. Pascal is named after the famous French mathematician Blaise Pascal, who in 1690 developed the first mechanical calculator. The language is well suited for algorithm generation and data structure definitions. It is known as a library extension language, since it allows the user to add subprograms consistent with the library format. The C language was developed in the 1970s. It enables the programmer to generate efficient and portable programs.

FORTRAN

This language uses a fixed format for statement and data entry, within an eighty-column field definition. Column 1 is used to denote a comment by inserting the letter C. Columns 2 through 5 are used to designate the statement number. Column 6 is used to indicate a continuation, by entering a digit with a value between 2 and 9. Columns 7 through 72 are used for the actual FORTRAN statement definition. Columns 73 through 80 are used to assign a program identification number. Data entry values may be placed anywhere within the eighty-column field.

There are seven basic FORTRAN statement types: input, output, assignment, control, specification, function, and subroutine. There are two kinds of operands: constants and variables. Each can be specified as either integer, floating-point, double precision, or logical types. An operand is defined using one to six alphanumeric characters, the first of which is always a letter. Integer operand definitions start with letters I through N, and the remaining letters are used to specify floating-point values. However, assignment statements may be used to redefine the various operand types, independent of initial letter restrictions.

READ is an example of an input statement type and has the following syntax:

$$S_n \text{ READ} (\text{I}, \text{J}) \ v_1, v_2, \ldots, v_m$$

where S_n is an optional statement number, I indicates the input device, J specifies the statement label associated with the input **FORMAT** specification statement, and v_i are the actual variable values.

WRITE is an example of an output statement type and has the following syntax:

$$S_n \text{ WRITE } (\text{I, J}) \ v_1, v_2, \ldots, v_m$$

where S_n is an optional statement number, I indicates the output device, J specifies the statement label associated with the output **FORMAT** specification statement, and v_i are the actual variable values.

The assignment statement equates an expression to a variable and has the following syntax:

$$S_n \ variable = expression$$

The order of expression evaluation is done in accordance with the left-to-right rule. Parenthetical expressions have the highest priority, followed by exponentiation, multiplication and division, and addition and subtraction. The corresponding operator symbols are **, *, /, +, and −.

There are several control-type statements that perform either conditional or unconditional program transfers. The **GO TO** statement is used for unconditional transfer of control and provides either single- or multiple-branch operation. There are two variations, the simple and the computed. Their associated syntax is shown below:

$$S_n \text{ GO TO } S_i$$
$$S_n \text{ GO TO } (S_i, S_j, S_k, \ldots, S_l), \ variable$$

The simple **GO TO** transfers control to a specific location indicated by the statement number. The computed **GO TO** transfers control to one of several possible locations, determined by the value of the associated integer variable at the time of statement execution. The **STOP** and **END** control statements are used to indicate program termination and compiler completion, respectively. Conditional transfer of control is accomplished with the **IF** statement. The **IF** statement can be defined with either arithmetic or logical operators. The arithmetic version provides for a three-way conditional branch. Its syntax is shown below:

$$S_n \text{ IF } (arithmetic \ expression) \ S_i, S_j, S_k$$

The arithmetic expression is computed and compared to zero. If the result is less than zero, control goes to the S_i statement number. If the result equals zero, then control is transferred to the second statement number. Finally, if the result is greater than zero, control passes to the third statement number. The logical **IF** statement provides a conditional branch using a logical relationship to compare to expressions. The syntax associated with this statement is shown below:

$$S_n \text{ IF } (expression_1 \ .logical \ operator. \ expression_2) \ statement$$

where   .logical operator. can be one of the following: .LT., .LE., .EQ., .NE., .GE., or .GT., and the statement must be an executable type.

In addition, the structured FORTRAN-77 version allows for a compound **IF** statement with the following syntax:

$$S_n \ \textbf{IF} \ (expression_1) \ \textbf{THEN} \ (expression_2) \ \textbf{ELSE} \ (expression_3) \ \textbf{ENDIF}$$

Another control statement that has numerous uses is the **DO** statement. It is used mainly for iterative operations with controlled termination. The basic **DO** statement syntax is shown below:

$$S_n \ \textbf{DO} \ S_l \ \text{I} \ = N_1, N_2, N_3$$

where S_l is the last statement in the loop, I is the loop index, N_1 is the initial index value, N_2 is the final index value, and N_3 is the index stepsize.

The **CONTINUE** is normally used as the last statement in the loop. The index values must be set outside the loop and prior to the first pass. The initial index is incremented by the index stepsize on each completed loop pass. The loop is executed a minimum of one time. A transfer out of the loop is permissible, but not into an arbitrary part of the loop. If the loop terminates normally, the index values are lost. Loop nesting is permitted under the guidelines above.

Specification statements are used to define the variable types as either integer, real, double precision, or logical, as shown below:

$$\textbf{INTEGER} \ V_1, V_2, \ldots, V_N$$

$$\textbf{REAL} \ V_1, V_2, \ldots, V_N$$

$$\textbf{DOUBLE PRECISION} \ V_1, V_2, \ldots, V_N$$

$$\textbf{LOGICAL} \ V_1, V_2, \ldots, V_N$$

A **FORMAT** statement is used to specify the variable type and field width associated with I/O data. The statement syntax is provided below:

$$S_n \ \textbf{FORMAT} \ (f_1, f_2, \ldots, f_m)$$

where f_i is keyed to a corresponding **READ** or **WRITE** statement variable, and is one of the following:

nX	Skip n spaces
In	Integer variable width
F$n.d$	Real variable width
D$n.d$	Double precision variable width
Ln	Logical variable width
An	Alphanumeric field width
"	Character string printing
/	Line skip
1H	Single line spacing
1H0	Double line spacing

`1H1`	Page skip
`1H+`	No space

The **DIMENSION** statement is used to specify arrays for one, two, or three dimensions and has the following syntax:

$$S_n \text{ DIMENSION } \textit{array name } (\texttt{I}, \texttt{J}, \texttt{K})$$

where   the array name is consistent with the stored data type, and the indices specify the array size in the corresponding dimension.

An array must be specified with either a **DIMENSION**, a **COMMON**, or a variable specification statement. The array values are entered using either a **READ** or an assignment statement. The indices must be positive integers and their values bounded by the array size.

The **COMMON** statement is used to enable either a variable or an array to be shared by other subprograms. The statement must appear in the main program and also in any subprogram that uses it. The statement syntax is listed below.

$$S_n \text{ COMMON } \textit{variable}, \textit{array name } (\texttt{I}, \texttt{J}, \texttt{K})$$

where   the variable and array names are defined as common.

The **FUNCTION** statement is used to define a subprogram that is invoked by its name and returns a value upon completion. The statement syntax is provided below:

$$S_n \text{ FUNCTION } \textit{name } (A_1, A_2, . . ., A_m)$$

where   the name consists of up to six alphanumeric characters, and the first determines the data type if it is not defined by a specification statement.

The **FUNCTION** contains at least one argument in parentheses, which cannot be a constant or a subscripted variable. A **FUNCTION** cannot call itself, or part of itself, and there must be a one-to-one relationship between its variable list and the calling statement. A **RETURN** statement is required to transfer the flow of control to the main program. It should be noted that FORTRAN has a large library of predefined **FUNCTION** routines available to the user.

The **SUBROUTINE** statement is used to define a subprogram, invoked by a **CALL** statement, which may or may not return a value upon completion. The statement syntax is given below.

$$\text{SUBROUTINE } \textit{name } (A_1, A_2, . . ., A_m)$$

where   the name consists of one to six alphanumeric characters and an argument list in parentheses.

The argument list must agree in type, number, and order with the **CALL** statement. A **COMMON** statement can be used to eliminate the need for an argument list. This essentially makes the variable global, rather than local to each module. Subscripted variables are permitted, and a **RETURN** statement is required to transfer the flow of control to the calling program. SUBROU-

TINES are generalized **FUNCTION** routines written by the user to minimize code redundancy. The following example combines the salient FORTRAN features into a single program.

EXAMPLE 5.3

FORTRAN Program

```
C       EXAMPLE PROGRAM
        INTEGER TABLE,BASE
        COMMON TABLE (10,10)
        READ (5,10)((TABLE (I,J),J = 1,10),I = 1,10)
10      FORMAT (I4)
        CALL LARGE (I,J)
        WRITE (6,20) TABLE (I,J),I,J
20      FORMAT (5X,'MAX=',I4,3X,'I=',I2,IX,'J=',I2)
        READ (5,10) BASE
        K = TABLE (I,J)
        IF (K-BASE) 30,50,40
30      FUNCTION ISUM (K)
        WRITE (6,35) ISUM
35      FORMAT (5X,'ISUM=',I6)
        GO TO 50
40      FUNCTION IPROD (K)
        WRITE (6,45) IPROD
45      FORMAT (/,5X,'IPROD=',I10)
50      STOP
        END
C       SUBROUTINE
        SUBROUTINE LARGE (II,JJ)
        COMMON TABLE (10,10)
        II = 1
        JJ = 1
        INIT = TABLE (1,1)
        IMAX = INIT
        DO 10 I = 1,10
        DO 10 J = 1,10
        NEXT = TABLE (I,J)
        IF (NEXT.LE.IMAX) GO TO 10
        IMAX = NEXT
        II = I
        JJ = J
10      CONTINUE
        RETURN
        END
C       FUNCTION ISUM
        FUNCTION ISUM (N)
        ISUM = 0
        DO 10 I = 1,N
        ISUM = ISUM+1
```

```
10   CONTINUE
     RETURN
     END
C    FUNCTION IPROD
     FUNCTION IPROD (N)
     IPROD = 1
     DO 10 I = 1, N
     IPROD = IPROD*I
10   CONTINUE
     RETURN
     END
```

The program begins by specifying the variable names TABLE and BASE as integers and by defining a two-dimensional array TABLE(10,10) as **COMMON** so that it can be used by the subroutine. The **READ** statement and its associated **FORMAT** statement are used to enter values into the array. Next, a subroutine call is made to LARGE, which searches and finds the largest numerical element in the array. The **WRITE** statement is used to print the element and its location in accordance with the **FORMAT** statement. Then the integer variable BASE is entered, using a **READ** statement, and the largest array element is assigned to the variable K. The arithmetic **IF** statement provides a conditional three-way branch in the program flow. If the largest array element value is less than the variable BASE, then the function ISUM is invoked. This returns a value equal to the sum of all consecutive integers from 1 to K. If the variable BASE equals K, then the program terminates. Finally, if K is greater than the variable BASE, the function IPROD is invoked. This returns a value equal to the product of all consecutive integers from 1 to K. If either of the above functions is invoked, then a corresponding **WRITE** statement is used to output the function's value in the specified format. The subroutine LARGE returns to the main program the index variables I and J, which indicate the location of the largest array element. The **COMMON** statement is used to access the TABLE array in the subroutine. The array indices are initialized as ones to begin the search at location TABLE (1,1). Using two nested **DO** loop statements, the array elements are systematically compared, and the variable **IMAX** represents the largest value on every loop pass. When the **DO** loop terminates, after one hundred passes, the subroutine returns control to the main program. The two functions are very similar in operation. They both accept an integer variable to define the upper limit of a **DO** statement that evaluates a mathematical expression; then they return the result to the main program.

BASIC

This is an extension-type language, in the sense that new revisions add statements and functions to make it more versatile. It uses free format for statements and data entries. Variables are defined by either a single letter or a letter followed by a decimal digit. A value is assigned to a variable by either a **READ** or a **LET** statement. Comments are inserted using the **REM** statement. Numerical values are self-defining and usually expressed in either decimal or scientific notation. The arithmetic operators are the same as in FORTRAN. The order and precedence of mathematical evaluations adhere to the same algebraic rules. Relational operators are also provided to compare mathematical expressions for conditional program branching. Line numbers are used with every statement and must be in ascending order of magnitude. The types of statements available are similar to those in FORTRAN.

The **READ** statement is used in conjunction with a **DATA** statement for data input. A read statement contains a list of variables that are assigned values specified in the **DATA** statement. Their syntax is listed below:

$$L_n \text{ READ } (V_1, V_2, \ldots, V_m)$$
$$L_n \text{ DATA } (D_1, D_2, \ldots, D_m)$$

A **PRINT** statement is used to transfer data to an output device and has the following syntax:

$$L_n \text{ PRINT } (list\ of\ expressions)$$

The **LET** statement assigns the value of an expression to a variable and has the following syntax:

$$L_n \text{ LET } variable = (expression)$$

The **GOTO** statement provides unconditional program transfer of control within a program and has the following syntax:

$$L_n \text{ GOTO } (line\ number)$$

The **IF** statement provides conditional program transfer of control within a program and has the following syntax:

$$L_n \text{ IF } (expression_1)\ relational\ operator\ (expression_2)$$
$$\text{THEN } (expression_1)\ \text{ELSE } (expression_2)$$

The **ON** statement provides multiway branching to one of several specified line numbers within a program and has the following syntax:

$$L_n \text{ ON } (expression)\ \text{GOTO } (L_i, L_j, \ldots, K_m)$$

The relative position of the line number, from left to right, is keyed to the expression's value, in order to perform the branch operation. A value outside the limit results in an error condition.

The **STOP** statement halts program execution, and the **END** statement terminates the program. Program loops are constructed using the **FOR** statement, which has the following syntax:

$$L_n \text{ FOR } (variable = expression_1)\ \text{TO } (expression_2)$$
$$\text{STEP } (expression_3)$$
$$\vdots$$
$$\text{NEXT } (variable)$$

The variable is an integer type used for counting the loop iterations. *Expression$_1$* determines the initial value. *Expression$_2$* specifies the final value, and *expression$_3$* defines the stepsize. The **NEXT** statement is used to close the loop, and it becomes the decision point at which the variable is incremented and tested to determine the flow of control.

Subroutines can be defined in BASIC using the **GOSUB** and **RETURN** statements with the following syntax:

$$L_n \text{ GOSUB } (L_i)$$
$$\vdots$$
$$L_m \text{ RETURN}$$

There are no parameters passed since all variables in BASIC are considered global.

The **DIM** statement is used to specify table and array sizes and has the following syntax:

$$L_n \text{ DIM } variable \ (index), \ Variable \ (row \ index, \ column \ index), \ \ldots$$

The **INPUT** statement is used to process keyboard entries by providing an operator prompt. It has the following syntax:

$$\text{INPUT } \ "operator \ prompt"; \ variable$$

There are many built-in functions in BASIC, as in FORTRAN, that facilitate programming by eliminating cumbersome and tedious coding of commonly used operations. For example, the **PEEK** and **POKE** functions are used to read and write in a memory location. They have the following syntax:

$$\text{PEEK } (integer \ variable)$$
$$\text{POKE } (integer \ variable, \ data \ value)$$

BASIC provides a set of commands that enable source code editing, file operations, and program execution. These include the following:

EDIT *line*

DELETE *line_i, line_j*

LIST *line_i, line_j*

LOAD *filename*

RUN *filename*

SAVE *filename*

The following example program incorporates the main BASIC features.

EXAMPLE 5.4 BASIC Program

```
REM  EXAMPLE PROGRAM
 10  READ (A, B, C)
 20  DATA (3, 5, 9)
 30  LET Y=A*B*C
 40  PRINT A, B, C, "ANSWER IS", Y
 50  LET D = 1
 60  FOR X = 2 TO 20 STEP 2
```

```
 70  LET D = D*X
 80  PRINT D, X
 90  NEXT X
100  DIM LIST (10)
110  FOR I = 0 TO 9
120  READ LIST (I)
130  NEXT I
140  DATA 1, 7, 11, 17, 20, 21, 24, 28, 31, 45
150  GOSUB 200
        ⋮
200  LET J = 1
210  LET ID = 0
220  INPUT "ENTER ID NUMBER", I
230  IF (I=LIST (I)) THEN 280
240  PRINT "INVALID ENTRY"
250  IF (J=3) THEN 290
260  J = J+1
270  GOTO 210
280  LET ID = I
290  RETURN
```

This simple program starts by reading three variables and their defined values. Then it evaluates an arithmetic expression and outputs the result with the **PRINT** statement. Next, a control loop is defined that calculates the product of all even consecutive integers, from 2 through 20, and outputs the intermediate results. Also, an ID table named LIST is defined and initialized using the **DIM** and **DATA** statements, respectively. Finally, a subroutine is invoked that prompts the operator to input his ID number. The **IF** statement is used to determine its validity. An incorrect ID results in an INVALID ENTRY message. If a correct ID is entered, within three attempts, its value is passed to the main program. Otherwise an ID value of 0 is returned.

Pascal

This is a library extension language in which the user can augment the basic set using syntactically consistent functions and subroutines. The statements have a free format, and a semicolon delimiter is used to define statement boundaries. Comments are enclosed with the asterisk symbol, and the end of a program is indicated with a period.

Pascal accommodates a variety of data types, including scalar, structured, and pointer. Scalar data consist of standard integer, real, character, and Boolean variables. In addition, subrange and enumerated data can be user-definable. Structured data include sets, arrays, records, and files. Finally, pointer data are used to define and access linked data structures such as linked lists and binary trees. Arithmetic and relational operators exist for both integer and real variables. Standard functions are defined for integer, real, character, and Boolean variables. The standard integer operators include $+$, $-$, $*$, **DIV**, $>$, $>=$, $<$, $<=$, $=$, and $<>$. Examples of integer variable functions are the absolute value **ABS** (I), the square root **SQR** (I), the truncate **TRUNC** (I), and the roundoff **ROUND** (I). The standard real operators include $+$, $-$, $*$, and $/$, for addition, subtraction, multiplication, and division, respectively. Examples of real variable function types are the trigonometric, exponential, and logarithmic. The **ABS** (R) and **SQRT** (R) are equivalent real variable functions. A character is a member of the ASCII code set and is represented by a single byte. There are four common character functions: the **ORD** (C), which returns the decimal value representation of a character; the **CHR** (I), which performs the inverse **ORD** (C) operation; the **PRED** (C) = **CHR** (**ORD** (C) − 1); and the **SUCC** (C) = **CHR** (**ORD** (C) + 1). Boolean data consist of two constants, **TRUE** and **FALSE**, which are used with the three operators **AND, OR,** and **NOT.** Constants and variables are declared in Pascal using appropriate statements with the following syntax:

$$\textbf{CONST } name = constant;$$

$$\textbf{VAR } name : Data\ type;$$

Pascal is a strongly typed language in the sense that each scalar variable is associated with a single data type, and most operators and functions are defined for a specific data type. The typical operations on a Pascal variable are declaration, value definition, and reference. Arithmetic and Boolean expression can be defined, and their priority and order of operations are consistent with other languages. There are two basic input statements, the **READ** and the **READLN**. The latter advances to the next data line upon completion. These statements have the following syntax:

$$\textbf{READ } (variable_1,\ variable_2,\ .\ .\ .,\ variable_n)$$

$$\textbf{READLN } (variable_1,\ variable_2,\ .\ .\ .,\ variable_n)$$

The data values must conform to the syntax rules and be consistent with the variable type. Similarly, there are two output statements, the **WRITE** and the **WRITELN**, with the following syntax:

$$\textbf{WRITE } (variable_1,\ variable_2,\ .\ .\ .,\ variable_n)$$

$$\textbf{WRITELN } (variable_1,\ variable_2,\ .\ .\ .,\ variable_n)$$

The number of columns allocated per variable is a function of its type. Integer and Boolean variables have ten columns, real variables have twenty columns, and character variables have one column.

An assignment statement is used to evaluate an expression and equate it to a variable using the following syntax:

$$Variable := (expression)$$

Pascal is based on structured programming and has several flow of control statements. The block structure consists of a group of simple statements, with one entry and one exit point, using the following syntax:

$$\textbf{BEGIN}$$

$$Statement_1;$$

$$\vdots$$

$$Statement_n;$$

$$\textbf{END}$$

The conditional branch structure uses **IF** and **CASE** statements with the following syntax:

> **IF** (*expression*) **THEN** (*statement*) ;
>
> **IF** (*expression*) **THEN** (*statement₁*) **ELSE** (*statement₂*) ;
>
> **CASE** (*selection expression*) **OF**
>
> *label₁* : *statement₁*;
>
> ⋮
>
> *labelₙ* : *statementₙ*;
>
> **END**;

The **IF** statement provides a two-way branch, and the **CASE** achieves multiple-branch capability. The **WHILE** and **REPEAT** statements are used for conditional loop execution. **WHILE** does a precheck, and **REPEAT** a postcheck on the conditional expression. They have the following syntax:

> **WHILE** (*expression*) **DO** (*statement₁*, . . ., *statementₙ*)
>
> **REPEAT** (*statement₁*, . . ., *statementₙ*) **UNTIL** (*expression*)

The **FOR** statement provides controlled execution of program loops and uses the following syntax:

> **FOR** (*variable*) := (*initial value*) **TO** (*final value*) **DO** (*statement*)
>
> **FOR** (*variable*) := (*initial value*) **DOWNTO** (*final value*) **DO** (*statement*)

The two variations allow for increasing and decreasing control variables. Unconditional branching can be achieved using the **GOTO** statement (although this is discouraged in Pascal), with the following syntax:

> **LABEL** *value*;
>
> **GOTO** *label*;

First, a **LABEL** value declaration is defined. The **GOTO** specifies the statement label for an unconditional branch operation.

The **TYPE** statement is used to specify the structured and pointer data types. An array contains elements of the same type and can have up to three dimensions. The syntax for array data types is shown below.

> **TYPE** (*type name*) = **ARRAY** [*index*] **OF** *type*;
>
> **TYPE** (*type name*) = **ARRAY** [*index₁*, *index₂*] ; **OF** *type*;
>
> **TYPE** (*type name*) = **ARRAY** [*index₁*, *index₂*, *index₃*] ; **OF** *type*;

A record contains elements of different data types and is specified using the following **TYPE** statement syntax:

> **TYPE** (*record name*) = **RECORD**
>
> *field name₁* : *data type*;
>
> ⋮

> *field name$_n$* : *data type*;
>
> **END**;

The set is a structured data type whose elements are accessed as a unit rather than individually. The following syntax is used to specify a set of elements:

> **TYPE** (*set name*) = **SET OF** *type*;

There are three basic operations that can be performed on sets: union, intersection, and difference.

A file contains elements with identical data types. A file structure permits access to individual elements. This requires a search to locate the specific entry. The syntax for a file structure specification is shown below.

> **TYPE** (*filename*) = **FILE OF** *type*;

A file variable is associated with each file and is used to define the location of a single element window. There are five basic file operations: **RESET** (*filename*), **EOF** (*filename*), **GET** (*filename*), **PUT** (*filename*), **REWRITE** (*filename*). **RESET** and **EOF** set the file variable value to the beginning and end of the file, respectively. **GET** and **PUT** are used for read and write file operations, respectively. **REWRITE** is used to erase the file contents.

Pointer data types use dynamic variables that are referenced indirectly using a pointer. These variables are created and destroyed in the course of program execution. In contrast, static variables are defined for the duration of the executing program. The **TYPE** statement is used to specify pointers with the following syntax:

> **TYPE** (*pointername*) = ↑*type*;

where a variable of type pointername is a pointer of an element of the specified type.

Dynamic variables are created and destroyed using the **NEW** (P) and **DISPOSE** (P) statements, respectively. **NEW** will create a dynamic variable stored in a location specified by pointer P, and the actual location value is designated as P↑. Pointers are the building blocks of linked list and tree data structures.

Pascal supports functions as independent program units. A function is defined using the **FUNCTION** statement. Its actual computation takes place when the function is invoked by the main program. The function statement has the following syntax:

> **FUNCTION** *Name(variable*: *type*): *type*;
>
> **BEGIN**
>
> ⋮
>
> **END**;

A subroutine is defined using the PROCEDURE statement and has the following syntax:

> **PROCEDURE** *Name(variable*: *type*) ;
>
> **BEGIN**

$\vdots$

END;

Procedures do not require type specification since there is no explicit value returned, as is the case with the function. Procedure names need no value assignment within the block statement, as do function names. Finally, a procedure call is a standalone statement, whereas a function call is always a component of a larger expression. The procedure-invoking statement contains the actual parameters that positionally replace the formal parameters within the heading and body of the procedure. A parameter becomes global if it is defined in the main program and can then be accessed, used, or referenced by any part of the program, including functions and procedures.

The following example program serves to illustrate the main Pascal features.

EXAMPLE 5.5

Pascal Program

```
          PROGRAM EXAMPLE (INPUT, OUTPUT);
          LABEL     10;
          CONSTANT  MIN=1, MAX=10;
          TYPE      TABLE = ARRAY [1..10] OF INTEGER;
          VARIABLE  A, B :REAL;
          VARIABLE  C, D :INTEGER;
          PROCEDURE WEEK (VAR DAY: INT);
                    CASE DAY OF
                    6,0 :WRITE('WEEKEND')
                    1 :WRITE('PAYDAY')
                    2,3,4 :WRITE('WEEKDAY')
                    5 :WRITE('FRIDAY')
                    END;
          END;      (*WEEK*)
          FUNCTION  GMEAN (A, B: REAL) :REAL;
                    BEGIN
                    GMEAN:=SQRT(A*B)
                    END; (*GMEAN*)
          BEGIN
       10 READ      (A, B);
          READ      (C, D);
          IF        (C>D) THEN X:=3 ELSE C:=5;
          FOR       Z := MIN TO MAX DO
          BEGIN
                    MEAN:=GMEAN (X, Y);
                    WRITELN (MEAN)
          END;
                    WEEK (C);
          IF        (D=MAX) GOTO 10
          END;
          END.
```

The Pascal program starts with the main header, followed by the **LABEL** declaration statement. Next, the various data descriptions are accomplished using the **CONSTANT, TYPE,** and **VARIABLE** definition and declaration statements. The program declares two real and two integer variables. A procedure is defined to illustrate the use of a case statement, for multiple-branch operation. Next, a function is described to calculate the geometric mean of two real variables. The resident **SQRT** function is used in the evaluating expression. Finally, the main program body is listed and contained within the **BEGIN** and **END** statements. Then it proceeds with a conditional **IF** statement to assign a value to variable x. Next, a control loop is defined to calculate an arithmetic expression a number of times, as specified by the constant MAX. It should be noted that the function GMEAN is a part of the arithmetic expression. The procedure WEEK is invoked to print the day of the week as a function of the variable c. The conditional **IF** statement tests the value of the D variable and either repeats or terminates program execution.

In summary, Pascal is a highly structured language that employs top-down modular design methodology and in which the main program invokes the various procedures to perform specific tasks.

C

The C language was developed by Dennis Ritchie in the early 1970s, and it has evolved into one of the most popular computer languages. C provides the programmer with flexibility and efficiency. It is a general-purpose library extension language and supports structured, modular, and portable programs. Like Pascal, it uses free-format statements that end with a semicolon. Comments are denoted by a slash followed by an asterisk, and the program is contained inside a pair of brackets. The language is case-sensitive, with most keywords typed in lower case. The C language supports scalar, structure, and pointer data types. Scalar types are character, integer, and float. The integer can be qualified as unsigned, short, or long. The float is used to represent real numbers, and the double and long double versions can be used for added precision. The structure types include array, structure, and union. Finally, the pointer is used to access data in structures by performing operations on the address locations of the structures. In fact pointers are the essence of C, and they minimize data movement within the computer memory.

Arithmetic and relational operators exist for both integer and float variables. Boolean data types can be formed using integers, where a value of 0 indicates a false condition and all others indicate a true. Standard functions are defined for all data types. The arithmetic scalar type operations include $+$, $-$, $*$, and $/$, for addition, subtraction, multiplication, and division, respectively. The equals sign is the assignment operator. Relational operators include $>$, $<$, $==$, and $!=$, for greater than, less than, equal to, and not equal to, respectively. The logical operators include &&, ||, and !, for AND, OR, and NOT conditions. Like assembly languages, the C language also supports bitwise operators, such as &, |, ~, and ^ for AND, OR, complement, and exclusive-OR operations, respectively. Left and right bit shifting is also possible, using the $<<$ and $>>$ symbols, respectively.

A character is declared using the **char** keyword. A constant can be declared by either the **const** keyword or the **#define** directive. A variable is declared by specifying its type and then its name. The following samples illustrate the syntax:

> **char** x;
>
> **const float** pi = 3.414;
>
> **#define** value = 7.25;
>
> **int** k;
>
> **long int** speed;

The C language achieves flexibility and performance by relaxing the strongly typed requirements and checks found in Pascal. The basic operations in C are declarations, expressions, and statements. All operators have precedence and direction of association conventions. For example, parentheses have the highest precedence, and the direction of operation within them is from left to right. The equals sign has a low precedence, with a right-to-left direction.

C has three basic input functions: **scanf**, **gets**, and **getchar**. **Scanf** is used to read one or more keyboard inputs. **Gets** is used to read one or more characters—strings—from the keyboard. **Getchar** is used to read a single keyboard character. Each data value must be syntax- and type-compatible. These functions have the following syntax:

> **scanf** (*format*, &*name*) ;
>
> **gets** (*name*) ;
>
> **getchar ();**

An assignment statement is used to evaluate an expression and then equate it to a variable, using the following syntax:

> *variable = expression;*

Although developed prior to structured programming, the C language has the proper statements to implement the basic flow of control statements. The block structure consists of a group of statements, with one entry and one exit point, and has the following syntax:

> {   /* *comments* */
>
> *statement*$_1$;
>
> $\vdots$
>
> *statement*$_n$;   }

The conditional branch structure uses the **if**, **if-else**, or **switch** statements with the following syntax:

> **if** (*expression*)   **if** (*expression*)
>
> *statement*$_1$;   *statement*$_1$;
>
>   **else**
>
>   *statement*$_2$;

The **switch** statement achieves a multiway branch capability, in contrast to the **if**, which provides a two-way branch. The **switch** statement syntax is shown below:

$$\begin{aligned}
&\textbf{switch}\ (expression) \\
&\{\ \textbf{case}\quad constant_1; \\
&\qquad\qquad statement; \\
&\qquad\qquad \textbf{break}; \\
&\qquad\qquad\vdots \\
&\quad\textbf{case}\qquad constant_n; \\
&\qquad\qquad statement; \\
&\qquad\qquad \textbf{break}; \\
&\quad\textbf{default}; \\
&\qquad\qquad statement;\quad \}
\end{aligned}$$

The **while** and **do-while** statements are used for conditional loop execution. The **while** statement does a precheck and the **do-while** does a postcheck on the conditional expression. They use the following syntax:

$$\begin{aligned}
&\textbf{while}\ (expression) &\qquad &\textbf{do} \\
&\{\ statement_1; &\qquad &\{\ statement_1; \\
&\ \vdots &\qquad &\ \vdots \\
&\ statement_n;\ \} &\qquad &\ statement_n; \\
& & &\textbf{while}\ (expression)\quad \}
\end{aligned}$$

The **for** statement provides controlled execution of program loops and has the following syntax:

$$\begin{aligned}
&\textbf{for}\ (expression_1;\ expression_2;\ expression_3) \\
&\quad \{\ statement_1; \\
&\quad\ \ \vdots \\
&\quad\ statement_n;\quad \}
\end{aligned}$$

$Expression_1$ provides the initial count value, $expression_2$ checks the range limit, and $expression_3$ specifies the count modifier.

Unconditional branching can be achieved with the **goto** statement, using the following syntax:

$$\begin{aligned}
&label:\ statement; \\
&\qquad\vdots \\
&\textbf{goto}\ label;
\end{aligned}$$

An array contains elements of the same data type. The array declaration syntax is given below:

$$type\ name\,[size_1]\ldots[size_n];$$

A structure contains elements of different data types. Structures are defined using the following syntax:

$$\textbf{struct } name$$
$$\{ \; type \; member_1;$$
$$\vdots$$
$$type \; member_n; \; \};$$

The union defines a group of elements of different data types but stores only one, in location x, at any given time. The union has the following syntax:

$$\textbf{union } name$$
$$\{ \; type \; member_1;$$
$$\vdots$$
$$type \; member_n; \; \} \; x;$$

A pointer is used to hold the address of any data type or even another pointer, with the following syntax:

$$type \; *name;$$

Pointer notation makes the language powerful and portable. The following are some typical pointer-related operations:

```
int value = 123; /* variable value assignment */
int *pointer; /* pointer definition */
pointer = &value /* pointer assigned address of value */
*pointer; /* contents of address location stored in pointer */
int **ptoptr; /* pointer to pointer definition */
*ptoptr = &pointer; /* ptoptr assigned address of pointer */
```

A file contains elements with identical data types. A file provides a structure for accessing individual elements by searching within it. The C language does not have inherent file management capability. This is provided by the particular operating system. The file declaration syntax is given below:

$$\textbf{FILE } \; *file\_ptr;$$

The **FILE** declaration provides the necessary information on the present system, and file.ptr is a pointer to the **FILE**. The basic file operations are read, write, and append. These can be achieved with the **fopen** function, which has the following syntax:

$$\textbf{FILE } \; *file\_ptr, \; *fopen();$$
$$file\_ptr = \textbf{fopen} \; (filename, \; mode);$$

The *filename* is the actual name of a file. The *mode* specifies the required operation on the file data. To close the file, the **fclose** (*file_ptr*) function is used.

A program written in C consists of the main and one or more functions, which may or may not return a value and which have no hierarchical structure. The program source code is passed through a preprocessor prior to compiling. Its function is to include all required header files, provide macro or data definitions, and provide conditional compiling as needed. The three preprocessor directives are shown below.

```
#include <name>; /* for header file inclusion */
#define name value; /* for macro and data definition */
#ifdef and #endif /* conditional compiling options */
```

The following example provides some insight into the C language.

EXAMPLE 5.6

C Program

```
#include <stdio.h>;
#include <math.h>;
void week (int);
float gmean (float, float);
const int min = 1, max = 10;
int table [10];
main (void)
{ float x, y, yval;
start:  scanf ("%d, %d", &x, &y);
        scanf ("%d, %d", &c, &d);
          if (c > d) x = 3;
          else x = 5;
          for (z = min; z < max; z++)
          { yval = gmean (x, y);
            printf ("mean=", yval); }
          week(n);
          if (d = max) go to start;
        }
void week (int day)
{ switch (day)
{ case 0
  printf (Weekend.\n");
  break;
  case 6
  printf (Weekend.\n");
  break;
  case 1
  printf (Payday.\n");
  break;
  default;
```

```
    printf (Weekday.\n"); }
}
float gmean (float a, float b)
{ float mean;
  mean = sqrt (a*b);
  rtn mean;
}
```

The program starts with two header files, which provide description of the required C library functions. They are followed by function and global declarations. The main function is listed next, which has local declarations, followed by statements and other function calls. The week() and the gmean() functions are called from the main. The week() function does not return any values, while the gmean() returns a computed value. This example performs similar tasks as that of Example 5.5.

In summary, C is a compact and efficient language, with assembly-language features, for flexible and powerful programs.

5.5 SOFTWARE TOOLS

In order to facilitate and streamline the human-machine interface (HMI), a collection of specialized computer programs has been developed. They serve to handle the routine and tedious tasks associated with writing source code, generating object code, executing, and troubleshooting an application program. As a result the programmer can concentrate on the problem, devise an algorithmic solution, and rapidly implement it. These software tools, also called systems software, are coordinated and controlled using an executive program that is better known as the operating system. In addition, there are diagnostic programs available that exercise the hardware and provide a confidence status prior to actual system operation.

Systems Software

An *assembler* program is a software tool that converts symbolic language notation *source code* into a specific-MPU machine-language *object code*. Similarly, a *compiler* is a program that translates high-level language source statements into specific-MPU machine-language object code. The compiler frees the programmer from such chores as register assignment, addressing modes, and machine-language instructions. Compiler designs are based on a two-pass technique, as in the case of an assembler. The first pass operations are target machine–independent. First, a *lexical analysis* is conducted on each statement to ensure correctness and valid meanings of operands, operators, and identifiers. Second, a *syntactic analysis* is performed to examine the structural relationships among the statements. Third, a symbol table is generated. The second pass performs target MPU–dependent code optimization, memory allocation, and machine object-code generation. The compiler can generate object code for either the host or a specific target MPU. Some compilers provide an optional assembly-code generation capability.

An *interpreter* translates and executes source statements one at a time. Interpreters provide interaction between the user and the MPU. High-level languages are designed to provide a buffer between the user application and the MPU hardware resources.

Prior to any MPU operation, it is necessary to load programs into the MPU memory. This task is accomplished with a *loader* program. A *bootstrap loader* is a small program, permanently stored in memory, that transfers the loader into memory. A loader program is capable of storing byte-size instructions and data into specific memory addresses, performing error detection, and verifying the number of byte transfers. There are three types of loaders available: absolute, relocatable, and linking. An *absolute loader* is capable of loading an object program into a fixed area in memory. The *relocatable loader* is capable of loading an object program anywhere in memory. This is done by starting at a relative location and calculating address label offsets. The *linking loader* consists of two programs, a linker and a relocatable loader. The *linker* is used to bind two or more independent program modules into one that is suitable for loading. This binding is done by identifying and resolving external reference labels for each program.

An *editor* program is used to create, modify, or correct source program statements. The editor treats a source program as lines of text, organized into a file, that can be manipulated with various commands. The text-oriented commands include Search, Insert, Delete, Append, Revise, Move, and Renumber. The file-oriented commands include Create, Destroy, Copy, Save, and Rename. The I/O-oriented commands include Read, Write, Display, and Print. The *Search* command locates a specified text entry, which becomes the reference point for inserting, appending, deleting, or revising one or more lines of source code. The *Move text* command is used to transfer one or more lines of source code to another location within the file. The *Renumber* command is used to streamline the text after an edit session. The *Create* command is used to define a new source code file. The *Destroy* command purges a specified file from memory. The *Copy* command duplicates a designated file. The *Save* command stores a source file in a nonvolatile storage medium. The *Rename* command assigns a new name to a given source file. The I/O *Read* command transfers a file from nonvolatile storage to memory for editing. The *Write* command transfers a file to a nonvolatile storage device. The *Display* command allows the user to view a file on a display device. The *Print* command enables the user to make a hard copy of a specific file. An edited source code file is used as input to a compiler or assembler program. The resulting object code is linked with any library routines, available as part of the systems software, that are referenced by the application program. The library routines provide arithmetic, trigonometric, exponential, and other common mathematical functions, in object code form, that have been optimized for speed and accuracy.

A new program is likely to contain errors that can be detected, located, and corrected. A *debugger* program enables the user to perform controlled program execution. Typical debugger commands include Start, Stop, Set BreakP, Reset BreakP, Step, Examine, Modify, Search, and Move. These commands allow for single- or multiple-instruction execution, conditional program halt, MPU register, and memory read and write operations. Once a program is debugged and tested, it is stored in nonvolatile memory for later use. The object code development may or may not take place on the host MPU. If it does not, a target MPU simulator may be needed to verify program correctness.

A *simulator* program has the ability to duplicate a functional representation of the target MPU within the host. An *emulator* is a combination of hardware and software that achieves real-time simulation of the target MPU.

Figure 5.32 illustrates a typical application software development process.

Operating Systems

The executive is a program that integrates all the system software to create an operating system. As such it controls and coordinates MPU, memory, and I/O to provide a uniform and consistent interface between the user and the MPU. A typical operating system consists of a small program called the *kernel,* which manages the hardware and software resources. Its main functions are program control, MPU management, memory allocation, file operations, I/O control, and error handling. The operating system defines an environment for program development, execution, and modification. It establishes a concise set of procedures for accessing the various system resources.

A disk operating system (DOS), as the name implies, resides on a disk. It is loaded into memory at start-up time by a bootstrap loader. It is made up of three modules: the command monitor, the kernel, and the I/O handler. Figure 5.33 illustrates a simple disk operating system environment. The *command monitor* provides an interactive user interface for system control and status. It interprets and relays the high-level request to the kernel, via a subroutine call. The kernel responds by invoking the necessary software module to satisfy the request. The monitor commands include Enter, Cancel, Abort, Pause, and Reset. *Enter* identifies a text entry as a system command. *Cancel* deletes the text entry. *Abort* halts the execution of the last system com-

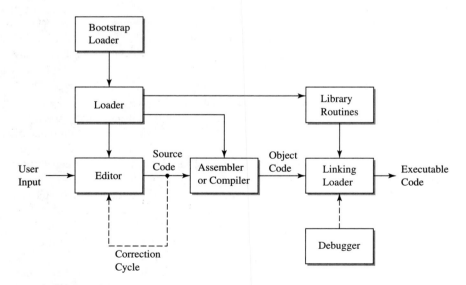

FIGURE 5.32
Software development process.

mand. *Pause* causes temporary interruption of the MPU program execution. *Reset* is used to initialize the operating system.

The flow of control goes from the application program to the kernel, via the command monitor. The kernel performs basic decisions, prior to invoking a software module, and provides proper hardware control via the I/O handler.

There are two types of system commands, resident and nonresident. Resident commands consist of frequent system calls and are loaded into memory at start-up. Nonresident commands consist of infrequent system calls and remain on disk. They are loaded into a designated memory area, upon request, in order to optimize memory use. Source code is stored as text files, and object code as binary or hexadecimal files.

The operating system also supports file management functions. These include editing, formatting, and transfer operations. A file is identified by a name formed by alphanumeric characters. A linked list structure is used to construct the file allocation table (FAT), which defines a cluster of blocks that make up a file. The table resides on track zero of a disk, and each block is associated with a sector number. Usually a filename has up to eight characters, with an optional three-character extension name following after a period. An asterisk is used to denote any filename. A question mark is used to denote any character within a name. These symbols serve to expedite certain file management operations.

Typical resident commands include Dir, Copy, Rename, Compare, Type, Print, and Erase. *Dir* displays a list of all resident files on a specified disk. A directory can be either flat or hierarchical. A hierarchical directory requires that a defined path be followed to locate a specific file. A binary tree structure is used as the basis for constructing a hierarchical directory. *Copy* is used to make a duplicate of a given file. *Rename* is used to assign a different name to a specific file. *Compare* is used to determine if two files contain identical data. *Type* is used to display the contents of a file on a cathode ray tube (CRT) screen. *Print* is used to output the

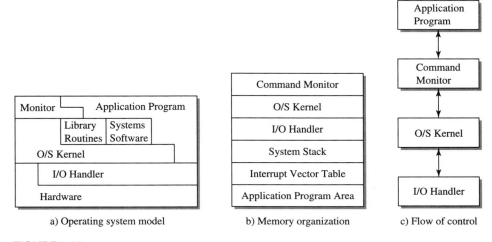

a) Operating system model b) Memory organization c) Flow of control

FIGURE 5.33
Disk operating system definitions.

contents of a file to a hardcopy device, such as a printer. *Erase* is used to delete a specific file-name from the directory file, effectively eliminating it.

Nonresident commands include Format, Dcopy, and Dcomp. *Format* is used to prepare disks so that they are compatible with the existing operating system file structure. *Dcopy* is used to duplicate the contents of the entire disk. *Dcomp* is used to compare the contents of two disks.

There are three basic file types: random access, linear list, and linked list. *Random access files* are referenced via a file directory table. *Linear list files* are stored in a contiguous memory area. *Linked list files* are sequentially indexed using pointers. Table 5.14 compares the access, overhead, and growth parameters of the three file types.

Memory can be partitioned into fixed regions in which only one program can reside at a given time. In addition, memory allocation can be either *static,* prior to program execution, or *dynamic,* during program execution. The allocation units can be either variable in size, called *segments,* or *pages* of fixed size. Three techniques are common for efficient memory utilization: overlay, swapping, and chaining. *Overlay* is used to define a common memory area for subroutine loading and execution, as required by the main program. *Swapping* is used to define a common memory space for storing the current executing program, in the case of multiple-program environments. Swapping can also be used to implement a *virtual memory* model. As such, data transfers are made from a large, slower memory to a small, faster memory on a demand basis. *Chaining* is used to define a common memory region in order to store the current executing module of a large program. Memory protection features ensure that application programs do not expand beyond operating system boundaries, thus "crashing" the system.

The I/O handler processes interrupts and contains hardware-dependent routines for external data transfers. These routines are also known as *drivers,* and they support either byte-oriented or block-oriented interfaces. They also initialize devices and provide both direct and buffered I/O capabilities. Buffered I/O is used to accommodate slower peripheral devices such as printers. It is also known as *spooling,* which stands for simultaneous peripheral operations on-line.

Operating systems come in designs of varying complexity to support multiple programs, multiple users, multiple MPUs, and even multiple MCUs. The simplest operating system supports a single-program environment and is rather inefficient in terms of resource management. A *batch-type operating system* can execute multiple programs sequentially, using a FIFO mechanism to store incoming programs. A *multiprogramming operating system* supports concurrent execution of several independent programs, by timesharing resource allocation. MPU scheduling is accomplished using equal-priority time slices. Thus, each program executes in a round-robin fashion for a fixed time interval. The time intervals may or may not be of equal length. A *multiprocessing operating system* supports simultaneous program exe-

TABLE 5.14
File type comparison

Type	Access	Overhead	Growth
Random	Fastest	Low	Easier
Linear	Faster	Lowest	Easy
Linked	Fast	Lower	Easiest

cutions on multiple MPUs within the same MCU, by judicious resource allocation. A *distributed operating system* supports simultaneous program execution on multiple MCUs in a coordinated fashion.

A *real-time operating system* supports a dedicated single-program environment that is external event–driven. This requires scheduling by priority of the various independent modules, known as *tasks*. A program consists of several tasks, independent of each other and ready to execute on demand. The real-time kernel provides task synchronization, task communication, priority scheduling, interrupt processing, memory allocation, and error handling. The object of a real-time operating system is to provide a predictable time response, from the occurrence of an external event to the completion of the associated task, such that the worst-case value falls within the specified limit. A real-time system supports a *multitasking environment,* in the sense that several tasks are capable of operating concurrently, with each performing a unique function. *Task synchronization* is a technique for coordinating the execution of two or more tasks, where information exchange or event response actions are required. *Task-scheduling mechanisms* ensure the timely execution of higher-priority tasks, thus providing real-time response. Interrupt processing links external events to corresponding task executions. Memory allocation mechanisms provide dynamic memory sharing among the various tasks on a demand basis. Error handling detects both hardware failures and software-related faults.

PROBLEMS

5.1 Develop a design-level flowchart that either converts °C to °F or vice-versa, consistent with the input parameters #, °C, °F, and independent of input order.

5.2 Develop a programming-level flowchart for Table 5.12.

5.3 Develop a PDL structured diagram for a binary tree search algorithm.

5.4 Develop a PDL structured diagram for an exchange sort algorithm.

5.5 Write an assembly-language program that finds the average grade in a class of twenty students. Hint: Use the ADD A and DIV A instructions.

5.6 Write a FORTRAN subroutine that compares two equal-size arrays, HOST and TARGET, and stores the resulting matches in a third array named LIKE. Also, calculate the total number of matches.

5.7 Write a FORTRAN program to implement the linear list search algorithm.

5.8 Write a BASIC program that calculates the number of payments for a loan, using the following formula:

$$N = [\log (M / (M - P * I)) / (\log I + 1)]$$

Where P is the loan amount, M is the monthly payment, and I is the annual interest rate.

5.9 Write a BASIC program that implements the binary list search algorithm.

5.10 Write a Pascal procedure that implements the linked list insert algorithm.

5.11 Write a Pascal procedure that implements the linked list delete algorithm.

5.12 Write a Pascal program that implements the selection sort algorithm.

5.13 Write a C program that implements the binary tree search algorithm.

5.14 Write a C program that implements the exchange sort algorithm.

5.15 Write a C program that implements the design flowchart of Problem 5.1.

REFERENCES

Dahmke, M. *Microprocessor Operating Systems.* New York: McGraw-Hill, 1982.

Gear, C. W. *Applications and Algorithms in Science and Engineering.* Chicago: SRA, 1978.

Kernighan, Brian, and Dennis Ritchie. *The C Programming Language.* 2d ed. Englewood Cliffs, NJ: Prentice Hall, 1988.

Koffman, E. B., and F. L. Friedman. *Problem Solving and Structured Programming in BASIC.* Reading, MA: Addison-Wesley, 1979.

Scheider G. M., Weingert S. N., Pearlman D. M. *An Introduction to Programming and Program Solving in PASCAL.* New York: John Wiley, 1978.

Tanenbaum, Andrew S. *Operating Systems Design and Implementation.* Englewood Cliffs, NJ: Prentice Hall, 1987.

Trembley, J. P., and P. J. Sorenson. *Introduction to Data Structures and Algorithms.* New York: McGraw-Hill, 1976.

Zwass, V. *Introduction to Computer Science.* New York: H & R, 1981.

———. *Programming in FORTRAN.* New York: H & R, 1981.

6

MICROPROCESSOR INTERFACE

An MPU combined with memory and I/O capability is a simple MCU. The system bus provides a well-defined boundary between the MPU and each external device to perform controlled data transfers. A typical MCU has a set of interface modules necessary to support a variety of general-purpose applications. These modules are optimized for system throughput and contain a system bus interface. Their primary function is to relax the MPU software requirements by performing detailed functions in hardware. The modules can be configured by the MPU for different modes of operation, by presetting their internal control registers. This results in higher system throughput and lower software complexity. However, this inherent programmable flexibility can contribute to program overhead if multiple modes are required within the same application. The basic system support modules associated with an MPU provide parallel interface, serial interface, timing, and interrupt control functions. In addition, sophisticated interface modules exist that provide peripheral device control. These include floppy disk drive and CRT display controllers. These devices can also require the use of dedicated direct memory access (DMA) controller modules to support the high data rate transfers.

Figure 6.1 is a typical MCU system block diagram that presents the above support modules. The system bus consists of address, data, and control signals. The RAM is used by the MPU to access and process stored data, load data from an external device, and buffer data to an external device. The ROM provides quick access to stored fixed data, such as look-up tables, and to application or systems programs. The parallel I/O interface enables byte- and word-oriented devices, such as keyboards and displays, to perform data transfer operations with the MPU. Similarly, the serial I/O interface provides MPU compatibility with bit stream–oriented devices for communicating with remote equipment. The timer provides an integrated method for generating device clocks, programmable delays, and system interrupts. The interrupt controller provides an interface between the MPU and all external devices, by setting priorities and generating address vectors. The floppy disk controller interfaces the disk drive with the system bus, to provide data storage. The CRT controller accepts ASCII data files, or keyboard entries,

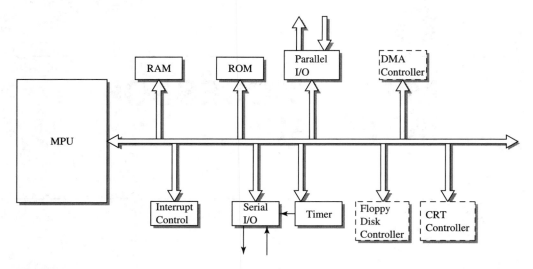

FIGURE 6.1
Typical microcomputer block diagram.

and displays them on a screen. The DMA controller enables high-speed block data transfers to and from disk, to enhance performance.

The objectives of this chapter are as follows: (1) to define the MPU modes of operation, (2) to explain the main interface logic functions, (3) to cover serial interface device operation, (4) to discuss parallel interface device operation, and (5) to cover the floppy disk and CRT peripheral device controllers.

6.1 MODES OF OPERATION

MPU operation modes can be divided into five types: internal, programmed I/O, polled I/O, interrupt I/O, and DMA.

Internal operation refers to the MPU execution of arithmetic and logic, program control, and memory transfer instructions. Since the main memory access time is closely matched to the MPU cycle, there is no appreciable loss in throughput when executing memory reference instructions.

Programmed I/O is used to provide data transfers between the MPU and an external device. This is achieved by setting up a test-and-wait loop. The loop continually reads the device status to determine its ability to perform a synchronized data exchange. This technique results in the inefficient use of MPU time and is therefore of limited use for systems with a single external device. Figure 6.2 illustrates the basic programmed I/O method in a high-level flowchart.

Polled I/O is an improvement over programmed I/O and can be extended to several external devices. The MPU performs periodic sampling of each device status, using a test-and-skip loop, to determine its readiness to perform data exchange. This approach makes better use

FIGURE 6.2
Programmed I/O operation block diagram.

of the MPU by spending minimal time checking each device status. Figure 6.3 shows a typical polled I/O software block diagram. In contrast to programmed I/O, this method uses a timer to determine the external device sampling period, T. Then it systematically queries each device, by a status read and test operation, to determine if a data transfer is required. As such it eliminates time-consuming test-and-wait loops that hinder MPU performance.

Interrupt I/O is associated with a break in the normal internal mode of operation by an external request. The requesting device causes the execution of an associated routine, and upon completion the MPU resumes its normal operation. The particular device makes asynchronous requests to the MPU, signaling its readiness for data transfer. In response the MPU acknowledges the request and saves the current state in the stack. Next, it processes the request by invoking the proper routine. At completion it restores the original MPU state, by popping the stack, and resumes normal execution. Interrupt I/O makes the best use of MPU time by halting operation only when actual data transfers are needed.

Multiple interrupt requests can also be supported. This is accomplished by a combination of techniques such as software-controlled blocking or masking, priority resolution, vector table usage, and interrupt queueing. Interrupt *masking* is a way of selectively enabling individual interrupts such that only one is processed at a time. *Priority resolution* enables a higher-urgency interrupt to preempt a lower one, thus expediting the MPU response time. The result is interrupt nesting using the system stack. A *vector table* eliminates the MPU's need to poll each device status, in response to an interrupt request, to pinpoint the source. Instead, the device provides a unique address on the data bus that is used by the MPU to invoke the proper routine, via a vector table look-up process. In the case of several interrupts, a unique routine is written for each one. However, as the number of interrupts grows, this solution may create a bottleneck and become impractical. A better solution would be to use a common interrupt handler routine that stores the device status and message in a FIFO buffer. Then, an input message handler routine

FIGURE 6.3
Polled I/O sequence block diagram.

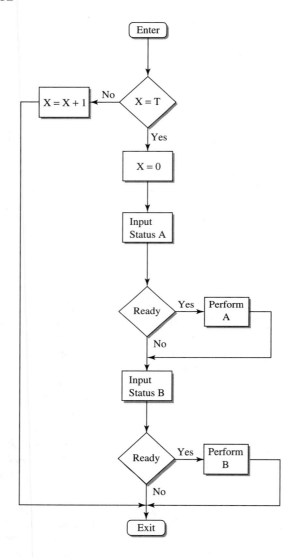

processes the FIFO buffer contents, between interrupts, to speed operation. This scheme as-signs equal priority to all interrupt requests. External interrupt requests occur at random inter-vals, although it is possible to implement periodic interrupts using a timer. Figure 6.4 illustrates the various interrupt I/O techniques discussed above.

The interrupt routine of Figure 6.4a represents a generalized approach to MPU interrupts. First, the current MPU state is saved in the stack. Next, all other interrupt requests are disabled, by appropriate control of the mask register. Then, the interrupt source is determined, either by device polling or via a vector table. The corresponding interrupt service routine is invoked and executed to satisfy the request. Upon completion, the MPU state is restored and the other inter-rupts are enabled prior to exiting the routine.

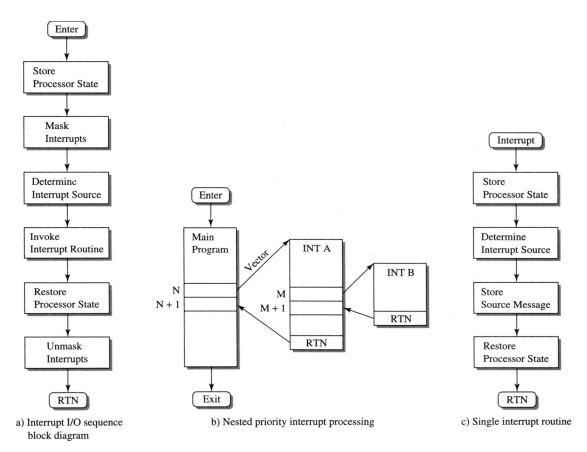

a) Interrupt I/O sequence
block diagram

b) Nested priority interrupt processing

c) Single interrupt routine

FIGURE 6.4
Interrupt I/O methods.

Figure 6.4b illustrates the use of interrupt nesting to handle multiple priority interrupts occurring at about the same time. Interrupt masking can be used to disable equal-priority interrupts. Masking of unequal-priority interrupts, however, can result in the delay of higher-priority requests; therefore, the handler does not provide masking, which makes lower-priority interrupt preempting possible. The system stack is used to accommodate multiple interrupt routine nesting capability so that a graceful return to the normal program execution is possible.

Figure 6.4c shows a generalized routine that handles multiple interrupts on a FIFO basis. First, the MPU state is saved in the stack. Then the requesting device is determined, usually by polling. Next, its status and output data register contents are transferred into the FIFO buffer for eventual processing. Finally, the processor state is restored, from the stack, and normal execution resumes.

DMA I/O is a technique that isolates the MPU from the system bus and allows an external device to perform high-speed data transfers directly to and from memory. This is an efficient method for block-oriented I/O devices, such as disk controllers, to achieve transfer rates close to their throughput. In this mode the device requests bus control from the MPU. In response the MPU yields control and provides an acknowledge signal to the device. In turn the device generates the required address, data, and control signals to perform block data transfers. Upon completion the device notifies the MPU and returns control of the bus. The DMA device is usually programmed by the MPU, prior to the actual transfer, with specific information such as source address, destination address, and block data size. A DMA controller may be a standalone module or integrated into the device. A variation of this technique, known as *cycle stealing,* achieves transparent data transfers between a device and memory. This is accomplished by periodically interrupting the MPU to transfer a single word. Cycle stealing is used in noncritical transfer time applications and results in a slight reduction of MPU throughput. In time-critical data transfer applications, DMA block transfers are essential to overcome the initial setup latency.

Figure 6.5 is a typical DMA operation block diagram. Initially, the MPU under program control sets up the DMA controller command and data registers. This configures the transfer mode, direction, source, destination, and block size. When the device is ready to perform a block transfer, it notifies the DMA controller by raising its *request* control signal. In response the controller raises its *bus request* signal to the MPU. The MPU responds by raising its *bus grant* signal, and the controller takes command of the system bus. Next, the controller raises its *acknowledge* signal to the device signifying the start of a DMA cycle. During each data word transfer, the controller increments a counter and pulses its acknowledge signal. Upon block transfer completion, the device lowers its request signal. In turn, the controller lowers its bus request signal to the MPU, which lowers its bus grant signal. The DMA controller lowers its acknowledge signal to the device, and the cycle is completed.

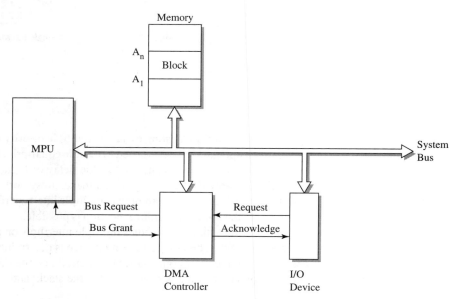

FIGURE 6.5
DMA operation block diagram.

6.2 INTERFACE LOGIC FUNCTIONS

The MPU and the external I/O devices are usually incompatible because of differences in word size, speed, protocol, data format, and control. In order to achieve compatibility, additional logic may be required along with specialized I/O routines. To relieve the MPU of this burden, a variety of specialized LSI modules have been developed that accept high-level commands and provide efficient, hardware-based interface solutions.

The basic peripheral device interface (PDI) module provides data buffering, address and command decoding, and timing and control functions. Buffering synchronizes data transfers between the MPU and a device. Address decoding selects a specific I/O device under program control. Command decoding selects the data transfer mode. Finally, timing and control coordinate the functions required to complete the transfer sequence. Figure 6.6 illustrates the internal architecture of a typical PDI module. The bidirectional data buffer provides a suitable interface to the MPU data bus. The address and control logic decodes the address bus lines that activate the device via software and selects and coordinates I/O operations with the MPU. It also contains a command register to hold the programmed configuration mode and supports interrupt operation. The status register provides the current device condition, which may be read by the MPU for programmed or polled I/O operation. The input and output data registers provide buffering and format conversion, to achieve peripheral compatibility. The timing and control section is used to coordinate the internal bus operation, provide proper protocol, and synchronize data transfers.

The programmable timer is a versatile module used to support a variety of time-related functions associated with the MPU. A typical timer architecture (shown in Figure 6.7) resembles a simplified version of a PDI module. The MPU interface consists of I/O data buffers, address bus decoders, and the required control logic to access and configure the device. An internal bus connects the status register and the programmable counters so that they are accessible by the MPU.

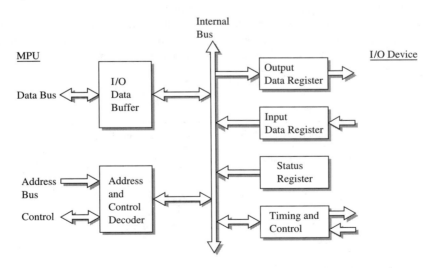

FIGURE 6.6
Typical peripheral device interface module block diagram.

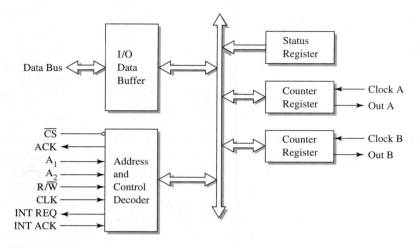

FIGURE 6.7
Programmable timer block diagram.

The control logic uses the chip select ($\overline{\text{CS}}$) and acknowledge control lines for system bus handshake prior to any data exchange. The $\overline{\text{CS}}$ signal is derived by a base address decoder that provides a reliable timer access, via software control. The A_1 and A_2 address lines are used to select one of the four internal registers. The Read/Write ($R/\overline{W}$) input specifies the type of register operation performed by the MPU. The interrupt request and acknowledge control signals support interrupt I/O capability. The counters can operate either with the system clock or by using an independent external clock signal.

The command register is a part of the control decoder and is used to store the mode of operation for each counter. The status register contains the internal state of the timer. The built-in register holds the initial count value to be loaded in the counter. Table 6.1 lists the typical timer command and status register bit definitions. The command register format defines each timer mode

TABLE 6.1
Programmable timer register definitions

Bit Number	Command Register Bit Definition	Status Register Bit Definition
0	Counter A EN/$\overline{\text{DIS}}$	Counter A state
1	Output SQUARE/$\overline{\text{PULSE}}$	Zero count
2	Cycle CONT/$\overline{\text{SINGLE}}$	Cycle mode
3	Clock INT/$\overline{\text{EXT}}$	Clock source
4	Counter B EN/$\overline{\text{DIS}}$	Counter B state
5	Output SQUARE/$\overline{\text{PULSE}}$	Zero count
6	Cycle CONT/$\overline{\text{SINGLE}}$	Cycle mode
7	Clock INT/$\overline{\text{EXT}}$	Clock source

using four bits per counter. One bit is used for count control by gating the clock source to each counter. The remaining three bits are used to define eight possible modes of operation for each counter section. The output control bit selects either a square wave or a pulse-type signal. The pulse signal causes the timer module to generate an interrupt signal. The cycle control bit selects either single or continuous mode of operation. In the single mode, the initial count value is loaded into the counter and a countdown sequence is performed once. In the continuous mode, the initial count value is loaded at zero count and the sequence is repeated. The clock-select bit seven picks either the internal or an external source clock signal. The status register reflects the state of the command register, so that the MPU can verify the programmed configuration. The zero-count status bit five is set when the zero count value is detected in a specific counter.

The eight possible configuration modes are summarized in Table 6.2. Timer applications are limited only by the programmer's imagination. Modes 0 and 4 are used in conjunction with a suitable initial count value to generate a programmable data rate clock source. Modes 1 and 5 are used to provide a periodic interrupt capability to the MPU for the polled I/O mode of operation. Mode 2 can be used for time interval measurements under software control. Mode 6 can be used to implement an event counter, under software control, using an external clock to keep track of each event occurrence. Modes 3 and 7 can be used to generate programmable time delay intervals for interrupting the MPU. Modes 1 and 5 can also be used to implement a watchdog timer under software control. In this application, one routine presets the count value and starts the countdown. Meanwhile a second routine, under normal execution, presets the counter to its initial value, preventing an interrupt condition. However, if the second routine execution is delayed past the countdown interval, an interrupt occurs.

An interrupt controller module serves to coordinate all interrupt calls to the MPU. It accomplishes this by resolving priorities and providing unique vector addresses to minimize latency and enhance throughput. Figure 6.8 is a typical interrupt controller functional block diagram. Its MPU interface is similar to that of the programmable timer. The MPU configures the mask and mode registers during initialization. It can also verify their contents by performing read operations. The mask register is used to selectively inhibit one or more external events from causing an interrupt request. The mode register is used to configure the priority logic to a fixed, rotating, or program-controlled priority sequence. The highest-priority active interrupt becomes the vector table pointer that generates the MPU interrupt service routine vector address.

The interrupt sequence begins with an external event activating the corresponding bit in the interrupt register. If its associated mask bit is not set, and no higher priority request is in

TABLE 6.2
Timer configuration modes

Mode	Description
0	Periodic square wave internal clock
1	Periodic pulse interrupt internal clock
2	Single square wave internal clock
3	Single pulse interrupt internal clock
4	Periodic square wave external clock
5	Periodic pulse interrupt external clock
6	Single square wave external clock
7	Single pulse interrupt external clock

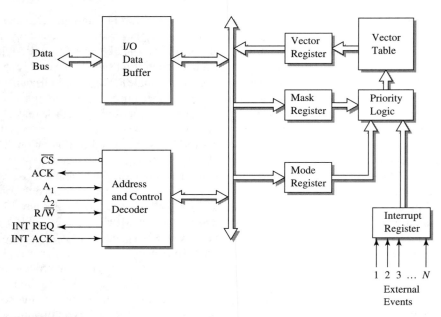

FIGURE 6.8
Interrupt controller block diagram.

progress, the priority logic generates a pointer to the vector table and activates the MPU interrupt request line. When the MPU responds with its acknowledge signal, the controller places a vector number on the data bus, which is used to invoke the corresponding interrupt service routine. Upon completion of the service routine, the controller is commanded to reset the initial interrupt condition. Nested interrupts result if a higher-priority request occurs during an ongoing interrupt service routine. Rotating priority service is suitable for equal-priority interrupt requests, in a round-robin fashion. Program-controlled priority service provides dynamic reordering for each device's relative urgency of request.

6.3 SERIAL INTERFACE

Serial information exchanges use a single data path between the MPU and the peripheral device. As such, data transfers occur one bit at a time, resulting in reduced throughput. Also, the need for data format conversion results in complex designs with built-in synchronization and error-detection features. The two basic data transfer methods are the asynchronous and the synchronous. Asynchronous data transfers occur on a character-by-character basis. The transmitter wraps each character with framing bits so that it is reliably detected by the receiver. Synchronous data transfers occur in character blocks. Each block is preceded by one or two framing or Sync characters. Figure 6.9 is a serial I/O interface module block diagram.

The serial I/O interface module is better known as a universal synchronous asynchronous receiver transmitter (USART). It has a standard MPU interface section for uniform and consistent system bus exchanges. The serial data out path consists of a transmit data buffer and a

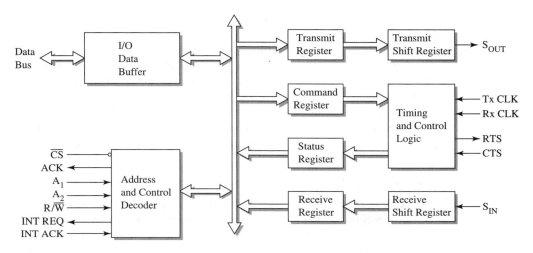

FIGURE 6.9
Serial transmitter receiver block diagram.

parallel-load shift register. Similarly, the serial data in path consists of a shift register and a receive data buffer. The command and status registers are used for configuration control and device monitoring. The timing and control logic coordinates and sequences the external device I/O operations.

The details of module operation are best explained using the command and status register bit definitions listed in Table 6.3. The command register bit 0 controls the request to send (RTS) signal to notify the external device that output data are available. Bit 1 is used to enable the module's interrupt logic. Bit 2 is used to define the number of Stop bits per character, for asynchronous mode, or the number of Sync characters per block, for synchronous mode. Bit 3 is used to specify either odd or even parity generation and detection for each transmitted character. Bits 4 and 5 define the number of data bits used to represent a character. Bits 6 and 7 are used to specify one of four possible modes of operation.

TABLE 6.3
Serial transmitter/receiver register definitions

	Command Register Bit	Status Register Bit
Bit Number	Definition	Definition
0	RTS ENABLE/$\overline{\text{DISABLE}}$	CTS SET/$\overline{\text{RESET}}$
1	INT ENABLE/$\overline{\text{DISABLE}}$	Sync Detect
2	Stop bits (Sync chars) ONE/$\overline{\text{TWO}}$	Tx Shift register empty
3	Parity select EVEN/$\overline{\text{ODD}}$	Tx Ready
4	Data bits (5, 4): 00, 01, 10, 11	Rx Ready
5	5, 6, 7, 8	Frame error
6	Mode bits (7, 6): 00, 01, 10, 11	Parity error
7	ASYNC, ISO, SYNC, SYNC SEARCH	Overrun error

The status register bit 0 indicates the state of the clear to send (CTS) input control signal. Bit 1, when set, indicates synchronous mode Sync character match completed. Bit 2 is set to indicate that the transmitter shift register is empty. Bit 3 is set to indicate that the transmitter buffer register contents have been transferred to the shift register. Bit 4 is used to generate an interrupt request when the receiver shift register contents have been transferred to the receiver buffer register. Bit 5 is set to indicate that the asynchronous character is missing a Stop bit. Bit 6 is used to indicate that there is a parity mismatch between the received character and the character specified by command register bit 3. Bit 7 is set to indicate that the MPU did not read the previous character in time; hence it was overwritten by the current character.

Asynchronous Operation

This mode of operation uses individual data characters preceded by a Start bit and followed by one or more Stop bits to maintain character-level synchronization. Figure 6.10 illustrates a typical asynchronous data transfer format. The *Start bit* is defined by a *Mark-* to *Space*-level transition and serves to alert the receiver that a data character is pending. The data bits following the Start bit are equally spaced and conform to the specified character length. A proper parity bit is added after the last data bit and is used by the receiver to detect any transmission errors. The *Stop bit* indicates the end of a character. It also compensates for transmitter and receiver clock variations by providing an idle time interval.

The MPU configures the serial interface module via the command register and loads data into the transmitter buffer register. The module adds a Start bit, inserts a parity bit, and appends the programmed number of Stop bits. The composite character is then shifted out at a rate equal to the transmit clock signal. The RTS/CTS handshake signals provide character transmission control between the module and the external device. As each character is transferred from the transmit buffer to the shift register, the Tx Ready bit is set in the status register, causing an interrupt request to the MPU. When the last character is flushed out of the transmit shift register, the Tx Empty bit is set in the status register to be read by the MPU.

Similarly, when the receiver Start bit detection logic senses the Mark- to Space-level transition, it synchronizes its clock with the event and generates a periodic timing signal to sample the bit's midcell position. If its state is still a Space, it continues to sample the incoming data bits at midcell; otherwise, the detection logic is reset. Next, the parity bit is sampled and checked for validity. When the Stop bit is detected, the character data bits are transferred to the receiver buffer register and the Rx Ready bit is set in the status register, causing an interrupt re-

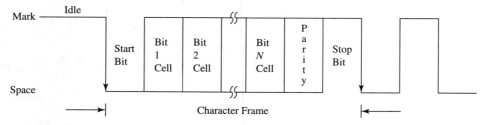

FIGURE 6.10
Asynchronous mode character format.

quest to the MPU. This sequence of events is repeated for each new incoming character. If the receiver sampling clock is sixteen times the data rate, bit sampling occurs within $\pm\frac{1}{16}$ or $\pm6.25\%$ of midcell position. The receiver clock rate is always greater than the data rate.

Isochronous transmission is identical to asynchronous, with the exception that data and clock rates are equal. Thus, the transmit and receive clocks must be synchronized for reliable operation. This can be accomplished by phase-locking the receive clock to the incoming data bit stream. The term *baud* is defined as the smallest signaling time interval. Hence, if the bit cell is 10 ms, then the corresponding baud equals 1 over 10 ms, or 100 baud. Character time equals the bit cell interval times the number of bits per character. Thus, if a character is made up of seven data bits, one Start, one parity, and one Stop, then the character time equals 10×10 ms, or 100 ms. This translates to a signaling rate of 10 characters per second (cps). The information transfer rate is defined as the number of data bits per character times the signaling rate, or 7 bits/char $\times$ 10 cps = 70 bits per second (bps). Thus, a 100 baud results in a signaling rate of 70 bps, achieving 70% transfer efficiency.

Synchronous Operation

This mode of operation groups characters in blocks. To maintain synchronization, one or two Sync characters are inserted at the beginning of each block. These characters can be either built-in or loaded from the MPU for added flexibility. The command register is used to specify either one or two Sync characters, parity, and data length. The Sync characters are inserted and transmitted automatically when the transmit buffer register is empty.

Figure 6.11 illustrates a typical synchronous data transfer format. Once the RTS/CTS handshake is satisfied, the transmitter will send out Sync characters until the MPU provides the actual formatted data block. If the interrupt bit is set in the command register, the Tx Ready status bit will generate an interrupt request to the MPU for a new data output character. The receiver is set initially in the synchronous search mode so that it will look for incoming Sync characters. In this mode each received data character is compared to the stored Sync character(s) until a match occurs. As a result, the Sync Detect bit is set in the status register, and an interrupt request is generated. In response the MPU programs the receiver for normal synchronous mode of operation. In this mode the receiver transfers each incoming character into the receive buffer register and provides parity and overrun status. Sync character detection is still available in this mode, but it occurs only at each block frame to accommodate the Tx Empty status. Also, the Sync Detect bit is updated to

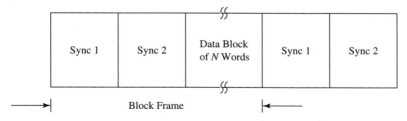

FIGURE 6.11
Synchronous mode character format.

reflect current status, but no interrupt is generated and the Sync characters are discarded by the receiver.

In synchronous mode the clock and data rates are equal. This requires that the transmit and receive clocks be phase-locked in order to achieve successful data transfers. The receiver timing logic usually contains a phase-lock loop circuit that uses the incoming bit stream for clock synchronization. In contrast, a typical asynchronous mode character has ten bits, seven of which are data, and a synchronous mode character has eight, one of which is for parity. Also, the synchronous mode requires at least one Sync character per block. Thus, it takes $10 \times N$ bits to transfer N characters asynchronously and $8 \times N + S$ bits to transfer N characters synchronously, where S is the number of Sync characters per block. Hence, the break-even point for data transfer efficiency becomes four and eight characters for one and two Sync characters, respectively. Usually, low-speed, character-oriented I/O devices use the asynchronous mode, while high-speed, block-oriented devices use synchronous instead.

Parity is used in both modes by adding an extra bit to detect a single-bit transmission error. Even parity is formed when the sum of all data bits, including a parity bit, is an even number. Similarly, odd parity is formed when the sum is an odd number. The transmitter has a parity generator that sums the data bits and sets the parity bit value to produce consistent output characters. For example, a seven-bit character 1011101 has five ones; hence, a parity bit value of zero or one produces odd or even parity, respectively. The receiver has a parity checker that performs an addition modulo 2 operation on the character bits to determine the parity. Figure 6.12 illustrates a typical parity generator and checker logic implementation. The generator is preset to either odd or even parity by the command register bit. As the character bits are received, the T flip-flop toggles each time it senses a one. At parity bit time slot, the parity enable signal gates the serial data output and inserts the flip-flop's output state as the parity bit. Similarly, the parity checker consists of a T flip-flop gated with the Start bit detect logic. The one-valued bits in the character toggle the flip-flop, and its final output state becomes the parity status for that input character.

Figure 6.13 is a simplified Sync search logic functional block diagram. This design will accommodate either single or double Sync character format. The received data are compared with the stored Sync character(s) on a bit-by-bit basis. If a perfect match occurs, the TC counter output sets the status register Sync Detect bit; otherwise the counter is reset and the search resumes.

6.4 PARALLEL INTERFACE

This information exchange method uses n signal lines to provide high-speed transfers between the MPU and external interface devices. This results in simple designs suitable for word-oriented I/O device architectures. There are three basic parallel data transfer techniques: direct, handshake, and bidirectional I/O. *Direct I/O* requires no control signals in order to coordinate data transfers. Thus, an output device must be available at any time to accept MPU data. Similarly, an input device must have data available on a continuous basis. *Handshake I/O* requires that an exchange of control signals take place prior to any actual data transfers. This technique provides for positive control of each data transfer. Both the direct and handshake transfers use a separate data path for each data direction, which is fixed upon module initialization. The *bidirectional I/O* technique uses the same data path, and the direction is determined dynamically by the handshake signals. As such, arbitration logic within the module prevents any possible contention problems from arising.

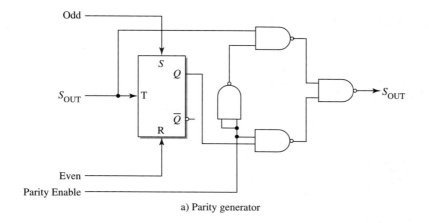

a) Parity generator

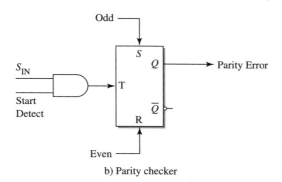

b) Parity checker

FIGURE 6.12
Parity generator/checker functional logic.

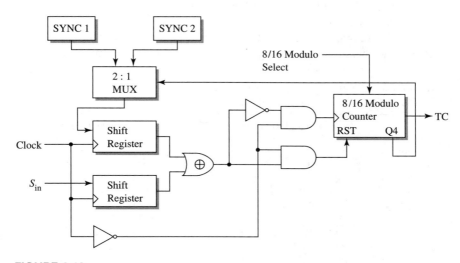

FIGURE 6.13
Sync search functional logic.

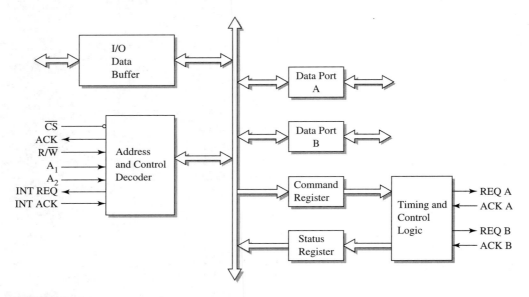

FIGURE 6.14
Parallel I/O interface functional block diagram.

A typical parallel I/O interface module block diagram is shown in Figure 6.14. The I/O data buffer, along with the address and control decoder, provides the required logic for MPU system bus interfacing. The MPU executes an initialization routine to configure the module. The module has two parallel data ports, or channels, which operate independently. The command and status registers hold the configuration mode and current state, respectively. Two sets of bidirectional signals are provided, via the control and timing logic, to accommodate input or output data transfers.

Table 6.4 provides detailed command and status register format definitions. This serves to provide a better understanding of the device's functional capability. The command register

TABLE 6.4
Parallel I/O interface register definitions

	Command Register Format	Status Register Format
Bit Number	Definition	Definition
0	Port A mode select bits (1, 0)	Port A mode (1, 0)
1	Direct In/Out, Handshake In/Out	00, 01, 10, 11
2	Port B mode select bits (3, 2)	Port B mode (3, 2)
3	Direct In/Out, Handshake In/Out	00, 01, 10, 11
4	Port A INT enable	Port A interrupt
5	Port B INT enable	Port B interrupt
6	Port A REQ/ACK enable	Port A Register full
7	Port B REQ/ACK enable	Port B Register full

bits 0 and 1 are used to define one of the four possible port A modes of operation. Similarly, bits 2 and 3 specify the mode for port B. Bit 4 serves as port A interrupt request control in the handshake mode. Bit 5 provides port B interrupt request control in the handshake mode. Bit 6 is used to enable the automatic generation of an output request control signal each time port A is loaded with a data word, in the handshake output mode. Similarly, it is used to generate an input acknowledge control signal each time port A accepts a data word, from the external device, in the handshake input mode. Bit 7 provides the same functions as bit 6, but for port B.

The status register bits 0 and 1 reflect the current mode of operation for port A. Similarly, bits 2 and 3 indicate the mode of operation for port B. Bits 4 and 5 identify the interrupt request source, ports A or B. Bit 6 indicates either an empty or full status for the port A buffer register. Bit 7 provides the same status for the port B buffer register.

Direct I/O

This mode of operation requires no handshake signals to perform data transfers. Thus, an output device is always accepting data and an input device provides data continuously. A simple application of the direct I/O technique occurs in an alarm system. Suppose that several independent sensors need to be polled periodically to determine their states. To make efficient use of the module data ports, the sensors are arranged in a matrix configuration. Sequential scanning is used to detect each sensor state. This is illustrated in Figure 6.15. The sensor matrix consists of N^2 individual single pole single throw (SPST) switches, arranged in N-rows-by-N-

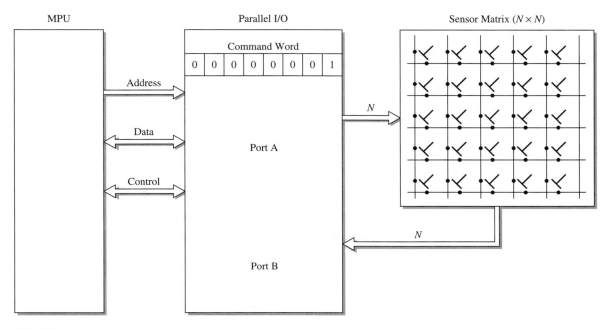

FIGURE 6.15
Direct I/O operation block diagram.

columns format. The parallel I/O interface module is configured with port A as output and port B as input. The MPU systematically selects each matrix row by sending an output data word into port A. Then it reads the corresponding column sensor input data word from port B. The input word reflects the instantaneous sensor states in the selected row. Thus, the MPU creates a table format of the matrix, which is used to detect subsequent changes as they occur. Figure 6.16 is a typical timing diagram of each matrix row scanning sequence. First, the MPU places the proper address value on the system bus to select the parallel I/O interface module. Next, it activates the R/$\overline{\text{W}}$ control signal to enable one data bus word transfer to the module. This data word, which specifies a unique matrix row, is loaded into port A. Then, using the R/$\overline{\text{W}}$ control signal, the MPU initiates a read cycle to the module and transfers the port B data to the system bus. This sequence is repeated N times in order to scan the matrix once. The scanning interval is in the order of 100 ms, which is fast enough to detect any sensor state changes.

Handshake I/O

This mode of operation requires that a control signal exchange sequence take place prior to any data transfers. A handshake output data transfer starts with the MPU sending a data word to the interface module. In turn the module raises its output request signal to the device. When the de-

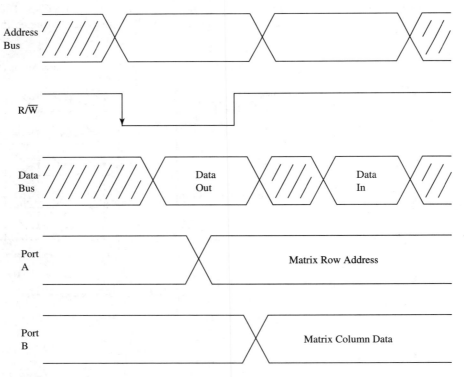

FIGURE 6.16
Direct I/O operation timing diagram.

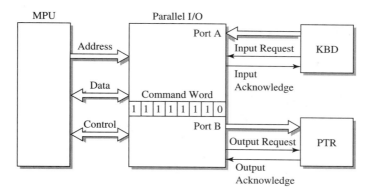

FIGURE 6.17
Handshake I/O operation block diagram.

vice accepts the data word, it raises its output acknowledge control signal to the interface module. Similarly, a handshake input data transfer begins with the external device raising its input request signal to the interface module. When the module accepts the data word, it raises its input acknowledge control signal. Next, the MPU, either by polling or interrupt request, reads the data and stores it in the system memory for processing. A common application of this technique is interfacing to a combination keyboard-and-printer external device. Port A can be configured for keyboard handshaking input. Port B can be configured for printer handshaking output.

Figure 6.17 provides a simplified interconnection block diagram. The mode control bits determine the data and control signal direction for each port. The interrupt enable bits provide an interrupt request signal to the MPU whenever an output data word is accepted by the device or an input data word is transferred in the module. The port enable bits enable the port buffer registers and provide automatic output request and input acknowledge signals to the external device.

Figure 6.18 is the basic timing diagram for output data transfers. The sequence begins with the MPU selecting the interface module, via the system address bus, and placing a data word on the data bus. Next, the parallel I/O interface module sends the data word to its output port B and raises its output request signal to indicate output data word available. The external device accepts the word and responds by raising its output acknowledge signal. This signal resets the output request signal and causes the module to generate an interrupt request to the MPU. In turn the MPU responds with its interrupt acknowledge signal and resets the original request. Then it invokes its interrupt service routine, reads the module's status, and transfers the next output data word. If polled operation is desired, the interrupt enable bit is initially reset. The MPU sends a data word to the module and enables its output B port. Then the MPU periodically reads the module's status to determine if the external device has accepted the output data word. The printer device accepts ASCII data and generates a hardcopy output. Hence, the handshake signals are essential to prevent any loss of data due to transfer speed differences and other printer-related parameters.

The keyboard section contains built-in scanning logic to detect key depressions, which it then encodes into ASCII characters. Each time a key is depressed, an ASCII character is gener-

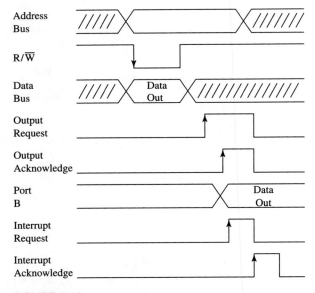

FIGURE 6.18
Handshake output timing block diagram.

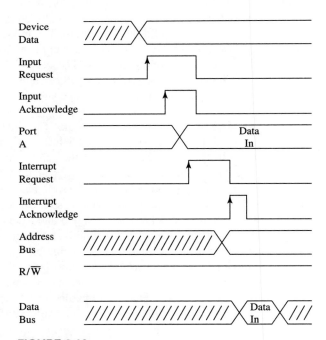

FIGURE 6.19
Handshake input timing block diagram.

ated. In response the keyboard logic activates its input request signal to the peripheral module. When the module accepts the ASCII character, it activates its input acknowledge signal, which resets the input request signal. The handshake input technique provides for positive control of data transfers from a device to the peripheral module. Figure 6.19 shows a typical handshake input timing diagram. The sequence begins with the device providing an input data word and activating its input request signal. The peripheral I/O module accepts the data word and responds with its input acknowledge signal. In addition, it generates an interrupt request to notify the MPU. In response the MPU invokes its interrupt service routine that reads the module's status and transfers the input data word to system memory for processing. If polled operation is desired, the port A interrupt enable is initially reset. The MPU enables port A and periodically reads the module's status to determine if the input data buffer is full.

Bidirectional I/O can be easily achieved by configuring one port as handshaking input and the other as handshaking output. The corresponding individual I/O data lines of each port are connected to form a data bus structure. The handshake signals provide the arbitration to coordinate data transfers in either direction.

Figure 6.20 contains a simplified bidirectional I/O functional logic diagram, using port A as output and port B as input. The output request control signal is activated each time the output data register is loaded, the request enable bit is set, and no input data is pending. In response, the output acknowledge control signal resets the output request and generates an inter-

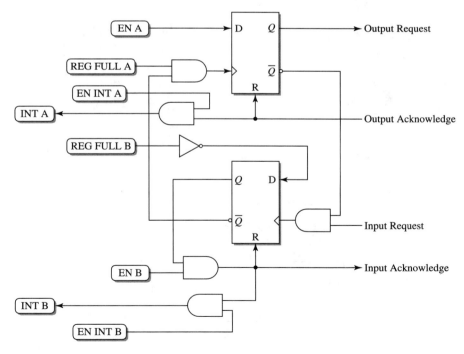

FIGURE 6.20
Bidirectional I/O functional block diagram.

rupt request, if the interrupt enable bit is set. The input request control signal is sensed if the input data register is empty and no output data is pending. Then, if the acknowledge enable bit is set, the input acknowledge signal is activated. Finally, an interrupt is generated if the interrupt enable bit is set.

6.5 PERIPHERAL DEVICE CONTROL

Specialized peripheral device controllers extend MPU performance and flexibility by implementing many functions in hardware. Such controllers can be configured for specific tasks by the initialization program, so that the MPU merely performs data transfers to and from the peripheral controller. In this section the discussion will be limited to the floppy disk and CRT controllers, which provide secondary storage and visual display capability, respectively.

Floppy Disk Controller

Figure 6.21 presents the physical characteristics and data storage organization associated with the floppy disk storage medium. The floppy disk consists of a thin, circular, plastic piece with a

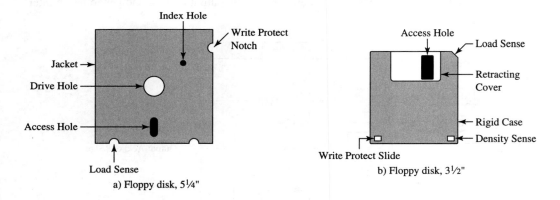

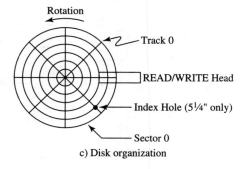

FIGURE 6.21
Floppy disk definitions.

magnetic coating, enclosed in a protective jacket. The disk has a hole at its center, which is used to rotate it at 360 rpm. A magnetic surface access opening is provided in the jacket, as is an index hole for synchronization. A write-protect notch is available for preventing accidental alteration or erasure of stored data. The load sense notch is used to ensure proper disk insertion. The circular inner surface is arranged in concentric rings known as *tracks*. The surface is also divided into wedge-shaped segments called *sectors*. Each sector can store a fixed number of data bytes. Disk sizes come in $5\frac{1}{4}''$ and $3\frac{1}{2}''$ diameter and can store data on both sides. The corresponding top and bottom tracks, on two-sided disks, are called a *cylinder*. A typical $5\frac{1}{4}''$ disk can be organized with up to eighty tracks per side and nine or fifteen sectors per track. A $3\frac{1}{2}''$ disk can be organized with up to eighty tracks per side and nine or eighteen sectors per track.

The floppy disk is inserted into a drive unit that rotates it at a constant speed. There are two types of disk configuration format, hard-sectored and soft-sectored. Hard-sectored disks sense the index hole, which marks the beginning of each track sector, on each revolution. Soft-sectored disks write a unique ID code at the beginning of each sector. Also, a read/write head assembly can be positioned over a track and then lowered to perform fast data transfers on each sector.

Figure 6.22 is a simplified block diagram of a floppy disk controller (FDC). The FDC basically provides the interface between the system bus and the disk drive unit. The FDC contains

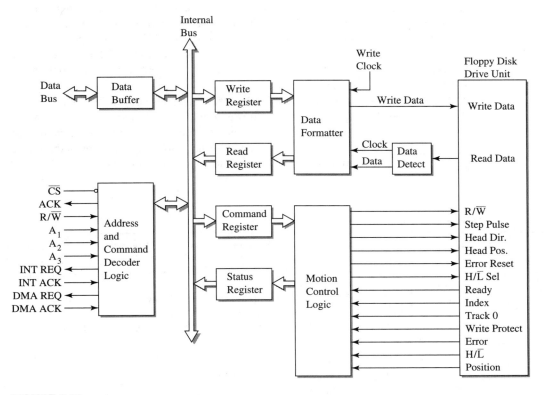

FIGURE 6.22
Floppy disk interface block diagram.

the MPU interface logic, which consists of a data buffer and the address and command decoder logic. The data formatter converts data words from the write register into a serial bit stream suitable for magnetic recording. It also detects a composite serial bit stream from the drive unit, extracts the clock, and loads the data into the read register. The motion control logic converts the MPU-initiated commands into signals required by the drive unit to execute each function. The $R/\overline{W}$ input signal specifies a read or write data operation. The step pulse signal is used to move the magnetic head assembly to the next track location. The head direction signal specifies the relative head movement, left or right. The head position signal is used to raise or lower the head assembly to and from the disk surface. The error reset signal is used to clear a sensed hardware error condition that may result in unreliable operation. The $H/\overline{L}$ signal is used to specify either high- or low-density storage. The disk drive ready output signal indicates that a disk has been properly loaded and is rotating. The index signal is activated each time the physical hole is sensed on each disk revolution. The track zero signal indicates when the head assembly is positioned over the outermost track. The write protect signal is used to determine if the disk data can be overwritten or modified. The error signal specifies a hardware fault of temporary or permanent nature. The $H/\overline{L}$ signal indicates the detected storage density. The position signal provides the head location status.

The interface controller has a total of eight addressable internal registers, used to command, configure, transfer data, and provide overall status. The read and write data registers are used for temporary storage of data transfers to and from the floppy disk. The command, status, and condition code registers are used to control and monitor the MPU-initiated operations. The configuration register is used to preset the stepsize and latency intervals of the magnetic head assembly. The track and sector address registers are used to specify a particular data block within the floppy disk data organization.

Table 6.5 provides a detailed format definition of the registers above. The command register bit 7 is used to enable DMA operation. Bit 6 is used to enable interrupt requests to the MPU. Bit 5, when set, enables the transfer of the configuration register contents to the motion control logic for parameter presetting. Bit 4 is used to format a specified track, by adding identification and framing information to it. Bit 3 is used to enable the movement of the head as-

TABLE 6.5

Floppy disk controller register definitions

Bit Number	Command Register Definition	Status Register Definition	Condition Code Register Definition	Configuration Register Definition	Track Register Definition	Sector Address Register Definition
0	Read	$R/\overline{W}$	Done	Head Latency	Address Value	Address Value
1	Write	High/$\overline{Low}$	Write Error	(4–64 msec)		
2	Head Position	Write Protect	Read Error	bits (3–0)	bits (6–0)	bits (5–0)
3	Track Select	Track 0	Track Error			
4	Format	Ready	Sector Error	Head		
5	Initialize	Data Request	Overrun Error	Stepsize		
6	Interrupt Enable	Interrupt	Hard Error	(1–16 msec)		
7	DMA Enable	DMA		bits (7–4)		

sembly to a specific track. Bit 2 is used to either raise or lower the head assembly over a track. Bits 1 and 0 are used to initiate a write and a read operation, respectively, on a location specified by the track and sector register values.

Status register bits 7 and 6 reflect the selected data transfer mode, as defined by the corresponding command register bits. In the DMA mode, an external controller is required. The MPU initializes the controller with the track and sector numbers and the starting memory address before actual data transfer. In the interrupt mode, the MPU initiates a command to the FDC, which in return generates an interrupt request when the FDC is ready. Bit 5 indicates that either the read data register is full or the write data register is empty, based on the state of the R/$\overline{\text{W}}$ bit 0. Bit 4 indicates that the floppy disk has been inserted properly and is rotating. Bit 3 indicates that the head assembly is located over track zero. Bit 2 is used to denote whether or not the disk is write-protected. Bit 1 is used to sense the storage density mode.

The condition code register is used to provide possible error status of each MPU-initiated command. Bit 6 is set to indicate either a temporary or a permanent drive unit fault. Bit 5 is set when the MPU is unable to respond to a data transfer request within a specified time interval. Bits 4 and 3 are set when the FDC is unable to read the sector and track values assigned during formatting. Bits 2 and 1 are set to indicate unsuccessful read and write operations, respectively. Bit 0 is set to indicate that the requested command has been successfully completed by the FDC.

The upper four bits of the configuration register are used to specify the head assembly lateral movement stepsize, in sixteen 1-msec increments. The lower four bits specify the head up and down motion latency interval, in sixteen 4-msec increments.

The track and sector address registers are loaded by the MPU, prior to any formatting or read and write operations, to specify the starting reference point. A typical floppy disk rotating at 360 rpm requires roughly 167 msec for each revolution. Using nine sectors per track, it takes about 18.5 msec to scan one sector length. If each sector contains 512 bytes, it takes 36 µsec to transfer each one, or 4.5 µsec per bit. Thus, a transfer rate of over 220 Kbps can be achieved.

CRT Display Controller

This controller provides the interface between the system bus and a CRT display unit. Also, it generates the necessary raster scan signals to provide a two-dimensional screen for alphanumeric character test. Figure 6.23 illustrates the basic raster scan system and related character display format. The raster scan display is formed by sweeping an electron beam across the CRT screen, as shown in Figure 6.23a. The n horizontal line scan signals and one vertical scan signal, shown in Figure 6.23b, make up a single *frame*. A horizontal line scan signal period of approximately 63.5 µsec corresponds to a sweep frequency of 15,750 Hz. The actual line scan duration is about 50 µsec, which leaves 13.5 µsec for the retrace interval. Similarly, the vertical scan signal period is approximately 16.7 msec, which corresponds to a frame rate of 60 Hz. The scan duration T_S is about 15.45 msec, which results in a retrace interval T_R of 1.25 msec. During both retrace intervals the electron beam is blanked off the screen.

An alphanumeric character can be represented using a column-by-row dot matrix format, as shown in Figure 6.23c. A typical 5×7 dot matrix provides sufficient resolution for displaying the ASCII character set. The display screen is arranged in n rows, each containing up to m

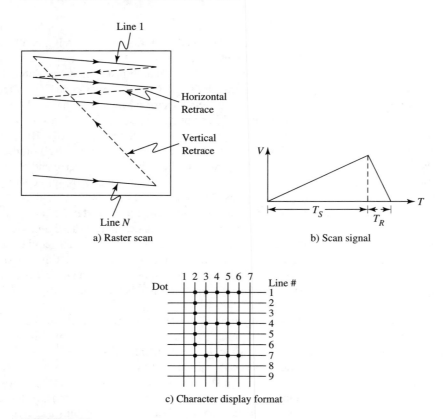

FIGURE 6.23
Raster scan character display definition.

characters. A character can be displayed anywhere within the screen format by using the intensity control signal to selectively illuminate the matrix character dots while blanking the rest. Similarly, a reverse video character can be generated by inverting the intensity control signal. A character can be highlighted by doubling the amplitude of the intensity control signal. A character can also be made to blink on the screen at a preset rate.

Using a display screen format of twenty-five rows, with up to eighty characters per row, requires a memory capacity of 2,000 bytes to contain one frame. Using a frame rate of 60 Hz, a data transfer rate of 120,000 bytes per second (Bps) must be maintained in order to support the screen format. The 5×7 dot matrix is placed in a 7×9 field, to enhance adjacent character recognition. This results in a total of 560 dots or *pixels* per horizontal line, which requires a bit-clocking rate of $560 \div 50$ μsec/line or 11.2 MHz.

Figure 6.24 is a CRT controller block diagram. The data buffer, along with the address and control decoder logic, provide the necessary system bus interface capability. The circular queue is used to store two lines of characters, such that as one is displayed, the other is updated by the MPU. The character column and row registers are used to define the cursor position, which is denoted by a blinking underline character. The command and status registers are used

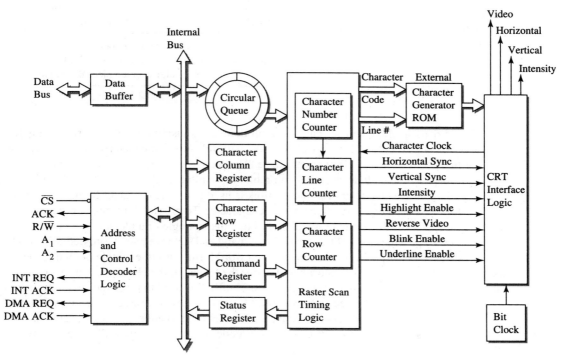

FIGURE 6.24
CRT controller functional block diagram.

to coordinate and monitor controller operation. The raster scan timing logic contains the character number, line, and row counters, which have a programmable modulo. The character number counter specifies the number, one through eighty, of displayed characters per row. The character line counter keeps track of the number, one through sixteen, of horizontal scan lines used to display a character. The character row counter specifies the number, one through sixty-four, of character rows displayed in each frame. An external character clock is used to enable counter operation.

The raster scan timing logic outputs a character code and its associated character scan line number to a character-generator ROM that provides the correct display dot pattern. The character code output is the circular queue data word value that is keyed to the character number counter value, and it is repeated once per horizontal scan line. In other words, the CRT controller provides display screen information as one horizontal scan line segment at a time. Also, the logic provides horizontal and vertical synchronization along with intensity control signals that are combined with the character dots to generate a composite display.

Table 6.6 provides the character data word bit definitions, using single word format. This format describes a monochrome CRT controller with sixty-four alphanumeric characters, using bits 0 through 5. Each character can be displayed in one of four possible modes: normal, reverse video, blinking, or highlighted.

TABLE 6.6

Monochrome CRT controller data format

Bit Number	Definition
0–5	Six-bit character code
6	Character attribute bits (7, 6)
7	Normal, Reverse video, Blink, Highlight

Table 6.7 lists the character data word bit definitions, using dual word format. This format defines a typical color CRT controller mode, with full ASCII character set display capability. The first word is the ASCII character code. The second word specifies the displayed character attributes. These include character color, highlight, blink, and underline. Highlight is used to double the relative character brightness. Blink is used to enable character blinking at a fixed rate. Underline is used to insert a line under the character. To provide for transfer efficiency, bit 6 is used to specify if the attribute word applies to either a single or a block of characters.

Table 6.8 provides the CRT controller command and status register word definitions. The command status bit 0 specifies the character data word format as either single or dual, to define the CRT controller mode. Bit 1 is used to transfer the values of the character and row registers into the raster scan logic for defining cursor position. Bit 2 is used to place the cursor in the upper left hand corner of the screen. Bit 3 is used to erase a row of characters from the circular queue. Bit 4 initializes the raster scan counters. Bit 5 is used to either blank or enable the display screen. Bits 6 and 7 are used to select the mode of data transfer, with the MPU, which takes places during the vertical retrace interval.

The status word bit 0 reflects the selected character format. Bits 1 and 2 signal the vertical and horizontal retrace intervals, respectively. Bits 3 and 4 provide circular queue condition status. Bits 5 through 7 reflect the corresponding command register bit states.

In summary, the displayed character row data words are stored in the queue. Each character code is sent to the character generator once for each character line. The next character row is transferred in the queue during the active row display interval. This process is repeated until a complete frame is displayed on the CRT and the frame rate is 60 Hz. The character data re-

TABLE 6.7

Color CRT controller data format

Word	Bit Number	Definition
One	0–6	ASCII character code
	7	Zero
Two	0	Green ON/$\overline{\text{OFF}}$
	1	Blue ON/$\overline{\text{OFF}}$
	2	Red ON/$\overline{\text{OFF}}$
	3	Highlight Enable
	4	Blink Enable
	5	Underline Enable
	6	CHAR/$\overline{\text{BLOCK}}$
	7	One

TABLE 6.8
CRT controller register definitions

Bit Number	Command Register Definition	Status Register Definition
0	SINGLE/DUAL	SINGLE/DUAL
1	Cursor Load	Frame End
2	Cursor Reset	Row End
3	FIFO Clear	FIFO Empty
4	FRAME Reset	FIFO Full
5	Display Enable	Display Enable
6	Interrupt Enable	Interrupt Enable
7	DMA Enable	DMA Enable

quired to construct a single frame are stored in the display block of the main system memory. Data transfers occur by either interrupt or DMA mode. If the character ROM is substituted with a dual port RAM, it is possible to provide different character fonts and graphics capability.

A video RAM (VRAM) is a customized dual port RAM that consists of a DRAM and a double-buffered shift register. The MPU can independently access the DRAM while the shift register is sending a serial bit stream to the CRT screen. As such, the MPU controls the individual dot or pixel states by dynamically modifying the DRAM contents. Also, a selected row of data can be loaded from the DRAM into one shift register buffer, while the other buffer is active. The ability to selectively alter each pixel in memory makes graphics displays possible. A typical 640×400 pixel graphics-display screen supports 256 colors with 256 KB of memory. A high-resolution display has a $1,024 \times 1,024$ pixel matrix and supports 256 colors with 1 MB of memory. In contrast, the 80×25 character display screen needs only 2 KB of memory.

PROBLEMS

6.1 Use Table 6.1 to determine the command word, in hex format, to configure the programmable timer for modes 0 and 5, as defined in Table 6.2.

6.2 Given command words A = 23_{16} and B = $A7_{16}$, determine the transmitter/receiver configuration modes using Table 6.3.

6.3 Given a bit cell of 1 msec and a character made up of seven data bits, one parity bit, and two Stop bits, calculate the baud rate and transfer efficiency.

6.4 Use Table 6.4 to determine the command word, in hex format, to configure the parallel I/O interface for the following mode: Port A handshake input, with interrupt, request, and acknowledge enabled; port B direct output, with all other controls disabled.

6.5 Use Table 6.5 to determine the command and configuration register words required for the following floppy disk controller mode: DMA enabled, initialized, format track zero, with stepsize of 10 msec and a latency of 28 msec.

6.6 A hard disk rotates at 3,600 rpm and has eighteen sectors per track. Determine its maximum data transfer rate in bits per second.

6.7 A $3\frac{1}{2}''$ hard disk rotates at 3,600 rpm. Determine its linear velocity at track zero and track eighty located $\frac{1}{2}''$ from the center. Also, determine the average sector length of the two tracks, assuming eighteen sectors per track.

6.8 A CRT display uses a horizontal sweep frequency of 31.5 KHz and a vertical frame rate of 60 Hz. Determine the horizontal and vertical scan durations for 15% retrace intervals. Also, calculate the bit frame rate and the bit clock frequency for a 7 × 9 character field format.

6.9 Use Table 6.7 to determine the CRT controller data word formats necessary to display the word "RBG." Each character should be highlighted and should have the corresponding initial letter color.

6.10 Using Table 6.8, determine the command word, in hex format, necessary to write the word "RGB" in the upper lefthand screen corner, using interrupt updates. Also, determine the corresponding status word in hex format.

6.11 Design a Start bit transition detector using gates, flip-flops, and a counter. A 16-times-the-data-rate receiver clock is present.

6.12 Using an 8 × 8 sensor matrix, determine the update period if the row sampling frequency is 120 Hz.

6.13 Design the arbitration logic for a bidirectional I/O data buffer, using the control signals from Figure 6.20.

6.14 Given the data words A = 1010101 and B = 0101010, determine their parity bit values for both even and odd parities.

6.15 Determine the pixel frame rate and the bit clock frequency for a sixteen-color graphics CRT controller, using a 640 × 480 resolution and the same scan frequencies used in Problem 6.8. Also, determine the display memory size.

REFERENCES

Intel. *Microsystem Components Handbook.* Santa Clara, CA: Intel, 1984.

———. *Peripherals Handbook.* Santa Clara, CA: Intel, 1990.

Korn, G. A. *Microprocessors and Small Digital Systems for Engineers and Scientists.* New York: McGraw-Hill, 1977.

Motorola. *Microprocessor Data Manual.* Phoenix, AZ: Motorola, 1982.

Texas Instruments. *MOS Memory Data Book.* Dallas, TX: Texas Instruments, 1993.

7

MICROPROCESSOR APPLICATIONS

Microprocessor-based design applications achieve a successful integration of hardware and software elements in order to accomplish a specific task. The development of such applications has both hardware and software phases. The hardware phases are architecture definition, functional description, logic design, and circuit realization. The software phases are machine organization, algorithm development, program design, and coding. The development process begins with defining the problem or identifying the need. In the requirements analysis phase, that need is examined and functions, performance parameters, and operational constraints are outlined. In the system design phase, how the need will be satisfied is determined and an overall solution is selected. In the start of this phase, the hardware architecture is defined, components are selected, and logical design is completed. Next, overall system organization is outlined; then an algorithm and data structure are developed. The design process continues with hardware and program module development and system integration. Finally, testing is conducted for debugging and performance verification. The objectives of this chapter are as follows: (1) to define the MPU system levels, (2) to explain the hardware components, (3) to discuss the software modules, (4) to present an example of conventional design, and (5) to cover multitasking design.

7.1 BASIC DEFINITIONS

The system design process can be broken into five hierarchical levels: system, component, register, logic, and circuit.

System-level definitions consist of operational requirements, functional description, performance criteria, architecture, and organization. These are used to generate design and testing specifications for the hardware and software elements. A system functional block diagram, shown in Figure 7.1a, is used to define the MCU system's interaction with its environment. A configuration block diagram, shown in Figure 7.1b, is used to define the

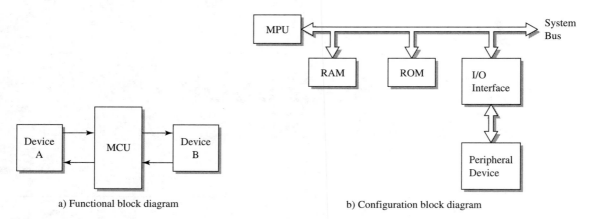

a) Functional block diagram

b) Configuration block diagram

FIGURE 7.1
System-level hardware block diagrams.

hardware component interconnections that make up the system. A memory map and a major flow diagram are used to define system-level software components. These provide built-in intelligence and decision-making capability. Figure 7.2a illustrates a typical system-level memory map that details the various program module locations. Figure 7.2b is a major flow diagram.

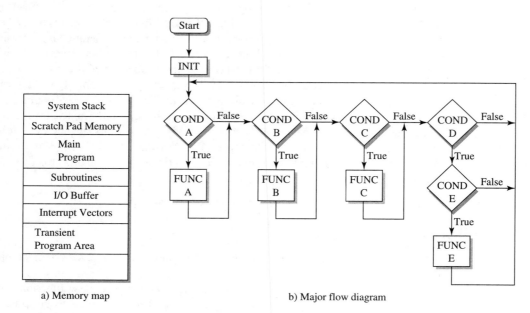

a) Memory map

b) Major flow diagram

FIGURE 7.2
System-level software block diagrams.

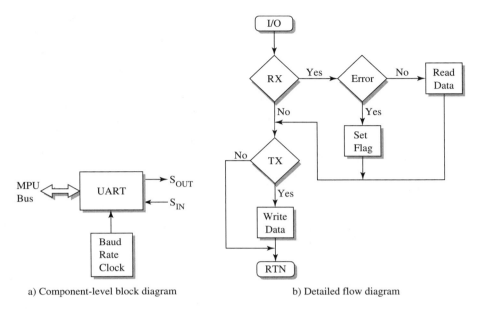

a) Component-level block diagram   b) Detailed flow diagram

FIGURE 7.3
Component-level definitions.

The component level addresses individual system elements and their interactions. Definitions such as response times, data formats, and exchange protocols are typical design parameters. Detailed flow diagrams and program design are developed at this level. Figure 7.3a is a typical component-level block diagram. A detailed flow diagram is presented in Figure 7.3b. At this level the system bus and peripheral device interfaces are detailed, along with corresponding software modules.

The register level addresses data transfers, register bit field definitions, and timing cycles associated with each component. Instruction-level module definition also takes place. The logic level addresses truth tables, Boolean equations, and Karnaugh maps, which are used to develop the interface to integrate the overall system functions. Finally, the circuit level specifies logic gates and functional blocks required for design realization.

7.2 HARDWARE ELEMENTS

The hardware design centers around the MPU, which is selected to reduce the building block component count, maximize programming flexibility, and minimize overall hardware element complexity. Time-critical operations, signal conditioning, and signal-level conversions are typical functions that require hardware element realization. Typical MPU selection factors include organization and design parameters such as instruction set, word size, I/O structure, execution speed, and power dissipation. The MPU internal architecture is optimized to execute its instruction set. To this end, multiple addressing modes are available, along with dedicated buses

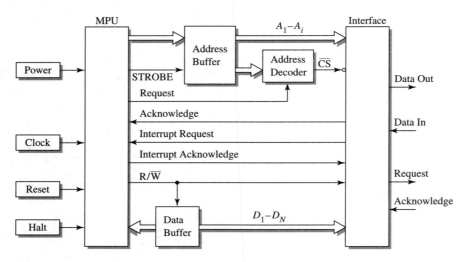

FIGURE 7.4
MPU system hardware block diagram.

and DMA capability. Also, synchronous internal and asynchronous external interrupt sensing are provided with priority and masking capabilities. Instruction prefetch and pipeline paths are provided to achieve enhanced throughput. The system bus links the MPU with other components, using address and data buffers and control signals. In addition, power, clock, external control, and decoding logic are required to form a complete system. Figure 7.4 is a typical MPU support hardware system configuration block diagram. Each block defines a major component necessary to support the MPU operation and system bus connectivity.

External Interface

The input power interface provides the MPU with a specified voltage level and current range values. A detailed block diagram of the power unit is shown in Figure 7.5. The power is derived from a nominal 115-VAC, 60-Hz source. A transient protector module eliminates high-amplitude voltage spikes, which can be extremely harmful to the sensitive MPU circuitry. The spikes are clamped by the protector to a safe voltage level. Next, a step-down transformer provides isolation and reduces the input voltage level to match MPU requirements. A rectifier circuit converts the low-level AC voltage into a pulsating DC waveform. Then a low-pass filter removes the inherent AC ripple, and a regulator provides a constant DC voltage-level output. In addition, the regulator has overvoltage and overcurrent protection capability.

The clock module uses a high-frequency, crystal-controlled oscillator as a reference to derive a highly stable and accurate clock signal. Figure 7.6 shows a typical clock generation module and its associated timing diagram. The crystal oscillator output, shown in Figure 7.6a, is fed into a modulo 16 counter to provide four square wave output signals of different frequencies. Two of the four outputs are fed into a decoder module to generate a four-phase clock. These waveforms, shown in Figure 7.6b, provide the system designer with a set of timing signals.

FIGURE 7.5
Power unit detailed block diagram.

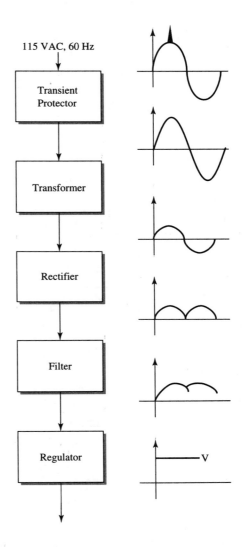

The external reset interface initializes the system upon power-on condition or manual input. In addition, a manual pulse generator can be used either to provide a halt pulse signal or to enable single-step clock operation. Figure 7.7 illustrates a typical external reset circuit implementation. The cross-coupled NAND gates form an RS flip-flop that serves as the S1 switch contact debouncer. The result is a clean output reset pulse, whose duration is a function of the switch dwell time. A similar scheme is used with switch S2, to generate the halt signal, but in addition a D-type flip-flop is used to latch the pulse and provide alternate action operation. The flip-flop is configured as a divide-by-two counter that alternates states on each input clock pulse. An RC time constant circuit is used to generate the power-on reset (POR) signal each time power is applied. A Schmitt-type inverting buffer converts the slowly changing signal into a fast transition output pulse to reset the flip-flop and set initial system conditions.

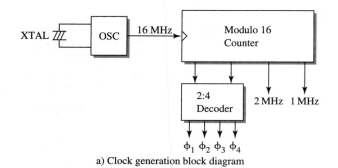

a) Clock generation block diagram

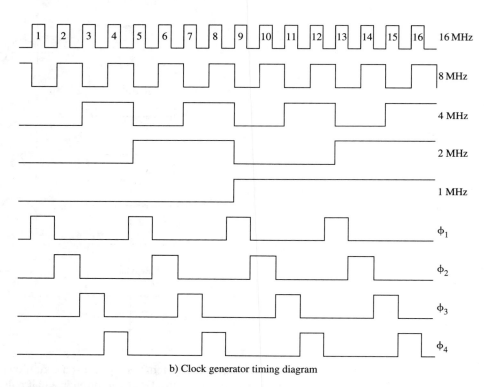

b) Clock generator timing diagram

FIGURE 7.6
Clock interface definition.

System Bus

The system bus consists of three types of signal groups: address, data, and control. The MPU output address signals need to be buffered in order to provide enough drive for the whole system. In addition, multiplexed address and data bus signals require a storage buffer. Figure 7.8 shows the two types of address buffers. These are usually packaged eight per module and have

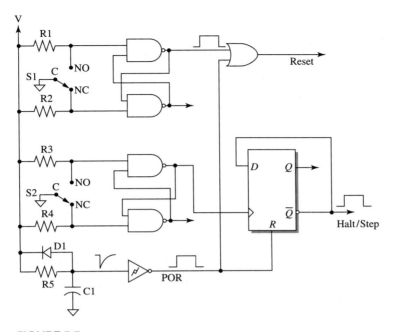

FIGURE 7.7
External reset circuit diagram.

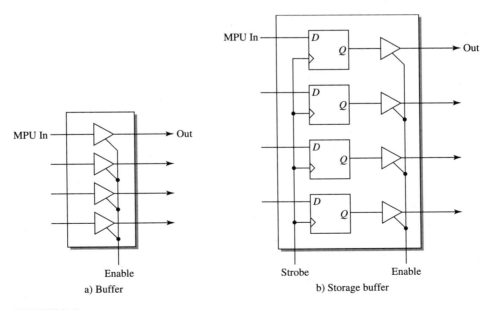

Enable

a) Buffer

Strobe   Enable

b) Storage buffer

FIGURE 7.8
Address buffer functional block diagram.

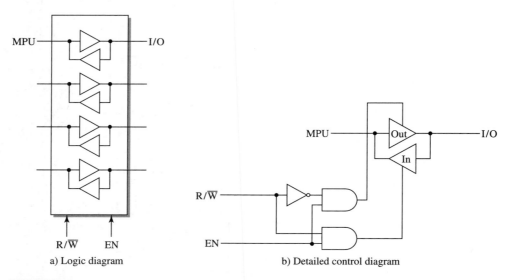

a) Logic diagram

b) Detailed control diagram

FIGURE 7.9
Data buffer functional block diagram.

an enable input control for tri-state operation. The storage buffer also has a strobe input to latch the valid address value.

The data bus requires a bidirectional buffer to support MPU I/O operations. Figure 7.9a is a typical data buffer logic diagram. The module contains eight individual buffers, with common $R/\overline{W}$ and EN control inputs. The $R/\overline{W}$ signal selects the buffer data path, and the EN signal enables the selected buffer and tri-states the other. Figure 7.9b is a detailed data buffer con-

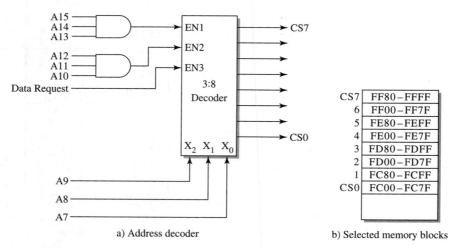

a) Address decoder

b) Selected memory blocks

FIGURE 7.10
Address decoding logic.

trol diagram. The control bus functions are mainly address decoding, interrupt sensing, and request and acknowledge operations.

Address decoding enables the MPU to select a memory location, an interface module, or a peripheral controller on the system bus. Figure 7.10 illustrates a typical address decoding scheme. Figure 7.10a shows a specific address decoding logic that selects one of eight memory space blocks in the range of $FC00_{16}$–$FFFF_{16}$. Each block location, as shown in Figure 7.10b, is selected by the lower seven address bits (A_6–A_0), and results in a block size of 128 locations.

Multiple interrupts are usually prioritized and encoded, as shown in Figure 7.11a, to accommodate MPU pin limitations. The MPU function code is decoded, as shown in Figure 7.11b, and provides status to the various system components. The request acknowledge signal, shown in Figure 7.11c, is provided to the MPU. First the MPU raises its request signal, along with address data, to select a source or destination location for data transfer. In response, the selected device replies with its acknowledge signal to complete the handshake sequence.

Peripheral Interface

A simple MPU peripheral consists of an input switch matrix and a visual output display matrix. A parallel I/O module can provide the necessary logic to achieve compatibility with the system bus timing requirements. Figure 7.12 illustrates this interface configuration. The MPU periodically scans the switch matrix and updates the display matrix. This is done at a fast rate to prevent missed switch closures and display flickering. The switch matrix consists of N switches in an X row, Y column arrangement. As each row is selected, the corresponding column switch states are read by the MPU. Similarly, display column data are provided by the MPU.

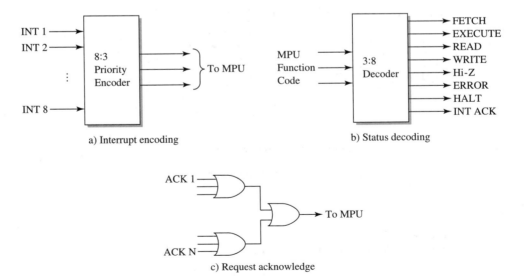

a) Interrupt encoding

b) Status decoding

c) Request acknowledge

FIGURE 7.11
MPU control bus interface.

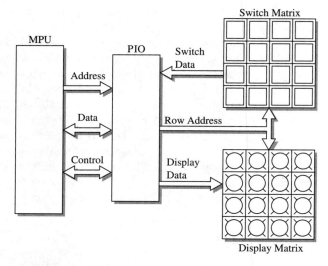

FIGURE 7.12
Switch/display matrix interface.

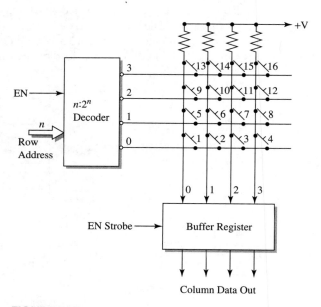

FIGURE 7.13
Switch matrix functional block diagram.

Figure 7.13 shows a detailed switch matrix design. The row address, provided by the MPU, is decoded to select the individual matrix row. The inactive switch state is set at logic one. A switch depression, in one or more columns, results in a logic zero state when the corresponding row is selected. A buffer register is used to store the selected switch states. For example, depression of switches 5 and 7 will result in a binary column data value of 1010_2 when row 1 is selected.

The display matrix consists of N visual indicators, arranged in an X row, Y column configuration. Its numbering convention is keyed to the switch matrix, such that switch and indicator positions have a one-to-one correspondence. Figure 7.14a is a typical display matrix logic diagram. A display element is illuminated when both its row and column are selected. In general, a de-

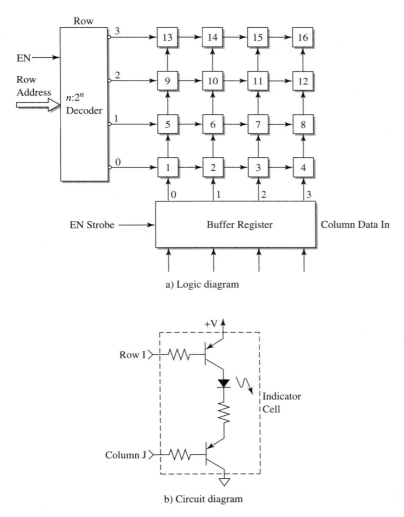

a) Logic diagram

b) Circuit diagram

FIGURE 7.14
Display matrix functional block diagram.

coder module is used for row selection. Similarly, a buffer register is used for column selection. For example, indicators 5 and 7 will be illuminated when row 1 and columns 0 and 2 are selected. This requires a display row address value of 01_2 and a column data value of 1010_2.

The display circuit diagram in Figure 7.14b provides a detailed view of a display indicator element. The row I and column J inputs are connected to the associated row and column matrix output lines. The circuit consists of two transistors, which serve as current drivers, and both must be ON for the indicator to illuminate. The voltage and ground terminals supply power to each element. The active data sense can be changed using inverting buffer registers.

7.3 SOFTWARE ELEMENTS

The software design process centers around the implementation of a specific program solution for a unique application. Existing systems software such as the editor, assembler, compiler, linker, and debugger are available to support and streamline the program development cycle. The basic application requirements dictate the program size, language selection, algorithm complexity, response time, and user interaction. Figure 7.15 illustrates a typical software de-

FIGURE 7.15
Application program development cycle.

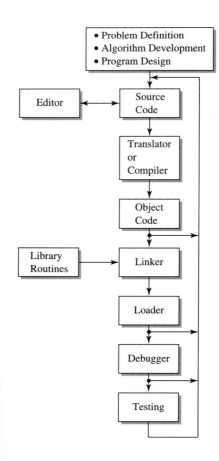

velopment process. Using the top-down design methodology, the problem statement defines the requirements.

The algorithm design provides a systematic approach to satisfy the requirements. Once the algorithm is refined, the program design gives a flowchart representation of the solution. Next, the editor is used to convert the flowchart into a source code program, consistent with the semantics and syntax of the chosen language. An assembler or compiler is used to generate the object code program. The linker is used to bind two or more object programs or built-in referenced routines. The loader transfers the composite object code program into a specified memory area. The debugger is used to exercise the program in order to detect and correct any possible design errors. The debugger selectively executes program segments by defining address or control signal state breakpoints. In addition, it supports single-instruction execution and memory or register content examine/modify operations. Program testing is performed to verify that the chosen solution satisfies the requirements.

Any program modification requires source code editing to reflect the resulting changes. High-level languages have a well-defined program organization that provides self-documenting source code. In contrast, an assembly language program requires that the designer define the organizing format. Figure 7.16 illustrates a typical assembly language program structure. The header usually contains the program name and date, the revision number, a brief description, and memory and I/O requirements. The constant block is used to assign symbolic labels to frequently used data values, MPU registers, memory addresses, and I/O device locations. The interrupt vector table contains the starting address location of all interrupt routines. The memory assignment section is used to specify reserved memory blocks for scratch pad, I/O buffers, and stack area. The data tables contain structured information for look-up solutions, to speed execution. The main program contains the initialization code and a small test-and-jump main loop that transfers control to the selected subroutine. The subroutines are the heart of the solution implementation. They operate in unison and interact so as to provide an integrated solution. The interrupts tem-

FIGURE 7.16

Application program structure block diagram.

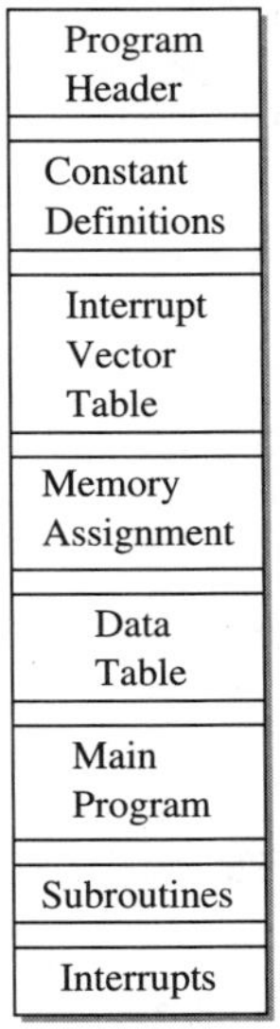

| Program Header |
| Constant Definitions |
| Interrupt Vector Table |
| Memory Assignment |
| Data Table |
| Main Program |
| Subroutines |
| Interrupts |

porarily halt the normal flow to process external requests or internal status conditions in the course of program execution.

Figure 7.17 provides a more detailed description of a typical main program code segment. The major block diagram in Figure 7.17a defines the individual code modules that make up the main program. The memory test code module functional block diagram, in Figure 7.17b, consists of the walk and gallop tests. In either test, if an error is detected, the corresponding status error bit is set and the module execution is terminated. If both tests are successfully completed, then the next code module is executed.

Figure 7.18 is a detailed memory test flow diagram. Each test is outlined at a level that allows a smooth transition to the specific programming language implementation. The walk test starts with address zero and performs N write-before-read operations in each memory location. The first data value is zero, followed by a one in the LSB position. As the process is repeated, the one value is shifted once towards the MSB position. A read operation at each step is followed by a comparison test. Once each memory location is exhaustively checked, the test is repeated for

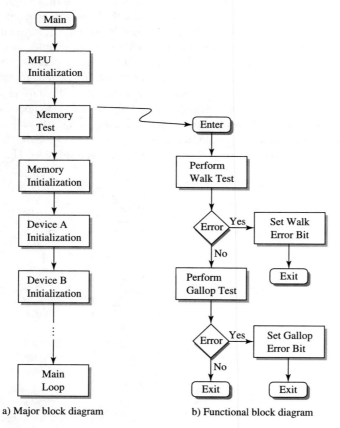

a) Major block diagram   b) Functional block diagram

FIGURE 7.17
Main program organization.

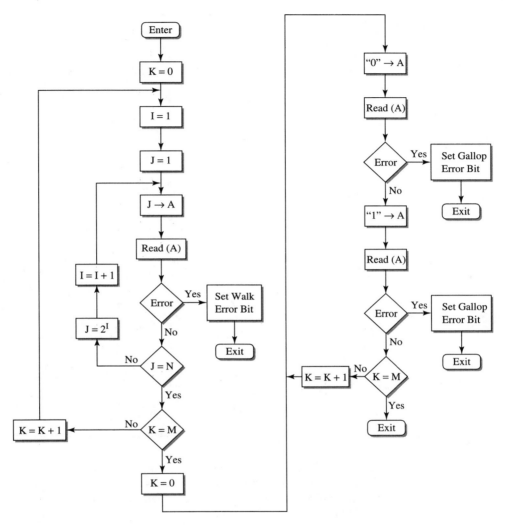

FIGURE 7.18
Memory test detailed flow diagram.

the next location until all memory is spanned. The test's objective is to detect any single-bit transition errors. The gallop test is similar, except a smaller set of data values is used—either all zeros and all ones or alternating ones and zeros. The objective of this test is to detect multiple-bit transition errors. The memory test is followed by the memory initialization module. Here program-related constants, variables, and data structures are assigned values or defined.

The main test-and-jump loop major block diagram is shown in Figure 7.19. Its operation is analogous to a finite state machine operation. At each loop state the status is checked and a condition is tested. In response, the program performs a function and transitions to the next

FIGURE 7.19

Main loop major flow diagram.

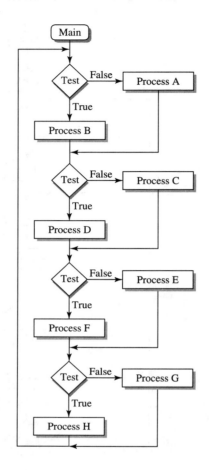

state. A given condition state may be altered by one of the following events: external interrupt, internal interrupt, or program subroutine. The process block denotes a generalized program module that may invoke subroutines and be preempted by interrupts.

Figure 7.20 depicts the different program modules for an I/O interface device. The initialization routine INIT, shown in Figure 7.20a, systematically exercises the device commands and monitors its status for proper response. Any error condition terminates routine execution and sets the appropriate status bit. Upon successful command testing, a read-after-write sequence is performed to verify data transfer operation. Again, any resulting errors terminate the test and set the corresponding status bit. Next, the device is configured, via its command register, for program-specific operation. Also, the device interrupt module starting address is loaded into the interrupt vector table.

On each data transfer request between the interface device and its peripheral, the interrupt module INT, shown in Figure 7.20b, is invoked. The routine saves the current MPU state into the system stack prior to any other action. Next, the associated device status is read to determine the requested action, in this case, either a read or a write operation. Then the corresponding program status flag bit is set, and the MPU state is restored for normal operation.

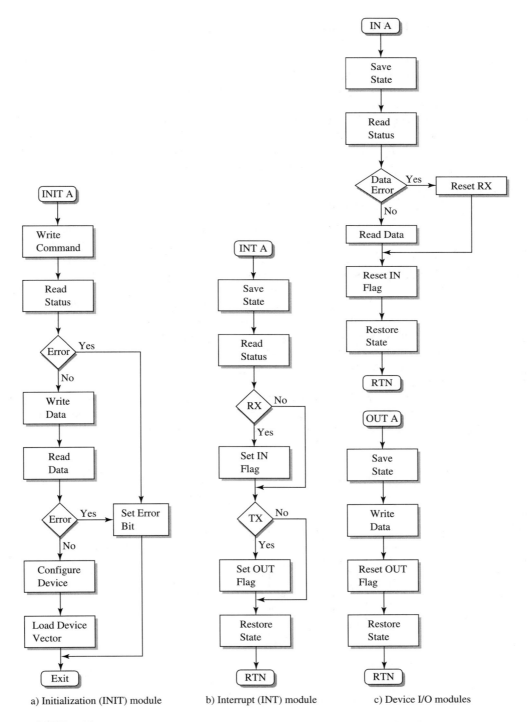

a) Initialization (INIT) module b) Interrupt (INT) module c) Device I/O modules

FIGURE 7.20
Program module definitions.

The device I/O modules, shown in Figure 7.20c, are executed when their corresponding program status flag, set by an interrupt, is tested in the main program test-and-jump loop. The IN subroutine module is invoked in response to an input data request from an external device A. The module structure is similar to the interrupt, in that they both save and restore the MPU state. The device status is read to determine if the received data is error-free. If no errors exist, the data is read by the MPU and the IN flag bit is reset. If, instead, an error is detected, the receiver is reset via the command register. The OUT subroutine module first writes a data word into the device output register, then resets the OUT flag big.

Switch/Display Update

The basic switch and display matrix operations require that a periodic display update is performed to maintain a current state and avoid flickering. A typical display frame update rate is 100 Hz, which translates to a display update period of 10 ms. A programmable timer is used to provide a periodic interrupt request to the MPU every 10 msec. The interrupt routine sets a flag bit that is tested in the main program loop to determine the update interval. Figure 7.21a is a switch and display matrix functional flow diagram. Each time a display update is required, the switch data word is read and tested for a non-zero value, which indicates a switch closure. If switch activity is detected, then the switch update code segment is executed first. The display update code segment is executed unconditionally. The main memory contains a stored image of the corresponding switch and display matrix words, as shown in Figure 7.21b, that are used to perform update operations.

Figure 7.22 provides a detailed flow diagram of the switch and display matrix update code module. The flow diagram describes the N-key rollover algorithm, which detects multiple switch closures. Each individual matrix switch closure is represented as an alternate action and

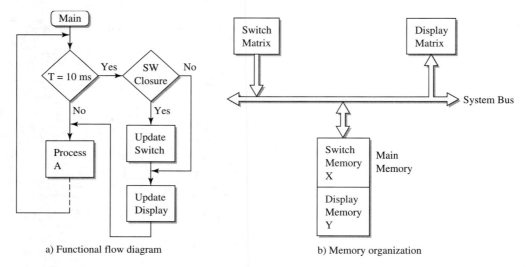

a) Functional flow diagram

b) Memory organization

FIGURE 7.21
Switch/display matrix configuration.

FIGURE 7.22
Display update detailed flow diagram.

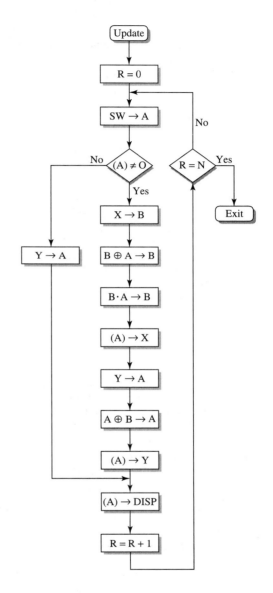

is reflected by the corresponding display element illumination state. Each new switch matrix row data word is read and tested for non-zero value status. In this implementation a non-zero value indicates one or more switch closures in the associated matrix columns. Next, the stored old switch matrix data word is fetched, and an exclusive-OR operation is performed on the old and new data words. The result is modified by an AND operation with the new switch matrix data word. Next, the old stored switch data word is updated with the new. Then, the old stored display matrix word is fetched and an exclusive-OR operation is performed with the modified switch data word. The result becomes the new display data word, which is used to update the display memory and matrix row locations. However, if no switch closure is detected, then the corresponding row display memory word is sent to the display matrix. The routine is repeated once for each matrix row, as indicated in the flowchart. The depicted flowchart shows a worst case instruction number of 13. For an instruction cycle time of 1 μsec, the resulting routine would be $13 \times N$ μsec long. The N-key rollover algorithm equation is given below.

$$DISP = Y \oplus [SW \cdot (X \oplus SW)] \tag{7.1}$$

where   DISP = the new display data word

Y = the old display data word

SW = the new switch data word

X = the old switch data word

Example 7.1 illustrates the N-key rollover process.

EXAMPLE 7.1

Given X = 0101, SW = 1011, and Y = 0110, find the new display word.

$$X \oplus SW = (0101) \oplus (1011) = 1110$$
$$SW \cdot (X \oplus SW) = (1011) \cdot (1110) = 1010$$
$$DISP = Y \oplus [SW \cdot (X \oplus SW)] = (0110) \oplus (1010) = 1100$$

The stored old switch word, X, indicates two previous switch closures, bits 0 and 2. The new SW data word detected three closures, bits 0, 1, and 3. The stored old display data word, Y, has bits 1 and 2 set. The N-key rollover algorithm results in a new display word with bits 2 and 3 set. These changes are directly attributed to the new switch matrix closures. For example, the display word bit 0 remained reset since there was no corresponding change in the two switch data words. Bit 1 was reset since there was a corresponding change in the new switch data word. Bit 2 remained set since there was no corresponding switch closure. Bit 3 was set as a result of a corresponding new switch closure.

7.4 CONVENTIONAL DESIGN

An MPU-based household alarm system will be used to illustrate the basic considerations involved in the design process. The following discussion provides an insight into the hardware architecture and software organization of the alarm system implementation. Also, the necessary hardware element and software module interactions are addressed.

A functional block diagram is shown in Figure 7.23a. The alarm system is designed around the integrated switch and display control panel, shown in Figure 7.23b. During power on, the MPU goes through its initialization codes, and upon successful completion it illuminates the READY indicator. The READY button is used to place the system in a self-test mode at any time. Once depressed, the READY indicator goes to an OFF state. It returns to an ON

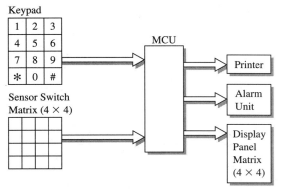

Keypad

1	2	3
4	5	6
7	8	9
*	0	#

Sensor Switch
Matrix (4 × 4)

MCU

a) Functional block diagram

Ready	Panic	Sound On/Off	Delay On/Off
Front Door	Back Door	Basement Door	Window 1
Window 2	Window 3	Window 4	Window 5
Window 6	Smoke Alarm 1	Smoke Alarm 2	Smoke Alarm 3

b) Control/display panel matrix layout

FIGURE 7.23
Functional system block diagram.

state upon successful test completion. The PANIC button, a momentary action switch, is used to activate the audio alarm. The PANIC button does not have an indicator associated with it; instead, the unused indicator is integrated with the keypad to show an error status. The SOUND button and indicator are used to enable or disable the audio alarm, but the sound button is overridden by the PANIC button. The DELAY button and indicator are used either to enable or to bypass the delay interval associated with entering or exiting the premises. The remaining panel consists of indicators associated with sensor switches distributed throughout the house and wired in a corresponding matrix configuration. The twelve-button keypad is used to control certain internal functions such as arm or disable alarm operation, set the clock, and command the MPU to print the status buffer. And built-in logic generates a serial output code.

Figure 7.24 provides the MCU configuration block diagram associated with the alarm system architecture definition. The MPU connects all the external I/O devices together via the system bus. The RAM is used for program data storage, buffer area, and other program functions. The EEPROM is used to store the actual program instructions. The parallel input/output (PIO) module provides the interface to the switch and display matrices. The serial input/output (SIO) module serves to transfer the serial data from the keypad to the printer, via the MPU. The timer module provides four distinct tone signals for the audio alarm. In addition, it implements two periodic interrupt timers, one for display update and another for time-of-day clock operation. The interrupt controller prioritizes and resolves multiple interrupt requests to the MPU. The interrupt priority is 10-msec timer, Rx Int, Tx Int, and 1-sec timer, respectively.

The alarm system software functional block diagram is presented in Figure 7.25. After initialization, the software centers around a main polling loop. The major software modules, listed in sequence, are invoked on demand from the main loop. After each module completes execution, it returns control to the loop.

The program begins with the initialization code module, followed by the built-in-test (BIT). Upon successful test completion, the flow of control transfers to the main loop, which contains a fixed sequence of four conditional branch instructions. An MPU register or a mem-

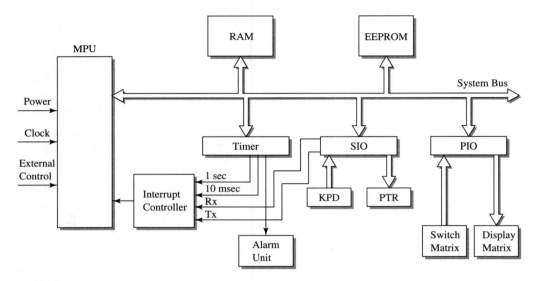

FIGURE 7.24
MCU configuration block diagram.

ory location are used to store specific bits, known as flags, that indicate the state of each condition. The DISP flag is set by the 10-msec periodic interrupt generated by the timer module. The KPD flag is set each time serial data are received by the SIO. The PTR flag is set each time the SIO output buffer is empty and its interrupt is enabled. The TIME flag is set by the 1-sec periodic interrupt timer. When the DISP service module is selected, the program checks for a matrix switch closure condition first. If no closure is detected, the display update function is performed and the DISP flag is reset prior to returning to the main loop. However, if a closure is detected, the current switch data is compared with the previous sample debounce operation, to eliminate the possibility of false alarms. Next, the four pushbutton states are examined to determine if any system configuration changes are required. The READY and PANIC buttons are implemented in firmware as momentary action switches. Similarly, the SOUND and DELAY buttons are implemented as alternate action switches. The individual sensors are implemented as single pole single throw (SPST)–type action switches.

When an alarm condition is sensed, the ALARM routine is invoked to determine the source and type, in order to provide the proper response. In addition, the RECORD routine is invoked, which stores time-of-day and alarm status information into a buffer. When the KPD service module is selected, the program retrieves the SIO data, decodes it, and performs the requested function. The request may be to arm or disarm the alarm, set the clock, program entry and exit delay, test the keypad, or print the status buffer contents. When the PTR service module is selected, the program writes one character at a time from the status buffer or the keypad input to the SIO, for a status hardcopy or keypad test, respectively. When the TIME service module is selected, the built-in clock is set to the proper time. The software context diagram,

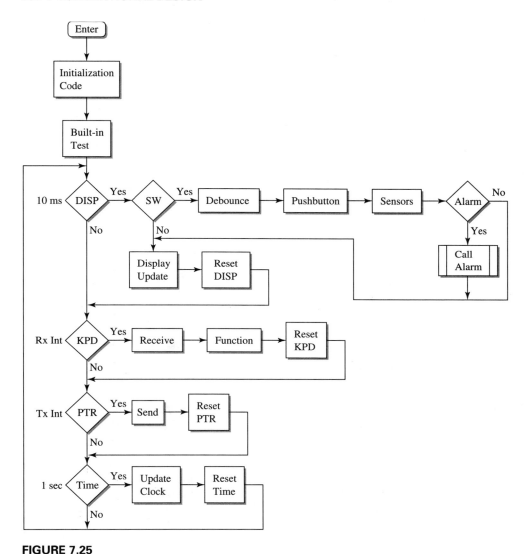

FIGURE 7.25
Alarm system software functional block diagram.

shown in Figure 7.26, depicts the main module interactions, with the external device interrupt routines.

Figure 7.27 provides a detailed flow diagram of the ALARM subroutine module. The PANIC button state is tested first, and if it is activated, then alarm tone D is sounded. Also, the RECORD subroutine is invoked to store the alarm status and time information. Otherwise, the DELAY button state is tested, and, if it is set, the delay loop operation takes place. The delay

FIGURE 7.26

Alarm system software context diagram.

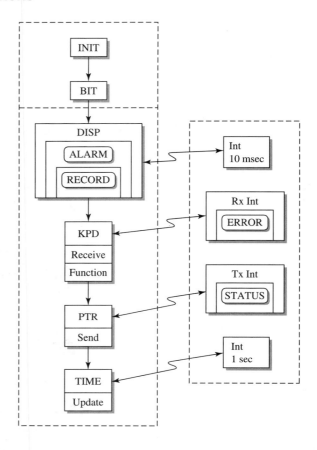

counter is incremented by one until its value reaches T, at which point the routine proceeds to determine which alarm was activated. Then if the alarm is still active the corresponding alarm tone is sounded. There are three possible tones available: A for window or door opening, B for smoke detection, and C for a combination of both conditions. The control panel SOUND button controls the type A alarm only. Again, after the specific alarm sound is activated, the RECORD subroutine is invoked to store the alarm type and time of day in the status buffer.

Figure 7.28 is a detailed description of the FUNCTION procedure that is used to decode the keypad input commands. A three-digit input code, preceded by the pound sign (#), is used to select the ARM function. When this code is entered, the program activates the switch matrix scan operation by enabling the 10-msec periodic interrupt timer and sets the DELAY flag. Similarly, a different three-digit input code, preceded by #, is used to select the DISABLE function. When selected, this function halts the switch matrix scan operation, resets any ongoing alarm, and disables the Tx interrupt. The remaining functions are accessed by unique three-digit codes followed by the asterisk (*). When the CLOCK function is selected, the operator enters the time-of-day data in an HHMMSS format to set the clock. As a result, the 1-sec interrupt timer is enabled. When the TSEL function is selected, the operator enters a two-digit number to se-

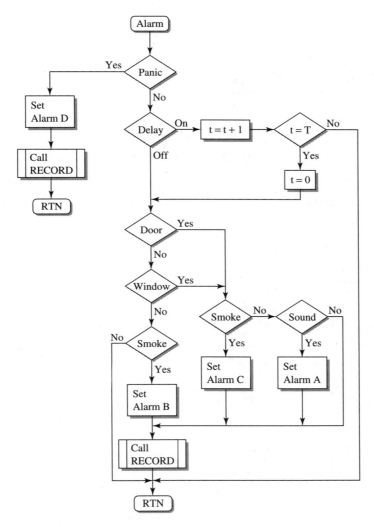

FIGURE 7.27
ALARM module flow diagram definition.

lect the delay value T in seconds. It also sets the delay register value to zero. When the STA-
TUS function is selected, the program sets the PRINT flag and enables the Tx interrupt to initiate the status buffer hardcopy output operation. When the TEST function is selected, the program sets the ECHO flag and enables the Tx interrupt to initiate keypad test operation. When
the STOP function is selected, the program resets the ECHO flag and inhibits Tx interrupt to
terminate the keypad test. Finally, when the BIT function is selected, the system executes the
built-in test module.

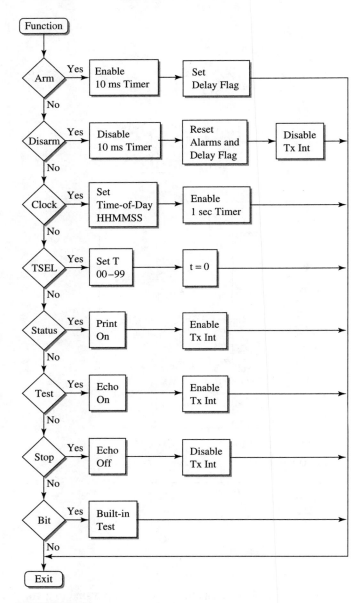

FIGURE 7.28
FUNCTION procedure detailed block diagram.

Figure 7.29 presents the detailed flow diagrams for the RECORD and STATUS subroutines. The RECORD subroutine, shown in Figure 7.29a, is invoked by the ALARM subroutine and is used to place into the status buffer, which is a FIFO structure, each alarm condition and the time of day it occurred. Initially the status buffer is empty and the FIFO flag is set to OPEN,

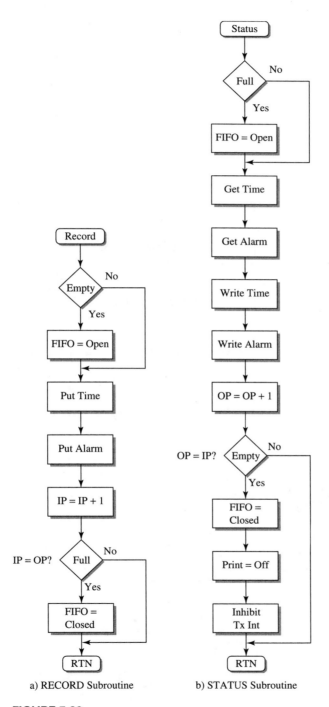

a) RECORD Subroutine   b) STATUS Subroutine

FIGURE 7.29
Buffer operation subroutines.

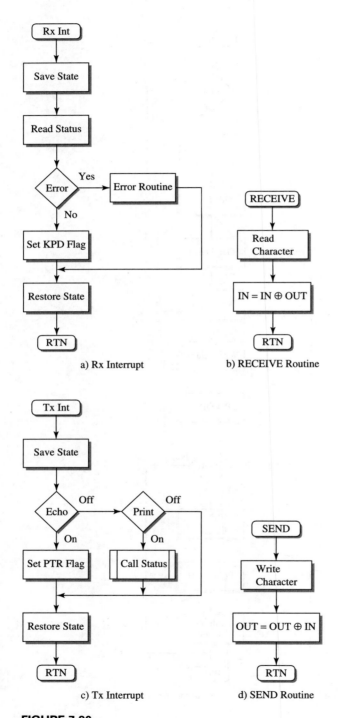

FIGURE 7.30
Input/output detailed flow diagram definition.

indicating that the buffer is active. When an alarm occurs, its status and time data are stored sequentially into the buffer. When the buffer fills up, the FIFO flag is reset to CLOSED to indicate the condition. The STATUS subroutine, shown in Figure 7.29b, is invoked by the Tx interrupt, provided the PRINT flag is set, in order to obtain a hardcopy of the status buffer data. The first step activates the buffer by setting FIFO to OPEN. Then one alarm and time data record per subroutine call is extracted. The record is sent to the printer, via the SIO interface. When all the status buffer contents have been printed, the subroutine resets the FIFO and PRINT flags and inhibits the Tx interrupt.

Figure 7.30 provides a detailed flowchart description of the Rx and Tx interrupts and the associated RECEIVE and SEND routines. The Rx interrupt, shown in Figure 7.30a, is executed each time there is a keypad entry character pending. Its main function is to set the KPD flag, whose state is examined by the main loop on every pass. First, the MPU state is saved in the stack. Second, the SIO status register is read to determine if any receive errors occurred. If the character is error-free, the KPD flag is set; otherwise, the error routine is invoked to turn ON the error indicator, the KPD. The MPU state is restored, prior to exiting the interrupt subroutine, and flow of control is returned to the main program. The RECEIVE routine, shown in Figure 7.30b, is executed in response to a set KPD flag in the main loop. The function of this routine is to read a character from the SIO input register and place it into a dual buffer structure. The structure consists of two memory locations, named IN and OUT. The Tx interrupt, shown in Figure 7.30c, is executed each time the SIO output register is empty and the Tx interrupt bit is enabled. Its main function is to either set the PTR flag or invoke the STATUS subroutine, in order to transfer data into the SIO output register. First, the MPU state is saved into the stack. Second, the states of the ECHO and PRINT flags are examined and appropriate action is taken. Then the MPU state is restored, and flow of control is transferred to the main program. The SEND routine, shown in Figure 7.30d, is executed during keypad testing to provide a hardcopy of each digit code. If the ECHO flag is set to ON, the routine transfers a data word from the dual buffer to the SIO output register.

Cyclic Executive

The heart of the alarm system software is a dedicated polling loop or *cyclic executive,* with a fixed priority sequence, which executes selective program modules. Periodic executed modules have two associated parameters, execution interval and repetition rate. The module execution period is the inverse of its repetition rate. The module duty cycle T_d is defined as the ratio of its execution interval, t_1, and its execution period, T, or $T_d = t_1/T$. The polling loop executive can call each module via a jump table structure. As such, each module has a chance to be executed once per loop pass. If the maximum loop execution interval, t_{max}, is less than the minimum individual module execution period, T_{min}, then the cyclic executive is acceptable. If the converse is true, then either the software must be modified or the MPU must be enhanced in order to meet the required performance criterion. Figure 7.31 illustrates the above definitions. For successful program operation, the relationship $t_{max}/T_{min} < 1$ must hold true. In other words, the module duty cycle must be less than one.

The priority sequence order is directly proportional to the module's repetition rate. In the previous example the display module has a repetition rate of 10 msec; hence it is assigned the highest priority. The keypad Rx interrupt has the second highest priority, due to the following assumptions and resulting calculations. The average data entry rate is 60 codes/min, with an

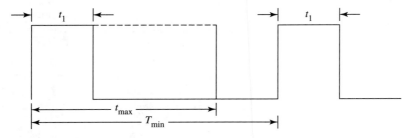

FIGURE 7.31
Module execution time definitions.

average code length of four digits. This results in 4 digits/sec or 250 msec/digit. Similarly, the printer Tx interrupt has the third highest priority. If, for instance, the SIO data transfer rate is 100 bps, then the digit transfer rate becomes 10 msec/bit $\times$ 10 bits/digit or 100 msec/digit. The printer format is 10 digits/line, with an output rate of 18 lines/min. This results in 3 digits/sec or 333 msec/digit. Finally, the TIME update occurs once a second; hence, it has the lowest priority. The dwell time of each module can be calculated as well. For example, using a 1-μsec MPU instruction cycle and a 100-instructions-per-row update results in a 100-μsec execution time. Multiplied by 4 rows/display, this becomes 400 μsec per frame update. In addition, if the DE-BOUNCE, PUSHBUTTON, SENSORS, ALARM, and RECORD routines use another three hundred instructions maximum, the DISP module execution interval, or dwell time, becomes 700 μsec. The actual KPD and PTR module execution intervals are in the microseconds range. The KPD module may require up to two hundred instructions in order to implement the RE-CEIVE and FUNCTION routines, which results in a maximum execution interval of 200 μsec. Similarly, the PTR module code may require up to fifty instructions, which results in an execution interval of 50 μsec. Finally, the TIME module requires up to thirty instructions, which results in an execution interval of 30 μsec. Table 7.1 lists the four modules and their associated execution time parameters. With a minimum module repetition period of 10 msec, the maximum loop execution interval must be less than 10 msec. In this case the maximum loop execution interval, four modules combined, is 0.98 msec, or one-tenth of the maximum.

Using a cyclic executive, a small change in one part of the program can affect the execution time of the entire loop. Polling loop operations are wasteful if external event occurrence is infrequent. Also, a linear increase in interrupts results in a nonlinear increase of loop execution time. Polling and interrupts are conflicting in the sense that if an event is just missed by the polling

TABLE 7.1
Module execution parameters

Module	t_1	T	$T_d = t_1/T$	Priority
DISP	700 μsec	10 msec	0.07	4 (highest)
KBD	200 μsec	250 msec	0.008	3
PTR	50 μsec	333 msec	0.00016	2
TIME	30 μsec	1 sec	0.00003	1 (lowest)

loop, a complete cycle occurs before the missing event is sensed. This results in poor interrupt response. Also, there is a chance that a subsequent event may occur that alters or destroys the previous event data. These effects become more noticeable as the module duty cycle, T_d, approaches unity and the loop execution interval, t_{max}, approaches the fastest module execution period, T_{min}. This design method is also known as module-driven, since each module passes control to the next logical module upon completion of execution. The execution period of each module becomes dependent upon the total number of modules and their individual execution intervals.

7.5 MULTITASKING DESIGN

MCUs have become integral parts of many products. They are buried or embedded within systems that do not have computing as a basic function. Often they require stringent response times to external stimulus. The software must provide a predictable response to external events such that its latency interval falls within a specified time window dictated by the application. As such the system can respond fast enough to control an ongoing process with a tolerable feedback delay. This feature is better known as *real-time processing*. Real-time processing can be achieved using conventional module-driven design techniques. These techniques are adequate if the fastest module execution period is less than the main-loop worst-case execution interval. In general, this approach makes inefficient use of hardware resources and does not provide the best solution to real-time processing. Thus, for borderline cases either a faster MPU is required or the program must be optimized to meet the constraints.

A technique known as *multitasking* can be used to provide the most efficient use of resources. With this technique the program is divided into a set of independent and functionally complete modules, called *tasks,* that can be scheduled and executed on a demand basis. Hence, the program speed equals the execution interval of the slowest task. Each task performs a unique function and has a well-defined interface with one or more other tasks. Task independence results in *concurrent execution* of individual tasks, by overlapping versus sequencing and efficient use of resources. Also, tasks are prioritized and event-driven. Hence, task execution is controlled by either an external request or an internal condition. The time interval between two consecutive executions of a given task depends upon its relative priority and the interrupt subroutine response time. Multitasking designs are based on a small, dedicated modular software component called the real-time executive (RTE). The primary function of the RTE is to manage tasks and provide a well-defined interface to external events. In doing so it achieves predictable time responses to specific requests. The RTE supports a multitasking environment that includes task control, task communication, task synchronization, scheduling, interrupt requests, task calls, error handling, memory allocation, and device arbitration. The user incorporates the commands associated with each of the above functions within the individual tasks as required by the specific application.

The control commands are used to transition a given task to one of its possible states, as shown in Figure 7.32. Initially all tasks are in the IDLE state. A task transitions to the READY state by issuing the ENTER command. When all necessary event or priority conditions are met, the task transitions to the ACTIVE state and takes control of the resources to execute its code. A task continues to execute until it is preempted, at which point it returns to the READY state. In addition, a WAIT, DELAY, or STOP command transitions an executing task to its HALTED

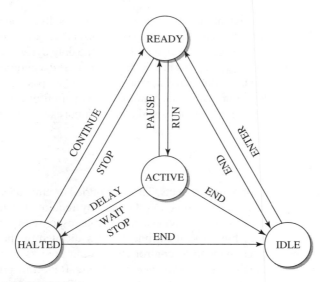

FIGURE 7.32
Task state flow diagram.

state. A halted task can transition to its READY state by issuing the CONTINUE command. A task can transition to the IDLE state from any of the other states by issuing the END command. Additional task control is achieved using specific commands to get status, reschedule, or alter priorities. The command parameters include task number, address, and data values. Similarly, the response parameters include address, data, and error codes.

The basic task structure consists of the initialization and the main cyclic code segments. When a task is created, its initialization code is executed prior to its main code segment being entered. If a task is preempted or stopped, the initialization code is bypassed upon reactivation. Each task has a task control table (TCT) associated with it, so that it can interface with the executive in a uniform and consistent manner. The TCT contains the minimal information required to control overall task operations. Figure 7.33 illustrates the task structure and associated TCT. The task structure shown in Figure 7.33a has an INIT code module and a main code module. The first TCT location, shown in Figure 7.33b, contains a link pointer that connects all tasks in a prioritized, dynamic linked list. The task number provides task identification. The priority, status, and delay parameters define the current task state. The task code, stack, and memory pointers provide a snapshot of the task execution environment.

Task communication is the exchange of data between two tasks. Task synchronization takes place when an event in task A causes a direct action in task B. A *mailbox* is an address location used for message transfers between two tasks. A *message* is an arbitrary unit of information. A message and a mailbox are the basic parameters needed for task communication and synchronization operations. Figure 7.34 defines intertask operations using the PUT, GET, and WAIT commands. Task communication, shown in Figure 7.34a, is achieved when the PUT command in task A places a message in a mailbox, located at X. Then task B retrieves it with the GET command. Task synchronization, shown in Figure 7.34b, is achieved when the PUT command in task A places a message, in location X. Then task B retrieves it with the WAIT

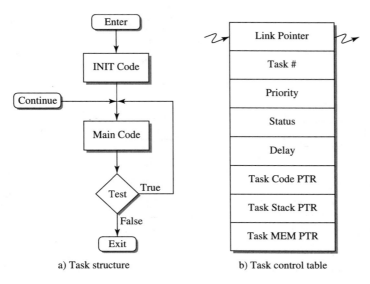

a) Task structure   b) Task control table

FIGURE 7.33
Task structure definitions.

command. As a result the presence of a message, location X may transition task B from the HALTED to the READY state.

There two basic types of tasks, the producer and the consumer. The *producer task* performs function A then sends a message to the consumer task, and awaits for reply. When the *consumer task* receives the message it performs function B, and then replies to the producer task. This cyclic task interaction continues until the required operation is completed. Figure 7.35 illustrates the process. The producer task A initiates the interaction with consumer task B. The process is implemented using a bidirectional task synchronization scheme shown in Figure 7.35a. The individual task flow diagrams are depicted in Figure 7.35b.

When two tasks are sharing a common area in memory it necessitates the use of mutual exclusion to prevent improper alteration of shared data. It also eliminates race conditions that result when two tasks attempt to access a single resource at the same time. Using *mutual exclusion,* a given task executes an uninterruptable test-and-set instruction to examine the status of an event flag or *semaphore*. Task A tests the flag status, sets it, if it is reset, and proceeds to access and alter the data. Similarly, task B follows the same procedure when accessing the shared data memory area. I/O device arbitration can also be achieved with mutual exclusion in order to ensure that a common peripheral is assigned to one task at a time. With I/O device arbitration,

a) Task communication   b) Task synchronization

FIGURE 7.34
Intertask operations.

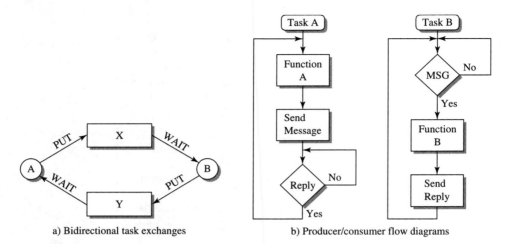

a) Bidirectional task exchanges   b) Producer/consumer flow diagrams

FIGURE 7.35
Producer/consumer task definitions.

other tasks are denied access to an I/O device that is assigned to an active task. *Deadlock* is a condition that arises when two tasks are attempting to control two resources, and each controls one while waiting for the other. This results in a cyclic race condition, and the program crashes. Program monitoring can be used to detect and avoid such situations.

Task execution is controlled by a preemptive scheduler routine that activates each task as a function of priority, event, and condition status. Task scheduling may be periodic in nature, or tasks may be scheduled after an interrupt request or within a fixed time window. With a preemptive scheduler, the active task may be paused for various reasons. For example, an interrupt request readies a higher priority task, releases a resource required by a higher priority task, sends a message to a halted higher priority task, or completes execution. This event-driven rescheduling results in a rapid succession of task executions that optimizes the real-time re-

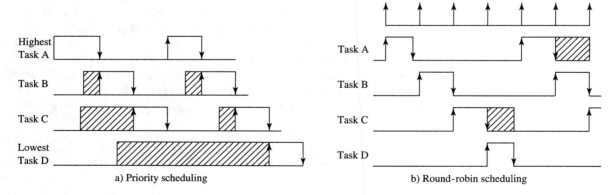

a) Priority scheduling   b) Round-robin scheduling

FIGURE 7.36
Task-scheduling methods.

sponse. Task priority may be fixed or variable since each TCT is arranged in an ordered linked list structure. *Starvation* is a condition that arises when a low-priority task never executes because it is denied the required resources. This condition can be corrected by priority reassignment. Equal-priority tasks are usually executed using time-slice allocation in a round-robin fashion. In this case, each active task yields control to the next one when its allotted time slice expires, regardless of its completion status.

Figure 7.36 illustrates both the priority and round-robin scheduling methods. Using priority scheduling, a higher priority task A will preempt a lower task, as shown in Figure 7.36a. Round-robin scheduling gives each task a fixed time slot to execute, as shown in Figure 7.36b. The shaded areas denote tasks in the READY state. Each task makes a command call to the executive, via the I/O handler, in a consistent format, as shown in Figure 7.37. On each call

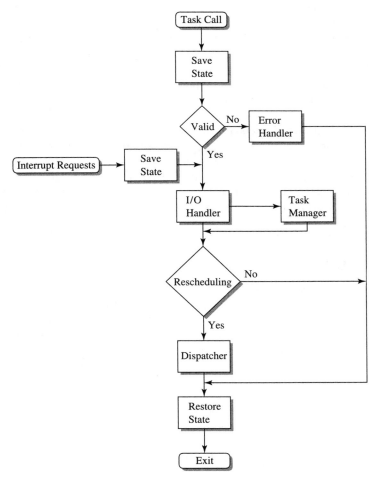

FIGURE 7.37
Command call processing.

the task state is saved, in its TCT, and the request is analyzed for validity. The I/O handler, based on the call request, passes control to either the task manager or the dispatcher. Rescheduling may be necessary as a result of the task call outcome. Upon completion, the next ready state task, which may or may not be the same, becomes active. The task switch time due to rescheduling is usually less than 100 μsec.

Interrupt requests in response to external events have their own priority and also invoke the I/O handler. Interrupts pass messages to waiting tasks and may invoke the dispatcher. In order to achieve real time response, an interrupt must be as short as possible. There are four basic factors that influence the overall response time of an interrupt: software delay, context switching, priority, and interrupt service code. Software delay is caused by either an uninterruptable instruction or critical region code. An *uninterruptable instruction* may be either an arithmetic or test-and-set instruction. A *critical region* is a section of task code that must execute to completion to prevent race conditions. *Context switching,* used to save and restore the current machine state, adds a fixed delay. Priority results in nested interrupts that add a variable delay. The length of the interrupt service routine causes an additional delay. Using these four delay values and the inherent hardware response delay, it is possible to predict the interrupt latency characteristics. Abnormal internal conditions, or exceptions, occur due to either logical or physical environment errors during the course of task execution. In such cases, the error handler resolves the problem, and if possible normal operation resumes.

Memory allocation is an essential function of the executive. There are two different parameters associated with it that result in four possible combinations. Memory allocation can be either static at task initialization, or dynamic upon demand of each active task. Also, the allocated unit of memory have either fixed or variable size. In a single program environment, static allocation of fixed size memory partitions provides a satisfactory solution. In a multitasking environment, dynamic allocation of either fixed size pages or variable size segments provides an efficient solution.

Multitasking Executive

The software structure block diagram for the alarm system design using multitasking is shown in Figure 7.38. The INIT code is executed upon power-on and places the MCU in a known state. Then it activates the BIT task by a command call to the executive. The BIT task exercises the hardware and identifies any system faults. It also defines and prioritizes the four main tasks and enables interrupts. Each task call to the executive has a common entry point and is processed by the I/O handler. Similarly, interrupt requests are interfaced to the I/O handler using a consistent format. The I/O handler, depending on the nature of the call, may invoke either the task manager or the dispatcher. The *task manager* supports task communication and synchronization, memory allocation, I/O arbitration, and time management. Also, it may invoke the dispatcher or pass messages directly to the tasks. The *dispatcher* supports task state control and scheduling functions. In a multitasking environment, the CPU idle time is minimized by eliminating polling and executing on a demand priority basis. However, the use of fixed-priority scheduling does not guarantee that all tasks will complete execution within their allotted time frames. There are two time param-

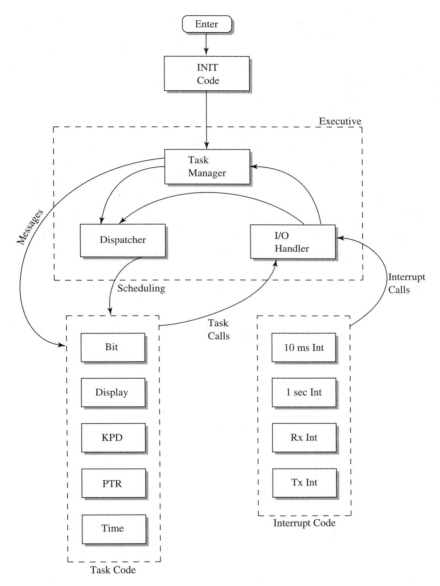

FIGURE 7.38
Multitasking software structure.

eters associated with each task execution interval and execution period. A higher-priority task may prevent a lower-priority task from completing within a given time limit. This condition is more prevalent when the execution interval approaches the execution period of the task.

For example, consider a system that monitors two input signals, analyzes them, and displays the results. Here, task A reads input data within 3 sec and requires 1 sec for analysis. Similarly, task B reads input data within 6 sec and requires 2 sec for analysis. Finally, task C requires 2 sec for analysis and outputs data to the display within 10 sec. If the three tasks are scheduled with a fixed priority sequence, based on their task execution period, then tasks A and B will be completed within their allotted time frames at the expense of task C. However, if the scheduling is designed to provide variable task priority as a function of the execution period, it is possible to achieve both fast and timely task execution. Figure 7.39 illustrates the fixed- and variable-priority scheduling schemes. Using fixed-priority scheduling, as shown in Figure 7.39a, task C does not complete its execution within the 10-sec time frame. Rather, it takes 2 sec longer, since it is preempted by task B. Since it is only a display function, the delay is not critical. In critical control applications, however, it could spell disaster. Using variable-priority scheduling, the priorities of tasks B and C are switched, at the proper interval, in order for task C to complete execution within its specified time frame. This scheme is shown in Figure 7.39b. Although this appears as a simple method, it may be necessary to place constraints on critical region code and task communications to achieve consistent results.

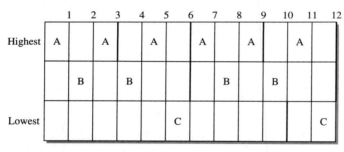

a) Fixed priority task scheduling

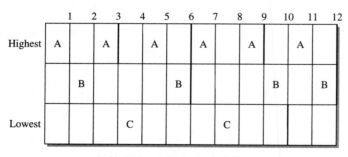

b) Variable priority task scheduling

FIGURE 7.39
Task priority scheduling methods.

PROBLEMS

7.1 Draw the equivalent structured diagram for Figure 7.3.

7.2 Determine the pulse width and duty cycle of ϕ_1 in Figure 7.6.

7.3 Design an address decoder for the range FC0000 to FFFFFF, with 32 KB page frames.

7.4 Given a thirty-two-bit MPU, determine the data values required to perform the walk and gallop memory tests.

7.5 Draw a design flowchart to emulate a momentary action switch/display with debounce logic.

7.6 Draw a programming flowchart to emulate a momentary action switch/display with debounce logic.

7.7 Given a sixteen-bit switch/display data word, determine the new display data, in hex format, if the new switch data word is 05AF and both the present switch and display data words are AAAA. Assume alternate action switch emulation.

7.8 Draw the equivalent structured diagram of Figure 7.22.

7.9 Using a 1-MHz clock source, determine the divide ratio for the 1-msec and 10-msec interrupt signals of Figure 7.24. Also, calculate the counter modulus for the 500-Hz, 1,000-Hz, 2,000-Hz, and 2,500-Hz alarm tones. Determine the divide chains using programmable modulo 10 counters.

7.10 Draw the design flowchart for the scheduler of Figure 7.36a.

7.11 Draw the design flowchart for the scheduler of Figure 7.36b.

7.12 Draw the design flowchart for the scheduler of Figure 7.39b.

REFERENCES

Brinch Hansen, P. *Operating System Principles.* Englewood Cliffs, NJ: Prentice Hall, 1973.

Dahmke, M. *Microprocessor Operating Systems.* New York: McGraw-Hill, 1982.

Deitel, H. M. *An Introduction to Operating Systems.* 2d ed. Reading, MA: Addison-Wesley, 1990.

Intel. *Microsystem Component Handbook.* Santa Clara, CA: Intel, 1984.

———. *Embedded Applications.* Santa Clara, CA: Intel, 1990.

Motorola. *Microprocessor Data Manual.* Phoenix, AZ: Motorola, 1982.

8

MICROPROCESSOR COMMUNICATIONS

Microprocessor data communications is the process by which information is transferred from a source *A* to a remote destination *B,* via a physical medium, at a uniform rate. The source is capable of generating a symbol sequence, from a finite set, with each symbol having a specific probability of occurrence. First, the sequence is passed through a source encoder, which formats the symbols into a specific code and inserts error checking. Next, the information bits are passed through a channel encoder, which transforms the information for efficient and reliable transfer. Then, the modified data stream is passed through a modulator that converts it into electrical signal waveforms compatible with the channel characteristics. The *channel* is the physical medium that connects the source and the destination points. The channel may introduce transmission errors or signal interference. The received information is passed through a demodulator, which detects the signal waveforms and converts them back into a data bit stream. Next, the channel decoder extracts information bits from the incoming data stream. Then, the destination decoder converts the bits into symbols, and detection/correction takes place prior to display.

Figure 8.1 is a typical data communications system block diagram. The individual blocks can be lumped into three distinct groups: the data terminal equipment (DTE), the data communication equipment (DCE), and the channel. The DTE is an integrated component that consists of a keyboard, a CRT display, memory, and control logic. It provides alphanumeric symbol formatting, error control, protocol, and data flow management. The DCE, better known as the Modulator/Demodulator, or modem, provides the necessary conversions between the DTE and the channel. It controls signal duration, bandwidth, and power in order to maintain efficient and reliable transfers. The channel can be either a cable link or a radio path. Cable types include coaxial, twisted pair, fiber, and telephone line. Radio paths include microwave and satellite links. A telephone system may contain one or more channels, of either or both types. The objectives in this chapter are to: (1) define channel and capacity, (2) explain modem and terminal operation, (3) present the various protocols, (4) cover error control techniques, and (5) discuss the available data communications standards.

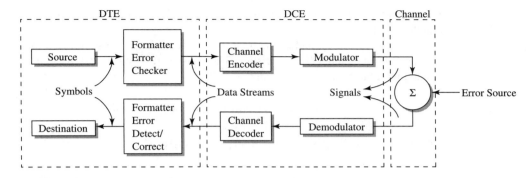

FIGURE 8.1
Data communications system block diagram.

8.1 CHANNELS

The physical channel may be either a unique path for transmitting information in electrical signal form or a band of frequencies available for modulation with a specific coding. The channel bandwidth, *W,* is defined as the difference between the highest and the lowest frequencies in that band. For example, the range of useful frequencies in the telephone network is from 300 Hz to 3,000 Hz. Hence, the telephone channel bandwidth is 2,700 Hz. The system was designed to carry voice signals, which are inherently analog signals. An *analog signal* is defined for a continuous range of amplitude and time values. In contrast, a *digital signal* is defined for a finite, quantized set of amplitude and discrete time values.

An ideal channel exhibits a uniform amplitude attenuation, $A(f)$, and introduces a constant phase shift, $\phi(f)$, over its frequency range *f,* as shown in Figure 8.2. *Attenuation* is defined as signal power loss due to absorption and dissipation by the channel medium. Power loss is measured in decibels (dB) and can be calculated with the following equation:

$$\text{Loss (dB) } A(f) = 10 \log_{10} (P_{\text{OUT}}/P_{\text{IN}}) \tag{8.1}$$

where *P* is expressed in watts.

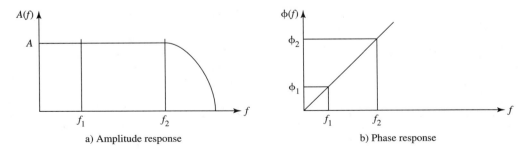

FIGURE 8.2
Ideal channel characteristics.

For example, if the send power is 10 watts and the received is only 5 watts, the attenuation loss equals −3 dB.

Phase shift is defined as the time difference between the source and the destination signals caused by channel characteristics. The phase shift is measured in radians and can be calculated with the following equation:

$$\text{Phase shift (radians) } \phi(f) = -\omega \cdot \tau \qquad (8.2)$$

where $\omega = 2 \cdot \pi \cdot f$ radians/sec and τ is a time constant.

Telephone networks introduce both amplitude and phase distortion. Amplitude distortion is caused by nonuniform signal attenuation across the frequency band. Phase distortion is caused when the phase shift rate of change is not constant over the channel bandwidth. Phase distortion is commonly referred to as envelope delay distortion. Both types of distortion are illustrated in Figure 8.3. The effect of these nonlinearities limits useful channel bandwidth to the center of the frequency range, where both amplitude and phase distortion are minimal. It is possible, however, using equalization techniques, to reduce channel amplitude and phase distortions. The *equalizer* is an electrical network that has inverse channel characteristics, such that when inserted in the path, it corrects distortion.

A channel contains noise, consisting of random signals, introduced by a variety of sources that may interfere with normal data transmission and result in errors. This occurs when the signal amplitude level is less than twice the noise level, which corresponds to a 3-dB higher signal power level. The least desired noise types are impulse noise and phase jitter. Impulse noise is caused by transient switching, which results in short-duration amplitude spikes that can be mistaken for data by the receiver. It effectively alters the amplitude and frequency of the signal waveform. Phase jitter is caused by variations in path delays or carrier signal instability, which results in random phase changes that can be mistaken as signal phase shifts by the receiver. The combined effects of bandwidth, noise, and channel imperfections place a higher limit on the signal-to-noise (S/N) ratio, of about 10 to 1. This corresponds to an S/N ratio of 10 dB. Figure 8.4 illustrates the types of noise interference.

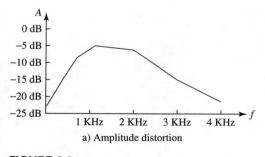

a) Amplitude distortion

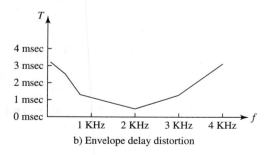

b) Envelope delay distortion

FIGURE 8.3
Real channel characteristics.

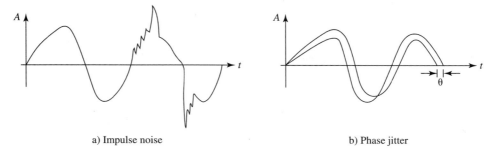

a) Impulse noise   b) Phase jitter

FIGURE 8.4
Transmission channel interference.

Capacity

The Nyquist theorem for a band-limited noiseless channel, with a bandwidth of W Hz, states that it is possible to send a maximum of $2 \cdot W$ symbols/sec. The term *baud* is used as the symbol rate unit. One baud corresponds to a rate of one symbol or one signal event per second. A binary digit or bit is the smallest information unit in a digital system. Thus, the symbol rate is defined in baud and the data rate is expressed in bits per second (bps). If each symbol represents a single bit, then the symbol rate equals the data rate. When a symbol is defined with n bits, then the data rate becomes the symbol rate times the number n of bits per symbol. Hence it is possible, through the use of coding, to effectively increase the channel data rate while limiting the maximum symbol rate to $2 \cdot W$ symbols/sec. The following equation defines the relationship between baud and data rates in terms of available discrete signal levels, M, that can be sent through the channel.

$$\text{Data rate (bps)} = \log_2 (M) \cdot \text{baud} \tag{8.3}$$

where $M = 2^n$ and n = bits/symbol.

For example, a 2,400-baud system, with sixteen possible levels, results in a data rate of $\log_2$ (16) · 2,400, or 9,600 bps. In general, a band-limited noiseless channel of W Hz can sustain a symbol rate of $2 \cdot W$ symbols per second. However, in a multilevel system with n bits/symbol, the maximum channel data rate, R, equals $2 \cdot W$ symbols/sec times n bits/symbol:

$$R = 2 \cdot W \cdot n \text{ bits/sec} \tag{8.4}$$

Table 8.1 lists data rates versus number of bits/symbol for a channel bandwidth of 2,400 Hz.
    The average information content, H, per symbol in a given message is defined as

$$H = \frac{I}{M} = \sum_{i=1}^{N} P_i \cdot \log_2 \left(\frac{1}{P_i}\right) \text{ bits/symbol} \tag{8.5}$$

where I is the total message information content, M is the number of symbols in the message, N is the number of unique symbols available at the source, and P_i is the probability of occurrence for each symbol in the message.

TABLE 8.1
Bandlimited noiseless channel characteristics

Bits/Symbol	Signal Levels	Data Rate (bps)
1	2	4,800
2	4	9,600
3	8	14,400
4	16	19,200
5	32	24,000

In the simple case of $N = 2$, a source sends either a 1 or a 0. The average information content is expressed by the following equation:

$$H = P_1 \cdot \log_2 \left(\frac{1}{P_1}\right) + P_2 \log_2 \left(\frac{1}{P_2}\right) \text{ bits/symbol} \tag{8.6}$$

The maximum value of H is reached when $P_1 = P_2 = \frac{1}{2}$, at which point H_{max} equals one bit/symbol. In general, if all available source symbols have the same P_i, then the expression for H_{max} becomes

$$H_{max} = \sum_{}^{N} \left(\frac{1}{N}\right) \log_2 (N) = \log_2 (N) \text{ bits/symbol} \tag{8.7}$$

The message coding efficiency is defined as the ratio of the average to the maximum information content per symbol. The coding redundancy is defined as one minus the coding efficiency. An efficiently coded message takes maximum advantage of the communication channel. However, redundancy may be intentionally introduced in the message in order to overcome the effects of channel noise. A balance must be reached between efficiency and redundancy so as to achieve optimum transmission between the source and destination. The message source outputs symbols at a uniform rate of r symbols/sec. The average source information transfer rate, R, is given by the following equation:

$$R = r(\text{symbols/sec}) \times H(\text{bits/symbol}) = r \cdot H \text{ bits/sec} \tag{8.8}$$

Shannon's theorem for a noisy channel states that if a message source has a transfer rate R and a capacity C, and if $R < C$, the coded source output can be sent and received over the channel without a high probability of errors. If, however, $R > C$, it is not possible to send and receive without a high probability of errors.

The Shannon-Hartley theorem defines the maximum noisy channel capacity, C, in bits/sec for a band-limited channel of W Hz with additive Gaussian noise. The *channel capacity* is defined in terms of channel bandwidth, W, and S/N ratio in the following equation:

$$C = W \cdot \log_2 \left(1 + \frac{S}{N}\right) \text{ bits/sec} \tag{8.9}$$

where S and N are the average signal and noise power, respectively, as measured at the channel input.

The following example elaborates on the maximum channel capacity concept.

EXAMPLE 8.1

Given W = 3,000 Hz and S/N = 1,023, find the maximum channel capacity C.

$$C = 3,000 \cdot \log_2 (1 + 1,023) = 30,000 \text{ bps}$$

However, coding and modulation methods necessary to achieve the maximum channel capacity are not described and may not be obtainable. The maximum noise channel capacity becomes a trade-off between bandwidth and signal-to-noise ratio, as expressed in the following equation:

$$\frac{S}{N} = 2^{c/w} - 1 \qquad\qquad \textbf{(8.10)}$$

In the previous example, an S/N ratio of 1,023 was required to achieve a channel capacity, C, of 30,000 bps for a channel bandwidth, W, of 3,000 Hz. If the S/N is doubled, then the required bandwidth becomes 2,727 Hz. Similarly, if the S/N is halved, the required bandwidth increases to 3,333 Hz. Thus, a 100% S/N ratio increase requires a 10% bandwidth reduction. A 50% S/N ratio reduction requires a 10% increase in bandwidth. According to Nyquist's theorem, the maximum data rate through a band-limited channel is limited to $2 \cdot W$ symbols/sec. In contrast, the Hartley-Shannon theorem indicates that the channel capacity can be expanded by increasing the S/N ratio.

Higher channel capacity is possible with the use of multilevel, or M-ary, coding. An M-ary system achieves a channel transfer rate of $2W \cdot (\log_2 M)$ bits/sec, where M is the number of possible signal levels. However, this is done at the expense of a reduced threshold. Thus, as the number of levels increases, the S/N ratio must be adjusted in order to maintain an acceptable bit error rate. The effect of M-ary coding on the S/N ratio is illustrated in the following example.

EXAMPLE 8.2

Given a bandlimited channel of 3,000 Hz, calculate the maximum data rate and required S/N ratios for M = 2, 3, 4.

    a. (M = 2)

        $C = 2W \cdot (\log_2 M) = (2 \times 3,000) \log_2 (2) = 6,000 \text{ bps}$

        $\text{S/N} = 2^{c/w} - 1 = 2^2 - 1 = 3$

        $\text{S/N (dB)} = 10 \log_{10} (3) = 4.8$

    b. (M = 3)

        $C = 2W \cdot (\log_2 M) = (2 \times 3,000) \log_2 (3) = 9,500 \text{ bps}$

        $\text{S/N} = 2^{c/w} - 1 = 2^3 - 1 = 7$

        $\text{S/N (dB)} = 10 \log_{10} (7) = 8.5$

    c. (M = 4)

        $C = 2W \cdot (\log_2 M) = (2 \times 3,000) \log_2 (4) = 12,000 \text{ bps}$

        $\text{S/N} = 2^{c/w} - 1 = 2^4 - 1 = 15$

        $\text{S/N (dB)} = 10 \log_{10} (15) = 11.8$

Thus, it can be seen that a three-level system requires an S/N that is 3.7 dB higher than that of a two-level system. Similarly, a four-level system requires an S/N that is 7 dB higher than that of a two-level system. Hence, the channel capacity gain is offset by the additional signal strength requirement.

8.2 MODEMS

The term modem is an abbreviation of Modulator/Demodulator. A modem is a DCE used to convert the digital data bit stream into a signal suitable for transmission over the telephone channel, and vice-versa. As such, the modem must provide proper encoding so as to contain the resulting signal within a typical 3,000-Hz channel bandwidth. Figure 8.5 is a simplified block diagram of a typical modem. A modem contains both the transmit and receive data paths, as well as the necessary logic to interface with a DTE.

Encoding is performed to minimize transmission bandwidth and to enhance signal detection. There are two basic methods for encoding binary data prior to carrier modulation, clocked and self-clocking. The raw binary code can be represented with one signal level for logic one and another for logic zero. This encoding technique, known as NRZ-L, is susceptible to channel attenuation and signal inversion, which results in data errors. A differential encoding technique, known as NRZ-M, minimizes errors by encoding the data as level changes instead. This is done by the addition modulo 2 of the bit stream and its one-bit-cell–delayed version. The RZ encoding technique uses the presence of a half-bit-cell pulse to denote a logic one and its absence to denote zero. This is accomplished by gating the data with the clock. The encoding techniques above require a synchronized receiver clock in order to extract the signal information. NRZ-L-encoded data can be combined with a clock, using addition modulo 2, to provide self-clocking capability. This scheme, known as Manchester encoding, uses a half-bit-cell pulse of one level to represent logic one and a half-bit-cell pulse of the inverse level to represent logic zero. In either case, pulse-level transitions occur at the mid-cell point. Similarly, NRZ-L data can be modified with a clock to provide self-clocking along with the advantages of NRZ-M encoding. The resulting encoding, known as biphase, has level transitions at the bit boundaries. Logic one is represented by an additional level change at bit mid-cell, and logic

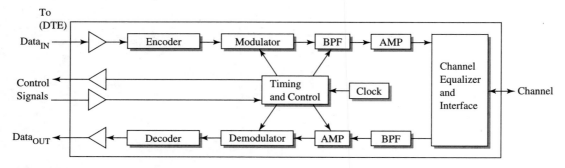

FIGURE 8.5
Modem: simplified block diagram.

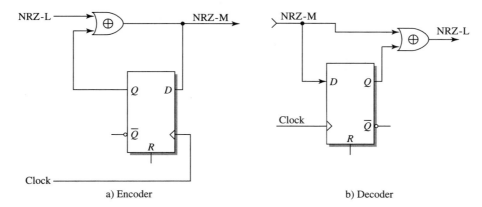

a) Encoder   b) Decoder

FIGURE 8.6
NRZ-L/NRZ-M encoding and decoding.

zero is represented by a constant level. Another self-clocking encoding scheme, known as Miller, represents logic one with a level change at mid-cell and uses no change for zero. If two consecutive zeros occur, a level change occurs at the bit boundary of the second zero. Figure 8.6 illustrates the relationship between NRZ-L and NRZ-M encoding.

These encoding techniques result in different channel bandwidth requirements, which are expressed in terms of the reference frequency, f_r, that corresponds to a specific data rate. For the channel to pass encoded data, it must exhibit certain frequency response characteristics. The channel bandwidth requirements for each of the encoding techniques above is listed in Table 8.2.

Figure 8.7 illustrates a binary data bit stream and its corresponding encoding formats. The example binary input is given as 10010110. The depicted timing waveforms are derived by applying the encoding rules for each technique on the binary logic states.

Modulation is the process of modifying one or more parameters of the reference carrier signal waveform by a digital data signal in accordance with a specific rule. There are three basic modulation methods: amplitude modulation (AM), frequency modulation (FM), and phase modulation (PM). Modems are designed to use either one or a combination of these methods. Data transmission using AM is limited to 5 bps, and the required channel bandwidth equals the data rate. The carrier frequency and phase remain constant, while the amplitude changes to one of two possible levels as a function of the input data bit states. Thus, channel noise can induce data errors as it combines with the composite signal. Data transmission using FM is capable of support-

TABLE 8.2
Channel bandwidth requirements

Code	f_1	f_2	Clock
NRZ-L	0	$0.75\,f_r$	External
NRZ-M	0	$0.50\,f_r$	External
RZ	$0.25\,f_r$	$1.0\,f_r$	External
Manchester	$0.20\,f_r$	$1.4\,f_r$	Self
Biphase	$0.50\,f_r$	$1.0\,f_r$	Self
Miller	$0.10\,f_r$	$0.75\,f_r$	Self

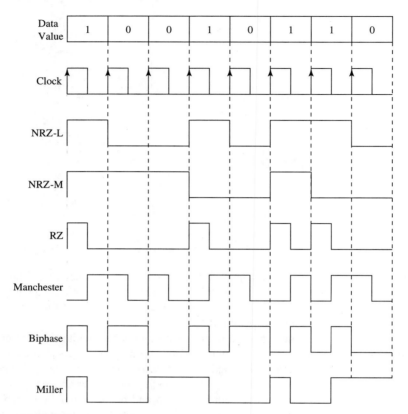

FIGURE 8.7
Encoded data formats.

ing data rates up to 1,200 bps. This requires a channel bandwidth of twice the data rate. The carrier amplitude remains constant, while the frequency is shifted to one of two possible values as a function of the input data bit states. This technique is better known as frequency shift keying (FSK). Using noncoherent FSK (FSK-NC), no phase continuity is provided between consecutive frequency shifts. In contrast, coherent FSK (FSK-C) provides a phase-continuous shift operation that eliminates spurious signals. This results in efficient bandwidth usage and higher data rate operation. Data transmission using PM is capable of supporting data rates of up to 9,600 bps. The carrier amplitude and frequency remain constant, while the phase shifts between two values as a function of the input data bit states. This technique is better known as phase shift keying (PSK). PSK modems have the highest implementation complexity, while AM modems have the lowest. Figure 8.8 illustrates these three basic modulation techniques.

Quadrature PSK (QPSK) is a modulation technique that encodes two consecutive data bit states to form a *dibit*. The dibit is represented by a discrete phase shift of the carrier signal. This two-bit grouping results in four possible unique phase shifts or signal states. In general, an M-ary modulation scheme groups n bits to represent $\log_2 (M)$ data bits/baud. The resulting M

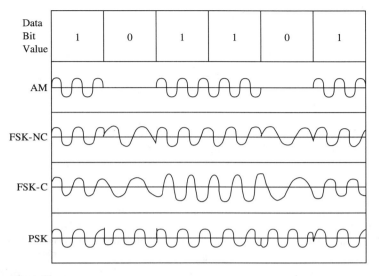

FIGURE 8.8
Data modulation techniques.

unique signal states provide a trade-off between bandwidth usage and S/N ratio. The effective data transfer rate equals the channel baud rate times the number of bits per baud, n. For QPSK, $n = 2$; hence the data rate becomes twice the channel baud rate and the bandwidth usage is reduced by a factor of two. However, the additional phase shifts effectively reduce the receiver detection threshold margin. This necessitates a higher S/N ratio in order to maintain the same low error rate as PSK. Figure 8.9 shows the PSK and QPSK phase diagrams.

A corresponding M-ary modulation scheme that sacrifices bandwidth to improve the S/N ratio is the multiple frequency phase shift keying (MFSK). In this approach, the bit group logic state combinations are represented by unique and equally spaced frequency values. The resulting greater bandwidth usage relaxes the required S/N ratio for a given bit error rate (BER). A

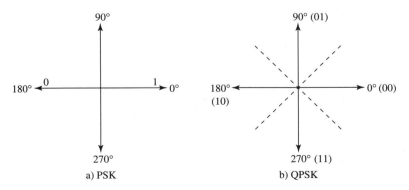

FIGURE 8.9
Phase modulation diagrams.

TABLE 8.3

Data modulation types

Modulation Type	n	M	Baud	S/N (dB)
AM	1	2	5	14.4
FSK-NC	1	2	300	13.2
FSK-C	1	2	300	11.7
PSK	1	2	600	8.4
QPSK	2	4	600	9.4
16-PSK	4	16	2,400	17.6
16-QAM	4	16	2,400	15.1

hybrid scheme that combines phase and amplitude modulation to increase the signal states is called quadrature amplitude modulation (QAM). For example, the 16-QAM can use both amplitude values and their phase values to define sixteen unique signal states. Thus, a 2,400-baud rate channel can transmit at an effective data rate of 9,600 bps. Table 8.3 provides a comparison of the various modulation schemes and their parameters. The indicated S/N ratios correspond to a bit error rate of 1×10^{-4}.

The basic modulator implementation consists of an electronic switch that is controlled by the input data bit stream. The AM modulator input consists of a carrier signal, f_c, that is switched ON and OFF as a function of the individual data bit states. The AM demodulator consists of a bandpass filter (BPF), which selects the carrier signal and enhances the S/N ratio, and an envelope detector circuit that recovers the signal. Figure 8.10 is a simplified block diagram

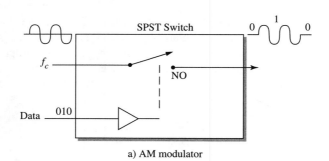

a) AM modulator

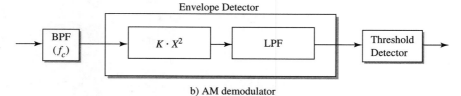

b) AM demodulator

FIGURE 8.10

AM modem block diagram.

of this scheme. The envelope detector consists of a square law device followed by a low pass filter (LPF), which enables it to sense the carrier signal energy. The threshold detector converts the detected signal into a bit stream.

An FSK modulator input consists of two carrier signals, f_1 and f_2, that are selected as a function of the individual data bit states. The FSK demodulator is composed of two envelope detectors, one for each carrier frequency, followed by a decision logic circuit to reconstruct the data bit stream. Figure 8.11 provides a simplified block diagram of the FSK technique.

A PSK modulator consists of a carrier signal, f_1, whose phase is selected as a function of the individual data bit states. The demodulator consists of a synchronous detector that senses the coherent phase shifts of the carrier signal. The basic synchronous detector consists of a multiplier followed by an LPF. Figure 8.12 is a simplified block diagram of the PSK process. The received signal is correlated with two possible, locally generated replicas of the carrier signal, and the decision logic selects the most likely one. As such it is necessary to have a stable local reference signal source in the demodulator that stays synchronized with the received signal.

Figure 8.13 shows a simplified block diagram of a 16-QAM operation. The modulator consists of two digital-to-analog converter (DAC) modules. Each module converts the specific input data bit states into analog signal levels. A quadrature modulator is used to combine the two independent signals into a common bandwidth. The demodulator consists of two synchronous detectors and two analog-to-digital (ADC) modules. The detectors extract the two inde-

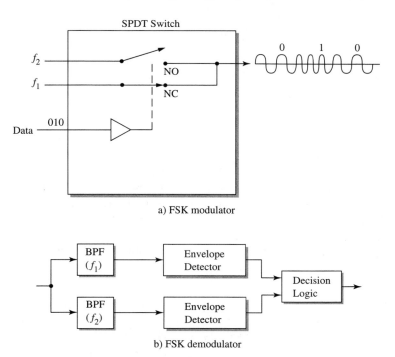

a) FSK modulator

b) FSK demodulator

FIGURE 8.11
FSK modem block diagram.

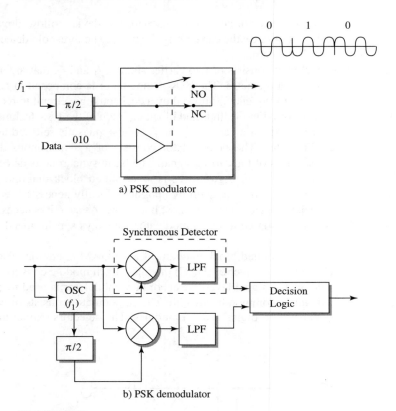

FIGURE 8.12
PSK modem block diagram.

pendent analog signals. The modules are used to convert the two received analog signal levels into corresponding data bit states.

Figure 8.5 showed an amplifier (AMP) and a bandpass filter (BPF) in the transmit and receive data paths. The amplifier is used to raise the sending signal level, within the passband, for a specific S/N ratio. The BPF is used to provide added selectivity and signal gain for optimum detection. Also, the channel equalizer provides both amplitude and phase corrections to compensate for nonuniform channel characteristics. Finally, the channel and DTE interfaces are provided to coordinate the modem's operation and ensure a reliable data transfer environment.

8.3 TERMINALS

The terminal acts as the data source, the data destination, or both. There are three basic types of terminal: the dumb, the smart, and the intelligent. A dumb terminal, such as a keyboard send/receive (KSR) unit, is able to transfer asynchronous character data, via a modem, to a remote terminal. A smart terminal is an MPU-based component with a keyboard, CRT display, data memory and built-in firmware functions to provide features such as editing, synchronous

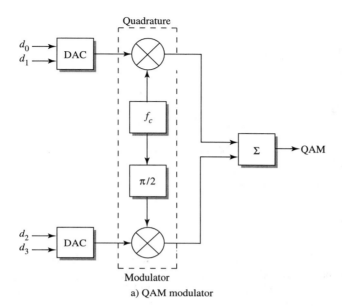

a) QAM modulator

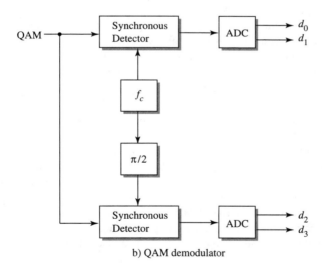

b) QAM demodulator

FIGURE 8.13
16-QAM modem block diagram.

block data, and error checking. An intelligent terminal is an MCU-based component that provides added data-processing capability and user-programmable functions.

Figure 8.14 is a functional block diagram of a dumb terminal. The transmit path contains a keyboard input device (KBD) and an ASCII encoder to generate alphanumeric data. The receive path contains an ASCII decoder and a printer device (PTR) to output alphanumeric

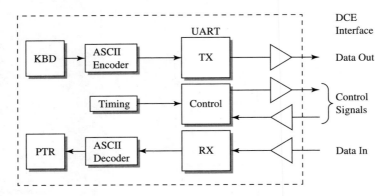

FIGURE 8.14
Dumb terminal block diagram.

characters. The heart of the unit is the universal asynchronous receiver transmitter (UART) module. It converts the ASCII code parallel data into a serial format prior to transmission. Similarly, it converts received serial data into parallel ASCII code prior to character decoding. Also, it has a DCE interface to facilitate remote data exchanges.

A terminal is capable of supporting one of three possible communication modes: simplex, half duplex, and full duplex. A simplex mode uses one terminal as the transmitter and another as the receiver, maintaining data flow in only one direction. In half duplex mode, one terminal either acts as the data source or destination, while the other acts as the destination or data source. This results in data flow in either direction, but not at the same time. In full duplex mode each terminal acts as both the data source and destination. This allows simultaneous bidirectional data transfers. A radio broadcast is an example of simplex communication mode. Communicating over a pair of walkie-talkies is an example of half duplex mode. A telephone conversation is an example of full duplex mode. These modes are shown in Figure 8.15.

There are two fundamental data formats available, asynchronous and synchronous. In asynchronous operation, each sent, fixed-length, data character contains a Start bit and a Stop bit. These are used by the receiver to maintain frame synchronization. This scheme allows characters to be sent at random intervals and results in variable data transfer rates. The Start bit transition activates the receiver's internal data rate clock, which samples each character bit at mid-cell point to determine its logic state. The Stop bit indicates the character's end and prepares the receiver for the next one. A logic one state is called Mark and a logic zero state is called Space.

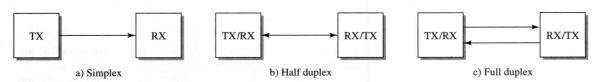

FIGURE 8.15
Communications modes.

Figure 8.16 illustrates the asynchronous data format. The Start bit is preceded by a Mark-to-Space transition that defines a new character frame. This is followed by the actual data bits representing the ASCII character code. Next, an optional parity bit is included for error detection. The Stop bit indicates the frame boundary. The parity bit provides redundancy to detect single data bit errors. There are four parity options: odd, even, Mark, and Space. The parity bit value is determined by the number of logic state one data bits in the character. For odd parity, if the number is odd, then the bit is set to 0; if the number is even, the bit is set to 1. The converse is true for even parity selection. If no parity is selected, the bit is held at either the Mark or the Space level.

The number of Stop bits can be one, one and a half, or two. The number of data bits per character symbols can be five to eight, depending on the code used. The five-bit code, known as Baudot, can define thirty-two unique character symbols. However, using the *letters and figures symbols* to select lower or upper case, it is possible to define a total of sixty-four characters. The six-bit code, known as BCD transcode, is used to define sixty-four unique character symbols such as alphanumeric characters, punctuation marks, and some control characters. The seven-bit code, known as ASCII, has attained widespread usage. It can define 128 unique combinations that are used to represent ninety-six printable character symbols, such as upper-case and lower-case letters, decimal digits, and punctuation marks. Also, thirty-two control characters are defined for device and data transfer operations. These include carriage return, line feed, form feed, acknowledge, and negative acknowledge. The eight-bit code, called EBCDIC, is used to represent 256 possible character symbols. Table 8.4 lists the upper-case letters and decimal digit representations in the four codes, using hexadecimal notation. In Baudot, for example, the letter A is represented as 03_{16} and is preceded by the letters symbol $1F_{16}$. Similarly, the digit 1 is represented as 17_{16} and is preceded by the figures symbol $1B_{16}$. In transcode, the letter A is represented as 01_{16} and the digit 1 as 31_{16}. In ASCII, the letter A is represented as 41_{16} and the digit 1 as 31_{16}. In EBCDIC, A is represented as $C1_{16}$ and 1 as $F1_{16}$.

A 3,000-Hz noisy channel with an S/N ratio of 128, 21 dB, has a theoretical channel capacity, C, of 21,000 bps. The use of ASCII-coded data results in an information content, H, of 7 bits/symbol. Hence, the maximum symbol rate $r = C/H = 3,000$ symbols per second. The bit cell interval, at 21,000 bps, becomes 47.6 µsec. Each send data character consists of seven code bits, a Start and Stop bit, and the parity bit, for a total of ten bits. The resulting character frame interval becomes 476 µsec, which translates into 2,100 symbols per second. Thus, the asynchronous data format overhead results in a 30% reduction of the maximum symbol rate.

A smart data terminal is an MPU-based component that supports both asynchronous and synchronous data formats. Figure 8.17 is a typical smart terminal functional block diagram.

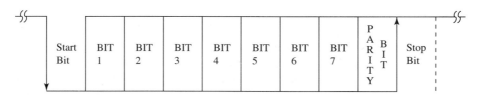

FIGURE 8.16
Asynchronous data format.

TABLE 8.4
Binary data codes

Symbol	Baudot	Transcode	ASCII	EBCDIC
A	03	01	41	C1
B	19	02	42	C2
C	0E	03	43	C3
D	09	04	44	C4
E	01	05	45	C5
F	0D	06	46	C6
G	1A	07	47	C7
H	14	08	48	C8
I	06	09	49	C9
J	0B	11	4A	D1
K	0F	12	4B	D2
L	12	13	4C	D3
M	1C	14	4D	D4
N	0C	15	4E	D5
O	18	16	4F	D6
P	16	17	50	D7
Q	17	18	51	D8
R	0A	19	52	D9
S	05	22	53	E2
T	10	23	54	E3
U	07	24	55	E4
V	1E	25	56	E5
W	13	26	57	E6
X	1D	27	58	E7
Y	15	28	59	E8
Z	11	29	5A	E9
0	16	30	30	F0
1	17	31	31	F1
2	13	32	32	F2
3	01	33	33	D3
4	0A	34	34	D4
5	10	35	35	D5
6	15	36	36	D6
7	07	37	37	D7
8	06	38	38	D8
9	18	39	39	F9

The MPU coordinates and controls all terminal operations. The CRT display is used for editing and viewing the data. The KBD is used for data entry and operator control functions. The PROM contains a set of function routines for BIT, data editing and formatting, and I/O functions. The RAM is used as a temporary message I/O buffer. The universal synchronous asynchronous receiver transmitter (USART) handles the serial communication data formats and protocols. The DCE interface provides the necessary control and I/O data signal levels.

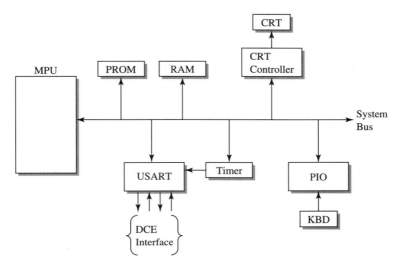

FIGURE 8.17
Smart terminal block diagram.

Synchronous data are sent in long blocks that contain multiples of n-bit character data. Frame synchronization occurs at the block level with special *Sync characters* preceding each block. The synchronous receiver is always looking for one or more of these Sync characters; the subsequent characters represent the actual data. The transmitter sends character data in a contiguous manner, and in the absence of data, it outputs sync characters to maintain link synchronization. Eliminating the need for character frame synchronization enables efficient high data rate transfers to occur. However, a transmit clock signal must be provided at the receiver to maintain bit cell synchronization. This clock is either sent via a separate channel or is derived from the input data bit stream.

Figure 8.18a illustrates the synchronous clock and data timing relationship. Each data bit is sampled at mid-cell, by the clock, to ensure a high degree of accuracy. The probability of error increases as a function of data block length; therefore error detection is required to ensure data transfer integrity. Figure 8.18b depicts a typical synchronous data block format. The send data are preceded by two special Sync characters and are contained between two control characters. The control characters indicate the start and end of the actual data. The last character provides data block error-checking information, similar to a parity bit, which is used by the receiver to determine data integrity.

The terminal contains firmware to support the various modes of operation. A typical software flow diagram is shown in Figure 8.19. Upon power-up, the terminal goes through its BIT routine to determine its health status. Next, the initialization routine presets all parameters to their default states. A terminal may be in either the offline or the online mode of operation. The offline mode provides user interaction, via the KBD, and may be used either to configure, to perform a function, or to compose and edit a message. The online mode supports both asynchronous and synchronous format data transfers between two terminals. Character-by-character data transfer is available only in asynchronous mode. Message, or block data, trans-

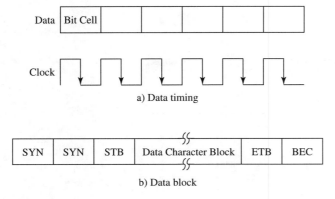

a) Data timing

| SYN | SYN | STB | Data Character Block | ETB | BEC |

b) Data block

FIGURE 8.18
Synchronous data definitions.

fer is available in either mode. Character transfers occur from the local KBD to the CRTs of the local and remote terminals. Message transfers occur between the local and distant terminals, from one buffer to another. In either case, an automatic error control function is provided.

The terminal interface to the DCE is defined by the Electronic Industries Association (EIA) standards. The most commonly used standard is the RS-232 physical layer interface description, which defines mechanical, electrical, and functional parameters for DTE and DCE serial binary data interchange. In order to provide performance enhancements, the RS-449 has been developed to address mechanical and functional parameters. Two additional standards, RS-422 and RS-423, define the electrical parameters to supplement the RS-449 standard. RS-232 specifies a twenty-five-pin connector and defines the pin assignments for each of the defined I/O signals. RS-449 specifies a thirty-seven-pin connector for the primary channel and a nine-pin connector for a secondary channel. The RS-485 standard is similar to RS-422, but it has tri-state drivers for multipoint connections—up to sixty-four of them. Also, the RS-530 standard combines the mechanical RS-232 parameters with the electrical RS-422 and RS-423 parameters.

The electrical parameters associated with the three basic standards are listed in Table 8.5. An unbalanced signal is referenced with respect to a common ground. A balanced signal consists of both the true and inverted polarity components, with respect to a common ground. The maximum distance refers to the physical separation between the signal source and the destination load. The distance is inversely proportional to the signal data rate. In the case of RS-232, a data rate of 20 kbps can be sustained at a maximum distance of 50 ft. However for RS-423, a data rate of 100 kbps can be sustained at a distance of 40 ft. To transmit at the maximum distance of 4,000 ft, it is necessary to limit the data to 900 bps. Similarly, RS-422 transmission at 10 mbps can be sustained up to 40 ft. To transmit at the maximum distance of 4,000 ft, it is necessary to limit the data rate to 90 kbps.

The main reason for these restrictions is the signal coupling, or crosstalk, between adjacent signal conductors, which can pose a major interference problem. Figure 8.20 illustrates both the time and frequency domain digital signal characteristics. A digital signal is defined in the time domain by its pulse duration, t_d, measured between two consecutive amplitude transi-

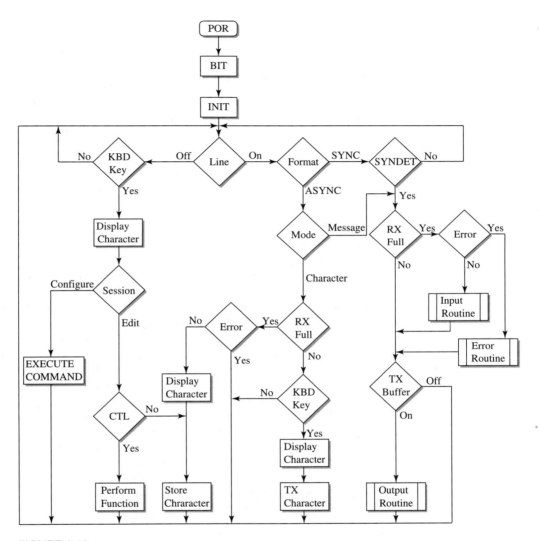

FIGURE 8.19
Terminal software flow diagram.

tions, and its period, T, which defines the start of a new pulse interval. The pulse leading edge and trailing edge transition times, from 10% to 90% amplitude values, are known as rise time, t_r, and fall time, t_f, respectively. A square wave is a special case of a digital waveform, in which pulse duration equals one-half the period. The frequency domain magnitude spectrum is a function of the above time domain parameters. The initial magnitude level, A, is proportional to the signal amplitude, X, and the duty cycle, t_d/T. The first rolloff breakpoint, f_1, is inversely proportional to the pulse duration, t_d. The second rolloff point, f_2, is inversely proportional to the pulse transition times, t_r or t_f, which are equal in general. By controlling the pulse transition

TABLE 8.5
EIA standards electrical parameters

Parameter	RS-232	RS-423	RS-422
Signal Type	Unbalanced	Unbalanced	Balanced
Maximum Distance	50 ft.	4,000 ft.	4,000 ft.
Maximum Data Rate	20 kbps	100 kbps	10 Mbps
Space Voltage	+5 V to +15 V	+4 to +6 V	+ 2 to +6 V
Space Threshold	+3 V	+200 mV	+200 mV
Mark Voltage	−5 V to −15 V	−4 to −6 V	−2 to −6 V
Mark Threshold	−3 V	−200 mV	−200 mV
Source Z	300 ohms	50 ohms	100 ohms
Load Z	3 to 7 kOhms	4 kOhms	4 kOhms

times, it is possible to reduce the magnitude of the higher frequencies and thereby control the crosstalk. In both RS-422 and RS-423, the pulse edge transition times are set for 10% of the pulse period, T. This reduces the crosstalk level to enable reliable signal transmission over the specified distances.

The minimum and maximum Space and Mark signal levels are specified as ±5 V to ±15 V for RS-232 and ±4 V to ±6 V for RS-423, with respect to a ground reference. The RS-422 Space and Mark signal levels, measured between the true and inverted outputs, are specified as ±2 V to ±6 V. The source impedance for the line driver and corresponding load impedance for the line receiver are also specified in each standard. Finally, the Space and Mark signal thresholds are listed in each standard. Figure 8.21 illustrates the electrical line driver and receiver interconnections for each of the three interface standards. The RS-232 standard uses an unbalanced line driver and receiver pair to transfer data to a maximum distance of 50 ft. The RS-423 uses an unbalanced driver and a balanced line receiver pair to transfer data over 4,000 ft. The balanced line receiver rejects any common mode noise and detects only the data signal across its input terminals. The received noise signal is rejected because it appears across both inputs in equal magnitude and polarity. The RS-422 standard achieves even higher data rate transfers by the use of a balanced driver-and-receiver pair. This configuration eliminates both noise and

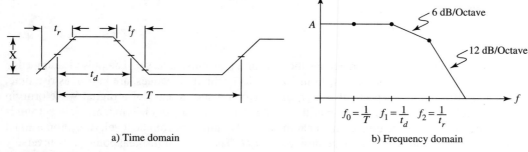

a) Time domain   b) Frequency domain

FIGURE 8.20
Digital signal characteristics.

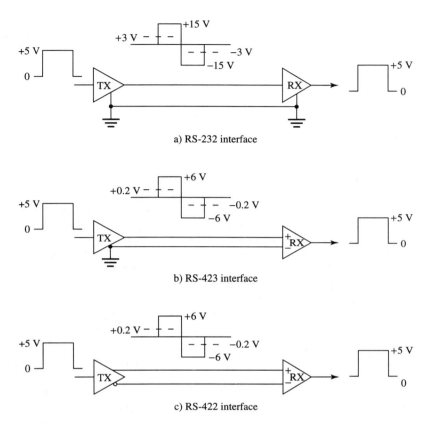

FIGURE 8.21
Serial electrical interface standards.

ground signal differences between the source and load locations. There is a similar functional exchange among these standards, called a handshake protocol.

Figure 8.22 illustrates a typical DTE-to-DCE handshake signal protocol. The DTE raises its data terminal ready (DTR) control signal to the DCE, which in turn responds with its data set ready (DSR) signal. When the terminal is ready to send data, it raises its request to send (RTS) signal to the DCE. When the DCE is ready to receive the data, it responds with its clear to send (CTS) signal. Then the DTE outputs data on its transmit data (TD) line. When the DCE is ready to send data, it raises its ring indicator (RI) signal to alert the DTE. Then it raises its carrier detect (CD) control signal to the DTE, indicating that valid data are present on its receive data (RD) line. In asynchronous data transfers, the DTE and DCE use their internal clock sources. In synchronous data transfers, the DCE provides both send and receive clocks to the DTE. If the data rate between two transfer nodes is far below the maximum channel capacity, then multiplexing techniques can be used to utilize all the available channel bandwidth.

The two basic multiplexing methods are frequency and time division. In frequency division multiplexing (FDM), the full channel bandwidth is statically allocated, in fixed bands, to

FIGURE 8.22
Handshake protocol.

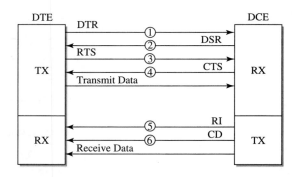

various users who in turn access their assigned subchannel on a normal basis. Time division multiplexing (TDM) can be either synchronous (STDM) or asynchronous (ATDM). STDM uses static allocation and deterministic access methods. ATDM, also known as statistical multiplexing, uses dynamic allocation and random access methods. STDM assigns the full channel bandwidth to a fixed number of equal time slots that make up a frame. Timing and synchronization are provided with each transmitted frame. If no data are available for a given time slot, then its bandwidth is wasted. ATDM overcomes the problem of unused time slots by allocating them to the various data sources on a demand basis. This may result in variable-length frames and requires source tracking with every frame. Also, the sum of the individual frame rates is greater than the total channel capacity. However, due to the random activity of each data source, the channel capacity is never exceeded, and channel bandwidth is wasted only when no source data are available.

Figure 8.23 illustrates a typical STDM configuration. Four DTEs with different data rates are multiplexed into a common 9,600-bps channel. If their data rates are equal, then the data slot sequence will be ABCD and the use of a 4-to-1 multiplexer will suffice. However, it is nec-

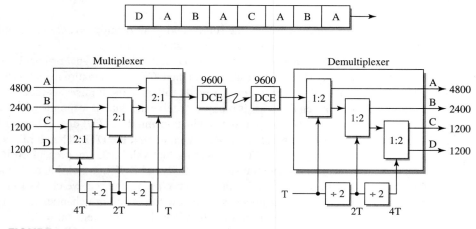

FIGURE 8.23
DTE multiplexing/demultiplexing.

essary to design a more elaborate scheme in order to accommodate different data rates. This is accomplished by cascading three 2-to-1 multiplexers, each with a corresponding slot time interval as a multiple of the source data rate $T = \frac{1}{9,600}$. As such each frame consists of two time slots. The send data slot sequence becomes ABACABAD, and it is repeated regardless of source data activity. At the receiving end, a demultiplexer routes the composite data bit stream to the corresponding DTEs in synchronization with the source DTEs. The T1 signaling is a high-speed multiplexing technique that combines twenty-four data channels, each operating at 64 kbps, into one 1.544 Mbps data bit stream. Each channel input contains 8 bits and is sampled every 125 μsec. Each T1 data frame consists of 193 bits (24 × 8) plus one framing bit. This results in 1.536 Mb of data and 8,000 framing bits per second. The T3 wideband multiplexing technique takes twenty-eight T1 data channels and combines them into one 44.736 Mbps data bit stream.

There are two communication approaches, point-to-point and multipoint. The point-to-point approach uses two physically separated nodes on the same channel. Each node may consist of a single or multiple DTEs using multiplexing. The multipoint-approach uses three or more physically separated nodes on the same channel. Point-to-point communications are in the form of simplex, half duplex, or full duplex modes. Multipoint communications are more elaborate and fall under three configurations: polled, netted, or broadcast. Using a polled configuration, one node is designated as the controller and operates in full duplex mode. The remaining nodes operate in half duplex mode and provide controlled responses as they are uniquely addressed. With the netted configuration, all nodes operate in half duplex. Whenever the channel is free, a pairwise data link is set up between two nodes. In broadcast each node operates in simplex mode, with one node transmitting and the others receiving.

8.4 PROTOCOLS

Protocols are procedures for defining the systematic data exchanges between two terminals. Data link protocols initiate and terminate logical connections, establish source and destination addresses, transfer data, provide framing and synchronization, perform error checking, and maintain link control. Framing is the process of determining the data segment of a transmitted bit stream. Framing may occur at the bit, byte, or block level. Synchronization is the method of establishing data segment boundaries by detecting unique bit patterns.

There are two basic protocol formats: asynchronous and synchronous. Asynchronous protocols are character-oriented. Synchronous protocols can be either bit-oriented or byte-oriented. A bit represents the smallest unit of information. A byte is a group of bits, eight of them, that may or may not represent meaningful information. A character is a group of bits that represents an alphanumeric symbol in a given code system. A block is a set of bits or bytes that collectively represent a message unit. Asynchronous protocols use the Start and Stop bit transitions to establish bit-level synchronization. These two bits define one character frame. Either single or multiple characters can be sent. In the former case, the time delay between consecutive characters exceeds one Stop bit in duration. This allows variable data transfer rates, as a function of the operator, up to the selected rate. When multiple characters are sent, a stored character sequence is sent at the selected data rate, with no delay between consecutive characters. Figure 8.24a illustrates the asynchronous data link protocol format. Each character is de-

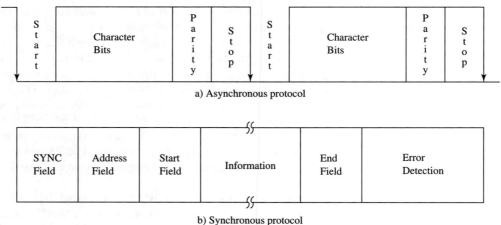

a) Asynchronous protocol

b) Synchronous protocol

FIGURE 8.24
Protocol formats.

fined by a Start bit, which is followed by a number of data bits, a parity bit slot, and the Stop bit(s). The basic difference between single and multiple character mode is the difference in time delay between consecutive characters. The Start bit is used by the receiving DTE to initiate frame synchronization, using its internal 16X or 32X clock. The incoming bits are sampled at mid-cell position to ensure data integrity. Similarly, the Stop bit is used to prepare the receiver for the next Start bit search.

Synchronous protocol uses encoded signal transitions to maintain bit-level synchronization. A fixed sync pattern is used to achieve byte-level synchronization. Block synchronization is achieved by searching for specific bytes that define block boundaries. The basic synchronous data protocol format is illustrated in Figure 8.24b. The SYNC field is used to establish transmitter and receiver synchronization, thus eliminating the need for Start and Stop bits at each data byte. The address field specifies the source and destination DTEs, in the case of a multipoint configuration. The start field precedes the actual information data fields, which are followed by the end field. Finally, the error detection field provides a reference check pattern that is used by the receiver to determine the presence of errors in the information data field.

There are two widespread transmission protocols, binary synchronous communication (BSC) and synchronous data link control (SDLC). BSC is a half duplex, byte-oriented protocol that uses specific control character codes to define various fields in each transmission block frame. SDLC is a full duplex, bit-oriented protocol that uses a set of bit patterns to define the various fields in each block frame. The BSC protocol uses either ASCII or EBCDIC character codes, without Start and Stop bits. With ASCII, a parity option of odd, even, or none can be specified. A special set of characters controls link access, data transmission, and link termination. Table 8.6 lists the main BSC control characters. The BSC frame starts with two consecutive SYN characters, followed by the SOH character, which denotes the start of header field. This field contains addressing information. The information data field is preceded by the STX character and followed by the ETX character. The BCC field is appended to provide error detection. Data transparency is achieved by ensuring that these special characters do not appear in

TABLE 8.6
BSC control characters

Control Character	Definition
SYN	Synchronization
SOH	Start of Header
STX	Start of Text
US	Unit Separator
ETB	End of Block
ETX	End of Text
ACK	Acknowledge
NAK	Negative Acknowledge
ENQ	Enquiry
DLE	Data Link Escape
EOT	End of Transmission

the data field. The special character DLE can also be used, as a delimiter, to achieve transparency when control characters are included or data encoding may create them.

Figure 8.25 illustrates a typical BSC protocol frame structure. This protocol describes a precise exchange sequence between the sender and the receiver. A data transmission is initiated with a message that contains the ENQ control character. In response, the receiver responds with a message that contains the ACK control character. Then the frame-by-frame mes-

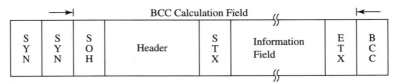

a) Basic message format

b) Transparent message format

c) Multiple message format

FIGURE 8.25
BSC protocol frame definitions.

sage transfers are controlled by the receiver's ACK and NAK responses. The ACK response enables the sender to transmit the next frame; the NAK response requests the sender to repeat the current frame. The transfer sequence is terminated by the presence of the EOT control character, which indicates "End of Transmission" to the receiver. The difference between the basic and transparent formats is the addition of two DLE characters at the data field boundaries in the transparent format. The multiple message format contains several information fields, with associated BCC fields. The information fields are separated with the US control character.

The SDLC uses a bit pattern, called a flag, to mark the start and end of each message frame. The message frame contains fields for address, control, information data, and frame check. Figure 8.26a illustrates the SDLC protocol basic message format. The flag has a fixed eight-bit pattern of six contiguous ones bounded by two zeros, which becomes 7E in hexadecimal notation. The address field contains one byte that specifies the destination DTE. The control field contains one byte for link commands, responses, and acknowledgments. The information field may be of any bit length and pattern. Data transparency is achieved by automatically inserting a zero bit after five consecutive one bits. This scheme eliminates the possibility that

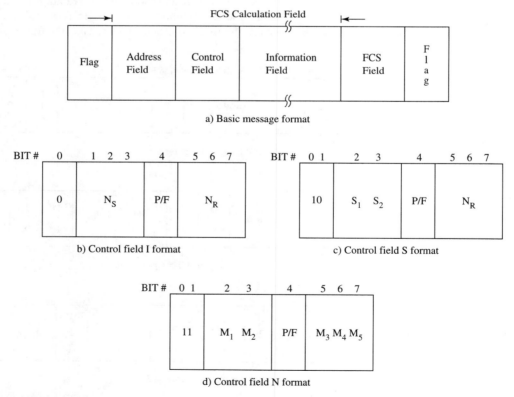

FIGURE 8.26
SDLC protocol frame definitions.

any data pattern within the field will resemble the flag. The frame check sequence consists of two bytes and is used by the receiver to ensure data field integrity.

There are three basic control field formats: the information (I), the supervisory (S), and the nonsequenced (N). The I format is used for normal sequence data transfers. The S format is used for initiating and controlling frame transfers, by either acknowledging or requesting retransmission. The N format is used to set up communication modes and initialize the link. Figures 8.26b, c, and d illustrate the three control field formats. The N_S and N_R subfields specify the number of frames—up to seven—that have been successfully sent and received, respectively. The P/F bit is set to one by the sender to request a response by the receiver. In turn, the receiver sets it to one to indicate its last frame response. The S_i subfield, in the S format, is used to indicate the receiver status: ready, nonread, or message rejection. The M_i subfield, in the N format, is used to specify one of thirty-two possible functions.

8.5 ERROR CONTROL

To maintain data integrity it is necessary to establish error control procedures. Such techniques, when used in conjunction with a data link protocol, transform the noisy channel into a reliable data path.

There are three basic error control methods: remote loopback checking, error detection and correction (EDAC), and forward error correction (FEC). Remote loopback checking requires a full duplex communications mode. In essence, the receiver echoes back the data to the sender for comparison. Since the data paths share the same medium, however, errors can occur in either direction. This makes the technique unattractive, although it is still suitable for channels with a low probability of error.

EDAC employs send message redundancy, which permits error detection. When an error occurs due to channel noise, it is detected by the receiver, which requests a message retransmission. The communication mode can be either half or full duplex. In the half duplex mode, the sender transmits the message and then waits for a receiver to either accept (ACK) or reject (NAK) it. In the full duplex mode, the sender transmits continuously while the receiver responds in sequence. Each message is tagged with a unique identification to facilitate possible retransmission. This technique is called automatic repeat request (ARQ). The three common error detection schemes available are vertical redundancy check (VRC), longitudal redundancy check (LRC), and cyclic redundancy check (CRC).

The VRC scheme is used primarily with asynchronous data transfers, using ASCII characters. The parity bit of each character code is set to either 1 or 0 by the transmitter, consistent with the selected parity mode. The VRC equation is provided below:

$$\text{VRC} = P_i \oplus \sum_{j=0}^{6} a_{ij} \tag{8.11}$$

where VRC = 0, 1 for even and odd parity, respectively.

For example, the VRC calculation for the first character becomes $P_1 \oplus a_{10} \oplus a_{11} \ldots \oplus a_{16}$. If a single data bit state is altered due to an error, the receiver senses the change and sets its parity error flag bit. In general, one and all multiple odd number errors will be detected. All even number errors go undetected with this scheme. The transmitter parity generator calculates the sum modulo 2 of the character code data bits and adjusts the parity bit value to produce the selected parity. Similarly, the receiver parity checker calculates the sum modulo 2 of the character bits to verify correct parity. Both the transmitter and receiver must be configured identically for this scheme to work. The following example illustrates VRC calculation using odd parity:

EXAMPLE 8.3

VRC Error Correction

Tx: 1 2 3 4 5 6 7 P   Rx: 1 2 3 4 5 6 7 P
     1 0 1 0 0 1 0 0   1 0 1 0 0 1 0 0 No error
                                 1 0 1 1 0 1 0 0 One error
                                 1 0 1 0 1 0 0 0 Two errors

If no errors occur, the parity check will be correct. If a single error occurs, the parity will be even; hence the error will be detected. If two errors occur, the parity will remain odd, and the parity check result will be correct.

The LRC scheme is used primarily with BSC protocol and ASCII character data coding. A check character is generated whose individual bit values are the sum modulo 2 of all the corresponding character data bit positions in the information field. The LRC equation is provided below:

$$\text{LRC} = C_j \oplus \sum_{i=1}^{N} a_{ij} \tag{8.12}$$

where LRC = 0, 1 for even and odd parity, respectively.

For example, the LRC calculation for bit zero, of N characters, becomes, $C_0 \oplus a_{10} \oplus a_{20} \ldots \oplus a_{n0}$. When LRC is used in conjunction with VRC, it is possible to detect all odd number bit errors and some even number errors as well. Error detection is performed by computing and inserting the check character in the BCC field prior to transmission. The receiver compares the BCC field against its computed version to detect any errors. Each seven-bit ASCII character data has its parity check bit appended during VRC generation. Similarly, each bit position in the BCC field is computed during LRC generation. The BSC protocol employs the send-and-wait ARQ scheme to transfer data reliably in a half duplex mode. The send DTE waits, after each message frame, for a reply from the receiving DTE. This idle time—the sum of the reply and turnaround times—reduces data transfer throughput. In addition, the channel bit error rate and message frame length have an adverse affect on the transfer rate.

The CRC error detection scheme is used primarily with BSC protocol, using EBCDIC code, or with SDLC protocol. Here the bits of an N-bit-long message are represented as the coefficients of an $N - 1$ degree polynomial in the variable X. Thus, an eight-bit-long message 10011001 is represented by the following equation:

$$\text{M}(X) = \sum_{i=0}^{N-1} a_i \cdot X^i = a_7 X^7 + a_4 X^4 + a_3 X^3 + a_0 X^0 = X^7 + X^4 + X^3 + 1 \tag{8.13}$$

It should be noted that the zero value coefficients are omitted. The transmitter computes the BCC polynomial $B(X)$, such that the transmitted polynomial $T(X) = M(X) + B(X)$ is exactly divisible by a fixed, binary CRC-generating polynomial $C(X)$. In the case of errors, the receiver sees a modified polynomial $T_e(X) = T(X) + E(X)$, where $E(X)$ is the error bit pattern. This results in a nonzero remainder, unless the error pattern is exactly divisible by $C(X)$. A CRC polynomial, when shifted one place in either direction, including end around, results in another CRC polynomial. This property enables the use of shift registers and modulo 2 adders, to implement coding and decoding operations. The judicious choice of CRC polynomials results in the detection of single, odd, and even number bit errors. In addition error bursts can be detected, provided their length is less than the degree of $B(X)$. In all, about 99% of all error patterns can be detected.

The CRC-16-generating polynomial $x^{16} + x^{15} + x^2 + 1$ is used to compute the BCC field in a BSC protocol. Similarly, the ITU-generating polynomial $x^{15} + x^{12} + x^5 + 1$ is used to calculate the FCS field in an SDLC protocol. Figures 8.25 and 8.26 illustrate the frame segments used for the computation of the BCC and FCS fields, respectively. The CRC error detection scheme is explained below. The message information field is represented by a polynomial $M(X)$ of degree $L - 1$, which consists of L binary bits. The $M(X)$ is first multiplied by X^{L-1}, which effectively shifts it $L - 1$ spaces to the left. The resulting polynomial, $M_1(X)$, is then divided by the CRC-generating polynomial, $C(X)$. The resulting modulo 2 division, without borrow or carry, produces the quotient, $Q(X)$, and remainder, $R(X)/C(X)$, polynomials. Next, the transmission polynomial, $T(X)$, is composed as the sum of the modified, $M_1(X)$, and the remainder, $R(X)$, polynomials. When the receiver divides $T(X)$ by $C(X)$, the remainder should be zero, unless an error has occurred. The resulting equations are

$$M_1(X) = M(X) \cdot X^{L-1} \qquad\qquad (8.14)$$

$$M_2(X) = M_1(X)/C(X) \qquad\qquad (8.15)$$

$$M_2(X) = Q(X) + R(X)/C(X) \qquad\qquad (8.16)$$

$$T(X) = M_1(X) + R(X) \qquad\qquad (8.17)$$

$$T(X)/C(X) = Q(X) \qquad\qquad (8.18)$$

The following example provides a detailed explanation of the CRC error detection procedure.

EXAMPLE 8.4

Given $M(X) = 100111010011 = X^{11} + X^8 + X^7 + X^6 + X^4 + X + 1$ and $C(X) = 10011 = X^4 + X + 1$, calculate the $T(X)$ polynomial for the CRC error detection procedure.

$M_1(X) = M(X) \cdot X^4 = X^{15} + X^{12} + X^{11} + X^{10} + X^8 + X^5 + X^4$

$M_2(X) = M_1(X)/C(X) = Q(X) + R(X)/C(X)$

$Q(X) = X^{11} + X^6 + X^4 + X^3 + X^2 + 1$

$R(X) = X^2 + X + 1$

$T(X) = M_1(X) + R(X) = X^{15} + X^{12} + X^{11} + X^{10} + X^8 + X^5 + X^4 + X^2 + X + 1$

$T(X)/C(X) = Q(X) = X^{11} + X^6 + X^4 + X^3 + X^2 + 1$, and $R(X) = 0$

Then, $[T(X) - R(X)] \cdot X^{-4} = M(X)$

The CRC computation is usually implemented with shift registers and exclusive-OR gates, as shown in Figure 8.27. Initially the CRC register is zeroized. Then the data bit stream is shifted through the register, and its final state, the remainder, becomes the error check field. When the data and error check fields are shifted through the receiver's CRC register, a final state of zero indicates an error-free message frame.

SDLC protocol uses full duplex mode for ARQ operation, which eliminates the idle time between message frames. The sender transmits message frames continuously, and the receiver responds to each with ACK or with NAK in case of error. When the sending DTE receives a NAK reply, it repeats the last two message frames, causing a two-frame delay, regardless of which frame caused the error condition. This technique enables the data throughput to approach 90% of the nominal transfer rate as a function of the frame length.

Forward error correction (FEC) schemes use redundancy to detect and correct errors at the receiver, thus eliminating the need for retransmission in case of error. The concept of Hamming distance is used to compose a message so as to reliably detect and correct errors. The *Hamming distance* between two n-bit-long sequences is the number of bit positions in which they differ. In order to detect k errors, it is necessary to have a Hamming distance of $k + 1$. Similarly, in order to correct k errors, it is necessary that the minimum distance be $2 \cdot k + 1$. Hence, a Hamming distance of two will detect one bit error, while a distance of three will also correct it. When a single parity bit is appended to a character code, it generates a coded sequence with a Hamming distance of two that enables single error detection.

There are several FEC codes that can detect and correct several errors at the expense of receiver decoder complexity. The Hamming (7, 4) code consists of four data bits and three check bits, for a total of seven bits. This code provides the capability of detecting and correcting one bit error. In general, the code has the following characteristics. The block length, L, equals $2^k - 1$. The number of check bits, P, equals k. The number of data bits, I, equals $L - P$. The minimum distance, D, equals 3. Each codeword is composed as $(P_1P_2I_1P_3I_2I_3I_4)$, so that each parity check bit is placed in the corresponding $2^{i-1}, i = 1, 2, \ldots, k$, position. In which case P_1 provides a parity check for data bits I_1, I_2 and I_4. Similarly, P_2 provides a parity check for bits I_1, I_3 and I_4. P_3 provides a parity check for bits I_2, I_3, and I_4. Thus, the sender takes a group of four bits, performs three parity checks, and then transmits the resulting codeword. Similarly, the receiver performs three parity checks to detect any errors. In the case of an error, the resulting parity check code becomes the codeword bit error position. The error is corrected

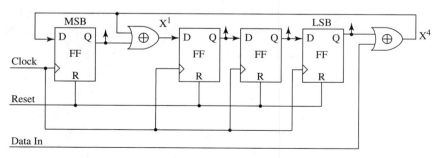

FIGURE 8.27
CRC hardware implementation.

by inverting the corresponding bit. Each parity check bit value is adjusted such that its modulo 2 sum, with the corresponding data bits, is consistent with the selected parity. The three parity check equations are shown below:

$$c_1 = P_1 \oplus I_1 \oplus I_2 \oplus I_4 \qquad c_2 = P_2 \oplus I_1 \oplus I_3 \oplus I_4 \qquad c_3 = P_3 \oplus I_2 \oplus I_3 \oplus I_4 \qquad \textbf{(8.19)}$$

If the actual bit positions are substituted in the above equations, they can be rewritten as

$$c_1 = b_1 \oplus b_3 \oplus b_5 \oplus b_7 \qquad c_2 = b_2 \oplus b_3 \oplus b_6 \oplus b_7 \qquad c_3 = b_4 \oplus b_5 \oplus b_6 \oplus b_7 \qquad \textbf{(8.20)}$$

The error position table, Table 8.7, is used by the receiver to pinpoint a single error location, using the vector notation $<c_3 c_2 c_1>$. The following example details the procedure:

EXAMPLE 8.5

Derive the Hamming (7, 4) codeword for $I = 0101$.
$P + I = P_1 P_2 I_1 P_3 I_2 I_3 I_4$
For even parity, $P = 010$ and $P + I = 0100101$
For odd parity, $P = 101$ and $P + I = 1001101$
If an error occurred in I_4, the vector $<c_3 c_2 c_1> = <111>$, which points to location 7 of the received codeword.

This technique works well for single random errors. However, burst error conditions can produce multiple errors. In order to reliably detect and correct errors under these conditions, data interleaving techniques are used. As such, each message block length is adjusted to the burst error duration, N, and a $N \times N$ matrix is formed using N consecutive blocks. Using this matrix, a new message is composed using the ith bit from each original message, where $i = 1, 2, \ldots, N$. Thus the burst errors affecting a single message are spread over N messages, effectively transforming them into single random errors. The receiver performs the inverse operation in order to reconstruct the original messages. This technique requires data buffering on both ends of the data link.

Another type of FEC is convolutional coding, used to correct random errors in a data bit stream. The basic encoder consists of an n-length shift register, the outputs of which have fixed connections to m XOR gates. Each set of connections between the shift register and the specific XOR gate is called the generator coefficient. An input data bit stream of length n, with the leading bit set to 1 and the rest to 0, results in the characteristic output sequence. A typical convo-

TABLE 8.7
Hamming code error position

Error Position	Bit Label	c_3	c_2	c_1
0	None	0	0	0
1	P_1	0	0	1
2	P_2	0	1	0
3	I_1	0	1	1
4	P_3	1	0	0
5	I_2	1	0	1
6	I_3	1	1	0
7	I_4	1	1	1

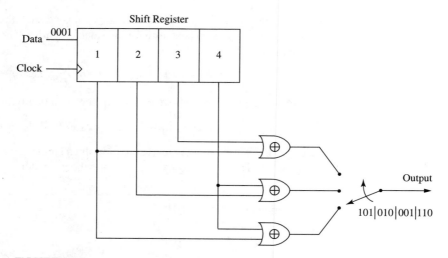

FIGURE 8.28
C(3, 2) convolutional encoder.

lutional encoder is shown in Figure 8.28. The depicted encoder has a four-stage shift register, the outputs of which are connected to a set of three exclusive-OR gates. The C(3, 2) designation indicates that three two-input XOR gates are used. Given an input data rate of X bps, the output code rate is $Y = X/m$ symbols per second, where m is the number of output code bits generated for each new input data bit. For example, if an input bit sequence of 0001 is shifted into the encoder, the output code will be 101 010 001 110.

A code tree diagram can be constructed to provide a graphic representation of the resulting output code. The tree is a binary structure that has two branches, one stemming from each node, to indicate the output state as a result of each input bit state. Because of the introduced redundancy, there are 2^{n-1} unique nodes possible. A single input bit affects the next $n \cdot m$ encoder output bit states. A convolutional decoder takes the received sequence, which may contain errors, and attempts to choose a binary tree path. A minimum-distance algorithm is employed to determine the most likely send data bit sequence.

8.6 STANDARDS

A standard is a set of rules that forms the basis for compatibility among the various types of communications equipment. There are four basic standard types: modulation, error detection and correction (EDAC), data compression, and file transfer. Modulation standards define the process by which a signal carrier frequency is altered to represent the information data bits. The International Telecommunications Union (ITU) recommendations have been widely accepted as the *de facto* modulation standards for modem communications. There are six basic standards available: V.21, V.22, V.22bis, V.32, V.32bis, and V.32terbo. All of these standards support full duplex operation on a two-wire telephone line.

The V.21 standard specifies a 300-bps data rate using FSK modulation. The V.22 standard specifies a 1,200-bps data rate using QPSK modulation at 600 baud. The V.22 standard is the first to employ the dibit concept, which encodes two bits per baud. The V.22bis standard specifies a 2,400-bps data rate, using QAM modulation at 600 baud. This results in an encoding scheme of four bits per baud. A two-dimensional graph of fixed-amplitude-versus-phase combinations is used to define a *constellation* of unique symbols. The V.22bis scheme results in a constellation of 16 unique points. Each symbol point represents a unique four-bit combination. The V.32 standard specifies a 9,600-bps data rate, with a fallback to 4,800 bps. It uses 2,400-baud QAM modulation with trellis coded modulation (TCM). It results in a constellation of 32 points and provides echo cancellation.

The V.32bis standard specifies a 14,400-bps data rate, with fallback to 12,000, 9,600, 7,200, and 4,800 bps as a function of line conditions. It uses 2,400-baud QAM modulation with TCM that results in a constellation of 128 points. It also provides echo cancellation and adaptive line equalization. Echo cancellation dynamically subtracts the transmitted signal return echo from the received signal. Adaptive line equalization compensates for any distortion by multiplying the channel response by its inverse characteristics. This standard supports data rate autoranging, as a function of line conditions, for optimum data throughput.

The V.32terbo standard specifies a 19,200-bps data rate, with fallback to 16,800 bps. It uses 2,400-baud QAM modulation with TCM that results in a constellation of 512 points. The latest standard, called V.34, specifies selectable modulation, baud rate, and carrier frequency parameters. This standard extends the maximum data rate from 19,200 to 28,800 bps. The above standards with the exception of V.21 provide for both synchronous and asynchronous data transmission.

Error detection and correction (EDAC) standards are used to ensure data integrity when a data transfer takes place between two modems. The two prevalent EDAC standards are the Microcom Network Protocol (MNP) levels 1 to 4 and the ITU V.42. Both standards operate on the principle of automatic repeat request (ARQ). In essence, this principle means that when a received data block is corrupted, the receiver sends an ARQ to the sending unit for that block. The MNP level 1 supports half duplex CRC-16 error control. Level 2 provides full duplex ACK/NAK error control. Level 3 speeds up the process by stripping any framing bits off each character. Level 4 creates variable-size blocks as a function of the line bit error rate (BER). The V.42 standard supports both MNP levels 1 to 4 and the Link Access Protocol for Modems (LAPM). The LAPM uses positive and negative acknowledgment (ACK/NAK) messages. In addition, it provides features such as selective retransmission and CRC-32 calculation. For error control, the sending modem appends a CRC value to each data block for data integrity checking. The receiving modem recalculates a CRC from each data block and compares it with the received value. If they don't match, it sends an ARQ back to the sending unit. The sending modem uses the ARQ log to adjust the data block size for optimum throughput in the presence of noise. Yet another scheme uses TCM to perform forward error correction. This approach adds an extra bit to provide data redundancy. The augmented constellation provides a dependency between successive encoded symbol points. The receiver uses the redundancy to perform error detection and correction.

Data compression standards increase the effective data throughput between two modems. This they achieve by reducing the number of bits needed to represent a specific unit of information. The two main compression standards are MNP level 5 and V.42bis. The degree of compression is a function of the inherent data redundancy. MNP level 5 uses modified Huffman coding to achieve a maximum compression ratio of 2:1. The V.42bis uses the Lempel-Liv dynamic dictionary algorithm and can achieve a compression ratio of up to 4:1. For example, a V.32bis modem operating at 14,400 bps can provide an effective data throughput of 57,600 bps.

File transfer standards define orderly procedures for modem-independent file exchanges. The following standards are commonly used: ASCII, KERMIT, XMODEM, YMODEM, and ZMODEM. The main parameters are communications mode, handshake method, block size, and error control. The ASCII standard operates in either half or full duplex mode and supports seven-bit code. It provides no inherent handshake control mechanism; however, ON/OFF software or RTS/CTS hardware flow of control may be used. There is no limitation on data block size. Parity can be used for limited error control. KERMIT was developed by Frank de Cruz at Columbia University. It supports either half of full duplex mode. It uses ACK/NAK for handshaking. It supports variable data block size, originally up to 90 bytes, but now up to 1,024 bytes long. It performs eight-bit to seven-bit code conversion, control character conversion and encoding, file compression, and file transfer abort. It uses either a one-byte checksum (CS) or a two-byte CRC-16 value for error control. XMODEM was developed by Ward Christensen. It supports only half duplex mode. It uses ACK/NAK exchanges for handshaking. It uses a fixed-length 128-byte block and supports eight-bit code. XMODEM can provide either CS or CRC-16 for error control. YMODEM provides enhancements over XMODEM. It supports only half duplex operation. It uses ACK/NAK exchanges for handshaking. It allows variable-size data blocks, from 128 to 1,024 bytes long. It supports multiple file transfers and eight-bit code. YMODEM can abort a file transfer and uses CRC-16 for error control. ZMODEM was developed by Chuck Forsberg. It supports only the full duplex mode of operation. It uses ACK/NAK exchanges for handshaking. It automatically adjusts block size, from 128 to 1,024 bytes, as a function of line BER for efficient data transfers. It has multiple-file transfers, file transfer stop, and restart capabilities and uses either CRC-16 or CRC-32 for error checking.

PROBLEMS

8.1 Design a sequential network that encodes the data of Figure 8.7 into a Miller format.

8.2 Design a sequential network that encodes the data of Figure 8.7 into a biphase format.

8.3 Given a channel bandwidth of 75 kHz and an S/N ratio of 2,047, determine the maximum channel capacity. Also, calculate the channel capacity for S/N ratios of 1,023 and 4,095.

8.4 Determine the maximum data rate and required S/N ratios for problem 8.3, using M-ary coding of 8 and 16.

8.5 Given the reference data rate frequency $f_r = 10$ kHz, determine the channel bandwidth requirements for the encoding techniques of Table 8.2.

8.6 Given a data rate of 57,600 bps, determine the actual symbol rate, bit cell interval, and transfer efficiency for eight-bit character transfers. Assume no parity bits and one Stop bit.

8.7 Design an STDM multiplexer that will operate at 19.2 kbps and handle eight input signals. The signal data rates are two 4,800-bps inputs, two 2,400-bps inputs, and four 1,200-bps inputs.

8.8 Calculate the even VRC for the ASCII characters "DIGITAL."

8.9 Calculate the odd LRC for Problem 8.8.

8.10 Calculate the T(X) polynomial for Example 8.4, using an error-checking polynomial C(X) = X^4 + X^2 + 1.

8.11 Calculate the Hamming code word of I = 1010, for both even and odd parity.

8.12 Given the input sequence 1010, determine the output of the convolutional decoder in Figure 8.28.

REFERENCES

Bennett, W. R., and J. R. Davey. *Data Transmission.* New York: McGraw-Hill, 1965.

Davenport, W. D. *Modern Data Transmission.* New Rochelle, NY: Hayden, 1971.

Hamming, R. W. *Coding and Information Theory.* Englewood Cliffs, NJ: Prentice Hall, 1987.

Intel. *Microcommunications Handbook.* Santa Clara, CA: Intel, 1990.

McNamara J. E. *Technical Aspects of Data Communications.* Bedford, MA: Digital Equipment, 1982.

Motorola Codex. *The Basics Book of Information Networking.* Reading, MA: Addison Wesley, 1992.

Racal-Datacom. *High Speed Dial-Up Modem Handbook.* Fort Lauderdale, FL: Racal-Datacom, 1991.

Racal-Vadic. *Data Communications.* Sunnyvale, CA: Racal-Vadic, 1984.

Roden, M. S. *Digital and Data Communication Systems.* Englewood Cliffs, NJ: Prentice Hall, 1982.

9

MICROPROCESSOR NETWORKS

Microprocessors form the heart of microcomputers and can be either standalone or embedded. Standalone microprocessors are used for general-purpose applications, while embedded microprocessors are used for dedicated control. MCUs can also be grouped together to enhance performance, provide connectivity, and share available resources. There are two basic microprocessor architectures available, the complex instruction set computer (CISC) and the reduced instruction set computer (RISC). A CISC machine uses a set of microprogrammed instructions and requires several clock cycles per instruction. A RISC machine uses an optimal subset of hardwired instructions and usually requires one clock cycle per instruction. The RISC machines are based on the 80-20 rule, which states that 80% of the time a program uses 20% of the instruction set.

These two architectures are collectively known as single instruction single data (SISD) machines. They basically fetch one instruction at a time and perform operations on a single data element. An SISD or scalar processor can execute either one program at a time or multiple programs concurrently. Its performance can be drastically improved by controlling the clock speed, instruction execution cycle, and system bus bandwidth. Also, the use of an internal high-speed cache memory reduces main memory access time, and pipelining speeds up instruction execution times. Performance is measured in either instructions or floating-point operations per second, the units of measure being millions of instructions per second (mips) or millions of floating-point operations per second (mflops), respectively. A group of processors that have both a local and a shared global memory is called a multiprocessor system. The objectives of this chapter are as follows: (1) to define the different multiprocessor architectures, (2) to explain local area networks, (3) to discuss the ISO/OSI reference model, (4) to present the main network standards, and (5) to cover switched networks.

9.1 MULTIPROCESSOR SYSTEMS

A simple multiprocessor system consists of two or more MCUs that share memory and I/O devices via an interconnection network. A *centralized configuration* contains all components in one physical location. Components in a *distributed configuration* reside at multiple locations and process and exchange data upon request. Figure 9.1 illustrates these two basic configurations and their variations.

A single instruction multiple data (SIMD) architecture executes a single instruction on a group of data or vectors. Similar data elements are stored in memory arrays and are fetched as a single entity. Hence, throughput is maximized by eliminating the need to fetch and execute a single instruction and element pair. Figure 9.2 depicts the differences between the SISD and SIMD architectures. The SISD, shown in Figure 9.2a, fetches and decodes an instruction, loads the required data operand, executes the function, and stores the results. In contrast, the SIMD, shown in Figure 9.2b, fetches and decodes an instruction and then executes it on a vector data set. This eliminates the fetch and decode overhead for each data operand. The SIMD architecture uses a central processor unit (CPU) and an I/O processor (IOP) that share a common memory. The CPU contains a memory management unit (MMU), which optimizes memory transfers by providing allocation, protection, and control of system memory. The CPU also has a dedicated vector processor unit and an independent scalar processor unit. Vector processing offers a speed advantage in problems that require calculation-intensive solutions, such as real-time simulation and image processing applications. The scalar processor is used to provide address calculations, pointer maintenance, and loop variable control.

The multiple instruction multiple data (MIMD) architecture performs simultaneous execution of multiple instructions on different data sets, using multiple processors to achieve a degree of parallelism. Traditionally, the von Neumann architecture creates a bottleneck because of the sequential nature of its instruction fetch, decode, and execute cycle. As a result, various attempts have been made to improve the machine's performance. Innovations have included faster cycle time, wider or dual bus, and pipelining for overlapped operation. The use of multiple processors in applications with inherently parallel solutions results in a dramatic increase in performance. However, a hybrid solution that requires both parallel and sequential algorithms may result in a marginal improvement.

There are three basic MIMD architectures: the bus-oriented, the switch-based, and the *N*-cube. The bus-oriented design, shown in Figure 9.3a, uses several processors with local memory to access a global memory via a common high-speed bus. This method permits

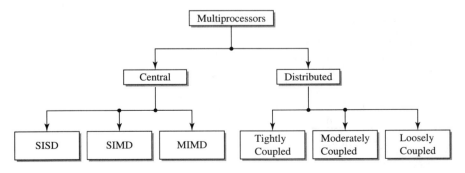

FIGURE 9.1
Multiprocessor architectures.

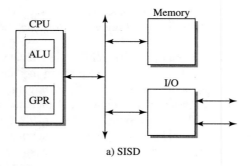

a) SISD

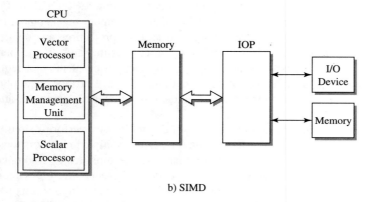

b) SIMD

FIGURE 9.2
Scalar and vector processor architectures.

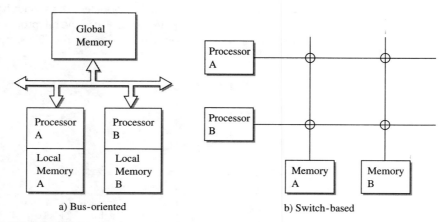

a) Bus-oriented

b) Switch-based

FIGURE 9.3
MIMD processor architectures.

parallel processor operation, but bus saturation limits the number of processors. The switch-based architecture, shown in Figure 9.3b, uses a crossbar switch to provide a unique path from each processor to each memory unit. This scheme becomes rather complex as the number of processors increases, but it maintains high-speed data transfers. In the event of a failure, a degraded mode of operation is possible. The N-cube configuration has 2^N nodes that each consist of a processor with local memory and that can communicate with each other. Each node has N dedicated interfaces to adjacent nodes. For example, a six-cube architecture has sixty-four processors, each of which is connected to six adjacent ones. This technique achieves very high speed transfer rates and can support a large number of processors. It uses message exchanges between adjacent processors to coordinate program execution and is referred to as *data flow processing*. Figure 9.4 depicts an N-cube architecture for $N = 2$.

Distributed processor architectures are classified in terms of interprocessor coupling as either tight, moderate, or loose. A tightly coupled architecture, shown in Figure 9.5a, uses common system memory. The bus arbitration logic resolves priorities and simultaneous accesses. This results in a data word level of communication between processors. Each processor uses an internal cache memory, acting as a prefetch instruction queue, to enhance throughput. A moderately coupled architecture, shown in Figure 9.5b, has processors with local memory that share a global memory via dedicated buses. The global memory can be a dual port disk drive. It permits independent access to any location and provides conflict resolution for simultaneous access to the same location by the two processors. This results in a high-speed data block level of communication between processors. The loosely coupled architecture, shown in Figure 9.5c, has no resource sharing, which results in a high degree of processor independence. Interprocessor communication takes place in the form of relatively high speed data-file level transfers via a common interface medium.

Multiprocessing provides enhanced system performance, modularity, and degraded-mode operation. At the same time, software complexity increases, and system testing becomes more difficult.

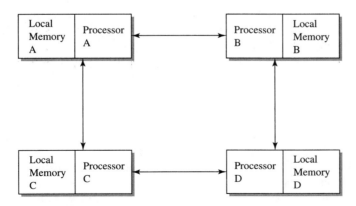

FIGURE 9.4
N-cube processor architecture ($N = 2$).

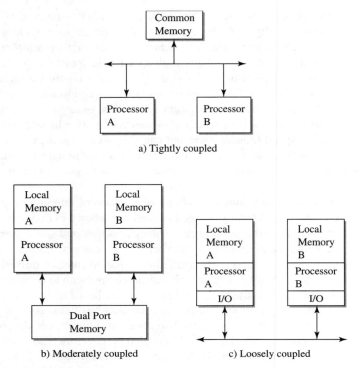

FIGURE 9.5
Distributed processor architectures.

9.2 LOCAL AREA NETWORKS

A local area network (LAN) is a methodology for uniformly linking two or more independent, standalone MCUs to achieve reliable data exchanges and facilitate resource sharing among them. The LAN is a form of loosely coupled distributed processor architecture that can extend for several miles and sustain data rates of greater than 1 Mbps. The user has access to all nodes on the LAN, which can be either computers or peripherals, independent of their relative physical locations. The LAN has added reliability because of its multiple resources, and it can support several users simultaneously. A LAN can be described in terms of topology, transmission medium, transmission method, and access control.

The connectivity arrangement among the various network nodes is referred to as the *topology*. There are three basic network interconnection schemes, the Star, the Bus, and the Ring. Figure 9.6 illustrates these three topologies. In addition, a hybrid network can be defined that combines elements of the basic schemes. The *star topology,* shown in Figure 9.6a, connects each node to a master control node, which is located at the network *hub*. A pairwise exchange between two nodes must be routed through the hub, which directs and controls all traffic. This topology provides ease of testability and expansion. The hub provides centralized network access control but slows down response times. In case of failure, all operations are

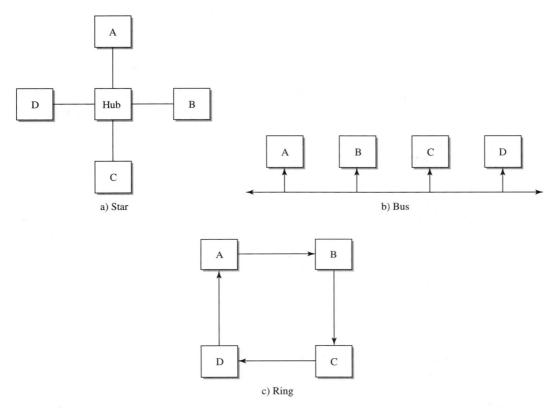

FIGURE 9.6
LAN topologies.

halted. The *bus topology,* shown in Figure 9.6b, connects all nodes via a common system bus. A pairwise exchange between two nodes is broadcast on the bus. This scheme allows for easy expansion, tolerates node failures, and offers a speed advantage over the star topology. However, it is increasingly susceptible to traffic congestion as the number of nodes increases. The *ring topology,* shown in Figure 9.6c, connects all nodes in a cascade that forms a closed loop. Pairwise exchange between two nodes takes place by broadcasting, in a fixed direction, and may pass through several nodes before reaching its destination. This scheme does not lend itself easily to expansion, but it can tolerate node failures if bypass techniques are applied.

Topology can be either physical or logical. Physical topology refers to the actual inter-connection scheme, and logical topology describes the data exchange paths within the network. Thus, it is possible to have a physical bus operating as a logical ring. This is accomplished by specifying a message-relaying sequence, from source to destination, via intermediate nodes.

The three main transmission media available are twisted-pair wire, coaxial cable, and fiber-optic cable. Twisted-pair wire has a maximum data transfer rate of about 10 Mbps, with a maximum distance of 4,000 ft. Coaxial cable, on the other hand, can support a maximum data rate of 300 Mbps, with a maximum distance of 10,000 ft. Fiber-optic cable provides a maximum data rate of 2.5 Gbps, over a distance of several miles.

The two basic data transmission methods are baseband and broadband. *Baseband transmission* uses digital signals to provide data exchanges. A user gains control of the network, on a demand basis, and transmits for a finite time interval. This is also known as time division multiplexing (TDM), since the medium is shared among various users at different times. *Broadband transmission* uses analog signals to provide data exchanges. This scheme supports simultaneous transmissions over the same medium, which is accomplished by frequency division multiplexing (FDM). This technique divides the bandwidth of the available medium into fixed channels and assigns them to individual users. Thus, a user can occupy a portion of the total bandwidth continuously, in contrast to baseband transmission, with which the total bandwidth is used by a single user for a short time interval.

Network medium access control is exercised either through random contention schemes or by deterministic polling rules. Using random contention, any LAN node may access the medium on demand. However, when two or more nodes happen to transmit concurrently, the data may become garbled. If two or more nodes transmit simultaneously, data collision occurs. In order to avoid these situations, collision detection and avoidance schemes have been developed to ensure that only one user transmits at a time, on a first-come, first-served basis. Deterministic access can be in the form of either token passing or time slots. *Token passing* is a special message that is circulated in the network, from one node to the next, in a fixed sequence. As the token travels through the LAN, a node requests transmission by altering the token's status field to reflect the condition and then releasing the token to inform the other nodes. The node then proceeds with the transmission of data. Upon completion, the node resets the token status to its original state, so that other nodes can gain access as required. A *time slot* gives each node a fixed and uniform time window during which it can transmit. This method provides each node with a periodic transmit capability that may or may not enhance throughput, depending on the consistency and amount of available transfer data.

9.3 ISO/OSI REFERENCE MODEL

A LAN is made up of layers and protocols. A layer is an elementary network building block in the form of a software module. Each layer module interfaces with its logically adjacent layers and performs well-defined functions. A protocol is a set of rules that are invoked by a given layer in one node to exchange information with its corresponding layer in another node within the same network. It also specifies the location and meaning of each data field within a given layer.

The International Standards Organization (ISO) has defined a seven-layer network architecture known as the Open Systems Interconnection (OSI) reference model. The OSI is to be used for developing uniform protocols and interfaces that ensure connectivity and compatibility among network nodes. The OSI is a hierarchical layer model, with each layer performing unique well-defined functions and layer boundaries regulating the amount of information flow between adjacent layers. The purpose of the OSI model is to simplify and streamline communication functions, support modular network implementation, and provide a flexible architecture capable of developmental changes. Figure 9.7 illustrates the ISO/OSI reference model.

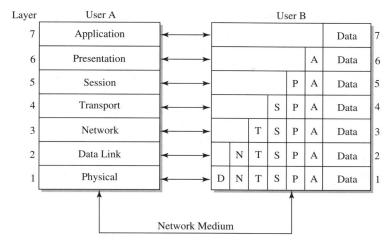

FIGURE 9.7
ISO/OSI reference model.

The layered architecture allows for changes within each level as long as the adjacent level interface functions remain intact. Information is exchanged between users A and B using packet switching. *Packet switching* breaks a message into variable size blocks called *packets* and attaches synchronization, address, and error-checking fields to generate independent data frames that are routed through the various links of the physical network medium. The destination node collects the frames sequentially and recomposes the message. The application layer provides user interface and is at the top of the hierarchy. Messages originate at this layer, are packetized, and are augmented by protocol fields as they pass through the lower layers, until they reach the physical layer. The *physical layer* defines the mechanical, electrical, and functional requirements necessary to establish a connection and access control to the network medium. It converts logical data bits into electrical signals that can transfer across the network medium, and vice versa. This layer also coordinates transmissions and provides a transparent interface connection between the network medium and the data link layer. The *data link layer* defines procedural requirements and protocols to reliably initiate, maintain, and terminate a link between two network nodes. It accepts packets from the network layer, attaches synchronization and frame boundaries, and then passes them to the physical layer. Similarly, it accepts data frames from the physical layer, acknowledges reception, detects and corrects any induced errors, and provides flow of control. The *network layer* defines the methodology to provide efficient path switching and data routing to the various nodes. It controls data packet transfers over multiple paths. It attaches actual source and destination node addresses to each data packet and then sends it to the link layer. It also provides traffic congestion control using adaptive routing. The *transport layer* ensures reliable end-to-end message transfer integrity between network nodes. It breaks messages into packets for transmission and assembles received data packets into messages. It creates, monitors, and deletes unique network connections between source and destination nodes, as requested by the session layer. It provides a virtual end-to-end routing, using logical addresses. The *session layer* manages the dialogue between two users by accessing, coordinating, and releasing the corresponding connections. These are usually accomplished with the logon, logoff, and user ID procedures. This layer performs received data formatting and passes those data to the presentation layer. It also provides recovery procedures to maintain connectivity. The *presentation layer* performs format and code conversions and data compression as required and supports optional network security. It also provides word processing, text formatting, and terminal control. The *application layer* provides the interface between the network and the user to support various functions such as file transfers, message exchanges, and terminal support.

LAN connectivity can be achieved at the three lower OSI layers. The physical distance boundaries of a given LAN can be extended by the use of repeaters; that is, the network can be split into segments that are interconnected via repeaters to eliminate the electrical signal distortions caused by the transmission medium. A *repeater* provides signal amplification, timing, and shaping. This method supports connectivity at the physical layer. Two similar LANs can communicate with one another at the data link layer using a protocol-independent *bridge* between them. In this case, the two LANs operate independently but exchange data frames through a common network node. The bridge stores and forwards data frames between the two LANs at the data link layer. Two dissimilar LANs can communicate, using a common protocol, at the network layer by using a protocol-dependent *router* between them. A *gateway* stores and forwards packets, provides protocol and data rate conversions, and provides connectivity between two dissimilar LANs using all seven layers.

9.4 NETWORK STANDARDS

The ISO/OSI reference model provides a framework for the development of standards and protocol specifications required for LAN implementation. The Institute of Electrical and Electronics Engineers (IEEE) 802 Committee has undertaken the task of developing standards based on the OSI network model. The bulk of the effort has been concentrated in developing well-defined standards for the physical and data link layers.

Figure 9.8 compares the IEEE 802 Committee LAN standards to the ISO/OSI reference model. The IEEE 802.1 addresses the upper layers, starting at the network level. The data link layer is represented by the 802.2 that defines data link control protocol and the medium access control methods outlined by specific standards. The physical layer is described by four well-

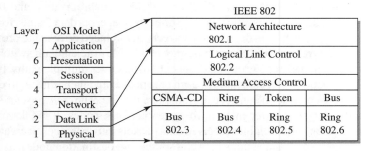

FIGURE 9.8
ISO/IEEE LAN standard relationships.

defined IEEE standards, the 802.3, 802.4, 802.5, and 802.6. These detailed standards, intended for interoperability, address topology, medium, transmission, and access control methods.

The 802.3 LAN standard is for *Ethernet*™-based networks with a bus topology, coaxial or fiber-optic cable, and baseband transmission using Manchester coding. (Ethernet is a trademark of Xerox Corporation.) The medium access control method is known as carrier sense multiple access with collision detection (CSMA/CD). Each node is required to monitor the medium and verify that no other transmission is in progress, that is, no carrier is sensed, before it initiates its own transmission. A carrier is sensed on the medium by the presence of an electrical signal. The transmitting node continues to monitor the medium during a transmission in order to detect any data collisions. Collisions are indicated by the presence of a higher-level electrical signal. When a collision is detected, the node terminates its transmission instantly and sends out a jamming signal to alert the remaining nodes. Then the transmitting node waits a random time interval before retransmitting the data frame that collided. Since each node uses a random waiting algorithm, the probability of repeated collisions is greatly reduced. A binary exponential backoff algorithm is used to calculate the waiting time interval. This LAN standard provides optimum data transfer performance at minimum loading conditions, provided that bus access latency is negligible. Because of the random nature of data frame collisions, medium access times and transfer intervals are not predictable at heavy load conditions. For example, a star network topology, using an active hub node, can achieve a data transfer time of $t_x = t_d + t_h + t_f$, where t_d is the source-to-destination signal path delay, t_h is the hub node latency interval, and t_f is the frame interval. Hence, the data throughput is the reciprocal of t_x. In comparison, the Ethernet bus topology average data transfer time is $t_x = (t_d/2) + t_f$, where t_d is the maximum bus propagation delay and t_f is the frame interval. Also, the average collision-related delay equals one-half the frame time interval.

Figure 9.9 illustrates the physical layout and logical frame format of the IEEE 802.3 LAN standard. The Ethernet bus, shown in Figure 9.9a, uses a baseband coaxial cable with a maximum length of 500 m and operates at a maximum data transfer rate of 10 Mbps. If the cable terminations are replaced with repeaters, then additional 500-m cable sections can be added to expand the network. A repeater provides signal amplification, retiming, and reshaping. The maximum number of nodes per section is limited to one hundred, with a minimum physical separation distance of 2.5 m. Each node is connected to the main cable with a passive tap arrangement. The cable connecting each node to its transceiver can have a maximum length of 50 m. The cable distance between any two nodes cannot exceed 1,500 m, and no more than 1,024 nodes can be tapped into one cable.

The frame size, shown in Figure 9.9b, can be anywhere from 72 to 1,526 bytes long. A minimum time gap, t_g, of 9.6 µsec is required between consecutive frame transmissions. The maximum two-way signal path delay is 51.2 µsec. In the event of a collision, a jamming signal consisting of 4 to 6 bytes of arbitrary data is sent out by the transmitter to alert all the other nodes. Up to sixteen retransmission attempts are permitted prior to a higher protocol intervention. The wait value for each attempt is computed using an algorithm to provide a uniformly random distribution between 0 and 1,023 units of delay. A unit delay is defined as 51.2 µsec. Each frame consists of a sequence of bytes, with the least significant bit (LSB) transmitted first. The preamble contains a pattern of alternating ones and zeros, ending with two consecutive ones in the last byte. The destination address field specifies the receiving node. Each listening node examines this field to determine if it should accept the frame. The first bit in this field de-

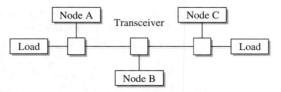

a) Ethernet physical configuration

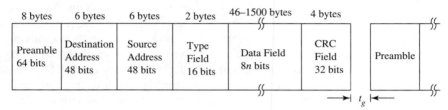

b) Ethernet frame format

FIGURE 9.9
IEEE 802.3 LAN standard definitions.

fines unique or group node addressing, with a zero or a one, respectively. If the field contains all ones, then the transmission is a broadcast transmission. The source address field specifies a unique transmission node address. The type field specifies a higher-level protocol associated with the frame, so that the data field is correctly interpreted. The number of bytes in the data field is an integer ranging from 46 to 1,500. The minimum imposed number guarantees distinguishability from any resulting collision segments. The cyclic redundancy check (CRC) field contains a unique check sequence for each frame. This sequence is used by the destination node to determine if the destination, source, type, and data fields are error-free. Each data bit cell occupies 100 nsec. The first half of the cell contains the false bit state, and the second half, the true bit state. This encoding scheme, known as Manchester coding, results in a data bit cell transition rate of twice the data transfer rate.

The IEEE 802.4 LAN standard, known as the *token bus,* is used with broadband coaxial cable in a bus topology. An analog carrier signal is modulated with the digital baseband data. The medium access control method is a deterministic technique, employing token passing protocol, that eliminates data collisions and provides message priorities. The data transfer rates are 1, 5, or 10 Mbps. Each network node is assigned an address independent of its physical location within the LAN. The token passing mechanism forms a logical ring by transferring the token in succession from the highest to the lowest address node. The *token* is a special bit pattern that is circulated from node to node in a fixed sequence. A node can transmit only if it gets hold of a "free" token. It then sets it to a "busy" status and attaches to it source, destination, and data fields. In return, the destination node accepts the data and returns the token to the source node. The source node resets the token to "free" and then releases it. A network node that is designated as a controller keeps track of the process and performs error checking to ensure reliable operation. There are fixed data transmission time periods, and each node can have up to four message priority levels. The broadband modulation scheme supports several signals, at different frequencies, on the cable simultaneously. As such, it provides independent channels that can be used to support multiple LANs on the same cable or to carry additional analog signals such as audio and video information.

There are two basic broadband systems, single cable and dual cable. Figure 9.10 illustrates them. Both use FDM to allocate a number of fixed bandwidth data channels. The single broadband coaxial cable is connected to the head end. The cable bandwidth is divided into two equal bands. All nodes are allocated transmission channels in the lower band. The head end contains a low-pass filter and a modulator to translate the transmission channels into the upper band. This is necessary in order for the nodes to receive the messages. Hence, all inbound head

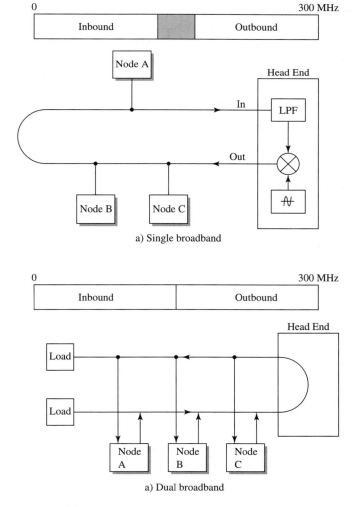

FIGURE 9.10
Broadband cable system definitions.

end traffic is in the lower band, and all outbound is in the upper band. This scheme requires that a guard band, of unusable channels, be defined to provide enough separation between the lower and upper bands to eliminate interference. The dual broadband cable system eliminates this constraint and makes optimum use of its available bandwidth. The single cable system, shown in Figure 9.10a, allows for a maximum of fifty 6-MHz channels. However, the guard band may require up to ten channels, reducing the number of usable channels to forty, or twenty independent channel pairs. The dual broadband cable system, shown in Figure 9.10b, results in twenty-five independent channel pairs, with the head end replaced by a passive loop. The token bus network is transformed into a logical ring with the use of token passing protocol.

The physical configuration and data frame format of the IEEE 802.4 token bus LAN standard are shown in Figure 9.11. The physical bus consists of a single broadband cable with a head end and in this case contains five nodes. Using token passing protocol, the logical ring equivalent (shown in Figure 9.11b) connects the five nodes in a descending address order. The token bus frame format (shown in Figure 9.11c), which is similar to that of Ethernet, contains additional frame boundary information.

The IEEE 802.5 *token ring* LAN standard uses either shielded twisted-pair cable of coaxial cable. The baseband digital data are transmitted using Manchester coding. Medium access control uses deterministic token passing protocol, which provides predictable performance and frame prioritizing. A node is assigned as the network controller to initiate and monitor the to-

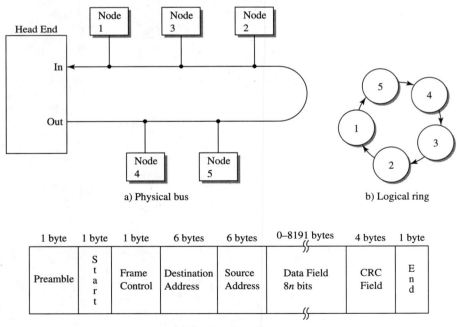

a) Physical bus

b) Logical ring

1 byte	1 byte	1 byte	6 bytes	6 bytes	0–8191 bytes	4 bytes	1 byte
Preamble	Start	Frame Control	Destination Address	Source Address	Data Field $8n$ bits	CRC Field	End

c) Token bus frame format

FIGURE 9.11
Token bus LAN standard definitions.

ken as it circulates through the ring, thus ensuring integrity. If a node needs to transmit, it seizes a "free" token as it passes through, sets it to "busy," and proceeds with sending data. Upon completion, or when a specified token holding time has passed, the node resets the token to "free" status so it is again available to the other nodes. Token holding times are specified and can be set no higher than 10 msec. Token passing is extremely fast because each node provides only a single bit delay prior to its retransmission. Information passes from node to node in frames of variable size. Each node checks the destination address field of each frame to determine if that frame is intended for it. If so, it copies the data and forwards the token back on the ring. Otherwise, it passes the whole frame to the next node. A node can be bypassed, in case of a failure, by use of passive switching. Ring topology requires more cable than a typical bus topology, but it can span longer distances because each node acts as a repeater. Deterministic priority-based token passing protocol provides the fastest data transfer rates at heavy loading conditions. The data transfer time t_x can be expressed as $t_x = t_p + (N \cdot t_n) + t_f$, where t_p is the source-to-destination propagation delay, N is the number of nodes, t_n is the node latency, and t_f is the frame interval. The propagation delay t_p is a function of the ring circumference, since the transmitter must receive its own message prior to releasing the token. Also, the data throughput is the reciprocal of t_x. The data transfer rate is 1 to 16 Mbps, on a coaxial cable medium. Assuming a data transfer rate of r bps and a propagation velocity of v_p meters/sec, a bit cell will occupy $x = v_p/r$ meters per bit. If the ring circumference is l meters, then the network capacity is l/x bits.

Figure 9.12 illustrates the physical layout and logical frame format of the IEEE 802.5 token ring LAN standard. Each node makes independent transmitter and receiver connections to

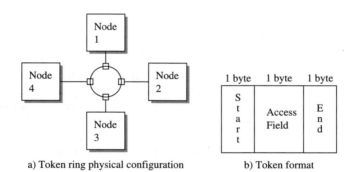

a) Token ring physical configuration   b) Token format

c) Token ring frame format

FIGURE 9.12
Token ring LAN standard definitions.

the ring. In case of failure these connections may be bypassed, using a passive switch, to permit LAN operation. A specific node is designated the LAN controller to issue and monitor token passing protocol. The token access field, shown in Figure 9.12b, contains the actual token bit, a token status monitor bit, and priority-related coding. Token passing flows from the higher to the lower address nodes, as tokens circulate through the ring. A given node that requires transmission seizes a "free" token, inserts a bit in its second byte, and attaches data to it, as shown in Figure 9.12c. The destination address node performs an address match and then copies the data field. The data frame goes around the ring until it reaches the source node. The source node examines the frame status bits, to determine whether the frame was received successfully, and either sends out a new frame or releases the token and passes it to the next node. If transmission was unsuccessful, it retransmits the original frame.

The IEEE 802.6 LAN standard, known as the distributed queued dual bus (DQDB), uses a fiber-optic cable in a physical ring topology, forming a logical bus with baseband modulation. It supports single fault tolerance, since each node can provide bus termination, and it allows variable data rates. This network standard is used with metropolitan area networks (MANs), which can extend over a 50-km area and provide LAN-to-LAN connectivity. The DQDB standard data rate is 155 Mbps.

The fiber-optic distribution data interface (FDDI) is a high-speed LAN standard that uses ring topology and a token passing access control mechanism. It complies with the ISO/OSI model. It is capable of a 125-Mbps data rate, with adjacent nodes located up to 2.5 km apart. It has maximum circumference of 200 km and can support up to 1,000 nodes. FDDI was developed for MAN applications, and provides reliable connectivity using a dual ring.

9.5 SWITCHED NETWORKS

Switched networks are distributed over a wide area and have multiple connections among them. Figure 9.13 illustrates a typical switched network configuration. There are three fundamental connectivity methods: circuit switching, message switching, and packet switching.

The *circuit switching* method provides a real-time, point-to-point electrical path, using a dedicated data channel between the source and destination locations. The procedure consists of three steps: path setup, data transfer, and path release. This method has minimum path delay and no message length restriction, and data flows without interruption. If, however, the path is already in use when a transmission attempt is made, multiple path setup attempts will be required. Also, circuit switching provides no data buffering or protocol conversion, which imposes compatibility restrictions. To request a path, a sender provides the receiver destination address to the circuit switch. In turn, the first switch passes the information to the second switch via an available link, and so on, until the message reaches the final receiver switch. If the receiver is sender-compatible, and not in use, then the connection is completed. A request acknowledgment is sent back to the sender, verifying the newly established path. Once the path is set up, message transfers can take place in one or both directions. Upon message completion, the end-to-end connection is released, and the individual links become available for future path requests. The overhead associated with path setup and release and the use of a dedicated path for each connection result in an overall message transfer rate reduction.

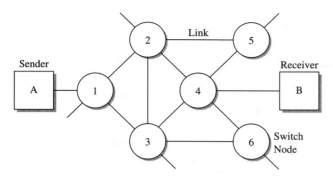

FIGURE 9.13
Switched network configuration.

The *message switching* method provides a non-real-time, indirect, store-and-forward message transfer mechanism between the source and destination locations. The procedure requires no path setup and has no message length restrictions. These properties result in a variable path delay, and the data flow occurs in a contiguous manner. The sender experiences no "busy" path conditions because each switch has memory for intermediate storage. Also, since protocol, code, and rate conversion are provided at each message switch, the compatibility restrictions are relaxed. Each message provides receiver destination address information, which can be either point-to-point or multipoint. To request a path, the sender transmits a message to the first switch with a header that contains the receiver destination address. The switch stores the messages, and as soon as a link is available to the next switch, it forwards the message. The process continues until the final receiver switch is accessed, which transfers the message to its destination address. Since no dedicated path setup takes place, the end-to-end path delay is offset by the efficient use of the links.

The *packet switching* method provides near real-time direct message forwarding between source and destination locations. Each message is broken into variable-length segments known as packets. Each packet switch provides protocol, code, and rate conversions. Using complex dynamic routing algorithms, the packets are sent through the various nodes on a link-availability basis. Each packet contains a header with receiver address information and a sequence number. Each packet may take a different path, which can result in out-of-sequence, noncontiguous packet reception. The variable-link path delays are offset by the packet size and routing flexibility, which result in high transfer rates. To request a path, the sender transmits a packet with a header. The first switch uses the header information to select an available link to the next switch, and then forwards the packet. This process continues until the packet arrives at the receiver. When all message packets are received, they are sorted according to their sequence number. The dynamic routing mechanism provides a multipath network for each message to speed its delivery.

The X.25 packet switching standard has been developed for interfacing data terminal equipment (DTE) and data communication equipment (DCE), when they are connected via a dedicated link to public data networks. The DTE can be a data sender, a receiver, or both. The DCE is used to set up, maintain, and terminate network path connectivity. The standard consists of three layers: the physical, the frame, and the packet. The physical layer defines the interface of a DTE and a DCE operating in a networked environment that provides packet switching to many different users. The frame layer defines data exchanges between the DTE and the DCE. It performs node-to-node management, flow and error control. The packet layer defines address, control, and data fields that make each packet unique and compatible with the network protocol. It performs end-to-end connections, routing, and error recovery. Figure 9.14 illustrates the packet and frame layers of the X.25 standard.

The X.25 physical interface standard, which is similar to the RS-232, is used to define the physical layer. The high level data link control (HDLC), operating in the link access procedure-balanced (LAP-B) mode, is used to manage data frame exchanges in the frame layer. There are three different frame types associated with the LAP-B mode: the supervisory (S-frame), the unnumbered (U-frame), and the information (I-frame). The I-frame, which contains packet data, starts and ends with a frame flag byte. It also includes address and control fields for node management and reliable data transfers. A frame check sequence (FCS) is provided for error detection. The actual packet consists of an information field and a data field. The information field defines the packet contents as control or data, provides transfer status, and specifies packet size. The group and channel fields provide a total of 4,096 possible user addresses on the network. The packet type field specifies network management, data transfer, flow of control, and diagnostic functions. As each frame is received by an intermediate node, it is stored and checked for errors. If error-free, it is forwarded to the next available node, and an ACK is sent to the previous node. If it has errors, a NACK with ARQ is sent to the previous node. Packet data size can range up to 4,096 bytes, with a usual size of 128 bytes. The data transfer rate varies from 9.6 to 56 kbps. The X.25 packet switching standard provides for a virtual circuit connectivity, via the network, between two users. A virtual circuit connection can use a different path for each packet transfer. Each packet of a given message follows the next available path bypassing any node and link failures.

The *frame relay* is an interface for packet switching networks. It is similar but considerably faster than X.25 and uses variable-length data segments, or frames, with six bytes of header information. A frame contains a header with address and control fields for routing, a

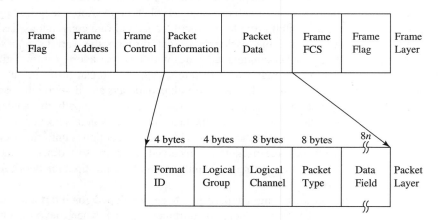

FIGURE 9.14
X.25 packet switching standard definition.

variable-length data segment, and a CRC-16 field. The frame relay can support rapidly changing frame sizes and data rates. Frames are dynamically routed from node to node until they reach their destination addresses. Error checking and retransmission are performed only between the source and destination nodes. By eliminating node-to-node error checking and ARQ, the frame relay interface can attain data transfer rates of up to 2 Mbps.

The Internet is a worldwide interconnection of an assortment of networks and computer architectures using gateways. A *datagram* is a universal, variable-size packet for information transfer on the Internet. Data transfer rates for datagrams vary from 56 kbps to 1.544 Mbps. Internet addressing consists of a uniform four-byte header that contains the network address field and the user address field. The field lengths are configured to one of three formats so as to match the user-to-network size ratio. The Transmission Control Protocol (TCP) performs the OSI transport layer four function. It has a twenty-four-byte header, followed by the data block. The Internet Protocol (IP) performs the OSI network layer three function. These two protocols provide a vehicle for communicating over the Internet. The TCP provides a reliable full duplex virtual circuit path and supports multiple connections. It adds a twenty-four-byte header to each new segment. It establishes and terminates source-to-destination node connections. It also disassembles messages into packets and reassembles received packets into messages. The IP provides routing and a store-and-forward function, converts packets into frames, and changes received frames into packets.

The Synchronous Optical Network (SONET) standard uses fiber-optic transmission medium technology to achieve extremely fast data transfers. These range from 51.84 Mbps (synchronous transport signal [STS-1]) to 2.488 Gbps (STS-48), in seven selectable rates. This technology is intended for wide area networks (WANs), which span large geographical areas. The SONET standard corresponds to the physical OSI layer one.

The asynchronous transfer mode (ATM) is a switching methodology. It corresponds to the OSI logical link layer two. It combines packet-switching techniques with short, fixed-length data frames, called *cells,* to transfer high-speed data over broadband networks such as SONET. This technique is also known as *cell relay*. Each cell consists of fifty-three bytes, five for address information and forty-eight for data.

PROBLEMS

9.1 Design a bus arbitration logic circuit to resolve the requests of two tightly coupled MPUs, using the bus request and bus grant signals.

9.2 Determine the possible number of host, destination address, and data type formats that can be defined in an Ethernet frame.

9.3 Given a propagation velocity of 1.98×10^8 m/sec, determine the minimum and maximum Ethernet frame intervals, bit length, and propagation delay on a coaxial cable.

9.4 An Ethernet CRC field polynomial is defined as $R(X) = X^{31} + X^{26} + X^{23} + X^{22} + X^{16} + X^{12} + X^{11} + X^{10} + X^8 + X^7 + X^5 + X^4 + X^2 + X + 1$. Determine its equivalent hexadecimal and octal formats.

9.5 Determine the backoff interval values $i = 2^{n+1}$, using the random number algorithm $k = (n \cdot a + b)$ mod 10, where n is the number of retransmissions (1 to 5), $a = 7$, and $b = 11$.

9.6 Determine the data throughput of a star topology LAN with the following parameters: a source-to-destination delay of 10 μsec, a hub delay of 2 μsec, and a frame interval of 120 μsec.

9.7 Determine the low pass filter (LPF) cutoff and modulator frequencies for Figure 9.10a.

9.8 Determine the data throughput of a bus topology LAN with the following parameters: a bus propagation delay of 10 μsec and a frame interval of 120 μsec.

9.9 Determine the data throughput of a ten-node ring topology LAN with the following parameters: a source-to-destination delay of 10 μsec, a node delay interval of 2 μsec, and a frame interval of 120 μsec.

9.10 Given a propagation velocity of 1.98×10^8 meters/sec and a data rate of 16 mbps, determine the capacity of a 5,000-m ring topology LAN.

9.11 Determine the various delays possible through the network of Figure 9.13. Assume each node link has one unit delay.

9.12 For Problem 9.11, determine the order of a received six-packet message. Assume that packets 1, 4, and 6 experience minimum delays; packets 3 and 5, maximum delays; and packet 2, an average delay.

REFERENCES

Schatt, Stan. *Understanding LANs.* 3d ed. Indianapolis, IN: H. W. Sams, 1992.

Schwartz, Mischa. *Computer Communications: Network Design and Analysis.* Englewood Cliffs, NJ: Prentice Hall, 1977.

―――. *Telecommunications Networks: Protocols Modeling and Analysis.* Reading, MA: Addison-Wesley, 1987.

Tanenbaum, Andrew. *Computer Networks.* Englewood Cliffs, NJ: Prentice Hall, 1981.

10

SIGNAL CONVERSION

Real-world signals are not compatible with the binary data formats used by the MCU, and thus they require conversion before and after processing. The majority of these signals are classified as analog. An *analog signal* is defined over a continuous time interval and assumes a continuous range of amplitude values. The required conversion functions are performed using specialized modules. These modules facilitate and integrate the process to achieve optimum performance. An analog-to-digital converter (ADC) module changes an analog input signal into a binary output code, compatible with an MCU data word format. A digital-to-analog converter (DAC) module performs the inverse function.

Figure 10.1 is a typical analog interface block diagram. The sensor converts a physical process parameter such as position, velocity, acceleration, temperature, or force into an electrical output variable. The magnitude of the parameter is represented as a voltage, current, resistance, or capacitance value. Signal conditioning of the sensor output ensures high conversion accuracy and provides uniform signal levels to the ADC module. For example, the variable may be converted into a voltage level and then amplified or attenuated so that the amplitude falls within a specific range. Also, filtering may be performed to reduce noise or eliminate undesired frequency components. In the case of slow, varying signals, a multiplexer can be used to select sequentially one of several input sources for conversion. The MCU performs signal analysis, formatting, display, and hardcopy printing of the data. In addition, binary output data may be converted to an analog signal via a DAC module, conditioned and used as a feedback parameter to control a process. The analog input signal is sampled every T seconds. This results in a signal defined for discrete time values and a continuous range of amplitude values. The sampled signal is then held at a constant level between sample intervals resulting in a time-continuous but discrete amplitude waveform. During the hold time the amplitude value is converted, using an ADC, into a set of n binary digits. The result is a digital signal defined for discrete time and quantized amplitude values. The discrete time values are multiples of the sampling period T, and the n-bit code represents the quantized amplitude values.

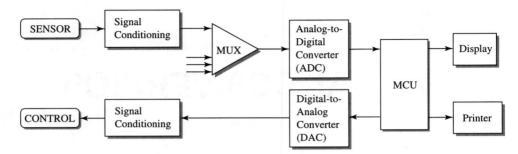

FIGURE 10.1 Analog interface block diagram.

This procedure is illustrated in Figure 10.2, using a sinusoidal analog input signal. An ADC module accepts an analog signal V_{IN}, bounded by upper and lower amplitude levels, and outputs a corresponding n-bit code. The code can represent a maximum of 2^n different input values, in steps of $V_{IN}/2^n$. The binary code can be converted back to an analog signal by first assigning a binary weight to each bit and then summing the active bit levels. A DAC module accepts an n-bit binary code and outputs a corresponding analog signal V_{OUT}. The signal can assume 2^n possible values, with a minimum step of $V_{REF}/2^n$, where V_{REF} is the DAC voltage reference level. Data conversion is needed to enable the MCU to analyze external input data and provide controlled feedback. The objectives of this chapter are as follows: (1) to review op-

Signal	Amplitude	Time	Example
Analog	Continuous	Continuous	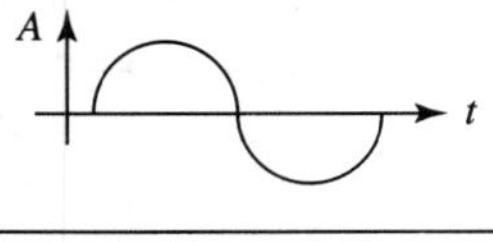
Sampled	Continuous	Discrete	
Held	Discrete	Continuous	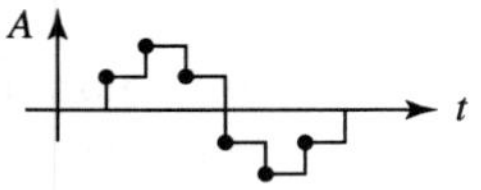
Digital	Quantized	Discrete	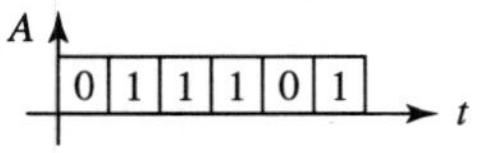

FIGURE 10.2 Signal definitions.

erational amplifier basics, (2) to explain sampling and quantization, (3) to discuss the different DAC types and their operation, (4) to cover the various ADC types and their operation, and (5) to present the angle-to-digital conversion techniques.

10.1 OPERATIONAL AMPLIFIERS

An amplifier is the basic building block for analog signal functions. The typical amplifier accepts an input signal, voltage or current, which is used to control a power source such that the enhanced output signal resembles the input. The magnitude ratio of the output to the input signal is called the *gain* and is denoted as A_v. The amplifier gain is usually a function of the input signal frequency. The *bandwidth* is defined as the range of frequencies $(f_2 - f_1)$, where the gain variation is within 3 dB. The *input impedance* is the ratio of the differences in input voltage to input current change. Similarly, *output impedance* is the ratio of the differences in output voltage to output current change. The *null voltage* is the offset input voltage value required to achieve an output value of zero with no input signal.

An *operational amplifier* (op amp) is a high-gain differential, two-input amplifier that has a wide bandwidth. Also, it has high input impedance and low output impedance, and its null voltage approaches zero. These characteristics enable the device, via feedback, to provide versatile and predictable performance and stability, independent of its internal parameters. Figure 10.3 shows an operational amplifier symbol and an equivalent circuit diagram.

The op amp has an inverting and a noninverting input, denoted by minus and plus signs, respectively. In the equivalent diagram the input impedance, Z_{IN}, approaches infinity, or open circuit, in the ideal case, but in practice it is measured in MOhms. Similarly, the output impedance, Z_{OUT}, approaches zero, or short circuit, in the ideal case, but in practice it is measured in ohms. The amplifier voltage gain, A_v, in the ideal case would be infinite. In practice, it can be as high as 1×10^5. Its bandwidth is infinite in the ideal case, but in practice it is several MHz wide. The null voltages of both inputs approach zero. The op amp is capable of performing mathematical operations on analog signals; hence its derived name. The most common configuration is the scaling amplifier, illustrated in Figure 10.4a.

Using Kirchoff's current law, which states that the sum of the currents entering a circuit node equals the sum exiting it, it is possible to define the following relationship:

$$I_1 = I_s + I_f$$

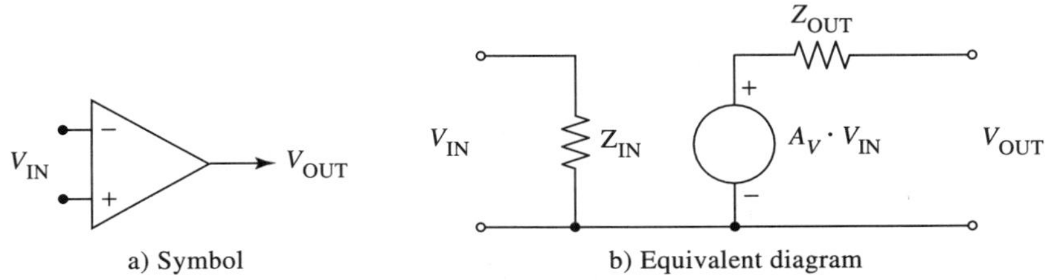

a) Symbol   b) Equivalent diagram

FIGURE 10.3 Operational amplifier definitions.

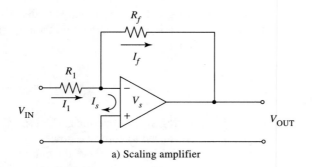

a) Scaling amplifier

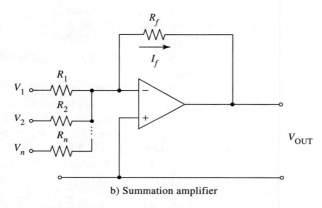

b) Summation amplifier

FIGURE 10.4 Operational amplifier configuration diagrams.

where I_s is the shunt current

I_f is the feedback current.

However, as the input impedance approaches infinity, I_s approaches zero and $I_1 \approx I_f$. Since

$$I_1 = \frac{V_{IN} - V_s}{R_1}$$

and

$$I_f = \frac{V_s - V_{OUT}}{R_f}$$

we have

$$\frac{V_{IN} - V_s}{R_1} \approx \frac{V_s - V_{OUT}}{R_f}$$

Also as the op amp gain approaches infinity, V_s approaches zero; hence

$$\frac{V_{IN}}{R_1} = \frac{-V_{OUT}}{R_f}$$

and the gain equation becomes

$$V_{OUT} = -\left(\frac{R_f}{R_1}\right) \cdot V_{IN} \qquad \qquad \text{(10.1)}$$

Therefore, the output voltage V_{OUT} is derived by multiplying the input voltage V_{IN} by the negative ratio of the two external resistors. If the resistor values are equal, the result is unity gain. If they are unequal, the op amp performs scaling on the input signal. In general, when complex impedances are used, the gain equation becomes

$$V_{OUT} = -\left(\frac{Z_f \underline{/\theta_2}}{Z_1 \underline{/\theta_1}}\right) \cdot V_{IN} \qquad \qquad \text{(10.2)}$$

This is a transfer function that performs frequency-dependent scaling and phase shifting of the input signal.

The summation amplifier shown in Figure 10.4b is a natural extension of the basic scaling amplifier. Using Kirchoff's current law, it is possible to define the following relationship:

$$V_{OUT} = -\left(\frac{V_{IN}}{R_{IN}}\right) \cdot R_f = -I_{IN} \cdot R_f \qquad \qquad \text{(10.3)}$$

where $I_{IN} = \dfrac{V_1}{R_1} + \dfrac{V_2}{R_2} + \ldots + \dfrac{V_n}{R_n}$

Thus, V_{OUT} is the linear sum of the individual scaled input signals. A scaling amplifier can be used to perform current-to-voltage conversion, as illustrated in Figure 10.5a. An input current signal I_{IN} develops a voltage V_{IN} across resistor R_s. Using the scaling amplifier equation, $V_{OUT} = -V_{IN} \cdot (R_f/R_{IN})$, where $V_{IN} = I_{IN} \cdot R_s$. Therefore, the current-to-voltage relationship becomes

$$V_{OUT} = -(I_{IN} \cdot R_s) \cdot \left(\frac{R_f}{R_{IN}}\right) \qquad \qquad \text{(10.4)}$$

where $R_{IN} > 10 \cdot R_s$

For very small input currents, the input resistors R_s and R_{IN} can be omitted, resulting in $V_{OUT} = -R_f \cdot I_{IN}$.

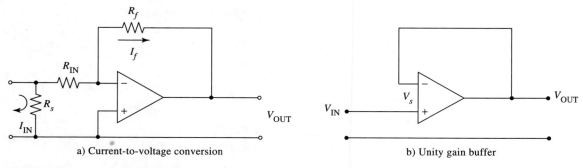

a) Current-to-voltage conversion   b) Unity gain buffer

FIGURE 10.5 Operational amplifier applications.

A unity gain, noninverting, buffer amplifier is shown in Figure 10.5b. Using Kirchoff's voltage law, which states that the algebraic sum of any closed loop voltages equals zero, it is possible to define the following relationships:

$$V_{IN} - V_s - V_{OUT} = 0$$

or

$$V_{IN} - V_s = V_{OUT}$$

However, as the voltage gain, A_v, approaches infinity, V_s approaches zero and results in $V_{IN} \approx V_{OUT}$ and $V_{OUT}/V_{IN} \approx 1$.

Op amps are frequently used to integrate or differentiate the input signal, and in effect behave as low pass filters (LPF) and high pass filters (HPF), respectively. Figure 10.6a illustrates an integrating amplifier, using a capacitor, $C,$ as the feedback element. Taking the scaling amplifier current relationship,

$$V_{OUT} = -V_{IN} \cdot R_f$$

where $I_{IN} = \dfrac{V_{IN}}{R}$ and $\dfrac{dV_{OUT}}{dt} = \dfrac{-I_{IN}}{C}$

By substituting and solving for V_{OUT}, the equation becomes

$$V_{OUT} = -\frac{1}{R \cdot C} \int_0^T V_{IN} \cdot dt \qquad \textbf{(10.5)}$$

The following example provides a detailed description of the integrator.

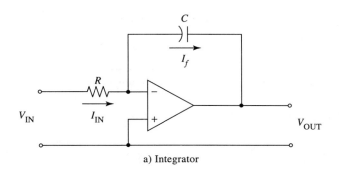

a) Integrator

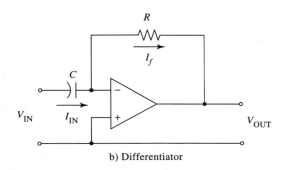

b) Differentiator

FIGURE 10.6 Operational amplifier operations.

EXAMPLE 10.1

Calculate the integrating amplifier output V_{OUT} for the following conditions:

$$V_{IN} = 5 \text{ V}, T = 4 \text{ msec}, R = 10 \text{ kOhms, and } C = 1 \text{ μF}$$

$$V_{OUT} = -\frac{(V_{IN} \cdot T)}{(R \cdot C)}$$

$$V_{OUT} = -\frac{(5) \cdot (4 \times 10^{-3})}{(10 \times 10^{3}) \cdot (1 \times 10^{-6})} = -2 \text{ V}$$

Hence a constant positive input voltage results in a steady negative ramp output voltage. The output starts at zero and 4 milliseconds later it ramps down to -2 V.

A differentiating amplifier is formed by exchanging the element positions as shown in Figure 10.6b. Again, using the scaling amplifier current relationship, $V_{OUT} = -I_{IN} \cdot R_f$, where $I_{IN} = C \cdot (dV_{IN}/dt)$. By substituting and solving for V_{OUT}, the following equation results:

$$V_{OUT} = -(R \cdot C) \cdot \frac{dV_{IN}}{dt} \qquad \textbf{(10.6)}$$

The following example serves to explain the differentiator.

EXAMPLE 10.2

Calculate the differentiating amplifier, V_{OUT}, for the following conditions:

$$R = 10 \text{ kOhms, } C = 1 \text{ }\mu F, \text{ and } \frac{dV_{IN}}{dt} = 0.3 \text{ V/msec}$$

$$V_{OUT} = -(R \cdot C) \cdot \left(\frac{dV_{IN}}{dt}\right) = -(1 \times 10^{-6} \cdot 1 \times 10^4) \cdot \left(\frac{0.3}{10^{-3}}\right) = -3 \text{ V}$$

Thus, a steady positive ramp input voltage results in a constant negative output voltage. The output will remain at -3 V as long as the input ramp of 0.3 V/msec is present.

The op amp transfer characteristics are of great importance for data conversion performance. The three basic parameters are rise time, slew rate, and settling time. The *rise time* is defined as the time it takes the output signal to change from 10% to 90% of its maximum value in response to a small input step pulse signal. The *slew rate* is defined as the maximum rate of change of the output signal in response to a large input waveform. In the case of a sinusoidal input signal, $V_{OUT} = V_{IN} \cdot \sin(\omega \cdot t)$, the signal rate of change expression becomes

$$\frac{dV_{OUT}}{dt} = \omega \cdot V_{IN} \cdot \cos(\omega \cdot t)$$

The slew rate equation becomes

$$\max\left(\frac{dV_{OUT}}{dt}\right) = [\omega \cdot V_{IN} \cdot \cos(\omega \cdot t)]_{t=0} = 2 \cdot \pi \cdot f \cdot V_{IN} \tag{10.7}$$

where $2 \cdot \pi \cdot f = \omega$

The *settling time*, T_s, is defined as the amount of time it takes for the output to attain a value, within a specified error limit, in response to a large input step signal. The settling time includes the inherent input to output propagation delay, T_d, and the slew rate interval, ΔT. The error limit is usually defined as 1% of the final value. These concepts are illustrated in Figure 10.7.

Data conversions require op amps with high slew rate, wide bandwidth, high gain, and fast settling time. An op amp can also be used as a level comparator. In this configuration no external elements are required. Its output voltage can assume one of two possible values, as a function of the amplitude and polarity of the input signal. Comparators are designed with high gain, low input threshold, and fast slew rate. Figure 10.8 illustrates a typical comparator symbol and transfer characteristic. The device has an input threshold level V_{TH} which must be exceeded, by the input signal V_{IN}, in order for its output to switch levels. If the input signal V_{IN} is less than V_{TH}, the comparator output will be $-V$. When V_{IN} is greater than V_{TH}, the output

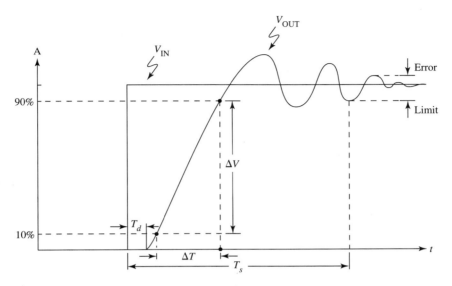

FIGURE 10.7 Operational amplifier settling time definitions.

switches abruptly to $+V$. Comparators are used to convert a range of analog input signal values into one of two possible digital output levels.

10.2 SAMPLE/HOLD AND QUANTIZATION

The analog input signal must go through several steps in order to be converted into corresponding digital signal. The first step is waveform sampling. Next, each individual sample is held constant at its initial level while it is amplitude-quantized. Sampling converts the analog input into a continuous amplitude but discrete time signal. Sampling can be viewed as the product of an analog input with a periodic pulse train of uniform amplitude and duration. This concept is illustrated in Figure 10.9. The resulting output signal envelope resembles the analog input signal.

The pulse train consists of a series of τ duration pulses, spaced at T intervals apart. The

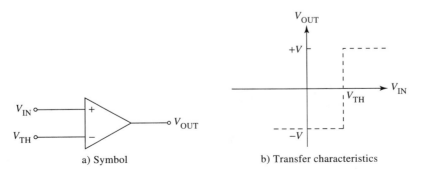

FIGURE 10.8 Comparator definitions.

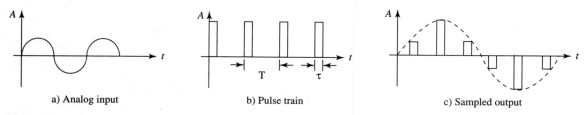

a) Analog input   b) Pulse train   c) Sampled output

FIGURE 10.9 Sampling process definitions.

corresponding sampling frequency $f_s = 1/T$ and cannot be picked arbitrarily. The Nyquist sampling theorem states that a continuous signal, containing frequency components no greater than f_{max}, can be reconstructed from its sampled form, provided that $f_s \geq 2 \cdot f_{max}$. This can be easily demonstrated with Figure 10.10, which shows the effect of the sampling frequency on the sampled signal spectrum. The resulting spectrum extends to f_{max} and forms a periodic waveform at multiples of f_s.

If the sampling frequency is at least twice f_{max}, then no interference exists. If it is less than twice f_{max}, however, then the periodically spaced components of the sampled signal spectrum begin to overlap, and distortion occurs. This effect is known as *aliasing*, and it takes place at integer multiples of $\frac{1}{2} \cdot f_s$. The resulting spectrum bears no resemblance to the original analog input spectrum, and thus reconstruction is not possible. The usual procedure is to pass the input signal through an LPF filter prior to sampling, which eliminates any undesired high-frequency components that may cause aliasing. These may be either transient signals or noise and are therefore unwanted. An ideal LPF passes all frequencies inside its passband from zero to its cutoff f_c and inhibits all others. Also, its transition from passband to stopband is abrupt, and the sampling rate can be as low as $2 \cdot f_{max}$. This value is also known as the *Nyquist rate*. However, the typical LPF exhibits a gradual rolloff attenuation, from passband to stopband, that necessitates a proportional sampling rate increase to reduce aliasing distortion.

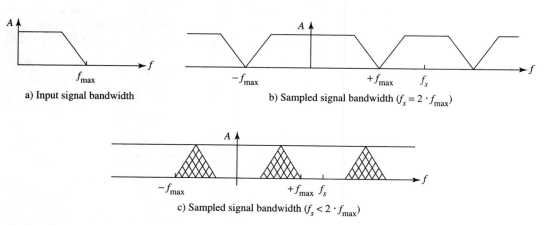

a) Input signal bandwidth

b) Sampled signal bandwidth ($f_s = 2 \cdot f_{max}$)

c) Sampled signal bandwidth ($f_s < 2 \cdot f_{max}$)

FIGURE 10.10 Frequency domain sampling.

The sampling pulsewidth, τ, is another source of error. The analog input signal amplitude can vary greatly during τ and can result in a related sample error. In the case of a sinusoidal input signal, $V = V_{peak} \cdot \sin(\omega \cdot t)$, and $dV/dt = (\omega \cdot V_{peak}) \cdot \cos(\omega \cdot t)$. As t approaches zero, the expression can be written as

$$\frac{\Delta V}{\Delta t} = 2 \cdot \pi \cdot f \cdot V_{peak}$$

By letting $f = f_{max}$ and $\Delta t = \tau$, the relative error equation becomes

$$e = \frac{\Delta V}{V_{peak}} = 2 \cdot \pi \cdot f_{max} \cdot \tau \qquad (10.8)$$

EXAMPLE 10.3

Given $f_{max} = 3$ kHz and $e = 0.1$, find τ.

$$\tau = \frac{e}{2 \cdot \pi \cdot f} = \frac{0.1}{6.28 \cdot 3 \times 10^3} = 5.3 \times 10^{-6} \text{ sec}$$

To minimize this error, a sample and hold (S/H) amplifier is used to track the input signal and hold it, at a constant value, during quantization. This operation is shown in Figure 10.11.

The *sampling time* duration t_s is the sum of the acquisition and aperture times. The *acquisition time* t_{ac} is the interval required by the S/H amplifier, going from hold to sample mode, to track the input signal, usually within 0.1% of its final value. This time starts at the sample command and includes switch closure delay, slew rate, settling time, and capacitor charge time. The *aperture time* t_{ap} is the interval required by the S/H amplifier to switch from sample to hold mode, usually 10% to 90% from the start of the hold command. The maximum aperture time variation, measured over a number of sample and hold operations, is called *jitter*. Sampling transforms the analog input into a continuous amplitude and discrete time signal. The hold function provides a discrete amplitude and time-continuous waveform, suitable for quantization. Quantization assigns each analog input sample the nearest possible value, from a finite set, using an n-bit code to represent each of the 2^n levels. The smallest possible input level, q, needed to cause a change in one LSB, in the output n-bit code, is called the step size and is calculated by

$$q = \frac{V_{max} - V_{min}}{2^n},$$

where V_{max} and V_{min} are the input voltage range limits.

In the typical case of a sinusoidal input signal, $q = (2 \cdot V_{peak})/2^n$.

There are two basic quantizing rules, the round off and the truncation. *Round off* quantizing assigns the analog input value to the nearest quantized level; *truncation* quantizing assigns it to the nearest quantized level that does not exceed the signal. The resulting transfer characteristics are illustrated in Figure 10.12. The round off rule threshold for assigning the next level

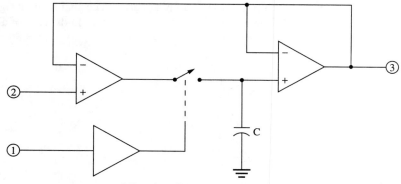

a) Sample and hold amplifier diagram

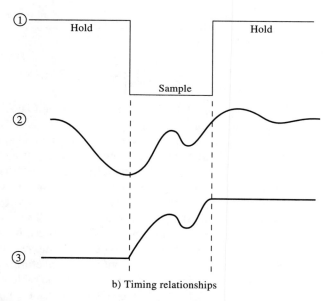

b) Timing relationships

FIGURE 10.11 Sample and hold operation.

is $\frac{q}{2}$. Hence if $\delta V_{IN} < \frac{q}{2}$, then the output becomes $k \cdot q$; otherwise it becomes $(k + 1) \cdot q$. The maximum round off error becomes $\pm\frac{q}{2}$, which results in an average error of zero. The truncation rule threshold for assigning the next level is q. The truncation error is either 0 or q, resulting in an average error of $\pm\frac{q}{2}$. Hence, round off is the preferred quantization rule. The number of bits, n, determines the amplitude resolution of the resulting binary number. For n bits, there are 2^n possible levels.

The quantizer dynamic range (DR) can be expressed in terms of resolution as DR (dB) $= 20 \cdot \log_{10}(2^n) = 6.02 \cdot n$. In other words, each additional bit increases the resolution by about 6 dB. Also, by taking into account the $\pm\frac{q}{2}$ round off error, the dynamic range equation becomes

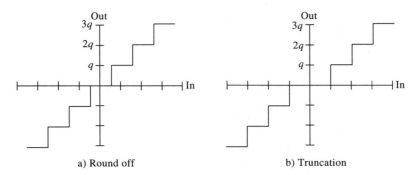

a) Round off   b) Truncation

FIGURE 10.12 Quantization rules.

$$DR \text{ (dB)} = 6.02 \cdot n - 3.01 \qquad (10.9)$$

For example, a ten-bit quantizer has a dynamic range of about 57 dB. The required digital data rate for an n-bit quantizer becomes rate (bps) $= n \cdot f_s$, where f_s is the sampling frequency. The sampled signal quantization must take place within the time interval t_q, which is the time it takes the input q to change one LSB. If the slew rate of a sinusoidal input signal is equated to the quantization rate q/t_q (V/sec), then the highest frequency element, for a specific quantization interval, can be determined as follows. Given that

$$\frac{dV}{dt} = 2 \cdot \pi \cdot f_{max} \cdot V_{peak} = \frac{q}{t_q},$$

solving for f_{max} results in

$$f_{max} = \frac{q}{(t_q \cdot 2 \cdot \pi \cdot V_{peak})}$$

By substituting $q = (2 \cdot V_{peak})/2^n$, the expression becomes

$$f_{max} = \frac{1}{t_q \cdot \pi \cdot 2^n}$$

EXAMPLE 10.4   Determine f_{max} for $t_q = 10$ μsec, $n = 10$, and $V_{peak} = 5$ V.

$$q = \frac{(2 \cdot 5)}{2^{10}} = 9.76 \times 10^{-3}$$

$$f_{max} = \frac{9.76 \times 10^{-3}}{(10 \times 10^{-6} \times 6.28 \times 5)} = 31.1 \text{ Hz}$$

or

$$f_{max} = \frac{1}{(10 \times 10^{-6} \times 3.14 \times 2^{10})} = 31.1 \text{ Hz}$$

If, however, the sampled input signal is held constant during quantization, the maximum frequency element is limited only by the Nyquist rate, so that $f_{max} = 1/[2 \cdot (t_q + t_s)]$, where $t_s = t_{ac} + t_{ap}$, the S/H amplifier sampling time.

In the previous example, if an S/H amplifier precedes the quantizer, assuming $t_s = 5$ μsec, the maximum signal frequency increases to $f_{max} = 1/[2(10 \times 10^{-6} + 5 \times 10^{-6})] = 33.33$ kHz.

It is also possible, using a multiplexer, to convert several analog input signals using the same devices. There are two basic sampling approaches, the sequential and the simultaneous. These two methods are shown in Figure 10.13. Using sequential sampling, the different inputs are selected, in a fixed sequence, and they share the same S/H and quantizer devices. The maximum channel frequency, f_{ch}, can be calculated using $f_{ch} = 1/[2 \cdot m \cdot (t_q + t_s)]$, where m is the number of input signals. The sampling time, t_s, is the sum of the multiplexer time, t_{acm}; the S/H acquisition time, t_{acs}; and the S/H aperture time, t_{aps}. The basic limitation is the cumulative delay among the various signal samples due to the multiplexer operation. The results are signal phase shift and related amplitude skewing relative to other inputs. *Phase shift* is the angle slippage between two adjacent channel input signal samples when one is held while the other is changing. This is a limiting factor in sequential sampling and can be calculated with the following equation:

$$\text{Phase shift } (\theta) = \left[\frac{(t_s + t_q)}{T_h} \right] \cdot 360° \tag{10.10}$$

where $t_s = t_{acm} + t_{acs} + t_{aps}$ and T_h is the reciprocal of the highest input signal frequency given by $T_h = \dfrac{1}{f_h}$

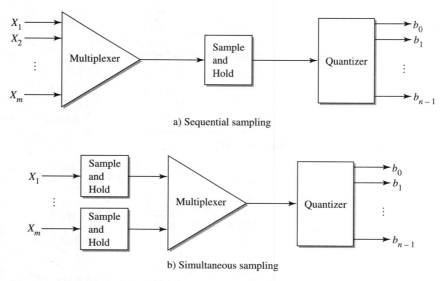

a) Sequential sampling

b) Simultaneous sampling

FIGURE 10.13 Multiple input signal quantization.

The limiting factor in simultaneous sampling is the S/H amplifier hold capacitor leakage rate. The leakage rate is the S/H output hold mode voltage change per unit time, during the hold mode of operation, and it is caused by the analog switch and capacitor leakages. The maximum number of channels, m_{max}, for one LSB error is given by

$$m_{max} = \frac{(f_s \cdot \text{LSB})}{(\text{leakage rate})} \tag{10.11}$$

where f_s = sampling rate and the leakage rate is in volts/sec.

The following example provides detailed calculations for both sequential and simultaneous sampling methods.

EXAMPLE 10.5

Determine the phase shift and m_{max} for the following parameters using sequential and simultaneous sampling: $n = 12$, $m = 4$, $t_q = 10$ μsec, $t_s = 5$ μsec, $f_s = 1 \times 10^4$, $f_h = 5 \times 10^3$, $V_{peak} = 5$ V, and leakage rate = 1 μvolt/μsec

Sequential sampling:
Phase shift $(\theta) = [(10 + 5) \times 10^{-6}/(200 \times 10^{-6})] \cdot 360° = 27°$ per channel

Simultaneous sampling:
LSB $= (5 \cdot 2)/2^{12}) = 2.44 \times 10^{-3}$ V
$m_{max} = (1 \times 10^4 \cdot 2.44 \times 10^{-3})/(1) \approx 24$

Sequential sampling may be acceptable for slow, varying input signals. For sampling high-speed signals, though, simultaneous sampling provides the required accuracy.

10.3 DIGITAL-TO-ANALOG CONVERSION

The aim of digital-to-analog conversion is to generate a consistently unique analog output signal value for a specific binary input data word. A DAC module consists of a binary input register, a switching matrix, a resistor ladder network, a voltage reference V_{ref}, and an op amp, as shown in Figure 10.14.

The digital input signal is usually expressed in its natural binary code. As such a binary number N is represented as

$$N = I + F = a_{n-1} \cdot 2^{n-1} + a_{n-2} \cdot 2^{n-2} + \ldots + a_0 \cdot 2^0$$
$$+ a_{-1} \cdot 2^{-1} + \ldots + a_{-n} \cdot 2^{-n} \tag{10.12}$$

The left half of the number is the integer part, I, and the right half makes up the fractional part, F. The binary coefficients a_i, $n - 1 \geq i \geq -n$, are called bits. Each bit has a corresponding power term that defines its relative weight. The leftmost bit has the highest weight and is called the most significant bit (MSB). Similarly, the rightmost bit has the lowest weight and is called

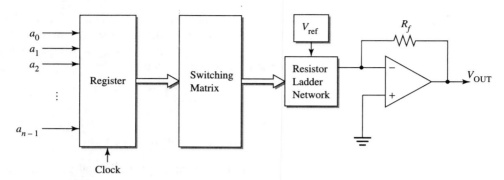

FIGURE 10.14 DAC module block diagram.

the least significant bit (LSB). The analog output voltage V_{OUT}, for an n-bit DAC, is expressed as a fraction of the voltage reference V_{ref} and is determined by the binary input code. The input code is written as an integer, but treated as a fraction whose value is defined between 0 and 1, to represent the analog output value in terms of V_{ref}. Therefore, the analog output expression for an n-bit DAC becomes

$$V_{OUT} = V_{ref} \cdot (a_{-1} \cdot 2^{-1} + \ldots + a_{-n} \cdot 2^{-n}) = V_{ref} \cdot \left(\sum_{i=1}^{n} a_{-i} \cdot 2^{-i} \right) \quad (10.13)$$

Using the above equation, the expressions for maximum, minimum, and half-scale output signal levels can be derived. The maximum output, for an all-ones input code, becomes

$$V_{OUT}(max) = V_{ref} \cdot \left(\frac{1}{2} + \frac{1}{4} + \frac{1}{8} + \ldots + \frac{1}{2^n} \right) = V_{ref}\left(1 - \frac{1}{2^n} \right) \quad (10.14)$$

Thus, the maximum attainable analog output value is one LSB less than V_{ref}. Similarly, the minimum output expression can be written as

$$V_{OUT}(min) = V_{ref} \cdot \frac{1}{2^n} \quad (10.15)$$

This corresponds to an input code with only its LSB set to one. Likewise, the half-scale expression becomes

$$V_{OUT}(H/S) = V_{ref} \cdot \frac{1}{2} \quad (10.16)$$

This corresponds to an input code with only its MSB set to one.

EXAMPLE 10.6 Determine the maximum, minimum, and half-scale output voltage values for a DAC with $n = 6$ and $V_{ref} = 10$ V.

$$V_{OUT} (max) = V_{ref} \left(1 - \frac{1}{2^n} \right) = 10 \times (1 - 0.015625) = 9.84375 \text{ V}$$

$$V_{OUT} (min) = V_{ref} \cdot \frac{1}{2^n} = 10 \times 0.015625 = 0.15625 \text{ V}$$

$$V_{OUT} (H/S) = V_{ref} \cdot \frac{1}{2} = 10 \times \frac{1}{2} = 5 \text{ V}$$

The reference voltage V_{ref} can be internal or external, fixed or variable, and unipolar or bipolar. The DAC transfer function is a graphical representation of the output level changes corresponding to the finite input binary codes.

Figure 10.15 illustrates the transfer functions of a unipolar and a bipolar reference voltage source for a three-bit DAC. In the unipolar case, there are eight equally spaced output voltage levels, ranging from zero to V (max). In the bipolar case there are also eight equally spaced output levels, but they range from $-V_{ref}$ to V (max). Assuming equal V_{ref} ranges, the output voltage step size of the unipolar is one-half that of the bipolar. In this case $\frac{1}{8}$ versus $\frac{1}{4}$.

Digital Input Codes

There are several different binary codes used for digital-to-analog conversion. They can be grouped as either unipolar or bipolar. Unipolar codes include the natural binary, complementary binary, and BCD. Bipolar codes include the offset binary, one's complement, two's complement, and sign magnitude representations.

The natural binary code is a weighted code that consists of n binary coefficients, a_i, and their associated weights, in a 2^i ordered sequence. The absence or presence of a signal level is denoted by a 0 or 1 coefficient, respectively. The DACs use the following code notation:

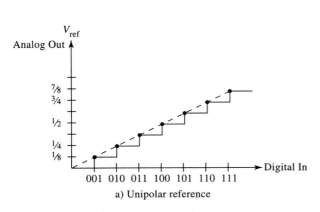

a) Unipolar reference

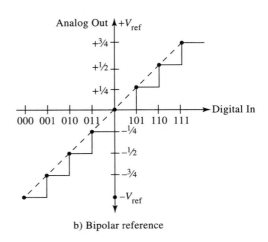

b) Bipolar reference

FIGURE 10.15 DAC transfer characteristics.

$F = a_{-1} \cdot 2^{-1} + a_{-2} \cdot 2^{-2} + \ldots + a_{-n} \cdot 2^{-n}$, where $0 < F < 1$. The complementary binary code, as the name implies, differs from the natural in that its coefficients are inverted. Hence, the presence of a signal level is represented by a 0, and the absence of it by a coefficient value of 1. The BCD code is normally used to format decimal numbers for digital display information. Each decimal digit, 0 through 9, is represented by a four-bit group 8-4-2-1 weighted binary code that uses ten out of the possible sixteen combinations. For example, the decimal number 2947 is represented in BCD format as 0010 1001 0100 0111.

The offset binary code is used to represent analog output signal values, using a bipolar reference voltage. This code is obtained by shifting the natural binary code such that the half scale value, 100 . . . 00, represents the analog output level zero. As a result, the minimum code value represents the analog output level of $-V_{ref}$, and the maximum code value represents the analog output level of $V_{ref}(1 - 1/2^n)$. The one's complement binary code is also used for bipolar representations. A property of this code is that the sum of two equal magnitudes of opposite sign results in all-ones coefficients. The two's complement binary code is the most popular for bipolar representations. This code can be obtained by simply complementing the MSB of the offset binary code. The sum of two equal magnitudes of opposite sign equals an all-zeros code plus a carry. This code is consistent with signed operations within the MPU. The sign magnitude code uses its MSB to specify either a positive (one) or negative (zero) magnitude polarity. This code exhibits equal magnitude symmetry and has single bit changes near the zero scale value.

Table 10.1 provides a tabulation of natural binary and BCD codes for a twelve-bit DAC with a $+10$-V voltage reference source.

Table 10.2 provides a tabulation of offset binary, two's complement, and sign magnitude codes for a twelve-bit DAC with a ±5-V voltage reference. It should be noted that the sign magnitude code has two zero-level representations. As a result, it never reaches the V_{ref} value in either magnitude polarity.

DAC Definitions

The DAC *resolution* is defined as the nominal analog output signal stepsize change in response to an adjacent binary input code change. Thus, an n-bit DAC will produce an output voltage change of $V_{ref}/2^n$ when the input code is altered by one LSB. Similarly, a d-digit BCD DAC

TABLE 10.1
Unipolar input codes

Scale	$V_{ref} = 10$ V	Binary	$V_{ref} = 10$ V	BCD
$V_{ref} - 1$ LSB	9.9975	1111 1111 1111	9.99	1001 1001 1001
3/4	7.5	1100 0000 0000	7.5	0111 0101 0000
1/2	5.0	1000 0000 0000	5.0	0101 0000 0000
1/4	2.5	0100 0000 0000	2.5	0010 0101 0000
1/8	1.25	0010 0000 0000	1.25	0001 0010 0101
1/16	0.625	0001 0000 0000	0.625	0000 0110 0010
1 LSB	0.0025	0000 0000 0001	0.001	0000 0000 0001
0	0	0000 0000 0000	0	0000 0000 0000

TABLE 10.2

Bipolar input codes

Scale	$V_{ref} = \pm 5$ V	Offset Binary	Two's Complement	Sign Magnitude
V_{ref} − 1 LSB	4.9975	111111111111	011111111111	111111111111
3/4	3.750	111000000000	011000000000	111000000000
1/2	2.50	110000000000	010000000000	110000000000
1/4	1.25	101000000000	001000000000	101000000000
1/8	0.625	100100000000	000100000000	100100000000
1/16	0.312	100010000000	000010000000	100010000000
1 LSB	0.0025	100000000001	000000000001	100000000001
0	0.00	100000000000	000000000000	X00000000000
−1/16	−0.312	011110000000	111110000000	000010000000
−1/8	−0.625	011100000000	111100000000	000100000000
−1/4	−1.250	011000000000	111000000000	001000000000
−1/2	−2.50	010000000000	110000000000	010000000000
−3/4	−3.750	001000000000	101000000000	011000000000
−V_{ref} + 1 LSB	−4.9975	000000000001	100000000001	011111111111
−V_{ref}	−5.00	000000000000	100000000000	------------

will produce an output voltage change of $V_{ref}/10^d$ when the input code is altered by one LSB. Resolution can be expressed in bits, digits, or $\%V_{ref}$. Hence for an n-bit DAC, there are 2^n possible uniform output voltage levels that can be produced with a minimum resolution of $(1/2^n) \times 100$ for an n-bit DAC and $(1/10^d) \times 100$ for a d-digit DAC. For example, a twelve-bit DAC has a minimum resolution of 0.024%, and a three-digit DAC has a minimum resolution of 0.1%, as a result of one LSB input code change. The DAC dynamic range is defined as the ratio of the maximum output voltage to the minimum and is expressed in dB as follows:

$$\text{Dynamic Range (dB)} = 20 \cdot \log_{10}\left[\frac{V_{ref} \cdot (1 - 2^{-n})}{V_{ref}(2^{-n})}\right]$$

This expression can be simplified to

$$\text{Dynamic Range (dB)} = 20 \cdot \log_{10} \cdot (2^n - 1) \approx 20 \cdot \log_{10} \cdot (2^n) \approx 6.02 \cdot n \quad \textbf{(10.17)}$$

Table 10.3 provides the resolution and dynamic range of a DAC for various values of n.

The DAC *accuracy* is a measure of the worst case variation from the ideal, straight line, transfer function drawn between zero and V_{ref}. Accuracy can be expressed as either $\%V_{ref}$ or a fraction of LSB, and includes the cumulative effects of offset, scale, and nonlinearity errors. The best accuracy possible is $\pm\frac{1}{2}$ LSB or $\frac{1}{2}^{n+1}$, due to the finite number of bits, and thus DAC resolution. An *offset error* results when an all-zeros input binary code does not result in the minimum output voltage value. It is defined as the maximum difference between the nominal and the actual output voltage values for a minimum input code combination. A *scale error* occurs when an all-ones binary input code does not result in the $V_{ref} \cdot (1 - 1/2^n)$ output voltage value. It is defined as the maximum difference between the nominal and the actual output voltage value for a maximum input code combination. The *nonlinearity error* is a combination of integral and differen-

TABLE 10.3
DAC parameters

Bits (n)	Resolution (%)	Dynamic Range (dB)
1	50	6
2	25	12
3	12.5	18
4	6.25	24
5	3.12	30
6	1.56	36
7	0.78	42
8	0.40	48
9	0.20	54
10	0.10	60
11	0.05	66
12	0.024	72

tial linearity variations. The integral variation, or macroscopic effect, is defined as the maximum difference between the nominal straight line transfer function and the actual transfer curve. The differential variation, or microscopic effect, is defined as the difference between the nominal and actual output voltage changes, for a one-bit input code change. An upper limit of ± 1 LSB differential nonlinearity error is required to ensure that the DAC has a monotonic transfer function. This results in a consistently changing input- to output-level relationship. The converter *settling time* is a measure of the delay interval required for the output to reach a new value, within a specified error limit, in response to an input code change. It is usually specified for the maximum input code change. Figure 10.16 illustrates the four DAC error definitions. DAC modules have external adjustment capability to minimize the offset and scale errors. The integral nonlinearity can be corrected by the use of a compensating lookup table in the MCU memory. However, differential nonlinearity must be kept below the tolerance limit by design.

DAC Types

There are three basic DAC modules available: the binary weight resistor ladder, the R-$2R$ resistor ladder, and the multiplying DAC (MDAC).

The binary weight resistor ladder DAC uses an internal precision voltage reference source, which may be either unipolar or bipolar. The ladder network consists of n resistors, whose values are related by the binary power progression and form the input summing junction of an op amp. Figure 10.17 is a simplified circuit diagram of a unipolar reference DAC module. Each resistor is either connected to the reference source or to a ground, via the switch matrix, based on the state of the corresponding input bit. As a result, the expression at the op amp output becomes $V_{OUT} = -I_{IN} \cdot R_f$ and results in the following equation:

$$V_{OUT} = -(R_f) \cdot \left(\frac{V_{ref}}{R} \right) \cdot \left[\sum_{i=0}^{n-1} \left(\frac{a_i}{2^{n-i}} \right) \right]$$ **(10.18)**

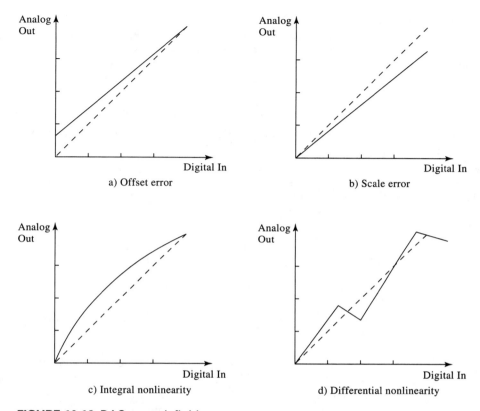

FIGURE 10.16 DAC error definitions.

a) Offset error

b) Scale error

c) Integral nonlinearity

d) Differential nonlinearity

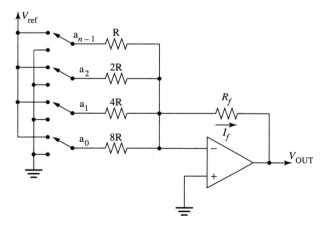

FIGURE 10.17 Binary Weight Resistor Ladder DAC.

The term I_{IN} represents the sum of the individual path currents, each of whose values is a function of the bit state and position of the corresponding input code. If the feedback resistor, R_f, value is equal to R, then the DAC output voltage expression becomes

$$V_{\text{OUT}} = -V_{\text{ref}} \cdot \left[\sum_{i=0}^{n-1} \left(\frac{a_i}{2^{n-i}} \right) \right] \tag{10.19}$$

The input MSB results in an output voltage value of $\frac{1}{2}V_{\text{ref}}$. Similarly, the input LSB results in an output value of $V_{\text{ref}}/2^n$.

EXAMPLE 10.7

Calculate the resulting output voltage of a four-bit DAC, with a 10-V internal reference, when the input code is $a_3a_2a_1a_0 = 1010$.

$$V_{\text{OUT}} = -10 \cdot \left[\frac{a_0}{2^4} + \frac{a_1}{2^3} + \frac{a_2}{2^2} + \frac{a_3}{2^1} \right]$$

$$V_{\text{OUT}} = -10 \cdot \left(0 + \frac{1}{8} + 0 + \frac{1}{2} \right) = -6.25\text{v}$$

In practice a unity gain inverting op amp can be added to provide the correct output polarity.

This type of DAC design is relatively simple, it requires one resistor per bit, and it can be used for high-speed conversions. However, resistor tolerance and temperature variation effects result in reduced accuracy due to the wide range of values.

The R-2R weight resistor ladder, as the name implies, uses only two resistor values, R and 2R. Figure 10.18 is a simplified circuit diagram of the module. The resistor ladder acts as a current divider network. The current entering point A splits into two equal resistance paths, each with a value of 2R. Hence, the resulting current for the input code MSB, a_{n-1}, will be $\frac{I}{2}$. Like-

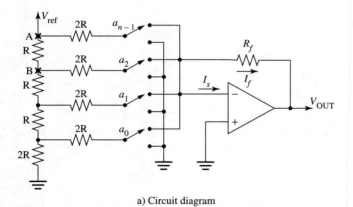

a) Circuit diagram   b) R-2R ladder equivalent diagram

FIGURE 10.18 R-2R weight resistor ladder DAC.

wise, at point B the current splits again into two equal parts of $\frac{I}{4}$ each. The resulting current for an n-bit input code LSB, a_0, will be $\frac{I}{2^n}$. The equivalent resistance from any point of the network to ground is constant and equals R. The individual path currents are summed at the amplifier input node, and the resulting current expression becomes

$$I_{IN} = \left(\frac{V_{ref}}{R}\right) \cdot \left[\sum_{i=0}^{n-1}\left(\frac{a_i}{2^{n-i}}\right)\right]$$
(10.20)

The converter output voltage expression is $V_{OUT} = -I_{IN} \cdot R_f$. By substituting Equation 10.20 for I_s and letting $R_f = R$, the converter output voltage expression becomes

$$V_{OUT} = -V_{ref} \cdot \left[\sum_{i=0}^{n-1}\left(\frac{a_i}{2^{n-i}}\right)\right]$$
(10.21)

which is the same expression as for the binary weight resistor ladder DAC. The R-$2R$ ladder DAC can perform very high speed conversions due to its constant resistance to ground and relatively low resistance values. However, it requires two resistors per bit.

The MDAC module consists of an R-$2R$ resistor ladder DAC with an external reference voltage source. The voltage can be either unipolar or bipolar, with a digitally controlled magnitude. As such it could be used as a programmable attenuator. For instance, the amplitude range of a sinusoidal reference voltage can be controlled by an input binary code. Similarly, a sinusoidal reference voltage can be multiplied by a table of stored binary values using the MDAC to generate an amplitude envelope. The input binary code is stored in the MDAC register.

The input binary code is latched into the DAC register using the leading edge of the clock pulse. In order to avoid any erroneous analog output voltage values during conversion, an S/H device can be placed at the output of the DAC. In this configuration, the first half of the clock cycle places the S/H in the hold mode and the second half switches it back to sample mode, as the output signal becomes stable.

10.4 ANALOG-TO-DIGITAL CONVERSION

The purpose of an analog-to-digital converter (ADC) is to generate consistently a unique output binary code for a specific analog input signal level. The ADC module consists of the analog section, the quantizer, the encoder, and the control logic. Figure 10.19 is a typical ADC simplified block diagram.

The analog section has a reference voltage source and either an integrating op amp or a DAC module. The quantizer consists of one or more level comparators. The encoder performs binary coding, consistent with DAC modules, and has a holding output register. The control logic coordinates the conversion process, using external clock and start signals, and provides a finish status output. The analog input voltage V_{IN} can be either unipolar or bipolar, but cannot exceed the ADC's internal reference voltage range. The digital output code for an n-bit ADC represents 2^n possible input voltage values. The output is expressed as a fractional number, between 0 and 1, which represents the ratio of the input to the internal reference voltage. The smallest detectable analog input voltage level is defined as $V_{ref}/2^n$ and is represented with a one in the LSB bit position and the other bits as zeros. The analog input level, which equals $V_{ref}/2$,

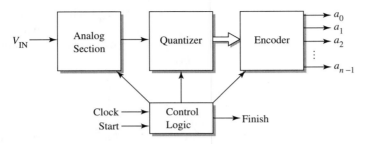

FIGURE 10.19 ADC module block diagram.

is represented with a one in the MSB bit position and the other bits as zeros. The output code of all ones represents an analog input level of $V_{ref} \cdot (1 - 1/2^n)$, as in the case of the DAC module. Figure 10.20 provides a graphical transfer function representation for a three-bit output ADC module, using both unipolar and bipolar reference sources. Using a unipolar input signal, there are eight possible output code values, representing eight equally spaced levels, ranging from zero to $V_{ref} \cdot (1 - \frac{1}{8})$. Similarly, for the bipolar input there are eight equally spaced levels ranging from $-V_{ref}$ to $V_{ref} \cdot (1 - \frac{1}{4})$. Assuming equal V_{ref} ranges, the unipolar input detectable level is one-half that of the bipolar.

ADC Definitions

The ADC *resolution* is defined as the minimum input voltage level increment necessary to change the binary output code to the next adjacent state. An n-bit resolution ADC has the ability to detect an input change of one part in 2^n. For example, a twelve-bit ADC can resolve 1 part in 4,096, or 0.024%, of its internal reference voltage V_{ref}.

The ADC *accuracy* is defined as the difference between the nominal and the actual input voltage level required to produce the same binary output code, due to the cumulative effects of quantization, offset, scale, and nonlinearity errors. Errors are expressed either in fractional LSBs or as a percent of the ADC reference voltage. At best, a quantizer, using the round off rule, exhibits a maximum quantization error of $\pm\frac{1}{2}$ LSB. Hence, as the number of bits is increased, the error magnitude is decreased. For example, a six-bit ADC exhibits a maximum error of $\pm 0.78\%$ of V_{ref}, while a twelve-bit ADC exhibits a maximum error of $\pm 0.122\%$ of V_{ref}. The *offset error* is the maximum deviation between the nominal and the actual input voltage necessary for the minimum output code combination. The *scale error* is the maximum deviation between the nominal and the actual input voltage necessary for the maximum output code combination. The *nonlinearity error* is a combination of both integral and differential linearity variations. Integral nonlinearity is a macroscopic measure of the maximum deviation between the nominal and the actual transfer function along any point of the curve. The differential linearity error is a microscopic measure of the maximum deviation between the nominal and the actual difference of any one LSB change along any point of the transfer curve. The nominal analog input level change of $V_{ref} \cdot (1/2^n)$ equals one LSB change in the binary output code. A differential linearity error of $\pm\frac{1}{2}$ LSB results in an equivalent analog input stepsize of $\frac{1}{2}$ to $\frac{3}{2}$ LSB along the transfer curve. Hence, if the error exceeds 1 LSB, then the

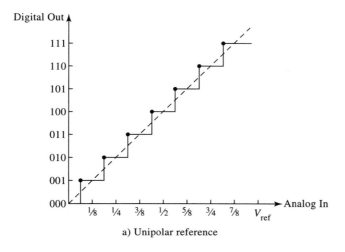

a) Unipolar reference

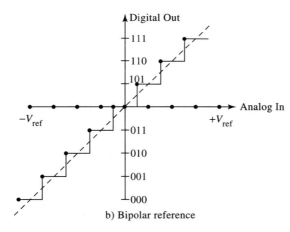

b) Bipolar reference

FIGURE 10.20 ADC transfer characteristics.

ADC will miss an output binary code combination. Figure 10.21 illustrates the four ADC error definitions.

The ADC *conversion speed* is defined as the time required for a single conversion cycle and is measured from the time a start command is given to the time a finish status signal is returned. The *conversion rate* is defined as the maximum number of conversions possible per second.

ADC Types

There are four basic analog-to-digital conversion techniques available: counter tracking, integrating, successive approximation, and parallel.

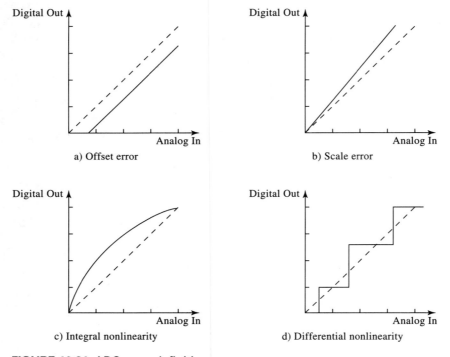

FIGURE 10.21 ADC error definitions.

A simple counter tracking ADC module block diagram is shown in Figure 10.22. The counter register serves as the input to the DAC and as the binary code output. When the start command signal becomes active, the counter is reset and then increments one LSB at a time at the input clock rate. The DAC converts the counter state into an equivalent analog level. The level is continuously compared against the unknown analog input by means of a comparator. When the two levels are equal, the comparator changes state and the control logic stops the counter. Also, the finish status output signal is activated to indicate the completion of the conversion. This ADC is suited for slowly changing input signals, since the conversion time is directly proportional to the input voltage magnitude. Its maximum conversion time is $2^n \cdot T$, where T is the clock period, with an average conversion time of $2^{n-1} \cdot T$.

An enhancement of this technique uses an up/down counter, as shown in Figure 10.23. The advantage of this approach is that the ADC output constantly follows input signal level changes. The average conversion time is twice as fast, and it is significantly faster for small input level variations. The converter accuracy is within one LSB, due to the counter action. Also, an external input control signal can be used to place the ADC in either track or hold mode by controlling counter operation.

Integrating-type DACs use an indirect conversion technique. The unknown analog input voltage is converted into a time interval, which is measured using a counter. The most popular type is the dual slope ADC. This measures the amount of time required for the integral of the reference voltage to equal the average input voltage level over a fixed time interval. A simpli-

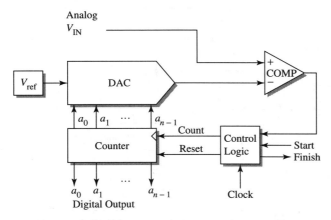

FIGURE 10.22 Simple counter ADC.

fied dual slope ADC module block diagram is shown in Figure 10.24a. Since the output binary code is the average of the analog input signal, the module is immune to instantaneous noise. The principle of operation is based on the charge and discharge of a stable capacitor and the comparison of the analog input with the reference voltage source.

There are three distinct steps in the conversion process: zeroizing, unknown input integration, and reference voltage integration. At the beginning of the start command, the integration capacitor is zeroized and the counter is reset during T_0. Next, the input analog signal V_{IN} is used to charge the capacitor during the fixed interval T_1. The resulting integrator output voltage V_{OUT} is proportional to the input signal level, or

$$V_{OUT} = - \frac{1}{R \cdot C} \int_0^{T_1} V_{IN} \cdot dt \tag{10.22}$$

FIGURE 10.23 Counter tracking ADC.

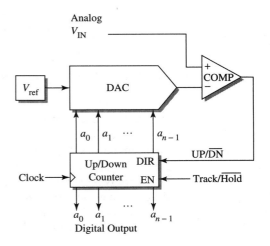

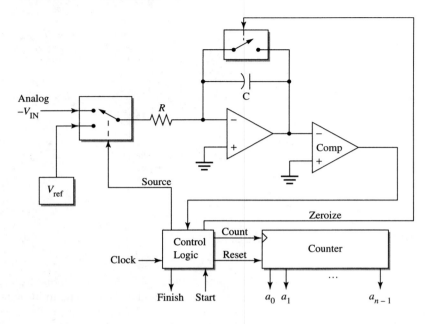

a) Block diagram

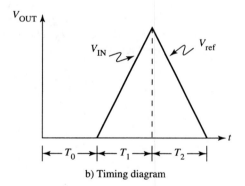

b) Timing diagram

FIGURE 10.24 Dual slope integrating ADC.

Finally, a fixed reference voltage of opposite polarity is applied to the integrator during T_2 until the capacitor is discharged to zero. This integration interval is a function of the analog input signal magnitude, as shown in Figure 10.24b. Also, the relationship between the two integration intervals, T_1 and T_2, satisfies the relation $V_{IN} \cdot T_1 = V_{ref} \cdot T_2$. Since V_{ref} and T_1 are fixed, the interval T_2 is directly proportional to the magnitude of V_{IN}. The counter is enabled at the start of T_2 and disabled when the comparator senses a V_{OUT} value of zero. The resulting binary counter state is proportional to the unknown analog input signal magnitude. Integrating-type ADCs offer high noise immunity and high resolution. The typical conversion speed is about 100 msec per cycle.

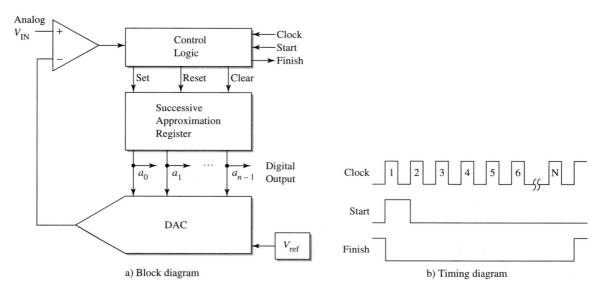

a) Block diagram   b) Timing diagram

FIGURE 10.25 Successive approximation ADC.

A successive approximation ADC compares the unknown analog input with exact fractional values of the internal reference voltage, starting at $V_{ref}/2$. The conversion process is optimized such that it takes n steps for an n-bit module to complete the conversion cycle. The converter output binary code represents the ratio of the input to the reference voltage magnitudes. Figure 10.25 is a simplified block diagram of a successive approximation ADC module.

The start command activates the conversion process. The control logic provides successively smaller voltage level trial increments to the internal DAC until its output equals that of the unknown input voltage. The successive approximation register (SAR) MSB is initially set to 1, which results in a DAC output level of $V_{ref}/2$. If the input level is greater than $V_{ref}/2$, the MSB remains set; otherwise it is reset. Then the next significant DAC bit is set, which results in an output level of either $\frac{3}{4}V_{ref}$ or $\frac{1}{4}V_{ref}$ depending on the previous outcome. Again, this bit either remains set or is reset, depending on the DAC output and input signal comparison outcome. This process repeats until the LSB is tested, at which point the SAR contains a binary code that represents the analog input voltage level. The clear control input signal resets all bits of the SAR. Figure 10.26 illustrates the intermediate conversion steps performed by an eight-bit ADC with a 10-V reference and a 3-V input signal. Table 10.4 lists the individual bit values in the order of conversion. The DAC successive output values and the associated SAR bit states are indicated for each clock pulse.

The conversion time equals $n \cdot T$. Successive approximation ADCs are very popular and provide high resolution and conversion speeds, typically 2 μsec for a twelve-bit ADC.

Parallel ADCs compare the analog input against $2^n - 1$ uniformly spaced voltage levels, using an equal number of comparators. Comparator thresholds are set one LSB apart, using a

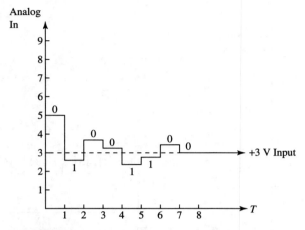

FIGURE 10.26 Successive approximation process.

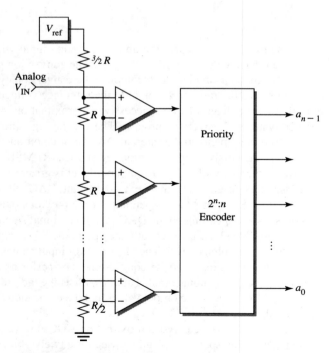

FIGURE 10.27 Parallel ADC.

440

TABLE 10.4
Successive approximation

Bit		Weight
MSB	0	5 V
	1	2.5 V
	0	1.25 V
	0	0.625 V
	1	0.3135 V
	1	0.1562 V
	0	0.0781 V
LSB	0	0.0390 V

stable voltage reference and a precision resistor divider network. Thus, for a given analog input voltage, all comparators that are biased below that level change state while those above remain at the same state. The comparator outputs are fed into a priority encoder, which performs a binary logic conversion and produces an output code. The conversion speed is determined by the slowest comparator switching time. Figure 10.27 is a typical parallel ADC module block diagram.

A parallel or flash converter exhibits high conversion speed but has low resolution, low noise immunity, and circuit complexity. For example, an eight-bit parallel converter has a typical conversion speed of 10 nsec but requires 255 comparators and a 255-to-8 priority encoder.

10.5 ANGLE-TO-DIGITAL CONVERSION

The prevalent form of angular position sensors consists of a variable coupled transformer made up of a fixed and a rotating coil. The output signal represents the angular position between the fixed and rotating coils, as a trigonometric function of the input signal. The turns ratio of the two coils is usually one-to-one. A *synchro* consists of a single rotor winding and three fixed stator windings positioned at 120° relative to each other. A *resolver* consists of a single rotor winding and two fixed stator windings positioned at 90° relative to each other. A rotor input vector signal is converted into its sine and cosine output components, whose amplitudes are functions of the stator coupling angle. Figure 10.28 shows a simplified resolver circuit diagram and its associated signal equations. The AC reference signal $V \cdot \sin (\omega \cdot t)$ is fed to the rotor and displays a constant amplitude versus angular position. The rotor signal is coupled to the stator windings, and its amplitude is weighted by either the sine or cosine of the coupling angle, θ. In this configuration the resolver acts as transmitter.

The stator windings of the sending resolver can be connected to those of a second resolver acting as a receiver. In this arrangement, the receiving resolver rotor will produce a signal whose amplitude is a function of the two resolver shaft angles. The signal can be expressed as

$$V_r = V \cdot \sin (\theta - \phi) \cdot \sin (\omega \cdot t) \tag{10.23}$$

The expression $V \cdot \sin (\theta - \phi) = V \cdot \sin \theta \cdot \cos \phi - V \cdot \cos \theta \cdot \sin \phi$, where θ and ϕ are the sending and receiving resolver shaft angles, respectively. A synchro also has an AC input ref-

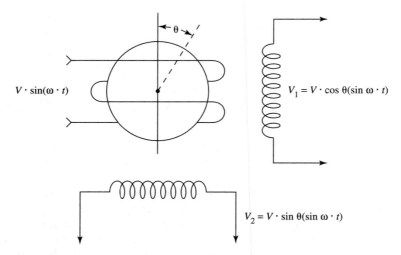

FIGURE 10.28 Resolver signal definitions.

erence signal fed to its rotor, and it produces three output signal waveforms that can be expressed as follows:

$$V_1 = V \cdot \sin \theta \cdot \sin (\omega \cdot t) \qquad \text{(10.24)}$$
$$V_2 = V \cdot \sin (\theta + 120°) \cdot \sin (\omega \cdot t) \qquad \text{(10.25)}$$
$$V_3 = V \cdot \sin (\theta - 120°) \cdot \sin (\omega \cdot t) \qquad \text{(10.26)}$$

A conversion between synchro and resolver devices is easily accomplished by the use of a Scott-T transformer. Figure 10.29 presents the circuit diagrams for a synchro device and a Scott-T transformer. The transformer is a bidirectional device that can perform synchro-to-resolver conversion and vice versa.

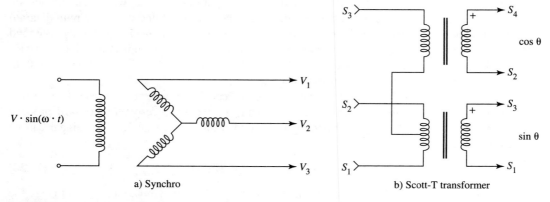

FIGURE 10.29 Synchro-to-resolver conversion.

TABLE 10.5
Digital angle representation

Bits (n)	Resolution (%)	Relative Angle (°)
1	50	180
2	25	90
3	12.5	45
4	6.25	22.5
5	3.12	11.25
6	1.56	5.62
7	0.78	2.81
8	0.40	1.40
9	0.20	0.70
10	0.10	0.35
11	0.05	0.175
12	0.024	0.088

A digital-to-angle converter, synchro or resolver, accepts a binary input code, along with an AC reference signal, and produces an equivalent analog angle output signal. Similarly, an angle-to-digital converter accepts an analog angle input signal, along with an AC reference signal, and produces an equivalent digital angle output binary code. The digital angle is represented with natural binary code. The range of angles lies between 0° and 360°. The binary code word is treated as a fraction whose value is defined between 0 and 1. Thus, the MSB bit position represents an angle of 180°. This is the product of the maximum angle value times one-half. Similarly, the LSB bit position represents a minimum angle of 360° · $(1/2^{n})$. The maximum angle representation is 360° − 1 LSB, due to the finite number of bits. The angle resolution is defined as $(1/2^n) \times 100$, where n is the number of bits used to define a digital angle. Table 10.5 lists the relative angle and resolution as a function of the number of bits.

Digital-to-Angle Converter

This converter module accepts an n-bit binary word, representing an angle, θ, and produces an equivalent analog output signal. The output signal's amplitude is attenuated as a function of the input angle. Its resolution is measured in fractional degrees corresponding to 1 LSB, and its accuracy is usually within ±3 LSB. The settling time, usually specified for a 90° step size, is several microseconds.

Figure 10.30 is a typical digital-to-angle converter module block diagram. The input register stores the digital angle value. The quadrant selection logic (QSL) makes it possible to reduce the conversion process from four quadrant operations to one, between 0° and 90°. The reference input voltage is transformer-isolated and converted into two equal signals of opposite polarity by centertapping the secondary winding. The upper two input register bits are used by the QSL to generate the sine and cosine signal polarities over the four quadrants. The two MDACs use a resistance ladder network and solid state switches to attenuate the input reference voltage. The resistor network values are chosen so as to attenuate the reference signal proportionally to either the sine or cosine of the input binary code word. The MDAC

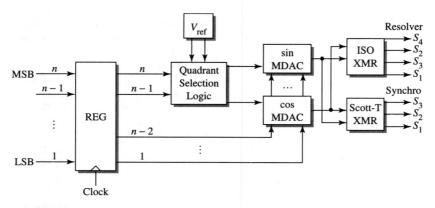

FIGURE 10.30 Digital-to-angle converter.

outputs are fed into either an isolation or a Scott-T transformer to provide either a resolver or a synchro output signal, respectively. The MDACs are basically single quadrant multipliers. However, when used in conjunction with the QSL, four-quadrant multiplication is in effect achieved.

Figure 10.31 is a simplified circuit diagram of the QSL. The QSL takes advantage of the sinusoidal waveform symmetry about 90°, and provides the proper reference signal sign to the MDACs for each quadrant. Table 10.6 lists the corresponding quadrant switch function.

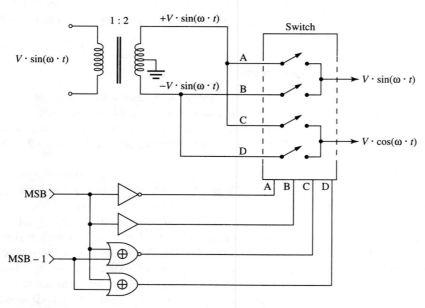

FIGURE 10.31 Quadrant selection logic definition.

TABLE 10.6
Quadrant switch function

MSB	MSB-1	Quadrant	Range	Sin θ	Cos θ	Switch On
0	0	1	0–90°	+	+	A and C
0	1	2	90–180°	+	−	A and D
1	0	3	180–270°	−	−	B and D
1	1	4	270–360°	−	+	B and C

Angle-to-Digital Converter

This converter module accepts either a resolver or a synchro input signal and produces an equivalent n-bit output binary code representing the coupling angle, θ. Its resolution is measured in fractional degrees corresponding to 1 LSB. Its accuracy is usually within ±1 LSB. The tracking rate is approximately equal to the reference voltage frequency divided by the number of output bits and is expressed in revolutions per second. Figure 10.32 is a typical angle-to-digital converter module block diagram.

This module is known as a tracking-type converter. The converter input can either be resolver or synchro, depending on the transformer interface. The QSL and the MDACs operate the same as in the digital-to-angle converter. Together with the difference amplifier they form a solid state control transformer (SSCT), which produces a signal proportional to the difference

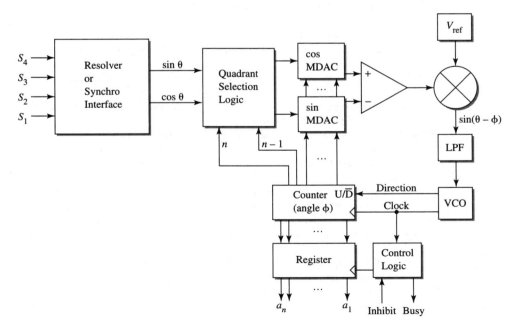

FIGURE 10.32 Angle-to-digital converter.

of the two input angles, θ and ϕ. The output difference signal $V \cdot \sin(\theta - \phi) \cdot \sin(\omega \cdot t)$ is demodulated, using the reference signal, and fed into the voltage-controlled oscillator (VCO) circuit. The VCO output controls the clocking rate and direction of the counter. When the input angle θ equals the digital angle ϕ, the VCO output voltage is 0 and the counter state becomes θ. The control logic is used to interface the module with an MCU and load θ in the register.

PROBLEMS

10.1 Given a scaling amplifier with $V_{IN} = 10$ mV, $R_{IN} = 10$ kOhms, and $R_f = 250$ kOhms, determine V_{OUT}.

10.2 Given a four-input summation amplifier with $V_1 = 10$ mV, $R_1 = 10$ kOhms, $V_2 = 20$ mV, $R_2 = 50$ kOhms, $V_3 = -10$ mV, $R_3 = 5$ kOhms, $V_4 = 50$ mV, and $R_4 = 100$ kOhms, determine V_{OUT} for $R_f = 100$ kOhms.

10.3 Given a current-to-voltage converting op amp with $R_{IN} = 200$ ohms, $R_s = 15$ ohms, and $R_f = 1$ kOhm, determine V_{OUT} for $I_{IN} = 50$ ma.

10.4 Given an integrating amplifier with $R = 100$ kOhms, $C = 0.01$ μF, $V_{IN} = 2 \cdot$ t, and $T = 5$ msec, determine V_{OUT}.

10.5 Given a differentiating amplifier with $R = 100$ kOhms, $C = 0.01$ μF, and $dV_{IN}/dt = 0.3$ V/μsec, determine V_{OUT}.

10.6 Determine the dynamic range and data rate for a twelve-bit quantizer with a sampling frequency of 20 kHz.

10.7 Determine the highest frequency for a 1-LSB error of a twelve-bit quantizer with $t_q = 4$ μsec, and $V_{peak} = 10$ V. Also determine the highest frequency if the quantizer is preceded by an S/H amplifier with $t_s = 2$ μsec.

10.8 Determine the channel frequency f_{ch} of a sixteen-input sequential sampling quantizer, if $t_{acm} = 1$ μsec, $t_{acs} = 1$ μsec, $t_{aps} = 0.5$ μsec, and $t_q = 4$ μsec.

10.9 Determine the maximum phase shift, using sequential sampling, for the following parameters: $m = 4$, $t_q = 5$ μsec, $t_s = 2$ μsec, and $f_h = 10$ kHz.

10.10 Determine the maximum number of channels, using simultaneous sampling, for the following parameters: $V_{peak} = 5$ V, $n = 16$, $f_s = 30$ kHz, and a leakage rate of 0.5×10^{-6} V/μsec.

10.11 Determine the maximum, minimum, and half-scale output voltage values, for a sixteen-bit DAC with $V_{ref} = 10$ V.

10.12 Express the values of Problem 10.11 in binary notation using a unipolar source of 10 V. Also, express them in two's complement notation using a bipolar ±5-V reference.

10.13 Determine the resolution and dynamic range of a sixteen-bit DAC.

10.14 Calculate the resulting output voltage of an eight-bit DAC, with a 10-V reference, for an input code of $a_7 \ldots a_0 = 10100101$.

10.15 Calculate the resulting output binary code for a 7-V analog input, using an eight-bit successive approximation ADC, with a 10-V internal reference.

10.16 Determine the resolution and relative angle for a sixteen-bit digital-to-angle converter.

10.17 Using Table 10.6, derive the logic of Figure 10.31.

REFERENCES

Burr-Brown. *IC Data Book.* Tucson, AZ: Burr-Brown, 1990.

The Engineering Staff of ILC Data Device Corporation. *Synchro Conversion Handbook.* Bohemia, NY: ILC Data Device Corporation, 1979.

Harris Semiconductor. *Linear and Data Acquisition Products.* Melbourne, FL: Harris Semiconductor, 1977.

National Semiconductor. *Data Acquisition Handbook.* Santa Clara, CA: National Semiconductor, 1977.

Schmid, H. *Electronic Analog/Digital Conversions.* New York: Van Nostrand–Reinhold, 1970.

Sheingold, D. H. *Analog to Digital Conversion Handbook.* Englewood, NJ: Prentice Hall, 1986.

11

SIGNAL ANALYSIS

Digital signal analysis systems consist of three sections. The input section performs analog input signal prefiltering and analog-to-digital conversion. The digital signal processor (DSP) performs a series of mathematical operations on the data, using specialized algorithms, to achieve signal modification and/or information extraction. The output section performs digital-to-analog conversion and postfiltering on the analog output signal. The output is suitable for display or control. Figure 11.1 is a typical signal analysis system block diagram.

The DSP is optimized to perform high-speed multiplication and addition on the input data. This is possible through the use of hardware multipliers, adders, pipelining, and a Harvard architecture. The hardware implementation of the arithmetic operations results in single-cycle instruction execution. Pipelining maintains a constant data flow stream to and from the ALU by dividing each computation into several smaller steps. At any given time the pipeline contains data that reflect the various stages of the computational process. The Harvard architecture of separate program and data storage enables instruction fetching and operant execution to take place concurrently. The signal-processing algorithms enable signal representation and modification in either time or frequency domain.

The three basic operations are convolution, correlation, and spectrum analysis. *Convolution* is a time domain operation that corresponds to frequency domain filtering. *Correlation* is a time domain operation that compares one signal to another for possible similarities. *Spectrum analysis* transforms a time domain signal to its frequency domain equivalent and provides magnitude and phase for each frequency component.

The objectives of this chapter are as follows: (1) to review basic definitions, (2) to discuss sampling and rate modification, (3) to explain discrete system concepts, (4) to present FIR digital filter design, and (5) to define DFT and FFT algorithm operations.

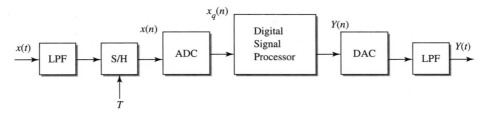

FIGURE 11.1
Digital analysis system.

11.1 DEFINITIONS

A *signal* is an electrical quantity—voltage or current—used to represent information in an electrical network. Signals that can be precisely defined as functions of time are called *deterministic*. Those that cannot be defined because of some parameter uncertainty are called *random*. A deterministic signal is *periodic* in nature if $x(t) = x(t + T)$, where T represents its repetition period. An example of such a signal is shown in Figure 11.2.

The signal function $x(t) = A \cdot \sin(\omega \cdot t + T)$ has a maximum amplitude, A, that varies periodically over time as specified by $\sin(\theta)$, where $\theta = \omega \cdot t = (2 \cdot \pi/T) \cdot t$. The signal frequency, f, is the reciprocal of its period, T. The signal average or mean value can be calculated over T by

$$A_{mean} = \frac{1}{2 \cdot \pi} \int_0^{2\pi} A \cdot \sin(\theta)\, d\theta \tag{11.1}$$

The signal mean value computed over T equals zero. If the signal mean value is computed over $T/2$, then it becomes $A_{mean} = (2 \cdot A)/\pi = 0.637 \cdot A$. The root mean square (RMS) value of the signal computed over T is determined by

$$A_{rms} = \left[\frac{1}{2 \cdot \pi} \int_0^{2\pi} (A \cdot \sin \theta)^2\, d\theta \right]^{1/2} = \frac{A}{\sqrt{2}} = 0.707 \cdot A \tag{11.2}$$

A group of electrical components forms a *system* that transfers a signal between two points or nodes. The system parameters interact with the signal to produce a specific response. A system is defined as *linear* if $Y_1(t) = f(x_1(t))$ and $Y_2(t) = f(x_2(t))$ imply $Y_1(t) + Y_2(t) = f(x_1(t) + x_2(t))$ and $k \cdot Y_1(t) = k \cdot f(x_1(t))$. If an input signal time shift results in a corresponding output response time shift, $Y_1(t - t_0) = f(x_1(t - t_0))$, the system is called *time invariant*. A *causal sys-*

FIGURE 11.2
Time domain waveforms.

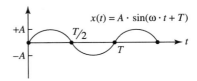

FIGURE 11.3
Linear time-invariant system block diagram.

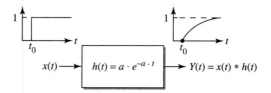

tem produces an output response that begins at or after the time an input signal is applied, or $Y_1(t_1) = f[x_1(t_0)]$ and $t_1 \geq t_0$. Figure 11.3 is a linear system block diagram.

The input-output relationship is analytically determined by the use of the following equation, known as the convolution integral:

$$Y(t) = \int_{-\infty}^{\infty} [x(\tau) \cdot h(t - \tau)]d\tau = x(t) * h(t) \qquad (11.3)$$

The function $h(t)$ defines the system impulse response, which is obtained by setting $x(t) = \delta(t_0)$ the unit impulse function. For example, if $x(t) = u(t)$ (the unit step function), and $h(t) = a \cdot e^{-at}$ then the output response $Y(t)$ becomes

$$Y(t) = u(t) * (a \cdot e^{-a \cdot t}) = \int_{0}^{t} (u(\tau) \cdot (a \cdot e^{-a \cdot (t-\tau)})d\tau = 1 - e^{-a \cdot t} \qquad (11.4)$$

A periodic time function $x(t)$, which is continuous over the entire interval T, can be expressed as the summation of harmonically related trigonometric or exponential functions, known as the Fourier series representation. Hence, $x(t)$ becomes

$$x(t) = \frac{A_0}{2} + \sum_{m=1}^{\infty} [(A_m \cdot \cos (m \cdot \omega \cdot t) + B_m \cdot \sin (m \cdot \omega \cdot t)] \qquad (11.5)$$

where t = time variable
   T = signal period
   $\omega = (2 \cdot \pi)/T$

Also, the A_0, A_m, and B_m coefficient equations are

$$A_0 = \frac{1}{T} \int_{0}^{T} x(t)dt \qquad (11.6)$$

$$A_m = \frac{2}{T} \int_{0}^{T} [x(t) \cdot \cos (m \cdot \omega \cdot t)]dt \qquad (11.7)$$

$$B_m = \frac{2}{T} \int_{0}^{T} [x(t) \cdot \sin (m \cdot \omega \cdot t)]dt \qquad (11.8)$$

If the function is even, or $x(t) = x(-t)$, then $B_m = 0$ and the series contains only cosine terms. Similarly, if the function is odd, or $x(t) = -x(-t)$, then $A_m = 0$ and the series contains only sine terms. Also, if $x(t) = x(t + T/2)$, then only even harmonics exist. If $x(t) = -x(t + T/2)$, then only odd harmonics exist. The Fourier series representation of $x(t)$ can also be represented in the following compact format:

$$x(t) = \frac{A_0}{2} + \sum_{m=1}^{\infty} [(C_m) \cdot \cos(m \cdot \omega \cdot t + \theta_m)] \tag{11.9}$$

where $\quad C_m = \frac{1}{2} \cdot [(A_m)^2 + (B_m)^2]^{1/2}$

$$\theta_m = -\tan^{-1}\left(\frac{B_m}{A_m}\right)$$

If both positive and negative values of m are included, then all the frequency components are effectively divided by two and A_0 can be included in the summation.

Figure 11.4 depicts a periodic square wave signal in the time domain and its corresponding line magnitude spectrum in the frequency domain for positive values of m. The time domain signal definition becomes $x(t) = A$ for $|t| < \tau$ and $x(t) = 0$ for $|t| > \tau$. Also, $x(t) = x(t + T)$. The Fourier series signal definition becomes

$$x(t) = \left(\frac{A \cdot \tau}{T}\right) \cdot \sum_{m=-\infty}^{\infty} \frac{\sin(m \cdot \omega \cdot \tau/2)}{m \cdot \omega \cdot \tau/2} \cdot \cos(m \cdot \omega \cdot t + \theta_m)$$

Since $\omega = 2 \cdot \pi \cdot f$, the sin x/x, or sinc, function argument becomes $\sin(m \cdot \pi \cdot f \cdot \tau)/m \cdot \pi \cdot f \cdot \tau$, but $\tau = T/2$ and $f = 1/T$; thus $x(t)$ can be written as

$$x(t) = \frac{A}{2} \cdot \sum_{m=-\infty}^{\infty} \frac{\sin(m \cdot \pi/2)}{m \cdot \pi/2} \cdot \cos(m \cdot \omega \cdot t + \theta_m) \tag{11.10}$$

Since the function is even, $B_m = 0$ and θ_m becomes $-(m \cdot \pi/2)$ due to a $\tau/2$ time shift. In general, it should be noted that $1/T = f$ the frequency component spacing. Also, $1/(m \cdot \tau)$ specifies the null frequency components. Lastly, the number of frequency components between nulls is

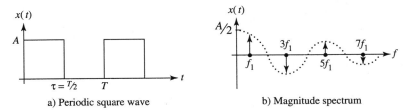

a) Periodic square wave

b) Magnitude spectrum

FIGURE 11.4
Fourier series spectrum of a square wave.

$(T/\tau) - 1$. Thus, a periodic analog time domain signal has a corresponding nonperiodic discrete frequency domain spectrum. The magnitude frequency spectrum representation, together with each component's phase information, uniquely defines a corresponding time domain signal.

A nonperiodic or transient time dom/ain function $x(t)$ that is defined over a continuous interval T can be represented as a frequency domain function $X(f)$ using the forward Fourier transform integral equation:

$$X(f) = \int_{-\infty}^{\infty} [x(t) \cdot e^{-j \cdot 2 \cdot \pi \cdot f \cdot t}]dt \qquad (11.11)$$

where $j = (-1)^{1/2}$

Similarly, a frequency domain signal definition $X(f)$ can be represented as a time domain function $x(t)$ by the use of the inverse Fourier transform integral equation:

$$x(t) = \int_{-\infty}^{\infty} [X(f) \cdot e^{j \cdot 2 \cdot \pi \cdot f \cdot t}]df \qquad (11.12)$$

where $j = (-1)^{1/2}$

Figure 11.5 illustrates the use of the Fourier transform pairs. A rectangular pulse in the time domain becomes a sinc function in the frequency domain. Similarly, a sinc function in the time domain becomes a rectangular pulse in the frequency domain.

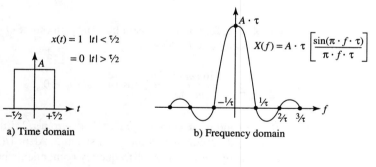

a) Time domain

b) Frequency domain

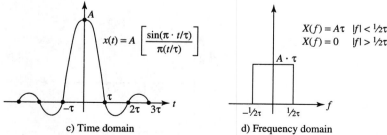

c) Time domain

d) Frequency domain

FIGURE 11.5
Fourier transform pairs.

TABLE 11.1

Fourier transform properties

Name	Time Domain	Frequency Domain
Addition	$x_1(t) + x_2(t)$	$X_1(f) + X_2(f)$
Constant Multiplication	$a \cdot x(t)$	$a \cdot X(f)$
Time Scaling	$x_1(t/a)$	$\lvert a \rvert \cdot X(a \cdot f)$
Time Delay	$x(t - t_0)$	$X(f) \cdot e^{-j \cdot 2 \cdot \pi \cdot f \cdot t_0}$
Frequency Shift	$x(t) \cdot e^{j \cdot 2 \cdot \pi \cdot f_0 \cdot t}$	$X(f - f_0)$
Modulation	$x(t) \cdot 2 \cdot \cos(2 \cdot \pi \cdot f_0 \cdot t)$	$X(f - f_0) + X(f + f_0)$
Time Multiplication	$x_1(t) \cdot x_2(t)$	$X_1(f) * X_2(f)$
Frequency Multiplication	$x_1(t) * x_2(t)$	$X_1(f) \cdot X_2(f)$
Time Sampling	$\sum_{n=-\infty}^{\infty} \delta(t - nT_s)$	$1/T \cdot \sum_{m=-\infty}^{\infty} \delta(f - mf_s)$

An aperiodic analog time signal has a corresponding aperiodic frequency spectrum representation, and vice versa. Due to the nature of the transform pair, each operation in one domain has a corresponding operation in the other. It turns out that certain operations are computed more easily in one of the two domains. Table 11.1 lists the most common Fourier transform properties. These properties make some signal analysis operations easier in time domain, while others in the frequency domain. For example, convolution in one domain becomes multiplication in the other, and vice versa. Figure 11.6 illustrates a system input-output relationship in the frequency domain. The system performs a mathematical operation on the input signal and produces an output. The impulse response $h(t)$ and the system transfer function $H(f)$ form a Fourier transform pair. The output signal frequency response $Y(f)$ is obtained by multiplying the input signal frequency response $X(f)$ by the system transfer function $H(f)$. The following example is used to explain the above concepts.

EXAMPLE 11.1

Let $x(t) = u(t) \leftrightarrow X(f) = \pi\delta(\omega) + 1/(j\omega)$, where $\omega = 2 \cdot \pi \cdot f$, and let $h(t) = e^{-a \cdot t} \leftrightarrow H(f) = 1/(j\omega + a)$.

Then,

$$Y(f) = H(f) \cdot X(f) = \frac{\pi\delta(\omega)}{j\omega + a} + \frac{1}{j\omega \cdot (j\omega + a)}$$

In general, since the frequency domain functions are complex, they can be expressed as magnitude and phase component spectra. As such,

$$Y(f) = \lvert H(f) \rvert \, \underline{/\theta}\,(f) \cdot \lvert X(f) \rvert \, \underline{/\phi}\,(f) = \lvert H(f) \rvert \cdot \lvert X(f) \rvert \, \underline{/\theta}\,(f) + \underline{/\phi}(f) \quad \textbf{(11.13)}$$

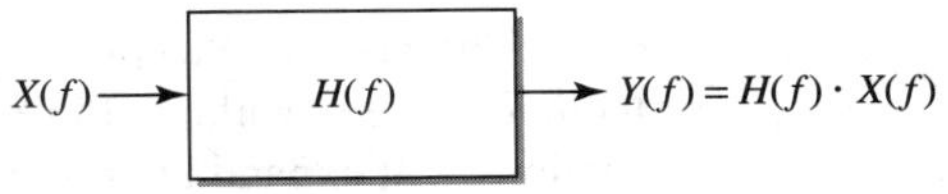

FIGURE 11.6
System transfer function block diagram.

$X(f) \longrightarrow \boxed{H(f)} \longrightarrow Y(f) = H(f) \cdot X(f)$

Another way to define signals is by their energy content, using the concept of correlation. The autocorrelation function of a signal is the integral product of itself and its time-shifted replica over an interval T and is written as

$$R_{xx}(\tau) = \int_{-\infty}^{\infty} [x(t) \cdot x(t - \tau)]dt \qquad (11.14)$$

A useful property of the autocorrelation function is that $R_{xx}(\tau) = R_{xx}(-\tau)$. The following example is used to calculate the autocorrelation function of an exponential signal.

EXAMPLE 11.2

Find the autocorrelation function of the signal $x(t) = e^{-a \cdot t}$.

$$R_{xx}(\tau) = \int_{-\infty}^{\infty} [e^{-a \cdot t} \cdot e^{-a(t-\tau)}]dt = e^{a \cdot \tau} \int_{\tau}^{\infty} [e^{-2 \cdot a \cdot t}]dt$$

$$R_{xx}(\tau) = (e^{-a \cdot |\tau|})/(2 \cdot a)$$

The signal energy, in (volts)^2, is defined as

$$<x^2(t)> = \int_{-\infty}^{\infty} [x^2(t)]dt = R_{xx}(0) \qquad (11.15)$$

For the previous example, the signal energy becomes, $<x^2(t)> = 1/(2 \cdot a)$ (volts)^2. The Fourier transform of the autocorrelation function $R_{xx}(\tau)$ becomes the energy spectral density function $S_{xx}(f)$ and is expressed in (volts)^2/Hz. The spectral density function for the previous example becomes

$$S_{xx}(f) = F[R_{xx}(\tau)] = \int_{-\infty}^{\infty} \left[\left(\frac{e^{-a \cdot |\tau|}}{2 \cdot a} \right) \cdot (e^{-j \cdot \omega \cdot t}) \right] dt \qquad (11.16)$$

which simplifies to $S_{xx}(f) = 1/(a^2 + \omega^2)$, where $\omega = 2 \cdot \pi \cdot f$.

If a system is defined in terms of the input and output spectral densities, then the following relationships exist: Since $Y(f) = H(f) \cdot X(f)$, the output spectral density $S_{yy}(f) = |Y(f)|^2 = |H(f) \cdot X(f)|^2$, which can be written as $S_{yy}(f) = |H(f)|^2 \cdot S_{xx}(f)$.

EXAMPLE 11.3

Find the output spectral density for $x(t) = u(t)$ and $h(t) = a \cdot e^{-a \cdot t}$.

$$R_{xx}(\tau) = 1 \qquad\qquad H(f) = a/(a + j\omega)$$
$$S_{xx}(f) = 2 \cdot \pi \cdot \delta(\omega) \qquad |H(f)|^2 = a^2/(a^2 + \omega^2)$$
$$S_{yy}(f) = [a^2/(a^2 + \omega^2)] \cdot [2 \cdot \pi \cdot \delta(\omega)] \text{ (volts)}^2/\text{Hz}$$

The above concepts also hold true in a digital system environment. Various tools and techniques are available to perform mathematical operations on digital signals. The following sections will expand upon selected equivalent digital signal analysis operations.

11.2 SAMPLING AND ALIASING

An analog signal must be sampled and quantized prior to performing any digital analysis operation. Ideal sampling is defined as the product of the analog time domain signal $x(t)$ and the periodic impulse function $s(t)$. This can be expressed mathematically as

$$Y(t) = x(t) \cdot s(t) = x(t) \cdot \sum_{n=-\infty}^{\infty} \delta(t - n \cdot T_s) = \sum_{n=-\infty}^{\infty} x(n \cdot T_s) \cdot \delta(t - n \cdot T_s) \quad \textbf{(11.17)}$$

where $\delta(t - n \cdot T_s) = \begin{cases} 1 & \text{if } t - n \cdot T_s = 0 \\ 0 & \text{otherwise} \end{cases}$

The term T_s is the sampling period of the analog input signal. By means of the Fourier transform, the sampling operation can be defined in the frequency domain as the convolution of the two individual signal spectra. Hence we have

$$Y(f) = X(f) * S(f) = f_s \cdot \sum_{m=-\infty}^{\infty} X(f - m \cdot f_s) \quad \textbf{(11.18)}$$

where $f_s = 1/T_s$, and it is called the sampling frequency.

Figure 11.7 illustrates the ideal sampling process, in both time and frequency domains. If the sampling frequency, f_s, is at least twice the highest input signal frequency, f_h, then the sampled signal can be reconstructed. This is done by using an ideal low pass filter whose bandwidth, BW, satisfies the relationship $f_h < \text{BW} < f_s - f_h$. From this expression, it can be seen that $f_s \geq 2 \cdot f_h$. However, in practice a sampling function $g(t)$ consists of a periodic pulse train, with finite amplitude and time duration. This can be expressed mathematically in the time domain as

$$g(t) = \sum_{n=-\infty}^{\infty} g(t - n \cdot T_s) \quad \textbf{(11.19)}$$

Substituting $g(t)$ into Equation 11.17 results in the following equation:

$$Y(t) = x(t) \cdot g(t) = \sum_{n=-\infty}^{\infty} x(n \cdot T_s) \cdot g(t - n \cdot T_s) = x(t) * g(t) \quad \textbf{(11.20)}$$

The corresponding frequency domain expression becomes

$$Y(f) = X(f) \cdot G(f) = G(f) \cdot f_s \cdot \sum_{m=-\infty}^{\infty} X(f - m \cdot f_s) \quad \textbf{(11.21)}$$

where $G(f) = k \cdot \dfrac{\sin x}{x}$

$$x = \frac{m \cdot \pi \cdot \tau}{T_s}$$

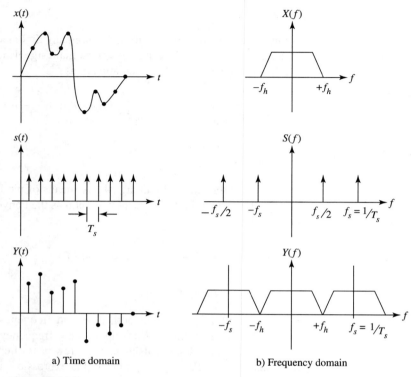

a) Time domain

b) Frequency domain

FIGURE 11.7
Ideal sampling process definition.

Figure 11.8 illustrates the time and frequency domain practical sampling signal function. The repetitive pulse signal frequency response results in the sinc, or $(\sin x)/x$ function. Figure 11.8b shows its absolute magnitude spectrum for positive values of m. Its major effect is attenuation of the sample signal's high frequency component. However, this can be minimized by ensuring that the sampling pulse duration, τ, is very small compared to its repetition rate, T_s.

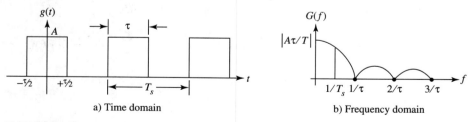

a) Time domain

b) Frequency domain

FIGURE 11.8
Practical sampling process definition.

The high frequency component attenuation is known as the *aperture effect*. If a continuous baseband signal contains frequency components no higher than f_h, then it can be recovered, without appreciable distortion, if it is sampled at a rate equal to or greater than twice f_h. When the sampling rate $f_s = 2 \cdot f_h$, the sampled waveform can be reconstructed using an ideal low pass filter whose bandwidth $BW = f_h$. Such a filter would pass all frequency components less than or equal to f_h and block all those greater than f_h. However, such a filter is difficult if not impossible to realize. Practical filters exhibit a transition band between the pass and stop bands, which results in a gradual attenuation of undesired frequency components. Therefore, in order to compensate for the filter, the sampling frequency is usually increased by a factor k. When the sampling rate, f_s, drops below the Nyquist rate, $2 \cdot f_h$, frequency folding or overlap into the original signal spectrum occurs, which causes aliasing distortion. The mathematical expression for calculating the alias frequency due to undersampling is as follows: $|f_{alias}| = m \cdot f_s - f_h$, where $m = 1, 2, \ldots, n$ and $0 < f_{alias} < f_s/2$.

EXAMPLE 11.4

Calculate the alias frequencies for the following conditions: $f_s = 100$ Hz and $f_h = 170$ Hz, 220 Hz.

a) $|f_{alias}| = m \cdot 100 - 170 = 2 \cdot 100 - 170 = 30$ Hz

b) $|f_{alias}| = m \cdot 100 - 220 = 2 \cdot 100 - 220 = 20$ Hz

---

Figure 11.9 illustrates the effect of frequency aliasing. If a continuous bandpass input signal contains frequency components between f_1 and f_2, then the original signal can be recovered, with negligible distortion, if it is sampled at a rate f_s determined by the relationship, $f_s = 2 \cdot f_2/(m + 1)$, where $m = \lceil (f_1/(f_2 - f_1)) \rceil = \lceil (f_1/BW) \rceil$. If either f_1 or f_2 is an integer multiple of the sampling frequency, then $f_s = 2 \cdot (f_2 - f_1)$. Also when $f_1 = 0$, then $f_s = 2 \cdot f_2$, which is the baseband signal sampling criterion. When the sampling frequency satisfies the above relationship, then the sampled bandpass signal can be reconstructed using an ideal bandpass filter whose $BW = f_2 - f_1$.

EXAMPLE 11.5

Calculate the sampling frequency f_s for the following bandpass signals:
a) $f_1 = 150$ Hz, $f_2 = 180$ Hz
b) $f_1 = 170$ Hz, $f_2 = 340$ Hz
a) $f_s = (2 \cdot f_2)/[(f_1/30) + 1] = 360/6 = 60$ Hz, and $f_s = 2 \cdot (f_2 - f_1)$
b) $f_s = (2 \cdot f_2)/[(f_1/170) + 1] = 680/2 = 340$ Hz, and $f_s = 2 \cdot (f_2 - f_1)$

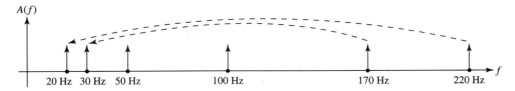

FIGURE 11.9
Frequency aliasing.

Rate Modification

When it becomes necessary to alter the signal sampling rate, within a system, either decimation or interpolation is used. *Decimation* is used in order to reduce the initial sampling rate by an integer factor, D. Similarly, *interpolation* is used to increase the sampling rate by an integer factor, I. In addition, rational sampling rate changes are possible by combining the two operations.

As shown in Figure 11.10, decimation is a two-step process. First, a low pass digital filter is used to remove the undesired input signal frequency components. Then the filtered signal is sampled at the reduced rate. The output signal sampling rate becomes f_s/D.

Interpolation is the inverse of decimation, and it is also achieved in two steps. First, the sampled signal is padded using $I - 1$ samples, between the existing sample points, of zero value. The resulting output signal has an effective sampling rate of $I \cdot f_s$. It is then passed through a low pass filter, as shown in Figure 11.11, to extract the interpolated signal.

By combining decimation and interpolation, it is possible to obtain rational sampling ratio changes, as shown in Figure 11.12. Also by performing interpolation prior to decimation, it is possible to use a single low pass filter for both operations.

Synchronous data rate modification is accomplished with an interpolator, followed by a low pass filter and a decimator in cascade. The input signal is unsampled by the interpolator. This is accomplished by inserting $I - 1$ zero-valued samples, increasing the sample rate by a factor of I. The digital LPF removes the image frequencies from the upsampled signal. Its cutoff frequency, f_c, is one-half the output sample rate, in this case $(I/D) \cdot (f_s/2)$, where I and D are integers and their quotient is a rational sampling ratio. The decimator eliminates $D - 1$ samples from the filtered signal. The effective output sampling rate becomes $f_{os} = (I/D) \cdot f_s$. The following example illustrates the synchronous rate modification, using a rational sampling ratio.

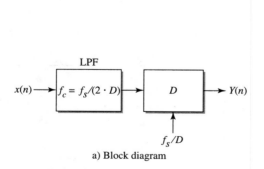

a) Block diagram

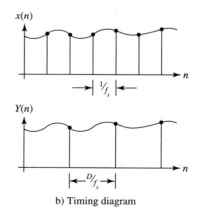

b) Timing diagram

FIGURE 11.10
Sampled signal decimation.

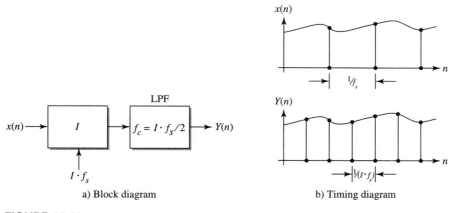

a) Block diagram   b) Timing diagram

FIGURE 11.11
Sampled signal interpolation.

EXAMPLE 11.6

Given $I = 9$, $D = 5$, and $f_s = 5{,}000$ Hz, find the interpolation rate, f_{os}, and f_c.

$$I \cdot f_s = 9 \cdot 5{,}000 = 45 \text{ kHz}$$
$$f_{os} = (I/D) \cdot f_s = (9/5) \cdot 5{,}000 = 9{,}000 \text{ Hz}$$
$$f_c = (I/D) \cdot (f_s/2) = (9/5) \cdot (5{,}000/2) = 4{,}500 \text{ Hz}$$

The synchronous data rate modification method can be extended to the asynchronous case, in which sampling ratios are irrational. This is achieved by increasing the interpolation factor N, such that $N = 2^n$, where n is the sample data resolution in bits. This ensures that adjacent data samples have a maximum of one LSB magnitude variation. This technique approximates an analog signal, which is in turn resampled at a new output data rate by the decimator.

11.3 DISCRETE PROCESSES

A system is a set of integrated elements that perform a specific function as a whole. A signal is a function of time that transfers data between two nodes within a system. A signal-processing

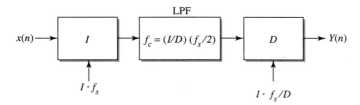

FIGURE 11.12
Sampled signal rational rate conversion.

system may perform filtering or spectral analysis. When a system filters, it removes selected signal frequency components. When it performs spectral analysis, it determines signal frequency components.

An arbitrary discrete time signal can be represented as a sequence of normalized and delayed unit samples. This can be expressed mathematically as

$$x(n) = \sum_{k=-\infty}^{\infty} [x(k) \cdot \delta(n - k)] \qquad (11.22)$$

where $x(k) \cdot \delta(n - k) = \begin{cases} a_k & \text{if } n = k \\ 0 & \text{otherwise} \end{cases}$

The index k represents the kth sample interval T, or $k \cdot T$, which is omitted for simplicity. Figure 11.13a illustrates an example of a discrete time signal, defined both for negative and positive values of time. The equation describing this particular signal is as follows:

$$x(n) = x(-2) \cdot \delta(n + 2) + x(-1) \cdot \delta(n + 1) + x(0) \cdot \delta(0) + x(1) \cdot \delta(n - 1) \\ + x(2) \cdot \delta(n - 2)$$

The mean value of a discrete signal is determined using the following expression:

$$\bar{X}_n = \frac{1}{N} \sum_{1}^{N} x(n) \qquad (11.23)$$

For the example signal it becomes $\bar{X}_n = \frac{1}{5} \cdot (2 + 4 + 3 + 2 + 4) = 3$

The mean square value of a discrete signal is calculated with the following expression:

$$\bar{X}_n^2 = \frac{1}{N} \sum_{1}^{N} x^2(n) \qquad (11.24)$$

For the example signal it becomes $\bar{X}_n^2 = \frac{1}{5} \cdot (4 + 16 + 9 + 4 + 16) = 9.8$.

The root mean square (RMS) value of a discrete signal can be calculated using the following expression:

$$X_n \text{ (RMS)} = [\bar{X}_n^2]^{1/2} \qquad (11.25)$$

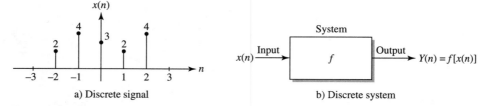

a) Discrete signal

b) Discrete system

FIGURE 11.13
Discrete process definitions.

By substituting the calculated value into this expression, the RMS value of the example signal becomes X_n (RMS) $= [9.8]^{1/2} = 3.13$.

A discrete system can be thought of as a computational process that produces an output signal as a function of the input. Systems can be classified according to their properties. In discrete signal analysis applications, the following system properties simplify mathematical calculations and physical realization. A system, as shown in Figure 11.13b, is said to be *linear* if it satisfies the following relationship:

$$f[a_1 \cdot x_1(n) + a_2 \cdot x_2(n)] = a_1 \cdot f[x_1(n)] + a_2 \cdot f[x_2(n)]$$

In other words, the output function of the sum of two input signals equals the sum of the individual signal output functions. Thus, a linear system satisfies the principle of superposition. A system is said to be *invariant* if it satisfies the following relationship:

$$Y(n - n_0) = f[x(n - n_0)]$$

for all values of n_0. That is, a time shift in the input signal results in an equivalent time shift in the output. A system is said to be *causal* if it satisfies the following relationship:

$$Y(n) = f[x(n_0)]$$

for $n \geq n_0$. Thus, a causal system outputs a signal in response to an applied input signal. A *stable* system produces a finite output signal in response to a finite input signal.

Discrete signal analysis is based on three fundamental operations: unit delay, summation, and multiplication. These operations are illustrated in Figure 11.14. Difference equations are used to describe discrete time systems. There are two basic system types, *recursive* and *nonrecursive*. A recursive system produces an output that is a function of both past output and the past and present input signal values. A nonrecursive system produces an output that is a function of the past and present input signal values. The following equation is used to describe arbitrary recursive discrete time systems:

$$Y(n) = \sum_{k=0}^{N} [a_k \cdot x(n - k)] + \sum_{k=0}^{M} [b_k \cdot Y(n - k)] \qquad (11.26)$$

FIGURE 11.14

Discrete operations block diagram.

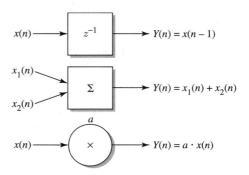

The following equation is used to describe arbitrary nonrecursive discrete time systems:

$$Y(n) = \sum_{k=0}^{N} [a_k \cdot x(n - k)] \tag{11.27}$$

The z transform is a mathematical method used to convert difference equations into a form suitable for algebraic manipulation. The z transform of a discrete time sequence $x(n)$ can be written as

$$X(z) = \sum_{n=0}^{\infty} x(n) \cdot z^{-n} \tag{11.28}$$

Table 11.2 lists the basic discrete time functions and their corresponding z transform equivalents.

The z transform of a recursive system equation becomes

$$Z(Y(n)) = Y(z) = \sum_{k=0}^{N} a_k \cdot z^{-k} \cdot X(z) + \sum_{k=0}^{M} b_k \cdot z^{-k} \cdot Y(z) \tag{11.29}$$

which can be written in terms of the ratio of the output to the input, also called the system transfer function, and written as follows:

$$H(z) = \frac{Y(z)}{X(z)} = \frac{\sum_{k=0}^{N} a_k \cdot z^{-k}}{1 - \sum_{k=0}^{M} b_k \cdot z^{-k}} \tag{11.30}$$

where z^{-k} = delay

$b_0 = 1$

Similarly, the nonrecursive system transfer function can be expressed as follows:

$$H(z) = \frac{Y(z)}{X(z)} = \sum_{k=0}^{N} a_k \cdot z^{-k} \tag{11.31}$$

TABLE 11.2
Z transform pairs

Function	Equation	Z Transform
Unit Sample	$\delta(n)$	1
Unit Delay	$\delta(n - 1)$	z^{-1}
Unit Step	$u(n)$	$z/(z - 1), |z| > 1$
Discrete Time	$n \cdot u(n)$	$z/(z - 1)^2$
Exponential	a^n	$z/(z - a)$
Delay	$x(n - 1)$	$z^{-1} \cdot X(z)$

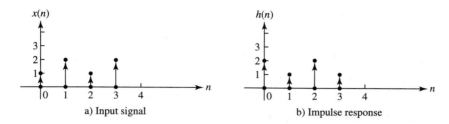

a) Input signal b) Impulse response

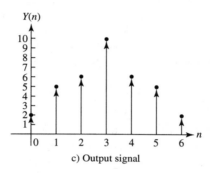

c) Output signal

FIGURE 11.15
Discrete signal convolution.

Discrete time convolution is the product summation of two discrete signal sequences, one of which is reversed and shifted in time. The time convolution results in a signal whose frequency spectrum is the product of the two individual sequence spectra. If $x(n)$ represents the input signal sequence and $h(n)$ the system impulse response sequence, then the resulting output $Y(n)$ becomes the time convolution function of the two and is defined as

$$Y(n) = \sum_{k=0}^{N-1} x(k) \cdot h(n - k) \tag{11.32}$$

where $h(n) = 0$ for $0 > k > N - 1$

Figure 11.15 illustrates a discrete signal convolution, which is detailed in the following example.

EXAMPLE 11.7

Let $x(n) = 1 \cdot \delta(0) + 2 \cdot \delta(n - 1) + 1 \cdot \delta(n - 2) + 2 \cdot \delta(n - 3)$ and $h(n) = 2 \cdot \delta(0) + 1 \cdot \delta(n - 1) + 2 \cdot \delta(n - 2) + 1 \cdot \delta(n - 3)$. Find their discrete time convolution function.

$$Y(n) = \sum_{k=0}^{3} x(k) \cdot h(n - k)$$

$$Y(0) = x(0) \cdot h(0) = 2$$
$$Y(1) = x(0) \cdot h(1) + x(1) \cdot h(0) = 5$$
$$Y(2) = x(0) \cdot h(2) + x(1) \cdot h(1) + x(2) \cdot h(0) = 6$$

$$Y(3) = x(0) \cdot h(3) + x(1) \cdot h(2) + x(2) \cdot h(1) + x(3) \cdot h(0) = 10$$
$$Y(4) = x(1) \cdot h(3) + x(2) \cdot h(2) + x(3) \cdot h(1) = 6$$
$$Y(5) = x(2) \cdot h(3) + x(3) \cdot h(2) = 5$$
$$Y(6) = x(3) \cdot h(3) = 2$$

The resulting output sequence is shown in Figure 11.15c.

Discrete time correlation is the product summation of two discrete time sequences, one of which is shifted in time. The time correlation of two such sequences results in an output whose spectrum is the product of the two individual spectra, and represents their cross power spectrum density function. If $x_1(n)$ and $x_2(n)$ represent the two sequences, their crosscorrelation function, $R(k)$, can be calculated using the following expression:

$$R(k) = \sum_{n=0}^{N-1} x_1(n) \cdot x_2(n - k) \qquad (11.33)$$

When $x_1(n) = x_2(n)$, $R(k)$ becomes the autocorrelation function in the time domain, and the auto power spectrum density function in the frequency domain. Correlation is used to perform time sequence comparisons for a possible match. Power spectrum implies a periodic sequence.

The following example illustrates discrete signal correlation.

EXAMPLE 11.8   Calculate the crosscorrelation function of the time sequences shown in Figure 11.15.

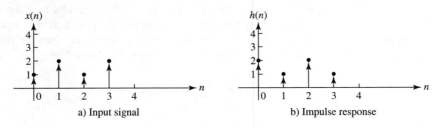

a) Input signal

b) Impulse response

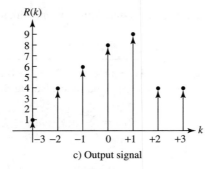

c) Output signal

FIGURE 11.16
Discrete signal correlation.

$$R(k) = \sum_{n=0}^{3} x(n) \cdot h(n - k)$$

$R(-3) = x(0) \cdot h(3) = 1$

$R(-2) = x(0) \cdot h(2) + x(1) \cdot h(3) = 4$

$R(-1) = x(0) \cdot h(1) + x(1) \cdot h(2) + x(2) \cdot h(3) = 6$

$R(0) = x(0) \cdot h(0) + x(1) \cdot h(1) + x(2) \cdot h(2) + x(3) \cdot h(3) = 8$

$R(+1) = x(1) \cdot h(0) + x(2) \cdot h(1) + x(3) \cdot h(2) = 9$

$R(+2) = x(2) \cdot h(0) + x(3) \cdot h(1) = 4$

$R(+3) = x(3) \cdot h(0) = 4$

The resulting crosscorrelation function is illustrated in Figure 11.16.

11.4 DIGITAL FILTERS

A digital filter is an algorithm, implemented in either software or hardware, that accepts a digital input and generates a modified output signal. There are two general filter types, the infinite impulse response (IIR) and the finite impulse response (FIR). IIR filters produce an infinite-duration output signal in response to a unit sample input, $x(n) = \delta(n)$. These filters are usually realized recursively, the filter output being a function of the weighted past output values and the past and present input values. The filter order is determined by the greater of n or m, which also equals the number of specified forward or feedback unit delay elements. Figure 11.17 is an IIR filter block diagram that shows the three basic operations of unit delay, summation, and multiplication. Each delayed signal sample is multiplied by a coefficient to produce a weighted value that is summed to generate the filter output signal. The filter equation becomes

$$Y(n) = \sum_{k=0}^{N} a_k \cdot V(n - k) \tag{11.34}$$

where

$$V(n) = x(n) - \sum_{k=1}^{M} b_k \cdot V(n - k)$$

FIR filters produce a finite-duration output in response to a unit sample input, $x(n) = \delta(n)$. These filters are usually realized nonrecursively, the filter output being the sum of the weighted past and present input signal values. Figure 11.18 is an FIR filter block diagram that shows the three basic operations of unit delay, summation, and multiplication. The filter order is determined by the number of specified unit delay elements n. The filter equation becomes

$$Y(n) = \sum_{k=0}^{N} a_k \cdot x(n - k) \tag{11.35}$$

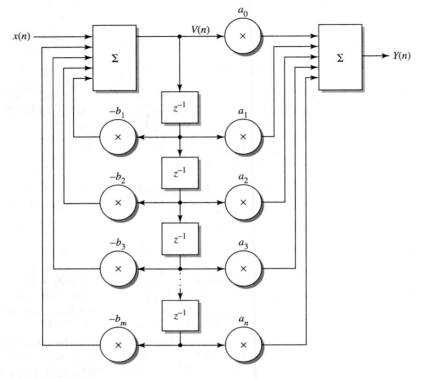

FIGURE 11.17
IIR filter block diagram.

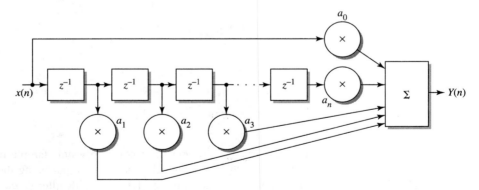

FIGURE 11.18
FIR filter block diagram.

FIR filters provide linear phase delay and stability, and demand less design effort than IIR filters. However, they require more delay elements than equivalent IIR filters. An FIR filter implementation is the time convolution of the impulse response coefficients, a_k, and the delayed input signal sample, $x(n - k)$. The integer k defines each sample point occurring at a rate of $1/f_s$. The coefficient index, k, ranges from 0 to N, the filter set size. The window method of FIR filter design is the easiest and provides the basis for all others. First, the filter's frequency response is defined as $H(\omega)$, which is used to derive its corresponding impulse response, $h(n)$. The abrupt sample termination, n-term truncation, results in excessive amplitude ripple in the filter's frequency response. The use of a weighting function, or *window,* to taper the time domain sample results in reduced amplitude ripple at the expense of frequency spreading. The truncated impulse response is multiplied by the window function $w(n)$, which is equivalent to a convolution in the frequency domain, to produce a modified frequency spectrum. The weighted filter impulse response becomes $H(n) = h(n) \cdot w(n)$, and it is time shifted by $\frac{N}{2}$ points so as to produce a causal filter implementation. Figure 11.19a illustrates a low pass filter (LPF) frequency response that can be realized with an FIR-type digital filter, using the window design method. The filter's frequency response is defined as

$$H(f) = \begin{cases} 1 & \text{if } |f| \leq f_1 \\ 0 & \text{if } |f| > f_1 \end{cases}$$

To realize a causal filter, it is necessary to time shift the filter's impulse response, $h(n)$. However, using the time delay theorem, which states that $h(n - n_0) \longleftrightarrow H(f) \cdot e^{-j \cdot 2 \cdot \pi \cdot f \cdot n_0}$, it is possible to achieve the same result by defining the filter's response as $H(f) = 1 \cdot e^{-j \cdot 2 \cdot \pi \cdot f \cdot n_0}$, for $|f| \leq f_1$. By assuming a rectangular window, the corresponding impulse response coefficients are calculated using the inverse Fourier transform

$$H(n) = \int_{-f_p}^{f_p} [e^{j \cdot 2 \cdot \pi \cdot f \cdot (n - n_0)}] df = \frac{\sin (2 \cdot \pi \cdot f_p \cdot (n - n_0))}{\pi \cdot (n - n_0)} \tag{11.36}$$

The number of coefficients, N, is determined by the relationship $N \geq (k \cdot f_h)/|f_1 - f_2|$. Since N is an even number, the number of coefficients, 0 through N, becomes odd. The constant, k, is a function of the window type used. The default window function is rectangular. The term f_h is the highest input signal frequency component; f_1 is the filter's cutoff frequency at -3-dB attenuation. Also, f_2 is the stopband transition frequency for a specified attenuation level. The

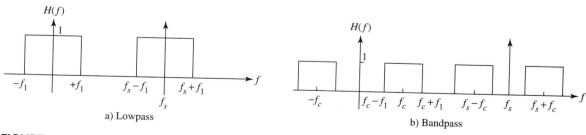

a) Lowpass

b) Bandpass

FIGURE 11.19
Digital filter definitions.

sampling frequency, f_s, must satisfy the relationship $f_s \geq 2.5 \cdot f_h$. Also, $f_p = f_1/f_s$, and $n_0 = \frac{N}{2}$. The following example elaborates on the concepts above.

EXAMPLE 11.9

Derive the impulse response of an LPF filter with the following parameters: $f_h = 5$ kHz, $f_s = 12.5$ kHz, $f_1 = 3$ kHz at -3 dB, $f_2 = 4.5$ kHz at -40 dB, and $k = 10$.

$$N \geq \frac{10 \cdot (5 \times 10^3)}{1.5 \times 10^3} \approx 34$$

$$f_p = \frac{3 \times 10^3}{12.5 \times 10^3} = 0.24$$

$$H(n) = \frac{\sin(0.48 \cdot \pi \cdot (n - 17))}{\pi \cdot (n - 17)}$$

A bandpass filter (BPF) can be realized easily using the modulation theorem, which states

$$x(n) \cdot 2 \cdot \cos(2 \cdot \pi \cdot f_0 \cdot n) \longleftrightarrow X(f - f_0) + X(f + f_0)$$

Figure 11.19b illustrates a BPF frequency response that can be implemented using a FIR type digital filter. The filter's frequency response can be defined as

$$H(f) = \begin{cases} 1 & \text{if } f_c - f_1 \leq |f| \leq f_c + f_1 \\ 0 & \text{otherwise} \end{cases}$$

The corresponding impulse response coefficients are calculated by

$$H(n) = \frac{\sin(2 \cdot \pi \cdot f_b \cdot (n - n_o)) \cdot 2 \cdot \cos(2 \cdot \pi \cdot f_m \cdot (n - n_o))}{\pi \cdot (n - n_o)} \tag{11.37}$$

where $f_{bw} = 2 \cdot f_1$

$f_b = f_{bw}/f_s$

f_c = filter's center frequency

f_s = sampling frequency

$f_m = f_c/f_s$

The following example provides insight into the definitions above.

EXAMPLE 11.10

Derive the impulse response of a BPF filter with the following parameters: $f_c = 10$ kHz, $f_1 = 3$ kHz at -3 dB, $f_2 = 4.5$ kHz at -40 dB, $f_s = 45$ kHz, and $n = 34$.

$$f_{bw} = 2 \cdot f_1 = 2 \cdot 3 \times 10^3 = 6 \times 10^3$$

$$f_{bw}/f_s = 6 \times 10^3/45 \times 10^3 \approx .13$$

$$f_c/f_s = 10 \times 10^3/45 \times 10^3 \approx .22$$
$$H(n) = \sin[(0.26 \cdot \pi \cdot (n - 17))] \cdot [2 \cdot \cos(0.44 \cdot \pi \cdot (n - 17))]/[\pi \cdot (n - 17)]$$

It should be noted that when $f_c = f_s/2$, the filter response becomes a high pass filter (HPF) definition. Also, a band reject filter (BRF) can be formed using an LPF and an HPF combination. By truncating the filter coefficients to N terms, it is implied that a window function is used. The window function multiplies each filter coefficient by a fixed weight, in this case 1, determined by the window's time domain function. There are several window functions available. The rectangular window is defined as

$$w_r(n) = \begin{cases} 1 & \text{if } |n| \leq N \\ 0 & \text{if otherwise} \end{cases}$$

Its corresponding frequency domain response becomes a $\dfrac{\sin x}{x}$ or sinc function. A triangular window is defined as

$$w_t(n) = \begin{cases} 1 - \dfrac{|n|}{N} & \text{if } n \leq N \\ 0 & \text{if otherwise} \end{cases}$$

Its corresponding frequency domain response becomes a $\left(\dfrac{\sin x}{x}\right)^2$ function. The Hanning window is defined as follows:

$$w_{\text{Hn}}(n) = 0.50 + 0.50 \cdot \cos(2 \cdot \pi \cdot n)/N \text{ for } n \leq N \qquad \textbf{(11.38)}$$

Similarly, the Hamming window is defined as follows:

$$w_{\text{Hm}}(n) = 0.54 + 0.46 \cdot \cos(2 \cdot \pi \cdot n)/N \text{ for } n \leq N \qquad \textbf{(11.39)}$$

As indicated earlier, the filter's impulse response and the window's time domain function must be time-shifted by $N/2$ points to realize a causal filter. The frequency spectrum of these two window functions consists of the main lobe, which contains most of the energy, and the side lobes. Table 11.3 lists the characteristics of the four basic window functions, in terms of main lobe spread relative to a rectangular and side lobe attenuation.

The ideal window function has a narrow main lobe and a maximum side lobe attenuation. Realizable window functions offer a compromise of main lobe width versus side lobe attenua-

TABLE 11.3
Window characteristics

Window	Main Lobe Width	Side Lobe Attenuation (dB)
Rectangular	1.0	−15
Triangular	1.8	−25
Hanning	2.0	−30
Hamming	2.0	−40

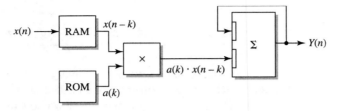

FIGURE 11.20
FIR filter hardware block diagram.

tion characteristics. The hardware realization of an FIR-type digital filter is shown in Figure 11.20. The weighted filter coefficients, which are stored in a ROM, are multiplied by the appropriately shifted input data samples. Each such partial product is then added to the previous one. The filter coefficients are cycled every N input samples, at which point a new output response is computed. A discrete signal is quantized to produce an input data sample.

11.5 DISCRETE FOURIER TRANSFORM

The discrete Fourier transform (DFT) is an algorithm that performs time-to-frequency domain transformation of discrete signal sequences. The DFT operation can be defined as

$$X(m \cdot \delta f) = \sum_{n=0}^{N-1} [x(n \cdot \delta t) \cdot e^{-j\omega/N) \cdot n \cdot m}] \tag{11.40}$$

where
n = time index from 0 to $N - 1$

m = frequency index from 0 to $N - 1$

$x(n \cdot \delta t)$ = finite duration sequence, $0 < n < N - 1$, periodic in T

$X(m \cdot \delta f)$ = finite duration sequence periodic over f_s

δt = sample interval

$j = \sqrt{-1}$

N = number of sample intervals in T

The following relationships also exist: $\delta f = 1/(N \cdot \delta t) = 1/T = f_s/N$; $\delta t = 1/f_s = T/N$; $N \cdot \delta f = 1/\delta t = f_s$, the sample frequency; and $1/(2 \cdot \delta t) = f_s/2$, the Nyquist frequency. If both δf and δt are implied, and W is defined as $W = e^{-j(\omega)/N} = e^{-j(2 \cdot \pi)/N}$, then the DFT operation can be rewritten as

$$X(m) = \sum_{n=0}^{N-1} x(n) \cdot W^{n \cdot m} \tag{11.41}$$

The term $W^{n \cdot m}$ is periodic in N, such that $W^{n \cdot m} = W^{(m+i \cdot N) \cdot (n+k \cdot N)}$ for $i, k = 0, 1, 2, \ldots$, and it exhibits a symmetry about $N/2$, such that $W^{n \cdot m} = -W^{(n+N/2) \cdot (m+N/2)}$.

The inverse DFT, which performs frequency-to-time transformation, can be written as

$$x(n) = \frac{1}{N} \sum_{m=0}^{N-1} X(m) \cdot W^{-(n \cdot m)} \tag{11.42}$$

Figure 11.21 illustrates the time and frequency domain parameters of a discrete signal sequence. The integers n and m represent the sample interval and frequency component indices, respectively. The actual time is the product of $n \cdot \delta t$ and the actual frequency is the product of $m \cdot \delta f$. For an arbitrary real periodic time sequence $x(n)$, the real part of $X(m)$ is symmetric about $f_s/2$, the Nyquist frequency. The frequency components between $f_s/2$ and f_s make up the mirror image, or negative frequencies, of $X(m)$. If a time series $x(n)$ contains frequency components no higher than f_h, then $f_s \geq 2 \cdot f_h$. Also, the number of sample points required for a given resolution of δf becomes $N = f_s/\delta f$.

EXAMPLE 11.11

Given a time sequence $x(n)$ with $f_h = 40$ kHz, $f_s = 2.5 \cdot f_h$, and $N = 256$, determine δf, δt, and T.

$$f_s = 2.5 \cdot (40 \times 10^3) = 100 \times 10^3 \text{ Hz}$$
$$\delta f = f_s/N = (100 \times 10^3)/256 \approx 390 \text{ Hz}$$
$$\delta t = 1/f_s = 10 \times 10^{-6} \text{ sec}$$
$$T = N \cdot \delta t = 2.56 \times 10^{-3} \text{ sec}$$

Since there are N points per sample period, each frequency component requires N complex multiplications and N complex additions for a total of $2 \cdot N$ complex computations per component.

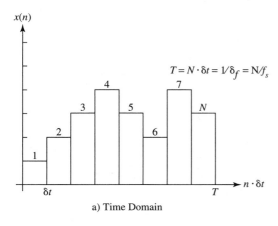

a) Time Domain

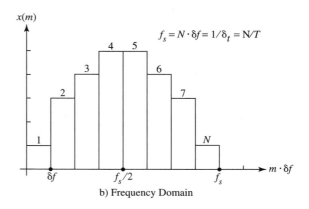

b) Frequency Domain

FIGURE 11.21
Discrete fourier transform definitions.

For a real $x(n)$ time sequence, the first $N/2$ frequency components uniquely define the discrete frequency spectrum. Hence the total number of computations for each N-point DFT becomes $(2 \cdot N) \cdot (N/2) = N^2$. Figure 11.22 provides a flowchart outline of the basic DFT procedure. The frequency components are used to derive the magnitude and phase.

The A(I) array contains the initial time domain sequence sample points. The output frequency domain components, COS and SIN, are placed in the A(I) and B(I) arrays, respectively. The following FORTRAN IV subroutine is an implementation of the flowcharted DFT procedure.

```
SUBROUTINE DFT (A(N), B(N), N, M(N), P(N))
C    INPUT A(N) TIME SEQUENCE
C    OUTPUT A(N), B(N) FREQ. SEQ.
C    OUTPUT M(N), P(N) MAGN. & PHASE
     THETA = 6.28/N
```

FIGURE 11.22
DFT procedure flowchart.

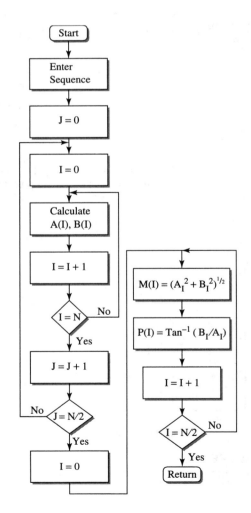

```
      DO 10 J=1, N/2
      DO 20 I=1, N
      TEMP = A(I)
      A(J) = A(J)+TEMP*COS(I*J*THETA)
      B(J) = B(J)+TEMP*SIN(I*J*THETA)
20    CONTINUE
10    WRITE(6,30) J
30    FORMAT ('HARMONIC',I3)
C     CALCULATE MAGN & PHASE
      DO 40 I=1, N/2
      M(I) = SQRT(A(I)*A(I)+B(I)*B(I))
      P(I) = ATAN(B(I)/A(I))
40    CONTINUE
      RETURN
```

The first part of the routine calculates the A_j, B_j coefficients, and the second generates the magnitude and phase values of each corresponding frequency component.

A class of algorithms designed to drastically reduce the total amount of DFT calculations is known collectively as the fast Fourier transform (FFT). When the number of sample points is chosen to be an integral power of two, the N-point DFT can be decomposed into a set of smaller equivalent DFTs. This results in a considerable reduction of DFT calculations. Using the *decimation* concept, each N-point input sequence can be divided into two sequences of $N/2$ points each. Each $N/2$ point sequence is further divided into two sequences of $N/4$ points each. The process continues until the original sequence is decomposed into $N/2$ sequences of two points each. The individual two-point sequence DFT can be calculated rapidly and combined successfully into 2^k-point DFTs, where $k = 2, 3, 4, . . .$, $\log_2 N$, until the N-point DFT is evaluated. Hence, the number of calculations reduces from N^2, in the DFT case, to $N \cdot \log_2 N$. The two-point calculation and combination process forms the heart of the FFT algorithm, and it is known as the *butterfly operation*. Table 11.4 lists the number of required calculations for a DFT, and a corresponding FFT, as a function of N. It also provides the ratio of their operations.

There are two basic FFT algorithms available, the decimation-in-time (DIT) and the decimation-in-frequency (DIF). They are both radix-2 type, since they successively halve the N-point sequence. They are also known as in-place algorithms because the output data of each intermediate step can be stored in the same memory location as the input data. This provides for

TABLE 11.4
DFT and FFT comparison

N	N^2	$N \cdot \log_2 N$	$(N^2)/(N \cdot \log_2 N)$
16	256	64	4
32	1,024	160	6.4
64	4,096	384	10.6
128	16,384	896	18.28
256	65,536	2,048	32
512	252,144	4,608	54.72
1,024	1,048,576	10,240	102.4

efficient memory use. However, in-place algorithms provide a predictable scrabbling of the output data points, and thus they require reordering of the results. The reordering procedure is called bit reversal and can be performed on either the input or the output data samples. Bit reversal begins by converting each data sample location index into its binary equivalent. Then, it systematically reverses the binary weight of each bit location, so that MSB = LSB, etc.

The DIT algorithm takes an input sample sequence, $x(n)$, and separates it into two sequences. The first sequence, $x_e(n) = x(2 \cdot n)$, contains all even points, and the second sequence, $x_o(n) = x(2 \cdot n + 1)$, contains all odd points. The two sequences are substituted into Equation 11.41, and after simplification, the resulting decimation-in-time FFT algorithm equation becomes

$$X(m) = \sum_{n=0}^{\frac{N}{2}-1} x_e(n) \cdot W^{2 \cdot n \cdot m} + W^m \cdot \sum_{n=0}^{\frac{N}{2}-1} x_o(n) \cdot W^{2 \cdot n \cdot m} \qquad \textbf{(11.43)}$$

where $\quad W^{2(n \cdot m)} = e^{-j(2 \cdot \pi/N)2 \cdot n \cdot m}$

$\qquad\qquad m = 0, 1, 2, . . ., (N - 1)$

Since $e^{-j(2 \cdot \pi/N) \cdot 2} = e^{-j(2 \cdot \pi/(N/2))}$, the two summation terms of Equation 11.43 have a periodicity of $N/2$. Hence, only the first $N/2 - 1$ frequency indices, m, need be calculated. The basic two-point DIT butterfly operation is defined as

$$X_{n+1}(i) = X_n(i) + X_n(j) \cdot W^m$$
$$X_{n+1}(j) = X_n(i) - X_n(j) \cdot W^m$$

The butterfly operation is illustrated in Figure 11.23, along with a 4-point DIT algorithm.

The DIF algorithm takes an input sample sequence $x(n)$ and separates it into two sequences. The first sequence, $x(n)$, contains the first $N/2$ points, and the second sequence,

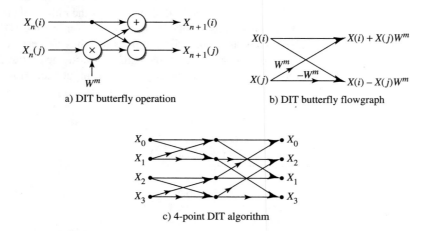

a) DIT butterfly operation

b) DIT butterfly flowgraph

c) 4-point DIT algorithm

FIGURE 11.23
DIT-FFT definition.

$x(n + N/2)$, contains the remaining $N/2$ points. These two sequences are substituted into Equation 11.41 and are simplified. The resulting equation is then used to derive the decimation-in-frequency FFT algorithm equations, by substituting $X_e(m) = x(2 \cdot m)$ and $X_o(m) = x(2 \cdot m + 1)$, respectively. The resulting, even- and odd-point, DIF FFT algorithm equations become

$$X_e(m) = \sum_{n=0}^{\frac{N}{2}-1} [x(n) + x(n + N/2)] \cdot W^{2 \cdot n \cdot m} \qquad (11.44)$$

$$X_o(m) = \sum_{n=0}^{\frac{N}{2}-1} [(x(n) - x(n + N/2)) \cdot W^n] \cdot W^{2 \cdot n \cdot m} \qquad (11.45)$$

where $m = 0, 1, 2, \ldots, \frac{N}{2} - 1$.

The basic two-point DIF butterfly operation is defined as

$$X_{n+1}(i) = X_n(i) + X_n(j)$$
$$X_{n+1}(j) = [X_n(i) - X_n(j)] \cdot W^m$$

and is illustrated in Figure 11.24, along with a 4-point DIF algorithm.

With either algorithm, an input sequence of N samples requires $\log_2 N$ passes, with $N/2$ iterations per pass. Also, the angular increment becomes $(2 \cdot \pi)/N$. For example, if $N = 64$ is the number of sample points, then the number of required passes is $\log_2 64 = 6$. The number of iterations per pass is $64/2 = 32$. The angular step is $(2 \cdot \pi)/64 = 5.6°$. Also, the number of computations is $64 \cdot \log_2 64 = 384$.

The detailed DIT butterfly operation is explained in the following example.

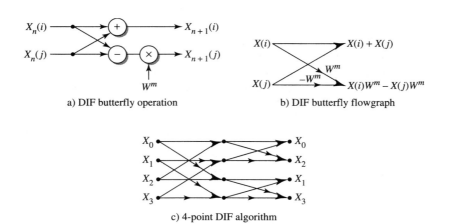

a) DIF butterfly operation

b) DIF butterfly flowgraph

c) 4-point DIF algorithm

FIGURE 11.24
DIF-FFT definition.

EXAMPLE 11.12

Given a pair of input sample data points $x_1 = a + jb$ and $x_2 = c + jd$, with the corresponding output sample data points $X_1 = A + jB$ and $X_2 = C + jD$, derive the DIT butterfly operation of Figure 11.23. Let

$$W = e^{-j(2\pi/N)} = e^{-j(\theta)} = (\cos \theta - j \sin \theta)$$

$$A + jB = (a + jb) + (c + jd) \cdot (W) = (a + jb) + (c + jd) \cdot (\cos \theta - j \sin \theta)$$

$$A + jB = a + jb + c(\cos \theta) - jc(\sin \theta) + jd(\cos \theta) + d(\sin \theta)$$

$$C + jD = (a + jb) + (c + jd) \cdot (-W) = (a + jb) + (c + jd) \cdot (-\cos \theta + j \sin \theta)$$

$$C + jD = a + jb - c(\cos \theta) + jc(\sin \theta) - jd(\cos \theta) - d(\sin \theta)$$

Separating real and imaginary terms,

$$A = a + c(\cos \theta) + d(\sin \theta) \quad (1)$$
$$jB = jb + jd(\cos \theta) - jc(\sin \theta) \quad (2)$$
$$C = a - c(\cos \theta) - d(\sin \theta) \quad (3)$$
$$jD = jb - jd (\cos \theta) + jc(\sin \theta) \quad (4)$$

Let $a =$ AR[I], $b =$ BI[I], $c =$ AR[J], $d =$ BI[J], $\cos \theta =$ AR, $\sin \theta =$ AI and, WR = AR[J]*AR + BI[J]*AI, and WI = BI[J]*AR − AR[J]*AI. Then the basic butterfly equations become

$$AR[I] = AR[I] + WR \quad (1)$$
$$BI[I] = BI[I] + WI \quad (2)$$
$$AR[J] = AR[I] - WR \quad (3)$$
$$BI[J] = BI[I] - WI \quad (4)$$

Figure 11.25 provides a flowchart for a DIT-type FFT algorithm implementation. First, the sample data points are entered into a real array A(N). Next, a bit-reversal routine is invoked to provide a predictable scrabbling of the input data. This compensates for the algorithm's inherent output data scrabbling. Then, the FFT routine performs the butterfly operation repeatedly, and the resulting output contains both real and imaginary data in the A(N) and B(N) arrays respectively. Finally, the magnitude and phase of each complex output frequency component is calculated. The following FORTRAN IV routine is an implementation of the algorithm above:

```
FFT  (A(N), B(N), M(N), P(N), M)
C    INPUT A(N) REAL TIME SEQUENCE
C    CALL BIT REVERSAL ROUTINE
C    FFT EVALUATION
     N = 2**M
     DO 10 IP = 1,M
     NEXT = 2**IP
     ISTEP = NEXT/2
     DO 20 K = 1,ISTEP
```

```
        Q = FLOAT(ISTEP)
        THETA = 3.14159265/Q
        AR = COS(THETA)
        AI = SIN(THETA)
        DO 20 I = K,N,NEXT
        J = I + ISTEP
C       DIT BUTTERFLY
        WR = AR[J]*AR + BI[J]*AI
        WI = BI[J]*AR - AR[J]*AI
        AR[I] = AR[I] + WR
        BI[I] = BI[I] + WI
        AR[J] = AR[I] - WR
```

FIGURE 11.25
DIT-FFT flowchart.

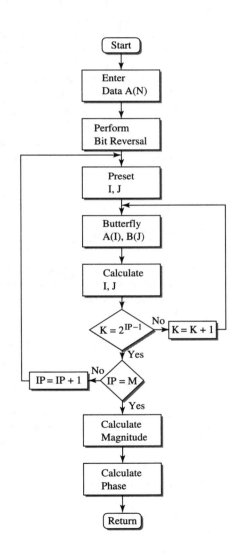

```
      BI[J]  =  BI[I]  -  WI
 20   CONTINUE
 10   CONTINUE
 C    MAGNITUDE AND PHASE
      DO 30 I = 1,N/2
      M(I)  =  SQRT(A(I)*A(I)  +  B(I)*B(I))
      P(I)  =  ATAN(B(I)/A(I))
 30   CONTINUE
      RETURN
```

There are three major problem areas associated with FFT evaluation: aliasing, leakage, and the picket fence effect. *Aliasing* is the result of input signal undersampling and can be easily corrected with an LPF to limit the input signal spectrum below its Nyquist frequency. *Leakage* is the result of abrupt termination of the input signal sample, which causes overall frequency spectrum distortion. The use of a suitable window, to provide a tapered signal sample termination, minimizes this effect. The *picket fence effect* is the result of discrete frequency component calculation. It can be minimized by choosing a window function that provides a slight spreading of each frequency component to smooth the overall signal spectrum. Comparing the two Fourier transform methods, it becomes apparent that the DFT is more flexible in the sense that it allows for individual frequency component calculation. In contrast, the FFT algorithm calculates all the frequency components at once. Hence, for a given subset of frequencies, k, if $2N \cdot k < N \cdot \log_2 N$, then the DFT calculation becomes faster than the FFT algorithm. It should be noted that the inverse FFT algorithm can be derived as well.

PROBLEMS

11.1 Given $x(t) = e^{-a \cdot t}$ and $h(t) = a \cdot e^{-a \cdot t}$, determine the output signal frequency response Y(f).

11.2 Find the autocorrelation function $R_{xx}(\tau)$ of the signal $x(t) = e^{-|a| \cdot t}$.

11.3 Find the output spectral density function, $S_{yy}(f)$ for $x(t) = e^{-a \cdot t}$ and $h(t) = a \cdot e^{-a \cdot t}$.

11.4 Calculate the alias frequencies for the following baseband conditions: $f_s = 100$ Hz and $f_h = 180$ Hz, 240 Hz.

11.5 Calculate the sampling frequency f_s for the following bandpass conditions: $f_1 = 180$ Hz, $f_2 = 240$ Hz.

11.6 Given $I = 21$, $D = 14$, and $f_s = 19.2$ kHz, find the output sample rate f_{os}.

11.7 Given $x(n) = 0 \cdot \delta(0) + 1 \cdot \delta(n - 1) + 2 \cdot \delta(n - 2) + 3 \cdot \delta(n - 3) + 4 \cdot \delta(n - 4)$ and $h(n) = 4 \cdot \delta(0) + 3 \cdot \delta(n - 1) + 2 \cdot \delta(n - 2) + 1 \cdot \delta(n - 3) + 0 \cdot \delta(n - 4)$, calculate their convolution Y(n).

11.8 Calculate the crosscorrelation function $R(k)$ for Problem 11.7.

11.9 Write a BASIC program to calculate the coefficient values for Example 11.9, using a rectangular and a Hanning window, respectively.

11.10 Given an HPF filter with $f_1 = 16.5$ kHz at -3 dB, $f_2 = 15.0$ kHz at -40 dB, $N = 34$, and $f_s = 45$ kHz, determine $H(n)$, using a rectangular window. Hint: let $f_{bw} = f_c - f_1$.

11.11 Given a discrete time sequence $x(n)$ with $f_h = 128$ kHz and $T = 8 \times 10^{-3}$ sec, determine δf, δt, and N.

11.12 Derive the DIF butterfly operation shown in Figure 11.24.

REFERENCES

Burdic, W. S. *Radar Signal Analysis.* Englewood Cliffs, NJ: Prentice Hall, 1968.

Oppenheim, A. V. and R. W. Schafer. *Digital Signal Processing.* Englewood Cliffs, NJ: Prentice Hall, 1975.

Rabiner, L. R. and B. Gold. *Theory and Applications of Digital Signal Processing.* Englewood Cliffs, NJ: Prentice Hall, 1976.

Rabiner, L. R. and R. W. Schafer. *Digital Processing of Speech Signals.* Englewood Cliffs, NJ: Prentice Hall, 1978.

Shanmugam, K. Sam. *Digital and Analog Communication Systems.* New York: John Wiley & Sons, 1979.

Stanley, W. D. *Digital Signal Processing.* Reston, VA: Reston Publishing, 1975.

Stearns, S. D. *Digital Signal Analysis.* New Rochelle, NY: Hayden Book Co., 1976.

Taub, H. and D. L. Schilling. *Principles of Communications Systems.* New York: McGraw-Hill, 1971.

TRW. *VLSI Data Book.* La Jolla, Ca: TRW, 1985.

12

SIGNAL SYNTHESIS

A signal can be expressed as a magnitude function of either time or frequency domain. Also, a signal can be defined as a frequency function of the time domain. These concepts are illustrated in Figure 12.1

Signal synthesis provides the means to generate arbitrary signal waveforms using the following basic equation:

$$x(t) = A \cdot \sin(\omega_0 \cdot t + \theta) = A \cdot \sin(2 \cdot \pi \cdot f_0 \cdot t + \theta)$$

where A = signal magnitude in volts

ω_0 = angular frequency in radians/sec

f_0 = frequency in Hz

θ = phase shift in radians

The analog sinusoidal function is periodic, with a period $T_0 = (2 \cdot \pi)/\omega_0$. When the above parameters are controlled independently, it is possible to produce a large number of different waveforms. In the discrete case, the above equation becomes

$$x(n) = A \cdot \sin(\omega_0 \cdot n + \theta)$$

where $\omega_0 = (2 \cdot \pi)/N$ radians per sample

$\theta = (2 \cdot \pi)/m$ radians

n = discrete sample variable

and m = integer constant

The discrete sinusoidal function is periodic, with a period

$$N = (2 \cdot \pi \cdot n)/\omega_0$$

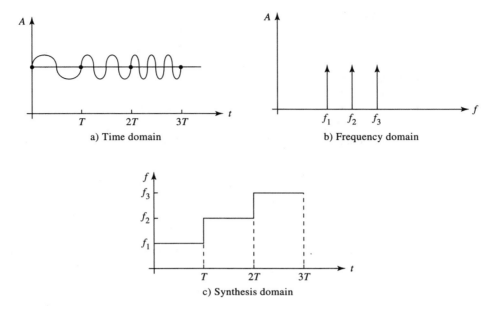

FIGURE 12.1
Signal domain definitions.

Figure 12.2 shows both the continuous and discrete time signal definitions.

The objectives of this chapter are as follows: (1) to define signal synthesis terms, (2) to discuss indirect synthesis using PLLs, (3) to explain direct synthesis using phase accumulators, (4) to present a multitone synthesis example, and (5) to cover pseudorandom noise sequence generation.

12.1 DEFINITIONS

Several basic definitions associated with signal synthesis are used to specify design parameters and to make comparisons.

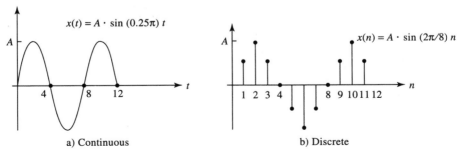

FIGURE 12.2
Sinusoidal function definition.

Frequency stability is the ratio of the nominal value plus any drift to the nominal value, due to temperature and component value variations, over a period of time. This can be expressed as $S = (f_0 \pm f_d)/f_0$, where f_0 is the nominal and f_d is the maximum drift frequency. Short-term stability is normally measured over a time interval of 1 second. Long-term stability is usually specified over a 24-hour period.

Resolution is the minimum possible distance between two adjacent frequencies produced by the same source. This is expressed by $\delta f = |f_2 - f_1|$, where f_2 and f_1 are the minimum adjacent frequencies.

Range, or bandwidth, is the total number of signal frequencies that can be produced by a given source. This can be expressed as $BW = N \cdot \delta f$, where N is the maximum number of frequencies possible.

Switching time, or delay, is the actual time required to change between two frequency values, and it is proportional to their relative distance. This can be expressed as $T_d = k \cdot |f_a - f_b|$, where k is the proportionality constant.

Spurious response is the measurement of the magnitude ratio, usually in dB, of the nominal frequency f_0 to the highest magnitude frequency component f_h, within a specified bandwidth about f_0. This is expressed as follows:

$$SR = 20 \cdot \log_{10} [A (f_h)/A (f_0)] \text{ dB/Hz}$$

where $A(f_i) = $ magnitude value

When switching between frequency values, phase control can be an important factor in applications such as FSK or PSK modulation. The signal phase can be either *continuous* or *coherent*. If it is continuous, the new frequency assumes the phase of the previous frequency at the time of the change. If the phase is coherent, it is altered to reflect the actual phase of the new frequency at the time of the change. These two concepts are shown in Figure 12.3.

Signal synthesis can be achieved either indirectly or directly. In the indirect approach an existing signal source is controlled to provide the desired output. In the direct approach the actual parameters are specified and realized. The phase lock loop (PLL) and the direct digital synthesis (DDS) methods will be discussed as examples of indirect and direct techniques, respectively. The former offers a simpler design, greater range, and a slightly better spurious response. The latter offers better resolution, faster switching times, and independent parameter control.

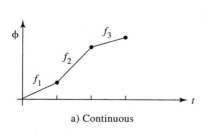

a) Continuous

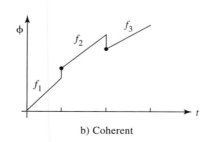

b) Coherent

FIGURE 12.3
Phase control definitions.

12.2 INDIRECT SYNTHESIS

The PLL forms the heart of indirect signal synthesis. It is an electronic closed loop feedback system that consists of a phase detector, an LPF filter, and a voltage-controlled oscillator (VCO). Figure 12.4 illustrates the basic PLL elements and parameters. With no input signal, the VCO operates at an arbitrary frequency, f_0, which is also known as its free running frequency. When an input signal, V_{IN}, is present with a frequency, f_1, the VCO output frequency becomes proportional to the control voltage, $V_f(t)$. This can be expressed as

$$f_0(t) = f_0 + k_v \cdot V_f(t)$$

where $\quad k_v$ = VCO gain constant in hertz/volt

$\qquad V_f(t)$ = filtered error signal $V_e(t)$ in volts

The phase detector generates an output error signal $V_e(t)$ that is proportional to the phase difference of its two input signals f_1 and f_0. This can be expressed as

$$V_e(t) = k_d \cdot [\phi_1(t) - \phi_0(t)]$$

where $\quad k_d$ = detector gain constant in volts/radian

The LPF filter smoothes the error voltage $V_e(t)$ to control the loop noise. A wide filter bandwidth reduces internal loop noise, while a narrow bandwidth reduces external input loop noise.

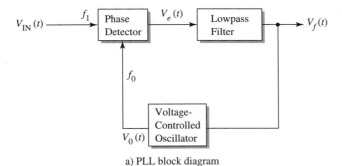

a) PLL block diagram

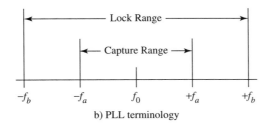

b) PLL terminology

FIGURE 12.4
Phase lock loop definitions.

The VCO responds to the filtered error voltage, $V_f(t)$, by changing its output frequency so as to minimize the phase detector output error voltage $V_e(t)$. When this minimal error condition is reached, the PLL is said to be locked or in sync, and the two signal frequencies are identical except for a small phase difference.

The range of frequencies over which a PLL can lock or acquire synchronization with an input signal is called the *capture range,* and it is symmetrical about f_0. Similarly, the range of frequencies over which a PLL can maintain a lock condition with an input signal is called the *lock range.* The capture range is always less than the lock range. The capture range is directly proportional to the LPF filter bandwidth, and the lock range is directly proportional to the loop gain. The loop gain is the product of the individual loop gain constants, or $K_l = k_d \cdot k_v$ in hertz/radian. The time interval required for a PLL to go from a free running state to a locked state is called the lockup time, and it is inversely proportional to the LPF bandwidth. Also, due to the random initial phase relationship of the two signal frequencies, the lockup time can be predicted within a time window.

The PLL transfer function is used to analyze the loop and determine its transient and frequency responses. Figure 12.5 provides a mathematical PLL block diagram definition. The corresponding transfer function can be derived as follows:

Given $e(s) = X(s) - Y(s)$, substituting $Y(s) = e(s) \cdot k_d(s) \cdot k_v(s)$ results in

$$e(s) = X(s) - [e(s) \cdot k_d(s) \cdot k_v(s)]$$

Solving for

$$X(s) = e(s) + e(s) \cdot k_d(s) \cdot k_v(s)$$

The transfer function equation can now be defined as the ratio of $Y(s)/X(s)$, or

$$\frac{Y(s)}{X(s)} = \frac{e(s) \cdot k_d(s) \cdot k_v(s)}{e(s) + e(s) + k_d(s) \cdot k_v(s)} = \frac{k_d(s) \cdot k_v(s)}{1 + k_d(s) \cdot k_v(s)} = \frac{K_1(s)}{1 + K_1(s)} \qquad (12.1)$$

There are two basic phase detector designs: the XOR gate and the RS flip-flop. Figure 12.6 presents both detectors for comparison. The phase difference between two periodic signals of the same frequency can be expressed as $\delta\phi = [(t_1 - t_2)/T] \cdot 2 \cdot \pi$, where $(t_1 - t_2)$ is the time delay between them and T is the period. The XOR detector requires symmetrical input signals and a 50% duty cycle, but it provides good noise immunity. The RS detector does not require symmetrical inputs, but it is noise-sensitive. It also exhibits greater capture and lock ranges than the XOR type.

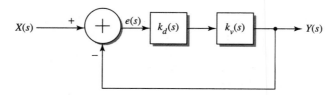

FIGURE 12.5
PLL model.

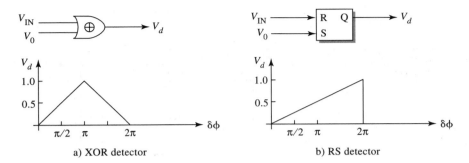

FIGURE 12.6
Phase detector characteristics.

The PLL can be used as the building block for generating a range of integer signal frequencies from a single, stable reference signal source. The simplest PLL-based synthesizer adds a binary counter with programmable modulus N to the feedback loop, as shown in Figure 12.7. When the PLL is in its locked state, the following relation holds: $f_r = f_{OUT}/N$ or $f_{OUT} = N \cdot f_r$. The frequency resolution or minimum step size becomes $f_{step} = f_r$, and the maximum number of different frequencies possible is N. For example, using a VCO with $f_0 = 10$ MHz, a reference source $f_r = 1$ kHz, and a counter with modulus $N = 10,000$ preset to $n = 1,250$ results in an output signal frequency of $f_{OUT} = n \cdot f_r$, or 1.25 MHz. There are 10,000 possible frequencies, spaced 1 kHz apart, from 1 kHz to 10 MHz. For reliable operation, the maximum VCO operation range should extend 25% above and below these limits.

If there is a requirement to generate signal frequencies that are noninteger multiples of f_r, then an additional counter with programmable modulus Q is inserted before the phase detector. This configuration is called fractional synthesis and is illustrated in Figure 12.8. When the PLL reaches a locked state, the following relation holds: $f_r/Q = f_{OUT}/N$, or $f_{OUT} = f_r \cdot (N/Q)$. The

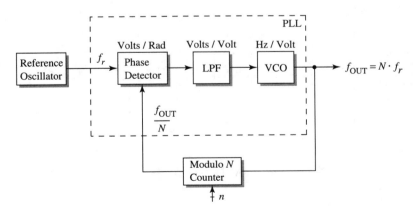

FIGURE 12.7
Integer PLL synthesis.

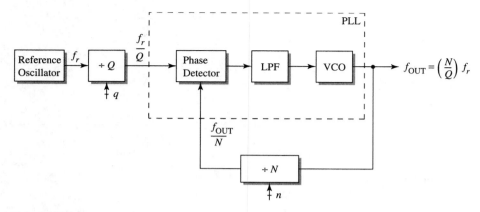

FIGURE 12.8
Fractional PLL synthesis.

frequency resolution or minimum step size becomes $f_{step} = f_r/Q$, and the maximum number of frequencies remains N. For example, using $f_0 = 10$ MHz, $f_r = 1$ kHz, $n = 1,250$, and $q = 1,000$ results in an output frequency of $f_{OUT} = f_r \cdot (n/q)$, or 1.25 kHz.

In applications where the VCO frequency operating range is beyond the programmable counter's toggle frequency, a high-speed counter with fixed modulus P is inserted in the feedback loop. This configuration is shown in Figure 12.9. When the PLL achieves a locked state, the following relation holds: $f_r = f_{OUT}/(N \cdot P)$, or $f_{OUT} = (f_r \cdot P) \cdot N$. The frequency resolution or step size becomes $f_{step} = f_r \cdot P$, and the maximum number of frequencies remains N. For example, using $f_0 = 100$ MHz, $f_r = 100$ Hz, $P = 10$, and $N = 1$–100,000 results in an output frequency range of $f_{OUT} = (f_r \cdot P) \cdot N = (100 \cdot 10) \cdot N$, or 1 kHz to 100 MHz, in 1-kHz step increments. Since the reference frequency $f_r = f_{step}/P$, the loop filter bandwidth must be narrowed by the same factor P, which slows the PLL response time.

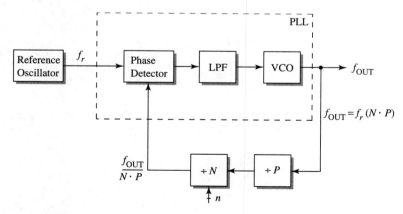

FIGURE 12.9
Prescaler PLL synthesis.

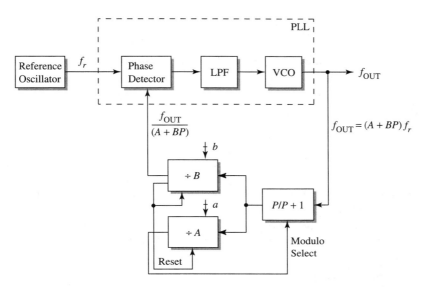

FIGURE 12.10
Dual modulo PLL synthesis.

Using the dual modulo approach, however, it is possible to make the step size equal to the reference frequency ($f_{step} = f_r$). This is shown in Figure 12.10. This method employs two variable-modulus counters, A and B, and one with dual modulus $P/P + 1$. When the PLL reaches a locked state, the following relationship exists: $f_r = f_{OUT}/(A + B \cdot P)$, or $f_{OUT} = f_r \cdot (A + B \cdot P)$.

The operation of the programmable, high-speed counter with dual modulus $P/P + 1$ is explained below. Initially, it counts in the $P + 1$ modulus for A cycles. Then it switches to the P modulus and counts for an additional $(B - A)$ cycles. This requires that $B \geq A$. Thus, the combined total divide ratio is $N = A \cdot (P + 1) + (B - A) \cdot P = A + (B \cdot P)$. For example, using $f_0 = 100$ MHz, $f_r = 1,000$ Hz, $P = 10$, $b = 7$, and $a = 4$ results in an output frequency $f_{OUT} = f_r(A + (B \cdot P)) = (1,000) \cdot [4 + (7 \cdot 10)]$, or 74 kHz. Also, there are 100,000 different output frequencies possible, with a minimum step size of $f_s = f_r = 1$ kHz. Hence, the added complexity of a dual modulus relaxes the LPF filter bandwidth requirement and speeds up the loop response.

12.3 DIRECT DIGITAL SYNTHESIS

Direct digital synthesis (DDS) can generate arbitrary signal waveforms with good resolution, fast switching time, and low phase noise. Figure 12.11 is a DDS synthesizer block diagram showing the four building blocks: the phase accumulator, the waveform table, the DAC module, and the LPF filter. The phase accumulator produces a fixed–step size, monotonically increasing binary number, representing the instantaneous signal phase, at a uniform sample rate. The sample rate is determined by the clock frequency f_c. The step size input value, k, is propor-

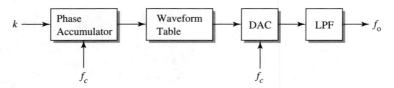

FIGURE 12.11
DDS block diagram.

tional to the desired output signal frequency f_o. The waveform table provides a phase-to-amplitude conversion for a specific output signal function generation. The table contents can be either fixed or variable, depending on the flexibility requirements. The DAC module is used to perform an analog approximation of the sampled waveform. Also, an MDAC module can be used to provide signal amplitude scaling. The LPF filter removes the higher harmonic components and provides smoothing between the quantized output sample transitions.

Phase Accumulator

The phase accumulator consists of a binary adder in a feedback configuration, as shown in Figure 12.12a. The initial phase angle, θ, can be preset into the output register. The phase angle step size, k, which is stored into the input register, is added to the accumulator contents every $T = 1/f_c$ seconds.

The output sum is continually added to the step size, which results in an equivalent linear ramp signal, as shown in Figure 12.12b. Each sum output sample corresponds to the instantaneous phase ϕ of the synthesized signal, from 0 to $2 \cdot \pi$. This can be expressed mathematically as $(\phi_2 - \phi_1)/[(2 \cdot T) - T] = \delta\phi/\delta T$, where $T = 1/f_c$. The accumulator overflow rate equals the output signal frequency f_o. If n represents the number of accumulator bits, k the phase step size, and f_c the sample clock frequency, then the signal output frequency is determined by $f_o = [(f_c/2^n)] \cdot k = (k)/(2^n \cdot T) = (k)/(N \cdot T)$, where $T = 1/f_c$ and $N = 2^n$, the accumulator modulus. The minimum output frequency is calculated by setting $k = 1$, or $f_o(\text{min}) = \delta f = f_c/N = 1/(N \cdot T)$. This value represents the synthesizer resolution. Hence, either the sample clock frequency f_c or the modulus N must be changed in order to achieve a given resolution limit. Similarly, the maximum output frequency can be calculated such that it satisfies the Nyquist criterion, which limits it to $f_c/2$. This is done by setting $k = 2^{n-1}$ and $f_o(\text{max}) = [(f_c/2^n)] \cdot 2^{n-1} = f_c/2 = 1/(2 \cdot T)$. There are $N/2$ different output signal frequencies possible, with a minimum spacing of $1/(N \cdot T)$ Hz. The following example elaborates on these concepts.

EXAMPLE 12.1

Given $f_c = 1.024 \times 10^6$ Hz and $n = 12$, find f_o (min) and f_o (max).

$$N = 2^n = 4{,}096$$
$$f_o \text{ (min)} = f_c/N = 250 \text{ Hz}$$
$$f_o \text{ (max)} = f_c/2 = 512 \times 10^3 \text{ Hz}$$

Also, there are $N/2 = 2{,}048$ different output frequencies possible.

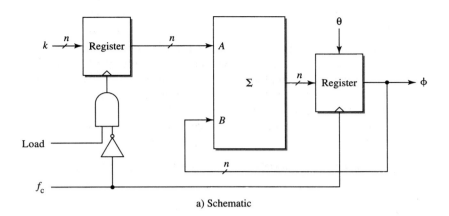

a) Schematic

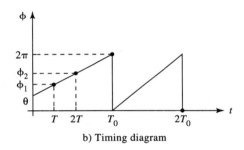

b) Timing diagram

FIGURE 12.12
Phase accumulator definition.

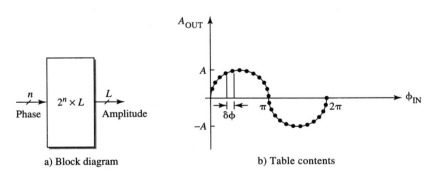

a) Block diagram

b) Table contents

FIGURE 12.13
Waveform table definitions.

Waveform Table

The waveform table consists of n input and L output bits. The total number of stored bits equals $2^n \cdot L$. Increasing the input phase bits by one doubles the table size, or $2^{n+1} \cdot L$. Similarly, increasing the output amplitude bits by one results in 2^n more bits in the table, or $2^n \cdot (L + 1)$. The waveform table values are stored in two's complement notation.

Figure 12.13 is the waveform table block diagram, which transforms the input linear phase data into an equivalent digital amplitude output function. For the simple case of a sinusoidal function, the following relationship exists:

$$Y(T) = A \cdot \sin(\omega_o \cdot T) = A \cdot \sin(2 \cdot \pi \cdot f_o \cdot T) = A \cdot \sin(\phi_k) \qquad \textbf{(12.2)}$$

where $A = 0$ to 2^{L-1}

$\phi_k = 2 \cdot \pi \cdot (k/N)$ radians

or

$\phi_k = 360° \cdot (k/N)$

The case of a single cycle lookup yields

$$Y(T) = \sum_{j=1}^{N/k} A \cdot \sin(j \cdot \phi_k + \theta) \qquad \textbf{(12.3)}$$

where θ is the initial phase shift and $j = 1, 2, 3, \ldots, N/k$

The minimum phase increment resolution, $\delta\phi$, is found by letting $k = 1$ and $\delta\phi = \phi$ (min) $= (2 \cdot \pi)/N$ radians or ϕ (min) $= 360/N$ degrees.

The number of table samples per cycle is determined by the following relation: samples/cycle $= (2 \cdot \pi)/\phi_k = f_c/f_k = N/k$. Table 12.1 shows f_k, ϕ_k, and samples/cycle as a function of k, given $n = 8$ and $f_c = 2,048$ Hz.

In general, the instantaneous phase value sample can be determined by

$$\phi_k = [(2 \cdot \pi \cdot k)/N \cdot i + \theta]$$

where $i = 1, 2, 3, \ldots, m$

TABLE 12.1
DDS parameters

k	f_k	ϕ_k	Samples/Cycle
1	8	1.406°	256
2	16	2.812°	128
4	32	5.625°	64
8	64	11.25°	32
16	128	22.5°	16
32	256	45°	8
64	512	90°	4
128	1024	180°	2

Synthesis Example

The following example shows how DDS can be used to generate precise and stable signals using an accurate clock source. Figure 12.14 is a typical DDS synthesizer block diagram. If $f_c = 256$ Hz, and n = 4, then it has the following capabilities: $f_{min} = f_c/2^n = 256/16 = 16$ Hz, $f_{max} = f_c/2 = 256/2 = 128$ Hz, and $\phi_{min} = 360°/2^n = 22.5°$.

In practice, due to the realization limitations of the LPF filter, the highest usable frequency, f_h, is approximately $0.45 \cdot f_c$, or in this case, 115 Hz. Its operation proceeds as follows. First, the frequency input register is loaded with the integer constant, k, which determines the output signal frequency. Also, the accumulator register may be preset to a nonzero phase value, θ, to introduce a phase shift. Once the synthesizer is enabled, the phase accumulator produces a linear sum with a uniform step size of k. For $k = 2$, the accumulator will overflow every eight clock cycles. This can be expressed as $2^n/k = N/k = 8$ samples/cycle. The resulting output signal frequency, f_o, becomes $f_o = f_k = k \cdot f_{min} = 2 \times 16 = 32$ Hz. And its phase increment becomes $\phi_k = k \cdot \phi_{min} = 2 \times 22.5° = 45°$. At the leading edge of each sample clock pulse, the accumulator contents are transferred to the accumulator output register. The register value is converted, via the waveform lookup table, into an equivalent amplitude value. The value is stored, by the next clock pulse, into the DAC input register.

The DAC module takes each amplitude value and produces a quantized output sample. Finally, the LPF removes all the undesired frequency components, and the result is a smooth

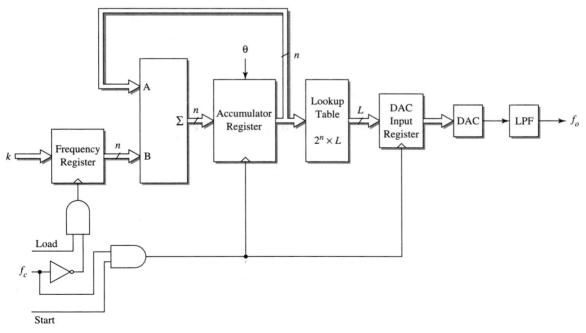

FIGURE 12.14
DDS functional block diagram.

sinusoidal signal. Figure 12.15 explains the overall operation by illustrating the signals at various points. The linear phase slope is determined by $\delta\phi/\delta T = 2 \cdot \pi \cdot f_k$, as shown in Figure 12.15a. The waveform table equivalent amplitude values are shown in Figure 12.15b. The DAC module output is shown in Figure 12.15c, and the filtered output signal is shown in Figure 12.15d. Table 12.2 provides further insight into the operation by listing the intermediate values for one complete output signal cycle.

The synthesizer switching speed, t_{sw}, is dependent on the number of registers in the pipeline. In this example there are only two registers. Hence, from the time a new k value is loaded to the time it will be reflected at the output, $2 \cdot T$, or 7.8 msec, will elapse. The DAC module should display good linearity and fast slew rate and settling time characteristics. Its settling time should be as a minimum less than $T/2$, or 1.95 msec, to prevent waveform distortion.

The DAC module output signal sample has a $\dfrac{\sin x}{x}$ envelope, where $x = (n \cdot \pi \cdot f_k)/f_c$. This results in an output signal spectrum of

$$f_o = f_k + (f_c + f_k) + (2 \cdot f_c + f_k) + \ldots + (n \cdot f_c + f_k)$$

where n represents the nth harmonic of f_c

The function of the LPF is to pass f_k and to attenuate all other frequency components, in order to minimize signal distortion. The LPF cutoff frequency is usually between $0.4 \cdot f_c$ and $0.45 \cdot f_c$.

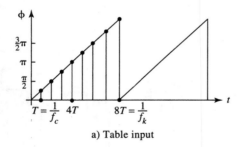

a) Table input

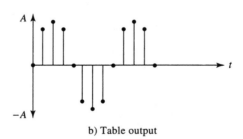

b) Table output

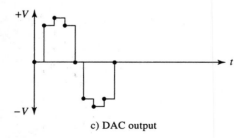

c) DAC output

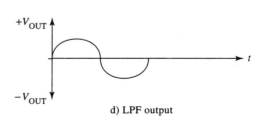

d) LPF output

FIGURE 12.15
DDS signal definitions.

TABLE 12.2
DDS signal values

Clock Pulse	Accumulator	Equivalent Phase	ROM Output	DAC Output
0	0000	0°	000000	0
	0001	22.5°	001100	+3.83
1	0010	45°	010110	+7.07
	0011	67.5°	011101	+9.24
2	0100	90°	011111	+9.69
	0101	112.5°	011101	+9.24
3	0110	135°	010110	+7.07
	0111	157.5°	001100	+3.83
4	1000	180°	000000	0
	1001	202.5°	101100	−3.83
5	1010	225°	110110	−7.07
	1011	247.5°	111101	−9.24
6	1100	270°	111111	−10.0
	1101	292.5°	111101	−9.24
7	1110	315°	110110	−7.07
	1111	337.5°	101100	−3.83
8	0000	0°	000000	0

However, there are physical realization parameters that place an upper limit on f_c. In this particular case the following relationship must be satisfied:

$$1/f_c = T > t_p + t_a + t_s$$

where t_p = accumulator register propagation delay time

t_a = lookup table access time

t_s = DAC input register setup time

In practice, the DAC module settling time requirement becomes the dominant limiting factor for f_c. The use of an S/H circuit after the DAC can relax this limitation. If the lookup table is bypassed, the resulting output signal is a sawtooth waveform whose period is $T_k = 1/f_k$. Also, if the value of k is incremented in equal steps and at a uniform rate, a linear signal frequency sweep is generated. The sweep rate becomes $\delta f/\delta T = (k_2 - k_1)/\delta T$ Hz/sec. The k_1 and k_2 constants determine the initial and final frequencies, respectively, and δT is the elapsed time between them.

In general, it is possible to modify all three signal parameters. This is accomplished by providing an MCU interface to each of the parameter registers, such that they are updated under software control. The interface is designed such that the synthesis operation takes precedence in case of a contention problem during updates. In Figure 12.14, the frequency number, k, update is done during the trailing edge of the clock pulse, where it does not interfere with normal operation. If phase shift θ capability is required for more than the initial signal, a second binary adder module is inserted at the output of the accumulator, so that instantaneous phase shifts can be produced. Finally, if amplitude A control is needed, an MDAC module is in-

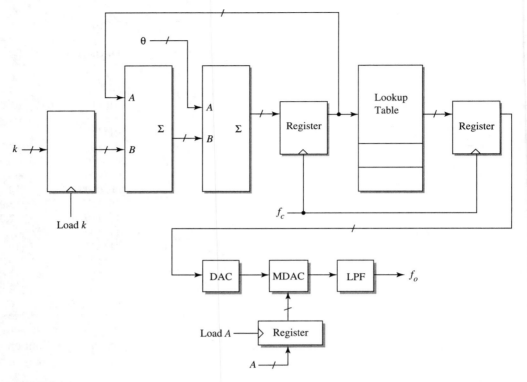

FIGURE 12.16
DDS parameter control.

serted between the DAC and the LPF filter. A DDS block diagram with these added features is shown in Figure 12.16. By proper design, independent control of each signal parameter can be achieved.

Is also is possible to generate an arbitrary waveform by either selecting one of several lookup table functions or by dynamically updating the table itself. Hence, the following generalized signal equation can be realized:

$$Y(T) = A(T) \cdot g((2 \cdot \pi \cdot f_k \cdot T) + \theta(T)) \tag{12.4}$$

where $A(T)$ = instantaneous amplitude level of the output signal, determined by the MDAC register value at each clock period T.

The function g is the selected periodic function in the lookup waveform table. The signal frequency, f_k, is controlled by the input constant, k. The instantaneous phase is determined by the sum of the phase step size, $\phi_k = 2 \cdot \pi \cdot f_k \cdot T$, and the offset, $\theta(T)$.

12.4 MULTITONE SYNTHESIS

The basic DDS techniques can be extended to include several multiplexed signals over a fixed interval, such that a composite waveform can be realized. This can be expressed in a compact mathematical notation as

$$Y(T) = \sum_{j=1}^{P} \sum_{i=1}^{M} A(i) \cdot \sin\left[j \cdot 2 \cdot \pi \cdot f(i) + \theta(i)\right] \qquad (12.5)$$

where $j = 1, 2, 3, \ldots, P$

The integer P represents the number of composite waveform output samples. The output waveform $Y(T)$ consists of M individual sinusoidal signals, each with a different amplitude value, $A(i)$, frequency value, $f(i)$, and initial phase value, $\theta(i)$. The individual signal samples are accumulated over a time index, i, interval from 1 to M. The i index increments for each signal to form a composite M signal waveform output sample.

The heart of this synthesizer is a multiplier accumulator (MAC) module, which is illustrated in Figure 12.17. The device consists of a parallel multiplier cascaded with a controllable accumulator. As such, M signal amplitude partial products can be summed and then transferred as a j composite waveform sample to its output register. The multitone synthesizer block diagram shown in Figure 12.18 will be used to describe waveform synthesis.

The synthesizer has three dedicated memories, one for each signal parameter. A reference frequency clock source, f_{ref}, is used to derive the four phases, one per clock period, that are re-

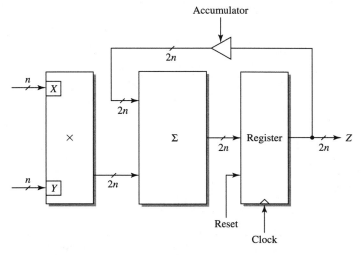

FIGURE 12.17
Multiplier accumulator block diagram.

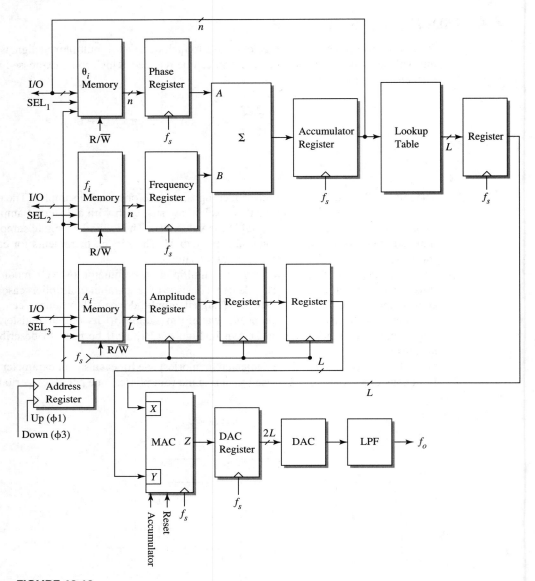

FIGURE 12.18
Multitone synthesizer.

quired to complete each signal sample element generation. The MAC module multiplies each signal sample with its corresponding $A(i)$. Since the four pipeline registers are clocked on a specific phase, the signal sample throughput rate becomes $f_s = f_{ref}/4$. The minimum time interval per signal sample calculation becomes $T_s = 1/f_s$. There are M such samples, and thus the time it takes to generate one complete waveform sample set P becomes $T = T_s \cdot M$ sec. The maximum clock frequency per waveform sample becomes $f_c = 1/T$, and it determines the highest output frequency component. That is, f_o (max) $\leq 0.5 \cdot f_c$ and f_o (min) $= f_c/2^n$ Hz. Similarly, the minimum phase increment ϕ (min) $= 360/2^n$ degrees. Finally, the corresponding minimum and maximum output voltage levels become V_o (min) $= |V_r|/2^{(L-1)}$ and V_o (max) $= |V_r| - V_o$ (min), where V_r is the DAC module reference voltage and L is the number of output bits in the lookup table.

The following example provides the synthesizer's specifications based on a given set of design parameters.

EXAMPLE 12.2

Using the listed parameters $f_{\text{ref}} = 4.096$ MHz, $M = 128$, $n = 12$, $L = 10$, and $V_r = \pm 10$ V, calculate the basic specifications.

$$f_s = f_{\text{ref}}/4 = 1.024 \text{ MHz} \qquad f_o \text{ (max)} \leq 0.5 \cdot f_c \leq 4 \text{ kHz}$$
$$T_s = 1/f_s = 0.976 \text{ μsec} \qquad f_o \text{ (min)} = f_c/2^n = 1.95 \text{ Hz}$$
$$T = T_s \cdot M = 125 \text{ μsec} \qquad \phi \text{ (min)} = 360°/2^n = 0.088°$$
$$f_c = 1/T = 8 \text{ kHz} \qquad V_o \text{ (min)} = |V_r|/2^{(L-1)} = 0.39 \text{ mV}$$
$$V_o \text{ (max)} = |V_r| - V_o \text{ (min)} = 19.961 \text{ V}$$

The basic synthesizer timing diagram is illustrated in Figure 12.19. The basic cycle starts with the incrementing of the address counter at phase 1. At phase 2 the contents of the $i^{\text{th}} + 1$ frequency, phase, and amplitude memory locations are transferred into the three input registers. At the same time the accumulator result for the ith memory locations is transferred to its output register. At phase 3 the address counter is decremented, and at phase 4 the output register contents are written into the ith phase memory location. The phase 2 clock is used as the pipeline signal sample clock, f_s. Therefore, each pipeline register contains a signal sample that corresponds to a different memory address. Since there are four such register stages, four contiguous memory address samples can exist at various processing stages. Also, the maximum switching time for a given signal sample becomes $4 \cdot T$. It should be noted that each amplitude memory

FIGURE 12.19
Synthesizer timing diagram.

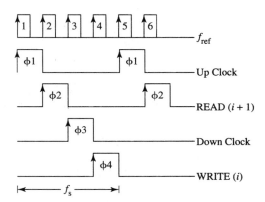

sample is delayed three clock periods so that it arrives at the MAC module input at the same time as its corresponding signal sample. Also, control signals are needed to select each memory and to control the MAC functions. For maximum performance, an MCU interface is needed to provide the required control and update the parameters on a non-interfering basis at the maximum transfer rate. The interface is designed to perform bidirectional data transfers with each signal parameter memory. A memory mapped I/O scheme is a good approach.

12.5   PRN SEQUENCE GENERATION

Pseudorandom noise (PRN) sequence generation complements DDS and makes it possible to simulate real-world signals with controllable signal-to-noise (S/N) ratios. An arbitrary n-length, linear binary sequence can be generated with shift registers, using XOR gates in a feedback configuration. This can be expressed as

$$P(X) = a_n \cdot X^n \oplus a_{n-1} \cdot X^{n-1} \oplus \cdot \cdot \cdot \oplus a_1 \cdot X^1 \tag{12.6}$$

where X_i represents the ith shift register stage, a_i represents the ith register coefficient, $a_i = 1$ stands for feedback connection, $a_i = 0$ stands for no connection, and $\oplus$ is the modulo 2 addition operator

The characteristics of each sequence are determined by the algebraic properties of its unique polynomial representation. To produce a maximum-length sequence (MLS), the n-tuple register state occurs once per cycle, and the feedback coefficients, a_i, must be chosen such that $P(X)$ is both irreducible and primitive. $P(X)$ is *irreducible* if it does not contain any factors with binary coefficients, and it is *primitive* if it is not a factor of $(X^k - 1)$ for $k < (2^n - 1)$. For an n-stage shift register, the MLS length equals 2^n. However, the all-zeros state results in a lockup condition and is therefore excluded. For a clock frequency f_c, the MLS period, T, becomes $T = N/f_c = (2^n - 1)/f_c = (2^n - 1) \cdot \delta T$, where $\delta T = 1/f_c$. An MLS sequence exhibits a certain degree of randomness. Although individual sequence states cannot be predicted, it is possible to extract certain overall pattern characteristics. Since the sequence repeats after a period T, it is referred to as cyclic and pseudorandom. Such sequences possess the following properties:

Each n-tuple state occurs once per cycle.

The number of ones per cycle is 2^{n-1}.

The number of zeros per cycle is $2^{n-1} - 1$.

To generate an MLS, the shift register must be configured with feedback paths that correspond to the coefficients of an nth-degree, irreducible, primitive polynomial over modulus 2. The number M of possible unique sequences for an n-stage shift register can be calculated using the following equation:

$$M = \frac{N}{n} \prod \frac{(P_i - 1)}{P_i} \tag{12.7}$$

where $N = 2^n - 1$, $\prod$ is the product operator, and P_i are the prime factors of N.

A sequence can be either forward or reverse. A reverse sequence occurs in the reverse order of a forward sequence. When the two are identical, the sequence is called a self sequence. If M is even, there are $M/2$ forward and $M/2$ reverse sequences. When M is odd, there exists one self sequence. The following example explains the use of the formula above to calculate M.

EXAMPLE 12.3

Given $n = 8$, calculate M.

$$N = 2^n - 1 = 255$$

$$M = (N/n) \cdot [\Pi(P_i - 1)/P_i] = (255/8) \times [(16 \times 4 \times 2)/(17 \times 5 \times 3)] = 16$$

Figure 12.20 shows the forward and reverse MLS sequence generator block diagrams for $n = 4$. The shift register transfers an input value using the clock, f_c, in its first stage, and then shifts it through each stage on each clock edge until it reaches the last stage.

Using the proper XOR feedback connections from the various shift register stages to the first stage, it is possible to produce a linear MLS binary output. The pattern repeats after $N = 2^n - 1$ bits; hence it is a cyclic pseudorandom sequence. The equations for a forward MLS become

$$D = X^3 \cdot \overline{X^4} + \overline{X^3} \cdot X^4 \text{ and } X_{i+1}(k + 1) = X_i(k)$$

where $i = 1, 2, 3 =$ register stage

$k =$ time index

Similarly, the reverse sequence equations become

$$D = X^1 \cdot \overline{X^4} + \overline{X^1} \cdot X^4$$

$$\text{and}$$

$$X_{i+1}(k + 1) = X_i(k)$$

Table 12.3 lists the two resulting sequences. Comparing the two reveals that the reverse sequence equals the forward sequence if it is read from bottom to top and the binary weights are reversed.

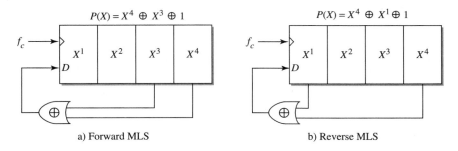

a) Forward MLS · b) Reverse MLS

FIGURE 12.20
MLS generators ($n = 4$).

TABLE 12.3
MLS sequences ($n = 4$)

Index	Forward	Reverse
k	1 2 3 4	1 2 3 4
1	1 0 0 0	1 0 0 0
2	0 1 0 0	1 1 0 0
3	0 0 1 0	1 1 1 0
4	1 0 0 1	1 1 1 1
5	1 1 0 0	0 1 1 1
6	0 1 1 0	1 0 1 1
7	1 0 1 1	0 1 0 1
8	0 1 0 1	1 0 1 0
9	1 0 1 0	1 1 0 1
10	1 1 0 1	0 1 1 0
11	1 1 1 0	0 0 1 1
12	1 1 1 1	1 0 0 1
13	0 1 1 1	0 1 0 0
14	0 0 1 1	0 0 1 0
15	0 0 0 1	0 0 0 1

Table 12.4 provides a tabulation of the key MLS parameters as a function of shift register length.

The following example provides a BASIC program to simulate the operation of an MLS sequence generator, shown in Figure 12.21, for $n = 12$.

EXAMPLE 12.4

Write an MLS simulation for $n = 12$.

```
    REM MLS SIMULATION
10  DIM SR(12)
20  SR(1) = 1
30  FOR I=1 TO 4095
40  IF SR(12) = SR(11) THEN BIT = 0 ELSE BIT = 1
50  IF SR(10) = BIT THEN BIT = 0 ELSE BIT = 1
60  IF SR(2) = BIT THEN BIT = 0 ELSE BIT = 1
70  FOR J = 11 TO 1 STEP -1
71  SR(J+1) = SR(J)
72  NEXT J
73  SR(1) = BIT
75  PRINT I;
80  FOR K=1 TO 12 STEP 1
81  PRINT SR(K)
82  NEXT K
83  PRINT
90  NEXT I
95  END
```

TABLE 12.4
MLS parameters

n	$N = 2^n - 1$	Feedback Stage
4	15	3, 4
8	255	2, 3, 4, 8
12	4,095	2, 10, 11, 12
16	65,535	11, 13, 14, 16
20	1,048,575	17, 20
24	16,777,215	19, 24
28	268,435,455	15, 28
32	4,295,967,295	17, 32
36	68,719,479,999	25, 36

The power spectral density of a linear MLS sequence results in a $\left(\dfrac{\sin x}{x}\right)^2$ function, where $x = (i \cdot \pi \cdot f_{min})/f_c$. Figure 12.22 illustrates the linear MLS power spectral density function. The term $f_{min} = 1/T = f_c/N = 1/(N \cdot \delta T)$, and the term $f_c = 1/\delta T$. Also, since $N = 2^n - 1$, $f_{min} = f_c/(2^n - 1)$. The highest frequency $f_h = 0.05 \cdot f_c$, with 0-dB attenuation relative to f_{min}. The maximum frequency $f_{max} = 0.45 \cdot f_c$, with -3-dB attenuation relative to f_{min}. The following example illustrates the concepts above.

EXAMPLE 12.5

Given $f_c = 10$ MHz and $n = 20$, find N, f_{min}, f_h, and f_{max}.

$$N = 2^{20} - 1 = 1,048,575$$
$$f_{min} = 10 \times 10^6/1,048,575 = 9.536 \text{ Hz}$$
$$f_h \text{ (0 dB)} = 0.05 \cdot 10 \times 10^6 = 500 \text{ kHz}$$
$$f_{max} \text{ (}-3 \text{ dB)} = 0.45 \cdot 10 \times 10^6 = 4.5 \text{ MHz}$$

In the previous example, the sequence period equals $T = N/f_c = 0.1$ sec. If the binary MLS signal is converted to analog and then bandlimited to f_h, it displays a flat power spectral density.

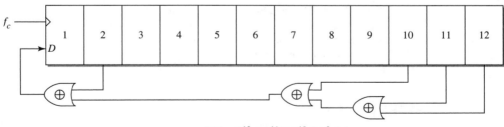

$$P(X) = X^{12} \oplus X^{11} \oplus X^{10} \oplus X^2 \oplus 1$$

FIGURE 12.21
MLS generator ($n = 12$).

FIGURE 12.22
Linear MLS PSD function.

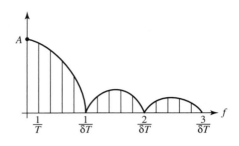

This is referred to as *white noise*. The random noise signal can be mixed with a deterministic signal, from a DDS synthesizer, to produce an arbitrary waveform with a controllable S/N ratio. Hence real-world signal simulation is possible.

PROBLEMS

12.1 For $x(n) = 2 \cdot \sin((2 \cdot \pi \cdot n/3) + (2 \cdot \pi/12))$ and $y(n) = 3 \cdot \sin((2 \cdot \pi \cdot n/4) + (2 \cdot \pi/18))$, determine the angle ϕ for continuous and coherent phase control. Assume $y(n)$ starts at $n = 5$.

12.2 Given an integer PLL with $f_o = 25$ MHz, $f_r = 5$ kHz, and $f_{OUT} = 17.5$ MHz, determine the counter modulus N.

12.3 Given a fractional synthesis PLL with $f_o = 5$ MHz, $f_r = 5$ kHz, $f_{OUT} = 19$ kHz, and $N = 475$, determine the counter modulus Q.

12.4 Given a prescaler PLL with $f_o = 100$ MHz, $f_r = 5$ kHz, and $P = 7$, determine the minimum and maximum f_{OUT} for a counter modulo $N = 2,048$.

12.5 Given a dual modulus PLL with $f_o = 120$ MHz, $f_r = 10$ kHz, $A = 150$, $B = 294$, and $f_{OUT} = 75$ MHz, determine the modulus P.

12.6 Given a DDS synthesizer with $N = 65,536$ and f_o (max) = 100 MHz, determine f_c, f_o (min), and n.

12.7 Given a waveform table with $n = 12$ inputs and $L = 10$ outputs, determine the number of stored bits and the additional bits for $n = 13$ and $L = 11$, respectively.

12.8 Given $A = 1$, $k = 128$, $\theta = 5°$, $n = 10$, and $f_c = 4,096$ Hz, find f_k, and evaluate Equation 12.3 for one complete cycle.

12.9 Given $x_i(k) = \sin((2 \cdot \pi \cdot k/16) + (\theta))$, calculate $Y(T) = x_1(k = 1, \theta = 5°) + x_2(k = 3, \theta = 10°) + x_3(k = 5, \theta = 15°)$, for one complete cycle of $x_1(k)$.

12.10 Given $n = 12$, calculate the number of possible linear MLS sequences.

12.11 Write a BASIC program to simulate an MLS generator for $n = 16$.

12.12 Given the MLS parameters $n = 24$ and $f_{min} = 5.9605$ Hz, determine f_c, f_{max}, f_h, and T.

REFERENCES

Gardner, F. M. *PLL Techniques.* New York: John Wiley & Sons, 1979.

Golomb, S. W. *Digital Communications with Space Applications.* Englewood Cliffs, NJ: Prentice Hall, 1967.

———. *Shift Register Sequences.* San Francisco: Holden-Day, 1964.

Gorki-Popiel, Jerzy. *Frequency Synthesis Techniques and Applications.* New York: IEEE Press, 1975.

Motorola Inc., *McMOS Integrated Circuits Data Book.* Phoenix, AZ: Motorola Inc., 1974.

———. *MECL Device Data Book.* Phoenix, AZ: Motorola Inc., 1987.

National Semiconductor. *MOS/LSI Data Book.* Santa Clara, CA: National Semiconductor, 1977.

Peterson, W. W. *Error Correcting Codes.* Cambridge, MA: MIT Press, 1961.

Rabiner, L. R. and B. Gold. *Theory and Applications of Digital Signal Processing.* Englewood Cliffs, NJ: Prentice Hall, 1975.

Signetics. *Linear Data Manual.* Sunnyvale, CA: Signetics, 1987.

GLOSSARY

ABEL (Advanced Boolean Expression Language): A software design tool for PLD design.

Access time: The time interval from the last input variable change to the time the output variable reaches a stable state.

Accumulator: An MPU register used to store data before and after ALU operations.

Acquisition time: The time required by a sample and hold device, going from hold state to sample state, to reach a final output value.

Addend: A number added to another to form a sum.

Address: A fixed group of bits used to specify the location of a data word in memory.

Aliasing: A condition caused by undersampling that results in an overlapped and distorted signal spectrum.

Algorithm: A sequence of operations that arrives consistently at a solution in a finite number of steps.

Alphanumeric code: A code that represents letters and numbers.

American Standard Code of Information Interchange (ASCII): A seven-bit character code used extensively for data communications.

Amplifier: An analog device used to increase the magnitude of an input signal within a certain bandwidth.

Analog: A signal defined for a continuous range of amplitude and time values.

Analog-to-digital converter (ADC): A module used to change an analog input signal to a corresponding digital output code.

Analysis: The examination of the detailed operation of a circuit, device, or system.

AND gate: A two-input logic device that produces a true or high-level output when both variables are true or high-level.

Angle-to-digital converter: A module used to change an analog input angle value into a corresponding digital output code.

Antifuse: An interconnection scheme for programmable devices that closes an open circuit when activated.

504

Aperture time: The time required for a sample and hold device, going from sample state to hold state, to reach a stable output level.

Arithmetic logic unit (ALU):   A section of the MPU that performs logical and arithmetic operations.

Array: A linear data structure that contains similar data types that are individually accessed by an address pointer.

Assembler: A program that translates mnemonic source code into machine object code.

Asynchronous transmission: The transmission of framed characters, bounded by Start and Stop bits, with variable intervals between them.

Asynchronous time division multiplexing (ATDM):   A dynamic channel bandwidth allocation and random access multiplexing scheme.

Asynchronous transfer mode (ATM):   A high-speed, packet-switching scheme using uniform-length cells.

Attenuation: The reduction of a signal's amplitude.

Attribute: Characteristic or property.

Augend: A number to which another is added to produce a sum.

Automatic repeat request (ARQ):   A scheme used to implement error detection and correction.

Autonomous network: A sequential network without input variables.

Backbone: A primary, wide-bandwidth network that interconnects various other networks and systems.

Bandwidth: The difference between the highest and the lowest frequencies, for a specified signal attenuation, in a communications channel or system.

Base: The number of unique values a digit can assume in a given number system.

Baseband: A LAN transmission method that uses a narrow bandwidth channel and is accessed by one node at a time.

BASIC (Beginner's All-purpose Symbolic Instructional Code):   A high-level language used to write interactive programs.

Batching: A scheme of grouping several similar programs and sending them to a computer for sequential processing.

Baud: A unit of signaling rate over a communications channel.

Baudot: A five-bit code used to represent alphanumeric characters.

Binary: Having two states or values.

Binary code: An assignment of unique combinations of n bits to represent a symbol.

Binary coded decimal (BCD) code: A four-bit binary code used to represent decimal digits.

Binary digit (Bit):   A digit whose value can be either 0 or 1.

Binary state: A given row of input combinations in a truth table.

Binary synchronous communications (BSC):   A half duplex, byte-oriented data protocol.

Bit error rate (BER):   The ratio of incorrectly to correctly received bits in a communications system.

Bit-slice: A modular MPU architecture that consists of an expandable RALU and a microcode sequencer.

Block: A group of contiguous data bytes usually 512, stored on a magnetic tape or disk.

Boolean algebra: A mathematical system of logic that forms the basis of digital systems.

Bridge: A protocol-independent device that interconnects two similar LANs at the data link layer.

Broadband: A LAN transmission method that uses a wide bandwidth channel and supports multiple-node access at the same time.

Buffer: A temporary data storage area between two devices operating at different data rates.

Bug: An error in a program.

Built-in-test (BIT):   A program module that tests the health status of a system upon power-up.

Bus: A group of conductors used to distribute data, address, and control signals throughout an MCU.

Butterfly: The basic FFT calculation.

Byte: A group of eight bits.

C language: An efficient, high-level language used to develop systems programs.

Cache: A small, high-speed memory used to store frequently accessed MPU instructions and data.

Canonical form: A switching function consisting of either all minterm or all maxterm expressions.

Capture range: The range of frequencies in which a PLL can achieve synchronization with an external input signal.

Carrier sense multiple access/collision detect (CSMA/CD):   A random access control scheme used with Ethernet.

Cell: A short, fixed-length packet.

Cell relay: A high-speed network transmission method using cells.

Central processing unit (CPU):   The MPU component that performs instruction fetch and execution and ALU operations.

Chaining: A process that uses a common memory region to store the currently executing module of a large program.

Channel: A physical data communications path and its assigned band of frequencies.

Character: A symbol such as a letter, number, or sign used to represent information.

Character code: A binary code that can represent a variety of characters.

Checksum: The addition modulo 2 of all bytes in a data block.

Chip select (CS):   A device input signal that enables device operation.

Circuit: A complete electrical path between two points.

Circuit switching: A real-time, point-to-point path between a source and a destination.

Clear: A sequential device input that places the device in a known initial state.

Clock: A digital circuit that produces a stable periodic reference signal.

Clock cycle: The time interval required to complete one period.

Code: A set of rules that is applied to represent a set of symbols.

Command: An executable MPU instruction.

Combinational: A switching function whose output value depends solely on the present input variable combinations.

Compact disk (CD):   An optical recording medium–based disk.

Compiler: A program that converts high-level language source code into machine object code.

Complement: The maximum range value minus the number in a given base system.

Complementary metal oxide semiconductor (CMOS):   A low-power integrated circuit technology.

Complex instruction set computer (CISC):   A computer with a large, variable-length instruction set.

Complex programmable logic device (CPLD): A programmable VLSI device consisting of PAL-based logic blocks.

Compression: A method of reducing the space required for data storage.

Computer-aided engineering (CAE): Use of software and hardware tools for automated design and simulation.

Concurrent: Overlapping or simultaneously occurring.

Contention: A condition in which two or more LAN nodes attempt to send data at the same time.

Context switching: The storing of the current MPU state in the stack in order to execute another task.

Control unit: The CPU section that decodes instructions and generates timing signals to control operation.

Conversion time: The interval required for a converter module to produce a stable output, measured from the start of the command.

Convolution: A time domain operation on two signals that corresponds to frequency domain filtering.

Constellation: A two-dimensional plot of amplitude against phase, used in QAM.

Correlation: A time domain operation that compares two signals for similarities.

Counter: A register whose contents are incremented using a clock signal.

Cover: A logical expression that represents a given switching function.

Crash: An MCU system failure due to either a hardware or a software error.

Critical region: A program segment that must be executed to completion without any other program or event interference.

Cycle: One complete interval of a periodic signal.

Cyclic redundancy check (CRC): An error detection scheme using division modulo 2.

Cylinder: The tracks on two or more magnetic disk sides that correspond in distance from the axis.

Daisy chain: A multiple-level, single-priority interrupt scheme.

Data: Information represented in binary form suitable for MPU interpretation.

Database: An orderly collection of data organized in a manner suitable for selective and quick access.

Datagram: A standard, variable-length packet for data transfer on the Internet.

Data communications equipment (DCE): An analog device that interfaces with the communications channel.

Data terminal equipment (DTE): A digital device that transmits or receives data.

Data structure: The arrangement of data elements in memory so as to facilitate access and manipulation.

Deadlock: A condition resulting when one task is waiting to access a resource that another is holding, and vice versa.

Debugger: A program that detects and corrects program errors.

Decimal point: The character separating the integer and fractional parts of a number.

Decimation: A method for reducing the system sampling rate.

Decoder: A digital device that converts a specific input code into a useful output format.

DeMorgan's theorems: Two Boolean algebra theorems used to simplify logical expressions.

Demultiplexer: A digital device that selectively distributes an input signal to one of several outputs.

Designation number: An input-variable column in a truth table.

Device driver: A program used to control the detailed operation of a peripheral device.

Diagram: A drawing illustrating a circuit or device.

Diagnostic: A program used to locate a specific hardware fault.

Dibit: A two-bit grouping that represents four possible signal states.

Digit: A symbol that represents one of the possible values in a number system.

Digital: A signal defined for quantized amplitude and discrete time values.

Digital-to-analog converter (DAC): A module used to convert a digital input code into an equivalent analog output value.

Digital-to-angle converter: A module used to convert a digital input code into an equivalent analog angle value.

Direct digital synthesis (DDS): A method of specifying the parameters and realizing a waveform signal.

Direct memory access (DMA): A technique for high-speed data block transfers between memory and an I/O device that bypass the MPU.

Directive: An assembler-specific instruction for controlling assembler operation.

Directory: A database containing information about a set of files.

Discrete: A signal defined over a discontinuous time interval.

Discrete Fourier transform (DFT): A mathematical operation that converts a time domain signal into its corresponding frequency domain.

Disk: A flat, circular surface, with either a magnetic or optical coating, used for high-density data storage.

Disk operating system (DOS): An executive program residing on a disk that is loaded in main memory during start-up.

Distributed Queue Dual Bus (DQDB): A fiber-optic, cable-based, ring topology network standard that operates at 155 Mbps.

Dividend: A number that is divided by another.

Divisor: A number by which another is divided.

Don't care: An input variable combination that will not occur or is of no concern.

Duplex: The ability to transmit independently in both directions on a communications channel.

Duty cycle: The ratio of a signal's active interval to its period.

Dynamic RAM (DRAM): A volatile, high-density semiconductor storage device that requires periodic refresh.

Dynamic range: The ratio of the largest to the smallest signal amplitude, expressed in dB, that a device or system can process.

Editor: A program that creates and modifies source code.

Electrically erasable PROM (EEPROM): An in-circuit programmable PROM that supports byte-level read and write operations.

Electronic Design Interchange Format (EDIF): A standard for exchanging design data files.

Electronic Industries Association (EIA): An organization that develops interface standards.

Emulator: A hardware and software component that simulates the functional and timing behavior of another.

Encoder: A logic device that converts a unique input variable combination into a compact output format.

Erasable PROM (EPROM): An out-of-circuit, programmable PROM that requires an ultraviolet light source for content erasure.

Error: A discrepancy between the sent and the received data.

Error Detection and Correction (EDAC): A method of ensuring transmission integrity by resending data with detected errors.

Ethernet: A coaxial cable–based, bus topology network standard.

Eulerian trail: An input-variable sequence that checks every state transition of a sequential network exactly once.

Exception: A condition caused by an attempt to perform an illegal MPU operation.

Excitation table: A tabulation of the input(s) required to cause a predictable next state transition in a sequential network.

Exclusive-OR gate: A two-input logic device that produces a true or high-level output when both input variable states differ.

Exponent: The integer part of a floating point number.

Execution phase: The interval during which a decoded instruction is executed.

Fast Fourier transform (FFT): An efficient algorithm to calculate the DFT of a time domain signal.

Fault: A hardware failure.

Fetch phase: The interval during which an instruction or data are accessed from memory.

Fiber-Optic Distribution Data Interface (FDDI): A dual ring topology network standard that operates at 125 Mbps.

Field: An area within a data record.

Field programmable cell array (FPCA): A programmable VLSI device that consists of interconnected universal logic cells.

Field programmable logic array (FPLA): A programmable LSI device made up of a two-level AND/OR logic matrix.

Field programmable logic sequencer (FPLS): An FPLA with programmable feedback registers.

File: An orderly collection of data records.

Filter: A circuit that passes a selective group of signal frequencies and attenuates the rest.

Finite input response (FIR) filter: A digital filter whose output signal is the sum of the weighted past and present input signal values.

Firmware: A computer program stored in nonvolatile memory.

First-in, first-out (FIFO) memory: A device that stores and retrieves data elements in the order in which they are written.

Fixed point: A real number notation in which the decimal point stays in a fixed position.

Flag: A status bit used as a condition or event indicator.

Flash EEPROM: An in-circuit, programmable PROM that supports byte-level read and entire array erase operations.

Flip-flop: A logic device that has two stable states as a function of the input data value.

Floating point notation: A real number notation in which the decimal point can move in either direction as a function of number's value.

Floating point unit (FPU): A logic device within an MPU that supports floating-point calculations.

Flowchart: A graphic representation of the sequence of steps that defines an operation.

Flowgraph: A directed graph model of a sequential network, in which nodes represent states and lines represent state transitions.

FORTRAN (Formula Translation): A high-level language used for scientific programming.

Forward error correction (FEC): A data integrity scheme using redundancy that enables the receiver to detect and correct errors.

Fragmentation: A condition that results in small, unequal, and noncontiguous free memory areas.

Frame: A data block that contains address, control, and error detection fields.

Frame relay: A high-speed, packet-switching network standard.

Frequency division multiplexing (FDM): Static allocation of fixed-size frequency channels.

Function table: A compact form of a state transition table.

Fundamental mode: An asynchronous sequential network using level inputs.

Fusible link: An interconnection for programmable devices that opens a closed circuit when activated.

Gain: The output-to-input signal magnitude ratio of an op amp over a specified bandwidth.

Gate: A two-valued logic device that provides an output level of either low or high, as a function of the input variable values.

Gateway: A device that interconnects two dissimilar networks by providing conversion at all seven layers.

Glitch: An erroneous, short-duration pulse, caused by race conditions, that results in abnormal operation.

Gallop test: A memory test that checks multiple data bit transitions in adjacent cells.

Hamiltonian path: An input-variable sequence that tests every state of a sequential network exactly once.

Hamming distance: The number of bit locations by which two data words differ.

Handshake: The exchange of control signals between two devices prior to data transfer.

Hardware: The physical components of an MCU, such as the MPU, the memory, and the I/O.

Hashing: A random method of determining a data storage location that uses the data itself.

Hazard: A glitch or error caused by the unequal propagation path delays of the input switching variables.

Hertz (Hz): A unit of frequency measurement that equals one cycle per second.

Hexadecimal: A base sixteen number system that uses digits 0 through 9 and letters A through F.

High: A voltage level indicating a true or "one" state in positive logic convention.

Hi-Z: A third logic state that results in a high impedance or virtual open output condition.

High level data link control (HDLC): A synchronous bit oriented protocol for managing data frames.

High-level language (HLL): A computer language that uses English-like statements to develop source code.

Hold time: The time required for an input variable to be stable after a clock transition in order for the output state to change.

Hybrid programmable logic device (HPLD): A programmable VLSI device that combines the best features of CPLDs and FPCAs.

Implicant: A minterm or P-term of a function that reflects the state of the function, whether true or false.

Impulse response: The output function of a system that is subjected to a unit impulse signal.

Inclusive-OR gate: A two-input logic device that produces a true or high-level output when both input variable states are the same.

Indirect digital synthesis: Signal synthesis accomplished by the control of an existing source in order to produce the desired output.

Infinite input response (IIR) filter: A digital filter whose output signal is the sum of the weighted past output values and the past and present input signal values.

Information: The presentation of knowledge in a useful manner.

Input/Output (I/O): The MCU component that interfaces with the real world.

Institute of Electrical and Electronic Engineers (IEEE): A committee that develops and proposes various standards.

Interface: A device or module used to interconnect MCU components.

Integrated circuit (IC): A complex logic circuit contained on a single silicon chip.

Interlaced: A scheme that uses an odd and an even scan field to produce one image frame.

Interleaving: A technique of rearranging contiguous data into noncontiguous patterns or locations to improve the BER.

Interpolation: A method for increasing the system sampling rate.

Interpreter: A program that converts source code into machine object code one line at a time.

Instruction: A codeword that the CPU decodes as a specific operation.

Instruction set: A list of all instructions that a given MPU can execute.

Interrupt: An external input signal that alerts the MPU that an external event has taken place.

Inverter gate: A single input logic device that produces the output complement of the input variable state.

International Telegraph Union (ITU): A committee that develops communications standards.

International Standards Organization (ISO): An organization responsible for the definition of the OSI networking standard.

Internet: An interconnection of large backbone networks that extends worldwide.

Internet Protocol (IP): An OSI network layer standard that has become a universal Internet packet format.

Isochronous: Asynchronous transmission using a clock rate that equals the data rate.

Iteration: The repetition of a subroutine or operation in order to derive the desired result.

Joint Electron Device Engineering Council (JEDEC) standard: An ASCII output file standard used for device programming.

Jitter: The maximum aperture time variation of a sample and hold device.

Karnaugh map: A two-dimensional diagram used to represent and simplify arbitrary logic functions of up to six switching variables.

Kernel: The main code module of an operating system.

Kilobyte (KB):   1,024 bytes.

Kilohertz (KHz):   1,000 Hertz.

Label: An alphanumeric character string used to represent an address value.

Land: The blank reflective area on an optical disk surface.

Large scale integration (LSI):   An integrated circuit technology that uses more than one hundred gates per package.

Last-in, first-out (LIFO) memory: A device that stores and retrieves data elements in the reverse order in which they are written.

Latch: A level-sensitive storage register device.

Latency: The time required for a spinning disk to make one-half of a revolution. Also, the time interval required to respond to an interrupt request.

Layer: One of several hierarchical levels of software that work in unison.

Leakage: Frequency spectrum distortion caused by the abrupt transition of the input signal sample. Also, a capacitive element's gradual loss of charge due to imperfections.

Least recently used (LRU):   A method of memory allocation that frees the infrequently used segments.

Least significant bit (LSB):   The rightmost bit of a digital word.

Least significant digit (LSD):   The rightmost digit bit of a number.

Level: A signal that has a duration of several clock pulse periods.

Lexical analysis: The process of ensuring that the source code is valid and correct.

Linear list: A data structure whose elements are contained in consecutive positions.

Light-emitting diode (LED):   A solid state indicator.

Linker: A program that binds multiple program modules so that they are suitable for execution.

Linked list: A data structure whose elements also contain pointers to specify the next non-contiguous element location.

Literal: A switching variable instance indicating either its true or false state.

Loader: A program used to load object code into a memory area.

Local area network (LAN):   A collection of independent MCUs and peripherals interconnected via a common physical medium.

Lock range: The range of frequencies in which a PLL can maintain synchronization with an external input signal.

Lockup: A condition in which a counter enters an unusable state and remains there indefinitely.

Logic: Based on the principles of Boolean algebra.

Logic diagram: A pictorial representation of a logic network using interconnected logic symbols.

Logic symbol: A graphical representation of a logic function that shows the input and output variable topology.

Logical address: An address consisting of the sum of two or more register values.

Longitudal redundancy check (LRC):   Bitwise parity checking for all characters in a given data block.

Low: A voltage level indicating a false or "zero" state in positive logic convention.

Machine code: The binary code that a specific MPU can decode and execute directly.

Machine cycle: One or more clock cycles required to complete a basic MPU operation.

Macro: A shorthand notation for a group of frequently used instructions.

Mailbox: An address location used by two tasks to exchange messages.

Mantissa: The fractional part of a floating-point number notation.

Mark: A data communications term corresponding to logic one.

Masking: The selective blocking of MPU interrupt requests.

Mass storage: A high-density, low-speed secondary memory device.

Matrix: A two-dimensional logic or data structure.

Maximum length sequence (MLS):   An n-bit shift register with feedback that can produce $2^n - 1$ states.

Maxterm: A sum of n switching variables that defines a unique combination.

Mealy machine: A sequential network whose outputs depend on the present state and present inputs.

Medium scale integration (MSI):   An integrated circuit technology that uses 10 to 100 gates per package.

Megabyte (MB):   One million bytes.

Megahertz (MHz):   One million cycles per second.

Magnetic disk: A magnetically coated disk used for high-density storage.

Memory: The MCU component used to store instruction and data words.

Memory management unit (MMU):   A device that manages, controls, and allocates system memory.

Memory allocation: A method of freeing and assigning memory space to various programs.

Merger diagram: A graph used to combine compatible states prior to state assignment.

Message: An arbitrary unit of information.

Message switching: A store-and-forward method of transferring data from source to destination.

Metropolitan area network (MAN):   A network extending over a large area that serves as a bridge between LANs and WANs.

Microcode: A sequence of microinstructions that make up one MPU instruction.

Microcomputer unit (MCU):   An MPU-based computer.

Microprocessor unit (MPU):   A CPU fabricated as a single IC package.

Million floating point operations per second (mflops):   A performance measurement unit for floating-point arithmetic operations.

Million instructions per second (mips):   A performance measurement unit for MPUs.

Minimal cover: A switching function cover that consists of all essential prime implicants and a small subset of prime implicants.

Minterm: A product of n switching variables that defines a unique combination.

Minuend: A number from which another is subtracted to form a difference.

Mnemonic: An abbreviation used to represent a machine instruction and designed to aid the human memory.

Module: A standalone computer program. A basic hardware unit.

Modulo: The capacity of measurement in a given number system.

Modulator/demodulator (Modem): A device used to transmit and receive digital data over an analog communications channel.

Modulation: The modification of one or more carrier signal parameters with information.

Monitor: A small MPU control program with limited capability.

Moore machine: A sequential network whose outputs depend only on the present state.

Most significant bit (MSB): The leftmost bit of a digital word.

Most significant digit (MSD): The leftmost digit bit of a number.

Multilevel network: A logic network that has more than two gates in cascade.

Multiple instructions multiple data (MIMD) computer: A computer that fetches and executes multiple instructions and data simultaneously.

Multiplexer: A logic device that selectively combines two or more input data signals paths into one output.

Multiplicand: A number to be multiplied by another.

Multiplier: A number that multiplies another.

Multiprocessing: The simultaneous operation of two or more MPUs in the same MCU.

Multiprogramming: The residence of two or more programs in main memory at the same time.

Multitasking: The concurrent execution of two or more independent program modules.

Mutual exclusion: The mechanism that ensures that common data are used by one program or task at a time.

NAND gate: A two-input logic device that produces a false or low-level output when both input variables are true or high-level.

Nesting: A technique that uses one subroutine to call another.

Netlist: A tabulation of device interconnections for design realization.

Network: A physical interconnection of computers, peripherals, and control software to enable high-speed data exchanges.

Network topology: The physical configuration of a LAN.

Next-state transition matrix: An encoded state table that is derived using the state assignment and a specific flip-flop excitation table.

Nibble: A group of four bits.

Node: A physical connection point in a network.

Noise: An electrical impulse that interferes with the normal reception of an intended signal.

NOR gate: A two-input logic device that produces a true or high-level output when both input variables are false or low-level.

Normalize: To adjust the exponent value in order to place the mantissa within a certain range.

Nyquist frequency: A frequency that equals one-half the Nyquist rate.

Nyquist rate: A sampling frequency that equals twice the highest input signal frequency.

Object code: The MPU-specific executable code generated by a compiler, interpreter, or assembler.

Octal number system: A base eight number system using digits 0 to 7.

Offline: Pertaining to operations not under direct MPU control.

One's complement: A number formed by inverting every bit in a binary data word.

Online: Pertaining to operations under direct MPU control.

Opcode: The part of an instruction that is decoded to determine the type of operation to be performed.

Open Systems Interconnection (OSI) reference model: A seven-level network protocol model made up of the physical, data link, network, transport, session, presentation, and application layers.

Operand: The part of an instruction that is manipulated by the ALU.

Operating system: A program used to control other programs, manage the MPU, memory and I/O, and provide error recovery.

Operational amplifier (Op amp): A high-gain differential amplifier with a wide bandwidth.

Optical disk: An optically coated disk that is used for high-density data storage.

OR gate: A two-input logic device that produces a true or high-level output when either input variable is true or high-level.

Oscillator: An analog circuit that generates a periodic signal.

Output Enable (OE): A device input signal that is used to control tri-state operation.

Overflow: A condition in which the mantissa of a floating-point number is greater than one or in which an operand value exceeds the capacity of the accumulator.

Overlay: The use of a common memory area for subroutine loading and execution as required by the main program.

Package: The physical layout of an integrated circuit device.

Packet: A variable-length block of data with addressing and control fields.

Packet switching: The routing of source node message segments via available network paths until they reach their destination node.

Paging: A memory allocation method that divides available memory into fixed-size segments.

Parallel I/O: The transfer of two or more bits of data simultaneously.

Parameter: A variable whose value defines a specific device or module characteristic.

Parity: An error detection scheme that uses an extra bit to make the number of bits in a character either odd or even.

Partition: A memory allocation method that divides available memory into fixed dedicated regions.

Pascal: A high-level language based on structured programming.

Path: The complete name needed to locate a file within a hierarchical directory.

Peripheral: An external I/O device that is connected to the MCU.

Picket fence: An FFT output spectrum characterized by discrete frequencies.

Pipelining: The use of registers between the MPU and memory to enable concurrent fetch and execute operations.

Pit: The data bit area on an optical disk.

Phase: The time shift between two time domain signals.

Phase detector: A device that produces an output error signal proportional to the phase difference of two input signals.

Phase lock loop (PLL): An analog device that adjusts its internal VCO frequency to compensate for an external input signal.

Physical address: The actual memory location of a data word.

Polling: A technique used by the MPU to determine device status.

Positional number system: A number system notation in which digit values are a function of each digit's relative location.

Preset: A sequential device input that places the device in a known high state.

Prime implicant: A minimized implicant.

Product-of-sums (POS): A product-of-maxterms representation of a switching function.

Program: A logical sequence of MPU instructions used to perform a predefined function.

Programmable array logic (PAL): A programmable LSI device consisting of a programmable AND and a fixed OR matrix.

Programmable folded gate array (PFGA): A programmable VLSI device using similar logic gates with programmable feedback paths.

Programmable gate array (PGA): A programmable LSI device consisting of similar logic gates.

Programmable logic array (PLA): A programmable LSI device made up of a two-level AND/OR logic matrix.

Programmable logic device (PLD): A generic programmable LSI device consisting of a two-level AND/OR matrix.

Programmable ROM (PROM): A one-time programmable, nonvolatile memory device.

Propagation delay: The time interval required for an input variable change to reach the device output.

Protocol: A set of procedures for defining reliable system-level data exchanges.

Pseudorandom number (PRN) sequence: A shift register–generated bit pattern that is effectively random for the purpose for which it is required.

P-term: A reduced maxterm that may not contain each variable.

Pulse: The active time interval of a periodic signal.

Pulse mode: Mode in which an asynchronous sequential network uses only pulse inputs.

Quadrant: The four symmetrical sections of a Cartesian coordinate graph.

Quadrature amplitude modulation (QAM): A hybrid modulation scheme that uses amplitude and phase carrier signal modification.

Quantization: A method of representing an analog input variable with a set of unique binary output values.

Queue: A data structure that is used to write data from one end and read them from the other.

Quine-McCluskey method: A tabular minimization procedure for switching functions.

Quotient: The result of a division operation.

Race condition: A condition in which two or more input signals arrive at different times at the output due to variable internal path delays.

Radix: The base value of a given number system.

Random access: The ability to uniformly access any next memory location.

Random access memory (RAM): A volatile storage device whose locations can be accessed within a short, fixed time interval.

Rate modification: The alteration of a system's sampling rate.

Read-only memory (ROM): An one-time programmed, nonvolatile memory device.

Real-time processing: The processing of an event as it occurs, or within a fixed time interval, so as to provide meaningful feedback to its source.

Record: A table that contains a group of dissimilar data fields.

Recursion: A scheme by which a subroutine calls itself in order to derive a result.

Reduced instruction set computer (RISC): A computer with a small uniform-size instruction set.

Reentrant code: An executable program segment that is not altered during execution.

Refresh: A periodic operation required to maintain DRAM data integrity.

Register: A group of flip-flops used to store, manipulate, and transfer data.

Register arithmetic logic unit (RALU): An expandable module that contains a register file and an ALU.

Repeater: A device that provides signal conditioning to extend the range of a LAN.

Reset: A sequential device input that places the device in a known low state.

Resolution: The minimum discernible distance between two levels or quantities.

Resolver: A two-phase analog device for angular position sensing.

Ring topology: A network configuration made up of a series of cascaded nodes.

Round off rule: A rule for assigning the next upper or lower value to an input level.

Round-robin: A scheduling method by which each task gets a fixed time slot to execute.

Router: A protocol-sensitive device for connecting dissimilar networks.

Sampling: The sensing and storing of an input signal value at discrete time intervals.

Sampling rate: The reciprocal of the sampling interval period.

Sample and hold device: A device that tracks and latches a sampled signal value.

Scheduler: A program that determines the task to be executed next.

Search: A process that determines the presence or absence of a specific data element in a list structure.

Sector: A wedge-shaped section of a formatted disk that holds blocks of data.

Seek time: The time it takes the head assembly to move one-third the distance across the tracks of a disk.

Segmentation: A memory allocation scheme that divides available memory into variable-size units.

Semaphore: An indicator bit used to control access to a shared resource.

Sequential switching function: A switching function whose output value depends on its present state and on input variable combinations.

Sequential access: The accessing of stored data in a specific order.

Sequential machine: A digital network whose next state output is a function of the present state and present inputs.

Serial I/O: The transfer of one bit at a time.

Settling time: The time it takes an op amp output to reach a final value within a specified error limit, in response to a large input signal.

Setup time: The time required for an input variable to be stable, before a clock transition, in order for the output state to change.

Shift register: A logic device whose contents can be displaced in either direction, one bit at a time.

Simplex: The ability to transmit through a communications channel in only one direction.

Single instruction multiple data (SIMD) computer: A computer that fetches a single instruction that operates on a group of data elements.

Single instruction single data (SISD) computer: A computer that fetches a single instruction that operates on one data element.

Signal: An electrical quantity used to represent information in an electrical network.

Signal-to-noise (S/N) ratio: The magnitude ratio of the desired signal to the undesired signal.

Simulator: A hardware-and-software component used to mimic the functional behavior of another component.

Slew rate: The maximum op amp output signal rate of change for a large input.

Small scale integration (SSI):   An integrated circuit technology using one to ten gates per package.

Software: A computer program stored in volatile memory and its documentation.

Sort: A method of arranging the elements of a list structure into ascending or descending order.

Source code: A user-generated list of instructions written in a programming language.

Space: A communications term for logic state zero.

Spectrum: The range of frequencies a signal occupies.

Spike: A short-duration, large-amplitude electrical signal.

Spool (Simultaneous peripheral operations online):   A method of interfacing an MPU to a printer using a data buffer to compensate for the transfer rate disparity.

Stack: A data structure in which data are written and read from the same entry point.

Standard: A set of rules that forms the basis of compatibility among various systems.

Standard form: A minimized switching function expression that may not contain every minterm or maxterm.

Star topology: A network configuration that connects each node to a central node called the "hub."

Start bit: A framing bit marking the beginning of a character.

Starvation: A condition in which a given task never is assigned a resource due to its low priority.

State: An internal, stable condition of a sequential network.

State assignment: A procedure for coding states.

State flow diagram: A graphical representation of a sequential network.

State table: A tabular representation of a sequential network.

Static RAM (SRAM):   A volatile, high-speed semiconductor storage device made up of flip-flop storage elements.

Status: A bit indicating the result of an operation.

Step size: The measurement of a signal-level increment.

Stop bit: A framing bit marking the end of a character.

String: A group of characters.

Strobe: A short-duration pulse that enables an action.

Structured diagram: A flowchart variant that uses logic control structures.

Structured programming: A methodology for developing programs using an elementary set of control structures.

Subtrahend: A number that is subtracted from another to form a difference.

Subroutine: A standalone sequence of instructions that can be invoked from the main program module.

Successive approximation: An adaptive search procedure for fast digital-to-analog signal conversion.

Superscalar: An MPU with multiple independent ALUs.

Sum-of-products (SOP): A sum-of-minterms representation of a switching function.

S-term: A reduced maxterm that may not include every variable.

Swapping: The use of a common memory space to store and execute the current program in a multiprogramming environment.

Switch: A device that opens (ON) or closes (OFF) a circuit path connection.

Switching variable: A binary variable that represents either an on or an off condition.

Symbol: A character that represents certain information.

Synchro: A three-phase analog device for angular position sensing.

Synchronous network: A network that uses a reference clock.

Synchronous data link control (SDLC): A full duplex, bit-oriented data transfer protocol.

Synchronous optical network (SONET) standard: A standard for very high speed data transmission over a fiber-optic cable.

Synchronous time division multiplexing (STDM): A static channel bandwidth allocation and deterministic access multiplexing scheme.

Synthesis: The process of designing a device, module, or system from a set of specified parameters.

Syntactic analysis: A process to ensure the proper structural relationship among source code program statements.

System: An arrangement of hardware components and/or software modules that performs a predefined function.

Table: A representation of data arranged in rows and columns.

Task: A standalone, functionally complete program module.

Terminal: A device for sending and receiving character data.

Thrashing: A condition in which the operating system spends excessive time swapping data to and from main memory.

Threshold: A reference level used to compare it against an analog input signal magnitude.

Time division multiplexing (TDM): The allocation of the full channel bandwidth in fixed time slots.

Timing logic: A logic circuit that generates reference signals at specified intervals.

Timing diagram: A graphic representation of the relationship between logic state and timing for a given switching function.

Toggle: To alternate between two states.

Token: A special message that is circulated from node to node for access control.

Token bus topology: A bus network topology that uses a token-passing access control method.

Token ring topology: A ring network topology that uses a token-passing access control method.

Track: A concentric ring section on a formatted disk that contains data sectors.

Transistor-transistor logic (TTL): A semiconductor technology used for SSI and MSI logic devices.

Trellis-coded modulation (TCM): A modulation scheme that also provides forward error correction.

Transmission control protocol (TCP): An OSI transport layer Internet protocol used in conjunction with IP.

Trigger: An input signal change that causes an action to take place.

Tri-state: A third logic state that results in a virtual open output condition.

Truncate rule: A rule for dropping off a number of bits from a data word.

Truth table: A tabular representation of all possible binary input variable combinations and their resulting output states.

Two's complement: A number formed by inverting every bit in a data word and then incrementing it by one.

Underflow: A condition in which the mantissa of a floating-point number is less than one-half.

Universal asynchronous receiver transmitter (UART): A logic module used to send and receive serial data characters.

User-specific integrated circuit (USIC): A programmable VLSI device that is custom-programmed by each user.

Vectored interrupt: A single-level, multiple-priority interrupt scheme.

Vertex: A directed line connecting two states in a flowgraph.

Very high speed integrated circuit (VHSIC): A specialized, high-performance VLSI logic device.

VHSIC Hardware Design Language (VHDL): A software tool for VLSI module synthesis, design, and simulation.

Vertical redundancy check (VRC): A character-by-character parity check in a data block.

Very large scale integration (VLSI): An integrated circuit technology using more than ten thousand gates per package.

Virtual memory: A technique that makes the cache, main, and secondary memories appear as one contiguous address space.

Voltage-controlled oscillator (VCO): An oscillator whose frequency is proportional to an input voltage level.

Wait state: An MPU condition that results in no operation.

Walk test: A memory test used to check single bit transitions of adjacent storage cells.

Waveform: A graphical representation of a signal in which amplitude is plotted against time.

Wide area network (WAN): A network that extends over a broad geographical area.

Wildcard: A character used in an editor command to perform generalized functions.

Window: A weight function for a digital filter.

Word: A group of sixteen bits.

X.25: A standard for communicating over a packet-switching network.

z transform: A mathematical operation that converts difference equations into a format suitable for algebraic manipulation.

INDEX